THE PAGEANT
OF AMERICA
R.K.

Independence Edition

VOLUME II

THE PAGEANT OF AMERICA

A PICTORIAL HISTORY OF THE UNITED STATES

RALPH HENRY GABRIEL
EDITOR

DIXON RYAN FOX   JOHN CHESTER ADAMS
ASSOCIATE EDITORS

EDWIN MIMS, JR.
ASSISTANT EDITOR

CHARLES M. ANDREWS
HERBERT E. BOLTON
IRVING N. COUNTRYMAN
WILLIAM E. DODD
DIXON RYAN FOX
ALLEN JOHNSON
WILLIAM BENNETT MUNRO
VICTOR H. PALTSITS
ARTHUR M. SCHLESINGER
NATHANIEL WRIGHT STEPHENSON
ADVISORY EDITORS

DAVID M. MATTESON
INDEXER

THE YALE PAGEANT OF AMERICA

THE LURE OF THE FRONTIER

A STORY OF RACE CONFLICT

BY

RALPH HENRY GABRIEL

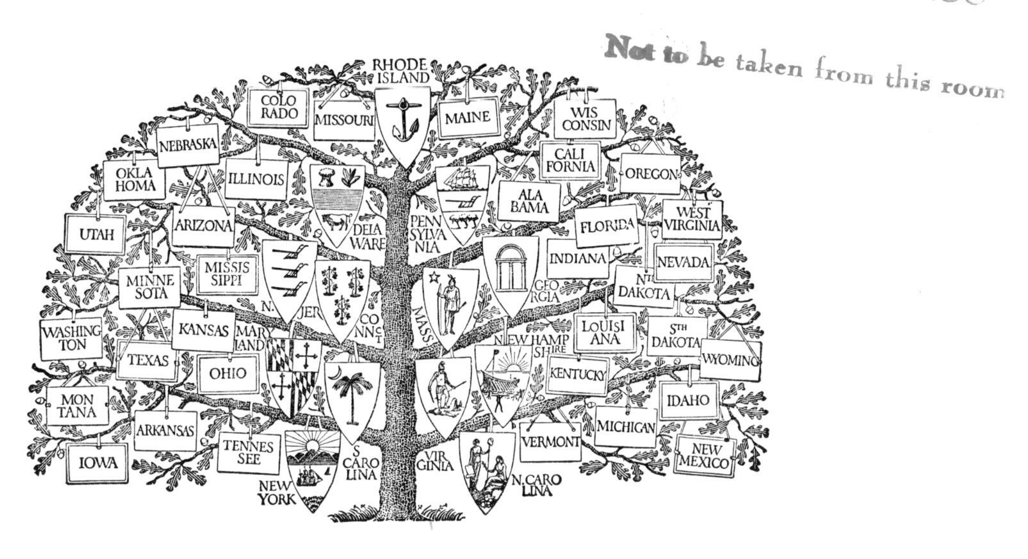

NEW YORK

UNITED STATES PUBLISHERS ASSOCIATION

TORONTO · GLASGOW, BROOK & CO.

1976

Printed in the United States of America

Library of Congress Catalog Card No. 29-22308

International Standard Book No. 0-911548-57-2

TABLE OF CONTENTS

THE AMERICAN FRONTIER

ONLY yesterday, as the geologist would reckon time, North America was in very truth "a lair of wild beasts." Then to this wilderness, through which no human voice had ever sounded, following a route which skirted the north Pacific, came men of the stone age. In course of time these people whose descendants were called Indians overran two empty continents. Theirs was the first American frontier. Only fragmentary records of this great human conquest remain — the evidence of graves and of long-forgotten village sites. Doubtless the chronicle of the sweep of this first frontier across America can never be written. Its triumphs and tragedies are lost in antiquity. But the retreat of the race which once claimed the continent is a matter of recorded history. These redskins who yielded sullenly to the white man were in many respects a gifted people. The Maya civilization which for above a thousand years cast its luster over Mexico and Central America was a brilliant intellectual achievement. The Pueblo and Mound Builder cultures within the area which was one day to be the United States were each accomplishments of a high order. But for the environmental handicap of a lack of domesticable animals in North America the race might have passed beyond the stone age and changed the history of the world. Its fate, however, was to bow to the superior power of the men of European origin.

In the fifteenth century, while the Mayas of Yucatan were slipping back into barbarism, the peoples of western Europe were embarking upon that marvelous age of expansion which carried their culture to the uttermost corners of the world. To the Americas, which Columbus stumbled upon just as the fifteenth century was drawing to a close, came in the decades that followed Spaniards, Frenchmen, Englishmen, Dutchmen, Portuguese, and many others. Before the white man had made the New World his own others of his race were overrunning Australia and New Zealand and were establishing a foothold in southern Africa. The story of the westward advance of the frontier within the area which is now the United States is but a phase of this broad movement, the struggle of the American Indians against the invaders but an episode in that conflict of the undeveloped peoples of the world to stay the advance of the conquering Caucasians.

In 1521 the potent and wide-flung Aztec empire, an afterglow of Mayan greatness, collapsed under the blows of the Spaniard, Cortez. In the West Indies, in Mexico, and in the country which stretched away to the south the Castilian found rich soil for great plantations, crude native mines for the acquisition of precious metals, and an Indian population to supply the needed labor. Lands, mines, and men were all exploited to make Spaniards rich and Spain great. Yet the subjects of Charles V and Philip II were not forgetful that the dark-skinned native of the New World possessed an immortal soul which might be saved to join the throng of the blessed in Paradise. Ruthless and cruel as were many of the white masters of New Spain, they did not expel the conquered race from its original habitat or seek to destroy it with fire and the sword. For them the Indian had value capable of being expressed in terms of economics, empire, and the glory of the Church.

Spain, moreover, sent relatively few men and fewer women to the New World. A mingling of racial blood resulted. Within the confines of that area where Montezuma had ruled, a stratified society emerged. White men were the masters, Indians the mudsills; and between the two a growing class of mixed-bloods developed. Beyond the borders of the old Aztec empire Spaniards pushed their frontier northward into Texas, New Mexico, and California. The policy of compromise with the Indian continued and an effort was made to tame the wild tribes into useful yet menial subjects of the Spanish king. A skirmish line of missionaries, shoulder to shoulder with whom marched small detachments of soldiers, comprised the edge of the northward advancing frontier of New Spain. Missions and the inevitable presidios marked the outposts of the Spanish culture area. In these stations the native was taught to worship and to work after the manner of the white man. Only in a few places did the Spaniard turn the New World into a white man's country. In much of that vast area which was once New Spain the mestizo of the twentieth century sits in the seat of the Castilian.

Seventeenth-century Spaniards watched with some uneasiness the rise of French power in the valley of the St. Lawrence and in the central lowland drained by the Mississippi system. Dreams of a mighty empire quickened the imagination of La Salle and of his king, Louis XIV. In spite of the grandiose visions of a handful the lure of New France enticed only a few thousand Frenchmen to the American wilderness. The Bourbon empire in the New World consisted of a vast expanse of primeval forest dotted here and there with forts and occasionally with tiny farming communities. The most important of the latter was the compact settlement of *seigneurs*, *habitants*, and merchants in the St. Lawrence Valley. Here was the heart of New France and here the peculiarities of the French phase of the expansion of European culture manifested themselves.

Larger than among the Spaniards was the proportion of French women who came to New France. The shores of the Bay of Fundy and the banks of the St. Lawrence were bordered by white communities from which the Indian, as a resident, was excluded. Yet the Frenchman was of all the European nations the most friendly to the strange race which peopled the New World. The tribes who dwelt in Canada or in the Mississippi Valley knew nothing of the empire of the Aztecs or the civilization of the Mayas. These northern peoples had achieved only a neolithic culture and the hunting stage of the arts. Without domestic animals they had been unable in their more rigorous northern environment to establish their food supply on the firm foundation of agriculture. Without the security and the leisure which spring from a surplus of food, advance to civilization had been impossible. The Frenchman displayed a genius for dealing with these untutored representatives of the stone age. French priests, the "black robes," threaded forest trails to villages in the heart of the continent seeking to bring the redskin into the Kingdom of God with the least possible change in his material life. If the black robes largely failed to make the light of the gospel penetrate the darkness of barbarism, they at least warmed the hearts of the Indians toward the French. This friendship between the races was strengthened and put on the sound basis of mutually profitable coöperation by the fur trader. The *courier de bois*, following the age-old traditions of successful traders, sought to adapt himself to the peculiarities of the people with whom he was doing business. He was not interested in changing the redskin's mode of life save in ways that would make for greater profits. The fur trade became the corner stone of the economic foundation of New France. The Spanish grandee turned the conquered native into a drudge and a serf; the *courier de bois* looked upon the forest hunter as a partner. The redskins should be encouraged to be hunters and trappers, exchanging their peltries for the goods of the white man. The French trader adopted the red man's garb and habitation, and married one or more dusky daughters of the wilderness. Though his success was great, the *courier de bois* never won the friendship of the Iroquois. To the end of the French régime the hostile Five Nations, who themselves had ambitions to control the trade of the tribes about the Great Lakes, menaced the flank of New France. In the agricultural and trading French community that centered in Quebec and Montreal the perpetual threat from beyond the Adirondacks brought about an adjustment unique in the annals of the white frontier in North America. The problems of the black robes with their converts helped also to shape this peculiar French adaptation to the conditions of the wilderness. The Iroquois whom the Jesuits had brought into the fold were driven into exile by their kinsmen and were settled on an island in the St. Lawrence near Montreal, where the Church could keep a watchful paternal eye upon them. The wretched remnants of the semi-Christianized Hurons, upon whom had fallen the murderous tomahawks of the Five Nations, were collected near Quebec. A protective fringe of converted Indians, therefore, helped to guard the heart of New France from enemies that lurked in the forest.

Between the French on the St. Lawrence and the Spaniards in Florida the English established in the seventeenth century their settlements. Unlike their white neighbors on the north and south the subjects of the Stuart kings came in relatively large numbers. They planted vigorous farming and fishing communities near the Atlantic shore. Like the French settlements in the valley of the St. Lawrence, Jamestown and Boston, Charlestown and Philadelphia were composed entirely of white inhabitants. Marriage across the race line such as that of Rolfe and Pocahontas was exceptional. English women came in large numbers with the men and aided in the firm establishment of white civilization on the eastern margin of the continent.

Both Spaniard and Frenchman had compromised for economic reasons with the native. The Englishman, though trade with the Indian was an important aspect of his life, founded his communities upon agriculture, fishing, and in course of time upon the sea trade. Indian labor, either as serf or hunter, was not an indispensable part of the economy of the English colonist. The English who migrated to the New World quickly learned to imitate the red man's adjustments to his forest environment. They also took over the cultivation of the maize plant. Having acquired, however, from the redskin whatever aspects of his culture were useful to them, they turned upon the native and began the task of expelling him from his original home. A few like John Eliot, Roger Williams, and William Penn looked upon the aborigines as potential friends rather than inevitable enemies. The mass of their fellow-colonists, however, regarded as axiomatic the proposition that the savage should make way for the advance of civilization. Rare indeed was the Englishman who, beholding in the primitive son of the forest his brother, considered himself his brother's keeper.

The race conflict which appeared almost from the inception of the English colonies helped to shape the official theory of the English with respect to their political relations to the native tribes. The French and Spaniards considered the redskins subjects of their respective kings; the English tended to look upon the tribes as independent nations. Tribal chieftains, like Powhatan, were sometimes referred to as "kings." The visit of Pocahontas to England caused a stir partly because she was regarded as an American princess. With the tribal sachems the English early found it expedient to enter into formal treaties. Some of these were mere arrangements of friendship; others had to do with land cessions. At first the English had considered the king the sole disposer of titles to that part of the New World claimed by England. One of the reasons for the banishment of Roger Williams from Massachusetts Bay Colony was his insistence that the company did not have a perfect title to its domain until the soil had been purchased from the Indians. By the middle of the eighteenth century, however, both colonists and the mother country had recognized the necessity of quieting the Indian title as a prelude to the advance of settlement.

The Government of the United States took as its own the British theory regarding the political relations between the races. The Indian tribes were considered independent yet subordinate nations, the members of which were governed by tribal law and custom. The only formal contact between the National Government and such tribes was by treaties negotiated by the President and ratified by the Senate. At the same time the government affirmed its complete sovereignty within its boundaries and also the right of eminent domain over the lands held by the Indians. The theory that the tribes were independent nations was, therefore, in effect a legal fiction. For the Indian the treaty was at best a vague concept. Private ownership in land was beyond the range of his experience and was an institution hard for him to grasp. Many times, when he sat down in solemn council with the representative of the United States, he had no clear idea of what he was bartering away. More than likely, moreover, the brave who was not present at the powwow would not feel obligated by the arrangements entered into by those present, so loose was the political organization of many of the tribes. The insatiable land hunger of the whites drove the more advanced tribes of the Old Southwest to threaten with the death penalty any tribesman who assisted in the further alienation of Indian lands. Such desperate measures, however, were of no avail against the advance of the white man.

On the border of settlement in the United States an intense hatred between the races came into being. Again and again fury and desperation drove the Indians to futile war. Two frontier types, the fur trader and the missionary, did not share in the active hostility to the redskin; but the farmers, chopping away the forest as they marched westward, were the deadly enemies of the red man. For the agricultural frontiersman the status of the redskin was somewhat below that of the negro slave. The latter had a definite value for society, but the interests of civilization would be furthered by the extermination of the former. The long-continued race conflict which, like a forest fire, burned its way westward across the continent produced some of the grossest abuses for which the American people and government have been responsible. The latter part of the nineteenth century, after the Indian had made his last stand and lost, witnessed the inevitable reaction. In communities far removed from the frontier sentimentalism created the conception of the noble savage with face turned in adoration toward the sun to take the place of the accepted picture of the skulking murderer of the wilderness whose reeking tomahawk fell with equal fury upon the fighting man and the defenseless babe. In the twentieth century, when the extremes of hatred and sentimentality have begun to pass, the Indian finds among his conquerors occasional wise and friendly councilors anxious to aid him in the difficult task of finding his place in the American commonwealth.

Race conflicts and adjustments, however, were not the only phases of frontier life. In the more than two centuries and a half in which the white man faced the wilderness within the area which is now the United States the fringe of settlement, like an advancing army, moved forward from position to position. The first frontier was the seventeenth-century chain of villages along the Atlantic Coast, in their day a portion of the periphery of the European culture area. By the middle of the eighteenth century the outpost cabins of the "back country" stood within the eastern shadow of the Appalachian Mountains. Progress across the coast plain and Piedmont plateau was slow, because the white population in the New World was as yet not large and also because transportation both across the ocean and within the continent was difficult. The last decades of the eighteenth century saw Americans in possession of a considerable area west of the Alleghenies — Kentucky, Tennessee, and a part of Ohio. The passing of the first third of the nineteenth century found in Missouri and Iowa the frontier established on the grasslands west of the Mississippi, with settlements dotting the Old Southwest and other settlements pushing northward against the forests of Wisconsin and Michigan. By the end of the first half of the century frontiersmen, crossing the Great Plains and the western mountains, were founding communities on the Pacific Coast. In the following forty years the mountains and the plains, an area of imperial extent, were occupied. The slow advance of the seventeenth and eighteenth centuries was transformed in the nineteenth to one of the most amazing population movements in modern history. Improvement of transportation and the development of the mechanic arts were fundamental causes for the acceleration.

From first to last earth hunger and the desire for profit were the two chief forces which caused men to detach themselves from civilized communities and to risk the uncertainties of the wilderness. There were other motives. Desire for greater religious freedom took the Pilgrims to Plymouth in the seventeenth century and the Mormons to Utah in the nineteenth. A belief that he could create an ideal social order which might become a model for all the world led Robert Owen to found New Harmony on the Indiana frontier. An interest in Indian culture and a compelling desire to pierce the mystery which lay behind the race was perhaps as important as the quest for gain in persuading James Adair in the eighteenth century to continue to live among his friends the Chickasaws, Creeks, and Cherokees. Desire to bring Christianity and civilization to the red man took Marcus Whitman in the nineteenth century to Oregon. Naturally many individuals who were unwilling to abide by the laws of civilized communities found in the wilderness an escape from retribution for criminal acts or from the burdens of social responsibility. Other individuals, shiftless and incompetent, gravitated to the low standard of living of the border and drifted aimlessly westward with the frontier. Thomas Lincoln was such a one. Finally many restless spirits found in the wild country with all its hardships and dangers a friendly environment where life offered the satisfactions they coveted. They lived vigorously, close to the heart of nature. The best of them carved out careers the romance of which has never ceased to stir the elemental emotions of the more domesticated Americans of city, town, and quiet farm. Usually the penalty for the escape from civilization was untimely death. The wilderness was no place for the maimed, the diseased, or the aged. Yet with full knowledge of the price at which their freedom was bought many of these worshipers of nature persisted recklessly, buoyantly to the end, living for the moment and letting the doubtful tomorrow care for itself.

Boone, who loved the freedom of the wilderness, had no conception of the freedom which civilization offers. The hunter-pioneer, who followed his calling for the love of it, could not comprehend the attitude of the best of the farmer-pioneers. The hunter saw only the hard, dull grind of tilling the soil and tending livestock. Vastly different were the emotions in the heart of Abram Garfield and of his wife, Eliza Ballou, both under twenty-one when they built their cabin in the Western Reserve. They sought the freedom born of economic independence. They coveted for themselves and for their children a greater share of that rich culture which man has created. They looked upon the frontier as a chance to get a start in life and viewed its hardships as temporary deprivations which would be compensated for by the richer years which would follow its passing. No barriers of social class confined their lives within narrow limits. For them the frontier was the door which opened upon opportunities unbounded. The hopes of Abram were destined to be blasted when disease struck him down while still in early manhood. His young wife carried on, reared the brood which had come to their cabin, and lived to share in the plaudits heaped upon her second son when he was elevated to the presidency of the United States.

Though many motives took Americans to the frontier the pioneers were all molded by certain common experiences. In the border zone on the edge of the wilderness the busy hum of civilized life was stilled. The market place, the college, and the seats of government were far away. Frontier life was isolated; the frontiersman enjoyed but the slightest contact with the thought-life of his race. Yet isolation did not of necessity bring mental stagnation. The mind of the pioneer was concentrated on the difficult task of adjusting himself to an untamed environment. The result was a certain mental alertness and an upstanding self-reliance. On the frontier the American people kept returning to an almost primitive struggle for existence where elemental virtues and the vices of the wilderness developed side by side. The artificialities of old communities disappeared in the lodge of the fur trader and the cabin of the pioneer farmer. During the century which elapsed between that time when the frontier lay in the eastern shadow of the Appalachian Mountains and when it finally disappeared, the people of the United States made great advances in the development of their civilization. Yet always on the frontier during this century social organization was being reduced to simple terms; American life was constantly starting afresh. Democracy and individualism were as inevitable on the edge of the wilderness as race conflict. Swiftly on every nineteenth-century frontier the crudities of the wilderness faded before the advance of civilization. Yet the frontier democrat carried the old attitudes with him as he took his place among the main body of the self-governing people of the nation. Democracy became a national characteristic, an ideal. Optimism, born of the swift progress which was forever obliterating frontier conditions, stimulated the nation to dreams of future greatness.

The frontier helped to make at least one American dream come true as the Government of the United States slowly changed its attitude toward the unoccupied land of the national domain. Hamilton, as a member of Washington's cabinet, seeking to establish the credit of an impoverished nation, looked to the western lands as a source of revenue. During the first half of the nineteenth century, however, the American people came to understand more and more clearly that growth of population would profit the nation more than revenues. In 1862, when the planter aristocracy of the South had embarked upon its struggle for independence, American democracy reached the acme of its development. The Homestead Act gave farms to all Americans who would take and improve them and to the nationals of other lands who announced their intention to become citizens of the republic. Never more truly was America a land of opportunity than during the years between 1862 and the passing of the frontier.

The summer of 1893 found the people of the United States commemorating in the World's Fair at Chicago the four hundredth anniversary of Columbus' epoch-making discovery. Not far from the fair grounds Indians, eighty-one years before, had wreaked a bloody vengeance upon the little garrison of Fort Dearborn. The exposition was America's notice to the world that a new age had dawned in the republic west of the Atlantic. In a quiet Chicago auditorium far from the blaring bands and gaping crowds of the Fair, Frederick J. Turner, in July 1893, addressed a small group of scholars. "What the Mediterranean Sea was to the Greeks, breaking the bond of custom, offering new experiences, calling out new institutions and activities, that, and more, the ever retreating frontier has been to the United States directly, and to the nations of Europe more remotely. And now, four centuries from the discovery of America, at the end of a hundred years of life under the Constitution, the frontier has gone, and with its going has closed the first period of American history."

Many phases of the march of the frontier across the continent lie within the provinces of other volumes in this series. Within the pages at hand an effort has been made to chronicle only the work of exploration which preceded the advance of civilization — the activities of the fur trader, the westward progress of the fringe of settlement, and the long, sad story of race conflict. Contact with civilization almost universally brought deterioration to the untamed children of the forest. Retrogression bred despair which, again and again, bore fruit in unavailing war. Thrice among the Indians despair brought forth new religions, those of Handsome Lake, the Prophet, and the Ghost Dancers. The narrative of the retreat of the red man has been coupled with that of the advance of the whites. Limits of space have prevented a discussion of the psychological and sociological aspects of the agricultural frontier behind the fringe of settlement.

Ralph H. Gabriel

CHAPTER I

IN THE SHADOW OF THE APPALACHIANS

A STRING of hamlets straggling along the Atlantic shore marked the seventeenth-century foothold of the English in the New World and the first white frontier within the region which was to become the United States. To the west of the pioneers stretched a vast and mysterious wilderness. In the middle of the seventeenth century, before the Carolinas or Pennsylvania had come into being, before New Amsterdam had been wrested from the Dutch, and while New England settlements still hugged the shore or clung to the navigable waterways, a Virginian turned his face to the West and sought to penetrate the wild country beyond the head of navigation of the rivers. As a result of an act of the House of Burgesses in 1646 Fort Henry at the falls of the Appomattox River, where Petersburg now stands, had passed into the possession of Abraham Wood. With it had gone "sixe hundred acres of land . . . with all houses and edifices belonging to the said Forte, with all boats and ammunition belonging to the said Forte, Provided that he the said Capt. Wood do maintayne and keep ten men constantly upon the said place for the terme of three years. . . ." Fort Henry was a post destined to become the most important that appeared on the fall line in Virginia, a frontier station and military and trading center. Across the river was situated the chief village of the Appomattox Indians, desirable neighbors who furnished Wood with messengers, hunters and guides.

Beyond this Appomattox town lay the rolling hills of the Piedmont covered with forests and grasslands and dotted with the habitations of the redskins. To the westward rose the rugged slopes of the Blue Ridge. When Wood assumed control at Fort Henry, this Blue Ridge country was scarcely known. Virginians dreamed that it might contain precious minerals and that the adventurer who crossed it might come ere long to the shores of the South Sea across which ships could sail to Asia. In August 1650, Wood with three other persons of importance, some servants, and an Appomattox guide drove their mounts through the gate of the stockade at Fort Henry and headed southwestward. In five days they had reached the falls of the Roanoke, where the Dan and Staunton unite to form that river. There they turned back to Fort Henry. They had passed through a pleasant country which they admired and had stopped at several Indian villages. But these people of the forest had looked upon the interlopers with distrust and an ill-concealed hostility. On the return trip the party slept on their arms and maintained a vigilant watch. The result of this exploring expedition into the interior was a little pamphlet, *The Discovery of New Brittaine*, by Edward Bland, a member of the party. It was published in London in 1651. The events of the expedition were recounted and the opportunities for settlement in a rich and promising land were laid before the Englishman of the day. As for Wood, he got a clearer view of the trading possibilities of the region and sent off to London orders for "Guns, Powder, Shot, Hatchets (which the Indians call Tomahawks), Kettles, red and blue planes, Duffields, Stroudwater blankets, and some Cutlary Wares, Brass Rings and other Trinkets." For Abraham Wood the wealth of the West was in furs.

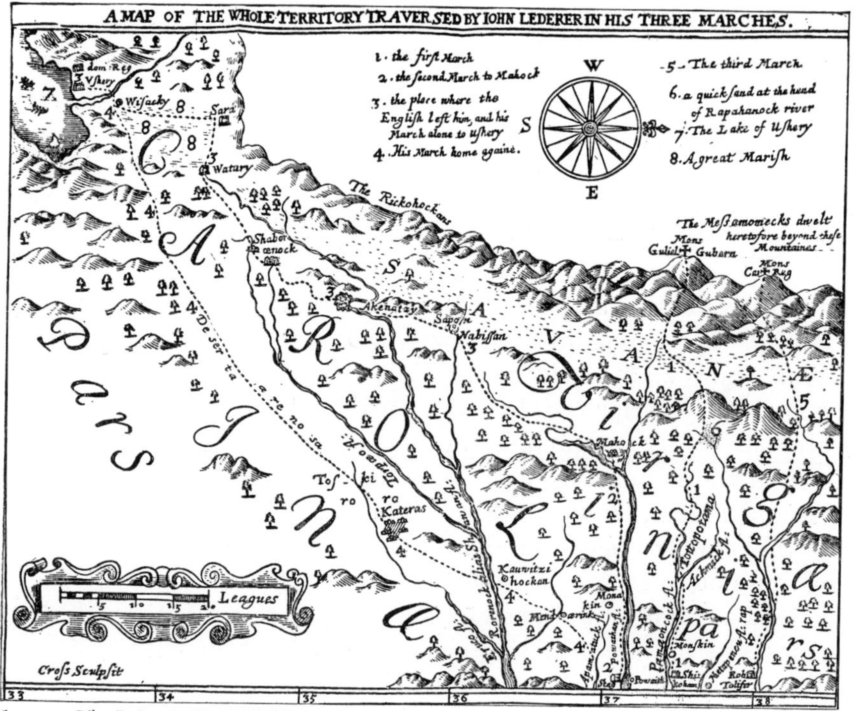

1 John Lederer's Map, 1669–70, from a facsimile of the original, in the Harvard College Library, Cambridge, Mass.

JOHN LEDERER

Abraham Wood, who as we have seen on page 7 owned Fort Henry, remained in control and waxed in importance. In 1669, twenty years after the journey into "New Brittaine," John Lederer, a German physician, joined the colony in Virginia. Lederer had a penchant for exploration in strange lands and Governor Berkeley had a great desire to learn more of the fabled wealth in the western country. The result was three expeditions led by the German doctor, the first in 1669 and the other two in the following year. While the Governor certainly sponsored the second expedition, his relation to the first and third is not clear. Thrice Lederer crossed the Piedmont and twice scrambled through the laurel up the steep eastern slope of the Blue Ridge. Looking to the west he saw beyond the valley the Shenandoah mountains. The first time he gazed over this expanse of wilderness spring was at hand; on his last trip he beheld the distant uplands transformed by the brilliant colors of autumn. When he returned from this final expedition, he left the colony in some haste and made his way to Maryland where he became friends with William Talbot, who turned Lederer's Latin notes into a book. One has but to turn the pages of this early writing to discover that the worthy doctor did not distinguish between fact and fancy. From the top of the Blue Ridge he had seen the Atlantic breaking on the Virginia shore, perhaps the honest illusion of a misty morning. On his second expedition he had skirted the eastern edge of the mountains until he had penetrated the back country of the Carolinas. From this remote region he brought back tales of silver tomahawks, Amazonian Indian women, peacocks, lakes "ten leagues broad," and barren sandy deserts. Lederer is the first white man whose ascent of the Blue Ridge is recorded. He found rugged uplands blocking his progress westward. On the first expedition his Indians had prostrated themselves before the mountain spirits; the white man paused before the mountain barrier. At the very time that Lederer was toiling painfully through the trackless undergrowth of the Virginia Piedmont, French adventurers from the valley of the St. Lawrence were making their way up the rivers that led into the continental interior. Traders and missionaries were beginning the task of winning an inland empire for France.

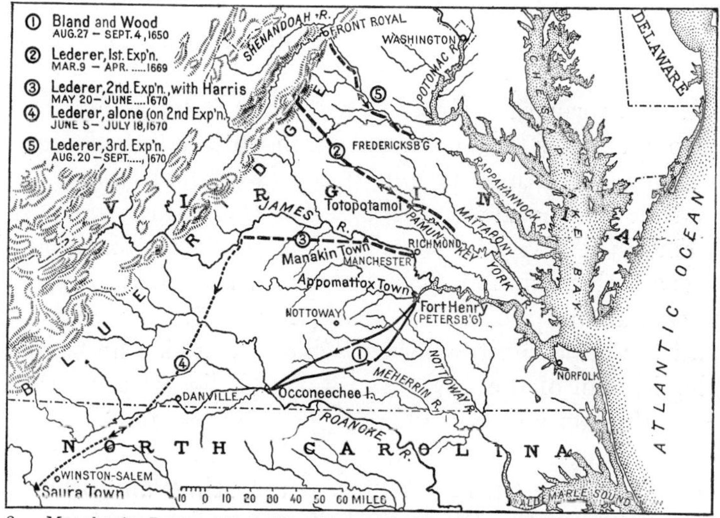

2 Map showing Routes of Early Expeditions to the Blue Ridge, drawn expressly for *The Pageant of America* by Gregor Noetzel, American Geographical Society, New York

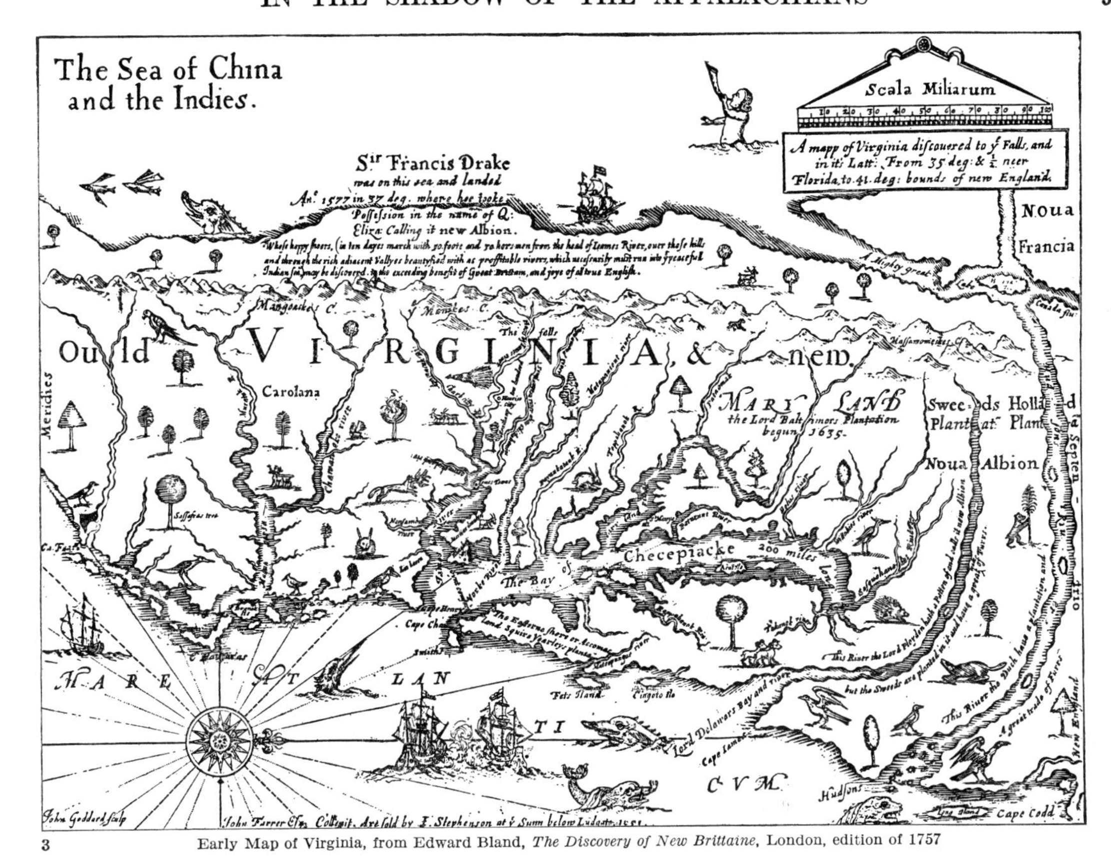

3 Early Map of Virginia, from Edward Bland, *The Discovery of New Brittaine*, London, edition of 1757

BATTS AND FALLAM

THE Indians of the Appomattox village across the river from Fort Henry were preparing for the autumn harvest when, on September 1, 1671, they saw a small mounted party leave the huts and turn their horses westward. In the group was one of their chieftains, Perecute, a man of courage and abiding loyalty. Captain Thomas Batts, Thomas Wood, and Robert Fallam were bound for the country beyond the Blue Ridge. The man who made the expedition possible and who listened with absorbed attention to the reports that came back was Abraham Wood of Fort Henry. Before the party reached the Blue Ridge Thomas Wood was left behind to die. The rest pushed on and twice crossed the Staunton River on September 8. They negotiated the Blue Ridge and built their camp at the foot of its western slope. The next day, after clambering over a small range to the west of the Blue Ridge, they came to a halt in the rich valley of the Roanoke. They were guests in a village of the Totero Indians. Here they remained two days, for Perecute was sick with fever and ague. Urged forward by the chief they resumed the trail and with a Totero guide crossed range after range that lay to the westward. On September 13, they passed the divide and came to a river flowing west. A little way to the west, according to the Bland map, they would reach the Pacific.

THE
DISCOVERY
OF
Nevv Brittaine.
Began August 27. Anno Dom. 1650.
By Edward Bland, Merchant, Abraham Woode, Captaine, Sackford Brewster, Elias Pennant, Gentlemen.
From Fort *Henry*, at the head of *Appamattuck* River in *Virginia*, to the Fals of *Blandina*, first River in *New Brittaine*, which runneth West; being 120. Mile South-west, between 35. & 37. degrees, (a pleasant Country,) of temperate Ayre, and fertile Soyle.
LONDON,
Printed by *Thomas Harper* for *John Stephenson*, at the Sun below Ludgate. M.DC.LI.

4 Title-page of Edward Bland, *The Discovery of New Brittaine*, London, 1651, from the original in the New York Historical Society

A Journal from Virginia beyond the Appallachian Mountains in Sept. 1671; Sent to the Royal Society by Mr. Clayton, & read Aug. 1. 1688. before the said Society.

Thomas Batts, Thomas Woods, & Robert Fallam having received a Commission from the honble Major General Wood for the finding out the ebbing & flowing of the Water on the other side of the Mountains, in order to the discovery of the South Sea, accompanied with Perecute, a great Man of the Apomatack Indians, & Jack Weason, formerly a servant to Major General Wood with five horses set forward from the Apomatacks town about eight of the clock in the morning, being Friday Sept. 1st 1671. That day we travelled about 40 miles, took up our quarters & found, that we had travell'd from the Okenechee path due West.

5 Facsimile of a page in *A Journal from Virginia Beyond the Appalachian Mountains in September, 1671*, from the original in the British Museum, London

ENGLISH IN THE OHIO COUNTRY

Four days more the adventurers toiled westward with provisions running low. They sent their Indians to range for food but these came back to report that the ground was so dry they could not approach the wary deer. At last they succeeded, but they were growing restive and wanted to return. So Batts and Fallam reluctantly brought their journey to an end. Under the date of September 17 Fallam wrote in his journal: "We found four trees exceeding fit for our purpose that had been half bared by our Indians, standing after one another. We first proclaimed the King in these words: 'Long live Charles the Second, by the grace of God King of England, Scotland, France, Ireland and Virginia and all the Territories thereunto belonging, Defender of the faith, etc.' firing some guns and went to the first tree which we marked thus with a pair of marking irons for his sacred majesty." The mark was the royal insignia. On another tree they put the initials of Governor Berkeley and on the third those of Abraham Wood. Their own, together with a P for Perecute who, despite his illness, was still with them, adorned the fourth. Theirs was the first recorded journey of Englishmen into the watershed of the Ohio, but only the day before they turned back they had found "two trees mark'd with a coal Mani. the other cut in with Ma and several other scratchments." They had conquered part but not all of the broad Appalachian barrier. The Virginians had no easy route like the St. Lawrence River up which they could paddle to the continental interior.

OPENING THE CHEROKEE TRADE

In April 1673 Wood sent a gentleman formerly of South Carolina, James Needham, and a clever but illiterate lad, Gabriel Arthur, into the fastnesses of the southern Appalachians where lived the powerful Cherokees. The travelers were prevented from even entering the mountains by the same treacherous and surly people who, twenty-three years before, had caused Wood himself to abandon his trip through "New Brittaine." Already Wood, through the Indians who lived in the Piedmont and who acted as middlemen, was trading with these distant redskins of the mountains. In May Needham and Arthur were off again and passed successfully the Occaneechi village which had caused their return the previous month. They crossed the towering Blue Ridge of North Carolina and reached in due course their objective, the habitations of the Cherokees. Clarence W. Alvord has described the scene. "The Cherokee village stood on a high bluff and was strongly fortified with a twelve-foot palisade and parapet on the landward sides. By the waterside were kept a hundred and fifty large war canoes, and in the magazines were large stores of dried fish. White men and horses had apparently never been seen in the town, so they were objects of respectful but intense curiosity. The one surviving horse was tied to a stake in the center of the town; and abundant food of whatever sort the Indians possessed, vegetable and animal, was offered it. The two white men and their Appomattox Indian — the single one of the eight who had been courageous enough to attempt the passage of the mountains — were placed on an elevated platform, that the multitude might see but not press upon them." — Alvord and Bidgood, *First Explorations of the Trans-Allegheny Region*, 82–83.

6 The country of the Cherokees in Western North Carolina, from a photograph in the United States National Museum, Washington

THE WANDERINGS OF GABRIEL ARTHUR

"Novel as were the English visitors, the Cherokees had long been acquainted with the Spaniards of Florida. They possessed, indeed, some sixty Spanish flintlock muskets, and other European implements, and must have traded with the Spaniards directly or through intermediaries for many years. This intercourse had recently ceased, because a party of Indians which had gone to Florida to trade had been half murdered, half enslaved. After a period of captivity two had succeeded in escaping and brought word to the tribe of their barbarous treatment. Since then the Cherokees had nursed a deadly enmity for the Spaniards, and on that account Needham had less difficulty in binding them in friendship to the English." —Alvord and Bidgood, 82–83. In the middle of September, having left Arthur in the Cherokee village, Needham was back at Fort Henry accompanied by a dozen of his new friends. With a Cherokee, he promptly set out to rejoin Arthur. In the shadow of the Blue Ridge he was killed by a treacherous Occaneechi brave who tore out his heart and, holding it aloft, bade defiance to the whole English nation. The lone Cherokee, who had been unable to prevent the tragedy, hurried with the news to his distant village. The chief of the Cherokees promised Arthur to escort him home in the spring and meanwhile, arming him in Indian fashion, sent him with several expeditions. Arthur was a member of a raiding party into West Florida against a Spanish mission and another against the Spaniards at Port Royal, South Carolina. Then the chief himself took Arthur to the friendly Mohetons, who lived on the banks of the Great Kanawha about a day's journey from where it flows into the Ohio. Returning from this visit, the Cherokees went out of their way to strike a blow at an old enemy, probably the Shawnees, living at the time on the Ohio. In this affray Arthur was wounded with two arrows and was captured. The Ohio Indians suspected that Arthur, because of his long hair, was no Cherokee. Scouring off the accumulated grime, they found his skin white. Gabriel promptly became a center of interest. The attentions bestowed upon him increased when he intimated by signs that he would return to the village to trade. His captors then set him on the way to the Cherokee country. Making the Cherokee camp in safety, Arthur journeyed in the following spring toward Fort Henry. With him were eighteen Cherokees laden with pelts for trading. The Occaneechi, particularly incensed at seeing their profits as middlemen disappearing with the opening of direct trade over the mountains, laid in wait for the party. But the white man eluded them and came home with his tale of adventure. He had penetrated farther than any of his countrymen into the Ohio country for the control of which England and France were to fight in less than a century a long and desperate war. Arthur is an example of the fur trader as explorer, a rôle which the trader frequently played in the advance of the frontier.

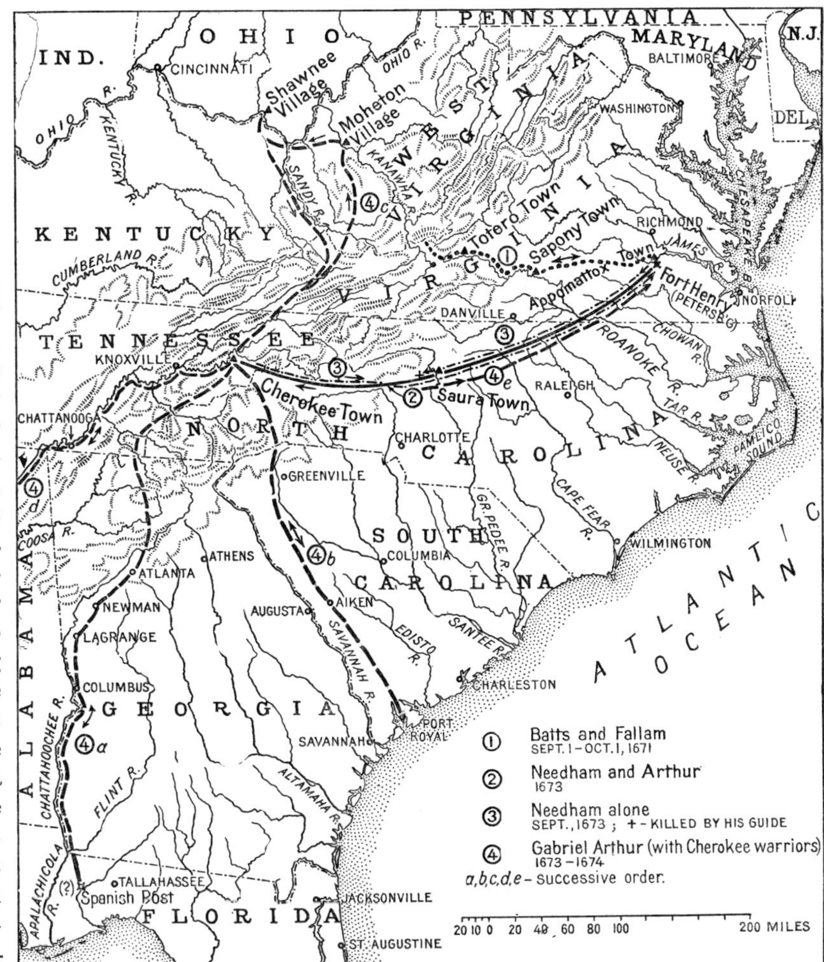

7 Map showing routes of early Appalachian explorers, drawn expressly for *The Pageant of America* by Gregor Noetzel, American Geographical Society, New York

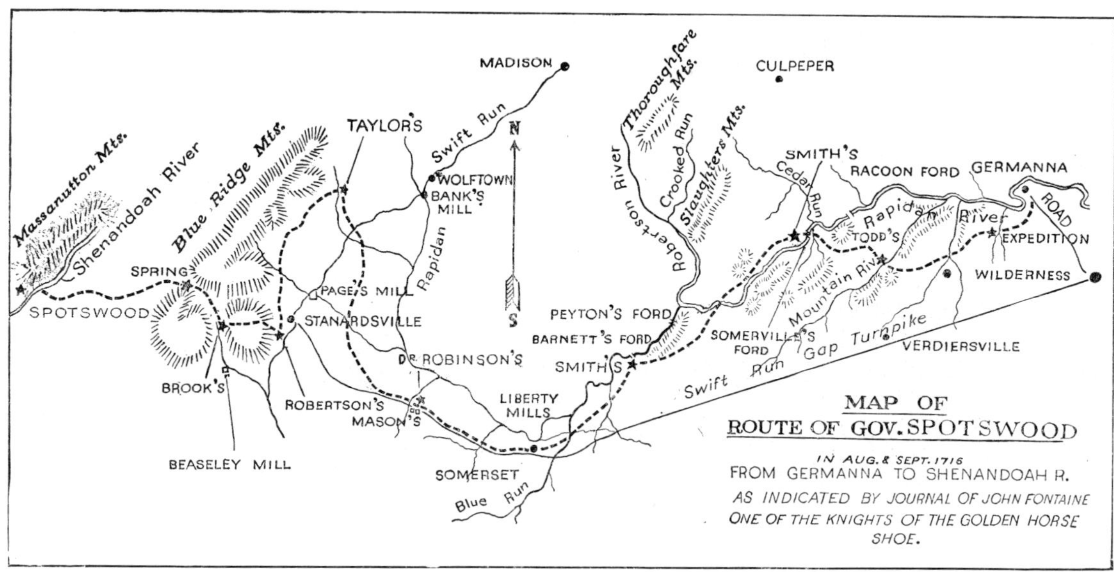

8 Redrawn from a map in Philip Slaughter, *A History of St. Mark's Parish*, 1877, from the original in the New York Public Library

GOVERNOR ALEXANDER SPOTSWOOD, 1676–1740

THE explorations sponsored by Abraham Wood had been primarily for purposes of trade. In the latter years of the seventeenth century Virginia's interest in them declined as the attention of the whole colony was then absorbed by Bacon's Rebellion (see Vol. VIII) and its aftermath. From time to time, however, rumors came across the mountains of the activities of the French and even the Spaniards. As a result Governor Spotswood in 1716 decided to make an official gesture to establish the English claim to the mountain region. With a band of Virginia gentlemen, servants and rangers he made his way to the Shenandoah valley. There "the Governor buried a bottle with a paper inclosed, on which he writ that he took possession of this place in the name and for King George the First of England. We had a good dinner, and after it we got the men together, and loaded all their arms, and we drank the King's health in Champagne, and fired a volley, the Princess's health in Burgundy, and fired a volley, and all the rest of the Royal Family in claret, and a volley."—A. MAURY, *Memoirs of a Huguenot Family*, 288–89. The Spotswood expedition did more than any previous event to turn the eyes of Englishmen to that region of forests and prairies beyond the mountains.

9 Governor Spotswood on the Blue Ridge, from an engraving after a drawing by William L. Shepherd, in W. A. Crafts, *Pioneers in the Settlement of America*, Boston, 1877

10 Governor Alexander Spotswood's Expedition over the Blue Ridge, Halting at a Mountain Stream, from an engraving in the possession of the publishers

11 Cherokee Burial Mound in East Tennessee, from a photograph, courtesy of The Museum of The American Indian, Heye Foundation, New York

12 Cherokee Method of Burial in East Tennessee, from a photograph, courtesy of The Museum of The American Indian, Heye Foundation, New York

ABORIGINAL MOUNTAINEERS

James Needham had made his way into the heart of the country of one of the greatest peoples of the eastern forests. The Cherokees were Indian mountaineers. In the dim past, they had migrated into the southern Appalachians from the north. Long before the advent of the whites they had separated, perhaps in the valley of the Ohio, from their kinsmen, the Iroquois of New York. Moving into the mountain country they had displaced an older and more primitive Algonquian people. Through many generations their culture had developed and undergone profound modifications. This is one theory to explain the fact that the graves and remains of the Cherokee country contain three culture levels denoting Indian occupation of the region for a great period of time. The oldest level is clearly not Cherokee; the second may or may not be. More in accordance with Cherokee tradition and with some of the evidence which the graves reveal is the theory that the "Second Culture" people, though similar to the Cherokees in many respects, were, in fact, a separate and distinct tribe. The Cherokees may have come in from the upper Ohio valley in comparatively recent times and found the people of the "Second Culture" in possession. These latter people may also have disappeared before the advent of the Cherokees, leaving the whole valley of the upper Tennessee depopulated except for a settlement of the Creeks. Whenever they came, the Cherokees made the region their own. When the whites found them, their territory covered more than fifty thousand square miles, almost half of which lay in eastern Tennessee, a small area in southwestern North Carolina and the remainder almost equally divided between Georgia and Alabama.

13 Typical Cherokee Country, Qualla Reservation, North Carolina, from a photograph in the DeLancey Gill Collection, United States National Museum, Washington

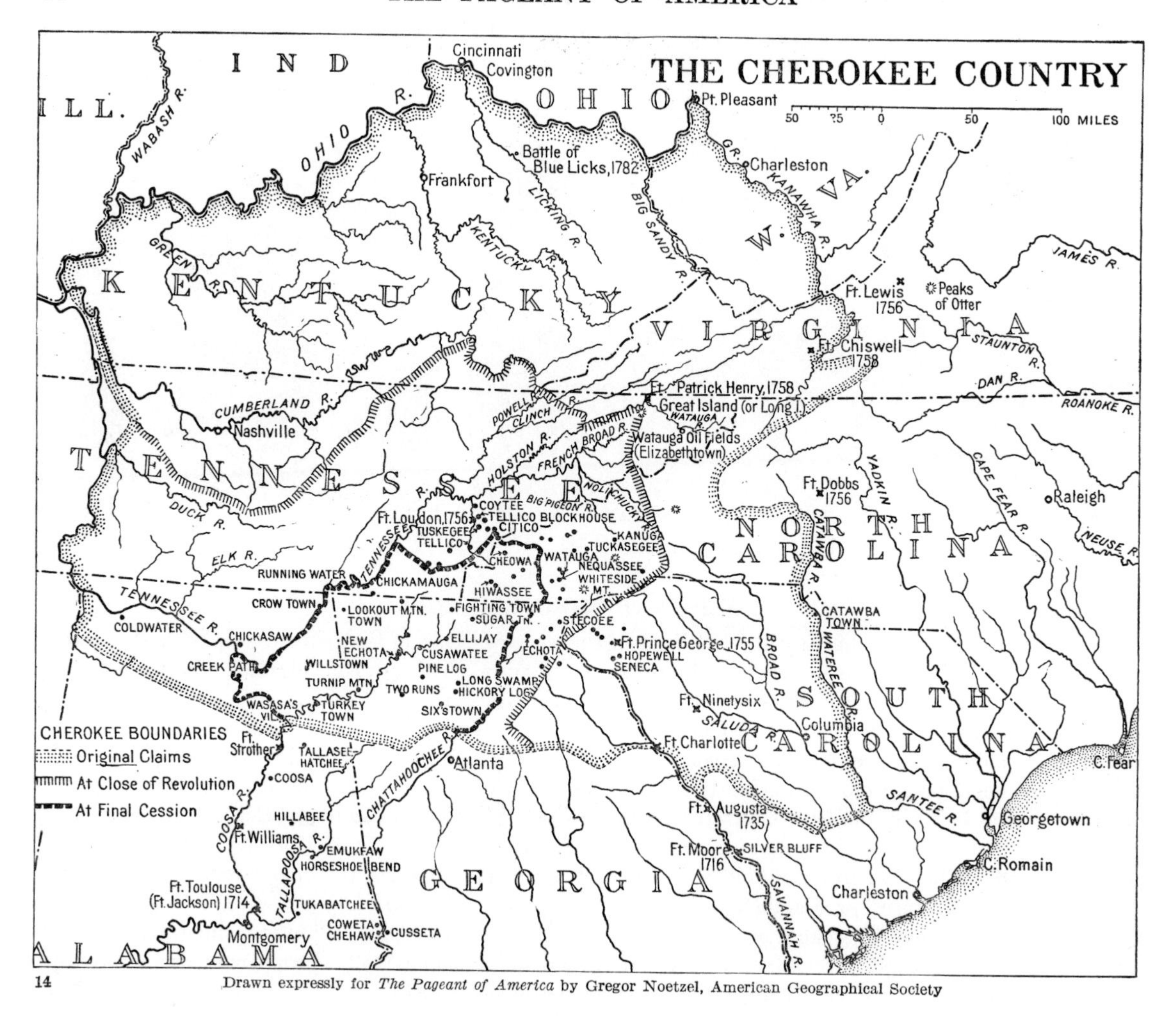

14 Drawn expressly for *The Pageant of America* by Gregor Noetzel, American Geographical Society

THE LAND OF THE CHEROKEE

AMID the majestic ranges of the Southern Appalachians lived this vigorous forest people. For most of their villages, the sun rose from behind the Great Smokies; some towns, however, lay to the east and south of the range. Long residence gave the Cherokees a barbaric attachment to the blue mountains that stretched away to the horizon in tumbled confusion, to the deep valleys where the night shadows gathered early, and perhaps most of all to the great Tennessee River stretching its lazy length across the northern part of their domain. The climate is favorable and invigorating; the winters are mild and an early spring covers the mountain slopes with blooms. Out of the Tennessee and its tributaries came fish, mussels, and turtles in abundance and the streams themselves furnished highways between the villages. The fertile bottom lands yielded abundant crops of corn while deer and other game in plenty lived in the forest. Cradled in such surroundings the legends and religion of the people became localized. The folk tales recounted in the evenings about the camp fires were associated with a familiar mountain peak, a prominent rock or tree, a well-known spring, a cave, or a river bend. Spirits dwelt in the mists of the mountains, in the unspoiled forests, and spoke through the twilight in the croak of a frog or the hoot of an owl. These were the tribal deities and the shades of the dead. The dead were precious to these Indians of the Appalachian valleys. The bones were laid to rest sometimes in round and sometimes in oblong graves in great mounds heaped up with infinite labor. These mounds were the sacred places of the Cherokee man, bonds that chained him to his mountain habitat. The grass-covered heaps of earth, moreover, were evidence of contact at some distant time with those shadowy, mysterious Indians, who left behind in the valleys of the Mississippi and the Ohio the remains from which the Mound Builder culture is being recovered. The Cherokee mounds are on the eastern periphery of the far-flung Mound Builder Culture.

THE GOVERNMENT OF THE TRIBES

In 1734 some sixty-four towns and villages were scattered throughout the Cherokee country populated with perhaps fifteen or sixteen thousand souls. Each village had its council house and its outlying fields of maize, beans, and squash, the common property of the community. The head man of the village, together with certain warriors distinguished for prowess, not only managed local affairs but represented the village in the General Council of the nation. A certain loose tribal unity was maintained by a principal chief and by certain general regulations binding all the members of the tribe. An English traveler at the end of the eighteenth century described this people as of larger stature and fairer complexion than their southern neighbors. "In their manner and disposition they are grave and steady; dignified and circumspect in their deportment; rather slow and reserved in their conversation, yet frank, cheerful, and humane; tenacious of the liberties and natural rights of man; secret, deliberate and determined in their councils; honest, just, and liberal, and ready always to sacrifice every pleasure and gratification, even their blood and life itself, to defend their territory and maintain their rights." — William Bartram, *Travels through North and South Carolina and Georgia*, 366.

15 Contemporary European Representation of a Cherokee, from an engraving, *Habit of Cunne Shote, a Cherokee Chief*, in Thomas Jefferys, *A Collection of the Dresses of the Different Nations*, London, 1757

THE TREATY OF DOVER, 1730

The trader first brought the Cherokees into contact with the whites. With the trader came knives, blankets, pots for cooking, guns for hunting, tawdry trinkets, and rum, the curse of the American aborigines. In 1721 a conference was held at Charleston between Cherokee chiefs and Governor Nicholson of South Carolina, one of the purposes being to hear at first hand the complaints of the Indians regarding the abuses of the traders. Nine years later North Carolina commissioned Sir Alexander Cummings to arrange a treaty of alliance with the tribe. After a preliminary conference he took seven of their head men to England. The caption of the portraits of these men reads as follows: "The above Indian Kings or Chiefs were brought over from Carolina by Sir Alexander Coming Bart. (being the Chiefs of the Cherokee Indians) to enter into Articles of Friendship and Commerce with his Majesty. As soon as they arrived they were conducted to Windsor, & were presented at the Installation of Prince William & the Ld. Chesterfield. The Pomp and Splendour of the Court, and ye Grandeur, not only of the Ceremony as well of the Place was what Struck them with infinite Surprize and Wonder. They were handsomely entertained at his Majesty's Charge, & Cloath'd with these habits out of ye Royal Wardrobe. When the Court left Windsor they were brought to Town and proper Lodgings & Attendance provided for them near Covent-Garden. They were entertain'd at all ye Publick Diversions of the Town, and carried to all Places of Note & Curiosity. They were remarkably strict in their Probity and Morality. Their Behaviour easy and courteous; and their Gratitude to his Majesty was often express'd in a publick Manner, for ye many Favours they receiv'd."

16 The Seven Cherokee Chiefs Carried to England in 1730, from an engraving by Basire, after a painting by Markham, in the Print Room, New York Public Library

17 Outacite, Chief of the Cherokees, 1723, from Samuel G. Drake, *Biography and History of the Indians of North America*, Boston, 1834

FRENCH INTRIGUE

"ON Monday September 7, 1730," continues the writer of the caption of the Cherokee portraits, "Articles of Friendship and Commerce were accordingly propos'd to them by ye Lds. Commissioners for Trade and Plantations, wch, were agreed on Two Days after . . . KETAGUSTA after a Short Speech, in Compliment to his Majesty, Concluded by laying down his Feathers upon ye Table & said; This is our way of Talking, wch is ye same Thing to us, as yr Letters in ye Book are to you; and to you, BELOVED MEN, we deliver these Feathers in Confirmation of all that we have said." They pledged themselves to trade with no nation but England and to allow none but Englishmen to build forts or cabins, or plant corn among them. In return for these concessions the chiefs carried home a generous supply of paint, a few pounds of beads and some other trinkets. Before some of them passed to the Happy Hunting Ground they perceived in the American subjects of this great King whom they had visited their bitter and implacable enemies. Six years after the return of the Cherokee chieftains from England, the French countered effectively. In 1736 they sent one Priber, "a gentleman of curious and speculative temper," to seduce the Cherokees from the British to the French interest. Making his way to Great Tellico, the principal town of the Cherokees, he changed his European garb for Indian clothing. "More effectually to answer the design of his commission, he ate, drank, slept, danced, dressed, and painted himself, with the Indians, so that it was not easy to distinguish him from the natives, — he married also with them, . . . soon learned their dialect, and by gradual advances, impressed them with a very ill opinion of the English . . . he at the same time, inflated the artless savages, with a prodigious high opinion of their own importance in the American scale of power. . . . Having thus infected them by his smoothe deluding art, he easily formed them into a nominal republican government — crowned their old Archi-magus, emperor, after a pleasing new savage form, and invented a variety of high-sounding titles for all the members of his imperial majesty's red court, and the great officers of state." — JAMES ADAIR, *The History of the North American Indians*, 1775, 240.

18 Trading with the Indians, from Bacqueville de la Potherie, *Histoire de l'Amérique Septentrionale*, Paris, 1722

THE TRADER

19 Rival Traders Racing to the Indian Camp, from an engraving after a painting by Frederic Remington, in the New York Public Library

BEFORE the end of the seventeenth century English traders had established themselves among the Cherokees. But the English were not alone. The Spaniards ruled in Florida and the French, holding the mouth of the Mississippi, extended their sphere of influence throughout the whole length of its valley and, through the region of the Great Lakes, to the country of the St. Lawrence. Rival white men came to Indian villages seeking profits. They brought with them the material objects of their civilization. Through these and the men who sold them the southern Indians gained their first contacts with the white man's culture. Nor did all the traders visit the Cherokees alone. East of the mountains in South Carolina dwelt the Yamasees, some three thousand warriors strong, their chief villages only sixty to eighty miles distant from the Spanish town of St. Augustine. West and south of the highlands in what is now Alabama and Georgia lived the Creeks, their scattered villages containing perhaps four thousand braves. Along the southern Mississippi were the habitations of the Choctaws. North of them in the region of the present western Tennessee lived the Chickasaws, the greatest fighters of any nation south of the Iroquois. In the eighteenth century this people followed their "best-beloved" trader, James Adair. "As the Chickkasah fought the French and their red allies, with the utmost firmness, in defense of their liberties and lands, to the very last . . . ," wrote Adair, "equity and gratitude ought to induce us to be kind to our steady old friends . . . I hope no future misconduct will alienate their affections. . . ." —*History*, 358. Adair was an educated and cultured Scotchman with a flare for writing, who found profit, adventure, and intellectual stimulus in the wilderness.

THE
HISTORY
OF THE
AMERICAN INDIANS;
PARTICULARLY
Thofe NATIONS adjoining to the MISSISIPPI, EAST AND WEST FLORIDA, GEORGIA, SOUTH AND NORTH CAROLINA, AND VIRGINIA:
CONTAINING
An ACCOUNT of their ORIGIN, LANGUAGE, MANNERS, RELIGIOUS and CIVIL CUSTOMS, LAWS, FORM of GOVERNMENT, PUNISHMENTS, CONDUCT in WAR and DOMESTIC LIFE, their HABITS, DIET, AGRICULTURE, MANUFACTURES, DISEASES and METHOD of CURE, and other Particulars, fufficient to render it
A
COMPLETE INDIAN SYSTEM.
WITH
OBSERVATIONS on former HISTORIANS, the Conduct of our Colony GOVERNORS, SUPERINTENDENTS, MISSIONARIES, &c.
ALSO
AN APPENDIX,
CONTAINING
A Defcription of the FLORIDAS, and the MISSISIPPI LANDS, with their PRODUCTIONS—The Benefits of colonifing GEORGIANA, and civilizing the INDIANS—And the way to make all the Colonies more valuable to the Mother Country.
With a new MAP of the Country referred to in the Hiftory.
By JAMES ADAIR, Efquire,
A TRADER with the INDIANS, and Refident in their Country for Forty Years.
LONDON:
Printed for EDWARD and CHARLES DILLY, in the Poultry.
MDCCLXXV.

20 Title-page of the original in the Yale Library

THE MESSENGER OF PEACE

ADAIR firmly believed that "a proper number of prudent honest traders dispersed among the savages would be better than all the soldiers, which the colonies support for their defence against them. The Indians are to be persuaded by friendly language; but nothing will terrify them to submit to what opposes their general idea of liberty. . . . When an Indian and trader contract friendship, they exchange the clothes then upon them, and afterwards they cherish it by mutual presents, and in general will maintain it to the death." —*History*, 371. Unfortunately Adair's few and honest traders were soon replaced by a conscienceless rabble. Moreover, successful traders were, at times, harassed by covetous colonial governors, until the agents of the latter more than once "hardly escaped from being tomahawked and cut to pieces on the spot by the enraged Indians, for the violence offered to their friendly traders." The child of the forest was bewildered by the white man's ways and by the enmities of traders speaking different tongues. Frequently the untutored savage became the victim of cunning and designing men.

21 A French Trader, from a sketch by Frederic Remington in *Harper's New Monthly Magazine*, February 1892

THE LESS DESIRABLE TRADER

"FORMERLY," wrote Adair, "each trader had a license for two towns, or villages; but according to the present unwise plan, two, and even three Arab-like pedlars skulk about in one of those villages. Several of them frequently emigrate into the woods with spirituous liquors, and cheating trifles, after the Indian hunting camps, in the winter season, to the great injury of a regular trader, who supplies them with all the conveniences of hunting: for, as they will sell even their wearing shirt for inebriating liquors, they must be supplied anew in the fall by the trader. At my first setting out among them, a number of traders who lived contiguous to each other, joined through our various nations in different companies, and were generally men of worth: of course they would have a living price for their goods which they carried on horse back to the remote Indian countries, at very great expences. These set an honest copy for the imitation of the natives. . . . As the trade was in this wise manner kept up to its just standard, the savages were industrious and frugal. But lowering it through a mistaken notion of regaining their affections, we made ourselves too cheap to them, and they despised us for it. . . . A mean and submissive temper can never manage our Indian affairs." — ADAIR, 367. The evils of the fur trade could only be cured by government regulation, then impossible.

THE TRADER'S INDIAN TRAITS

THE trader and, at times, the missionary composed the outer fringe of the frontier. Among the English as among the French in the St. Lawrence, young men plunged into the wilderness and spent their lives in facilitating the exchange of goods between cultures far apart. Occasionally a trader would be a man of superior intelligence. James Adair, scholar, who could use his Latin, Greek, and Hebrew, was unique. More often the men who cast their lot with the Indians were virile but ignorant and illiterate sons of the border. The "Indianization" of these latter men is one of the striking aspects of the intercourse between the races. Adair has left an account of his contact with one of these whom once he found in the forest "naked, except his Indian breeches and maccaseens [moccasins]." "On a Christmas day, at the trading house of that harmless, brave, but unfortunate man, I took the foot of a guinea-deer out of his shot-pouch — and another from my own partner, which they had very safely sewed in the corner of each of their otter-skin-pouches, to enable them, according to the Indian creed, to kill deer, bear, buffaloe, beaver, and other wild beasts, in plenty — but they were so infatuated with the Indian superstitious belief of the power of that charm, that all endeavours of reconciling them to reason were ineffectual: I therefore returned them, for as they were Nimrods, or hunters of men, as well as of wild beasts, I imagined, I should be answerable to myself for every accident that might befall them, by depriving them of what they depended upon as their chief good, in that wild sphere of life." — ADAIR, 239.

22 Typical Eighteenth-Century Frontiersman, from a statuette by Dwight Franklin (1888–), in the possession of the artist

THE BACK COUNTRY

23 Typical Piedmont Terrain, Pulaski, Virginia, from a photograph, courtesy of the Virginia State Chamber of Commerce

BETWEEN the mountain country of the Cherokees and the broad plantations laid out beside the sluggish rivers of the coast plain in the Carolinas and Virginia lies the rolling Piedmont, its hills the remnants of an ancient mountain range. Here where the soil is rich and the climate friendly appeared the first American frontier of the southern colonies. There were northward extensions of this in Pennsylvania, New York, and New England. In the seventeenth century, to be sure, a frontier had been established on the very shore of the Atlantic with Jamestown, Plymouth, and Boston as famous frontier towns. But those scattered settlements within sight of the sea were outposts of Europe. Out of them came the thirteen continental colonies of Britain, communities marked by great differences in the character of their people, in their economic foundations, and in social customs and religion. In the eighteenth century immigrants began coming to these seaboard colonies, in particular Germans and Scotch-Irish. The older inhabitants hurried the newcomers through their settled communities and established them on the edge of the wilderness — in New York in the Mohawk Valley, in Pennsylvania on lands to the west of Philadelphia. The immigrants kept coming, and on the frontier sons and daughters of the earlier English settlers joined them. In Pennsylvania westward expansion quickly found the mountains a barrier to further progress. Then the Germans and Scotch-Irish who had come in such large numbers into that province began to move southward. They went into the Shenandoah Valley and also took up farms to the east of it where Lederer had explored a hundred years before. They went on to North Carolina to found Mecklenburg county and to South Carolina where from their cabin doors they could watch the sun set behind the mountains of the Cherokees. In all these southern colonies the Germans and Scotch-Irish found English pioneers from the seaboard. So in the back country of the eighteenth century appeared a race which was the result of the fusion of blood of north European stocks. The creation of the "old American" had begun.

THE BORDERERS

IN this back country, many days' journey from the coast towns, appeared the first truly American type, the backwoodsman, known in his own day as a "borderer." In the eastern foothills of the Appalachians from Georgia northward he built his rude cabins and cleared a few small fields. His house was a single room of logs with an attic above, where the older children climbed at night to sleep. A broad-mouthed fireplace served for cooking and for heat. The floor was of dirt and the furniture the product of the borderer's ingenuity and skill with axe and knife. In the fields outside grew a crop of corn and some garden vegetables. A few scrawny sheep and cattle foraged where they could. A dog was usually within sight of his master, searching on his own for rabbits, woodchucks, or field mice. The first borderers to come into a region were, perforce, hunters who lived, like the Indians, on the game of the forest and cleared small patches of land for garden crops. Many of these hunter-pioneers could not brook the restraints of even a rude civilization and moved on into the wilderness when the farmer-pioneer appeared. The back country east of the mountains had by the middle of the eighteenth century been dotted by the habitations of this latter class. But their farms were small and badly tilled. The markets were far away and could only be reached with a few products. The pioneer was still dependent upon his rifle to supply his larder and to provide raiment.

24 The Buckskin Man, from a statuette by Dwight Franklin, courtesy of the artist

25 A Backwoodsman, from a sketch by Frederic Remington, in the Frederic Remington Scrap Book, New York Public Library

THE DRESS OF THE BACKWOODSMAN

In his dress as in his whole life the backwoodsman made a compromise between the culture of the whites to the east of him and the Indians to the west. A long hunting shirt of coarse cloth or of dressed deerskins together with pants and leggings of like material were his principal garments. The red man's barbarian love of display found its counterpart in the fringes and occasional ornamented collars of his clothing. On his feet he wore the Indian's moccasins of soft and pliant deerskin. In them he could pass noiselessly through the forest, but they were cold in winter even when stuffed with deer's hair or dry leaves, and the leather was so porous as to afford little protection against wet feet in foul weather. The hunter was wont to be an early victim to rheumatism. To the belt which encircled his waist he hung his powderhorn, bullet-pouch, scalping knife, and tomahawk. The breast of his hunting shirt served as a pouch for carrying food. His favorite head covering was a coonskin cap with a bushy tail dangling behind. So clad and equipped the borderer was a picturesque figure. His womenfolk, as was again the case among the Indians, were not so gaily attired. Their headgear was a huge sunbonnet in summer and a scarf in winter. Their loose gowns were of home-made cloth. When the weather was warm, they went barefoot and in the winter wore moccasins like their husbands. Life was crude and sometimes cruelly hard for both men and women. When disease came, there was little to fall back upon but a constitution toughened by a rough life out-of-doors.

THE EIGHTEENTH-CENTURY FRONTIER

For a generation the frontier paused in the eighteenth century in the eastern shadow of the mountains. As a consequence the backwoods made an unusually deep impress on the character of the borderers. Cut off largely from life-giving contact with the markets and the thought-life of the world the folk of the eighteenth-century frontier were thrown back upon themselves. They developed courage and resourcefulness. They amused themselves by telling stories and by singing old songs, some of which had been brought by immigrants across the Atlantic. Books were rare. Children were brought up with little or no schooling except that the boys learned to hunt and to cultivate the fields and the girls acquired the skill necessary for the varied household tasks. Within his narrow intellectual horizon the borderer developed the sharp wits of a man of action. He was a laborer; the antithesis of the modern workman who is chained to the deadening routine of the automatic machine.

26 Frontiersmen Viewing Kentucky, from a sculpture group by Dwight Franklin, courtesy of the artist

RELIGION AND THE BACKWOODS

27 A Frontier Religious Service, from The Chronicles of America Photoplay, *The Frontier Woman*

The borderer knew little or nothing of organized religion. In his faith European superstitions mingled with those of his Indian neighbors. He believed in omens, magic, witches and in the significance of bad dreams. Like the redskins he found evil portents in eclipses of the sun, the howling of dogs, or the croaking of ravens. He recognized the inadequacy of his own strength to deal with the mighty forces of nature which for him were embodied in the encircling forest. His kin had brought with them to the back country a belief in the Christian God. To Him they turned instinctively and without professional ministration, as the Cherokees turned to Yo He Wah, when the aspect of Nature became overwhelming. In the hearts of both was a childlike faith — "He will give his angels charge over thee, lest at any time thou dash thy foot against a stone." But this was the faith of emergencies. Religion languished on the frontier and deteriorated in the struggle of everyday life. When the circuit rider or the minister came and a revival of spiritual life occurred, the religion of the backwoods became a primitive mysticism. Terrifying manifestations of the immanence of the Deity occurred in the religious upheaval called the Great Awakening near the middle of the eighteenth century. Men and women swooned before the Mercy Seat. The frontiersman heard the voice of God speaking to him, saw Him in the clouds, and felt the quickening touch of His Holy Spirit. He was not a far way off, but near at hand to aid and to chastise. In like manner from the surrounding forest the Indian heard the voices of the spirits whom he worshiped.

SOCIAL CUSTOMS

For long periods there was "neither law nor gospel" in many backwoods areas. Justices of the peace had small authority. Nevertheless the folkways which governed this rude and isolated people were ways which made for clean and honorable living. The borderers respected and honored candor, honesty, hospitality, regular habits, and good behavior generally. They often visited harsh punishments on offenders. If a man proved himself a coward in time of war, if he shirked his full measure of duty to a community in which every man must at times coöperate with his fellows for the public good, if he failed to care for his womenfolk and children, if he was careless about debts or stole from his neighbors, if he failed to treat women respectfully, he was a marked man, shunned by his fellows or forced to leave the settlement. For the borderer life was full of danger and privation. He stood midway between civilization and barbarism. He was the vanguard of the white man's relentless assault upon the Indian and the wilderness.

28 A Frontier Homestead, from a sculpture group by Dwight Franklin, courtesy of the artist

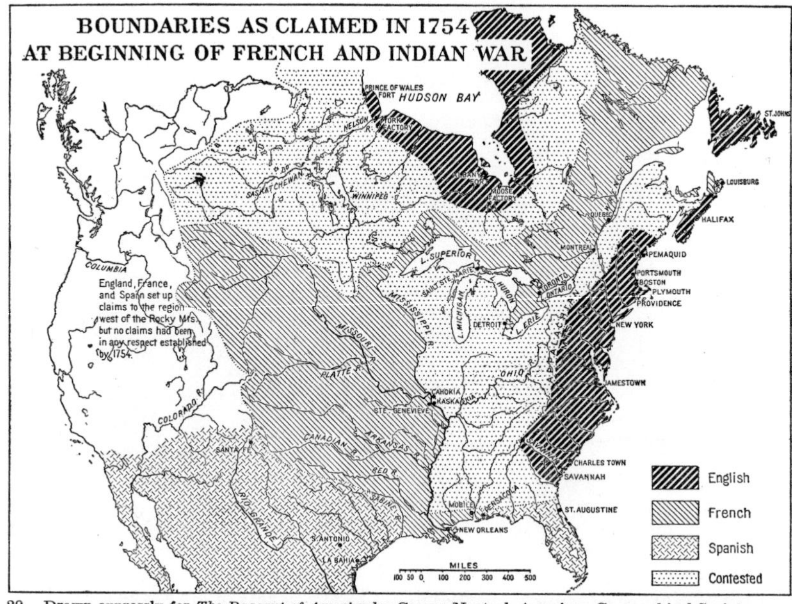

29 Drawn expressly for *The Pageant of America* by Gregor Noetzel, American Geographical Society, New York

THE FRENCH AND INDIAN WAR

To the borderers along the whole frontier came the news in the year 1754 of war with the French and of the defeat of a British army under General Braddock in the western forest near the forks of the Ohio. (See Vol. VI.) Before many weeks had passed the back country of Pennsylvania and Virginia felt the terrible aftermath of this defeat. "Ever since the tragical events of last July, on the banks of the Monongahela," wrote a contemporary, "our frontiers have been ravaged and dispeopled, great quantities of the stock of the back inhabitants driven off by the French and their Indians to Duquesne. Fire, sword, and perpetual alarms have surrounded them, persons of every age and sex have fallen a prey to the barbarians, and, in short, the most shocking outrages perpetrated on the western settlements of this colony, and our two next neighbors to the northward. By these means, our frontiers have been contracted in many places one hundred and fifty miles, and still are drawing nearer and nearer to the centre." — MAURY, *Memoirs of a Huguenot Family*, 403. The war for the control of a continent was on. The borderers who with axe and hoe and gun were struggling to make more secure a precarious foothold on the edge of the forest suddenly found a cataclysm upon them. The forest which had heard so often the crack of the hunter's rifle now saw the painted redskin creeping stealthily upon the lonely cabin. When the men of the region hurried in, too late, they found the scalped body of their neighbor stripped of everything that the Indian could use. Perhaps not far away lay the remains of his wife and children; but more likely these could not be found. Then the news passed from cabin to cabin that "John Bryan's woman and kids" had been carried off by the savages and were even then captives in Indian villages far in the forest. War, as well as trade, caused the mingling of racial blood.

THE OUTBREAK OF THE CHEROKEE WAR

THE French and Indian War made clear to the English colonies the progress of the French in winning the friendship of the Indians beyond the mountains. French influence again made its appearance among the southern Indians. From Virginia southward colonists began to cast anxious eyes toward those blue mountains from whose valleys rose the smoke of the Cherokee villages. Year after year, after the famous embassy to England, the Cherokees who lived to the east of the mountains had felt the pressure of the whites grow stronger. The year following Braddock's defeat they bargained away land to South Carolina for the building of a fort. In 1756 a chain of frontier fortifications was erected to guard the southern colonies against the mountain Indians: Fort Prince George on the upper waters of the Savannah, Fort Monroe one hundred and seventy miles farther down, and most important of all Fort Loudon in the heart of the mountains where the Tellico joins the Tennessee and not far from the Cherokee town of Great Tellico. (See No. 14.)

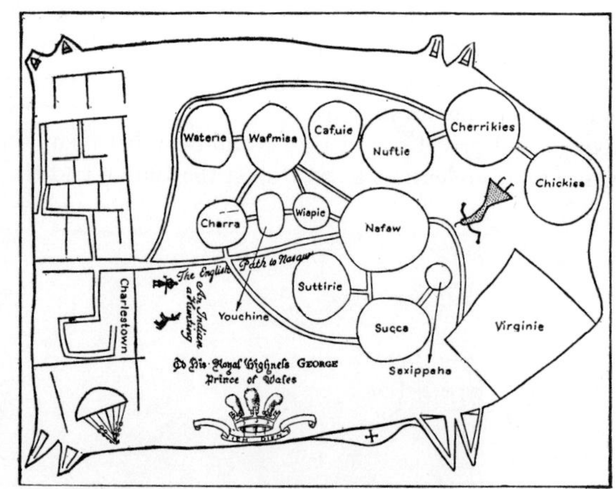

30 Cherokee Map of South Carolina drawn on deerskin, from the original in the British Museum, London

LITTLE CARPENTER

The treaties which made possible the building of the forts led to trouble, for the English claimed vastly more land than they had bargained for. Still the Cherokees remained at peace but the name Little Carpenter was heard again and again along the southern border. This was the designation which the English gave one of the seven Cherokees who as a young man had gone to England to be received by the King. Little Carpenter had felt the influence of the French and had seen the advantage to his people of balancing them against the English. Shrewdly divining the strength of the latter, however, he had chosen to remain friendly with them. In 1759 parties of Cherokees went northward to aid General Forbes in his toilsome advance against Fort Duquesne. The Indians were not well treated and slipped away into the forest. Making their way southward, they passed through the back country of Virginia. Here quarrels arose and German settlers murdered forty of the redskins. "The lying over the dead, and the wailing of the women in their various towns, and tribes, at the dawn of day and in the dusk of the evening, proved . . . a strong provocative to them to retaliate blood for blood." — Adair, 246. The young men of the Cherokees got out of hand and their raiding parties left a trail of blood and ashes across the North Carolina border.

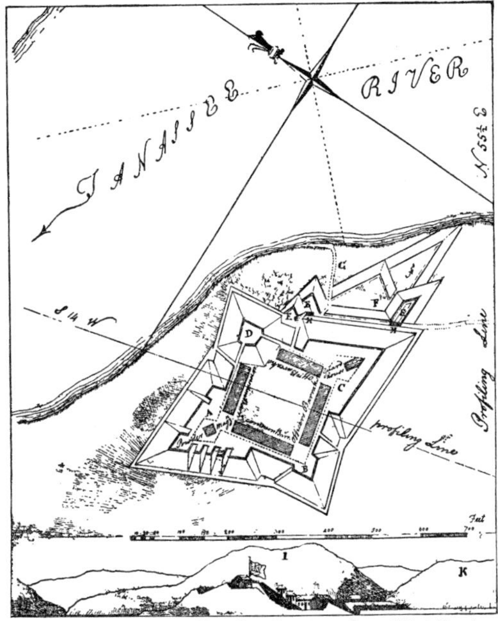

31 English Fort in the Cherokee Country, plan of Fort Loudon, from the manuscript of J. G. W. De Brahm, *History of the Three Provinces, South Carolina, Georgia, and East Florida*, in the Harvard College Library, Cambridge, Mass.

THE CHEROKEE DEFEAT

In the spring of 1760 war flamed up along the frontier. The Cherokees were defying the English. There were victories on both sides. In April Colonel Monckton with twelve hundred men sent from the regular British forces in New York marched into the southern part of the Cherokee country. He caught the Indians short of ammunition. Practically unopposed he destroyed the villages and crops east of the mountains, and returned to New York as quickly as he had come. His departure sealed the fate of Fort Loudon where Captain Demere and a small garrison were undergoing a siege. Before the Virginia militia, who had been called out for the purpose, could come to its relief, the fort surrendered. All but one of its defenders were put to death. Such was the Cherokees' revenge for the wanton murder of twenty of their people who had been left as hostages with the English at Fort Prince George the year before. The next year another regular British force under Colonel Grant together with a regiment of South Carolina militia ravaged the middle Cherokee country till all its towns were smoking ruins and its inhabitants slain or driven across the mountains. Then Little Carpenter sued for peace. Sadly he journeyed to Charleston, where Governor Bull met him in a kindly spirit. After mutual friendship had been pledged, the Cherokee chieftain returned to help his people to recover from their wounds.

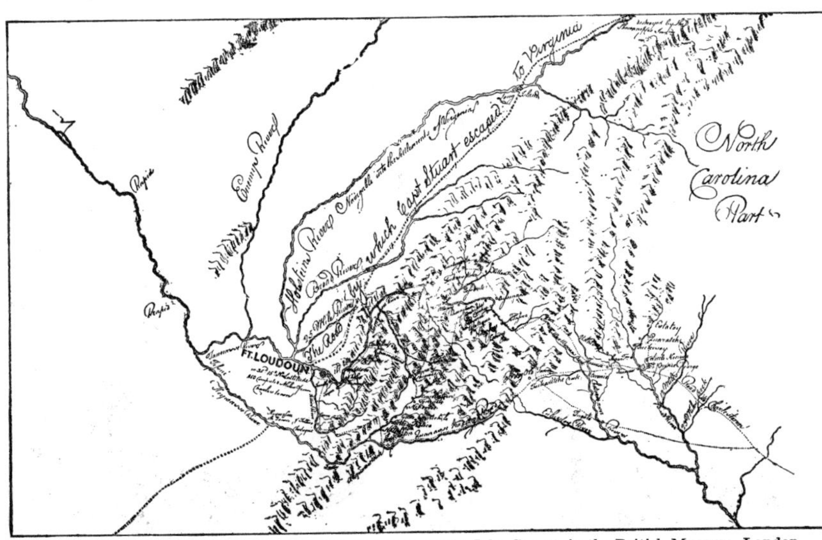

32 Detail from *A Map of the Cherokee Country*, by Captain John Stuart, in the British Museum, London

33 The Pioneer Woman, from a statue by Hermon A. McNeil (1866–), courtesy of the Reinhardt Galleries, New York

THE AFTERMATH OF WAR

THE fight with the Cherokees brought out in sharp relief the characteristics which marked Indian wars from the first contact of the races till the final passing of the free red man. It was a savage and ruthless struggle where women and children met the same fate as the soldier. Passion ran high on both sides and hate inspired cruel and bloody deeds. The Cherokees had felt the power of the white man and gloom pervaded their councils. But their spirit was not broken. They still had the strength and will to fight for that homeland of rich valleys and blue mountains. Returning to their ruined villages, they passed in the forest occasional heaps of stones, rude monuments which they or their ancestors had raised above the places where great men of their people had died in hunt or battle. Dropping yet other stones on these reminders, they filled their hearts with the courage of those leaders of other days. The white man should never desecrate the mounds where lay the bones of vanished heroes. Sad also was the southern border where the glare of burning cabins had lighted the summer nights. Doggedly the borderers who had been driven off returned. Half hunter, half farmer, the white man on the fringe of settlement had little to lose except his life in conflicts with his redskin neighbor. A new cabin could be quickly built above the ashes of the old. For the trader the Indian was a source of profit but for the borderer the red man was no better than the lynx or the panther; all three must be exterminated together. But "Cherokee" had become a dread word along the frontier, causing men to pale and sending terrified children scurrying into the cabins. Women were torn with anxiety when their men folk were slow in returning from the forest. Yet the borderer pressed ever westward. When the French and Indian War was over, he crossed the eastern ridge and entered the mountain valleys.

34 Cherokee Country in North Carolina, from a photograph, courtesy of the United States National Museum, Washington

And whereas it is juſt and reaſonable, and eſſential to Our Intereſt and the Security of Our Colonies, that the ſeveral Nations or Tribes of *Indians*, with whom We are connected, and who live under Our Protection, ſhould not be moleſted or diſturbed in the Poſſeſſion of ſuch Parts of Our Dominions and Territories as, not having been ceded to, or purchaſed by Us, are reſerved to them, or any of them, as their Hunting Grounds; We do therefore, with the Advice of Our Privy Council, declare it to be Our Royal Will and Pleaſure, that no Governor or Commander in Chief in any of Our Colonies of *Quebec*, *Eaſt Florida*, or *Weſt Florida*, do preſume, upon any Pretence whatever, to grant Warrants of Survey, or paſs any Patents for Lands beyond the Bounds of their reſpective Governments, as deſcribed in their Commiſſions; as alſo, that no Governor or Commander in Chief in any of Our other Colonies or Plantations in *America*, do preſume, for the preſent, and until Our further Pleaſure be known, to grant Warrants of Survey, or paſs Patents for any Lands beyond the Heads or Sources of any of the Rivers which fall into the *Atlantick* Ocean from the Weſt and North Weſt, or upon any Lands whatever, which, not having been ceded to, or purchaſed by Us as aforeſaid, are reſerved to the ſaid *Indians*, or any of them.

And We do further declare it to be Our Royal Will and Pleaſure, for the preſent as aforeſaid, to reſerve under Our Sovereignty, Protection, and Dominion, for the Uſe of the ſaid *Indians*, all the Lands and Territories not included within the Limits of Our ſaid Three New Governments, or within the Limits of the Territory granted to the *Hudſon's Bay* Company, as alſo all the Lands and Territories lying to the Weſtward of the Sources of the Rivers which fall into the Sea from the Weſt and North Weſt, as aforeſaid; and We do hereby ſtrictly forbid, on Pain of Our Diſpleaſure, all Our loving Subjects from making any Purchaſes or Settlements whatever, or taking Poſſeſſion of any of the Lands above reſerved, without Our eſpecial Leave and Licence for that Purpoſe firſt obtained.

35 Extract from the Proclamation of George III, Oct. 7, 1763, prohibiting settlement in the royal lands reserved for the Indians, from the copy in the Library of Congress

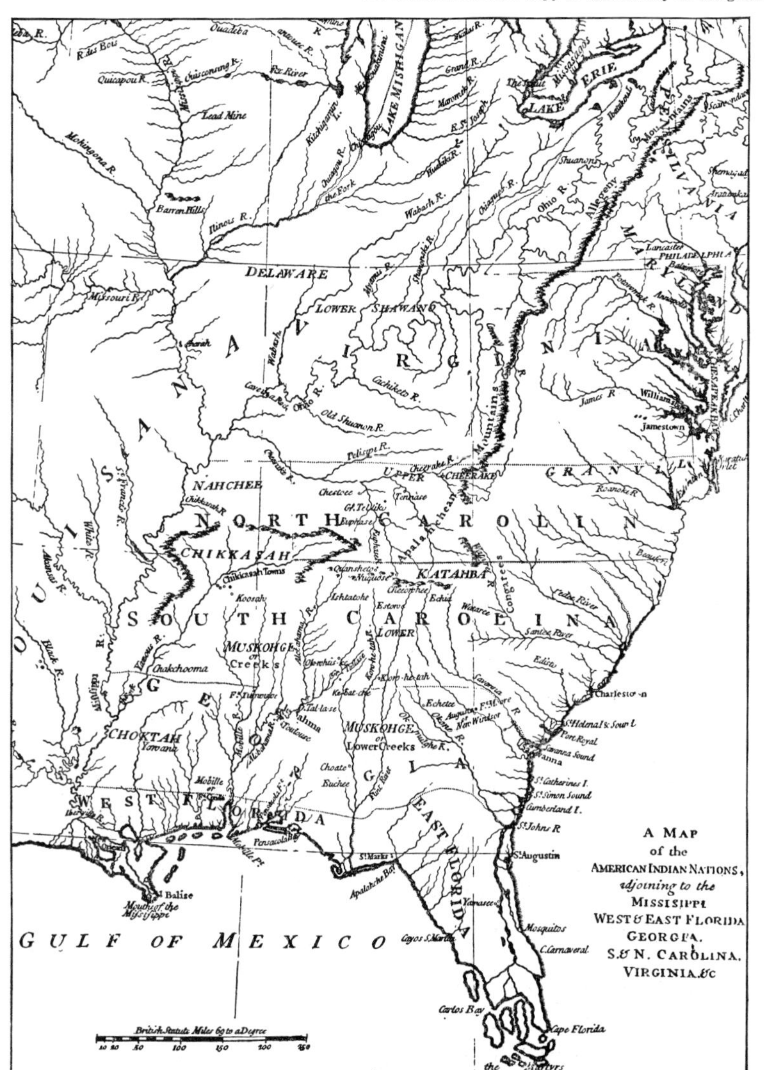

36 From James Adair, *The History of the American Indians . . . with a new map of the country referred to in the history*, Edward and Charles Dilly, London, 1775

THE PROCLAMATION LINE

THE French and Indian War marked the passing of hostile French influence in the valley of the Ohio and in all the country between the Appalachians and the Mississippi. With the signing of the peace of 1763 the British Government began to turn its attention to this new territory. Heretofore, when the western lands were in dispute, the crown had permitted easy extension of settlement. Speculation in the lands across the barrier had already begun. Powerful nations like the Iroquois and the Cherokees lived in the territories affected by the Treaty of Paris. The government must deal with them in its own way and not be embarrassed by adventurous settlers squatting on Indian lands, inevitable harbingers of interracial war. East of the mountains was land enough for all. At his own good pleasure and after he had made suitable arrangements with the redskin owners, the King would permit his subjects to build their homes beyond the mountains. So, in 1763, George III proclaimed that "all the lands and territories lying to the westward of the source of the rivers which fall into the sea from the west and northwest are reserved under the sovereignty, protection, and dominance of the king." Perhaps, as Washington at the time suggested, this proclamation was merely intended to allay the fears of the Indians until the English were ready to advance again.

37 Carolina Emigrants, detail from an engraving after the drawing by Harry Fenn, in *Picturesque America*, New York, 1872

SETTLERS IN THE MOUNTAIN VALLEY

ALMOST with the royal promulgation of the famous "Proclamation Line" borderers from North Carolina began moving across the Blue Ridge to build their cabins in the valley of the Holston, a thin skirmish line making a tentative advance. Those scattered settlements did not survive. But in 1768 backwoodsmen were again on the Holston, this time to stay. They were joined by a few discontented families from near the present Raleigh, North Carolina. About the same time logs were cut for the first cabin on the Watauga by one William Bean (or Been), an old hunting companion of Boone and a frontier soldier from Pittsylvania County, Virginia.

JAMES ROBERTSON, 1742–1814

To the Watauga valley three years later, in the spring of 1771, came a young man, James Robertson, with his wife and a little band of settlers. He had been in the region the year before, had hunted, and had raised a field of corn. Under Virginia law this gave him a cabin claim to four hundred acres of land. He found the soil good and the land suitable for settlement. Like Boone, the pioneer of Kentucky, Robertson was a child of the frontier reared amid its dangers and toughened to its hardships. But unlike his friend from the Yadkin he was first a settler and then a hunter. That he was a man of courage needs no better demonstration than that he dared to raise his cabin in the mountain country not far north of the sullen Cherokees. He had a quiet, masterful way in dealing with men and just that blend of caution and daring that marked the natural leader of the border. The Watauga settlers thought they were within the limits of Virginia but time was to prove that their territory was a part of North Carolina. Robertson was willing to accept for a time the low standard of living of the border because of his conviction that better days would follow the conquest of the wilderness.

38 James Robertson, from the portrait by Washington B. Cooper, in the Tennessee Historical Society, Nashville

JOHN SEVIER, 1745–1815

39 John Sevier, from a portrait attributed to Charles Willson Peale (1741–1827), in the possession of John H. DeWitt, Nashville

"Sevier, who came to the Watauga early in 1772, nearly a year after Robertson and his little colony had arrived, differed widely from his friend in almost every respect save highmindedness and dauntless courage. He was a gentleman by birth and breeding, the son of a Huguenot who had settled in the Shenandoah Valley. He had received a fair education, and, though never fond of books, he was to the end of his days an interested and intelligent observer of men and things, both in America and in Europe. He corresponded on intimate and equal terms with Madison, Franklin, and others of our most polished statesmen; while Robertson's letters, when he had finally learned to write them himself, were almost as remarkable for their phenomenally bad spelling as for their shrewd commonsense and homely, straightforward honesty. Sevier was a very handsome man; during his lifetime he was reputed the handsomest in Tennessee. He was tall, fair-skinned, blue-eyed, brown-haired, of slender build, with erect military carriage and commanding bearing, his lithe, finely proportioned figure being well set off by the hunting-shirt which he almost invariably wore. From his French forefathers he inherited a gay, pleasure-loving temperament, that made him the most charming of companions. His manners were polished and easy and he had great natural dignity. Over the backswoodsmen he exercised an almost unbounded influence, due as much to his ready tact, invariable courtesy, and lavish, generous hospitality, as to the skill and dashing prowess which made him the most renowned Indian fighter of the Southwest." — Theodore Roosevelt, *Winning of the West*, I, 180–81.

WATAUGA

Settlers came steadily to the valley of the Watauga and spread out into the country of the Nolichucky and Carter's Valley. With the solid backwoodsmen who sought lands and homes was a lawless, turbulent element from the seaboard communities, run-away redemptioners or fugitives from justice. The little communities, so far separated from the eastern capitals, needed a form of government. Tennessee historians have recorded that these over-hill people met in general conclave, entered into the Watauga Association and elected five commissioners to govern the valley settlements. James Robertson and John Sevier were two of these. So appeared the first self-governing community in the region beyond the Blue Ridge. The ancient Anglo-Saxon predilection for law and order reasserted itself in these cabin settlements in the midst of the mountains. In August 1776 was received at the state capital of North Carolina a petition from the Watauga people who had discovered that their settlement lay to the south of the Virginia line. "Finding ourselves on the frontiers, and being apprehensive that for want of proper legislature we might become a shelter for such as endeavored to defraud their creditors; considering also the necessity of recording deeds, wills, and doing other public business; we, by consent of the people, formed a court for the purposes above mentioned, taking, by desire of our constituents, the Virginia laws for our guide, so near as the situation of affairs would permit. This was intended for ourselves, and was done by consent of every individual. . . . We pray your mature and deliberate consideration in our behalf, that you may annex us to your Province . . . in such manner as may enable us to share in the glorious cause of Liberty; enforce our laws under authority and in every respect become the best members of society. . . ." Not without significance were their defense measures. They enlisted "a company of fine riflemen" under the command of "Captain" James Robertson and stationed them "on our frontiers in the defense of the common cause, at the expense and risque of our own private fortunes. . . ." In the following year Watauga became Washington county of North Carolina.

40 Reconstruction of the Watauga Stockade, made for The Chronicles of America Photoplay, *The Frontier Woman*

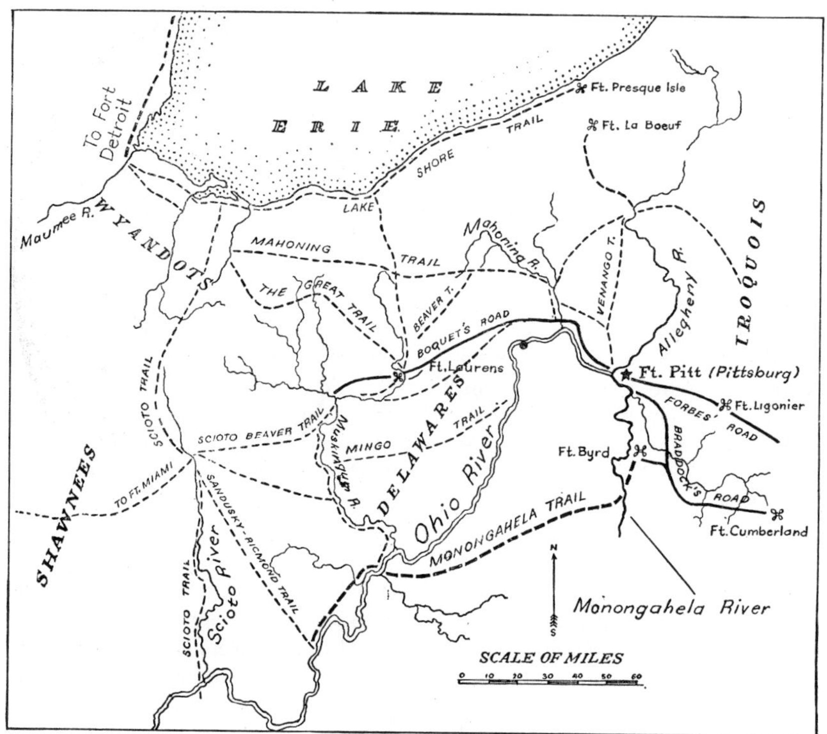

41 Indian trails in Eastern Ohio and Western Pennsylvania, redrawn from a map in Archer B. Hulbert, *Historic Highways of America*, Vol. II. © Arthur H. Clark Co., Cleveland, O., 1902

THE MENACE OF WAR

WELL might the people of Watauga look to their defenses. The Indians of the region north of the Ohio were growing restive. They had not been crushed by the defeat of Pontiac's Conspiracy immediately following the close of the French and Indian War (see Vol. VI, Chapter IV). The Shawnees, powerful and desperate fighters, had in particular watched the advance of the whites with growing apprehension and resentment. Since 1763, when the treaty of peace had been signed, the whites had crowded into the frontiers of Virginia and Pennsylvania. In the war Braddock had cut one road and Forbes another through the Pennsylvania forests. From the Monongahela a trail had been chopped to the Ohio where Wheeling Creek empties into the river. An island at this point was developed into a trading post and settlement, and below it the clearings of settlers began to dot the left bank of the Ohio. Surveyors were coming into the country to lay out tracts for men who had served in the war.

PANIC ON THE BORDER

THERE were mutterings about the camp fires of the Shawnees in the winter of 1773–74. Traders coming into the settlements reported that the Indians were sullen and that they were taking their pelts to Detroit tc exchange for powder and ball. It was a winter of apprehension on the border. Cornstalk was the Shawnee war chief and men could not forget that occasion not far back when he had come in the guise of friendship into the valley of the Greenbrier only to murder the unsuspecting settlers there. In the border cabins from Watauga through the Shenandoah as far as Pittsburgh men gathered on winter evenings to talk in low tones before the roaring fires and to clean and refit their rifles by the light of the burning logs. Spring found the frontier tense but the surveyors went again into the forest. A canoe belonging to one of these was fired on in April on the lower Kanawha by Shawnees. Five days later the Pittsburgh agent of Lord Dunmore, Governor of Virginia, issued an incendiary circular declaring that a state of war already existed. The most advanced frontier along the Ohio was seized with panic and refugees began fleeing across the Monongahela. Folk who had straggled into the Indian country scurried back to safety.

42 Contemporary English Representation of Indian Barbarities, from an engraving in Thomas Anburey, *Travels Through the Interior Parts of America*, London, 1789

DUNMORE'S WAR

In April 1774, the circular came to a band of borderers waiting near the site of the modern Wheeling to go down the Ohio. George Rogers Clark was among them and later recounted what happened. "The war post was planted, a Council called and the Ceremonies used by the Indians on so important an occasion acted, and war was formally declared. . . . The same evening two scalps were brought to camp." On April 30, a tragedy occurred, best told in the words of a man who as a boy of sixteen was not far away. "In the spring of the year 1774 a party of Indians encamped on the Northwest of the Ohio, near the mouth of Yellow Creek. a party of whites called Greenhouse's party, lay on the opposite side of the river, the Indians came over to the white party — I think five men, one woman and an infant babe, the whites gave them rum, which three of them drank, and in a short time became very drunk. the other two men and the woman refused, the Sober Indians were chalenged to shoot at a mark, to which they agreed, and as soon as they emptied their Guns, the whites shot them down, the woman Attempted to escape by flight, but was also shot down. She lived long enough however to beg mercy for her babe, telling them that it was a Kin to themselves, they had a man in the Cabbin, prepared with a tomahawk for the purpose of killing the three drunk Indians, which was immediately done. . . . I very well recollect my mother, feeding and dressing the Babe, Chirping to the little innocent, and it smiling." — Thwaites and Kellogg, *Documentary History of Dunmore's War*, 9–10.

43 The Grievance of the Indian, from a lithograph of a drawing, *Discovering the Murdered Chief*, by Felix O. C. Darley (1822–88), in *Scenes in Indian Life*, Philadelphia, 1843

Shortly before the massacre on the banks of the Ohio the famous chieftain Logan had played a conspicuous part in a council of his tribe where many demanded war on the Long Knives, as the Virginians were called. He admitted the Indians' ground of complaint but reminded them "that the long Knife would come like trees in the woods, and that ultimately, they would be drove from their good land that they now possessed; he therefore strongly recommended peace, to him they all agreed . . . when behold, in came the fugitives from Yellow creek; Logan's father, Brother and sister murdered; what is to be done now; Logan had lost three of his nearest and dearest relations, the consequence is that this same Logan, who a few days before was so pacific, raises the hatchet, with a declaration, that he will not Ground it, untill he has taken ten for one, which I believe he completely fulfilled, by taking thirty scalps and prisoners in the summer of 74." — Thwaites and Kellogg, 13. Still the Shawnees did not go to war. As late as July 21, Logan stated in a letter to the whites: "The Indians are not angry, only myself." But the border was in terror and, as the weeks passed, the Indian menace increased. The people of the frontier huddled within fortified stockades whence they sallied out to tend their cornfields. Scouts scoured the country toward the Indian villages. But in spite of all precautions came numerous reports of plunderings, burnings, captures, and massacres at the hands of stealthy redskin marauders.

44 John Muir, First Earl of Dunmore, 1732–1809, from the portrait by W. L. Shepherd (1833–1912) in the Virginia State Library, Richmond, after an original in England

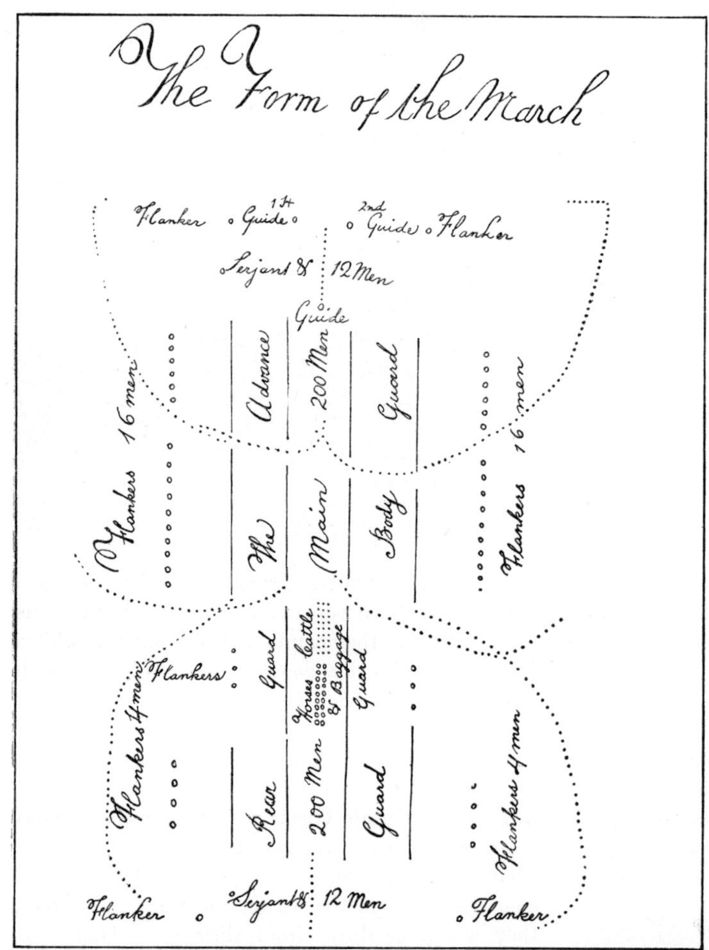

45 Dunmore's Form of March, redrawn from the original in the Draper Manuscripts, the State Historical Society of Wisconsin, Madison

DUNMORE PREPARES FOR BATTLE

VIRGINIA by virtue of her charter claimed the region which is now western Pennsylvania, and Dunmore was vigorously asserting the Virginia title to Pennsylvania lands. He was, therefore, deeply interested in the border situation and in July prepared to take the offensive against the Shawnees. He gathered a force of more than a thousand of which he took command in person. He sent orders to Colonel Andrew Lewis to call out the backwoodsmen. Lewis raised the standard on the Big Levels of the Greenbrier (in West Virginia). Thither came company after company of borderers, clad in their fringed shirts and coonskin caps, rifle on shoulder and knife in belt. They were volunteers who had turned out with alacrity at the call to carry war and destruction into the country of the hated Indian. Through the back country echoed the words of a recruiting officer: "The opportunity we have so long wished for is now before us . . . this useless People may now at last be obliged to abandon their country."

THE BATTLE OF POINT PLEASANT

WITH a little above a thousand men Lewis moved swiftly down the Great Kanawha. Meanwhile Dunmore followed the course of the Ohio until he reached the Hockhocking when he turned northward up this stream toward the heart of the Shawnee country. Cornstalk gathered his warriors and matured his plans. Like a good soldier he decided to strike before his enemy could unite. On October 6 Colonel Lewis camped at Point Pleasant where the Great Kanawha joins the Ohio. That night Cornstalk led some twelve hundred Shawnee and other braves across the silent river. Just before dawn he attacked. All day the fight continued. Both red and white men fought in Indian fashion. Toward evening Captain Shelby led his men from the Holston about the Indian flank. Cornstalk was defeated. The next day found him across the Ohio sending a white man who was in his party to Dunmore with a request for peace.

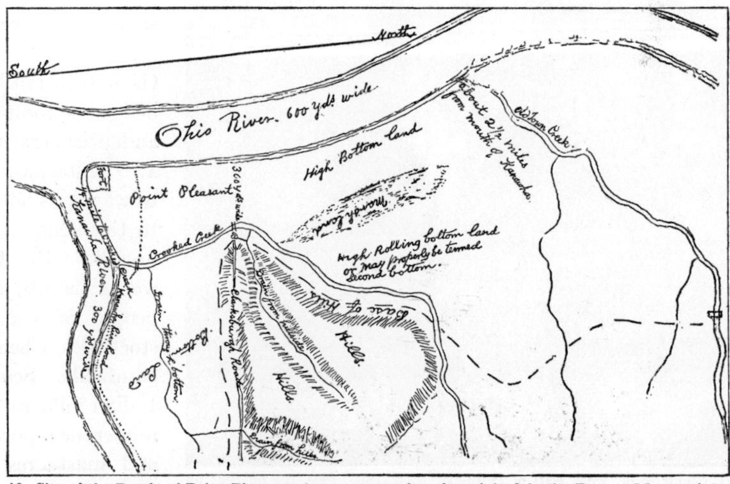

46 Site of the Battle of Point Pleasant, from a map, after the original in the Draper Manuscripts, in Reuben G. Thwaites and Louise R. Kellogg, *Documentary History of Dunmore's War*, the State Historical Society of Wisconsin, Madison, 1905

47 Logan, from a portrait reproduced in Franklin B. Sawvel, *Logan the Mingo.* © Richard G. Badger, Boston, 1921

LOGAN'S DEFIANCE

Lord Dunmore was quick to accept the offer. He smoked the pipe of peace with Cornstalk and his chieftains. He halted the borderers of Colonel Lewis bent on ravaging the country of the hostiles and sent them grumbling home. He missed, however, the figure of Logan at the council and dispatched a messenger for that chieftain. Logan's famous answer is probably the white man's memorandum of the chief's talk. "I appeal to any white man to say if ever he entered Logan's cabin hungry and he gave him not meat; if ever he came cold and naked and he clothed him not? During the course of the last long and bloody war, Logan remained idle in his camp, an advocate for peace. Such was my love for the whites that my countrymen pointed as I passed and said, 'Logan is the friend of the white man.' I had even thought to have lived with you, but for the injuries of one man. Colonel Cresap, the last spring, in cold blood and unprovoked, murdered all the relations of Logan, not even sparing my women and children. There runs not a drop of my blood in the veins of any living creature. This called on me for revenge. I have sought it. I have killed many. I have fully glutted my vengeance. For my country I rejoice at the beams of peace; but do not harbor a thought that mine is the joy of fear. Logan never felt fear. He will not turn on his heel to save his life. Who is there to mourn for Logan? Not one." Dunmore's tall frontiersmen listened to the reading of Logan's speech with eager interest. They knew that Greathouse, not Cresap, was responsible for the outrage. Indian haters though they were, they respected this one-time friend whose bloody revenge had not quenched the anguish of his sorrow. Dunmore returned to Williamsburg without making peace with Logan.

48 The Old Capitol at Williamsburg, from an illustration accompanying an article, "At Home in Virginia," by Woodrow Wilson, in *Harper's New Monthly Magazine,* May 1896

CHAPTER II

THE FOOTHOLD ACROSS THE MOUNTAINS

AT the outbreak of the Revolution the American frontier was just beginning to top the Appalachian mountains, though in Georgia it had not yet reached the eastern foothills. The southern Appalachians with their lofty ridges presented a barrier which could be crossed only with the greatest difficulty. The time had not yet come for settlers to skirt its southern end. For the time being the very inaccessibility of their habitat defended the Cherokees. If physical obstacles prevented the crossing of the southern mountains, an Indian confederacy blocked the way through the great pass of the Mohawk Valley at the northern end of the mountain barrier. Here stood the Iroquois, friends and allies of the English, yet guarding jealously their ancient tribal domains. So, when the frontier crossed the uplands, it did so in the middle regions. Here the mountains were broad but not so high nor tumbled in such confusion as the southern highlands. In Virginia and Pennsylvania the wooded ridges were parallel and of roughly uniform height. Between them ran broad valleys. The streams in these passed through the ridges in gaps. To the first men who penetrated the region the country seemed confused but in the latter half of the eighteenth century pioneers blazed a fairly level trail that meandered through valleys and gaps and about the ends of ridges. The Wilderness Road was long and arduous but it presented no impossible declivities and crossed no great heights. At first it was but a winding and turning line of blazed trees. Then it developed into a footpath where men and pack animals could walk. Many years passed before it became even a primitive wagon road. Into the rough mountain borderers advanced. Other settlers began to pass through to the plains beyond.

In this central mountain highland and that to the south, where the Cherokees built their villages, the border of the eighteenth century has persisted into the twentieth century. Gone is the Indian menace, but isolation, though rapidly passing in the second quarter of the twentieth century, still remains. Here is used the language of another day and here sound the folk songs that were brought from across the Atlantic. Here is the same primitive husbandry that was once to be found in the back country east of the mountains. Here live in sturdy independence, out of touch with the modern world, cousins of families that have risen to importance in the work of the nation. Those who climbed the rough slopes and built their cabins high on the sides of the Blue Ridge or the Great Smokies faced stagnation in their isolated communities. But those pioneers who passed through the mountains to the great central plain of the continent faced a future that offered boundless opportunity. They paid, however, a heavy price for their opportunity, for the mountains behind them cut them off from economic and cultural contact with the older communities as effectually as the Atlantic isolated seventeenth-century Virginia or New England.

49 Drawn expressly for *The Pageant of America* by Gregor Noetzel, American Geographical Society, New York

THE FRONTIER OF 1790

In 1790 the American people were for the first time officially counted. For the most part the population was of English origin, though many Germans and north-of-Ireland folk were mingling with the older stock on the frontier. One hundred and eighty-three years had elapsed between that day when the *Susan Constant* had moored beside the bank of the James and the taking of this first census. The passing decades had seen the frontier creeping slowly westward like the tide rising imperceptibly on the beach. The Appalachian Mountains did not, however, as some have thought, play the rôle of a gigantic dam impounding a growing population between its uplands and the sea. The foothills of the Blue Ridge and the Great Smokies were barely reached when tiny trickles of hunters and settlers began flowing through the gaps that notched the forest-covered ridges. Though Americans at the end of the eighteenth century were for the most part poor in money and material equipment, they would not be balked by the Alleghenies. Pack animals and their own legs were the first means of transport for the pioneers who threaded the mountain valleys to the beckoning plains of Kentucky. The first census takers found vigorous and thriving communities in the blue grass country where Boone had hunted. Other settlers were cultivating their corn crops near the confluence of the Muskingum and the Ohio. In 1790, when the American people looked at themselves for the first time through the eyes of the statistician, the fringe of settlement lay in several places west of the mountains. The majority of the citizens of the new republic, however, paid little heed to the progress or the needs of the border. The folk of the older communities were toiling on their fields and in their counting houses to make a living and were watching the effort at the National Capital to turn a paper constitution into a living government. Washington, the victorious leader of revolution, was President.

50 Beech tree where Daniel Boone killed a bear, 1760, from a photograph, courtesy of the United States Forest Service, Washington

THE DANIEL BOONE TREE

In the year 1760 a young man of the back country lived with his family near the banks of the Yadkin in western North Carolina in the shadow of the forest-covered ridges of the Appalachians. Like his neighbors he followed his plow across the fields of his clearing where charred stumps shouldered his wheat and corn. Much work remained for the young husbandman before his acres would be brought to that well-groomed state which marked the established farm. But Daniel Boone had little aptitude for the quiet life of a farmer. On a leaning beach tree well over the mountain west of the Yadkin settlement could be traced until a few years ago the rough inscription: "D Boon cilled A Bar on this tree 1760." Boone was at heart a hunter, characteristic of that first distinctive American type, the backwoodsman in whose life mingled the culture of the Indian and the white man.

CUMBERLAND GAP

The mountain wilderness to the west of the Yadkin drew Boone with an irresistible power. In the autumn of 1767 with one companion he climbed over the Blue Ridge and plunged into the labyrinth of parallel ridges and streams that characterizes the central Appalachians. Mountain hill, and valley bottom were covered with forest. The only sounds the two men heard were the noises of the wild country; the only trace of human kind they saw was the warpath that lay between the villages of the Cherokees and the northern Indians. The hunters crossed the Holston River and the Clinch, turned northeast, then northwest and came into the edge of the rugged country now known as the Kentucky Mountains. They hunted and trapped through the winter and in the spring brought back to the Yadkin the results of their winter's work. But Boone was not satisfied. His hunter friend, John Finley, had told him of a gap that he had learned about in the western edge of the mountains, leading out to a rich plains country beyond, where deer and elk filled the forest and herds of bison trampled broad trails among the trees. On the first of May, 1769, Boone, Finley, and John Stewart, with three others mounted their horses in the Yadkin settlement and started for the Cumberland Gap through forests decked out with the green of spring.

51 Cumberland Gap from Eagle Cliff, from an engraving, after a drawing by Harry Fenn, in *Picturesque America*, New York, 1872

52 Daniel Boone and his companions viewing "The beautiful level of Kentucky," from the lunette by T. Gilbert White, in the Kentucky State Capitol, Frankfort

VIEWING THE LAND OF KENTUCKY

"On the 7th day of June, 1769, Daniel Boone, in company with John Stewart, John Finley, Joseph Holden, James Holden, James Money and William Cool, found himself on Red River (the North branch of the Kentucky), and from the top of an eminence saw with pleasure the beautiful level of Kentucky." So wrote, soon after the Revolutionary War had ended, John Filson, "the first historian of Kentucky."

BOONE IN KENTUCKY

For Boone the trip into Kentucky was both to hunt and to explore. The party was amazed at the quantities of bear, deer and elk and at the herds of bison that crashed through the undergrowth. Panthers and wild cats watched stealthily from the trees. Wolves howled in the distance. But danger was greatest from the Indian. The white men had penetrated a land where no tribe built its villages, but where the Creeks and Cherokees on the south and the Iroquois on the north came to hunt. It was for the Indians a No-Man's-Land given over to war and the chase. In December 1769, a band of roving redskins attacked the white hunters from over the mountains and captured Boone and Stewart. But the white men escaped, weaponless, and finally found their party who had given them up for lost. Meanwhile Squire Boone, Daniel's brother, had come from the settlements with supplies. The large party now separated into small bands. Before the end of the winter the two Boones were alone in the woods. The next spring, 1770, Squire returned to the Yadkin with the catch, leaving Daniel to hunt and explore in solitude. By July the two brothers were again united and hunted through another fall and winter. When the snow melted in the spring of 1771 they started home richly laden with pelts. But just as they passed out of Kentucky through the Cumberland Gap a band of Indians pounced suddenly upon them and stripped them of their wealth.

53 Statue of Daniel Boone by Enid Yandell, in Cherokee Park, Louisville, Ky., courtesy of the Filson Club, Louisville

THE FIRST ATTEMPT TO SETTLE KENTUCKY

In the year 1773, when the autumn frosts were beginning to tinge the mountain slopes with red and gold, a group of emigrants passed the Watauga settlements going to Kentucky. Boone was the leader of the party. He had sold his farm on the Yadkin and had persuaded several neighbors to pull up stakes and take their families, as he was taking his, to the rich country beyond the Appalachians. A number of his wife's kinsfolk, the Bryans of the Valley of Virginia, were to join the party at Powell's Valley near the Cumberland Gap, and William Russell, a leader in the settlements on the banks of the Clinch, was also to go to Kentucky. The party reached the rendezvous and Boone's eldest son, but sixteen years of age, set out with two men to bring word to Russell. Returning with supplies and accompanied by Russell's son, two slaves and some white work people, young Boone missed the way to his father's camp and stopped for the night. In the dim light of the early morning a band of Shawnees crept stealthily on the two boys and their followers. Later in the day a frightened negro and a white workman burst into Boone's camp with the news that the redskins had killed the party and that they only had escaped. This event was an opening shot in Lord Dunmore's War. Boone's was the only voice urging the emigrants to go on. The group broke up and all returned to their respective homes save the Boone family, which went back a few miles to a little cabin on the Clinch. The next spring came news of the war on the border. Boone found his knowledge of Kentucky of value. Before Lord Dunmore opened hostilities, he sent the hunter of the Yadkin into the over-hill wilderness to warn the surveying parties of the approaching conflict. The advance agents of the frontier of settlers were therefore able to withdraw to safety before the conflagration broke out.

54 Daniel Boone escorting a Band of Pioneers into the Western Country, from the painting by George Caleb Bingham (1811–79), in the St. Louis City Art Museum, St. Louis, Mo.

55 Judge Richard Henderson, detail from the sketch in the Kentucky Historical Society by T. Gilbert White for his painting, *The Great Treaty* (see No. 57)

RICHARD HENDERSON, 1734–1785

THE defeat of the Shawnees in Lord Dunmore's War dispelled for the moment the menace of the northern Indians which hung over Kentucky. Richard Henderson of North Carolina was quick to take advantage of the opportunity and to begin the founding of a colony in the fertile plains beyond the mountains. His friend, Boone, had told him of the wealth that lay in Kentucky. He dreamed of a great colonial empire such as William Penn had founded in the province that bore his name. Henderson would be the proprietor of a vast tract of land; he would establish settlements; he would grant land generously to his settlers who should pay him a small quit rent. He would buy Kentucky from the southern Indians. The treaty of Fort Stanwix had wiped out the claim of the Iroquois, and Lord Dunmore's War had extinguished that of the Shawnees. With high hope in the early spring of 1775 he went down to the Sycamore Shoals of the Watauga to meet the assembling warriors of the southern nations.

A COMPANY of Gentlemen of *North Carolina* having, for a large and valuable Conſideration, purchaſed from the Chiefs of the *Cherokee Indians*, by and with the Conſent of the whole Nation, a conſiderable Tract of their Lands, now called *Tranſylvania*, lying on the Rivers *Ohio*, *Cumberland*, and *Louiſa*; and underſtanding that many People are deſirous of becoming Adventurers in that Part of the World, and wiſh to know the Terms on which Lands in that Country may be had, they therefore hereby inform the Public, that any Perſon who will ſettle on and inhabit the ſame before the firſt Day of *June* 1776, ſhall have the Privilege of taking up and ſurveying for himſelf 500 Acres, and for each tithable Perſon he may carry with him and ſettle there 250 Acres, on the Payment of 50s. Sterling *per* Hundred, ſubject to an yearly Quitrent of 2s. like Money, to commence in the Year 1780. Such Perſons as are willing to become Purchaſers may correſpond and treat with Mr. *William Johnſton* in *Hillſborough*, and Col. *John Williams* of *Granville*, *North Carolina*, or Col. *Richard Henderſon* at *Boonſborough*, in *Tranſylvania*.——This Country lies on the ſouth Side of the Rivers *Ohio* and *Louiſa*, in a temperate and healthy Climate. It is in general well watered with Springs and Rivulets, and has ſeveral Rivers, up which Veſſels of conſiderable Burthen may come with Eaſe. In different Places of it are a Number of Salt Springs' where the making of Salt has been tried with great Succeſs, and where, with Certainty, any Quantity needed may be eaſily and conveniently made. Large Tracts of the Land lie on Lime-ſtone, and in ſeveral Places there is Abundance of Iron Ore. The Fertility of the Soil, and Goodneſs of the Range, almoſt ſurpaſs Belief; and it is at preſent well ſtored with Buffalo, Elk, Deer, Bear, Beaver, &c. and the Rivers abound with Fiſh of various Kinds. Vaſt Crowds of people are daily flocking to it, and many Gentlemen of the firſt Rank and Character have bargained for Lands in it; ſo that there is a great Appearance of a rapid Settlement, and that it will ſoon become a conſiderable Colony, and one of the moſt agreeable Countries in *America*. (6)

56 Notice to attract settlers to Transylvania from the Eastern Colonies, from the *Virginia Gazette*, Williamsburg, September 30, 1775

THE TREATY OF SYCAMORE SHOALS

ON March 17, 1775, the Transylvania Land Company of which Henderson was the head purchased from Oconostota and other chiefs all lands lying between the Ohio and the Cumberland rivers. The price was ten thousand pounds, to be paid largely in merchandise. The agreement was not reached without a crisis. Chief Dragging Canoe of the Cherokees in an impressive speech pictured the relentless encroachment of the whites upon the land of the Indians, and asked how the children of the Cherokees would live when all their hunting grounds were gone. But the Indians, after a careful reading of the treaty in open council, signed. One of the signers was Little Carpenter. When Henderson was done, the Watauga Association purchased for two thousand pounds the land on which their settlement rested. The activity of Henderson was but a single manifestation of the interest in western lands among colonials not averse to speculation. Samuel Wharton, Benjamin Franklin, William Johnson, and a London banker, Thomas Walpole, formed a company in 1773 to promote a proposed domain west of the mountains, to be called Vandalia. The project was warmly opposed by Virginia and was wrecked by the early outbreak of the Revolution.

57 Cherokees selling Kentucky to the Transylvania Land Company, from the lunette by T. Gilbert White, in the Kentucky State Capitol, Frankfort

OLD FORT AT HARRODSBURG

In 1774, on the eve of Lord Dunmore's War, when Virginia had sent Boone through Kentucky to warn hunters and surveyors, he had notified among others James Harrod, who had led a handful of settlers into the region and was building a fort at Harrodsburg. Harrod withdrew before the storm broke but returned the next year to the unfinished cabins that he had hastily abandoned. So it fell to his lot rather than to Boone's to found the first permanent settlement in Kentucky. Harrod's people looked to Virginia as the owner of Kentucky. They scorned the pretentions of Henderson to the overlordship of the region. The individualism and aggressive independence of the frontiersman would brook no feudal control such as the land speculator from North Carolina sought to establish. Other settlers, Benjamin Logan and the McAfees, felt as Harrod did and Henderson was unable to enforce his claims.

58 Old Fort at Harrodsburg, from a drawing in the Kentucky State Historical Society, Frankfort

FORT BOONESBOROUGH

While Henderson was powwowing with the Cherokees at Sycamore Shoals, Boone had gone on ahead to open a trace into the heart of Kentucky and to build a fort which should be the center of the Transylvania colony. He planted Boonesborough at Big Lick on the Kentucky River just below Otter Creek. Henderson with his first band of tenants was on the trace to Boonesborough fort when Massachusetts Minute Men at Lexington and Concord met the British regulars in the skirmishes that brought on the Revolution. For long Boone's people knew nothing of the outbreak of war. Many miles of mountain wilderness separated Kentucky from the seaboard settlements. Not without significance for the future of America was the fact that the year which saw the first blood spilled by the thirteen colonies and the mother country witnessed also the first population movement across the mountain wilderness into the central lowland of the continent that lay beyond it.

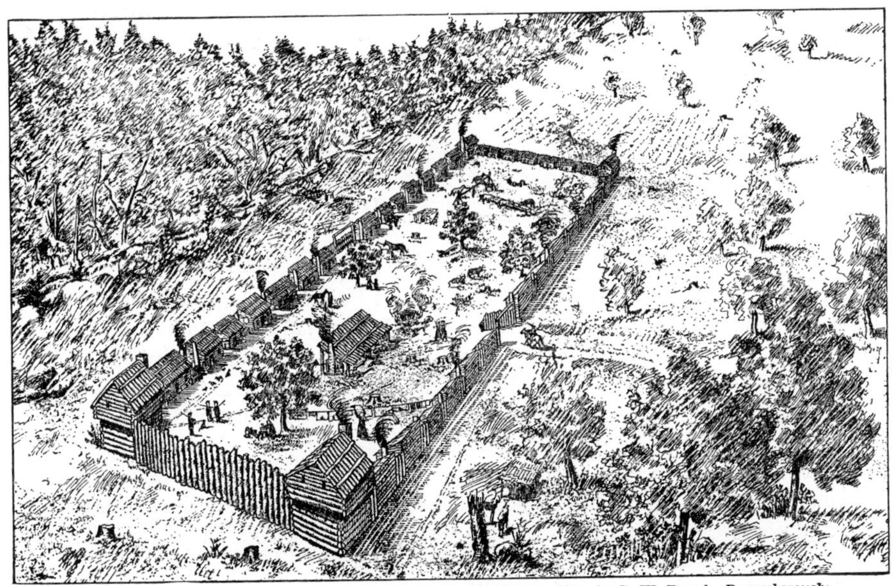

59 Plan of Fort Boonesborough, drawn from data in the Henderson Plan, in G. W. Ranck, *Boonesborough*, Filson Club Publications, No. 16, Louisville, 1901

60 Daniel Boone in hunter's garb, from an engraving by Chappel in the possession of the publishers

DANIEL BOONE, 1734–1820

Daniel Boone "was a tall, spare, sinewy man, with eyes like an eagle's and muscles that never tired; the toil and hardship of his life made no impress on his iron frame, unhurt by intemperance of any kind, and he lived for eighty-six years, a backwoods hunter to the end of his days. His thoughtful, quiet, pleasant face, so often portrayed, is familiar to everyone; it was the face of a man who never blustered or bullied, who would neither inflict nor suffer any wrong, and who had a limitless fund of fortitude, endurance, and indomitable resolution upon which to draw when fortune proved adverse. His self-command and patience, his daring, restless love of adventure, and, in time of danger, his absolute trust in his own powers and resources, all combined to render him peculiarly fitted to follow the career of which he was so fond." — Roosevelt, *Winning of the West*, 137–38. To Boone the wilderness which he loved and to which his life was so perfectly attuned brought immortality. He was not a typical borderer but a personification of the hunter-pioneer type at his best.

61 Daniel Boone, from a statuette by Dwight Franklin, courtesy of the artist

62 From a mural painting *Colonel Henderson calling to order the first Legislature of Kentucky*, by Arthur Thomas, in the Seelbach Hotel, Louisville

THE FIRST KENTUCKY LEGISLATURE

Three other settlements, Harrodsburg, Logan's Station and Boiling Spring, were established at about the same time as Boonesborough. Henderson, soon after his arrival, called an election of delegates to the "Legislature of Transylvania." Under a great elm tree outside the stockade of Boonesborough Henderson met seventeen representatives from the four Kentucky settlements. He explained to them the nature and regulation of the proprietary colony of Transylvania and read them its constitution. The clauses by which the reality of power was reserved to the Proprietors and those which required quitrents of all settlers in Transylvania fell upon unfriendly ears. The settlers doubted if Henderson could make good his claims in case Virginia chose to exercise her charter rights. The Legislature of Transylvania never met again. In 1778, in reply to a remonstrance drawn up by the men of Harrodsburg, Virginia disallowed Henderson's title but in recompense for his most important services in founding Kentucky granted him two hundred thousand acres between the Kentucky and the Green Rivers.

DANIEL BOONE IN THE CUMBERLAND GAP

BOONE returned to the settlements and brought his family to Boonesborough, the first white women on the banks of the Kentucky. In Powell's Valley wagons had to be abandoned and the journey continued on pack animals. Over the trail which Boone and Finley had years before used to go hunting in Kentucky came the immigrant harbingers of a new day. During the years of the Revolution each succeeding summer saw pack trains moving westward over the Wilderness Trail. Some folk chose to go to Fort Pitt and float down the Ohio to the plains of Kentucky. But this route passed too near the villages of the northern Indians. The Revolution had sent the redskins on the warpath. The longer journey through the Cumberland Gap was the safest.

63 From a painting *Daniel Boone and The Kentucky Settlers in Cumberland Gap*, made expressly for *The Chronicles of America* by C. W. Jefferys (1869–)

64 From the painting *Pioneers in the Alleghenies*, by Stanley M. Arthurs (1877–), courtesy of the artist

PIONEERS IN THE ALLEGHENIES

THEY were hardy folk in the main who made the long journey over the Wilderness Trail. Their lives were shaped by the rough environment in which they had lived. The men were strong of muscle, good hunters and bold Indian fighters. Their ears were trained to catch the sound of a distant animal and to detect the fraud when an Indian used the gobble of a wild turkey or the hoot of an owl to decoy them into danger. Their eyes were schooled to follow the trail of the redskins through the forest undergrowth. They were hunter-pioneers, the forerunners of the husbandmen who got their living from the soil rather than the hunting rifle and who soon abandoned the rough log cabin for the more pretentious frame house. Brave women shared the hard lot of their hunter husbands, kept house in the little cabins, made the clothes that the family wore, and reared children, ten, twelve and often more, to carry on the fight against the wilderness. The borderers of the frontier east of the mountains were peopling Kentucky. Life was desperately hard for these advance agents of civilization but they were daunted neither by poverty nor adversity.

65 Immigrants crossing the Alleghenies, from a woodcut in the *Western Miscellany*, Dayton, Ohio, April 1849

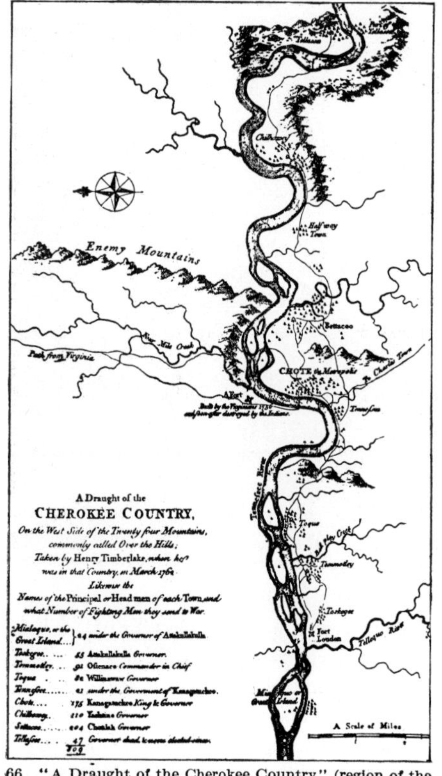

66 "A Draught of the Cherokee Country" (region of the Tennessee River), from *The Memoirs of Lieut. Henry Timberlake*, London, 1765

THE RESTIVE CHEROKEE

IN 1776 warning came to the outlying cabins of the Watauga settlement to be on their guard; there was war talk in the villages of the Cherokees. With growing fear this people had watched the white settlements advance like the tide to the very foot of the eastern slopes of their mountains and then come flooding into the upland valleys just north of them. They heard of the white man's determination to push his settlements down the Holston River to the mouth of the Broad (where Knoxville now stands). Such an advance would wipe out the northern Cherokee towns. Sadness was mixed with anger in the voice of young Dragging Canoe when in the spring of 1776 he told Stuart, an English agent who had come with powder and ball, that the Cherokees "were almost surrounded by the white people, that they had but a small spot of ground left for them to stand upon and that it seemed to be the intention of the white people to destroy them from being a people." Stuart's mission was to keep the Indians friendly toward the English by providing them with the hunting supplies that had been cut off by the outbreak of the Revolution. So dependent upon the white man's weapons had the Indians become that the interruption of the trade threatened the Cherokees with starvation. The revolting Americans also sent munitions to them. Dragging Canoe had not erred in his judgment of the temper of the borderers. Stuart warned the Watauga people. He also tried to dissuade the Indians. Among the latter was a division of sentiment. The old warriors had acquired wisdom in their wars against the whites. They raised their voices in council to urge against taking up the hatchet. They knew that no good could come of it and that it meant defeat on the field of battle and the wailing of women in the villages.

A COMMISSION FROM THE NORTH

THE old men of the Cherokees received their answer from an unexpected quarter. Fourteen Indians, delegates from the Iroquois, the Delawares, and the Shawnees, came to hold council with the Cherokees. They said that everywhere on their journey southward they had seen armed whites living in the country where not long before the deer and the shaggy-maned bison had moved among the trees. Then arose the representative of the Shawnees. Perhaps this was Cornstalk; the Kentucky settlers had heard that that dread chieftain "had gone to the Cherokees on some bad design." "He produced a War Belt about nine feet long and six inches wide of purple Whampun strewed over with Vermilion. He began with pathetically enumerating the distresses of his own and other Nations. He complained particularly of the Virginians who after having taken away all their lands and cruelly and treacherously treated some of their people, had unjustly brought war upon their Nation and destroyed many of their people; that in a few years their Nation from being a great people were now reduced to a handful. That the lands where but lately they hunted close to their Nations were thickly inhabited and covered with Forts and armed men; that wherever a fort appeared in their neighborhood, they might depend there would soon be towns and settlements; that it was plain there was an intention to extirpate them, and that he thought it better to die like men than to diminish away by inches."

67 Chiefs in Council, from a lithograph of a drawing by Felix O. C. Darley, in *Scenes in Indian Life*, Philadelphia, 1843

THE DECISION TO FIGHT

STUART heard and reported the speech of the Shawnee chief. He saw the Shawnee brave hand the war belt to Dragging Canoe, who was already painted black in token of his determination to fight. The Cherokee held the belt in silence — waiting. Then the Iroquois, led by the Mohawks, grasped the belt and sang their war song. They were followed by the Delawares, the Shawnees, and by the young men of the Cherokees. The mission had been successful. With rare courage Stuart stood up and urged against war, but his words did not avail. Youth rose with the fervor and abandon that has always characterized it to fight for the ancient homeland, for the women and children of the villages, for all that made life worth living. The old men shook their heads; it was glorious but futile.

68 Spreading the News, from a painting *The Indian Courier*, by Frederic Remington. © Curtis and Cameron

THE CHEROKEE DEFEAT

THE year of 1776 was a terrible one for borderer and Cherokee alike. The Indians, instead of concentrating their braves into one or two formidable forces, opened hostilities with scattered war parties which struck the frontier along a great arc stretching from Georgia to Watauga. Never before had their enemies, the border settlers, suffered so heavily. Terror, hatred, and the mad determination for revenge swept in turn through the back country of South and North Carolina. The over-hill settlements at Watauga on the first line of battle stood fast. At Long Island Flats, where the Watauga joins the Holston, the hardy men who had followed Robertson and Sevier defeated Dragging Canoe himself. Farther up the river the Watauga fort withstood the three weeks' siege; but a lad of the Watauga settlements was captured by a band of redskins. A few days later the people of the Cherokee village, Tuskega, saw him burned alive. The vengeance of the white man was sure and heavy. Expeditions from South Carolina, North Carolina, and Virginia ravaged the lower towns of the Cherokees east of the mountains and carried the war to their upland villages. The Cherokees, although their genius surpassed that of practically all the eastern forest Indians, were but mediocre warriors. There was sharp fighting in this war but no stubbornly fought battle like that of Cornstalk at Point Pleasant. When the autumn covered the green slopes of the Cherokee mountains with color, that proud nation had suffered disaster. Town after town lay in ruins, among them Tuskega, which had been singled out for particular punishment. In the spring of 1777 the Cherokee headmen again made peace and again yielded up territory on the borders of Georgia and the Carolinas and in the country south of Watauga. The failure to destroy Watauga meant that the Wilderness Road to Kentucky remained open. So the stand of the Watauga men protected the pioneers across the mountains. But their southern enemies were not destroyed. Dragging Canoe would not make peace. Taking the fiercest of the young men with him, he left the tribe and retired to the Chickamauga fastnesses.

69 Scene of the Defeat of Dragging Canoe, Long Island Flats, Tennessee, from a photograph, courtesy of E. W. Palmer, Kingsport, Tenn.

70 Contemporary French Representation of a Shawnee, from an engraving, by Tardieu l'ainé in Victor Collot, *Atlas to A Journal to North America*, Paris, 1826

THE SHAWNEES

FROM time to time during the summer of 1776 echoes of the Cherokee War came to the settlers in Boonesborough and Harrodsburg. But these pioneers in isolated Kentucky had scant time to consider the troubles of the Watauga people. They had problems of their own. To the north of them across the Ohio and in the valley of the Scioto River lived the Shawnees, bitter haters of the whites. These Indians had been toughened by hardship long before they faced Lord Dunmore or the Kentuckians. In the seventeenth century this Algonquian people were divided into a western and an eastern tribe. The western Shawnees lived on the Cumberland River with their principal village near Nashville. From here they carried on intermittent war with their most bitter enemies, the Cherokees. The eastern branch built their habitations in South Carolina. The power of the mighty Iroquois of New York may be gauged by the fact that they at times made war on both branches of the Shawnees. The eastern people were driven from their habitat by the whites in the latter part of the seventeenth century. Adair ascribed the withdrawal to "our own misconduct." They went to eastern Pennsylvania where, with the permission of the Governor, they settled in the lands of the Delawares. The early years of the eighteenth century saw the western Shawnees moving northward out of the Cumberland Valley. They could no longer withstand the powerful blows of the Cherokees aided by the Chickasaws. Crossing the Ohio the migrant Shawnees finally came to rest about 1730 on the north side of the Ohio, their villages extending from the Allegheny to the Scioto. Chillicothe became their principal town. These people who had come from the Cumberland were the survivors of infinite hardship. In 1748 their braves were estimated to number one hundred and sixty-two. A few years later they were joined by their kindred from Pennsylvania who had quarreled with the Delawares. For the first time in recorded history the Shawnees were a united people.

THE DELAWARES

THE Shawnees have been called the Ishmaelites among the western Indians, cruel, crafty, treacherous, known among their redskin neighbors as trouble makers. They had not been settled long in the Scioto region when their former friends, the Delawares, moved into the country near them in what is now the eastern part of the state of Ohio. The Delawares began to come about the middle of the eighteenth century. The pressure of the whites had driven them from their original home and, with the permission of the Iroquois, they had retreated up the Susquehanna to the region about Wyoming. Again the whites had crowded them out and they had crossed the mountain country to the headwaters of the Allegheny. From there they went to eastern Ohio. Looking southward the Delawares soon saw the whites crossing the upland barrier into the Kentucky region. These redskins called themselves Leni-lenápe, meaning "real men." In their days of greatness, before the coming of the whites, they had been the most important confederacy of Algonquian stock, and all the Algonquian people out of respect for their position called them, "grandfather." Their cognate tribes along the coast far up into New England were known among them as Wapanachki, "eastern land people," a term which in the case of the Abnakis of Maine appeared as a specific tribal designation. In the seventeenth century most of the "eastern land people" had bowed to the power of the whites. In the next century the Leni-lenápe began their retreat westward.

71 Contemporary English Representation of a Delaware, from an engraving in Thomas Jefferys, *A Collection of the Dresses of the Different Nations*, London, 1757

72 An Old French Trapper, from a drawing by E. S. Paxson in O. D. Wheeler, *The Trail of Lewis and Clark*. © G. P. Putnam's Sons, New York, 1904

THE FUR TRADE

Many miles southwest of the Ohio habitat of the Leni-lenâpe were the rude stockades of Boonesborough, Harrodsburg, and the other "stations" of the Kentucky borderers. To the westward and northwestward lay the old forest forts and towns of the French, now in the hands of the British. Detroit was at the western end of Lake Erie, Michilimackinac at the juncture of lakes Huron and Superior, Vincennes on the Wabash River, and Kaskaskia and Cahokia on the Mississippi in what is now southwestern Illinois. About many of these log forts there had grown up in the days when New France was still a reality tiny hamlets of traders and *habitants*. With the passing of French power the British had been quick to grasp these wilderness outposts. They lay within a country almost incredibly rich in furs, a country peopled by vigorous and able Indians of whom the Miamis were perhaps the most powerful. From this people, whose principal towns were in the valley of the river which bears their name, the fugitive Shawnees and Delawares obtained permission to settle in the Ohio region. Many a British subject derived fat profits from the pelts which the redskins brought into the forts which had fallen from the grasp of the French. To defend this trade and to supervise the traders came Lieutenant-Governor Henry Hamilton to Detroit on November 9, 1775, several months after Massachusetts had embarked upon open rebellion.

73 Henry Hamilton, from an engraving after a portrait (artist unknown), in Clarence M. Burton, *The City of Detroit, Michigan, 1701–1922*. © S. J. Clarke Publishing Co., Detroit, 1922

OLD DETROIT

At the outbreak of the Revolutionary War, Detroit numbered some fifteen hundred souls. Hither came the Indians in large numbers to trade, Miamis, Potawatomis, Ottawas, and Wyandots. A trader, one Smith by name, a member of an Indian village, has left a vivid account of the results for the Indians of contact with the whites. The tribes were camped about Detroit. "At length a trader came to town with French brandy. We purchased a keg of it, and held a council about who was to get drunk, and who was to keep sober. I was invited to get drunk, but I refused the proposal. Then they told me I must be one of those who were to conceal the arms, and keep every dangerous weapon we could out of their way, and endeavor, if possible, to keep the drinking club from killing each other, which was a very hard task. Several times we hazarded our lives, and got ourselves hurt, in preventing them from slaying each other. Before they had finished the keg, near one-third of the town was introduced to this drinking club. When they were done with the keg, they applied to the traders, and procured a kettle full of brandy at a time which they divided with a large wooden spoon — and so they went on and on and never quit whilst they had a single beaver skin. When the trader got all our beaver, he moved off to the Ottawa town about a mile above the Wyandot town. When the brandy was gone, and the drinking club sober, they appeared much dejected. Some of them were crippled, others badly wounded; five Ottawas were killed." — Quoted in Barce, *The Land of the Miamis*, 17–18.

74 View of Detroit in 1796, from an engraving, after the original in Paris, in Clarence M. Burton, *The City of Detroit, Michigan, 1701–1922*. ©S. J. Clarke Publishing Co., Detroit, 1922

75 Monument to George Rogers Clark, by Robert Aitken (1878–), at the University of Virginia, Charlottesville

GEORGE ROGERS CLARK, 1752–1818

A FEW months after Hamilton established his headquarters at Detroit a young Virginian, George Rogers Clark, definitely cast his lot with the Kentucky settlers. He had already been much on the border; was one of Captain Cresap's men in 1774; had marched with Dunmore into Cornstalk's country; had been part of the Harrodsburg enterprise in 1775; and now in 1776 was carrying to Williamsburg the Harrodsburg remonstrance which included a petition that Virginia establish Kentucky as a western county. Clark brought back with him powder, that commodity indispensable to a community whose very life still depended upon hunting and fighting. The outbreak of the Revolution had unsettled the Indian tribes. The year in which Clark made the long trek over the mountains to Virginia was the same in which Dragging Canoe was leading the Cherokee young men in their futile attack upon the border. While Watauga was withstanding the mountain Indians, Shawnee parties were prowling through the Kentucky forests, committing depredations and keeping the settlers in constant apprehension. But for Kentucky 1776 was merely a year of harassing raids. The testing time was yet to come.

CLARK'S PLAN

THE year 1777 found Clark in Kentucky aiding in the beating off of Indian raids and revolving important projects in his mind. During the hot summer days he, like his fellow Kentuckians, kept within rough stockades, knowing full well that Shawnees or Delawares lurked in the forest outside waiting to spring from ambush upon any unwary borderer. Birds were flocking for their autumn journeys southward when two hunters knocked at Clark's cabin to report to the chief who had sent them out the previous spring that Kaskaskia and Cahokia were lightly held. Saying no word to his border friends, the young Virginian joined a company of discouraged settlers who were returning across the mountains. On December 10, Clark walked into the office of Patrick Henry, Governor of Virginia, and laid before him a plan for conquering the Northwest. As he had passed through the familiar plantation country he had heard elated patriots tell the story of Burgoyne's defeat and surrender. Henry shared the hopeful spirit of the hour. At Redstone on the Monongahela in the following May, Colonel George Rogers Clark took command of a volunteer force of something more than two hundred men that he had recruited with considerable difficulty. Floating past Pittsburgh and Wheeling, he received the supplies that had been concentrated at those points. With him, as he drifted on flat boats down the Ohio, was a band of settlers seeking homes in the West. On Corn Island, at the falls of the Ohio, Clark left the settlers after having built for them a stockade and cabins. Such was the origin of Louisville, Kentucky. Here Clark erected a storehouse for his excess supplies and left ten soldiers as a guard. Then, as the sun suffered a total eclipse, he ran the falls with about a hundred and seventy-five men and turned his face toward Kaskaskia.

Instructions to Colo Clarke Jany 2d 1778.
(7 Companies – 50 men each.) No 1
Sir/
You are to proceed with all convenient speed to raise seven Companies of Soldiers to consist of 50 men each officered in the usual manner and armed most properly for the enterprise and with this force attack the British post at Kaskaskias – It is conjectured that there are many pieces of Cannon & military Stores to considerable amount at that place the taking & preservation of which would be a valuable acquisition to the State. If you are so fortunate therefore as to succeed in your expedition you will take every possible measure to secure the artillery & Stores & whatever may advantage the State.
For the transportation of the Troops provisions &c down the Ohio you are to apply to the Commanding Officer at Fort Pitt for Boats, and during the whole transaction you are to take especial Care to keep the true destination of your force secret. Its success depends upon this. Orders are therefore given to Capt Smith to secure the two men from Kaskaskia. Similar Conduct will be proper in similar cases. It is earnestly desired that you shew humanity to such British Subjects & other persons as fall in your hands. If the white Inhabitants at that post and the neighbourhood will give undoubted evidence of their attachment to this State (for it is certain they

76 Private Instructions given to George Rogers Clark by Patrick Henry, January 2, 1778, from the first page of the original in the Virginia Historical Society, Richmond

77 Ft. Gage, Kaskaskia, from a lithograph in the Illinois State Historical Society and Library, Springfield, Ill.

THE CAPTURE OF KASKASKIA

Clark had not fought the Indian in vain. More than a hundred miles above Kaskaskia he left his boats. Striking overland through tangled forests and over rolling prairies he crept upon his enemy with a stealth that Cornstalk could not have surpassed. The evening twilight of July 4, 1778, was graying into night when Clark threw a shadowy cordon about the fort and with half his men passed swiftly through the unguarded gate. Kaskaskia was taken by surprise. A few days later Cahokia was occupied without resistance. The French habitants pledged allegiance to the new United States the more easily when Clark told them that France was an ally of the American Government. Then Father Pierre Gibault, whose extended parish stretched from Lake Superior to the Ohio, set out for Vincennes to win his flock at that frontier post to the new flag. For two days he talked unmolested, for Fort Sackville beside the village was for the moment without a garrison. Then the French folk came to the church and took the oath. Lieutenant-Governor Hamilton at Detroit was astounded, but he lost no time in setting on foot preparations for an overwhelming counter-attack.

THE COUNCIL

The pounce of the Long Knives on Kaskaskia and Cahokia spread confusion and consternation among the prairie tribes. From far and near their headmen took the forest trails that led to Cahokia, until the tiny streets of that isolated frontier village were thronged with redskins. They came to see the white chief who had done this amazing thing and to talk with one another to discover what they should think and do. Vaguely they knew of the war between the Long Knives and the Great Father across the mighty water. The former were settlers pressing over on their hunting grounds; the servants of the latter were traders bringing them supplies. Their interest lay in remaining friendly with the traders and driving back the settlers. But here were the Long Knives with a victorious army in the very heart of their country; prudence demanded caution. For days they watched the white chief, a brave of twenty-five, as he walked with dignity and unconcern among them. Some chiefs sought to take him while he lay asleep only to find themselves seized and put in irons by his guards and to see the French of Cahokia rush to arms in his defense. Then he met them, the great tribes of the western country: Ottawas, Chippewas, Potawatomis, and Sauks and Foxes. The council was one of the most dramatic and most important in the annals of the Ohio country. Upon its outcome depended the success of Clark's far-reaching plans. In one hand he held the war belt, in the other that of peace. He warned the redskins that, if they did not wish their own women and children massacred, they must stop their forays against his people in Kentucky. He offered them the war belt and challenged them to see which would make it more bloody. He offered them the peace belt and told them that he would gladly be their friend. They bowed before a dauntless spirit and smoked the pipe of peace. On that day George Rogers Clark reached the greatest moment of his life save one.

78 From a mural painting *General Clark Signing a Treaty with the Indians*, by T. Gilbert White, in the Seelbach Hotel, Louisville

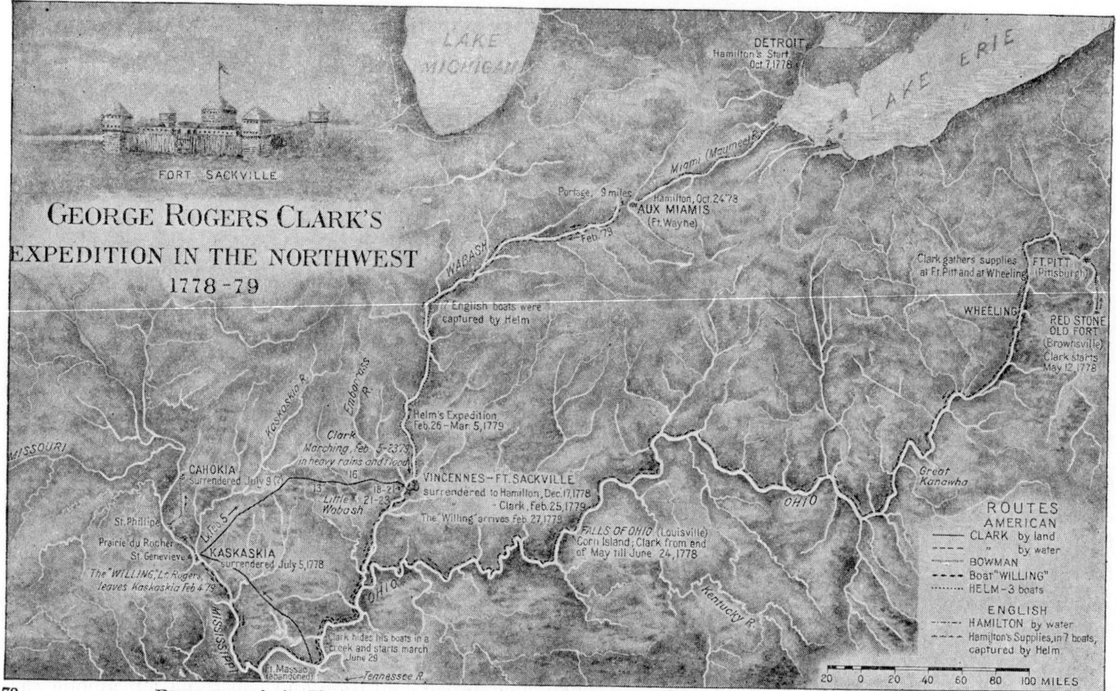

79 Drawn expressly for *The Pageant of America* by Gregor Noetzel, American Geographical Society, New York

THE WINTER MARCH

Word came to Clark about the end of the year 1778 that Hamilton had descended upon Vincennes with a force of more than five hundred men and reoccupied the fort. The news found the conqueror of Kaskaskia in an anxious plight. Most of his men had returned to Kentucky or Virginia because of the expiration of their terms of enlistment. He recruited some volunteers from among them and added to this force Frenchmen from the captured settlements. He expected an attack and prepared for a stubborn defense. Then came news through Colonel François Vigo, a Spanish merchant of St. Louis, that Hamilton had sent his Indians to their winter camps and the greater part of his militia to Detroit. He held Vincennes with eighty men. Promptly Clark determined upon the stroke which has made his fame secure in the annals of frontier war. A boat, the *Willing*, with forty-six men was sent to a point on the Wabash ten leagues below Vincennes. On February 7, with a hundred and seventy followers Clark started upon his overland march of sixteen weary and painful days to the fort of his enemy. His plan was brilliantly conceived and his leadership without a flaw. It was a rainy season and the streams were vastly swollen. Through swamps where the water was sometimes breast high the force toiled hour after hour and found no dry place at night to rest or cook their food. Always ahead was the colonel, leading the way or dropping back only to encourage those who weakened under the physical strain. In the camp at night his was always the guiding spirit. On February 23, after wading the flooded Wabash, Clark was within striking distance. Feeding his men on bison meat and corn from a captured Indian canoe, the leader prepared for immediate attack, though there was as yet no news of the *Willing*.

80 From the mural painting *General Clark and his Men in the Attack on Vincennes*, by T. Gilbert White, in the Seelbach Hotel, Louisville

CAPTURE OF VINCENNES

HATRED of "Hamilton, the hair-buyer" burned deep in the hearts of the borderers. His practice of paying for scalps made him a marked man. Clark warned the French inhabitants to stay within their houses and moved with avidity to the attack. All night from cleverly placed rifle pits his men poured a deadly fire into every porthole that the adversary opened. So well placed were the attackers that Hamilton could not train his cannon upon them. In the morning Clark summoned his enemy to surrender. He met Hamilton in the parish church and sent him back to the fort with an hour to make up his mind, and with the warning that, if Clark were obliged to storm the works, the commander would receive the treatment due a murderer. Meanwhile a party of Indians had returned from the Ohio country with fresh scalps. In full view of the fort they were tomahawked and their bodies thrown into the river. Then Hamilton capitulated. The Northwest had been won. Though he tried again and again Clark was never able to reach Detroit. But with the treaty of peace that post passed to the United States. Clark's conquest was confirmed by the able diplomatic maneuvers of the American representatives who brought home the treaty of 1783.

81 The Surrender of Vincennes, from a painting by Frederick C. Yohn. © Perry Mason Co., Boston

A BOONE STRATAGEM

IN January 1778, while Clark was beginning preparation for his expedition, that genial hunter, Daniel Boone, took a party of thirty men to the lower Blue Lick to make salt for the settlements with the new salt kettles which the Virginia government had just sent to the Kentucky people. Already three pack loads had gone off when Boone, returning alone to camp from a hunt, was caught in a blinding snowstorm and surprised by four Shawnees. They took him to their nearby camp where he found that Black Fish, the most powerful of the Shawnee sachems, was hurrying southward in the dead of winter to surprise Boonesborough. Boone knew that the stockade was not completed; such was the shiftlessness of border habits. He also knew the redskins. He persuaded them to turn aside to capture the party at the Lick. This was done and the Shawnees returned in triumph to their villages. Boonesborough had been saved from almost sure annihilation. Boone and sixteen others were adopted into the Shawnee tribe, the famous hunter becoming the son of Black Fish himself. "In the crowded, slightly built wigwams, filthy to the last degree, the lack of privacy, the ever-present insects, the blinding smoke of the lodge-fire, the continual yelping of dogs, and the shrill, querulous tones of old women as they haggled and bickered through the livelong day, all these and many other discomforts were intensely irritating to most white men. In order to disarm suspicion, Boone appeared to be happy. He whistled cheerfully at his tasks, sharing his game with his 'father' and pretended not to see that he was being watched." — THWAITES, *Boone*, 153–54. He was taken to Hamilton who tried unsuccessfully to ransom him. In May, Johnson, a captured comrade, escaped to warn the settlements. In June he was back, making a raid that netted several horses and scalps. In the same month Boonesborough men made a similar foray. On the sixteenth Boone escaped and made home, one hundred and sixty miles away, in four days.

82 Reconstruction of a Shawnee Village, from The Chronicles of America Photoplay, *Daniel Boone*

THE SIEGE OF BOONESBOROUGH

83 A Corner inside the Boonesborough Stockade, from a reconstruction for The Chronicles of America Photoplay, *Daniel Boone*

Boone had learned from the Shawnees of an expedition to be launched against Boonesborough and Harrodsburg. Once home he took the lead in completing the defenses of Boonesborough so that in September, when about four hundred warriors, Shawnees, Wyandots, Delawares, and Mingos, appeared before the stockade, they found it impregnable. With the redskins were some forty French-Canadians. Black Fish was the leader of all. Weeping freely over the ingratitude of his runaway "son," Black Fish in the parleys he had with Boone presented letters and proclamations from Hamilton offering pardon to all who would swear allegiance to the king. When these offers were rejected, the siege began in earnest. For nine days it lasted while the Indians sought by every device they knew to destroy the defenders. The whites with the Indians even attempted to undermine the stockade. At last the attackers withdrew, discomfited. Kentucky had passed its gravest crisis. Had Boonesborough fallen, the Kentucky frontier must, in all probability, have been driven in. Such an event would undoubtedly have brought to an end the expedition of Clark, who was even then holding the forts on the distant Mississippi.

84 Simon Kenton, from an engraving by R. W. Dodson after the portrait by L. W. Morgan, in the Fridenberg Collection, New York

SIMON KENTON, 1755–1836

The giant figure of Simon Kenton is almost as picturesque as that of his good friend Boone. He saved Boone's life one day in an Indian fight outside the Boonesborough stockade, when he brought down a redskin about to tomahawk the first hunter of Kentucky. His adventures form a tale of romance unsurpassed in backwoods history. Like Boone he had hunted in Kentucky before the settlement. With George Rogers Clark he was a scout in Lord Dunmore's army. In the fall of 1775 he had come out to Boonesborough and made it his home.

KENTON'S RIDE

Characteristic of Kenton is the old story of his horse-stealing escapade. In 1777 he had been one of a raiding party led by Boone against the troublesome Indians of the Scioto valley. On the return he and a companion, lagging behind the rest, had stolen four horses from the Indians and brought them home. Spurred on by this success, with two others he tried the feat again. This time, according to the account, he drove off no less than a hundred and sixty horses. But the Ohio was rough when the marauders reached it and they could not make their booty swim across. The pursuing Indians fell upon the three, killed one and captured Kenton. The angry redskins, with a somewhat savage humor, bound the captive hand and foot to an unbroken horse and then let the terrified animal dash madly through the underbrush until exhausted by his efforts to shake off the unwonted burden. Thus Kenton rode for three days to the Indian camp whence the horses had been stolen. The story is completed with the tale of how he was taken from camp, compelled again and again to run the gauntlet, tied to a post to be flogged by the squaws, sentenced to be burned at the stake and saved by the intercession of the chief, Logan, and finally ransomed by some traders who took him to the British fort at Detroit in the hope that they would get some valuable information from him. Here he recovered from the wounds he had received at the hands of the Indians. Then, in company with two other Kentucky captives, he escaped and made his way back to the settlements south of the Ohio.

85 Simon Kenton's Ride, from the painting by William Walcutt in the Kentucky State Historical Society, Frankfort

BRYANT'S STATION

86 Bryant's Station, from a drawing by Jean H. McHenry, after the ground plan of General George Rogers Clark, in the Durrett Collection of the University of Chicago Library

NEITHER the repulse at Boonesborough nor Clark's victory in the Northwest stopped the Indian raids against Kentucky. Summer after summer the hostiles from across the Ohio continued to harass this advanced frontier. In August 1782, nearly a year after Cornwallis surrendered at Yorktown, a force of redskins with some British rangers appeared before Bryant's Station, five miles from modern Lexington. The settlers were warned and held the stockade against attack. But they saw most of their cattle, hogs, and sheep either killed or driven off. After a day of heavy fighting the Indians withdrew and retired slowly northward. Then occurred an episode characteristic of the border. From the neighboring stations mounted men came hurrying in. Under the nominal leadership of John Todd and Daniel Boone they set out in hot pursuit without waiting for reinforcements which they knew were not far distant. At Blue Lick they caught up with the Indians who greatly outnumbered them. Older leaders counseled caution and advised waiting for help. But undisciplined, impetuous men demanded a fight. The result was an unexpected and terrible disaster. When the redskins turned the backwoodsmen's flank, they fled in panic, rallied and then retreated again. Seventy men were killed on that summer day, a heavy toll that brought mourning into every Kentucky station. As the story of Blue Lick sped from settlement to settlement, the frontier was plunged into deep dejection.

CAPTAIN BLAND W. BALLARD, 1761–1853

GEORGE ROGERS CLARK, commander of the Kentucky forces, upon hearing the news of Blue Lick, called the men of the Kentucky settlements to arms. They came, old and young, sinewy backwoodsmen hardened by life in the open, perennial Indian haters smarting under the humiliation of defeat. They knew that even as they assembled, the Shawnee village of Chillicothe where Boone had been a prisoner was echoing with the jubilant chant of the scalp dance. The powerful Miamis were also exulting. Young Bland Ballard was in the group that rallied to Clark. Though only twenty-one, he was embarking on his third campaign into the Indian country. Stamped on his face were the characteristics of the Kentucky borderer. Since Dunmore led his troops against the Shawnees the Kentucky country had had no respite from Indian raids. Their form of settlement was an adjustment to the ever-present danger from the hostiles. Their clearings did not dot the forest at random; there were few isolated cabins. The pioneers huddled together in stations and built their cluster of cabins behind stout stockades. Here the borderer clung tenaciously to his holding. Though he often heard the war whoop and the crack of the redskin's rifle, he did not retreat across the mountains. He refused to accept defeat. Burying his dead after the battle of Blue Lick, he joined Clark. Kentucky settlements saw a thousand angry men in hunting shirts and homespun turn northward toward the Ohio. They struck into the country of the Miamis, but the watchful Indians eluded them. So they tramped from village to village, burning the habitations and the winter stores of corn. They left behind a smoking waste, and Indians cowed for the moment but nursing in their hearts a bitter hatred.

87 Bland W. Ballard, from the portrait by Chester Harding (1792–1866), courtesy of the Filson Cub, Louisville

88 John Filson, from the copy of a portrait (artist unknown), in the Filson Club, Louisville, Kentucky

JOHN FILSON, 1747–1788

In 1783 peace came to the people of the United States; even the western Indians gave up their organized drives into Kentucky. Then suddenly the Wilderness Trail through Cumberland Gap seemed full of people trudging westward. Great flatboats dotted the Ohio on which they floated down from Pittsburgh to the end of the trail that led to the Blue Grass. For Kentucky the great immigration had begun. Many of the old time hunters who throughout the weary years of the Revolution had held Kentucky against the Indian and the British ranger now moved uncomfortably in villages developing rapidly toward the urbanity of towns east of the mountains. In the year that peace was established came a schoolmaster, John Filson, from Pennsylvania to Kentucky. He caught the romance of the rough lives of the borderers and at the same time recognized that the Kentucky settlements must one day grow into a community of great importance. He determined to write the history of the Blue Grass and make a map of its settlements, as his contribution. In 1784 he crossed the mountains with both map and manuscript, which he published that easterners might know the opportunities and the men beyond the Alleghenies. At the top of the map appears the following: — "While this work shall live let this inscription remain a monument of the gratitude of the author to Col'ls Dan'l Boone, Levi Todd, and Jas. Harrod; Capt. Christ. Greenup, Jno. Cowan, and Wm. Kennedy, Esq'rs. of Kentucke. . . ." To Filson more than to any other man posterity owes that full knowledge of the Kentucky border which has made the genial, happy-go-lucky, improvident Boone a national figure.

FILSON'S MAP OF KENTUCKY

Filson's map shows Kentucky divided into the three counties which Virginia had established in her western domain. In these lived, roughly, thirty thousand people. Seven little villages dotted the region, but most of the Kentuckians did not dwell in them. Nor did they live on isolated farms. More than fifty forts marked on the map in the heart of Kentucky are mute evidence of what the Revolutionary War meant to the people of this distant frontier. Within range of the rifles of these fortifications the corn was cultivated. There was no going out from the stockades during the "Indian Season" without danger. The industry of Filson has resulted in this imperishable record of the stoicism and the tenacity of purpose of the men and women who first built their cabins in the Kentucky forest. Before such folk the Indian could do nothing but retreat and retreat again until he reached the end of the journey.

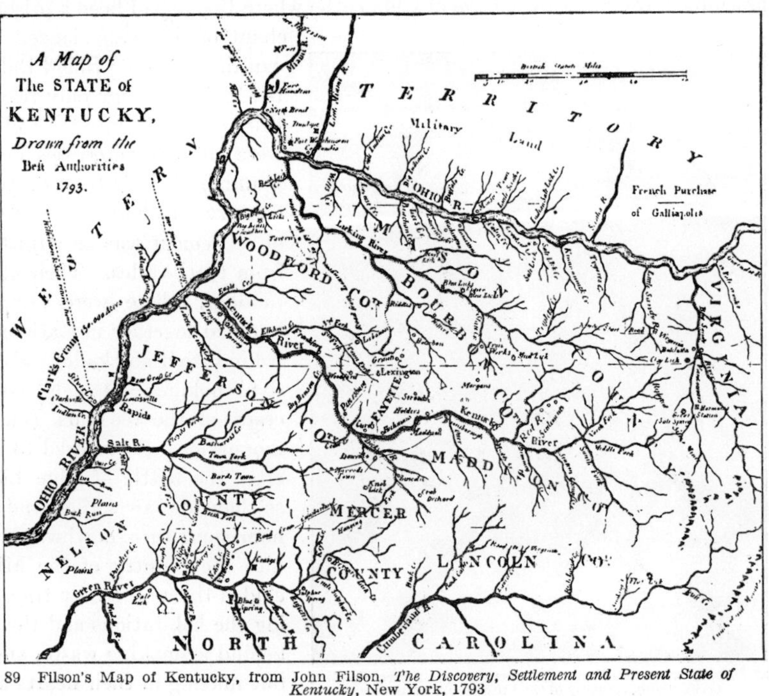

89 Filson's Map of Kentucky, from John Filson, *The Discovery, Settlement and Present State of Kentucky*, New York, 1793

SETTLERS DESCENDING THE OHIO

As the Revolution receded and the memories of its sufferings grew dim, settlers continued to pour into the rich plains of Kentucky. The Wilderness Road still brought many, but the great flood came by way of the Ohio. By thousands and tens of thousands they floated downstream past the mouths of alluring tributaries. Some turned aside to pole up streams like the Greenbrier and the Great Kanawha, where their descendants were one day to live within the jurisdiction of West Virginia. But for the most part they kept on to Limestone whence they made their way over the well-beaten road to the valleys of the Licking and the Kentucky. By 1787, when the delegates to the Constitutional Convention assembled at Philadelphia, the population of distant Kentucky numbered more than a hundred thousand souls. The Convention sought to make more perfect the union between the thirteen commonwealths that had freed themselves from England. As it deliberated, another state was taking form beyond the mountains. Kentuckians heard with deep interest the news of the formation of the new National Government and of the inauguration of Washington.

90 Emigrants Descending the Ohio, from an engraving by A. R. Waud in *Picturesque America*, New York, 1872

Patrick Henry Esq; Governor of the Commonwealth of VIRGINIA, to all to whom these Presents shall come, Greeting: KNOW YE, that [illegible] there is granted by the said Commonwealth, unto the said [illegible] a certain Tract or parcel of Land, containing [illegible]

with its Appurtenances; to have and to hold the said Tract or Parcel of Land with its Appurtenances, to the said [illegible] and his Heirs for ever. IN WITNESS whereof, the said Patrick Henry Esquire Governor of the Commonwealth of Virginia, hath hereunto set his Hand, and caused the lesser Seal of the said Commonwealth to be affixed, at Richmond, on the [illegible] Day of April in the Year of our Lord, One Thousand Seven Hundred and Eighty five and of the Commonwealth the Ninth

P. Henry

91 Kentucky Land Patent, from the original in the possession of R. C. Ballard Thruston, Louisville, Kentucky

PATENT OF A KENTUCKY SETTLER

In 1785 the old Virginia law governing the acquisition of land by settlers still prevailed in Kentucky. Actual settlement gave the settler four hundred acres of land with a presumption to a thousand acres about it. The patent here reproduced is a legal confirmation of John Clark's claim. It reads in part: "Patrick Henry, Esq; Governor of the Commonwealth of Virginia, to all to whom these Presents come, Greeting; Know Ye, that by Virtue of a Certificate in Right of Settlement given by the Commissioners for adjusting Titles to unpatented Lands in the District of Kentucky; and in Consideration of the ancient Composition of two pounds Sterling paid by John Clark into the Treasury of this Commonwealth there is granted by the said Commonwealth, unto the said John Clark, assignee of John Bailey a certain Tract and parcel of Land containing Four Hundred Acres by Survey. . . ." Clark later claimed and received a patent for the thousand acres about his original holding.

JOHN BRADFORD, EDITOR

The years that followed the Revolution saw great changes in Kentucky. Fewer and fewer of the settlers pouring in were of the backwoods type. Kentucky emerged swiftly from a land of clearings into a community of farms and plantations. In 1785 came John Bradford, a printer. Two years later he published from a printing house of logs in Lexington the first number of *The Kentucke Gazette*, the first newspaper west of the mountains. Kentucky was achieving self expression. Bradford proved himself an editor of honesty and common sense, and became a person of consequence. Tradition relates that he spent many late evenings at the gaming table with his good friend and political opponent, Henry Clay, the brilliant young lawyer from Virginia who, in 1798, hung out his shingle in Lexington.

92 John Bradford, from an engraved portrait in the Filson Club Publications, No. 3, Louisville, 1878

AS the Indians whenever they make incurſions into our ſettlements call at the evacuated houſes of Mr. Coppage on Dry run and Mr. Wilſon on M'Crackins run aboutfour miles from Col. Johnſons mill, and ſupply themſelves with wheat corn and potatoes. &c. as there is every probability that if ther were Articles impregnated with Arſenic or any other Subtil poiſon we might trap them. We therofore requeſt all perſons not to touch or in any manner moleſt any article left there, as we man to make the experiment.

JOHN PAYNE
ARCH. CAMPBELL

93 From the *Kentucke Gazette*, Lexington, March 15, 1788

THE MOVEMENT FOR STATEHOOD

VERY early Kentuckians began to chafe a little under their connection with the seaboard commonwealth of Virginia. The interests and the outlook of Kentucky were not those of the Old Dominion east of the mountains. As the population grew, the rich soil of the Blue Grass brought forth more than the inhabitants could use. The surplus could neither be carried on pack trains over the Wilderness Road nor poled up the Ohio to Pittsburgh to be transported across the Pennsylvania uplands. The Kentuckians must look to the Mississippi for the transportation of their goods to the outer world. But Spain held New Orleans and the river mouth. The Spanish monarch must give his consent before the backwoods Americans about Harrodsburg and Lexington could put their corn and hemp on the high seas for shipment to the eastern market. Indian fighters, who in the hardest campaign would brook little discipline from their officers, were not likely to sit by supinely while the Spaniard forbade them access to the ocean. Nor would they long be satisfied to see the government of contended, tobacco-raising Virginia state their case in the councils of the nation. They demanded statehood. There were those who feared they might abandon the new United States and fight their battles on their own. Kentuckians discussed statehood in a convention in 1785. The *Gazette* published the resolutions of the convention of 1787 after the Congress of the Confederation had voted that Kentucky be a state.

ISAAC SHELBY, 1750–1826

IN 1792 Isaac Shelby became the first Governor of Kentucky admitted to the Union in that year. He had fought at Point Pleasant and at King's Mountain. In 1782 he had left the Watauga settlements and cast his lot with Kentucky. Partly because they looked upon him as being able to protect them from the raids of the northern Indians, the farmers of the Blue Grass and the travelers on the Wilderness Road, his fellow citizens, elected him to high office. In him the independent spirit of the West found full expression. Shelby, the product of the border, rose to direct the affairs of a new state in which the old-time borderers were becoming a small minority.

94 Isaac Shelby, from a painting on wood by Matthew H. Jouett, owned (1916) by William R. Shelby, Grand Rapids, Mich. Photograph from the Tennessee Historical Society, Nashville

BOONE'S LAST DAYS

To one man Kentucky's growth and prosperity brought no sense of triumph, no feeling of contentment. The spirit of the wilderness had become his spirit; he must live his life in the solitude and the freedom of Nature where man had not entered to spoil the handiwork of God. So, in 1799, Boone said good-bye to his old friends of Kentucky, knowing well that he would never see them again. With his face turned toward the west he floated down the Ohio to the Mississippi and made his way up the Missouri. On the bank of that great stream beyond the settlements of the whites he built his cabin. He had left behind the forest country that he knew so well. Before his door stretched grasslands as far as the eye could reach. But their surface was not scarred by plow or harrow. On their rolling swells grazed deer and bison without number. In the distance rose the smoke of fires about Indian tipis. If not in blood, certainly in heart, Boone was kin to them. Like them he fled before the civilization of the white man.

95 The Nathan Boone House, Charette, Missouri, in which Daniel Boone died, from a photograph, courtesy of the Missouri Historical Society, St. Louis

CHAPTER III

IN THE COUNTRY OF THE IROQUOIS

WHERE the Alleghenies slope into the lowland which is partly filled by Lake Erie and Lake Ontario the white man found the Iroquois. Whence came these forest warriors fiercer than any of their neighbors, these statesmen skilled in the art of organizing government and in the devious ways of diplomacy, these people who held tenaciously to the peculiarities of their own culture and would seldom permit the arts of their Indian neighbors to take root among them? They left no written record. The archæologist digging in ancient village sites and long-forgotten graves has sought an answer. He has not, as yet, achieved certainty, but his hypothesis is strongly buttressed by evidence. They arrived in New York about 1400. "Let us suppose that the one, two, or more, related tribes of Huron-Iroquois lived in a portion of a region embraced within a circle having a radius of two hundred miles and with its center at the mouth of the Ohio River. Here they were in contact with the Caddos, the Muskhogees, the Sioux, and some of the Algonquins. They were more or less agricultural and sedentary and familiar with village life. They knew how to erect stockades and build earthen walls for their enclosures. Some movement of intruding immigrants or other influence caused them as a body to push northward up the Ohio River. Some went eastward into the Carolinas, but the main body migrated in a north-easterly direction. The tribes of the Cherokees were the first to lead the way and crowded upon the mound-building Indians of the Ohio, whom they fought for a long time. They finally overcame the Mound Builders, absorbed a large number into their own tribal divisions, and possessed themselves of a Mound Builder country. . . . They then took upon themselves various characteristics of the Mound Builders, but endeavored to blot out some of their arts, to the extent of mutilating objects they regarded as symbolic of their former enemies. Other Iroquoian tribes then pushed northward and endeavored to pass through the Cherokee Mound Builder country. Jealousies arose and the newcomers began a general war against them, finally driving them southward across the Appalachian ranges. This estranged the two branches and led to wars well up into the historic period. The victorious branch then moved into the habitat where the whites found them; the Hurons north of Lake Ontario, the Neutrals southeast of them in the region west of Niagara, the Eries south of the lake which received its name from them, the Senecas and other tribes in the country of the Finger Lakes, the Mohawks and the Onondagas stretching from the Mohawk River into the valley of the St. Lawrence. The Conestogas and Susquehannocks lived in Pennsylvania. There was constant intercourse between the various tribes who were well aware of the seats of one another. Often the various bands were at war, and often there were loose alliances, as of the Tuscaroras with the northern Iroquois. The Cherokees and Iroquois, especially the Senecas, were constantly at war. To the north the chief enemies of the Iroquois were the Adirondacks. The Huron-Iroquois pushed the eastern Algonquins to a narrow strip along the coast and so separated them from their western kinsmen that they exercised a dominant influence over their material culture and to some extent their social organization." — A. C. PARKER, *The Archæological History of New York*, 155–56.

96 Typical Iroquois flexed burial, with a pottery vessel and a pipe before the face, from Arthur C. Parker, *Archæological History of the State of New York*, University of the State of New York, Albany, 1922

THE FIVE NATIONS

To the east of the Iroquois who lived in central New York rose the wooded Catskills and the lake-studded Adirondacks. To the south the Allegheny plateau merged into the broken mountains of Pennsylvania. On the west and north were inland seas. Within this natural fortress was game in abundance and a rich soil. Here lived the tribes who entered into the famous league of the Five Nations. Before this was formed, somewhere between 1570 and 1600, the Mohawks whose habitat had been in the St. Lawrence returned to the region of New York state. They became the defenders of the eastern gateway. Far to the west in the valley of the Genesee the Senecas guarded the western portal. Between the two lived the Cayugas, the Oneidas, and the Onondagas. The Neutrals never joined the confederacy. They were considered the parent stock from whom all the Huron-Iroquois peoples were sprung. Within one of their villages near Niagara lived Jigonsaseh, "the Mother of Nations," a woman looked upon as the lineal descendant of "the first woman of earth." The Neutrals saw no need of entering the league for they were not engaged in local wars and their Huron and Iroquois kinsmen respected their ancient authority and the prestige given them by the "Mother of Nations."

HIAWATHA AND DEKANAWIDAH

The true figure of Hiawatha is almost obscured in mists of tradition that have gathered about him. He has sometimes been turned into a culture god who, after founding the league of the Iroquois and teaching his people to make wampum, ascended to heaven in his white canoe. A story much nearer the truth follows: "Hiawatha, He who seeks his Lost Mind which he knows where to find, (the Onondaga interpretation) was an Onondaga who wished the kindred nations of New York to abolish war among themselves. The Onondaga chief, Wathatotarho, opposed this, being a grim and ferocious warrior, jealous of his own power. At a national council he defeated the project. A second followed with the same result, and at the third one Hiawatha was alone. Then he went to the Mohawks, meeting with many adventures on the way. In his camp, near the Mohawk town, some young men found him stringing a kind of wampum, made of quills, the use of which he explained. Then he and the great chief Dekanawidah met. The Mohawk chief approved the plan of union, and the Mohawks ratified it in council. The Oneida chief, Otatshehteh, was consulted, but deferred the question for a time. On his approval another council was held at Onondaga with the old result. Then the Cayugas were approached and gave a quick consent. Another council met at Onondaga and a new proposal was made. Tadodaho was to be the head of the confederacy, and the Onondagas were to keep the great council fire. This made both desirous to extend the league. The Senecas were consulted, and the office of military commanders was offered to two of their great chiefs, Ganyadariyo and Shadekaronyes. On their acceptance the final steps were taken at Onondaga Lake." — W. M. Beauchamp, *A History of the New York Iroquois*, 156. The establishment of the Iroquois confederacy was a great intellectual and political achievement.

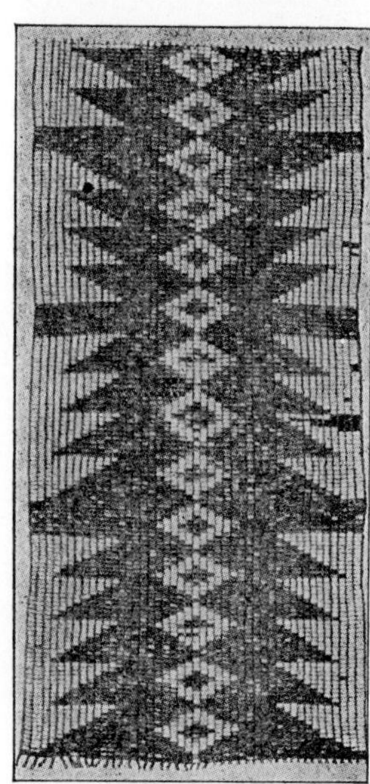

97 Belt of the Covenant displayed by the speaker of the confederate council, from Arthur C. Parker, *The Constitution of the Five Nations*, Albany, 1916

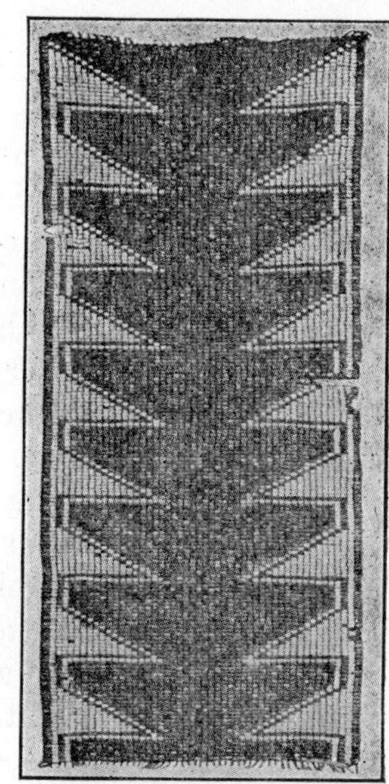

98 Great Belt of the Confederacy, symbolizing the Gayänesshä gowä as an ever-growing tree, from Arthur C. Parker, *The Constitution of the Five Nations*, Albany, 1916

99 A Central Council House of the Iroquois, from Lewis H. Morgan, *Houses and House Life of the American Aborigines*, Washington, 1881

THE TREE OF THE GREAT PEACE

Among the Iroquois generally the figure of Dekanawidah stands first in the creation of the confederacy. He is the culture hero of the Mohawks. Hiawatha takes second place. The prefatory articles of the Great Immutable Law which created the league show his position and importance. "I am Dekanawidah and with the Five Nations confederate lords I plant the Tree of the Great Peace. . . . I name the tree the Tree of the Great Long Leaves. Under the shade of this Tree of the Great Peace we spread the soft, white, feather down of the globe thistle as seats for you, Atotarho [Wathatotarho] and your cousin lords. There shall you sit and watch the council fire of the Confederacy of the Five Nations. Roots have spread out from the Tree of the Great Peace, and the name of these roots is the Great White Roots of Peace. If any man of any nation shall show a desire to obey the laws of the Great Peace, they may trace the roots to their source, and they shall be welcomed to take shelter beneath the Tree of the Long Leaves. The smoke of the confederate council fire shall ever ascend and shall pierce the sky so that all nations may discover the central council fire of the Great Peace. I, Dekanawidah, and the confederate lords now uproot the tallest pine tree and into the cavity thereby made we cast all weapons of war. Into the depths of the earth, down into the deep underearth currents of water flowing into unknown regions, we cast all weapons of strife. We bury them from sight forever and plant again the tree." — A. C. Parker, *The Constitution of the Five Nations*, 8–9. From generation to generation the Great Immutable Law was handed down orally by chiefs who learned it word for word. To give it more material form belts of wampum symbolized its various parts. The Constitution turned the Five Nations into a peace group and freed the member tribes from mutual fear.

100 Reciting the laws of the Confederacy, from an engraving in Joseph F. Lafitau, *Moeurs des Sauvages Ameriquains*, Paris, 1724

101 Return of the Mohawk Warriors, from the group in the State Museum, Albany, by Caspar Mayer and Henri Marchand, background painted by David C. Lithgow

CONQUEST

PEACE within, but war, determined and terrible, against their foes was the code of the Iroquois. War brought them territory, a veritable imperial domain. They crushed the Hurons who opposed them; they established their influence over the Indians of the Ohio country and the shadow of their power fell across Kentucky. The people of Pennsylvania looked upon them with dread and were much under their influence. The forests of Tennessee and the Carolinas heard the war cries of their braves. They were the Romans among the eastern forest Indians. Their men were tall, often six feet in height, well proportioned, with regular features and comparatively light complexions. "Their senses," wrote an early Jesuit missionary, "are most perfect, they have exceedingly acute vision, excellent hearing, an ear for music, and a rare sense of smell. With this sense they frequently discover fire long before seeing it." — *Jesuit Relations*, XXXVIII, 259. Active life in the open air, the severe military training, and the temperance and self-control necessary in the life of the good hunter and warrior, all contributed to make the Iroquois fine specimens of physical manhood.

IROQUOIS LIFE

THE Iroquois were a sedentary people, living by agriculture and the chase. Of the two husbandry was the more important, and husbandry was the task of the women. The men were hunters and warriors. The environment was a rich one permitting the Indians, even though they had no domestic animals and hence only primitive agricultural methods, to pile up a small surplus of wealth. This freed them a little from the desperate and grinding struggle for existence and made it possible for them to advance a little way along the road of intellectual and æsthetic progress. The status of women among them was the outgrowth of their economic power, they being the chief producers and controlling the agricultural surplus. So the women councilors, the Oyanders, held positions of great dignity and power. The council of the women's clan first took up important matters of state; in the general life of the community the voice of the women was of greater importance than that of the warriors. But the Council of Elders made the final decisions. "Even those chiefs who are most honored both for their ability and for their age, defer to such an extent to the authority of the senate, that they do not go further than to announce or to have announced the subject to be deliberated upon, after which they always cease to speak, saying, 'Think it over — you other Old Men; you are the masters, do you order.' The manner of deliberating is characterized by great self-restraint and maturity. Each speaker first restates the proposition in a few words, and gives all the arguments which have been brought forward for or against by those who have spoken first. After that, he expresses his own individual opinion." — LAFITAU, I, 477–81.

102 The Corn Harvest, from the group in the State Museum, Albany, by Caspar Mayer and Henri Marchand, background painted by David Lithgow

103 Iroquois picture writing, depicting Native Dance, redrawn by Seth Eastman for Henry R. Schoolcraft, *Information Respecting the Indians*, 1851–57

IROQUOIS RELIGION

CHILD of the wilderness, the Iroquois worshiped the manifestations of nature that he saw about him. On expeditions he addressed great rocks that towered above his path. He believed that the beaver, the bear, and all the living things of the woods had each an "elder brother" from whom they were sprung and to whom the hunter must give heed. Should the sleeping Indian meet such an "elder brother" in his dreams, he was sure that fortune would smile upon his hunt. The Iroquois beliefs had their origins in ancient times when particular families came to look upon particular spirits as their especial protectors, hence the Bear clan, the Beaver clan, and others who worshiped the Snipe, the Deer, the Wolf, the Tortoise, and the Eel. These were the totems of the clans. Each individual hunter worshiped that spirit which manifested itself to him after he had withdrawn in the solitude of the forest, had fasted, and had observed his dreams. Beside the animal deities were those of the plants, particularly the "Three Sisters," the spirit of maize, of beans, and of pumpkins. Beyond these particular objects of nature the Iroquois bowed before the sky, the sun, the rejuvenating power of nature, rain and warm winds as blessing-bringing deities and sought to propitiate those harbingers of evil, cold winds, frost, and hail. The Iroquois, like the American Indian in general, was deeply religious. He moved through his cornfields and through the forests which surrounded them, conscious of the presence of friendly and hostile spirits. To them, he sought to adjust himself through ritual acts of propitiation or exorcism of hostile spirits and through ancestor worship.

104 Indian Feast Dance, from David Pieterszen de Vries, *Voyagiens in de vier deelen des Werelts-Ronde*, Amsterdam, 1655

CONTACT WITH THE WHITES

EARLY in the seventeenth century news of a strange people with white skins passed from village to village of the Five Nations. There were perhaps twenty-four or less of these between the Genesee and the Mohawk. To them, as the years passed, came the Black Robes from the Frenchman's towns in the valley of the St. Lawrence, then Dutch, and after that English traders from the Hudson River country. The Indian was quick to grasp the advantages to him of trade with the white man. But only a few embraced the religion of the Black Robes. These latter moved to the region about Montreal and were ultimately cast off by their brethren as traitors. From the beginning the Iroquois, as a people, were hostile to the French and friendly to the rival English. In this relationship they were to play no small part in determining the fate of the North American continent. The white man's gun in their hands made them many times more terrible to their forest enemies. The seventeenth century, after the coming of the whites, was their golden age, the time when their conquests were most widely extended. Their villages increased in number. Many of their conquered enemies were adopted into their tribes. A few years before the outbreak of the first French and Indian War in 1689 the Iroquois were estimated at sixteen thousand souls. Then came heavy losses from war, disease, and the defection of the Catholic Iroquois. The eighteenth century was still young when the Five Nations had been reduced by half. They remained, however, a proud, independent, and powerful people, masters of the domain ruled by the Long House. In 1729 they added to the confederacy the Tuscaroras from the Carolinas, upon whose hunting grounds white settlements were pressing.

105 A Meeting of Whites and Iroquois, from a miniature sculpture group by Dwight Franklin, courtesy of the artist

106 Sir William Johnson, from a portrait (artist unknown), painted at Fort Johnson about 1750, in the Albany Institute of History and Art

SIR WILLIAM JOHNSON, 1715–1774

FOURTEEN years after the accession of the Tuscaroras to the Iroquois confederacy a young man of twenty-three summers journeyed from England to the province of New York and made his way into the Mohawk Valley. William Johnson had come to manage a tract of land belonging to his uncle, Admiral Sir Peter Warren. Johnson, like James Adair, proved himself to be one of those rare Britons of culture who could adapt his life to the customs of the Indians. Nor was his friendliness for the Iroquois feigned. The powerful Mohawks adopted him and elected him a sachem. Indian guests were welcome at his house. He married, after the Indian fashion, Mary Brant, sister of Joseph Brant, the greatest of the Mohawk war chiefs. He came to wield an influence over the Six Nations greater than that of any man since Dekanawidah. He acquired a vast estate in the valley of the Mohawk some twenty-five miles west of the present Schenectady. He was a successful colonizer and so developed his domain that in his later years he was able to live in Johnson Hall in the style of an English baron. For many years he was a councilor of the province. He organized and led military expeditions against the ancient enemy in the French and Indian wars. His influence held the Iroquois to the British side in these conflicts and prevented them from joining Pontiac's Conspiracy in 1764. His reward for services of inestimable value to his king was a baronetcy in 1755. On July 11, 1774, Johnson addressed a great council of the Iroquois assembled amid passion and excitement to discuss the murder by Greathouse of Logan's relatives. Two hours after his plea for peace the great white sachem died.

THE FIRST TREATY OF FORT STANWIX, 1768

IN October 1768, Sir William Johnson had performed one of his most important services. Meeting a council of some three thousand Indians he negotiated the first treaty of Fort Stanwix. He recognized the Iroquois claim to the country which stretched away to the south as far as the border of the Cherokees and to the hunting grounds which lay both north and south of the Ohio. He purchased for a little more than fifty thousand dollars the land south and east of the Ohio and of a line which ran across the northern part of Pennsylvania to the Delaware River where it turned northward to Fort Stanwix. (See map, No. 111.) The treaty was primarily the result of the westward extension of the white frontier in the province of New York. In the Mohawk Valley German and English settlers had pushed as far to the west as German Flats. Before the close of the last French and Indian War cabins had begun to dot the country, in the valleys of the Scoharie and the upper Susquehanna and east of Otsego Lake. Following the Stanwix purchase settlers began to come rapidly into this region. Villages like Cherry Valley and Unadilla increased in size and assumed an air of permanence. Here as in the frontiers to the southward the English mingled with the Scotch-Irish and the Germans.

107 The Home of Sir William Johnson, from an engraving, *A North View of Fort Johnson drawn on the spot by W. Guy Johnson Sir Wm. Johnson's Son*, in the Emmet Collection, New York Public Library, after a copperplate in the *Royal Magazine*, London, 1759

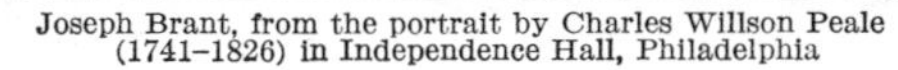

108 Joseph Brant, from the portrait by Charles Willson Peale (1741–1826) in Independence Hall, Philadelphia

109 Brant's Son, John, from an engraving, after a painting by Hoxie, in William M. Stone, *Life and Times of Sagoyewathe*, New York, 1867

JOSEPH BRANT, 1742–1807

DOUBTLESS among those present at the great council which resulted in the treaty of Fort Stanwix was Joseph Brant, a Mohawk chief, and a protegé of Sir William Johnson. In 1742, when his people were on a hunting expedition in the country of the Ohio, Thayendanagea (pronounced Tai-yen-da-nay-geh) was born. His father is believed to have been a Mohawk chief of the Wolf clan; his mother may have been a Shawnee woman. As a boy he showed promise and in his teens followed with credit the warpath in the last French and Indian War. In 1761 he with two comrades and with the backing of Sir William Johnson made his way on horseback through the hills of Connecticut to the village of Lebanon, where Doctor Eleazar Wheelock had a school for Indians. When two years later he was called back to his tribe by the outbreak of Pontiac's war, Brant had won the golden opinion of his masters. "Joseph," wrote Wheelock, "is indeed an excellent youth, he has much endeared himself to me." Joseph was a friend of the British and an enemy of Pontiac. When that chieftain had fallen, the years of peace that followed saw Thayendanagea wax in importance among his people. He became a Pine Tree chief, one who acquired his position not by inheritance but, like the towering pine, by his manifest excellence. When Colonel Guy Johnson became Superintendent of Indian Affairs in the place of the dead Sir William, Joseph Brant became his secretary. During the Revolution these two men worked desperately to keep the Six Nations loyal to the English crown.

110 Reputed portrait of Guy Johnson (artist unknown), from an engraving, after a mezzotint by E. Bartolozzi (1727–1813), in *The Sir William Johnson Papers*, Vol. II, University of the State of New York, Albany, 1922

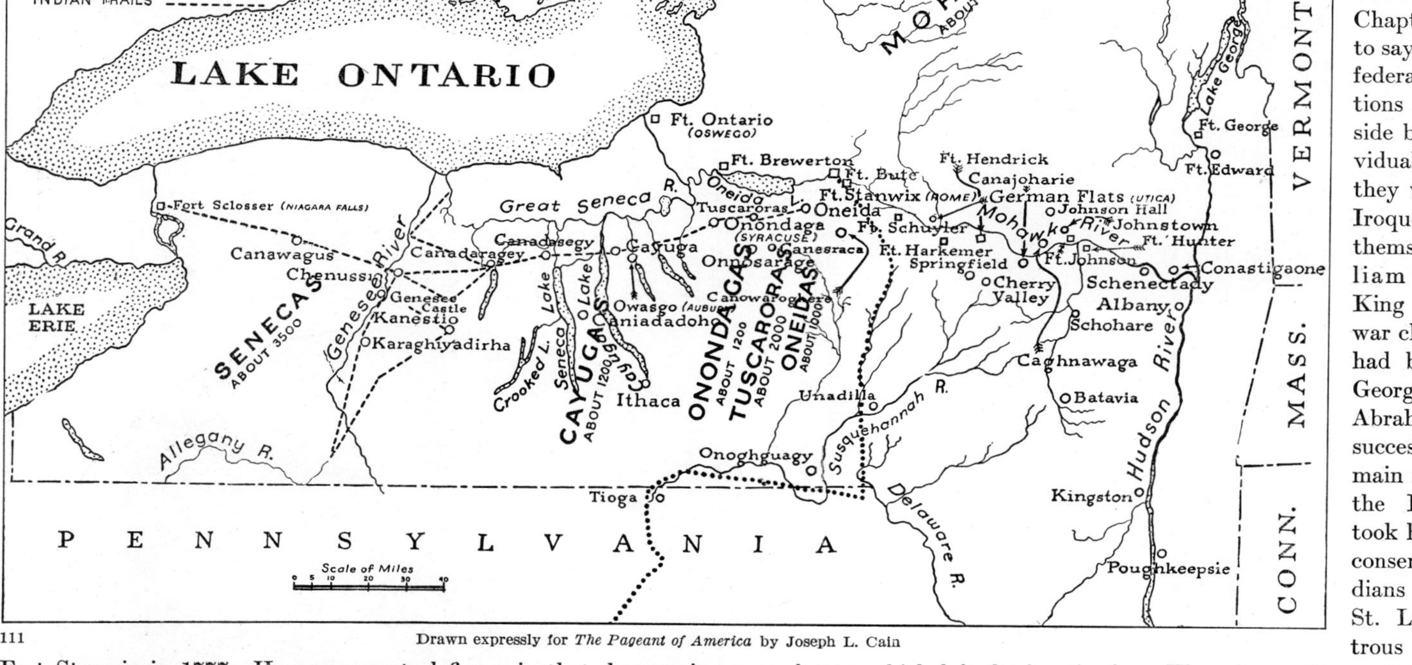

111 Drawn expressly for *The Pageant of America* by Joseph L. Cain

THE IROQUOIS IN THE REVOLUTION

THE story of the long war of the Iroquois against the pressing American frontier belongs to another volume (Volume VI, Chapter VIII). Suffice it to say here that, as a confederation, the Six Nations did not join either side but allowed the individual tribes to choose as they would. Most of the Iroquois, however, allied themselves with Sir William Johnson's King. King Hendrick, the old war chief of the Iroquois, had been slain at Lake George in 1755. Little Abraham, his hereditary successor, desired to remain neutral in the war of the Revolution. Brant took his place by common consent and led the Indians who accompanied St. Leger on his disastrous expedition against Fort Stanwix in 1777. He was a central figure in that devastating war of 1778 which left the frontier from Wyoming to Cherry Valley a smoking ruin. He was the leader of the desperate Iroquois on that fatal day late in August 1779, when the power of the Six Nations collapsed at Newtown before the disciplined army of General Sullivan. During the next few weeks his ears were assailed with the doleful tidings of burning villages and trampled cornfields, even as far west as the Genesee, the country of the Senecas. In 1780 he swept through the Mohawk River settlements exacting a terrible revenge. The next year news came to him in his forest stronghold that the great war chief, Cornwallis, had surrendered to the enemy. Two years later he heard of a treaty of peace between England and the United States, but neither he nor any of his people ever heard of any articles which sought to protect the interests of those Iroquois allies who had fought so stubbornly and so long against the American frontier.

THE MOHAWKS IN CANADA

112 Mohawk village on the Grand River, Canada, from a print in The Dominion Archives, Ottawa, Canada, after a drawing, 1793, in the British Museum

When the guns of the Revolution were silenced, the wigwams of the Mohawks were pitched for the most part on the west bank of the Niagara River; their ancient habitat was in the hands of the enemy. The Senecas, seeing them defeated and homeless, sent word that they might settle in the rich land of the Genesee. But Brant and the Mohawks declined. They remembered those words of General Haldimand in 1775. "The war has commenced. Assist the King now, and you will find it to your advantage. Go now and fight for your possessions, and, whatever you lose of your property during the war, the King will make up to you when peace returns." Brant journeyed to the St. Lawrence with the tale of the misfortunes of his people. The Canadian leaders, among them Haldimand himself, welcomed him with friendship and asked him where he would settle. He chose a territory on the Bay of Quinté. It was promised him. When he returned with the news, the Senecas were discontented. They feared the aggressions of the people of the United States in whose territory their villages stood. They looked to the Mohawks for help should it be necessary again to take up the hatchet. The Bay of Quinté was too far away. So Brant went again to the St. Lawrence. The Senecas had fought loyally beside the Mohawks and the latter must not abandon their friends. This time Brant brought back a promise of land on the Grand River, six miles on either side from its source to its mouth on the northern shore of Lake Erie. The Senecas were satisfied; this country was but forty miles from their own frontier. The promise received legal confirmation. Gradually the Mohawks together with other people of the Six Nations moved into the new habitat. Though much of the territory has been sold (it is in the heart of one of the richest agricultural regions of Canada), portions of all the Six Nations still live there with a full corps of chiefs.

THE SECOND TREATY OF FORT STANWIX, 1784

When the war was ended, the Americans, who could not forget the terrible tragedies of Wyoming and Cherry Valley, showed a disposition to expel the New York Iroquois. But both Washington and Schuyler opposed this. In 1784, the year following the treaty of peace, the Iroquois again met in council at Fort Stanwix. Here Lafayette addressed to them some plain-spoken words. Cornplanter, one of the principal chiefs of the Senecas, took a leading part in bringing about an accord. The hatchet was buried by all. In a brief treaty the Oneidas and Tuscaroras were secured in the possession of their lands. The Six Nations unwillingly gave up most of the territory not actually occupied by them. It had been gained and lost by the sword. At this council of Fort Stanwix, Pennsylvania commissioners were present and began the series of negotiations which resulted in the purchase of all the land owned by the Six Nations in Pennsylvania, except Cornplanter's reservation. Six years later Cornplanter stood before President Washington pleading for his people. "When your army entered the country of the Six Nations we called you the Town Destroyer; and to this day, when that name is heard, our women look behind them and turn pale, and our children cling close to the knees of their mothers. Our councilors and warriors are men, and cannot be afraid; but their hearts are grieved with the fears of our women and children, and desire that it may be buried so deep as to be heard no more. When you gave us peace, we called you father, because you promised to secure us in the possession of our lands. Do this and so long as the lands shall remain, that beloved name will live in the heart of every Seneca." (Quoted in Beauchamp, *History of the New York Iroquois*, 367–68.) Most of the lands, however, were destined to slip from the grasp of the Iroquois.

13 Cornplanter, a Seneca Chief, from a lithograph published by F. W. Greenough, Philadelphia, 1836

114 Map showing Military Land Grants, detail from *Map of the Middle States of North America with part of Canada*, 1791, in the Manuscript Room, New York Public Library

THE MILITARY TRACT

Two years before the second treaty of Fort Stanwix the state of New York set aside by law a certain portion of its western lands for the payment of military bounties to soldiers of the state who had served in the Revolution. "The Military Tract," which lay south of Lake Ontario and east of the lands ceded to Massachusetts (see below), comprised something more than one million six hundred thousand acres. Its southern boundary was the head of Seneca Lake. Seven years elapsed before the Indian title was extinguished. In 1789 surveyors entered the region and began laying out twenty-eight townships each containing one hundred lots of six hundred acres. To every private soldier and non-commissioned officer was assigned one lot. Officers received larger amounts varying with rank. The soldiers in many cases realized very little from the arrangement. In the long and uncertain period which elapsed before the lands were actually assigned and made ready for settlement many a man sold his patent for a pittance. In the end the Phelps-Gorham Purchase was settled more rapidly than the Military Tract. The latter, however, when pioneers once began coming in filled up swiftly.

THE PHELPS-GORHAM PURCHASE, 1787

As the Indian title to the lands of New York, Pennsylvania and Ohio began to fade, the imperial domain of the Six Nations caught the eye of the covetous land speculator. In the first two states the ownership of the soil was taken over by the states themselves; in the latter region it went to the central goverment. The claims of New York and Massachusetts clashed in that remote country south of Lake Ontario. To settle the dispute which arose from Massachusetts' charter, New York in 1786 granted to its eastern neighbor something more than six million acres of land in the western part of the state. On this Massachusetts quickly sought to realize a profit, for in the eighteenth century unoccupied wilderness was looked upon as a source of public revenue as well as the future abode of citizens. Massachusetts promptly disposed of the New York lands to two partners, Oliver Phelps and Nathaniel Gorham, for one million dollars. In 1788 Oliver Phelps left Massachusetts with men and means for exploring the vast territory of which he was part owner. At German Flats in the Mohawk Valley he left behind the white frontier. Pushing on through a hundred and thirty miles of wilderness known only to the Indian, he halted on the shores of Canandaigua Lake. Here with the help of Samuel K. Kirkland, a missionary among the Six Nations, he assembled a council of the Indian owners of the land.

115 Nathaniel Gorham, from an engraving after a mezzotint by Max Rosenthal, in the Emmet Collection, New York Public Library

respecting Rhode Island would have been injurious — and I am not clear that it would do any good to publish them at present — every thing that tends to irritate is by every means to be avoided —

Mr Oliver Phelps & myself have made the State an offer for the Western Land — viz.t £230000 in State paper — but as they expect a much larger sum we have no expectation of purchasing — the Assembly have spent two or three days in disputing how to conduct that business & have not yet come to a conclusion —

I have not to add but that I am very sincerely & respectfully Yours —

Nath.l Gorham

116 Last page of a letter from Nathaniel Gorham, describing his offer to purchase land in western New York, Boston, March 25, 1788, in the Emmet Collection, New York Public Library

THE SPEECH OF RED JACKET

Two days of negotiations followed and the contract was nearly completed when suddenly arose Red Jacket, one of the greatest of the Iroquois orators, and a man whose popularity had grown because of his opposition to Cornplanter at the second council of Fort Stanwix. Impressive in appearance, perfectly poised, he adjusted the silver bracelets on his arms and spoke to his countrymen. He recalled their former happy state, the usurpations of the white man, the suffering which followed in the wake of Sullivan's army. While he spoke he was master of his Indian audience. They wept with him; they echoed his demand for vengeance. When he sat down a thrill of fear ran through the little group of whites who had penetrated so far into the Indian country. Immediately rose a chief called Farmer's Brother, a more important leader than Red Jacket, a practical man and no demagogue. Though commending the eloquence of Red Jacket, he caused a cessation of the council, and, before the meeting had reassembled, with the aid of other prudent chiefs had moderated the fury of his nation. Then followed the arrangement of a satisfactory treaty.

117 Red Jacket, from the painting by Charles Willson Peale, in Independence Hall, Philadelphia

118 Oliver Phelps, 1749–1809, from the portrait (artist unknown), in the Ontario County Court House, Canandaigua, New York, courtesy of Oliver Phelps VI, Detroit

THE CANANDAIGUA SETTLEMENT

When Phelps had concluded the treaty, he began surveying his land into tracts called ranges, running north and south, subdivided these into townships, six miles square, and designated each by numbers. In 1789 he opened a land office at Canandaigua, said to have been the first in the United States for the sale of forest land to settlers. In 1797 that indefatigable compiler of gazeteers, Horatio Gates Spafford, made his way to the office at Canandaigua. "I found it [the Canandaigua settlement] but feeble, contending with innumerable embarrassments and difficulties. The spring of that year was uncommonly wet and cold. Besides a great deal of sickness, mud knee-deep, mosquitoes, and gnats, so thick that you could hardly breathe without swallowing them, rattlesnakes, and the ten thousand discouragements everywhere incident to new settlements, surrounded by all these, in June of that year, I saw, with wonder, that these people, all Yankees, from Massachusetts, Connecticut and Vermont, were perfectly undismayed, 'looking forward in hope,' 'sure and steadfast.' They talked to me of what the country would be, by-and-by as if it were history, and I received it as all *fable*. In order to see the whole 'power of the country,' a Military Muster of all the men capable of bearing arms, I waited a day or two, and attended 'the training.' Major Wadsworth was the commanding officer, and including the men who *had guns*, and who *had not*, the boys, women and children, it was supposed that near 200 persons were collected. This same territory, the 'old County of Ontario,' embraced a population in 1820, of two hundred and seventeen thousand three hundred and twenty-seven inhabitants divided into 10 Counties! But, as to the sagacity of any man foreseeing this, that is entirely out of the question." — Spafford, *Gazeteer of the State of New York,* 1824, 80.

LAND SPECULATION

The years from 1787 to 1796 saw wild speculation in land on more than one frontier. A wave of buoyant optimism was spreading over the country founded upon the possibilities of expansion during the next few decades. Many men, both Americans and foreigners, sought to make fortunes on western lands which they never expected to see and in which they had no interest beyond selling them in large blocks to other speculators for a larger price than that which they had payed. The year after the opening of the Canandaigua land office Phelps and Gorham sold a large part of their surveyed territory, something more than a million and two hundred thousand acres, to Robert Morris of Philadelphia for eight pence an acre. Phelps and Gorham, unable to fulfill their contract with Massachusetts, compromised, and surrendered the part of the land to which the Indian title was not extinguished. Morris sold his purchase to Sir William Pultney of England. In 1796 Morris, the "financier of the Revolution," purchased of Massachusetts the tract which Phelps and Gorham had surrendered. He extinguished the Indian title, sold off several large tracts along the Genesee, and mortgaged the residue to a group of Dutch bankers known as the Holland Land Company.

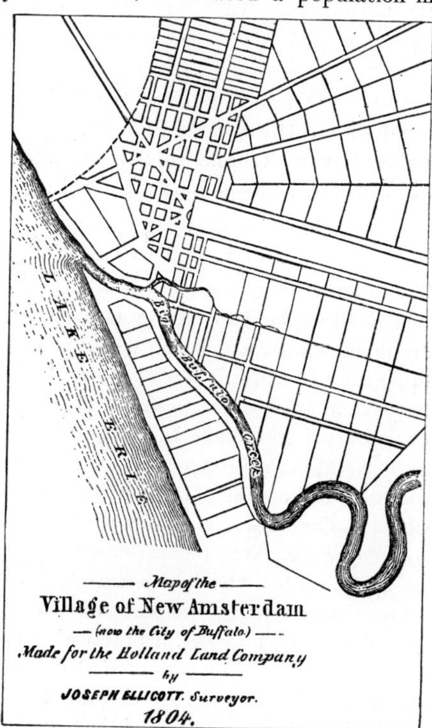

119 Laying out Townships in Western New York, from the original in the Map Room, New York Public Library

THE HOLLAND LAND COMPANY

120 Office of the Holland Land Company, from an engraving in J. Warner Barber, *A Pictorial History of New York*, Cooperstown, N. Y., 1846

"The men of the early 'nineties in the Eighteenth century sought to reap even before the seeding was complete. Rich and poor alike bought excitedly of wild lands wherever credit could be had and as excitedly sought to resell before time for repayment should arrive. It was in such circumstances, in 1792, that the Dutch bankers, later to be known as the Holland Land Company, were drawn into the maelstrom of American land speculation. Within a few years they had acquired title to more than five million acres in central and western New York, and in northern and western Pennsylvania. Unlike most American speculators they paid cash for their lands, intending to retain part of them at least for the large profits which they were assured would arise from resales to settlers. Even that portion which might have been resold quickly at wholesale had in the end to be held for sale in small lots, for in 1796 the land bubble broke and large sales thereafter were impossible. It was an imposing domain which these Dutch gentlemen had acquired. Five and a half million acres were indeed by no means an unprecedented holding for a small group or even for a single man. Whatever their original intentions, they found it necessary to retain much of their land for years and to sell it at retail to a multitude of actual settlers, poor men to whom they must extend credit. In carrying through this process they were confronted by a host of complex social problems. They were no longer mere cogs in a machine that constantly transferred wild land from one owner to another; they became guardians of a people's rights and interests, promoters of a people's life." — Paul D. Evans, *The Holland Land Company*, 12–13.

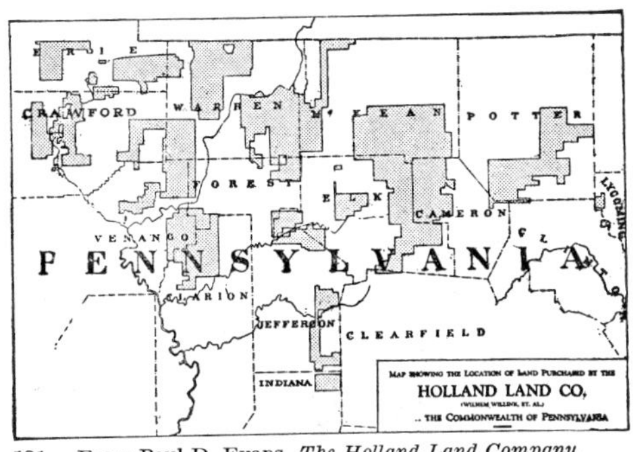

121 From Paul D. Evans, *The Holland Land Company*, Buffalo Historical Society, Buffalo, 1924

THE GENESEE ROAD

After the upper reaches of the Mohawk River were passed the Yankee settler going west to buy land from the Holland Company found his journey a difficult one. He might take the old military road from Fort Stanwix to Oswego and skirt the southern shore of Lake Ontario to the mouth of the Genesee, but there was no regular transportation service on the lake. So great was the rush of settlers to the fertile lands of the Finger Lakes region that in 1794 a road was authorized from Fort Stanwix to the Genesee River and four years later a law was passed extending it to the western boundary of the state. This was known as the "Main Genesee Road" until 1800, when the New York legislature incorporated a turnpike company known as "The President and Directors of the Seneca Road Company." The old name, however, still clung to it and lingers to the present day in the "Genesee Street" of both the large cities through which it passes, Syracuse and Utica. Over it jolted the wagons of the New England farmers seeking a more friendly soil in what had been the country of the Iroquois. The incorporation of a turnpike company to improve it, while the region was yet so young and only six years after the building of the first turnpike in the United States at Lancaster, Pennsylvania, is evidence of its vital significance for the settlement of western New York. West of the Appalachians in the valley of the Ohio a multitude of streams offered transportation to the pioneer, and the first settlers followed their courses. In New York, in contrast, the newcomers made their way westward over land routes that had to be constructed by the hand of man.

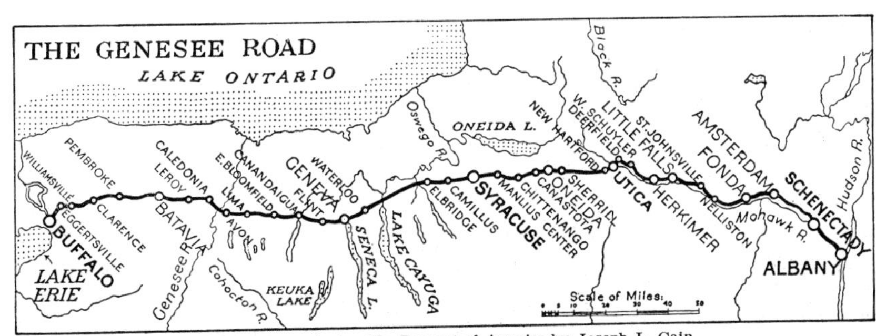

122 Drawn expressly for *The Pageant of America* by Joseph L. Cain

123 William Cooper, from the portrait by Gilbert Stuart (1755–1828), in the possession of Paul F. Cooper, Albany

WILLIAM COOPER, 1754–1809

THE operations of Phelps and Gorham and of the Holland Land Company were far to the west of the old New York frontier of the Mohawk and upper Susquehanna valleys. To this ruined region where brush had sprung up in the cleared fields, following the ravages of Brant and the Iroquois, settlers returned as soon as the Revolutionary War was over. Here came also in 1785 one William Cooper destined to be known in history as the father of a famous son. He took up land in the hitherto undeveloped country about Otsego Lake which James Fenimore subsequently immortalized as Lake Glimmerglass. The elder Cooper proved himself a successful colonizer. The problems which he faced are characteristic of the frontier in the forest.

EARLY EFFORT

"IN May 1786, I opened the sales of 40,000 acres, which in sixteen days were taken up by the poorest order of men. I soon after established a store, and went to live among them; the country was mountainous, and there were neither roads nor bridges. But the greatest discouragement was in the extreme poverty of the people, none of whom had the means of clearing more than a small spot in the midst of the thick and lofty woods, so that their grain grew chiefly in the shade; their maize did not ripen, their wheat was blasted, and the little they did gather they had no mill to grind within twenty miles' distance; not one in twenty had a horse, and the way lay through rapid streams, across swamps or over bogs. I resided among them and saw too clearly how bad their condition was. I erected a storehouse, and during each Winter filled it with large quantities of grain, purchased in distant places. I procured from my friend, Henry Drinker, a credit for a large quantity of sugar kettles; he also lent me some potash kettles. By this means I established potash works among the settlers, and made them debtor for their land and laboring utensils. I also gave them credit for their maple sugar and their potash [made from the ashes of burned logs] at a price that would bear transportation, and the first year after the adoption of this plan I collected in one mass forty-three hogsheads of sugar and three hundred barrels of pot and pearl ash, worth about nine thousand dollars. This kept the people together and at home, and the country soon assumed a new face. I had not funds of my own sufficient for the opening of new roads, but I collected the people at convenient seasons, and by joint efforts we were able to throw bridges over the deep streams, and to make, in the cheapest manner, such roads as suited our then humble purposes."

124 Otsego Hall, Cooperstown, built by William Cooper 1797–99 and destroyed by fire 1853, from an engraving in Francis W. Halsey, *The Old New York Frontier*. © Charles Scribner's Sons, New York, 1901, used by permission

— Quoted in HALSEY, *The Old New York Frontier*, 361–63. Such was the founding of Cooperstown in the land of the Deerslayer. Cooper's account brings into sharp relief the poverty of the average frontier family and the desperate struggle for a bare existence that characterized the fringe of settlement.

125 Newly Cleared Land in America, from Basil Hall, *Forty Etchings with the Camera Lucida in North America*, Edinburgh, 1829

126 Southwest view of the central part of Canandaigua, New York, from an engraving in John Warner Barber and Henry Howe, *Historical Collections of the State of New York*, New York, 1851

PIONEERS OF WESTERN NEW YORK

James H. Hotchkin, a Presbyterian minister, described in 1848 the people who were flooding into western New York during the first quarter of the nineteenth century. "The first emigrants . . . were from different parts of the United States; but mostly from New England. Those who were from the same neighborhood, frequently located themselves together in the same township. Not unfrequently, however, the case was otherwise. . . . Emigrants from Connecticut intermingled with emigrants from Massachusetts and other New England states, were found in the same neighborhood. Not unfrequently, emigrants from the New England States, and emigrants from New Jersey and Pennsylvania, located themselves side by side. A few from States south of Pennsylvania, and some from Europe, were among the early settlers of Western New York. . . . But in most cases the New England character was the prevalent trait. In consequence, however, of the intermixture of emigrants from different parts of the country, there was in many places a great diversity in their habits, tastes, and modes of thinking on a variety of subjects, and especially on the subject of religion and religious institutions. . . . A vast tract of wild land lay before them, on any part of which they might locate themselves. Diversity of soil and timber, and adaptedness to different branches of husbandry existed. Contiguity to roads, streams of water, places where water-power might be employed, and where centers of business might be expected to be formed, constituted attractions to different individuals. . . . Hence, for a considerable period after the commencement of the settlement, but few families were to be found in any one neighborhood. In many instances, a single family lived at a distance of some miles from any other for a year or two. Under these circumstances, it was not practicable to form religious societies, and congregations for divine worship, in most places, for a considerable period. . . . Sickness in the early period of the settlement greatly prevailed. The common disorders prevalent were fevers, and ague and fever. The seasons of 1793 and 1794 were very sickly seasons. 'At one time,' says Dr. Coventry, 'in the village of Geneva, there was but a single individual who could leave her bed, and she, like a ministering angel, went from house to house, bestowing on the sick the greatest of all boons, a drink of cold water." — *A History of the Purchase and Settlement of Western New York*, 18, 24–25.

127 View in the central part of Manlius, N. Y., from an engraving in J. W. Barber and Henry Howe, *Historical Collections of the State of New York*, New York, 1851

128 Buffalo Harbor From The Village, from a lithograph by Imbert, after a drawing by George Catlin, in *A Memoir presented at the Celebration of the Completion of the New York Canals*, New York, 1825

EARLY BUFFALO

In 1804 Timothy Dwight, President of Yale College, made a trip through the settlements of his fellow New Englanders in far-away New York. He traveled even to Buffalo. "The village consists of about twenty houses. The Holland company owns the soil. Hitherto they have declined to sell it; and, until very lately, to lease it. Most of the settlers have, therefore, taken up their ground without any title. The streets are straight, and cross each other at right angles; but are only forty feet wide. What could have induced this wretched limitation in a mere wilderness I am unable to conceive. The habitants are a casual collection of adventurers; and have the usual character of such adventurers, thus collected, when remote from regular society; retaining but little sense of Government, or Religion. We saw about as many Indians in this village, as white people. The period is not distant, when the commerce of this neighbourhood will become a great national object; and involve no small part of the interests and happiness of millions."

THE BROKEN IROQUOIS

In 1804 President Dwight at Buffalo looked toward the west where lay the destiny of his country. Behind him in the Genesee valley and in the lake country of New York still lived the proudest of the eastern forest Indians. The tribes who had conquered and held a domain larger than England and who had played an important part in the conflict between the British and the French for the continent of North America had at last been brought down. Their hunting grounds were controlled by land speculators and overrun by New England farmers. Their domain was rapidly shrinking to a few small reservations in New York, Cornplanter's reservation in Pennsylvania, and the holdings in Canada. The aged Red Jacket, dying in 1832, carried with him to his grave the spirit of the forest barbarian who was born to the wild freedom of nature and who would not bow to the white man nor acquire his civilization. When an old man he tottered from cabin to cabin of his friends to pay them a last ceremonial visit. "I am about to leave you," said he, "and when I am gone and my warning shall no longer be heard or regarded, the craft and the avarice of the white man will prevail. Many winters have I breasted the storm, but I am an aged tree, and can stand no longer. My leaves are fallen, my branches are withered, and I am shaken by every breeze. Soon my aged trunk will be prostrate, and the foot of the exulting foe of the Indian may be placed upon it in safety; for I leave none who will be enabled to avenge such an indignity. Think not I mourn for myself. I go to join the spirits of my fathers, where age cannot come; but my heart fails when I think of my people, who are soon to be scattered and forgotten." — Quoted in Barber, *Pictorial History of New York*, 1846, 94.

129 Red Jacket as an old man, from the portrait by John Ferguson Weir (1841–1926), in the New York Historical Society

A SENECA PROPHET

Time was to prove the despairing Red Jacket a poor prophet. The twentieth century found the Iroquois equal in number to those great days in the seventeenth century when they reached their apogee with an estimated sixteen thousand souls. Red Jacket had despised the man who, more than any other individual, saved his people from the white man. Handsome Lake, like Red Jacket a Seneca, was born in 1735, a half brother to Cornplanter. He was not a warrior and leader of men like Farmer's Brother and, unlike that powerful personality, he could not abstain from the white man's devastating liquor. Handsome Lake was for many years a drunkard. As the eighteenth century neared its end he was laid low by a wasting disease aggravated by his excesses. For four years in poverty, nursed by a married daughter, he lay on his bed. Then he arose and passed out of his lodge to preach a new religion to his people. In his sickness he had seen a vision; three men stood before him. "Their cheeks were painted red and it seemed that they had been painted the day before. Only a few feathers were in their bonnets. All three were alike and all seemed middle aged. Never before have I seen such handsome commanding men and they had in one hand bows and arrow as canes. Now in their other hands were huckleberry bushes and the berries were of every color." — A. C. Parker, *The Code of Handsome Lake*, 24.

130 Tne Sick Man Meditating, from a drawing by Jesse Cornplanter in Arthur C. Parker, *The Code of Handsome Lake*, University of the State of New York, Albany, 1913

THE PASSING OF AN OLD CULTURE

Handsome Lake devised a formula which helped the Iroquois to make the transition from barbarism to civilization. The time came at the end of the eighteenth century when the flood of white people coming into the country of the Finger Lakes forced the Indian to abandon the forest ways of his ancestors. His material culture was rapidly passing; long ago he had given up the bow for the rifle and the flint knife for the blade of steel. Now his habitations were built after the white man's model and with the white man's tools. When he laid his dead to rest few were the articles of Indian origin and make that were placed reverently beside the body; into the grave went the utensils and the ornaments fabricated by the white man's hand. As the Iroquois saw the forest melt away, he found his old manner of living, his old folkways, out of harmony with the new conditions. A woodland changed to an agricultural environment in two decades. The memories, the traditions, the religion of the past helped him but little. His "elder brothers" of the forest were harried even as himself; they could no longer help him in the hunt. He faced a revolution — perhaps extinction — for the white man had brought him a deadly poison. Fire water was threatening to become the master of his people, a destroyer of both spirit and body.

131 An Iroquois Home, from a sketch in Edward S. Ellis, *The Indian Wars of the United States*, New York, 1892

132 Reciting the Ritual of Handsome Lake at Tonawanda, from a drawing by Jesse Cornplanter in Arthur C. Parker, *The Code of Handsome Lake*, University of the State of New York, Albany, 1913

THE WORK OF HANDSOME LAKE

To Handsome Lake belongs the credit of drawing together those new aspects of the Iroquois life which made for a sound adjustment to the new conditions, of crystallizing this body of folkways into a new religion which the Indian could understand, and of making his code the most powerful force for good among his people because of its appeal to the Indian's highly developed religious instincts rather than to his reason. In 1802 Handsome Lake visited Thomas Jefferson, President of the United States, and received from that apostle of religious freedom the following letter. "Brothers — The President rejoices in his heart that one of your own people has been employed to make you sober, good and happy; and that he is so well disposed to give you good advice, and to set before you so good examples. Brothers — if all the red people follow the advice of your friend and teacher, the Handsome Lake, and in the future will be sober, honest, industrious and good, there can be no doubt but the Great Spirit will take care of you and make you happy." — Parker, *The Code of Handsome Lake*, 10. The letter was interpreted as giving Handsome Lake the right to teach. The accompanying picture is an excellent representation of a modern teacher reciting the *Gai wiie*, the ritual of the religion of Handsome Lake.

THE CODE OF HANDSOME LAKE

The teachings of this Indian prophet were, in the main, a body of moral precepts. Men should abjure strong drink, that monstrous evil which "has reared a high mound of Bones." They should remain constant to wife or husband and should be fruitful. They "should rear their children well, love them, and keep them in health." "The Creator forbids unkindness to the old." The people should refrain from pride and from speaking evil of one another. "Tell your people that petty thieving must cease." The old worship of the "elder brothers," the totem animals, must be given up. People must forget their old "compelling charms" because of which "a great pile of human bodies lies dead." Witches must stand before the people and say: "I am doing this evil thing but now I cease it forever, as long as I live." The people should give up the custom of mourning "at each recurring anniversary of the death of a friend or relative." They should know that in the world beyond the grave is punishment for evil done on earth and happiness for those who live aright. Twice a year, at the September meeting of the Six Nations and at the midwinter thanksgiving, the ritual of Handsome Lake was to be repeated. At dawn on three successive days the "holder" should rise before the people assembled in the "long house" and say the ritual for the particular day.

133 The Death Chant and March at the Newton Long House, from a drawing by Jesse Cornplanter in Arthur C. Parker, *The Code of Handsome Lake*, University of the State of New York, Albany, 1913

134 So-Son-Do-Wa or Edward Cornplanter, Seneca teacher of Handsome Lake's Code, from Arthur C. Parker, *The Code of Handsome Lake*, University of the State of New York, Albany, 1913

THE CODE TO-DAY

Into the twentieth century the worship has come. In the "long houses" the women still wear shawls over their heads and during the affecting parts of the story hide their faces to conceal their tears. The men sit with bowed heads, tears coursing down their cheeks. They do not worship Handsome Lake but the "Creator" of whom he taught. Reverently they listen to the last words of the ceremony of the third day and picture in their minds the teacher who has gone before. "Soon I will step into the new world, for there is a plain pathway before me leading there. Whoever follows my teaching will follow in my footsteps and I will look back upon him with outstretched arms inviting him into the new world of our Creator. Alas, I fear that a pall of smoke will obscure the eyes of many from the truth of *Gai wiie* but I pray that when I am gone all may do what I have taught." — Parker, *op. cit.*, 27–80.

135 The tomb of Handsome Lake, near the Onondaga Council House, from Arthur C. Parker, *The Code of Handsome Lake*, University of the State of New York, Albany, 1913

THE IROQUOIS OF THE PRESENT

Handsome Lake died in 1815. Past his tomb on the Onondaga reservation runs a broad macadam highway crowded with the motor cars of the twentieth century. This Indian son of the eighteenth century showed his people the way to preserve their ancient and peculiar moral strength in the midst of the white man's country. His name ranks with that of Dekanawidah; these two were the outstanding benefactors of their nation. But the world moves on and the code of Handsome Lake is now the "old religion." Many of the Indians are Christianized and "whitemanized" but on the reservations of the Senecas and the Onondagas the Indian folkways and manner of thinking still struggle for supremacy with the white man's civilization. "The Indian of the old way is arrayed against the Indian of the new way. The conservative Indian calls his Christian brother a traitor to his race, a man ashamed of his ancestors, a man who condones all the wrongs the white man has done his people, and a man who is at best an imitator and a poor one. On the other hand the Christian Indian calls his 'feather wearing' brother, 'a blind man in the wilderness,' a nonprogressive, behind the times, a man hopelessly struggling against fate, a heathen and a pagan. How long can they oppose their way to the overwhelming forces of the modern world and exist? Many Indian friends will answer, 'Of these things we know nothing; we know only that the Great Ruler will care for us as long as we are faithful.' Asked about the clothes they wear, the houses they live in, they reply, 'All these things may be made of the white man's material but they are outside things. Our religion is not one of paint and feathers; it is a thing of the heart.' That is the answer; it is a thing of the heart — who can change it?" — Parker, *op. cit.*, 14–15. The Indian may accept the white man's ways but, so long as his blood remains unmixed, his must continue to be a race apart with ideals and aspirations peculiar to itself.

136 Onondaga Long House, Onondaga reservation (+ marks the site of Handsome Lake's tomb), from Arthur C. Parker, *The Code of Handsome Lake*, University of the State of New York, Albany, 1913

CHAPTER IV

THE OLD NORTHWEST

IN the same year that the council of the Six Nations was negotiating the second Treaty of Fort Stanwix the Congress of the Confederation was considering the question of establishing a land policy to govern the settlement of that domain stretching from the boundary of Pennsylvania westward to the Mississippi and known as the Northwest Territory. The versatile Thomas Jefferson was chairman of a committee which brought in a report that led directly to the Ordinance of 1784. As the time for active settlement had not yet arrived, the significance of this legislation was chiefly in preparing the way for the famous enactment of three years later. In 1785, however, the Congress put on the statute books of the Confederation the Ordinance of 1785 by which the principle of rectangular surveys was established in the national land system. All land belonging to the United States before being opened for settlement was to be surveyed into townships six miles square, each containing thirty-six sections. From this time dates the checkerboard appearance of the land survey maps of the United States.

Two years later, in May 1787, the most distinguished Americans of the day assembled at Philadelphia to undertake the deliberations which were to eventuate in the Constitution of the United States. Sitting at the same time and struggling to hold a quorum was the Congress of the Confederation, a feeble body quite discredited after years of impotence. While the Constitutional Convention was debating in secret the issues which led to the "Great Compromise," the Congress was forging an enactment destined to take a place among the few basic pieces of legislation that have shaped the destinies of the American people. The Ordinance of 1787 established what was virtually a colonial policy. Its provisions have been spread on the pages of practically every textbook of American history. They included a scheme for the partition of land into territories, a plan of government, and a bill of rights. The Northwest Territory was to be divided into five parts each of which should ultimately become a state. Statehood was the third and last stage through which the government of the frontier settlement should pass. The first was that period in which the population of the territory was sparse and small in number, under which circumstances the Congress should appoint a governor, secretary, and judges, competent to make the laws and administer them without consulting the wish of any settler. The second stage was reached when the number of adult males in the territory reached five thousand. Then a legislature should be set up to assume control of lawmaking and the public purse. When the population numbered sixty thousand or was equal in number to that of the smallest state, the territory, which up to this time had been a colony, should become a member of the parent nation and assume a place in its councils on an equal footing with every other state. No more liberal colonial policy has ever been devised. The bill of rights was much like that which later was added to the Constitution, with the striking difference that the Ordinance abolished slavery in the Northwest Territory. More than a year before the Ordinance was passed surveyors went into the western country to prepare for the flood of settlers that soon pressed on their heels.

137 Drawn expressly for *The Pageant of America* by Gregor Noetzel, American Geographical Society, New York

THE FRONTIER OF 1800

THE second census of the United States was taken in a year of political strife. The stiff-necked Federalists were trying with evident lack of success to check the onslaughts of the followers of Jefferson. To the aristocrats who followed the leadership of those incompatibles, Adams and Hamilton, the victory of the author of the Declaration of Independence seemed nothing short of revolution. Political wiseacres among them did not fail to observe that the frontier had gone solidly for Jefferson. Thoughtful observers noted the appearance beyond the mountains of a menace to the ancient ideal of aristocracy. When the census returns were published New England politicians, who were willing to take the trouble, could visualize the political menace to their section which was rising in the West. Kentucky and Tennessee were in the Union and Ohio was on the verge of statehood. With the fringe of settlement pressing steadily westward New England's eighteenth-century importance in the councils of the nation was bound to wane. Many of the folk of this section, however, looked to the western country with hope rather than apprehension. A rich soil lying close to lakes and navigable rivers offered opportunities which New England could rarely match. Eighteenth-century farmers in Connecticut and Massachusetts had often chopped away the forest with more vigor than wisdom. Much of the land which had been stripped was stony and infertile. The opening years of the nineteenth century revealed to many a farmer that the hill fields where he and his oxen labored could not be cultivated with profit and that the wise husbandman allowed a friendly nature to cover the nakedness of his slopes with a mantle of trees. The force of the economic drive away from stony hillsides was augmented by the lure of the frontier. The young New England farmer found in the census returns from the country beyond the mountains a rough measure of the opportunity in unoccupied land which the West offered.

138 Louisville and Clarksville, from Gilbert Imlay, *A Topographical Description of the Western Territory of North America*, London, 1793

CLARK'S GRANT

THE story of the settlement of the Northwest Territory begins with George Rogers Clark. To him and to his men, as compensation for their great services to the commonwealth, Virginia voted one hundred and fifty thousand acres of land on the north bank of the Ohio. In addition Clark received an engraved sword and the formal thanks of the legislature. The conqueror of Vincennes chose the region immediately across from Louisville for the location of "Clark's Grant." When the Old Dominion surrendered to the central government all claim to the Northwest Territory, a saving clause provided for the confirmation of the grant to Clark. The country was wild. Indian villages were not far away to the north and the clouds of Indian war lay on the horizon. In course of time Clark built a cabin on his domain. Poverty overtook him; the intrepid leader in war could not adjust himself to the conditions of peace. He began to feel aggrieved that his military services had not received a greater financial recognition. He, "the conqueror of the Northwest," was given but a paltry six thousand acres in a remote wilderness. Had General Washington reasoned after the manner of Clark, one wonders what his compensation should have been. More and more Clark turned to drink. The strength of the old days was dissipated and the fire of former times burned low.

BRITISH NORTHWEST POLICY

THE treaty of 1783 gave to the United States a northern boundary which ran through the middle of the Great Lakes, save Michigan which was wholly American. The old French fort, Mackinac, guarded the entrance to the latter, while Detroit stood on the banks of the river of the same name. Other forts reared their palisades on the south shore of Ontario, the south bank of the St. Lawrence, and on Lake Champlain. All were on soil to which the sovereignty of the United States was extended by the treaty of 1783. They controlled the main trade routes into the fur-bearing country. They served as places of deposit and distribution for the merchants engaged in the trade. Here the men who traded directly with the Indians purchased their outfits and returned with their pelts. Here middle men carried on their business of importing goods from Montreal and selling them on credit to the traders. Detroit and Mackinac were of particular importance. At these posts the small ships on the inland seas gave up their supplies for the redskin. The goods were transferred to canoes for transport by river and portage to the tribes far in the forests. The fur trade was an important source of profit to both Canadians and Britons. Because of their strategic location, control of the forts enabled the British virtually to exclude American trading interests. It made possible also the retention of that alliance between the British and the western Indians which, as well as being commercially profitable, had been of some military importance during the Revolution. The forts were not surrendered.

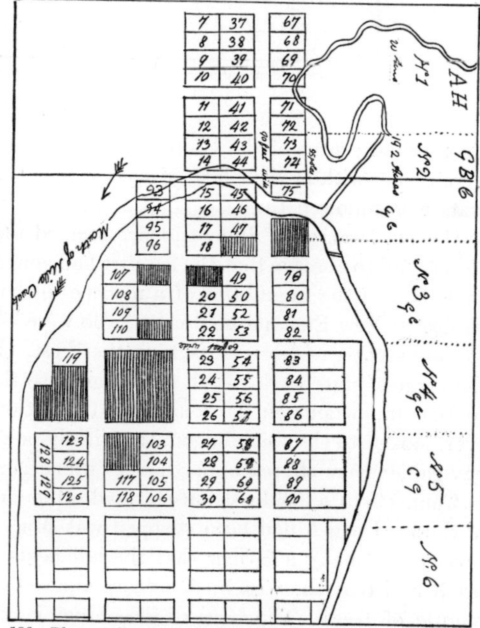

139 Plan of the town of Clarksville made by George Rogers Clark about 1805, from the original in the possession of R. C. Ballard Thruston, Louisville, Ky.

THE MIAMIS

North of Clark's Grant lived the Miamis. Little Turtle, their only famous chief, once remarked: "My fathers kindled the first fire at Detroit; thence they extended their lines to the headwaters of the Scioto; thence to its mouth, thence down the Ohio to the mouth of the Wabash, and thence to Chicago over Lake Michigan." The upper Wabash and the valley of the St. Joseph River were the regions of their chief settlement. In the early eighteenth century the fathers of Little Turtle had abandoned the Scioto region and the Shawnees had come in. The Miamis were the most powerful of the Indians of Ohio and Indiana and were looked upon by the whites as being the owners of the soil in this country, the Shawnees and Delawares being considered as holding their regions by the sufferance of the Miamis. In the eighteenth century, in the days of their prosperity, the total number of the Miamis varied around fifteen hundred. They were Algonquins and they showed an unusual discipline for Indians of that family. They respected their chiefs who had considerable authority over them. In 1718 their men were described as "of medium height, well built, heads rather round than oblong, countenances agreeable rather than sedate or morose, swift on foot, and excessively fond of racing." — Hodge, *Handbook of the American Indian*, I, 853. The women were generally well clad in deerskins, while the men used scarcely any covering and were tattooed all over the body.

140 Little Turtle, from an engraving, after a portrait painted from life, in Calvin M. Young, *Little Turtle*. © Sentinel Printing Co., Indianapolis, Indiana, 1917

NEIGHBORS OF THE MIAMIS

Near neighbors to the Miamis were the Potawatomis and the Ottawas. According to Indian tradition these two, together with the numerous Chippewa people whose villages were to be found all the way from the Dakota country to the region south of the Great Lakes, were sprung from a common origin in what is now Wisconsin. At the end of the seventeenth century the Potawatomis were conquering their way into northern Illinois where the Miamis had once been located, and extending eastward across southern Michigan. American pioneers, pushing the frontier westward, found their villages north of the Miamis, who occupied the valley of the Wabash. The Ottawas lived to the north of the Potawatomis in the country west of Lake Huron. The two tribes were close in culture and were sometimes bound together by a loose confederation which also, upon occasion, included the Chippewas. They were Algonquins with a culture essentially similar to that of the Miamis. The Ottawas produced in historic times one great leader, Pontiac. (See Volume VI, Chapter VIII.) They were the traders among the Indians of the region, their very name coming from an Indian root meaning "to buy and sell." They were found at times four and five hundred miles away from their home villages trading in corn meal, sunflower oil, furs and skins, rugs or mats, tobacco, and medicinal roots and herbs. The Potawatomis were early described as more disposed toward Christianity and more humane and civilized than the other tribes.

141 Location of Indian Tribes of the Northwest, redrawn from a map in Elmore Barce, *The Land of the Miamis*. © Fowler Press, Benton, Indiana, 1922

142 A full-blood Ottawa Type, from a photograph in the De Lancey Gill Collection, United States National Museum, Washington

143 A full-blood Miami Type, from a photograph in the De Lancey Gill Collection, United States National Museum, Washington

TRADING WITH THE WHITES

THROUGH the country of the Miamis passed one of the principal trade routes of the interior of North America in the seventeenth and eighteenth centuries. Detroit in the old French days was the chief trading post located in the plains country of the continental interior. From here goods were paddled up the Maumee and from thence carried across the short portage to the upper Wabash. Once on the waters of this south-flowing stream they were taken to the Ohio and perhaps down the Mississippi. Often they continued southward by way of the Cumberland or more commonly the Tennessee that flowed through the heart of the Cherokee country. From this great river portages would take the traders to the upper waters of streams flowing into the Gulf — to Mobile or to Pensacola. South of the Wabash the trade routes tended to diverge, to reach southern points distant from one another, but north of the Ohio they tended to converge in the Wabash-Maumee route which took them to Detroit. The Miamis, therefore, and their neighbors the Potawatomis, the Ottawas, and the Wyandots, had for many decades before the advance of the American frontier been accustomed to contact with the white man. And this contact had demoralized the forest people. French brandy and English rum had destroyed many of the fine qualities of the old-time barbarians. They were rapidly deteriorating when settlers began coming into Clark's Grant. But they had not lost entirely their pride of race. They were not to be driven finally from their hunting grounds without a fight.

144 A full-blood Potawatomi Type, from a photograph in the De Lancey Gill Collection, United States National Museum, Washington

145 Ste. Anne Street, now Jefferson Avenue, Detroit, 1800, from a drawing in George B. Catlin, *The Story of Detroit.* © *The Detroit News*, 1923

THE BRITISH IN THE LAKE COUNTRY

British imperial officials in Canada read the treaty of 1783 with some dismay. By the terms of that document the Ohio and Great Lakes tribes, with whom the British had maintained alliances since the passing of the French, came under the control of the United States. If the treaty was carried out, the profits from the fur trade of Upper Canada would be vastly reduced. Americans, moreover, in possession of the fortifications at Mackinac, Detroit, and Niagara would offer a serious threat to that province. Retention of the forts seemed necessary for the defense of Canada. Retention of the friendly alliances with the Indians was vital to the defense of the forts, for the British Government, burdened with war debts, could not afford to maintain adequate garrisons on the frontier. Watching with growing apprehension the determined advance of American settlers Canadian officials, Governor-General Dorchester and Lieutenant-Governor Simcoe, cultivated the friendship of the redskins. The Canadians desired to establish a No Man's Land between their own provinces and the settlements of the aggressive Americans. "The great object," wrote Dundas, the Colonial Secretary, in 1792, "is to interpose a barrier by means of Indians or where they are thinly scattered, by the strength and situation of the country so as to prevent encroachment on either side."

146 Pittsburgh in 1796, from a drawing in Victor Collot, *Voyage dans l'Amérique Septentrionale*, Paris, 1826

PITTSBURGH

The close of the Revolutionary War turned the minds of many eastern Americans toward the West. Pittsburgh at the confluence of the Allegheny and the Monongahela was being laid out as a town of some thousand inhabitants as the conflict ended. To it came the immigrants making their way westward through the valley of the Juniata. Past its warehouses floated the flatboats and arks which had been built at Redstone farther up the Monongahela. At first the westward moving folk were on their way to Limestone and Kentucky. Later the immigrant stream turned northward into Ohio. Pittsburgh became the gateway to the West.

147 Fort Harmar in 1790, from a lithograph in *The American Pioneer*, Chillicothe, Ohio, 1842

FORT HARMAR

THE year following the Ordinance of 1784 saw the beginning of governmental activities looking toward the management of the Northwest Territory. The Congress was hurried because of the fact that Kentuckians were beginning to venture across to the Indian side of the Ohio to take up tomahawk claims in the forests through which ran the Scioto and the Muskingum. At first they came singly, then in small parties. They had no legal right to enter. They were trespassers upon the national domain and upon the unceded lands of the Indians. Colonel Josiah Harmar commanded the federal garrison at Fort Pitt. When he learned from agents whom he sent into the region that Kentuckians were crossing the Ohio in considerable numbers, he promptly set about surveying the "Seven Ranges," as the country immediately west of the Pennsylvania line was called. The land survey Ordinance of 1785, therefore, as a result of the initiative of Harmar, began to operate in the very year of its passage. To protect his surveyors from the hostile squatters and to make a refuge for traffickers on the Ohio River the colonel built Fort Harmar at the mouth of the Muskingum in the same year, 1785. On the opposite bank of the smaller stream was an elaborate system of mounds, relics of the intriguing Mound Builder culture.

GENERAL RUFUS PUTNAM, 1738–1824

IN the year following the building of Fort Harmar, General Rufus Putnam and several other officers of the Continental Army met at the "Bunch of Grapes" tavern in Boston and decided to exchange the almost worthless paper money with which Congress had paid them for a tract of western land. The result of the meeting was the founding of the Company of the Ohio Associates.

148 Rufus Putnam, from a miniature painted in 1790 by John Trumbull (1756–1843), in the School of the Fine Arts, Yale University, New Haven

MANASSEH CUTLER, 1742–1823

ONE of the most interesting figures of the Ohio Company was the Reverend Doctor Manasseh Cutler, "preacher, lawyer, doctor, statesman, scientist, land speculator." Cutler, together with Putnam and Parsons, was sent to the Congress in New York to lay the company's request before the central government of the Confederation. He was in the National Capital during those momentous weeks in which the Constitution of the United States was being forged. Few lobbyists have ever worked with better success or have left their activities hidden behind deeper shadows. He argued that the sale of the Ohio land would bring much money into the sadly impoverished national treasury. He suggested that the transaction involving the Ohio Company would be the forerunner of many sales. He called attention to the fact that distant Kentucky, populated by vigorous and independent pioneers, was in danger of slipping from the hold of the United States and suggested the desirability, for the purposes of maintaining the territorial integrity of the nation, of having a settlement across the river from that outlying frontier. The cynical have implied that more persuasive than these arguments was the offer to General St. Clair, president of the Congress, of the governorship of the western country in case the deal succeeded. When Dr. Cutler returned to Boston, his colleagues were astonished to find that he had not only purchased land for the Ohio Company — land which turned out to be just under a million acres in area — but had secured in the name of Winthrop Sargent five million acres to the west of it. Among those interested in this second speculation, the Scioto Company, were some of the members of the Continental Congress who had voted the deal through. So land speculation on a gigantic scale came to the Ohio country. The Ohio Company, however, was destined to play an important part in the settlement of the state.

149 Manasseh Cutler, from a portrait by N. Lakeman in the Essex Institute, Salem, Mass.

MAP OF THE OHIO COMPANY'S LAND

THE Ohio Company chose for its site the mouth of the Muskingum and the valley of the Hockhocking. As they studied their maps of the Ohio country some of these enterprisers must have remembered that only thirteen years before Lord Fenmore had led an army up that same Hockhocking against the powerful Shawnees led by the able Cornstalk. They must have been aware that during the years of the Revolution these same Indians had continually harassed the Kentucky settlements and that, although they had been repulsed again and again in their attacks against Kentucky stations, no counter thrust had broken their power. Perhaps with these considerations in mind General Putnam picked the mouth of the Muskingum opposite Fort Harmar as the location for the first town in Ohio.

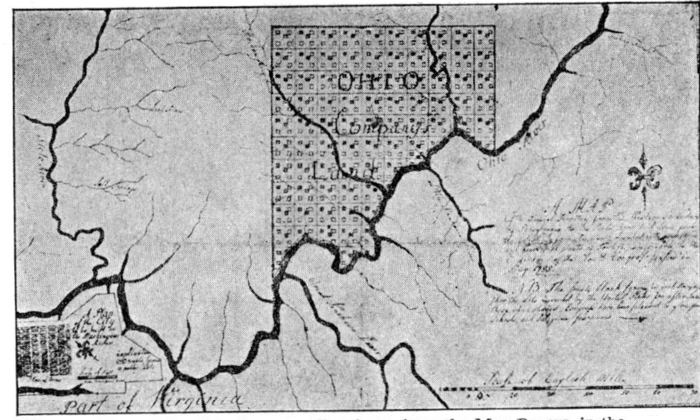

150 Map of the Ohio Company Purchase, from the May Papers, in the *Marietta College Collections*, 1917

151 From the painting *The Landing of General Putnam at Marietta, 1788*, by Philip Clover, in the Ohio State Archæological and Historical Society, Columbus, Ohio

PUTNAM AT THE MOUTH OF THE MUSKINGUM

ON April 7, 1788, Putnam with his party stepped ashore at the mouth of the Muskingum. In the previous autumn he, with Cutler and the others, had been busy persuading settlers to undertake the Ohio venture. In the dead of winter Putnam with a small band plowed through the snow of the mountain valleys of Pennsylvania to join a group that had gone a little earlier to the banks of the Youghiogheny to build boats for the descent of the Ohio. When spring came, the builders launched a great barge and named her the *Mayflower*. As she drew into the Muskingum on that April day the officers at Fort Harmar sent men across to help bring her to the bank. Delaware Indians came down to look curiously at the newcomers.

THE SETTLEMENT OF MARIETTA

CABINS quickly began to appear on the river bottom across the Muskingum from Fort Harmar. The first settlers went into the woods girdling the trees in preparation for a summer's crop of corn. There was little underbrush because of the annual autumn fires of the Indians. Before many weeks the green shoots of the young corn were appearing among the dead trees. With true pioneer enthusiasm one of the settlers wrote to a friend in New England: "This country, for fertility of soil and pleasantness of situation, not only exceeds my expectations, but exceeds any part of America, or Europe, I was ever in. The climate is exceedingly healthy; not a man sick since we have been here. We have started twenty buffaloes in a drove. Deer are as plenty as sheep with you. Beaver and otter are abundant. I have known one man to catch twenty or thirty of them in two or three nights. Turkies are innumerable; they come within a few rods of us in the fields. We have already planted a field of one hundred and fifty acres in corn."

152 View of the Ohio Company's garrison at the mouth of the Muskingum in 1792, from a drawing based on the recollections of John Matthews and Q. Stanley, inmates of the garrison, in the Stimson Collection, Marietta College Library

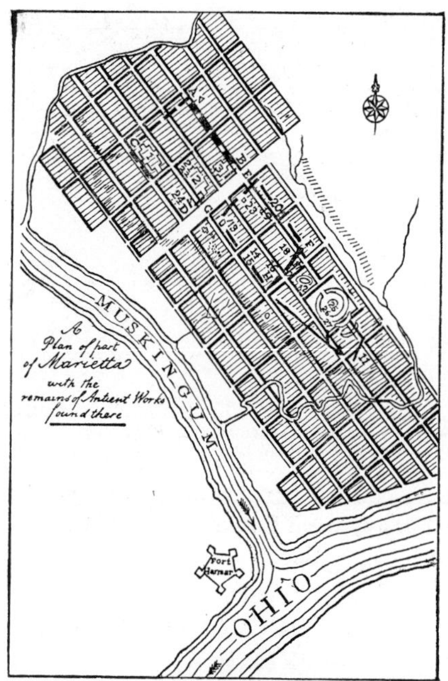

153 A Plan of a Part of Marietta, from Thaddeus Mason Harris, *A Tour of the Country Northwest of the River Ohio*, Boston, 1805. LEGEND: A B C D, Largest Ancient Fort; E F G H, Smaller Fort; 1, 2, 3, Elevated Squares; 11, Rampart at the end of the plain; 12, Oblong Elevated Mound; 13–24, Raised Mounds; 25, The Great Mound; 26, Circular Ditch round it; 27, A Surrounding Wall or Bank

PLAN OF A PART OF MARIETTA

OVER the ancient Indian mounds, long since abandoned and overgrown with trees, Putnam's surveyors laid out the plots of the town which, in honor of the French queen, Marie Antoinette, they named Marietta. Here came in July 1788, the elderly General Arthur St. Clair whom Congress the year before had chosen to be the first Governor of this western country. Here also came Manasseh Cutler to see the settlement whose existence depended so much upon his efforts. He dined with Governor St. Clair and with General and Mrs. Harmar at the fort. A little later Francis Vigo, the same trader who had welcomed Clark when he took Kaskaskia, came by, making his way up the Ohio in a keel boat propelled by ten oars and a square sail. Cutler joined him on his trading trip to Pittsburgh and so went back to the East to encourage new settlers to come out to Marietta.

PLAN OF THE CAMPUS MARTIUS

PUTNAM and most of the men with him were Revolutionary soldiers. They knew that they were building their colony in the edge of a forest haunted by some of the fiercest Indians that the backwoodsmen of the frontier had encountered. Although Fort Harmar was just across the little Muskingum, they did not long depend upon it. With great skill and thoroughness Putnam laid out and built a frontier fortress, unlike any that Kentucky had ever seen, which he called the Campus Martius. Settlers struggling over the Wilderness Road into the Blue Grass country had been individualistic and hard to control. They were the typical borderers who faced the risks of Indian attack behind little stockades, flanked by blockhouses. But Putnam's followers came as a group. Many of them were accustomed to army discipline; their leaders were men of large caliber. These pioneers established a stronghold capable of resisting the fiercest Indian attack. So they made known to spying redskins and to the British at Detroit their determination to remain. A contemporary observer wrote of Campus Martius. "It consists of a regular square, having a block house at each angle, eighteen feet square on the ground, and two stories high; the upper story on the outside or face jutting over the lower one, eighteen inches. These block houses serve as bastions to a regular fortification of four sides. The curtains are composed of dwelling houses two stories high, eighteen feet wide, and of different lengths. The block houses and curtains are so constructed by high roofs, etc., as to form one complete and entire building. The timber of which they are built is either sawed or hewed, four inches thick, so that the walls are very smooth, and when the seams are pointed with mortar will be very warm and comfortable. On top of three of the block houses are very handsome watch towers, which are to be made musket proof; and are large enough to hold four men, their arms, etc. On top of the fourth (in the northwest corner), above the watch tower, is a balcony with a cupola, spire, etc., for the reception of a bell, which we are told is coming on as a present from a gentleman in Boston." Running from corner to corner of the blockhouses was a row of palisades sloping outward. Twenty feet in front of these was another row of very strong palisades standing upright. Outside of this was an abatis made of the tops of trees sharpened and pointing outward. It was estimated that in case of emergency the fort would contain eight hundred and sixty-four people. Campus Martius was the reply of the white farmer to the menace of the red hunters of the Ohio forests, the Shawnees, Delawares, and Miamis.

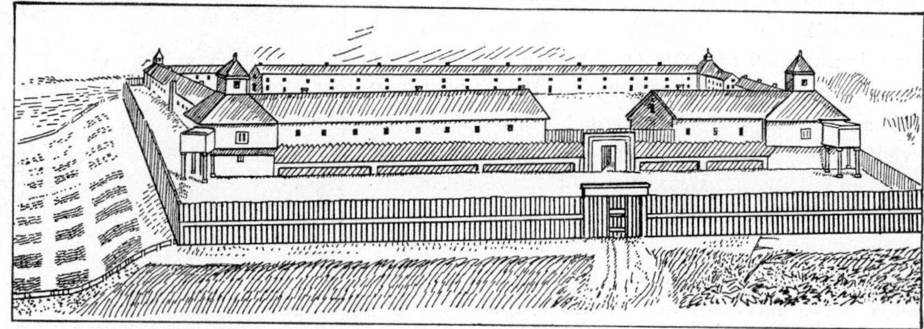

154 Campus Martius, from an original drawing in the Marietta College Collections, Marietta, Ohio

FARMER'S CASTLE

A FEW miles down the river from Marietta and opposite Blennerhasset's Island, Farmer's Castle was laid out soon after the founding of Marietta. Settlers were coming rapidly into the Ohio region. "Within a few seasons, something like twenty thousand souls floated down the Ohio to such expectant, law-abiding communities, and it remained to be seen whether these novel conditions of civilized life in the western wilderness would have a beneficent effect upon the five thousand savage warriors who made their homes between the Ohio and the Lakes." — JUSTIN WINSOR, *The Westward Movement.*

155 Farmer's Castle, from a print of a sketch made in 1791, in the Stimson Collection, Marietta College Library, Marietta, Ohio

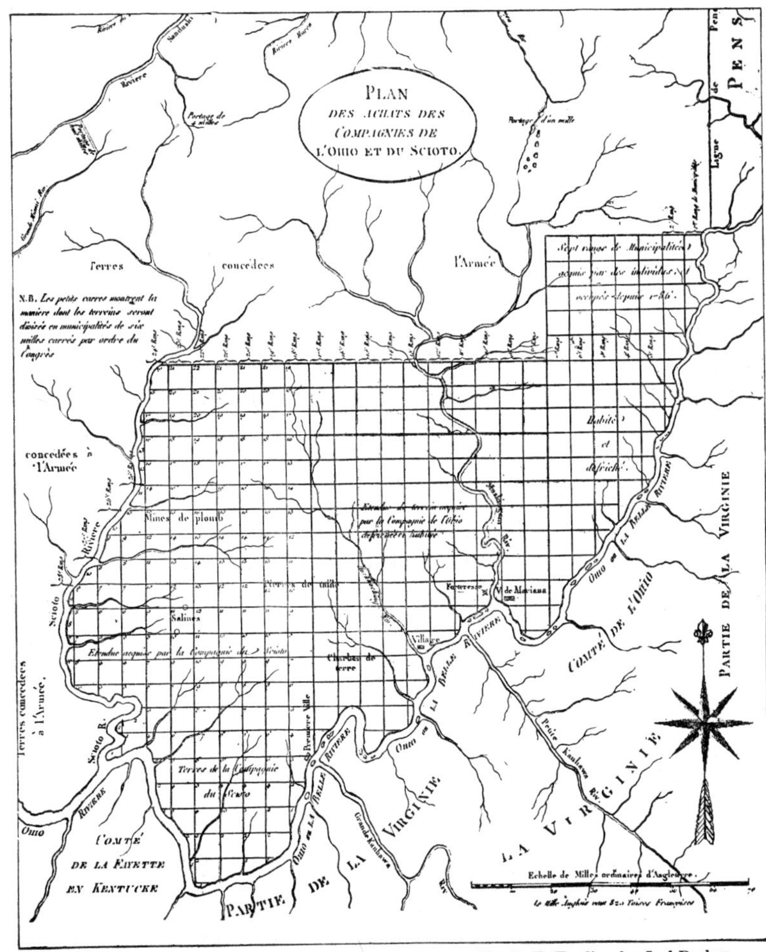

156 Map of the Ohio and Scioto Companies' Lands, engraved by P. F. Tardieu for Joel Barlow, 1788, from the original in the Harvard College Library, Cambridge, Mass.

THE SCIOTO COMPANY'S LANDS

THE Reverend Manasseh Cutler's purchase from Congress of five million acres of land to the west of the Ohio Company marked the beginning of the activities of the Scioto Company backed largely by a New York speculator by the name of Colonel Duer, who in his turn represented "some of the principal characters in the city." The company sought to people its lands with immigrants from Europe, a custom already known in the settlement of the West. Joel Barlow, famous as one of the "Connecticut Wits," was sent to Paris as foreign representative. Armed with an alluring description of Ohio adapted from Cutler's own pamphlet, he set out to interest French investors and French colonists in the enterprise. He had prepared and printed the "*Plan des Achats des compagnies de l'Ohio et du Scioto.*" With superlative dishonesty this showed the lands of the Ohio Company and those which lay to the east as cleared and inhabited.

157 A contemporary French cartoon, *Sale of the Deserts of the Scioto by a Group of Anglo-Americans*, from the Massachusetts Historical Society *Proceedings*, Boston, 1873

CARTOONS

Barlow could not have been in Paris at a more opportune time. The city was in the throes of the French Revolution which had broken out in 1789. Many folk fearing the outcome of the Revolution or suffering from the disturbed conditions were ready to look to America as a haven where they might live in peace and mend their fortunes. There were some, however, who sensed the fraud that lay behind the offer of the persuasive Barlow and hostile caricatures were printed to warn people against him. But they proved of little avail. He gathered a group of colonists and dispatched them to America. Strange indeed were their sensations when floating down the Ohio they found the "settled land" of Barlow's map, save for two small villages, a wilderness.

GALLIPOLIS

In 1790 some six hundred French immigrants reached America and prepared to make the long journey to the Ohio. They arrived at Gallipolis in October minus many of their number who had given up, and found eighty huts prepared for them. The cabins were cheering. But when they read the deeds which they received in return for their hard-earned savings, they discovered that these passed on to them such "right, title, interest and claim" as was possessed by the Scioto Company. This speedily proved to be no title at all, for Duer, the backer of the enterprise, failed and was clapped into a debtor's prison. Governor St. Clair wrote candidly to General Knox, the Secretary of War, that "an interested speculation of a few men, pursued with too great avidity, will reflect some disgrace on the American character, while it involves numbers in absolute ruin in a foreign land." Some of the luckless settlers made their way to the French settlements at Kaskaskia and Detroit. Others stayed, a miserable and disillusioned band. The land of the Scioto Company had reverted to the government. In 1795 Congress made partial amends when it distributed twenty-four thousand acres among the French folk in Gallipolis eighteen years of age and older.

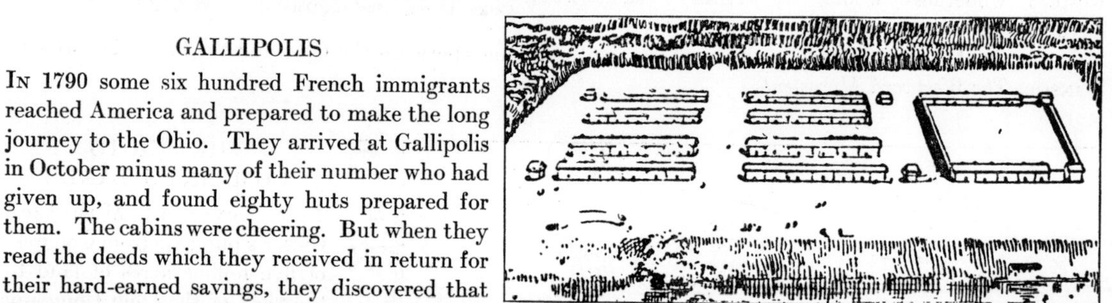

158 Huts Built in 1790 by Major John Burnham on the site of Public Square, Gallipolis, from a sketch in *The Centennial Anniversary of Gallipolis, Oct. 16–20, 1890*, the Ohio State Archæological and Historical Society, Columbus, Ohio

159 First Log Cabin Built in Cincinnati, 1788, from a photograph in Charles F. Goss, *Cincinnati, The Queen City, 1788–1912*. © S. J. Clarke Publishing Co., Cincinnati, 1912

CINCINNATI

Of quite a different character was the enterprise of John Cleve Symmes, who, in August, 1787, purchased from Congress the land far to the west of the grant to the Ohio Company, between the Great and Little Miami Rivers. The summer of the following year found Symmes on the Ohio with about sixty persons in a fleet of barges. They passed the mouth of the Muskingum, where the Marietta cabins were building. They passed Limestone where so many immigrants had formerly left the river for Kentucky. In September they moored the barges on the north shore opposite the broad mouth of the Great Licking. They had scarcely begun to build a town when the prowling of redskins decided them to return to Limestone. Here they waited until November, when a party returned and built a blockhouse. In December the settlers came down, pushing their boats through cakes of floating ice. John Filson, the Kentucky surveyor and historian, was employed to survey the town, but, venturing inland, was killed by Indians.

160 Fort Washington, from a lithograph after a drawing, 1790, by Captain Jonathan Heart, U.S.A., in the possession of the publishers

FORT WASHINGTON

Other settlements sprang up along the Ohio and General Harmar moved to protect this outlying frontier. In September 1789, his soldiers were busy cutting the logs that were built into the stout walls of Fort Washington beside the village of Cincinnati. In December, bringing half his force of six hundred men, he established his headquarters at the new station. Harmar wrote to General Knox, "this will be one of the most solid, substantial fortresses when finished, of any in the Western Territory. It is built of hewn timber, a perfect square, two stories high, with four blockhouses at the angles. On account of its superior excellence, I have thought proper to honor it with the name of Fort Washington." Governor St. Clair came also to Cincinnati and made it the seat of government in the Northwest Territory.

161 Arrival of the Pioneers at Youngstown, 1797, from the mural painting by Alonzo E. Foringer (1878–), in the Courthouse, Youngstown, Ohio, courtesy of the artist

THE OHIO IMMIGRANTS

As the nineteenth century opened, immigrants came flooding across the Ohio country. Eastern farmers, whose fields had grown less fruitful under unintelligent cropping, sold out their places for what they would bring, bundled their families and a few belongings into Conestoga wagons, and set out for Ohio. They started life over in the West. The country was new to them and the people about them were strangers. While they were getting their land, they lodged perhaps in the cabin of a neighbor whom they had never seen before. When they were ready to build, the people of the community turned out for the "raising." The folk who came to Ohio were farmers in the main, born and reared in old and well established communities. Frontier life was a new experience and a great adventure to them. They were unlike the seasoned backwoodsmen who laid out Watauga and the early stations of Kentucky. Those folk were hunter-pioneers, restless, roving, unruly, individualistic. The Ohio people were farmer-pioneers, following after the hunters, consolidating and holding the gains which were made against the forest.

162 A Flatboat on the Ohio, from an engraving by George H. Cushman, after a drawing by W. T. Russell Smith, in the possession of the publishers

FLATBOATS ON THE OHIO

The years that followed the opening up of the Ohio country saw the flood of immigrants on the great river increase. In the first half of the year 1787, one hundred and forty-six boats, bearing a little more than three thousand people, passed Fort Harmar. The next year the figures for twelve months grew to nine hundred and sixty-seven boats and more than eighteen thousand people. The time to travel was in the spring when the river was high. Yet even then there was grave danger from the ever-shifting sand bars. Both skillful and lucky was the pilot who, guiding the clumsy flatboat from Pittsburgh to Cincinnati, did not run afoul of a snag planted in the sand, become entangled in the branches of the overhanging trees, or find his craft swept against the bank by the swift current of a bend. If all went well the journey might be made in about a week. Accident sometimes spelled disaster.

INDIAN ATTACK DOWN THE OHIO

With grave forebodings the Indians watched the settlers pouring into their hunting grounds. From the trees along the banks parties of braves observed the boats float by and, when opportunity offered, attacked them. They sent captured or renegade whites down to the water's edge to call to the passers-by and beg for rescue. So they lured boats ashore, only to pour a deadly fire into the would-be rescuers. The time soon came when the voyagers shunned whites along the bank as they would a pestilence. But, though they killed a few, the red men could not stem the tide that was sweeping over their country.

163 Indian Attack Down the Ohio, from the painting by Stanley M. Arthurs, courtesy of the artist

164 Indians Watching the Advance of the Whites, from a painting by Stanley M. Arthurs, courtesy of the artist

THE INDIAN POINT OF VIEW

In January 1789, several months before that impressive ceremony in New York City when Washington was inaugurated the first President of the United States, Governor St. Clair, held two different councils at Fort Harmar. In one the Wyandots, Delawares, Ottawas, Chippewas, Potawatomis, and Sauks participated and established certain boundaries and reserves. But the treaty was never carried into effect owing to the uninterrupted hostilities on the part of the Indians. In the other the Six Nations renewed and confirmed the provisions of the second treaty of Fort Stanwix.

GENERAL HARMAR, 1753-1813

By 1790 Indian attacks along the river and against the Ohio and Kentucky settlements had become unbearable. Reluctantly Washington's new government, already struggling with stupendous problems, made ready to defend the frontier. Pennsylvania and Kentucky were asked for militia which was to assemble at Fort Washington in the summer of 1790. Governor St. Clair was ordered to inform the British in the posts along the lakes that the expedition was not directed against them. In September General Harmar started northward with three hundred and twenty regulars and some eleven hundred militia. With his motley force of raw and untrained men Harmar reached, sixteen days out, the villages of the Miamis. But he found the Indians gone and the storehouses of the Detroit traders empty. He burned the huts and many thousand bushels of corn. Three times he sent out small detachments beyond the support of the main body and each time the warriors of Little Turtle, including some Senecas, closed about them and destroyed them. Then Harmar retreated ingloriously to his base. St. Clair reported a "terrible stroke" against the redskins, but a wiser observer remarked: "The Indians can never be subdued by burning their houses and corn, for they can make themselves perfectly comfortable on meat alone, and they can build houses with as much facility as a bird does his nest." (See Map No. 169.)

165 General Joseph Harmar, from a mezzotint by John Sartain after the painting by Raphael Peale, in the possession of the publishers

GENERAL ST. CLAIR, 1734-1818

The United States was anxious to keep the Iroquois out of the war that had developed in the Ohio region. The June following the Harmar expedition saw a council assembling at Newtown, now Elmira, at which were present nearly a thousand Indians—Onondagas, Oneidas, and Senecas. Timothy Pickering acting for the government arranged a satisfactory understanding. That he had not been entirely successful, however, was evident in September when it was reported that "all Cornplanter's young people had left him and gone to the Miami to take part in the war." In October 1791, General St. Clair led another nondescript army into the Indian country. Without adequate scouts or patrols in front the commanding general plunged toward the Indian villages. On the morning of November 4, the war whoop echoed through the thick woods about St. Clair's camp on the Wabash. A band of redskins charged the tents. The Americans were surprised and surrounded. Undisciplined and untrained, they tried to form. Their muskets and their artillery availed little against a foe that crept from tree to tree. The Indians inflicted heavy losses. They were exultant as they saw the great white army helpless before them. They came yet nearer. The terror-stricken troops caught glimpses through the smoke of battle of flitting figures painted black and red, the feathers of the hawk and eagle braided in their long scalp locks. In desperation St. Clair ordered a charge through the Indian circle. Once outside, the retreat degenerated into a headlong flight. Only the allurement for the redskins of the booty of the camp saved the army from utter destruction. St. Clair's defeat was overwhelming. It profoundly disturbed the President.

166 General Arthur St. Clair, from the portrait by Charles Willson Peale in Independence Hall, Philadelphia

167 Little Turtle, from a copy by Ralph Dille of a portrait, 1797, attributed to Gilbert Stuart, in the Chicago Historical Society

LITTLE TURTLE

In a Miami village on the Eel River Little Turtle was born in 1752. His father was a Miami chief and his mother a Mahican. According to the Indian rule he was, therefore, a Mahican and received no advantage from his father's rank. His superior ability early manifested itself and, while still a young man, he was made a chief of the Miamis. He had been the principal leader of the redskins who had defeated Harmar. On November 4, 1791, he achieved the distinction, almost unique among Indian war chiefs, of driving out of his country a second white army defeated and demoralized.

GENERAL WAYNE, 1745–1796

St. Clair's defeat was a heavy blow to the prestige of the Washington administration and a disaster for the border. Indian raiding parties, fierce and exultant, harassed the settlements far into Kentucky. The redskins, ignorant of the vast power arrayed against them, believed for the moment that they could achieve their desire and establish the Ohio River as the boundary between them and the whites. General Anthony Wayne was recalled from private life and the task of reorganizing the Regular Army was entrusted to him. The agitated Knox, Secretary of War, informed him that "another defeat would be inexpressibly ruinous to the reputation of the government." During the summer of 1792 Wayne was at Pittsburgh recruiting and organizing his army, known as the "Legion." But men were loath to volunteer for service against Little Turtle. The dead who fell at the time of St. Clair's defeat still lay in the forest unburied. Detachments of recruits on the way to join the army at Pittsburgh became panicy and lost half or more by desertion. Wayne settled to the task of turning his raw material into soldiers. In both discipline and training he was thorough. He had made enough progress to feel able to spend the winter in camp some twenty-seven miles below Pittsburgh, nearer to the seat of hostilities. Meanwhile he tried to negotiate with the enemy but met with rebuff. After a busy winter his army of about twenty-five hundred was finally taking shape. At the close of March, 1793, he wrote: "The progress that the troops have made both in manoeuvering and as marksmen astonished the savages on St. Patrick's day." There was no campaign throughout the summer of 1793. The Government was making every effort to treat with the Indians. Little Turtle, wise counselor as well as able warrior, advised peace with this new "chief who never sleeps." But his braves would not heed his voice. The episode is characteristic of the slight control which the tribal leaders had over their braves.

168 General Anthony Wayne, from a portrait, artist unknown, in the New York Historical Society

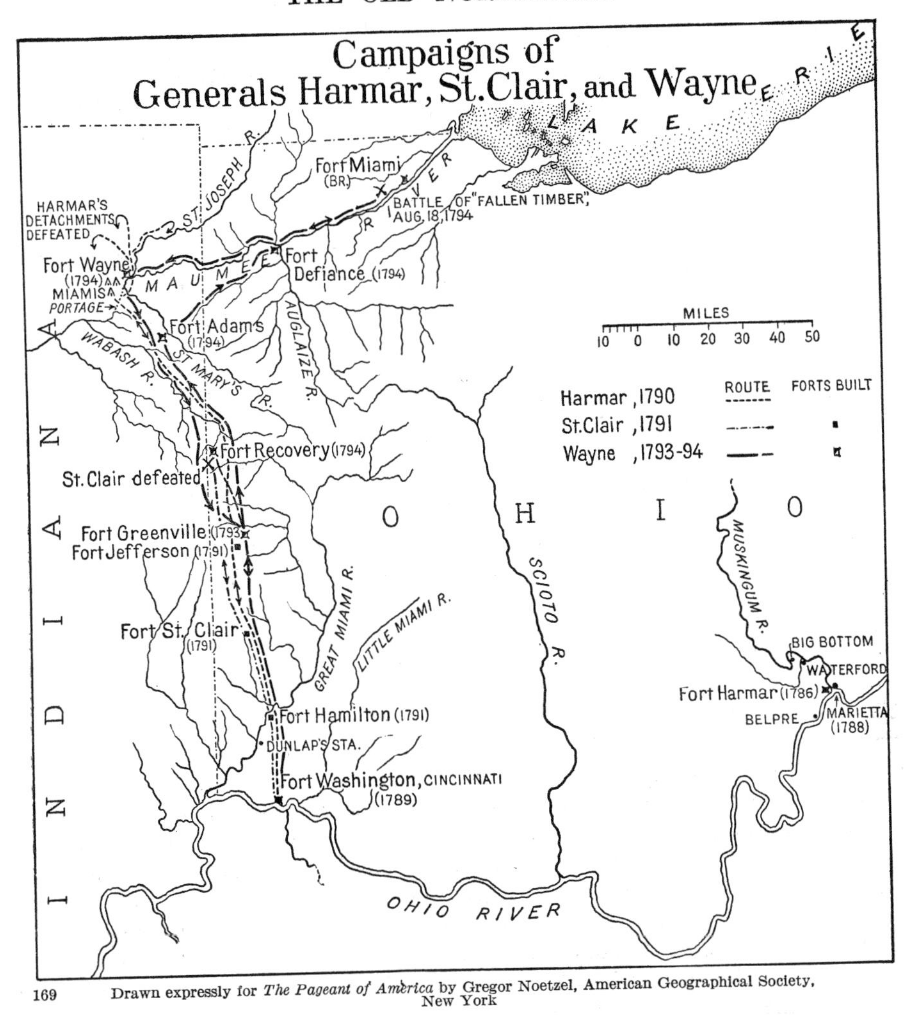

169 Drawn expressly for *The Pageant of America* by Gregor Noetzel, American Geographical Society, New York

FORT RECOVERY

In September Wayne, then near Cincinnati, heard from Knox that all hope of treating with the Indians had been abandoned. Again the Secretary expressed apprehension: "Let it therefore be again, and for the last time impressed deeply upon your mind, that a defeat at the present time, and under the present circumstances, would be ruinous to the interests of our country." Wayne replied: "You may rest assured that I will not commit the Legion unnecessarily." In the autumn of 1793 he pushed some eighty miles north of Cincinnati, took up a strong position, and went into winter quarters at Fort Greenville. Here, well advanced into the Indian country and surrounded by hostiles, he quietly and methodically continued the drilling of his troops and used his position to accustom them to Indian warfare. The redskins were harassing his supply trains, but the panics of 1792 had long since disappeared. Discipline and training had brought confidence and a desire to take up the tomahawk in deadly earnest. The nickname of "Mad" Anthony Wayne, like that of "Stonewall" Jackson, was singularly inappropriate. Few men were ever less mad than the conqueror of Stony Point as he prepared to break the power of the Miamis. From Fort Greenville, his winter camp, he sent a detachment to St. Clair's battlefield to bury the dead and to build Fort Recovery. In June 1794, a small American force was driven into Fort Recovery and the fort itself heavily attacked. There were Englishmen with the Indians. The defenders beat off the assault and inflicted heavy losses. At the rapids of the Maumee, on American soil, stood an English fort built since the beginning of hostilities between the United States and the Ohio Indians. So great was the confidence that the administration had come to have in General Wayne that Secretary Knox gave him the following significant authorization. "If in the course of your operations . . . it should become necessary to dislodge the party [the English garrison at the rapids of the Maumee] you are hereby authorized in the name of the President of the United States to do it."

170 Fort Defiance, looking southeast across the Maumee and up the Auglaize, from a drawing based on researches and surveys by the author, in Charles E. Slocum, *History of the Maumee River Basin*, Defiance, Ohio, 1905

THE BATTLE OF FALLEN TIMBERS

In July 1794, Wayne greeted at Fort Greenville General Scott, his old friend and comrade of Monmouth, who had come up with a heavy reinforcement of Kentucky volunteers. The commanding general then promptly took the offensive and pushed northward into the heart of the Indian country. At the junction of the Auglaize and the Maumee he built Fort Defiance, a name not without its significance for the little English garrison at Fort Miami farther down the river. At Fort Defiance the American commander made a last effort to treat with the Indians and failed. Then he advanced cautiously down the Maumee, determined to fight a decisive battle. Before him were braves, estimated to number between fifteen hundred and two thousand, from all the Ohio tribes together with Chippewas and Iroquois. In addition were some seventy whites of the Canadian border under Captain Caldwell. The enemy fell back but halted close to Fort Miami at a place where a tornado had once swept through the forest and left the earth covered with fallen trees. Here on ground which, according to Wayne, "rendered it impracticable for cavalry to act with effect, and afforded the enemy the most favorable convert for their savage mode of warfare," Little Turtle chose his battlefield. No white commander could have done better. His left flank was protected by the Maumee and his front covered by a tangle of logs. Not far in his rear lay an English fort upon which, if necessary, he could retire. Anxiously he awaited battle with the sleepless chief. The battle of Fallen Timbers established for all time Wayne's reputation as an Indian fighter. At eight o'clock on the morning of August 20 the advance guard of his marching army was attacked and driven back. He at once deployed in two lines with his Kentucky volunteer cavalry on his left flank. He sent these under General Scott "to gain and turn the [Indian] right with spirit and prompitude." But this movement did not determine the outcome of the fight. In the main line of battle Wayne went into action with the tactics which he had devised and had spent many months teaching to his men. "I ordered the front line to advance with trailed arms, rouse the Indians from their coverts at the point of the bayonet and, when up, to deliver a close and well directed fire on their backs followed by a brisk charge so as not to give time to load again . . . [s]uch was the impetuosity of the charge by the first line of infantry that the Indians and Canadian militia and volunteers were driven from all their coverts in so short a time that, although every exertion was used by the officers of the second line of the legion, and by Generals Scott, Todd, and Barber of the Mounted Volunteers to gain their proper positions, yet but a part of each could get up in season to participate in the action, the enemy being driven in the course of an hour more than two miles through the thick woods already mentioned by less than one half of their numbers. . . . From every account the enemy amounted to two thousand combatants, and the troops actually engaged against them were short of nine hundred." — Official report quoted in Stillé, *Major General Wayne and the Pennsylvania Line*, 331–32.

171 The Battle of Fallen Timbers, drawn expressly for *The Pageant of America* by C. W. Jefferys

172 Fort Wayne, 1794, from a lithograph made in 1795, in the Chicago Historical Society

FORT WAYNE

LITTLE TURTLE'S force was scattered and irreparably defeated. The next day Wayne, with his staff, reconnoitered so closely the British fort as to give offense to its commander, who informed the American that "it becomes my duty to inform myself as speedily as possible in what light I am to view your making such near approaches to this garrison." Wayne's reply breathed the old hatred of the Revolutionary days. "Without questioning the . . . propriety, Sir, of your interrogatory, I . . . may . . . observe to you that were you entitled to an answer, the most full and satisfactory one was announced to you from the muzzels of my small arms yesterday morning in the actions against the hordes of savages in the vicinity of your post. . . . But had it continued until the Indians *etc* had been driven under the influence of the post and guns you mention they would not have much impeded the progress of the Victorious Army under my command. . . ." — Official report quoted in STILLÉ, *Major General Wayne and the Pennsylvania Line*, 331–32. Following the battle of Fallen Timbers, Wayne fell back to Fort Defiance. In September he led his troops to the Miami villages near the scene of Harmar's disaster, and for six weeks the army was employed in the relentless destruction of the towns and crops of the hostiles. Here also the army built Fort Wayne. When the work was done, the commander returned to Fort Greenville to go into winter quarters. Wayne had destroyed the power of the northern Ohio Indians and brought the first real peace to the border beyond the Appalachians.

TREATY OF FORT GREENVILLE

IN the summer of 1795, Wayne met the representatives of the Indians at Fort Greenville. The braves began assembling in June. On July 30, after long days of speeches and explanations, the treaty was read again as Wayne had originally prepared it. The old warrior had refused to concede a point. When the reading was done he put the question: "Do you approve these articles?" One by one the spokesmen of the beaten tribes answered "Yes" — Ottawas, Potawatomis, Wyandots, Delawares, Shawnees, Miamis, Chippewas, Kickapoos, Weas, Piankashaws, Kaskaskias, and the Eel River tribe. In the old painting made after an officer's sketch the central figure in epaulets is Wayne with William Henry Harrison, whom Wayne had cited for bravery in the campaign, on his left. Chief Little Turtle is speaking and behind him stands Tark the Crane, a sachem of the Wyandots. As Little Turtle signed he remarked: "I am the last to sign it, and I will be the last to break it." Faithful to his promise he remained passive and counseled peace on the part of his people until his death at Fort Wayne on July 14, 1812. Before he passed away he had seen the rise of his successor as leader of the northwest Indians, the Shawnee, Tecumseh.

173 The Treaty of Fort Greenville, from the painting after a sketch by an officer on Wayne's staff, in the Chicago Historical Society

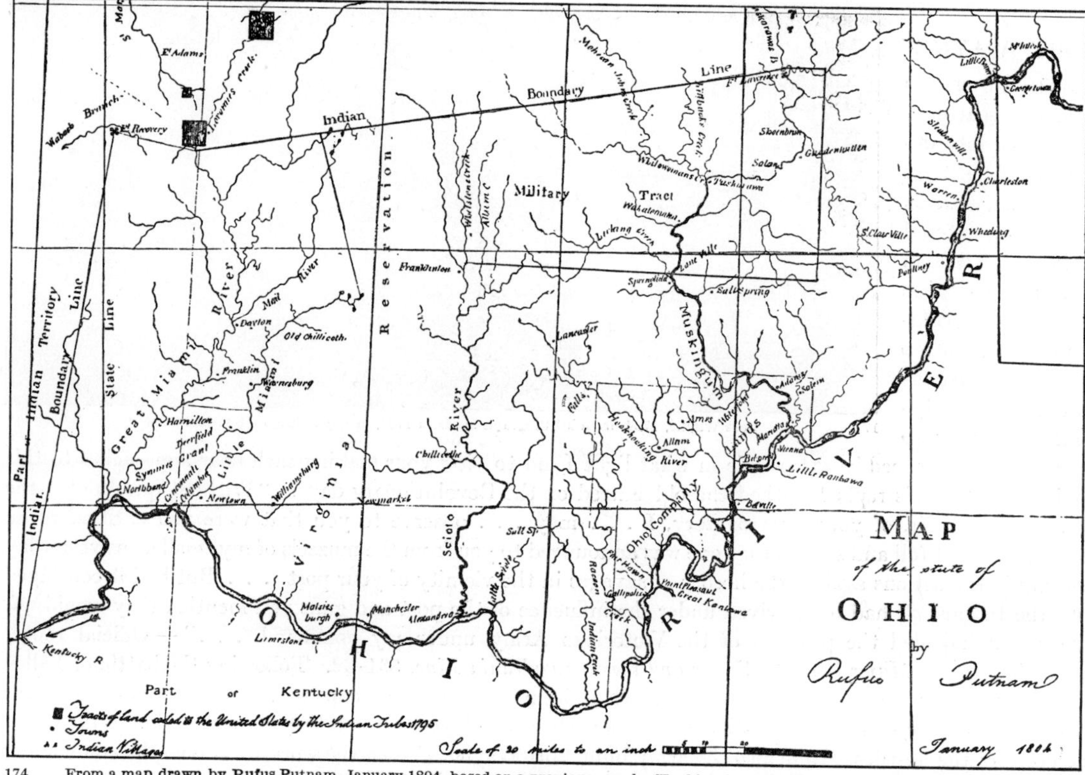

174 From a map drawn by Rufus Putnam, January 1804, based on a previous map by Huckins, in Archer B. Hulbert, *Historic Highways of America*, Vol. IX. © The Arthur H. Clark Company, Cleveland, 1903

MAP OF OHIO SHOWING THE LINE OF THE TREATY OF GREENVILLE

WAYNE demanded and secured from the Indians the land of southern Ohio and southeastern Indiana. In addition he required the tribes to grant reservations of varying size about such outlying posts as Fort Wayne, Fort Defiance and Detroit. The grant to Clark and his soldiers across from Louisville was also recognized. The United States recognized the Indian title to the remaining lands. Twenty thousand dollars worth of presents were distributed when the treaty was ratified and the Government undertook to pay certain annuities to the tribes. In midsummer of the following year Wayne came back to the scene of his great fight to receive for his government the surrender of the western posts. In accordance with the provisions of Jay's treaty, 1794, these frontier fortifications on American soil which the British had held for thirteen years after the treaty of peace were turned over to their rightful owners.

175 Moses Cleaveland meeting an Indian Chief, 1790, from the mural painting by David C. Lithgow in the Public Auditorium, Cleveland

THE FOUNDING OF CLEVELAND

IN the summer of 1796 a boatload of men, skirting the southern shore of Lake Erie, rounded a sand bar at the mouth of the Cuyahoga River and landed where the Indians had been wont to beach their canoes. Surveyors set to work to mark out a settlement. Homestead lots bordered the lake with ten-acre lots farther back. Still more distant farms of a hundred acres each were laid out. In October, 1796, the settlement was established. The people were from Connecticut. They had built their first town on the eastern bank of the river marking the boundary of the land that Wayne had forced the Indians to give up in the treaty of Fort Greenville.

MOSES CLEAVELAND, 1754–1806

MOSES CLEAVELAND, a general of the militia, was the leader of the party on the Cuyahoga. Behind him was an association known as the Connecticut Land Company, which had purchased from Connecticut three million acres of land on the south shore of Lake Erie. Connecticut's charter had carried her borders west to the South Sea. In the latter years of the Revolution, when all the states had ceded to the central government their claims to the region north of the Ohio River, Connecticut had reserved a tract in what is now the northeastern corner of the state of Ohio. Thither Connecticut people began to turn their eyes when the Indians were brought to terms.

176 Moses Cleaveland, from a carte de visite after a miniature (artist unknown), in the possession of the Western Reserve Historical Society, Cleveland

PROBLEMS OF THE WESTERN RESERVE

BEFORE the Connecticut Land Company had made its purchase east of the Cuyahoga, Connecticut had set aside the western part of the Reserve, the "Fire Lands," to recompense those citizens who had suffered a loss of property in the Revolution. The total number of "sufferers" was reported as eighteen hundred and seventy and the aggregate losses something over eight hundred thousand dollars. In 1796, the "sufferers" were incorporated in Connecticut, and seven years later in Ohio, under the title, "The Proprietors of the Half-Million Acres of Land lying south of Lake Erie." The land was surveyed and divided among the "Proprietors" according to each one's proportion. When the settlers came, their Connecticut origin was manifest in the names which they gave to their towns — New Haven, East Haven, New London, Norwalk, Greenwich, Fairfield, Danbury, and Ridgefield. Cleaveland's settlement in the Western Reserve did not grow rapidly. The reason was not that there were no immigrants who wished to come. The Western Reserve was in truth a no-man's land. Connecticut had reserved her charter claim. But Virginia also had a charter claim to this same land and had ceded it to the central government. Connecticut could not give a clear title to Cleaveland and his settlers. The Connecticut assembly did not extend its jurisdiction to this remote country and the settlers refused to recognize that of the central government. As the first years of settlement passed, the situation of the pioneers became difficult. They had no magistrates, no courts, no law. Finally the National Government granted to Connecticut ownership of the soil and Connecticut yielded its claims to political jurisdiction. So the problem was solved.

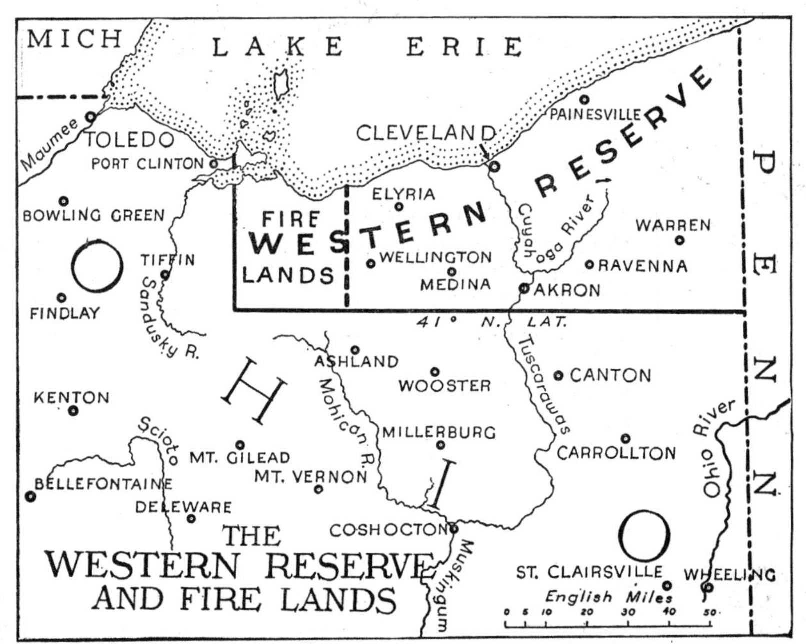

177 Drawn expressly for *The Pageant of America* by Joseph L. Cain

178 Emigration of Connecticut Pioneers, from a painting by Howard Pyle in Alfred Mathews, *Ohio and her Western Reserve*, D. Appleton & Co., New York, 1902

EMIGRATION

WITH the clearing up of title difficulties in 1800 emigrants from distant Connecticut began pouring into the Western Reserve. Most of them took the long hard route across the New York frontier. In this section south of Lake Erie appeared a replica of New England. The sons and daughters of the Puritans had moved inland. The stony hillsides had been exchanged for fertile fields. The code which had governed many successive generations was transferred to a more friendly environment, where it was to come into contact with the codes of people from other parts of the United States. The result was a cultural development of great significance for the Middle West.

REACTION IN NEW ENGLAND

NEW ENGLAND became alarmed at the exodus of her people. The rich, virgin soil of the West seemed robbing her of her very life blood. Pamphlets declaiming against emigration appeared in the villages of Connecticut and Massachusetts. The West was pictured as a place where men and women went with high hopes only to be disappointed and disillusioned. The pamphlets told of many who returned sadly to take up life again in the old familiar communities. But the propaganda failed. Year after year canvas-covered wagons set out from the greens of New England villages and a little knot of friends waved good-bye as a familiar neighbor passed out of their lives.

179 Dr. Cutler's church and parsonage at Ipswich Hamlet, Mass., from which the first company started for Ohio, December 3, 1787, from a sketch in Henry Howe, *History of Ohio*, Cincinnati, 1888

180 Nathaniel Massie, from a portrait, artist unknown, in the Public School Library, Chillicothe, O.

NATHANIEL MASSIE, 1763–1813

CONNNECTICUT was not the only eastern state to stamp the impress of its civilization in Ohio. In 1795, Nathaniel Massie, a Virginian, led a band of settlers into the Scioto Valley. On Brush Creek they unexpectedly met a band of surly Shawnees, who had refused to attend the great pow-wow with Wayne even then going on at Fort Greenville. In a sharp fight the Indians drove off the white invaders. The next year Massie was back and founded the town of Chillicothe. Before winter the village had "several stores, taverns and shops for Mechanics." The people came from Virginia and Kentucky, the latter in nearly all cases being natives of the Old Dominion. So the country in which Boone had spent months of captivity among the Shawnees heard the war whoop no more. Farms quickly replaced the hunting grounds.

THE PEOPLE OF OHIO

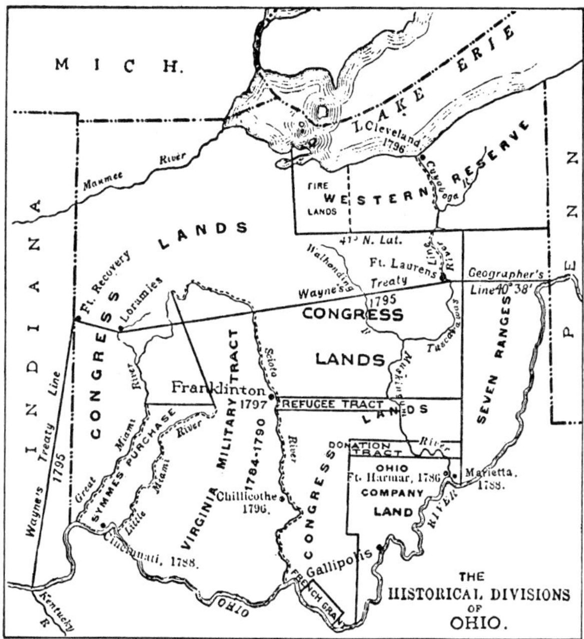

181 From a map in Emilius O. Randall and Daniel J. Ryan, *History of Ohio*, Century History Co., New York, 1912

In Ohio many different population elements were finally fused into a single commonwealth. There were "five principal nerve centers of the nascent state: 1. The Ohio Company, on the Ohio River, mainly from Connecticut and Massachusetts, representing perhaps the more liberal element of the New England Puritanic stock; 2. The Symmes Purchase, between the Miamis, whose immigrants were designated as a band of New Jersians, with a mixture of Scotch-Irish and Hollanders; 3. The Virginia Military District, between the Scioto and the Little Miami Rivers, in which the racial inflow was partly Marylandic, but mostly Virginian — the hardy, rollicking, fighting Anglo-Saxon stock, whose venturesome representatives brought with them the flavor of the old world aristocracy with its dignity, luxury and courtesy; 4. The Western Reserves, with its distinctively austere indomitable Puritan type, a colony, whose foundations were hewn from the granite rock of New England Calvinism; 5. The 'Seven Ranges,' consisting of the tract extending west from the Pennsylvania Line between the Ohio Company on the south and the Western Reserve on the north. The settlers in this section were not a few native born Quakers; a few settlers from the German Palatinate; many Germans, of the stock which has produced the variety known as "Pennsylvania Dutch"; and many Scotch-Irish, the people that prevailed in Western Pennsylvania. Swedish and French colonists located west of the Seven Ranges. The five chief centers of settlement were long separated by intervening forests, but slowly the paths of travel and channels of commerce brought them into closer and closer contact; gradually the tics of common purposes and a similar effort began to unite them." — Randall and Ryan, *History of Ohio*, II, 598–99.

CINCINNATI

Ohio grew with almost incredible rapidity. The forests that had so long been the hunting grounds of the northern Indians melted away as fields of corn and grain began to cover the hills and fill the valley bottoms. In the older settlements the rude cabins of the pioneers gave place to substantial frame houses. Five years after the treaty of Greenville extinguished the Indian's title to southern Ohio, young William Henry Harrison, a delegate to Congress from the Northwest Territory, succeeded in persuading the Government to divide that vast extent of land into two parts. North and south through Fort Recovery, which Wayne had built in the field where St. Clair had met disaster, ran the line that set off the territory of Ohio from that of Indiana stretching westward to the Mississippi. Harrison became the Governor of the wild country beyond Fort Recovery. Two years later Ohio became a state, and its representatives took their places in Congress beside those of Kentucky and Tennessee.

182 Cincinnati in 1800, from a painting based on authoritative data, by A. J. Swing, 1880, in the Historical and Philosophical Society of Ohio, Cincinnati. Fort Washington is shown in the right background

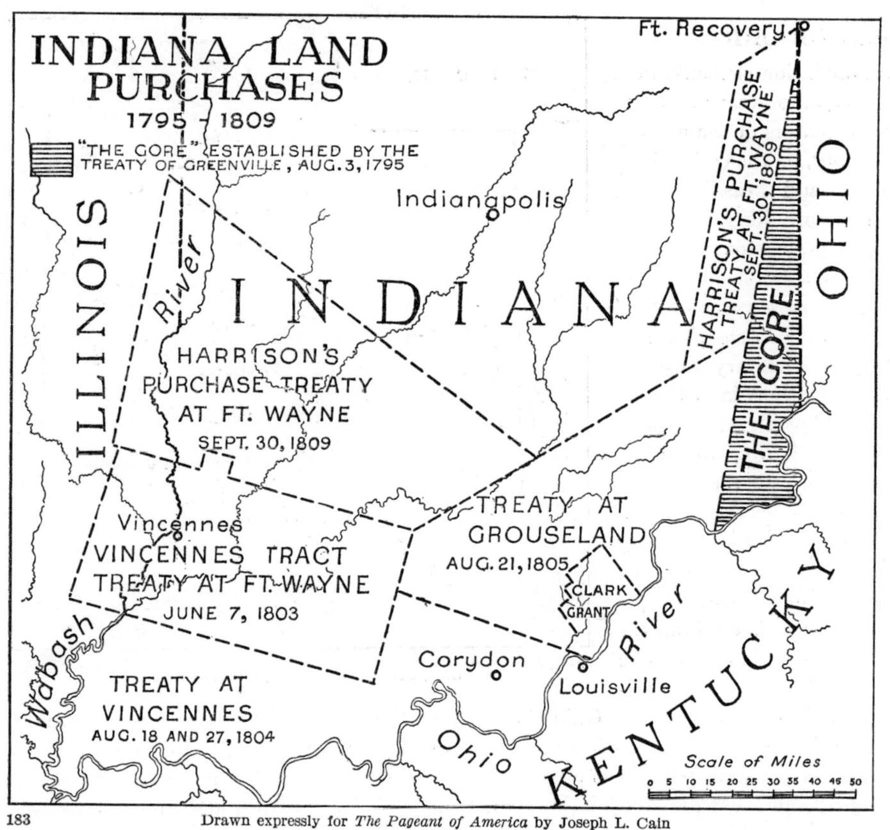

183 Drawn expressly for *The Pageant of America* by Joseph L. Cain

INDIANA SETTLEMENTS

The peopling of Ohio meant that the Shawnees must again take up their wanderings. Abandoning their towns in the valley of the Scioto, they turned their faces westward. Some crossed the Mississippi to join, in Missouri, a band of their people who, with some Delawares, had gone west in 1789. The remainder retired to the headwaters of the Auglaize. Many tribes still lived in the valley of the Wabash. The territory included in the present state of Indiana was Indian country save in two places. A narrow strip known as the "gore" in the southeastern corner lay between the western boundary of Ohio and the line of the treaty of Fort Greenville; settlers could also come into Clark's Grant. Governor William Henry Harrison sympathized with the land hunger of the pioneers. Like St. Clair he had difficulty in keeping the settlers within the boundary established by the treaties. Steadily he pressed the Indians for further sales of land. His redskin neighbors were becoming a degraded lot. More than once they bartered away great areas of their domain for a little rum and a few presents judiciously distributed. The story of the making of treaties between the United States and the Indians is a sorry and discreditable tale. In 1804 and 1805 Harrison extinguished the Indian title to a strip of land some thirty miles wide along the north bank of the Ohio. In 1809 he called the tribes into council at Fort Wayne where he procured from them the addition of a twelve mile strip along the western side of the "gore." The treaty of Fort Wayne, however, brought him face to face with an Indian crisis.

184 Indiana Pioneers Beginning a Cabin, from a drawing by J. Minton in Henry Howe, *One Hundred Years of Progress*, Cincinnati, 1871

185 A Pioneer's Wagon in Indiana, from *The Ohio Archæological and Historical Publications*, Vol. VIII, Columbus, 1900

THE OPEN DOOR, THE PROPHET

186 The Open Door, The Prophet, from a copy by Henry Inman (1802–46), of a painting by Charles B. King, (1786–1862) in the Fogg Museum of Art, Cambridge, Mass.

Four years before the treaty of Fort Wayne great excitement had stirred the people of the chief Shawnee village on the Auglaize. A young man had announced himself the bearer of a new revelation from the Master of Life. "He declared that he had been taken up to the spirit world and had been permitted to lift the veil of the past and the future; had seen the misery of evil doers and learned the happiness that awaited those who followed the precepts of the Indian god. He then began an earnest exhortation, denouncing the witchcraft practices and medicine juggleries of the tribe, and solemnly warning his hearers that none who had part in such things would ever taste of the future happiness. The firewater of the whites was poison and accursed; and those who continued its use would be tormented after death with all the pains of fire, while flames would continually issue from their mouths. This idea may have been derived from some white man's teaching or from the Indian practice of torture by fire. The young must cherish and respect the aged and infirm. All property must be in common, according to the ancient law of their ancestors. Indian women must cease to intermarry with white men; the two races were distinct and must remain so. The white man's dress, with his flint and steel, must be discarded for the old-time buckskin and the firestick. More than this, every tool and every custom derived from the whites must be put away, and the Indians must return to the methods the Master of Life had taught them." — Hodge, *Handbook of the American Indian*, II, 729–30. The Prophet adopted the name of The Open Door. His gospel of returning to the ancient ways of the forest held out to his defeated brothers the hope of saving themselves from the demoralizing effects of contact with the whites. He located himself at a new town on the Wabash below the mouth of Tippecanoe Creek and thither came ultimately more than a thousand of his converts.

TECUMSEH, 1768–1813

Twin brother to the Prophet was Tecumseh, known sometimes as the Crouching Panther, and sometimes as the Shooting Star. From early childhood these two Indian leaders had felt the destructive power of the white man. Their father, a Shawnee chief, was killed in 1774 at the battle of Point Pleasant when they were six years old. The village where they lived was raided by Kentuckians in 1780 and destroyed. The elder brother who had assumed responsibility for them at the time of their father's death was slain in a battle with the whites on the Tennessee frontier in 1788 or 1789. Still another brother fell at Tecumseh's side when Wayne crushed the Indians at Fallen Timbers. Tecumseh's hatred of the Americans crowding into the lands of the Indians dominated his life. He distinguished himself as a young man in the border wars but was also noted for his humane character, evinced by persuading his tribe to discontinue the practice of torturing prisoners. With the abandon of a patriot and the ability of a statesman Tecumseh devoted his life to the cause of his people. In spite of Wayne's victory he determined that the Ohio should be the boundary between the Indians and the white settlements. He sought to establish the theory that the land of the Ohio country was owned by all the Indian tribes in common and could not be alienated by any single tribe. Then like the Iroquois, Dekanawidah, he strove to unite the Indian peoples, but his dream reached far beyond that of the father of the Confederacy of the Six Nations. In person he went to the southern Indians, and his emissaries visited every tribe from Florida to the headwaters of the Missouri. The fame of Tecumseh was great but his influence failed to destroy those ancient tribal hatreds which had ever been the military weakness of the Indians.

187 Tecumseh, from a drawing in the Durett Collection, University of Chicago

188 Tecumseh and Harrison at the Council at Vincennes, 1810, from the painting by Stanley M. Arthurs, courtesy of the artist

THE INDIAN CHALLENGE

In the village which they established at Tippecanoe, Tecumseh and the Prophet sought to carry into effect the ideals which they held. Both were men of personal magnetism. The Indians at Tippecanoe tilled the soil diligently and abstained from the white man's firewater. They were realizing the wish of President Jefferson as expressed to Handsome Lake. In 1808 the Prophet visited Harrison at Vincennes. His speech in the public council remains the only record of his words. "I told all the redskins that the way they were in was not good, and that they ought to abandon it; that we ought to consider ourselves as one man, but we ought to live agreeable to our several customs, — the red people after their mode, and the white people after theirs; particularly that they should not drink whiskey; that it was not made for them, and that it is the cause of all the mischiefs which the Indians suffer. Determine to listen to nothing that is bad; do not meddle with anything that does not belong to you, but mind your own business, and cultivate the ground, that your women and your children may have enough to live on. I now inform you that it is our intention to live in peace with our father and his children forever." — Henry Adams, *History of the United States*, VI, 80–81. In spite of the Prophet's protestations of peace and in spite of Tecumseh's principle that the land was owned by all tribes in common, a principle which had been recognized by the treaty of Fort Greenville, Harrison, in 1809, dickered with individual village chiefs, gathered together some of "the most depraved wretches on earth," and bought land extending practically to the Wabash. Harrison was busy securing treaties before the power of Tecumseh became so great that the local chiefs would not dare oppose the great Indian leader. The year after Harrison had secured a considerable portion of the best remaining hunting ground of the Indians, south of the Great Lakes, Tecumseh met the white Governor. Armed guards protected the principals because each feared treachery. Behind Tecumseh was a real, though somewhat nebulous, confederacy which had been greatly strengthened by Harrison's purchase in 1809. Behind him also was active British support. He spoke boldly. "Brother, since the peace was made in 1795 you have killed some of the Shawnees, Winnebagos, Delawares, and Miamis, and you have taken our land from us; I do not see how we can remain at peace with you if you continue to do so. You try to force the red people to do some injury; it is you that are pushing them on to do mischief. You are continually driving the red people; and at last you will drive them into the great lake where they cannot either stand or work. Since my residence at Tippecanoe we have endeavored to level all distinctions, to destroy village chiefs by whom all mischief is done; it is they who sell our lands to the Americans. In the future we are prepared to punish those chiefs who may come forward to propose to sell their land. If you continue to purchase of them, I do not know what will be the consequence to the white people." — Henry Adams, VI, 86–87. The picture, No. 189, is a propagandist document for the uproarious presidential campaign of 1840 when Harrison was elected.

189 Tecumseh and Harrison, from an engraving in *The Life of Major-General William Henry Harrison: comprising . . . an accurate description of the Council at Vincennes*, Philadelphia, 1840

THE ADVANCE OF THE WHITES

YET Tecumseh did not want war. His plan was the organization of a confederacy and passive resistance. It was completed by the teachings of the Prophet who, as Handsome Lake was doing at the same time, gave his social program power among his people by making it into a religion. Only by giving divine sanction to the new customs and ways of life which he proposed could the Prophet hope to achieve his ends. With the spirit world on his side he might succeed. The religion which he taught and the political organization which Tecumseh advocated represented together an almost theoretically perfect defense for adjustment to the westward progress of white civilization. These leaders of a lost cause aimed to conserve the peculiar virtues of their race and to insulate their culture from the corroding effects of contacts with the hostile whites. Tecumseh was one of the greatest men the Indian race has produced and his brother shared his genius. But in trying to organize the Algonquins of the Northwest Territory they were doomed to failure. Those tribes had not the genius of the Iroquois or the Cherokees, of the Sioux or the Pueblos, of the once mighty Aztecs or the brilliant Mayas. Tecumseh tried to give strength and power to a people who had never had it, and he could not. During 1810 and 1811 Tecumseh's braves were restive. Rumors of depredations ran along the border. Harrison, in complete sympathy with the desires of the settlers for more land and itching for a military reputation, assembled at Vincennes in the summer of 1811 something under a thousand men. For the most part they were regulars but their training and their quality were inferior. Tecumseh had for the time being left to continue the work of organizing his confederacy among the southern Indians. His brother was in charge of Tippecanoe on the Wabash one hundred and seventy miles above Vincennes. Harrison took advantage of the absence of the great chief to march into the Indian country. The movement was an act of pure aggression as there was no war. He started in September. In October he paused to build Fort Harrison on the present site of Terre Haute. In November he pushed on to the Prophet's town. As he progressed into the Indian country, redskins were observed hanging on the flanks of the army, sullen and defiant. Reaching Tippecanoe on November 6, Harrison was urged to attack immediately but preferred not to. He would attack after his vigorous demands had been refused. He encamped for the night on a rise of ground where Tippecanoe Creek flows into the Wabash, a place to which he was led by some of the Prophet's braves. The conference was to be on the morrow.

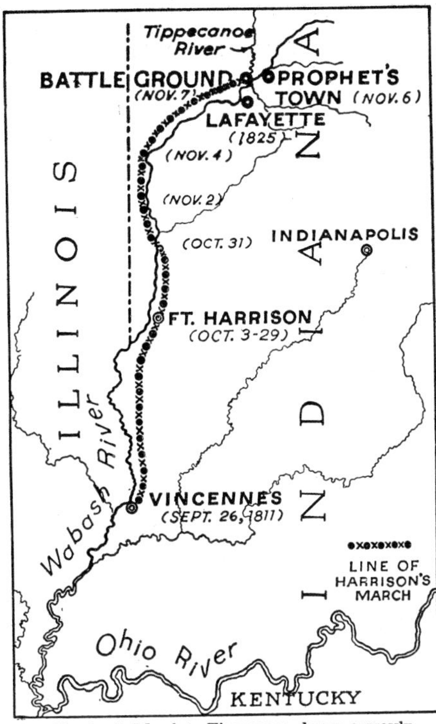

190 Harrison's March to Tippecanoe, drawn expressly for *The Pageant of America* by Joseph L. Cain

191 From a lithograph, drawn for the Presidential Campaign of 1840, by M. H. Wirton, in the Indiana State Library, Indianapolis

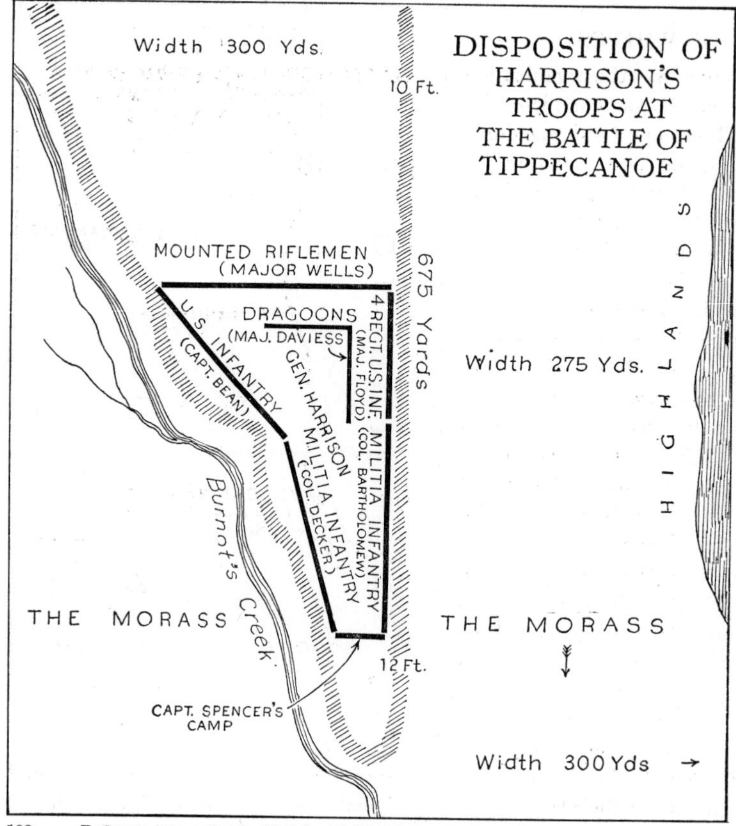

192 Redrawn from a sketch, 1840, by M. H. Winton, in the Indiana State Library

CONFUSED FIGHTING

The camp site afforded excellent opportunity for an enemy to approach under cover to the very edge of the encampment; yet Harrison considered a single line of sentries sufficient security. This fact alone suggests the measure of his military incapacity. About two hours before dawn a party of Indians rushed the camp and drove back the sentries on one side. There was confused fighting in the dark. Soon after daylight the attackers were beaten off and withdrew. The American loss was one hundred and eighty-eight, of whom sixty-one were killed or mortally wounded. Harrison stood to arms in camp all day and did not venture to send out a scout for twenty-four hours. When he did he found the Prophet's town abandoned; he promptly proceeded to burn it. The general said that he was opposed by six hundred warriors. Tecumseh said that a few young braves gave battle.

THE AFTERMATH OF TIPPECANOE

Harrison, short of supplies and burdened with wounded, retired to his base. The battle of Tippecanoe has bulked large in American history; colorful accounts of it helped, twenty-nine years later, to make the American commander President of the United States. In spite of the doubtful character of the tactical victory, however, it was in a strategic sense decisive. Tecumseh's prestige was irreparably impaired. That his confederacy should collapse under such a feeble blow as Harrison had given it was evidence of the poor quality of the Indians he sought to organize and of the utter hopelessness of his task from the outset. Six months after the battle the United States and England were again at war. Tecumseh was commissioned a brigadier-general in the British army. He fought in the campaigns of 1812 and 1813 and was killed in the latter year at the battle of the Thames (see volume VI, p. 318). When the war was over, the United States without opposition advanced its claim to land as far west as Lake Michigan. Following the war the Prophet, discredited by the reverse at Tippecanoe, his religion shorn of its power, lived in Canada where he enjoyed a British pension. In 1826, after an absence of twelve years, he rejoined his people in Ohio and the following year trekked with them to the country beyond the Mississippi. In 1837, after he had lived nearly a decade in Kansas, his spirit departed to join those of his relatives who had fallen in battle against the Long Knives.

OFFICIAL ACCOUNT

Of Gov. Harrison's battle with the Indians.

The following message from the President of the United States, enclosing Gov. Harrison's two letters to the Secretary at War, on the subject of the late engagement with the Indians on the Wabash, was laid before Congress on Thursday last.

To the Senate and House of Representatives of the United States.

I lay before Congress two letters received from Gov. Harrison of the Indians Territory, reporting the particulars and the issue of the expedition under his command, of which notice was taken in my communication of November 5.

While it is deeply lamented that so many valuable lives have been lost in the action which took place on the 7th ult. Congress will see with satisfaction the dauntless spirit and fortitude victoriously displayed by every description of the troops engaged, as well as the collected firmness which distinguished their commander on an occasion requiring the utmost exertions of valour and discipline.

It may reasonably be expected that the good effects of this critical defeat and dispersion of a combination of savages which appears to have been spreading to a greater extent, will be experienced not only in a cessation of the murders and depredations committed on our frontier, but in the prevention of any hostile incursions otherwise to have been apprehended.

The families of those brave and patriotic citizens who have fallen in this severe conflict, will doubtless engage the attention of Congress.

JAMES MADISON.

Washington, Dec. 18, 1811

193 President Madison's Tribute to Harrison and Harrison's Troops, in the New York *Evening Post*, December, 27, 1811

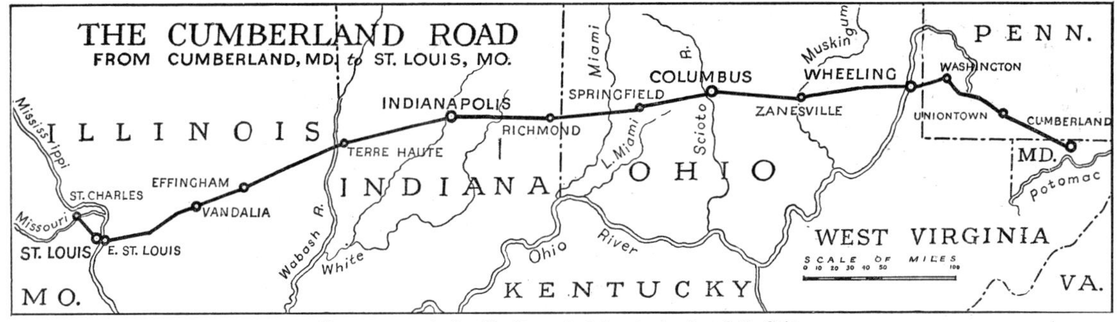

194 Drawn expressly for *The Pageant of America* by Joseph L. Cain

THE CUMBERLAND ROAD

NINE years before the Prophet's people set out for the land beyond the Father of Waters, East and West alike had hailed the completion of a project of profound interest to both. Before the close of the eighteenth century men, following Braddock's road through Pennsylvania, had discussed the possibility of its development into a great artery between East and West. In the Enabling Act of 1802 which made Ohio a state was a provision for establishing a fund out of the receipts from the sale of public lands which should be used for road building. The next year this was dedicated to a road to be built across the mountains. From this small beginning the movement for a national road grew until in 1811 contracts were let and work was actually begun. Into the building of the road went the knowledge obtained from the building of hundreds of miles of turnpikes in the Atlantic states by private companies in the first decade of the nineteenth century. The National Road was to be four rods wide with a surface of crushed stone for vehicles, and was to have ditches, culverts, and permanent bridges. Steep grades wherever possible were to be eliminated. It was a difficult engineering undertaking for its day in the United States. It was to run between Cumberland, Maryland, the head of navigation on the Potomac, and Wheeling on the Ohio. Here it would connect with Zane's Trace which, though unimproved, permitted communication across southeastern Ohio. The War of 1812 delayed construction, but three years after the signing of the Treaty of Ghent the great way was open. The first important link of improved transportation binding the people of the Atlantic seaboard to those who lived on the plains of the continental interior had been forged. The Cumberland Road was the first important attempt to solve the American problem of great distances.

195 Looking down on the Old National Road, near Cumberland, Maryland, from a photograph, courtesy of the Office of Public Roads, Department of Agriculture, Washington

196 The Cumberland Road, Richmond, Indiana, from a photograph, courtesy of the Office of Public Roads, Department of Agriculture, Washington

197 Iron Mile Post on the National Road, from a photograph, courtesy of the Office of Public Roads, Department of Agriculture, Washington

TRAFFIC ON THE CUMBERLAND ROAD

Few highways have so soon demonstrated the wisdom of their building as the Cumberland Road. The stage-coach companies operating on the eastern turnpikes immediately put stages on the new route. Mails were rushed from Washington to Wheeling in the amazing time of thirty hours. The stage-coach traveler witnessed a variegated scene. Hour after hour, as he journeyed, he passed or met occasional droves of cattle and what seemed an endless stream of great wagons drawn by straining teams carrying loads of a ton and a half or more. The wagoners were a rough and picturesque product of this early nineteenth-century freight traffic. At night they halted at the "wagon houses" to be found in almost every mile of the way. When the weather was warm they camped in the broad yards of these and tied their horses to the wheels. When snow was on the ground and cold winds swept the mountains, they slept rolled up in their blankets on the floor of the great common room of the wagon house at one end of which yawned a gigantic fireplace. The inns where the stage-coach passengers stayed were fitted with more luxuries and charged higher rates. Here of an evening after a hard day's jolting the chance acquaintances of a day warmed to the music of an old-time dance and obeyed the musical calls of a fiddler, "Salute your partner" and "Balance all." Past these hostelries plodded the immigrant families with all their worldly goods in their Conestoga wagons, where rode also the women folk and smaller children. Hidden somewhere about the persons or in the belongings of the family group was the little money they had managed to get together for the new start in the West. They were the typical Americans of their generation and the hope and determination written on their faces expressed the spirit of the nation.

THE NATIONAL ROAD IN THE WEST

At Wheeling a passenger could take a wheezy steamboat down the Ohio (see Vol. IV, ch. IV). Waterways were easier than landways and the immigrant followed them. The banks of the Ohio and its tributaries, the Hockhocking, the Muskingum, the Scioto, the two Miamis, and the Wabash saw the first cabins and the fields of the pioneers. The years after the close of the War of 1812 witnessed an unprecedented number of people crossing the mountains. Times had been hard and uncertain since the Embargo of President Jefferson in 1807; after the war they went from bad to worse until the climax was reached in the financial disaster of 1819. The manufacturing establishments that had sprung up during the war period were suffering from the competition of English goods dumped, often without regard to price, in the American market. The West beckoned the Easterner whom disaster had overtaken. Here was opportunity for all who had the strength and the will to grasp it. Never was the ideal of democracy more fully realized. The river lands were soon exhausted and settlers pushed farther and farther from the waterways. The demand for the extension of the National Road west of Wheeling grew loud. In 1820 Congress appropriated ten thousand dollars for laying out a road between Wheeling and a point on the left bank of the Mississippi between St. Louis and the mouth of the Illinois River. Five years later the building of the road to Zanesville began. The decade of the 'thirties witnessed the extension of the highway into Indiana. But new methods of communication, the canal and the railway, were engaging public interest. Ultimately, more by state than national aid, the road was carried to Vandalia, where it connected with St. Louis.

198 Old National (Cumberland) Road near Vandalia, Illinois, from a photograph, courtesy of the Office of Public Roads, Department of Agriculture, Washington

199 The Erie Canal at Lockport, from an engraving by W. Tombleson, after a drawing by W. H. Bartlett, in the possession of the publishers

THE ERIE CANAL

THE Cumberland Road retained for only seven years the unique distinction of being the one improved channel of communication across the Appalachian barrier. In 1825 Buffalo, found but twenty-one years before by President Dwight to be but a handful of frontier cabins, celebrated a great event. Governor Clinton took from Lake Erie a cask of water and started on his triumphal progress along the new Erie Canal which ran through the heart of the Iroquois country. In due time he poured the water from the inland lakes into the sea. The Erie Canal traversed the best pass across the Appalachian Highlands. Its completion meant that passengers and freight could be carried by water from New York to Cleveland, to Detroit, and even to that distant settlement, Chicago. Like the Cumberland Road it became an artery of trade. On its canal boats thousands of settlers moved to the West and with them went the products of the eastern factories. In due time the goods of the East met the commodities of the continental interior flowing toward the great port at the mouth of the Hudson. The Erie Canal was the second strand binding the West and East together. (See Vol. IV, ch. III.) Its completion ushered in a "canal era" in which waterways were completed or projected across the Appalachian barrier in Pennsylvania and Maryland. Canals were also begun and built in Ohio and Indiana connecting the Mississippi River system with the Great Lakes. In course of time it became possible to journey by inland waterways from New York or Philadelphia to New Orleans. When this occurred the frontier had long ceased to exist in the Ohio country and Indiana and Illinois had joined the union of states.

200 Western end of the Erie Canal, from a drawing in Basil Hall, *Forty Etchings Made with the Camera Lucida in North America*, Edinburgh, 1829

201 Drawn expressly for *The Pageant of America* by John L. Philip, American Geographical Society, New York

THE OLD NORTHWEST

George Rogers Clark, whose brilliance and courage had cowed the redskins and defeated the British in the days of the Revolution, lived to see the eastern portion of the wilderness which he had conquered dotted with farmsteads where dwelt men and women absorbed in the grateful tasks of peace. To his fireside was doubtless brought the news of the death in battle of Tecumseh in 1814. Perhaps the embittered leader of the Long Knives pondered the tragic fate of this Indian patriot who had been but a child when Hamilton, the hair-buyer, surrendered to Clark. Before the passing of the old warrior of Clarksville the Cumberland Road had crossed the mountains and the Erie Canal had been begun. The region with whose destiny his name was so closely linked was already in the midst of swift development. The rising tide of immigration which followed the close of the War of 1812 was pouring into the Old Northwest through every practicable channel. Wagons and boats of all descriptions were pressed into service to transport goods and people westward. When in 1818 death came to George Rogers Clark, Illinois, which had witnessed some of his greatest triumphs, was just becoming a state. On October 5 of the same year Nancy Hanks died of milk-sickness in the squalid cabin of Thomas Lincoln on Pidgeon Creek in Indiana. The boy Abraham was left to grow up with the country.

CHAPTER V

THE CONQUEST OF THE OLD SOUTHWEST

IN the spring of 1782 Benjamin Franklin was at Paris preparing for the negotiations that were to bring the American Revolution officially to an end. Fighting in America had practically ceased with the surrender of Lord Cornwallis at Yorktown the previous autumn. Doubtless with much satisfaction Franklin, in contemplating his lordship's defeat, remembered his own successful diplomacy four years before, which had played no small part in bringing about the overthrow of the doughty earl. France had come into the war and had been followed by Spain, hopeful to win back Gibraltar. John Jay was at Madrid in this same spring of 1782. Jay, Franklin, and John Adams were to be the active peace commissioners. Franklin urged Jay to hasten to Paris to aid in the preparation for the negotiations, a request with which that gentleman was quite ready to comply.

During some two years at the Spanish capital the suspicions of John Jay had been thoroughly aroused. He was aware that Spain would demand the return of Florida, lost to England by the Treaty of 1763. The Spanish flag already flew over New Orleans and that vast expanse of territory west of the Mississippi known as Louisiana. Possession of Florida meant the complete control of the Gulf coast, and the ownership of the forts at Pensacola and Mobile, whence could be carried on a highly lucrative trade with the powerful and populous Indian tribes of the Southwest, the Creeks, Cherokees, Choctaws, and Chickasaws. If Spain were to secure Florida, nay even if that effort failed, the Madrid Government would not be anxious to see the boundaries of the United States extend to the Mississippi River. There was too great a possibility that the young nation might one day become an aggressive and an unpleasant neighbor. Jay, sensing all this, was, at the same time, more than half persuaded that France intended to support the Spanish position regarding North America.

Jay mildly shocked the elderly Franklin when he proposed that the American commissioners disregard their explicit instructions and enter into separate negotiations with England. The philosopher of Philadelphia was won over, however, when that stanch Puritan, John Adams, arriving from the Hague, sided with Jay. Franklin agreed to test cautiously this policy, with results little short of amazing, when the real weakness of the United States at the moment is taken into consideration. Ultimately it became known that Spain and France would have preferred to establish the southern boundary of British America at the Ohio River and desired the western border of the United States to be the Appalachian Mountains. They were willing to concede an American "protectorate" over the country of Kentucky and eastern Tennessee. But this was primarily to be Indian country, as was that vast territory comprising most of Mississippi and Alabama and more than half of Tennessee, which was to be a Spanish protectorate. The scheme failed as a result of the maneuvering of the American commissioners. Jay, Franklin, and Adams came home with national boundaries established at the Great Lakes and the Mississippi. There was a sting in the accusation made against the British Government by its enemies that it bought rather than made a peace.

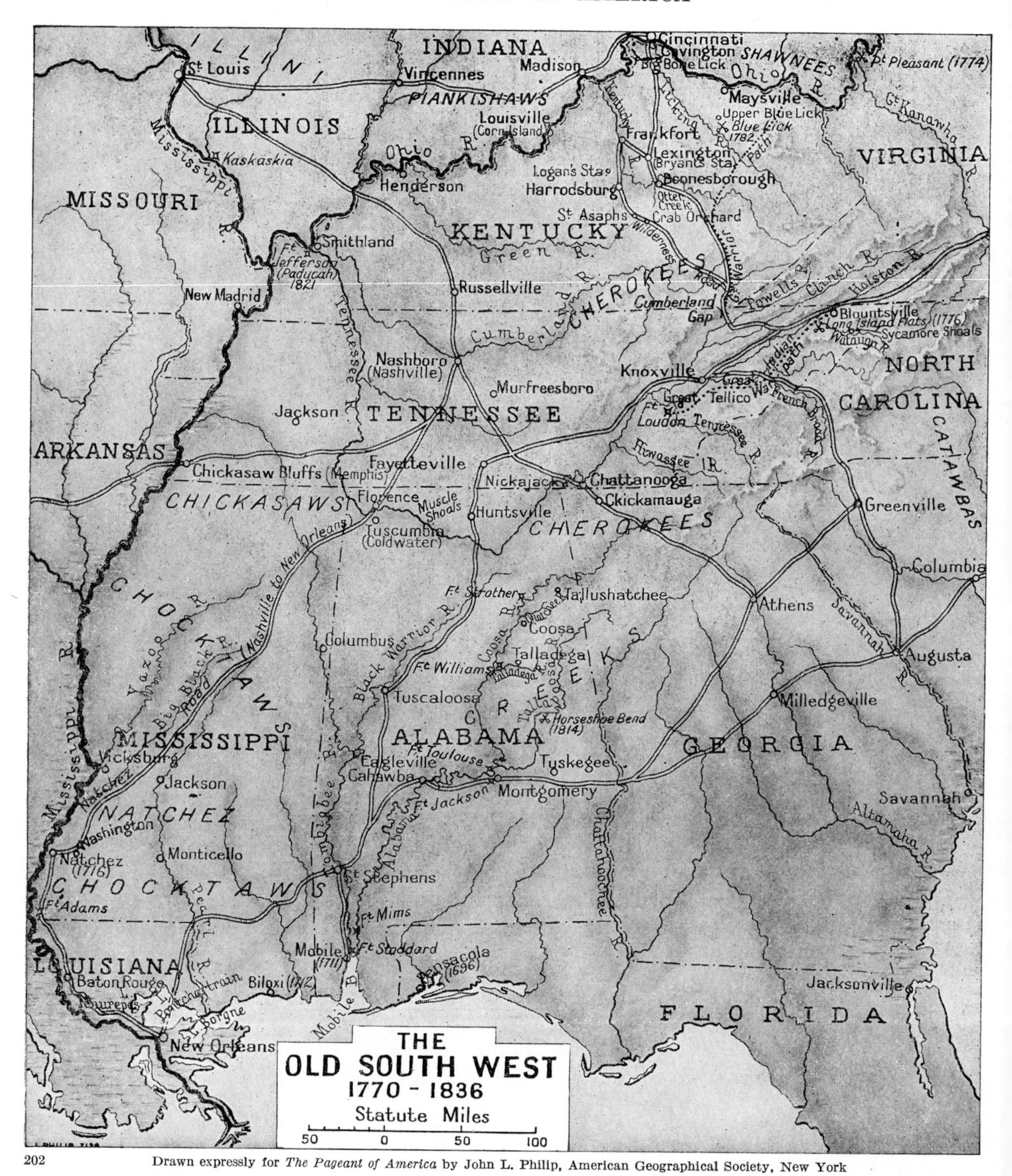

202 Drawn expressly for *The Pageant of America* by John L. Philip, American Geographical Society, New York

THE OLD SOUTHWEST

THE men of 1783 knew but little of that broad plains country which lay south of Kentucky and between the Appalachians and the Mississippi. Fur traders, to be sure, had been active in the region for many decades, but their knowledge of its physiography and climate had not been communicated to the public of either England or America. The immense extent of fertile soil in the country was only vaguely realized. Ignorance regarding the plains of Alabama and Mississippi at the end of the eighteenth century was inevitable because of their isolation. East of them lay the high southern Appalachians. The harbors on the south which gave access from the sea were held by a foreign power, Spain. The whole region was controlled by powerful and well-organized Indian tribes. These obstacles retarded settlement.

203 Fort at Natchez, Miss., from an engraving after a sketch by Tardieu l'ainé, in the Louisiana State Museum, New Orleans

THE TREATY OF 1783

OVERLOOKING the broad expanse of the lower Mississippi from its eastern bank was the old Spanish town of Natchez. Here was a center for trade with the Choctaws to the east and south and with the Chickasaws, whose habitat was northern Mississippi and western Tennessee. Spanish officials reading the Treaty of 1783 between the United States and Great Britain noted that the northern boundary of West Florida was placed at the thirty-first parallel, which line crossed the Mississippi somewhat south of Natchez. A mere scrap of paper, however, did not persuade the Spaniards to withdraw from that highly desirable place and abandon it to the rough borderers of the American frontier. There was still less likelihood of Natchez being given up when alert Spanish officials later discovered that the treaty between England and the United States contained a secret article framed to the disadvantage of Spain. This provided that, in case England was successful in retaining possession of East and West Florida, the northern boundary of the latter should be a line which should pass through the junction of the Yazoo and the Mississippi, and, therefore, above the town of Natchez. Spain was not slow to claim this same line as the northern boundary of Spanish West Florida. As for the clause in the treaty that the navigation of the Mississippi should "forever remain free and open," Spanish officials shrugged their shoulders and called attention to the fact that the agreement containing these words was one merely between England and the United States, and that Spain, who controlled both banks of the Mississippi in its lower reaches, had had nothing whatever to do with it.

THE NASHVILLE SETTLEMENT

IN the year which saw the promulgation of the Treaty of 1783 North Carolina had organized the Nashville settlement on the Cumberland River as its most western county. For this rich region, known as French Lick, whither came thousands of bison in the course of a year, James Robertson started from Watauga with a band of men in November 1779. These pioneers promptly began the building of a stockade and laid out a town. Late in the winter of 1779–80 Colonel Donelson, a sharer with Robertson in the movement, brought on the women and children and the less hardy men. Between two and three hundred people in thirty boats made their way from Watauga down the Tennessee, past the villages of the Cherokees, through the heart of the country of the northern Creeks, and along the borders of the Chickasaw hunting grounds until they came to the Ohio.

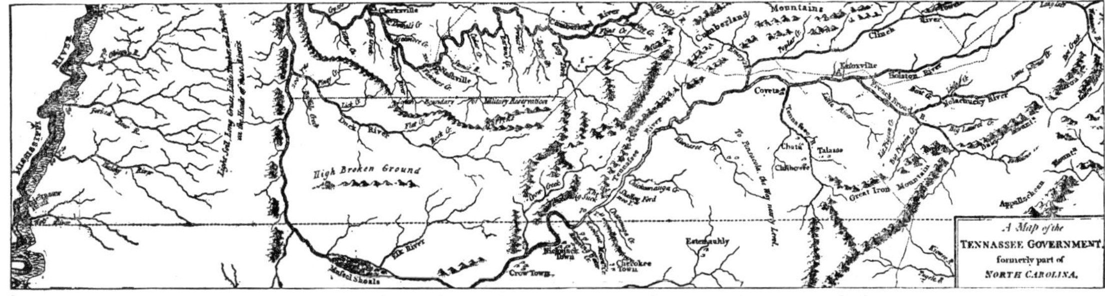

204 Map of Tennessee, 1795, from Gilbert Imlay, *A Topographical Description of the Western Territories of North America*, London, 1797

205 Extract from the Cumberland Compact, showing signatures, from the original in the Tennessee State Archives, Nashville

THE CUMBERLAND CONTRACT

THE party wearily worked their boats against the current of the great river until they left it to make their way up the Cumberland. At last on April 24, 1780, they poled their bateaux up to the Cumberland bluffs, where Robertson and his men were waiting for them. The travelers told of the treacherous currents of the Tennessee which more than once had swept their flotilla for the moment out of control. They recounted their desperate adventures in running past the Chickamaugas, a tribe of the Cherokees ruled by Dragging Canoe, who, concealed on the banks, had opened a heavy fire upon the boats. They told the sad story, so common on the border, of the appearance of that dread scourge, small pox. So the settlement of central Tennessee was begun. Three hundred miles of forest separated Nashborough, as it was called at first, from neighborly succor. Seven days after the arrival of the boats the people of Nashville entered into a voluntary association to "restrain the licentious and supply the blessings flowing from a just and equitable government." There were two hundred and fifty-six signatures to this document, mostly those of men in vigorous early manhood. How desperate was the business of pushing back the wilderness was never more vividly shown than by the fact that, after the lapse of a dozen years, scarcely a score of these signers were alive.

THE STATE OF FRANKLIN

THE settlement of Nashville was a warning to Spain of what might be expected of the vigorous Americans bent on chopping farms out of the forest. But its extreme isolation from the more settled parts of the United States gave rise to Spanish speculation as to whether all the overhill settlements might not be beguiled from their allegiance to the new republic. Developments in Watauga the year after the treaty of peace strengthened the Spanish hopes. In 1784 North Carolina ceded to the United States its charter lands lying west of the mountains, giving the central government two years in which to accept. The Watauga folk heard the news of this with considerable resentment. Quite obviously they could no longer count on North Carolina militia to aid them in the event of Indian war and until the cession was accepted Federal troops would not be available. From the beginning these borderers beyond the mountains had been an independent lot and the act of North Carolina increased their independent spirit. Though North Carolina repealed the cession in June 1784, the Watauga people in August organized under the presidency of Sevier and decided to set up a sovereign state. When this news passed out of the little courthouse at Jonesboro to the crowd of hunters and backwoodsmen outside there was turbulent joy. These frontier folk had not learned in vain the lesson of the Revolution. But Governor Patrick Henry of Virginia saw in the event the outcropping of nefarious Spanish designs. The following spring the state of "Franklin" took more definite shape and a letter was sent to the Congress of the Confederation asking recognition. The capital of the Wataugans was a log cabin, their currency fox and mink skins, their number perhaps twenty-five thousand. Congress studiously ignored the existence of this backwoods state. North Carolina promptly took measures to strengthen its own jurisdiction in its three mountain counties. Division appeared among the Watauga people. Finally, in 1787, the movement died. It served, however, as a warning to the East that the folk beyond the mountains might be very difficult to handle and might even, if provoked, separate from the republic.

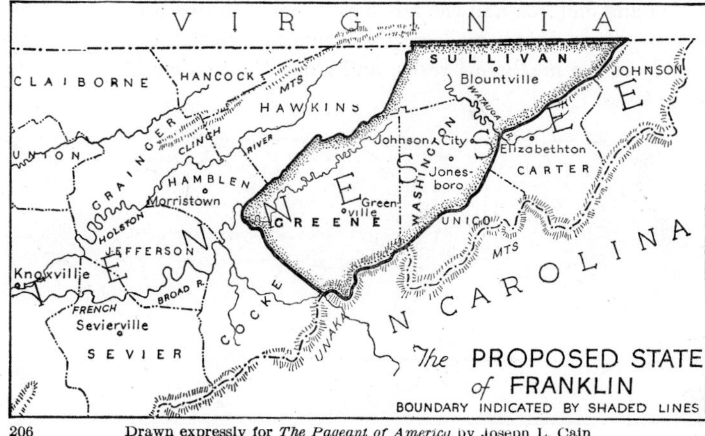

206 Drawn expressly for *The Pageant of America* by Joseph L. Cain

JAY AND GARDOQUI

In 1786, when the State of Franklin was tottering to its fall, the westerners beyond the mountains were excitedly discussing rumors which, if proved true, might lead to an act which would cause disaster to the United States. John Jay, as Secretary of Foreign Affairs for the Confederation, was negotiating with the official representative of Spain, one Diego de Gardoqui. Spain offered to the United States an alternative: on the one hand a commercial treaty; or, on the other, free navigation of the Mississippi. Under no circumstances would both be yielded. It was a move of Machiavellian astuteness. New England and the middle states, excluded from their former lucrative trade within the British Empire, were seeking the world over for new trading connections, and their efforts were spurred on by the financial depression that followed in the wake of the Revolution. In Congress the delegates of every state north of Mason and Dixon's Line were a unit in demanding the acceptance of the Spanish offer to make a commercial treaty. Jay estimated the situation carefully and proposed to Congress the negotiation of such a treaty. After all, he argued, there were but a handful of people, relatively considered, west of the mountains. There was more logic in sacrificing the interests of a small minority rather than those of a great majority. The United States was weak; perhaps even was on the point of dissolution. The states were quarreling with one another and the central government was impotent before Shays' rebellion in this very year of 1786. The unsettled boundary of West Florida was a source of danger and might lead to war unless the United States made a treaty with Spain — and war would bring disaster. Jay urged that the navigation of the Mississippi be yielded for a period of years until the West grew more populous; then they might negotiate again. A vote of nine states was required to ratify the Jay proposal. The vote was seven northern states in favor to five southern states opposed, and the plan was defeated. The United States had passed, without fully realizing it, one of the gravest crises of its early history. The Confederation must have been impotent before a secession movement on the part of the transmontane settlements.

207 John Jay, 1745–1829, from a mezzotint, 1783, by William Richardson, after a drawing from life by Du Simetière, in the possession of the publishers

208 Don Diego de Gardoqui, from an engraving of a miniature by Francisco Goya y Lucientes (1746–1828), owned, 1892, by Cesareo de Gardoqui, Valladolid, Spain, in *The Centennial of Washington's Inauguration*, New York, 1892

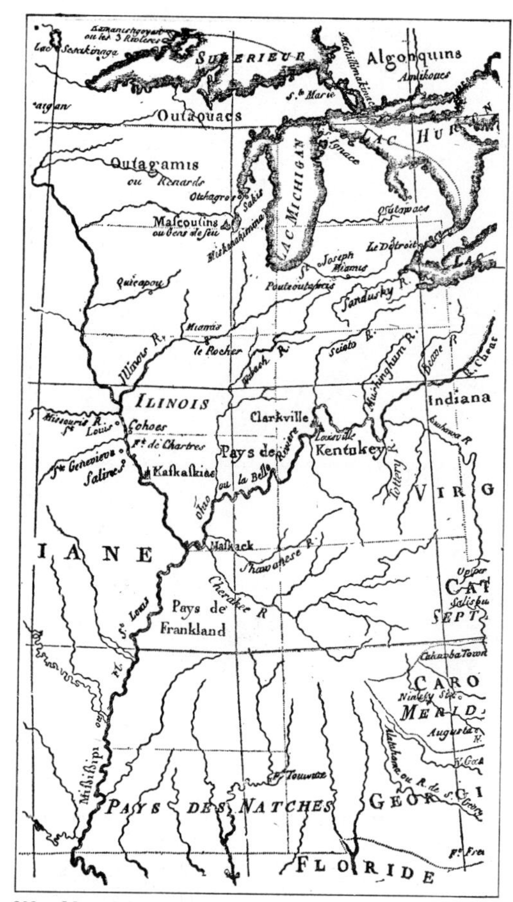

209 Map of the Mississippi and Ohio Valleys, in St. John de Crèvecœur, *Lettres d'un Cultivateur*, Paris, 1787

EXCITEMENT IN THE WEST

In the days before the channels of communication across the mountains were improved, the western people were dependent almost entirely upon the Mississippi and its tributaries for their commercial outlet. When rumors of the Jay negotiations were broadcast through the communities of Kentucky and Tennessee, excitement became intense. A report that Jay's plan had been accepted was widely believed. An anonymous letter from Louisville, Kentucky, to an eastern man expressed the temper of the section. "Shall all this country now be cultivated for the use of the Spaniards? Shall we be their bondmen as the children of Israel were to the Egyptians? Shall one part of the United States be slaves, while the other is free? We can raise twenty thousand troops this side of the Allegheny and Appalachian mountains; and the annual increase of them by emigration from other parts is from two to four thousand. We have taken all the goods belonging to Spanish merchants of the post Vincennes and the Illinois, and we are determined they shall not trade up the river, provided they will not let us trade down it. Preparations are now making here (if necessary) to drive the Spaniards from their settlements at the mouth of the Mississippi. In case we are not countenanced and succored by the United States (if we need it), our allegiance will be thrown off, and some other power applied to. Great Britain stands ready with open arms to receive us and support us. They have already offered to open their resources for our supplies. When once reunited with them, 'farewell, a long farewell, to all your boasted greatness.' The province of Canada and the inhabitants of these waters, of themselves, in time, will be able to conquer you. You are as ignorant of this country as Great Britain was of America. These hints, if rightly improved, may be of some service; if not, blame yourselves for the neglect."

SPANISH INTRIGUE

Investigation of the evidence that has come to light long after the years in which the fate of the western settlements was shrouded with uncertainty has made it clear that Gardoqui at the National Capital and Miro, the Spanish Governor at New Orleans, were not always in harmony in the designs which they set on foot in the western country. James Wilkinson, of doubtful fame, was at the time a prominent citizen of Kentucky and was but one of a considerable group of Kentuckians with whom either one or the other of the Spanish officials was having secret communication.

From the Spirit of '76.

WILKINSON.

GEORGETOWN, Dec. 8, 1811.

Messrs. Printers,

I inclose you a document, short indeed, but of a nature calculated to throw greater light on the real character of General James Wilkinson, than all the evidence that has hitherto been brought against the man.

I shall barely mention that I received this scrip, which is at present in the hands of the Acting-Judge Advocate, Mr. W. Jones, enclosed in a letter from the General dated 22d April, 18 3; at the very time that the Spanish minister Yrujo, and the administration were negotiating for the re-opening of the port of New-Orleans; and if I had succeeded in carrying into effect the General's wishes, even during one week, Louisiana would have been deluged in blood, and the two countries would most assuredly have been involved in a war. Let such as may read the following lines, reflect seriously on what would have been the result.

[" Private and strictly confidential."]

" Should a change of circumstances, which are talked of but not expected by me, produce a change of policy in the councils of Spain, and the opening of the port be contemplated, I beg you to interest yourself in my name, (confidentially) to prevent the measure, until I arrive near you— You can speak freely to the Marquis de Casa-Calvo or the intendant from me.

" I have strong motives for
" this request !"

Ah! Judas! Judas! Thou worse than thy companion and friend Benedict Arnold, and thy much admired Prototype Judas Ischariot! The one sold his country, the other betrayed his *Master only*—but thou, thou hast sold thy country and betrayed thy *Friend!*

It is a subject of sincere regret and sad lamentation to the General's friends that he possesses not the sensibilities of the jew; that like him, he might anticipate the future duty of some officer of *high executive justice* and elevate to Erasmus's Paradise, between Heaven and Earth, such a monstrous compound of every ingredient that can degrade and debase human nature.

Thomas Strickland Power.

210 Later Stricture on Wilkinson's Intrigue with Spain, from a Communication in the New York *Evening Post*, December 17, 1811

THE AMERICAN MENACE

THE suggestion was made that the westerners might be able better to secure navigation rights on the Spanish-controlled part of the Mississippi if they were not a part of the United States. At the same time Spain was to take steps to protect the down-river settlements from the wrath of the borderers if such a course should become necessary. In the summer of 1788 Spanish troops were sent to fortify New Madrid on the west bank of the Mississippi nearly opposite the mouth of the Ohio. The defenses of Natchez were strengthened and a flotilla of patrol boats was placed on the river to guard against piratical inroads of the Americans. A Spanish attempt to bring American settlers to New Madrid with the inducement of free land and the right of free navigation of the Mississippi failed. Meanwhile the flood of eager immigrant families across the mountains continued and grew apace.

211 Detail from a *Plan of the Fort of New Madrid or Anse à La Graisse*, in Victor Collot, *Voyage dans l'Amérique Septentrionale*, Paris, 1826

ALEXANDER McGILLIVRAY, 1739–1793

ONE of the most interesting recipients of attention from the Spanish officials was Alexander McGillivray, head chief of the Creek nation. His father, Lachlan McGillivray, had been a wealthy Scotch trader who had married Sehoy, a famous Creek beauty in whose veins ran both French and Spanish blood. Alexander had been educated at Charleston and at the age of seventeen had been placed in a counting house in Savannah. But he soon cast his lot with his mother's people. During the Revolution, at the head of the Creeks, he actively sided with the British, holding a colonel's commission. His bitterness against the Americans was intensified when Georgia confiscated important lands which he had inherited from his father. After the treaty of peace he entered into an agreement with the Spaniards at Pensacola. Recognizing his power, the United States made several unsuccessful overtures for peace. Finally, in 1790, the year after Washington's inauguration, he was persuaded to journey to New York, the National Capital for the time being. After a conference with the President he left with treaties favorable to his people and for himself a commission as brigadier-general in the army of the United States with the pay of twelve hundred dollars per annum. His oath of allegiance to the United States did not, however, prevent his intrigue with Spain by which government he was appointed superintendent-general of the Creek nation at a salary of two thousand dollars a year. The year before his death he was agent for the United States, superintendent-general for Spain, "emperor" of the Creek and Seminole nations, and the mercantile partner of Panton, a Scotch trader. The annual importations of the two were estimated at forty thousand pounds. McGillivray was a wealthy man for his day. He received one hundred thousand dollars indemnity for his confiscated Georgia lands. At the time of his death he owned two or three plantations and some sixty slaves. A man of such ability at the head of the Creeks was justly feared by the borderers. To James Robertson, who knew him well, he was altogether "Creek scoundrel."

212 Scene of Agreement between McGillivray and the Spaniards, from the engraving *A Perspective View of Pensacola*, by J. Hinton in *The Universal Magazine*, London, 1764

LEGEND: 1. The fort. 2. The church. 3. The Governor's house. 4. The Commandant's house. 5. A well. 6. A bungo.

213 Thomas Pinckney, 1750–1828, from an engraving by W. C. Armstrong of the miniature by John Trumbull (1756–1843) in the Yale School of the Fine Arts, New Haven, Conn.

THE TREATY OF SAN LORENZO

THE question of the navigation of the Mississippi continued unsettled. Finally, in 1795, Thomas Pinckney was sent to Spain to bring an end if possible to the difficulty. He chanced upon favorable times. For two years Europe had been in the throes of war following the French Revolution. Spain had been worsted by France, and the Spanish prime minister, Don Manuel Godoy, had extricated his country from the conflict in the month following Pinckney's arrival in Madrid. Godoy was hailed as "prince of peace" and was in a mood to settle the difficulties with the United States. News of the Jay Treaty with England, negotiated the year before, was coming to the Spanish capital. Spain feared that this was but the prelude to an alliance and that England would again become active in the Mississippi Valley. Godoy considered it good policy to placate the Americans. Spanish evasiveness, however, finally drove Pinckney to demand his passports. Three days later, October 27, 1795, Godoy signed the surprising Treaty of San Lorenzo. He agreed to the thirty-first parallel as the boundary of West Florida; he granted to the Americans free navigation of the Mississippi "from its source to the ocean"; and he yielded them the privilege for three years "to deposit their merchandise and effects in the port of New Orleans, and to export them thence without paying any other duty than a fair price for the hire of the stores." Spain was soon to rue the liberal terms of the treaty. The agreement did not make the westerner appreciably more friendly to the Spaniard. Spanish troops were not withdrawn from Natchez for two years after its signing. Any nation that controlled the mouth of the Mississippi was inevitably the enemy of the folk beyond the mountains.

THE STATEHOOD OF TENNESSEE

THE year following the promulgation of the Treaty of San Lorenzo a group of frontier delegates met at Knoxville on the Holston River to consider matters of public import. Five years before, chiefs of the Cherokee nation had gathered at this place, then known as White's Fort, to confer with Governor Blount of the Territory of Tennessee. They had yielded much land which the whites had already occupied, and had guaranteed that travelers crossing their domains, either by road or by the Tennessee River, would not be molested. Soon after the treaty Blount had begun to sell town lots for eight hundred dollars each. In the autumn of 1791 the *Knoxville Gazette* was started. Now in 1796 came representatives from Watauga and from Nashville. Mountain men from the east sat down with plainsmen from about Nashville to seek a solution for the political problems of the isolated settlements. A frame of government was decided upon and the name, Tennessee, chosen for the new state. A delegation was sent to the National Capital to demand the admission of the new commonwealth to the union of states.

214 Blockhouse, Knoxville, Tenn., from the painting by Lloyd Bronson in the Court House; Knoxville. Photograph, courtesy of the S. J. Clarke Publishing Company, Chicago

A sharp debate followed in Congress regarding the propriety of the people of a territory calling a convention under the general terms of the Ordinance of 1787 without waiting for specific leave from the National Government. The friends of the West were in the ascendancy, however, and Tennessee became a state on June 1, 1796. John Sevier, a leader in civil government as in Indian fights since almost the earliest settlements in the Watauga watershed, became the first governor. Tennessee was still a true frontier, but in the Kentucky blue grass region to the north frontier conditions were rapidly passing and life was assuming an aspect much like that of the Old Dominion whence so many Kentuckians had come.

ANDREW JACKSON, 1767–1845

THE sole representative of the new state in the lower house was, in the words of Albert Gallatin, "a tall, lank, uncouth-looking personage, with long locks of hair hanging over his face, and a queue down his back tied in an eel-skin; his dress singular, his manners and deportment those of a rough backwoodsman." For some seven years Andrew Jackson had been practicing law in Nashville whither he had come as a young man when the settlement was but eight years old. He knew little law but men of his profession were so few in this isolated region that he speedily had all the clients he could serve. No great legal knowledge was required to meet the simple needs of the frontier. Qualities in a lawyer that were prized were personal courage and moral strength. In this respect Jackson was preëminent. He was passionately devoted to a "square deal," he worked hard and was conscientious. His business kept him constantly traveling over wretched roads and through the forests, in danger from marauding Indians and threatened by vindictive wrongdoers; for he soon became a public prosecutor. After years of contact with this energetic frontier attorney, his neighbors came to place implicit confidence in him. Never, to the day of his death, though his fortune took him to the presidency of the United States, did he impair that confidence by any word or deed. Jackson was of the frontier; his faults, many and glaring, as well as his virtues were those of frontier people.

215 Andrew Jackson as a Country Lawyer, from the painting by Stanley M. Arthurs in *The Chronicles of America*, Vol. XX, *The Reign of Andrew Jackson*, Yale University Press, New Haven, 1920

THE YAZOO LAND FRAUDS

THE year in which Tennessee was made a state found the people of Georgia seething with indignation. On January 7, 1795, the Governor of the state had affixed his signature to an act by which the state of Georgia sold to four land companies a domain comprising the larger part of the present states of Mississippi and Alabama. The price was five hundred thousand dollars. The region was still in dispute with Spain, for Pinckney had not yet reached Madrid. Some time after the transaction it became known that with one exception every member of the Georgia legislature who had voted for the grant was a member of one of the companies. It was the grossest case of political corruption that had been exposed since the independence of the United States. In 1795 Georgia people fought a bitter fight in the election of a new legislature. On February 13, 1796, a rescinding act was passed. To give to the movement for vindication a dramatic climax the vicious act of 1795 was publicly burned, the fire which ignited the paper being "brought from heaven" with a burning-glass. In the picture the figure with the burning-glass represents James Jackson, who resigned from the Senate of the United States to lead the fight for vindication. He remarked later that he was "fired at in the papers, abused in the coffee-houses and furnished a target for all the Yazoo scrip-holders — but I have the people still with me." So bitter was the opposition to him that he was forced into several duels, in one of which ten years later he was killed.

216 *Burning The Yazoo Act*, from the original drawing by C. H. Warren for L. B. Evans, *History of Georgia*. © University Publishing Co., New York, 1900

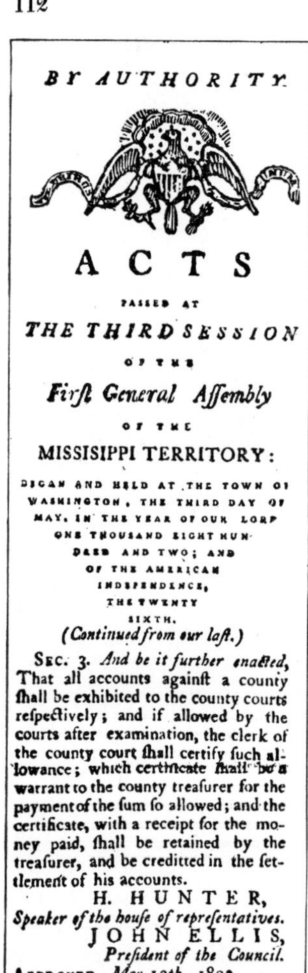

BY AUTHORITY.

ACTS

PASSED AT

THE THIRD SESSION

OF THE

First General Assembly

OF THE

MISSISIPPI TERRITORY:

BEGAN AND HELD AT THE TOWN OF WASHINGTON, THE THIRD DAY OF MAY, IN THE YEAR OF OUR LORD ONE THOUSAND EIGHT HUNDRED AND TWO; AND OF THE AMERICAN INDEPENDENCE, THE TWENTY SIXTH.

(Continued from our last.)

SEC. 3. *And be it further enacted,* That all accounts againſt a county ſhall be exhibited to the county courts reſpectively; and if allowed by the courts after examination, the clerk of the county court ſhall certify ſuch allowance; which certificate ſhall be a warrant to the county treaſurer for the payment of the ſum ſo allowed; and the certificate, with a receipt for the money paid, ſhall be retained by the treaſurer, and be credited in the ſettlement of his accounts.

H. HUNTER,
Speaker of the houſe of repreſentatives.
JOHN ELLIS,
Preſident of the Council.
APPROVED, *May 13th, 1802.*
WILLIAM C. C. CLAIBORNE,
Governor of the Miſſiſippi territory.

217 From the *Mississippi Herald*, Natchez, August 10, 1802

THE TERRITORY OF MISSISSIPPI

In 1798, the year in which President John Adams presented to the astonished American people the famous X.Y.Z. letters which precipitated a conflict with France, Congress established the Territory of Mississippi. The old town of Natchez, looking down from its bluffs upon the lazy Mississippi, was the most important settlement in the wilderness which now received territorial status. The Territory of Mississippi included the country south of the border of Tennessee and north of Spanish West Florida. It extended from the Appalachian Mountains to the Father of Waters. From a geographical point of view, the Territory of Mississippi was an anomaly. It provided an organization for the upper portions of several river systems, the mouths of which were controlled by a foreign power. Perhaps the most important of these rivers were the Alabama and the Tombigbee, flowing into Mobile Bay where stood the Spanish town of Mobile. The Territory of Mississippi, moreover, included the lands of some of the most powerful Indian tribes within the United States. Under the circumstances the settlers who began coming to the region soon after its organization tended to establish themselves near Natchez and the Mississippi River. Settlements far from friendly aid appeared, however, in the Tombigbee country. In spite of the Spanish control of the river mouths and of the presence of powerful Indian nations, the Territory of Mississippi appealed strongly to men from the states of the south Atlantic Coast. The Territory contained cotton land of unsurpassed richness and within reach of cheap transportation.

THE FIRST CAPITAL

The son of William C. C. Claiborne whom President Jefferson in 1801 appointed the second Governor of the Territory of Mississippi, has left a detailed and somewhat highly colored account of Washington, the territorial capital, "six miles east of Natchez in a rich, elevated and picturesque country." Claiborne's picture illustrates the contrast between the settlers, who sought the cotton lands of the southwest, and the small farmers, who founded their homes north of the Ohio River. "The Land Office, the Surveyor-General's office, the office of the Commissioner of Claims, and the Courts of the United States, were all there. In the immediate vicinity was Fort Dearborn, and a permanent cantonment of United States troops. The high officials of the Territory made it their residence, and many gentlemen of fortune, attracted by its advantages, went there to reside. There were three large hotels, and the Academical department of Jefferson College, established during the administration of Governor Claiborne, was in successful operation. The society was highly cultivated and refined. The conflicting land titles had drawn there a crowd of lawyers, generally young men of fine attainments and brilliant talents. The medical profession was equally well represented, at the head of which was Dr. Daniel Rawlings, a native of Calvert county, Maryland, a man of high moral character and exalted patriotism, eminent in his profession, and who, as a vigorous writer and acute reasoner, had no superior and few equals."

PRICES CURRENT,

NATCHEZ, AUGUST, 10, 1802.
Bacon, per lb. 10 to 12½ cents, briſk
Bar Iron, per cwt. 16 dollars.
Caſtings, ſmall, per do 10 dollars.
Cordage, per cwt. 12½ to 15 dollars
Corn, per buſhel 50 cents very dull.
Corn, meal per bbl. 3 dolls. dull.
Flour, per bbl. 4 dolls. dull.
Lime, per buſhel 25 to 37½ cents, great quantities at market.
Peach brandy, per gallon, 1 dollar.
Whiſky, per do 75 to 100 cents, ſcarce
Pork, ſalted, per bbl 10 dollars.
Tobacco, per cwt. 3 to 3½ dolls. dull.
Walnut and cherry plank, per 100 feet 4 dollars;

NEW-ORLEANS.
Cotton, per cwt. 18 to 20 dols.
Flour, per bbl. 4 to 5 dols.
Tobacco, per cwt. 3 1-2 to 4 dols.
Bacon per cwt. 15 dols.
Sugar, brown, per cwt. 7 dols.
Logwood, per cwt. 28 dols.
Iron, bar, per cwt. 10 dollars.

☞ *Advertiſements, &c. omitted for want of room, will be inſerted in an extra paper to-morrow.*

218 Scale of Prices in Frontier Mississippi, from the *Mississippi Herald*, Natchez, August 10, 1802

LIFE IN FRONTIER MISSISSIPPI

"The immigration from Maryland," continued Claiborne, "chiefly from Calvert, Prince George and Montgomery counties, consisted, for the most part, of educated and wealthy planters, the Covingtons, Chews, Calvits, Wilkinsons, Graysons, Freelands, Wailes, Bowies and Magruders; and the Winstons, Dangerfields and others from Virginia, who for a long time gave tone to the society of the Territorial capital. It was a gay and fashionable place, compactly built for a mile or more from east to west, every hill in the neighborhood occupied by some gentleman's chateau. The presence of the military had its influence on society; punctilio and ceremony, parades and public entertainments were the features of the place. It was, of course, the haunt of politicians and office hunters; the center of political intrigue; the point to which all persons in the pursuit of land or occupation first came. It was famous for its wine parties and its dinners, not unfrequently enlivened by one or more duels directly afterward. Such was this now deserted and forlorn looking little village during the Territorial organization. In its forums there was more oratory, in its *salons* more wit and beauty than we have ever witnessed since, all now mouldering, neglected and forgotten, in the desolate graveyard of the ancient capital of Mississippi."

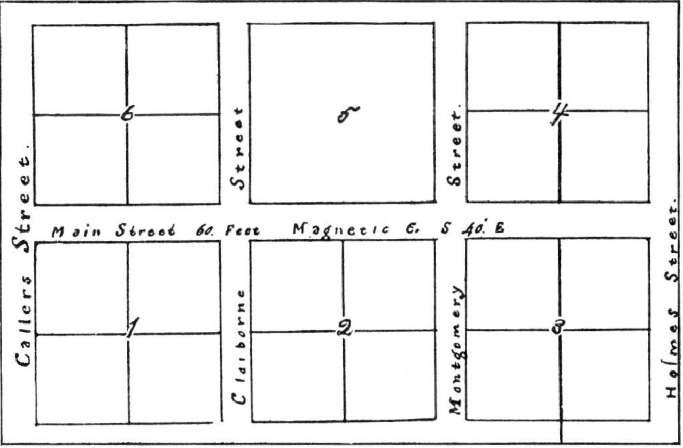

219 Plan of Washington, Mississippi, from Dunbar Rowland, *History of Mississippi; the Heart of the South*, S. J. Clarke Publishing Co., Chicago, 1925

THE CHICKASAWS

The Yazoo grants included lands which were still in the actual possession of the Indians of the Southwest, the Creeks, the Choctaws, and the Chickasaws. All these peoples belonged to the Muskhogean family and doubtless have a common origin. James Adair had spent most of his life with the Chickasaws and the memory of that brave and friendly trader-scholar was fresh among them when Tennessee became a state. Their villages lay in northern Mississippi between the upper reaches of the Yazoo and the Tombigbee. Here the ill-fated De Soto had found them in 1540 and had called them "Chicaza." They were gardeners, and hunters over a domain which stretched northward to the Ohio, eastward far toward the country of the Cherokees, and southward to the lands held by their inveterate enemies, the Choctaws. The Chickasaw people, numbering somewhere between three and six thousand, lived in four settlements. A traveler in 1775 found one of these, a narrow line of straggling habitations a mile and a half long in the center of "an uneven and large nitrous savannah." From this settlement a trail of one hundred and sixty miles led to the Mississippi at Chickasaw Bluffs, the modern Memphis, where they had their main landing place. The Chickasaws were belligerent and warlike Indians, noted from antiquity for their bravery and their independence. In 1715 they combined with the Cherokees and drove the Shawnees from the region of the Cumberland River (see page 42). Seventeen years later they cut to pieces a war party of Iroquois who had invaded their country. Between 1736 and 1740 they defeated all efforts of the French to conquer them. Like the Iroquois they were from the first to last the Frenchman's implacable enemies. In 1769 they put their former allies, the Cherokees, to utter rout. At the opening of the nineteenth century these fiery braves faced in the advancing frontier a menace surpassing any in their history.

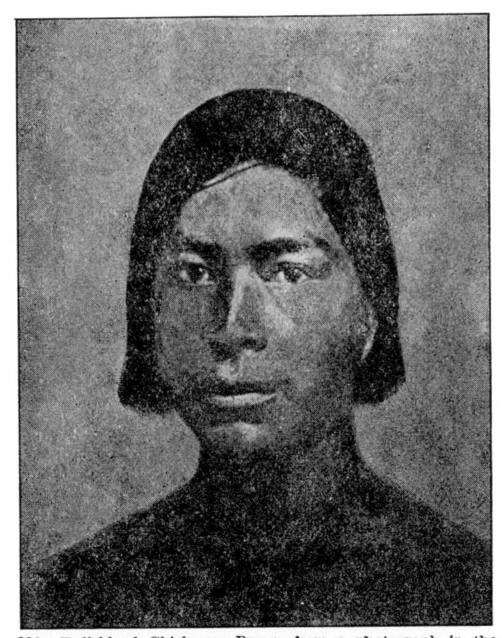

220 Full-blood Chickasaw Brave, from a photograph in the De Lancey Gill Collection, United States National Museum, Washington

221 The Land of the Choctaws in the Forests of Long Leaf Pine, from a photograph in the United States National Museum, Washington

CHOCTAWS

Cousins to the fiery Chickasaws were the Choctaws who lived in the country of the Long Leaf Pine in central and southern Mississippi, their eastern villages extending as far as Georgia. They were a powerful and numerous people with a population of between fifteen and twenty thousand living in fifty villages. Preëminently agriculturists, they were less warlike than their northern neighbors, with whom, however, they were almost constantly engaged in defensive strife. Other inveterate enemies were the Creeks who assailed them from the east. The Choctaws early became friends with the French, which fact may be the reason why the Chickasaws remained hostile to the subjects of the Bourbon monarchs. When English traders weaned the eastern villages from the French attachment, civil war raged intermittently in the Choctaw nation until 1763, when the Frenchman was driven from the North American continent. With them the Spanish successors of the French sought to establish close relations. The Choctaws early began moving across the Mississippi into what is now the state of Louisiana.

CREEKS

Most powerful of the Muskhogean peoples was the Creek confederacy, occupying most of Alabama, southern Georgia, and a part of Florida. They were not in origin a single nation; six languages were spoken within the confederacy but Muskhogee was the dominant and official tongue. The name "Creeks" was given them by the English who found them living in a country filled with small streams. The Cherokees and later the whites recognized two great divisions known as "Upper" and "Lower" Creeks, emigrants from the latter finally developing into the Seminoles of northern Florida. In 1789 the Seminoles and Creeks were estimated to number twenty-four thousand people living in about a hundred towns. Their women were short of stature but their men were taller than the average European and invariably well formed. They were Indians more than usually devoted to ornament and decoration, fond of music and ball play, proud, and brave. There were many ranks of chieftains among them. In the center of their important villages was an open square for the performance of ceremonies. "Red towns" were set apart for war ceremonials and "white towns" were consecrated to peace. Each year, as the crops of corn matured, the Creek villages celebrated the harvest festival and cleansing ceremony when the building of a new fire symbolized the coming of the new year. The villages were swept and cleaned; old clothing was discarded and new garments donned; the utensils of the past months were thrown away and new procured. There was feasting and dancing. As the nineteenth century opened, the conversations at these ceremonies turned more and more to the steady encroachment of the whites on the Indian lands. The Creeks had always been friends with the English. They were suspicious of the Americans. The former were traders while the latter were farmers, implacable enemies of hunting peoples whose lands they desired.

222 John, a Creek, from an engraving after the pencil sketch from life, by Trumbull, New York, 1790, in John Trumbull, *Reminiscences of His Own Times*, New York and New Haven, 1841

223 Creek House in 1791, from an engraving after a drawing by J. C. Tidball, U. S. A., published by J. B. Lippincott & Co., Philadelphia, courtesy of the Bureau of American Ethnology, Washington

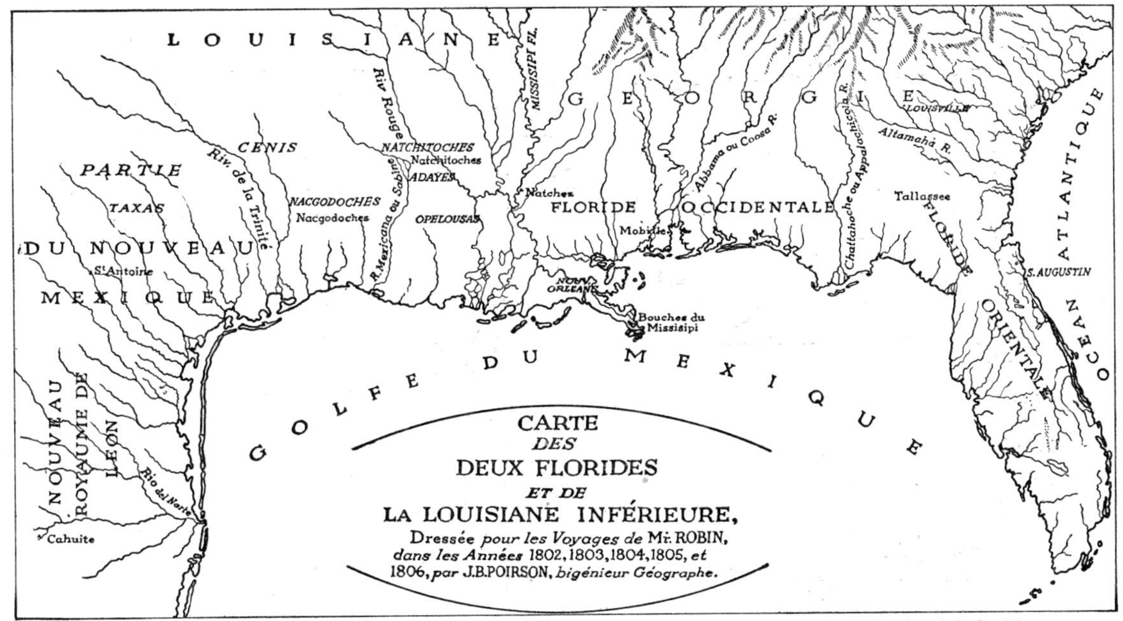

224 Map of the two Floridas and of lower Louisiana, redrawn from a map in Claude C. Robin, *Voyages dans l'Interieur de la Louisiane*, Paris, 1807

LOUISIANA AND FLORIDA

THE first years of the nineteenth century saw vast changes in the outlook of the eastern white settlers. In 1803 Louisiana was purchased (see Chapter VII) and the American boundary extended to the far distant Rockies. Quite characteristic of President Jefferson was a scheme to "validate" the purchase and justify himself in the eyes of his strict-constructionist friends. He drew a rough draft of an amendment to the Constitution which would give him the power to purchase the area and also power to buy Indian lands. Jefferson visualized the removal of all the Indian tribes to the newly acquired territory. The President persuaded Congress to grant fifteen thousand dollars as a preliminary step toward bringing about the removal. Some of the Cherokees were interested and before 1817 between two and three thousand of that nation had migrated to their present habitat in Oklahoma. The greater part of the people, however, clung tenaciously to the old home. The Choctaws ever since the fall of New France in 1763 had been crossing the river into what is now the state of Louisiana. The retreat of the great tribes of the Old Southwest had begun. The acquisition of Louisiana was of inestimable importance to the United States but Florida still remained in the hands of Spain. Certain Americans, among whom was Thomas Jefferson, persuaded themselves, however, that West Florida had been acquired with the domain west of the Mississippi. Acting on a hint from the Executive, Congress coolly passed an act giving the President authority to erect Mobile Bay and River into a separate revenue district and to designate a port of entry. The Spanish minister, Don Carlos Yrujo, quite pardonably lost his temper and delivered himself of some undiplomatic language directed toward the Secretary of State, James Madison. The securing of West Florida become an obsession with President Jefferson but from first to last he bungled the effort to get it. When he left office, the Gulf littoral east of the Mississippi was still Spanish. Along this shore, at Baton Rouge, at Mobile, and in scattered settlements, lived perhaps a hundred thousand people — a miscellaneous lot, speculators and home seekers, Spaniards, French, and probably a majority of Americans. Taking advantage of a change in the Spanish dynasty brought about by the Napoleonic wars, a so-called "movement for self-government" started at Bayou Sara and Baton Rouge in 1810. The population of this region was nine-tenths American. On September 26 the people of West Florida, "appealing to the Supreme Ruler of the World," declared their independence and hastily dispatched a message to Washington asking immediate incorporation into the United States. In this situation, the apparent consummation of desires long held by him and his predecessor, President Madison was harassed by both timidity and constitutional scruples. With an effort he conquered both. In October he authorized Governor Claiborne of New Orleans to govern the region and in the following January secretly sought and obtained the approval of Congress for the temporary occupation by force of East Florida should that become desirable. Before the matter was finally settled, the War of 1812 had begun.

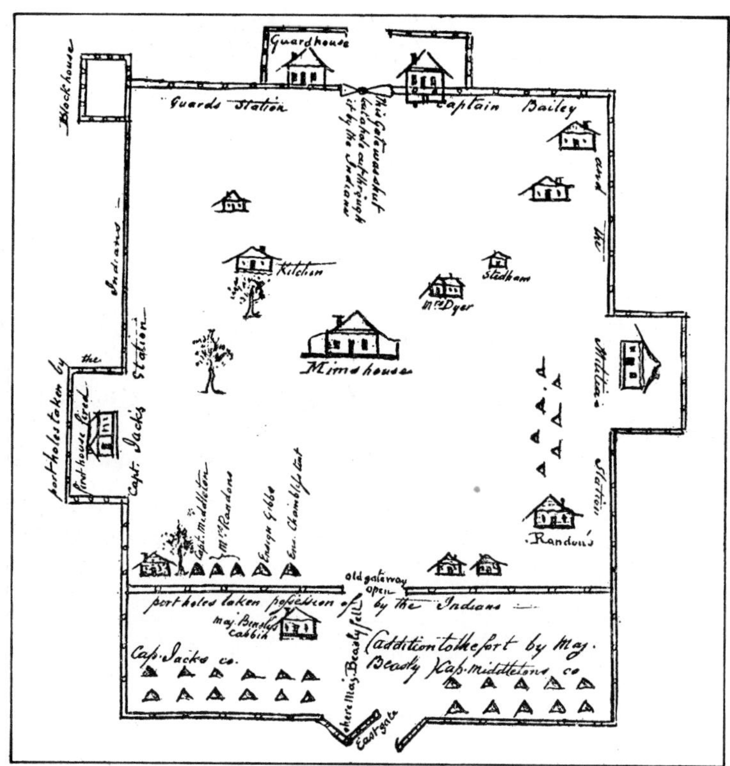

225 Plan of Fort Mims, from the drawing in Claiborne's manuscript, in the Pickett Collection, Department of Archives and History, State of Alabama, Montgomery, Ala.

FORT MIMS

WHILE Governor Claiborne, in 1811, was extending the jurisdiction of the United States to that part of West Florida near the Mississippi River, Tecumseh was visiting the Indians of the Southwest. Before his mission was completed, he was compelled to hurry north to retrieve the disaster of Tippecanoe. The Chickasaws, Choctaws, and Cherokees would have nothing to do with war. But the case was different among the Creeks. When the news of the fall of Detroit filtered southward, the young men of that confederacy became restive. There was talk of taking up the hatchet, and war dances were held in the "red towns." The "Red Sticks," as the war party among the Creeks was called, were incensed at the decision of their eastern neighbors to remain neutral and began to perpetrate outrages upon the Cherokees. This led to retaliation. The Cherokee nation placed its forces at the command of the Federal Government. In 1813 the Creeks were definitely on the warpath and the frontier from Tennessee to Georgia was apprehensive. The Creeks were numerous and powerful; other tribes of the Old Southwest might join them. Terror seized the white settlers along the Mobile River; their position was exposed and they were far from help. To protect them the government sent a certain Major Beasley with one hundred and seventy-five militia. The threatened borderers gathered for protection within a stockade called Fort Mims near the junction of the Alabama and the Tombigbee rivers.

THE MASSACRE

HERE five hundred and fifty-three persons awaited the passing of the war cloud. Beasley proved quite unfit for his responsibility. In spite of warnings he left the gates unguarded. He permitted the enemy to creep within striking distance without ever a patrol bringing him word of the movement. On August 30, 1813, a thousand Creeks rushed and gained the open gates as the occupants of the fort were beginning dinner. Then occurred one of the most terrible massacres of border history. The negroes were spared to be taken off as slaves. When the Creeks withdrew, the bodies of two hundred and fifty persons, men, women, and children, lay dead within the stockade. Twelve whites only cut their way to safety.

226 A Conventional Mid-Nineteenth Century Representation of Indian Warfare, from an engraving, *Massacre At Fort Mims*, after the painting by Chappel, in the possession of the publishers

PUSHMATAHA, 1764–1824

THE war begun by the Creeks was an act of madness. The Red Sticks comprised but four thousand out of the seven thousand warriors of the confederacy. Not more than a third of the hostiles had guns. Ammunition was scarce, because the Spaniards, whence the supply came, sold only enough for hunting. In addition to fighting the Americans the Red Sticks were at war with the Cherokees, and many of their own Creek people. Finally they faced the might of the Choctaws led by the great chief, Pushmataha. He had actively opposed Tecumseh, when that chieftain visited the Choctaws. In 1813 he led about a hundred and fifty warriors in joint actions with the whites against the Creeks. In this campaign he proved a strict disciplinarian and turned his wild braves into efficient soldiers. Andrew Jackson frequently expressed the opinion that Pushmataha was the greatest and bravest Indian that he had ever known. When in Washington on a mission in 1824, the Choctaw chieftain suddenly died. John Randolph of Roanoke said of him in the Senate: "He was wise in council — eloquent in an extraordinary degree, and on all occasions, and under all circumstances, the white man's friend."

227 Pushmataha, from the portrait by Charles Bird King (1785–1862) in the Redwood Library, Newport, R. I.

THE CAMPAIGN AGAINST THE CREEKS

TENNESSEE rose to avenge the murders at Fort Mims and to break the power of the Creeks. Jackson, with a commission as major-general of militia, led the expedition. In October 1813, he reached the great bend of the Tennessee, where he erected Fort Deposit to serve as his base of supplies. He made ready to cross the menacing ridges of the Raccoon and Lookout Mountains preparatory to the plunge into the heart of the Creek country. Bad as was the organization of the quartermaster department for the regular troops in the War of 1812, the service of supply for such expeditions as Jackson's was worse — in fact had to be created largely by the commanding general. At the Tennessee Jackson's contract wagoners failed him. He met the emergency by impressing wagons and horses in the neighboring region. In November he was across the mountains and had built Fort Strother on the Coosa. He commanded some three thousand men. On November 3 his subordinate, General Coffee, won a minor victory over the enemy at their village at Tallushatchee. Five days later Jackson marched with the larger part of his army to the relief of a friendly Indian village besieged by a thousand hostiles. Jackson's scheme of maneuver was perfect. He attacked with his army in the form of a crescent, the flanks well in advance of the center. In front of the center was a party of skirmishers who engaged the Indians hotly and then retreated, drawing the exultant braves into a trap. The flanks closed behind the Indians, who were caught in a circle of fire. Jackson might possibly have ended the Creek war on that day in this battle of Talladega had not one detachment of infantry fled, leaving an opening through which most of the Indians escaped before the reserves could be brought up to fill it. The blow, however, was severe, for three hundred fallen Creeks were left behind.

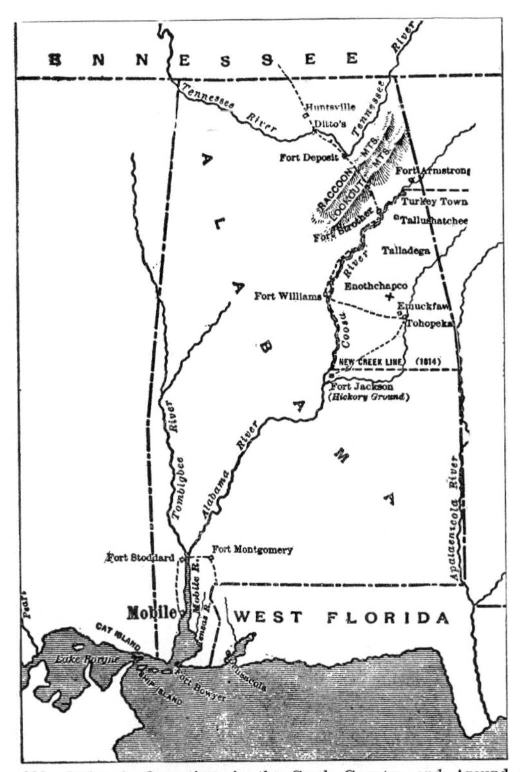

228 Jackson's Operations in the Creek Country and Around Mobile, 1813–14, from a map in John Spencer Bassett, *Life of Andrew Jackson*, Doubleday, Page & Co., New York, 1911, Courtesy of Doubleday Doran, Garden City, L. I.

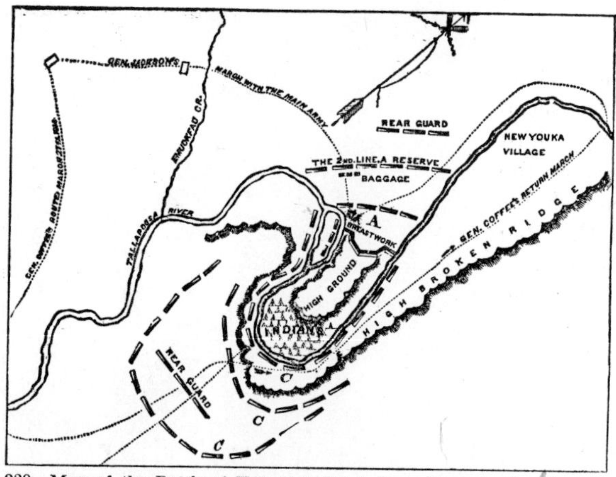

229 Map of the Battle of Horseshoe Bend, from *Harper's Encyclopaedia of United States History*, Harper & Bros., New York, 1901

THE BATTLE OF HORSESHOE BEND

In December and January Jackson was forced to see the greater part of his army go home as their terms of enlistment expired. The characteristics of the commander never showed more clearly than when, on December 31, 1813, he sat in camp with only a handful of disaffected troops left, raging impotently at a detachment of departing militia and wishing for each "a petticoat as a coat of mail to hand down to posterity." Another army of raw levies quite untrained began to arrive. In February six hundred regulars came in. With this force to fall back upon Jackson announced that the next case of mutiny among the militia would result in execution. On March 14, John Woods, a youth of eighteen, paid the penalty. The measure was, perhaps, unduly harsh but its effect on discipline was salutary. Thirteen days later Jackson was before the fortification at the Horseshoe Bend on the Tallapoosa River where the Creeks had prepared to make their last stand. They deemed their defenses impregnable — the broad river on three sides and on the fourth a zigzag breastwork of logs from five to eight feet high with a double row of portholes. A thousand warriors and three hundred women were within the enclosure of one hundred acres. Again Jackson's strategy was impeccable. He sent Coffee with mounted troops to cut off retreat while he disposed the main body to rush the works. Coöperating Cherokees, among whom was young John Ross, went with Coffee. These swam across the river to the fort, carried off the canoes of the Creeks, and rushed among the houses setting fire to them. At this moment Jackson charged, carried the breastwork, and fought hand to hand inside the enclosure. When night came on, eight hundred Creeks lay dead; only four of the three hundred captured were men. In August the victorious Jackson dictated a treaty which deprived the Creeks of a large part of their rich Alabama lands.

THE AFTERMATH OF THE WAR OF 1812

Jackson's overwhelming victory at Horseshoe Bend broke the power of the Creek nation. Much of the lands of that numerous people was ceded to the United States. Horseshoe Bend was the first step in the process which ended with the removal of the Creeks to the country west of the Mississippi. The Treaty of Ghent, which brought the War of 1812 to an end, was the signal for a great influx of people into the Alabama-Mississippi territory. An early Alabama historian has commented: "The flood-gates of Virginia, the two Carolinas, Tennessee, Kentucky and Georgia, were now hoisted, and mighty streams of emigration poured through them, spreading over the whole territory of Alabama. The axe resounded from side to side, and from corner to corner. The stately and magnificent forests fell. Log cabins sprang, as if by magic, into sight. Never, before or since, has a country been so rapidly peopled." — A. J. Pickett, *The History of Alabama*, 1851, II, 385. In 1817 Congress divided Alabama from Mississippi and permitted the people of the latter territory to form a constitution preparatory to their admission as a state. Mississippi struck a blow for democracy by adopting the then novel procedure of submitting this constitution to the voters of the territory for ratification. In 1819 Alabama joined the union of the states. The American was not yet, however, in full possession of the Old Southwest.

230 A Settler's Home on the Pascagoula River, Mississippi, from an engraving after a drawing, in *Our Native Land*, D. Appleton and Company, New York, 1882

THE ACQUISITION OF FLORIDA

AFTER the conclusion of the War of 1812 the question of the status of Florida continued to embarrass the Government of the United States. The eastern portion of West Florida had never been taken over by the United States. Effective Spanish control, on the other hand, was almost wholly lacking. The colonial empire of Spain, which had once been the greatest in the world, was crumbling. Florida swamps had become the refuge for a motley host of undesirables of all races while pirates' nests developed on its coasts. John Quincy Adams, Secretary of State to President Monroe, took up the task of negotiating for the cession of all of Florida. The state of Georgia began to grow restive as fugitive slaves fled beyond the international border. At this stage Andrew Jackson, since his victory over the Creeks a major-general in the Regular Army, was sent in 1818 to protect the southern frontier against outrages from Florida. He suggested to the President that the most effective defense was to cross the line and break up the concentrations on Florida soil. He believed that he received Monroe's authorization. With an army of nearly three hundred white troops and two thousand Indian allies he swept across Florida. The Seminoles fled before him leaving their villages to be burned and their provisions destroyed. Jackson confronted and took St. Marks on Apalachee Bay. At the latter place two Englishmen, Ambrister and Arbuthnot, who had been captured, were brought before a court-martial, condemned for inciting Indian uprisings, and executed. The next year Spain, under strong pressure from the United States, sold Florida, though the treaty was not finally ratified until 1821.

Sir, Department of War
Decr 26th 1817

You will repair, with as little delay as practicable, to Fort Scott and assume the immediate command of the forces in that section of the Southern Division

The increasing display of hostile intentions, by the Seminole Indians, may render it necessary to concentrate all the contiguous and disposable force of your Division, upon that quarter. The regular force now there is about Eight hundred strong; and One thousand militia of the State of Georgia are called into service. General Gaines estimates the strength of the Indians at two thousand seven hundred. Should you be of opinion that our numbers are too small to beat the Enemy, you will call on the Executives

231 First page of an order, dated December 26, 1817, from Secretary of War Calhoun to General Jackson instructing him to assume command of troops along the Florida border, from the original in the Library of Congress, Washington

WILLIAM MACINTOSH, 1775–1825

FOUR years after the ratification of the Florida purchase William MacIntosh, on May 1, 1825, found his house surrounded by Creek warriors who killed him as he tried to escape. The band was executing a formal sentence of death passed in accordance with tribal law. The story of MacIntosh is significant of many things in the history of the frontier. He was the son of a Scotch trader and a Creek woman. In 1811 he was made chief of the Lower Creeks. In 1802, six years after the revocation of the notorious Yazoo grants, Georgia had relinquished to the Federal Government the state's claim, derived from its colonial charter, to what is now Mississippi and Alabama, on the condition that the United States would extinguish the Indian title as rapidly as it could be done peaceably. By the treaty of 1805 millions of acres of Creek lands were turned over to Georgia. The Georgia people pressed for more territory, with the result that in 1811 MacIntosh moved in the tribal council the passage of a law forbidding the sale of any further land under penalty of death. In the Creek war MacIntosh sided against the Red Sticks and held a major's commission in the American army. He was prominent at the battle of Horseshoe Bend. In 1818 land, in addition to that confiscated as a result of the battle, was by treaty acquired from the Creeks by the United States. Three years later, while in the pay of the whites MacIntosh, with a dozen other chiefs controlled by him, alienated more Creek land to the United States over the protest of thirty-six chiefs present. MacIntosh had his price. When he tried the same maneuver in 1823, his people reënacted the death penalty which he had originally moved. The domain of the Creeks had been reduced by 1825 to ten million acres. This remainder MacIntosh sold in the early months of the year. On May 1, 1825, he suffered his punishment.

232 William MacIntosh, from Thomas L. M'Kenney, *History of the Indian Tribes of North America*, Philadelphia, 1872

233 Chiefs of the Creek Nation and a Georgia Squatter, from Basil Hall, *Forty Etchings From Sketches Made with the Camera Lucida in North America*, Edinburgh, 1829

REMOVAL OF THE CREEKS

CONDEMNATION of MacIntosh for his venality and his treachery to his people is easy. White men, representing the United States, bribed him. They were determined to drive the Creeks off the rich lands of the cotton belt. The Creeks clung tenaciously to their lands because they were rapidly becoming civilized, had slaves, and were themselves raising cotton. John C. Calhoun, Secretary of War under President Monroe, had declared that he would not accept a treaty to which the chiefs of the Creek nation did not acquiesce. Nevertheless, at the very end of his administration, Monroe submitted this infamous last treaty of MacIntosh to the Senate for ratification. That august body, fully expecting the desperate Creeks to rise in revolt as a result of their action, ratified the arrangement. But the Creeks did not rise. They were a defeated people and the sorrow born of the last war had not been forgotten. For ten years more they remained on their ancestral lands. Then, without resistance, they suffered themselves to be herded by the Federal Government across the Mississippi to their present habitat in Oklahoma. The migration took four years, 1836–1840. The policy of Thomas Jefferson was being put into operation.

234 Foke-Luste-Hajo, a Seminole, from a portrait by Charles Bird King in Thomas L. M'Kenney, *History of the Indian Tribes of North America*, Philadelphia, 1872

THE SEMINOLES

THE word "Seminole" means "separatist" or "runaway." About 1775 the Creeks who migrated to the Florida country began to be called by this name. They were never numerous; at the end of the eighteenth century they had but seven towns. These ultimately increased to twenty. As fugitive slaves fled to their villages, they began to show a mixture of negro blood. They were allies of the Spaniards so long as Spain retained control of Florida, and were enemies of the United States. When the latter nation gained control of their hunting grounds, they began to feel the heavy pressure of the white frontier. Two years after Spain ratified the Florida Purchase Treaty most of their lands were taken from them by an arrangement made at Fort Moultrie in Florida in 1823. They were left with a central reservation. Within ten years this was coveted. In 1832 the chief, Emathla, signed it away and promised that his people would, like their Creek cousins, submit to removal beyond the Mississippi.

235 A Seminole Village Group, Florida, from a model in the Department of Ethnology, United States National Museum, Washington

OSCEOLA, *ca.* 1804–1838

Osceola of the Seminoles was a young man when the treaty of 1832 was signed. In his veins ran white blood inherited from his Scotch grandfather. He was not a chief by descent nor even by formal election. He became, however, the leader of his people in their last war with the whites. Standing up in the councils of his nation he demanded the repudiation of the treaty and resistance to the aggressor. The Seminoles rallied to him. Emathla was killed, as was General A. R. Thompson who had been instrumental in applying pressure to those Indians who opposed the treaty. Secreting the women, children, and old men in the fastnesses of inaccessible swamps, Osceola began his harassing campaign. The war opened with a surprise attack upon Major Dade in 1835 and the killing of some hundred soldiers. Year after year the war lasted, while the army dragged itself after the Indians who flitted from covert to covert, who pounced upon settlements far from the defending troops, and who could never be brought to a general battle. Under a flag of truce Osceola came into the camp of General Jesup for a conference. Here with the grossest treachery he was seized. A few months later, broken in spirit and brooding over his betrayal, the young chief died in January 1838, a prisoner at Fort Moultrie. His death did not end the war which dragged on until August 1842. Fifteen hundred lives, lost mostly by disease, and twenty million dollars was the price which the United States paid for the removal of the Seminoles to lands in the West.

236 Osceola, Chief of the Seminoles, from the statue in painted plaster by Achille Collin, courtesy of the Division of Ethnology, United States National Museum, Washington

CHANGES AMONG THE CHEROKEES

About 1817 a considerable group of the Cherokees left their old homes and migrated to the country beyond the Mississippi. A majority of the nation, however, remained on their tribal lands in the shadow of the Appalachians. Theirs was a rich country. They began to adopt the farming methods of the white man. They raised cotton and shipped considerable quantities of the staple in boats of their own make to New Orleans. They exported hides and live stock. The traveler through their country found log cabin homes, grist mills, saw mills, looms, and cotton mills. One such traveler, B. Gold, a citizen of Cornwall, Connecticut, journeyed to the Cherokee country in 1829 to visit his daughter who had married Elias Boudinot. ". . . the people all appear to be perfectly friendly," he wrote home, "and many places we have seen look indeed like civilization and they tell us that many parts that we have not seen are much better. . . . New Echota [the Cherokee capital] has a Council House and Court House and two or three Merchant Stores, about half a dozen handsome frame dwelling houses in sight . . . and very decently furnished to be in any country. . . . I have been in most of the houses and find the families very polite and agreeable and fit associates for any country. The National Council and Superior Court is now here in session and I have yesterday and to-day attended both and seen important causes before them — have observed much order and decorum — in their Council and Court are quite a number of learned polished and well qualified gentlemen. . . . I . . . have been introduced to most of the members of the Council and the Court — am much pleased with the acquaintance I have already had — to be sure some of the gentlemen are full blood Cherokees and in a rude State and easily to be seen of great natural powers of mind." — From a manuscript in the possession of Dudley L. Vail.

237 A Modern Cherokee Cabin on the Qualla Reservation, North Carolina, from a photograph in the De Lancey Gill Collection, United States National Museum, Washington. This picture represents with reasonable accuracy conditions among more advanced Cherokees about 1825

Cherokee Alphabet.					
Ꭰ a	Ꭱ e	Ꭲ i	Ꭳ o	Ꭴ u	Ꭵ v
Ꭶ ga Ꭷ ka	Ꭸ ge	Ꭹ gi	Ꭺ go	Ꭻ gu	Ꭼ gv
Ꭽ ha	Ꭾ he	Ꭿ hi	Ꮀ ho	Ꮁ hu	Ꮂ hv
Ꮃ la	Ꮄ le	Ꮅ li	Ꮆ lo	Ꮇ lu	Ꮈ lv
Ꮉ ma	Ꮊ me	Ꮋ mi	Ꮌ mo	Ꮍ mu	
Ꮎ na Ꮏ hna Ꮐ nah	Ꮑ ne	Ꮒ ni	Ꮓ no	Ꮔ nu	Ꮕ nv
Ꮖ qua	Ꮗ que	Ꮘ qui	Ꮙ quo	Ꮚ quu	Ꮛ quv
Ꮜ sa Ꮝ s	Ꮞ se	Ꮟ si	Ꮠ so	Ꮡ su	Ꮢ sv
Ꮣ da Ꮤ ta	Ꮥ de Ꮦ te	Ꮧ di Ꮨ ti	Ꮩ do	Ꮪ du	Ꮫ dv
Ꮬ dla Ꮭ tla	Ꮮ tle	Ꮯ tli	Ꮰ tlo	Ꮱ tlu	Ꮲ tlv
Ꮳ tsa	Ꮴ tse	Ꮵ tsi	Ꮶ tso	Ꮷ tsu	Ꮸ tsv
Ꮹ wà	Ꮺ we	Ꮻ wi	Ꮼ wo	Ꮽ wu	Ꮾ wv
Ꮿ ya	Ᏸ ye	Ᏹ yi	Ᏺ yo	Ᏻ yu	Ᏼ yv

238 The Cherokee Syllabary, from a copy in the Bureau of American Ethnology, United States National Museum, Washington

CHEROKEE EDUCATION

Economic change among the Cherokees underlay a veritable social and intellectual revolution. Trade schools managed by missionaries flourished among them and a beginning was made in the teaching of the academic branches. In 1819 a tract of land twelve miles square was sold, the proceeds of which were invested by the President of the United States and the income used for the education of Cherokee boys. Three years later seven Cherokees studied at the mission school at Cornwall, Connecticut. Of these John Ridge, Elias Boudinot, and Richard Brown were to play important rôles in the politics of their nation. Once the Cherokees had caught the meaning and significance of the white man's culture, their hopes and ambitions ran high. There is a childlike aspiration as well as naïveté in the circular letter which they sent to the adjoining states in 1813, declaring that many of their youth of both sexes "had acquired such knowledge of letters as to show the most incredulous that our mental powers are not, by nature, inferior to yours, and we look forward to a period of time when it may be said 'this artist, this mathematician, this astronomer is a Cherokee.'" — *Niles Register IV*, 125.

SEQUOYA

In 1821 the development of the Cherokee people received a sudden and dramatic impetus as a result of the work of a tribesman known as Sequoya. He had been born about 1760, son of a German father and a mixed-blood mother. As a boy he lived at Chota, the peace town of the Cherokees, and heard the wailing of the women following the fighting of Revolutionary times. George Guess (or Guest) as he was called among the white people, never went to school. Like most of the friends of his boyhood, he became a hunter and a trader in furs. He was also a silversmith in which work his inventive turn of mind had a limited opportunity. An accident befell him and he became a cripple for life. When about forty years of age, a chance conversation turned his attention to the importance for the white man's civilization of the arts of writing and printing. For some twelve years he worked on a syllabary for the Cherokee language. In 1821 he submitted it to the chief men of the nation who promptly endorsed it. Sequoya's invention should rank as one of the important intellectual achievements of the nineteenth century. It was not, as has sometimes been implied, the invention of writing by a primitive people; its inspiration by the writing of the white man is clear. The brilliance of the achievement lies in the perfect adaptation of the syllabary to the Cherokee language. The memorizing of eighty-six characters enabled the Indian to read and write. The immediate result of the invention was adult education on a vast scale, a veritable intellectual revolution. Before a year had passed, thousands of Cherokees who could not speak English and who were, therefore, cut off from the opportunities of an education had learned to read and write their own tongue.

239 Sequoya, Inventor of the Cherokee Syllabary, after a sketch made at Washington in 1828, from Thomas L. M'Kenney, *History of the Indian Tribes of North America*, Philadelphia, 1872

PROTECTION

ᏣᎳᎩ ᏧᎴᎯᏌᏅᎯ.
CHEROKEE PHŒNIX.

VOL. I. NEW ECHOTA, WEDNESDAY JUNE 4, 1828. NO. 15.

EDITED BY ELIAS BOUDINOTT
PRINTED WEEKLY BY
ISAAC H. HARRIS,
FOR THE CHEROKEE NATION.

of said river opposite to Fort Strother. on said river; all north of said line is the Cherokee lands, all south of said line is the Creek lands.

William Hambly, (Seal)
his
Big ⋈ Warrior, (Seal)
mark.

mitting murder on the subjects of the other, is approved and adopted; but respecting thefts, it is hereby agreed that the following rule be substituted,

240 From the *Cherokee Phœnix*, June 4, 1828, in the New York Public Library

THE *CHEROKEE PHŒNIX*

SEQUOYA had the missionary spirit. In 1823 he traveled to the western Cherokees, who had migrated some years before beyond the Mississippi, and introduced his syllabary among them. Here he settled down to spend the remaining years of his life. His intellectual interests broadened. He dreamed of a common Indian language and visited tribes of various stocks in a fruitless search for the elements of a common speech and grammar. In the Mexican Sierras seeking to trace a lost tribe of the Cherokees, which according to tradition had crossed the Mississippi before the Revolution and had wandered into the western mountains, he met his death, striving to the end to serve the interests of his people. Meanwhile, the National Council of the eastern Cherokees had caused the setting up of a printing press at New Echota. In 1828 Elias Boudinot began to edit the *Cherokee Phœnix*. "My duties are complicated," wrote Boudinot to Connecticut friends. "I have to prepare what little editorial may be seen in the *Phœnix* in English and Cherokee . . . one can't write fast in Cherokee. . . . I have also to receive all communications on business made to this establishment. . . . If I have what may be called a leisure day, I have . . . work . . . preparing tracts in the Cherokee language, with the Rev. S. A. Worcester. We are now publishing a small Hymn Book. . . . It is the first Cherokee book ever published." — From a manuscript in the possession of DUDLEY L. VAIL.

THE CHEROKEE COUNCIL

THE National Council of the Cherokees in the 'twenties and 'thirties was a body of interesting and able men. One of the younger members was John Ross, son of a Scotch immigrant and his Cherokee wife who was herself three-quarters white. Senior to him on the Council was Major Ridge, whose son John Ridge went to the Cornwall School. The elder Ridge was a full-blood Cherokee and one of the most able men that that nation has produced, a broad-minded and public-spirited individual, keen of intellect and commanding in appearance. His magnetic personality and his strength of character made him a natural leader of men. By sheer native ability he had forged his way to the front of the Cherokee nation and for thirty years wielded a strong influence over the affairs of his people. Above him in the 'twenties was the principal chief of the Cherokees, the aged and venerable Path Killer. In his lifetime he had seen the white sea, rising like the tide, inundate more and more of the lands of his people. His own mark stood at the bottom of the treaties of Tellico in 1804 and 1805 and of Turkeytown in 1816. He was an Indian born and reared in the days when the Cherokees still retained the greater part of their primitive culture. His fortune was to lead his people in days when they were awakening to a new life and were quickened with new aspirations. He beheld Sequoya make the Cherokees a literate people in scarcely more moons than elapsed from winter to winter. He shared fully in the passionate desire of his nation to live in the lands where the landmarks were associated with the great men and the great deeds of their people and where the tumbled Appalachians cast shadows over the graves of their dead. In 1827 his spirit went to join those of his forefathers.

241 John Ridge, d. 1839, from a lithograph in Thomas L. M'Kenney, *History of the Indian Tribes of North America*, Philadelphia, 1872

242 Major Ridge, 1771–1839, from a lithograph in Thomas L. M'Kenney, *History of the Indian Tribes of North America*, Philadelphia, 1872

PRESSURE BY THE UNITED STATES

THE fate of the Cherokees was sealed as far back as 1802 in the agreement between the United States and Georgia when the Federal Government assumed the obligation to remove the Indians from the lands of the state as soon as it could be peaceably done. In 1817 the United States obtained a land cession. Two years later the National Council of the Cherokees, imitating the Creeks, decreed the death penalty to any individual signing a treaty ceding more lands. In 1822 the question came up in the House of Representatives, when it was decided that the Federal Government was not living up to its obligations to Georgia and the sum of thirty thousand dollars was voted to extinguish Indian land titles within that state. The Cherokee Council, hearing of the action of Congress, voted unanimously to negotiate no more treaties with the United States for the purpose of making cessions of lands and despatched a copy to Calhoun, the Secretary of War. The reply of the United States was the sending of two commissioners, Campbell and Meriweather, to New Echota in the fall of 1823. They met the National Council, where Campbell made a diplomatic speech in praise of the Cherokee civilization and concluded with the remark that time and deliberation were essential for the wise expenditure of the appropriation at their disposal. The meaning of this was not lost on the Indians who discomfited the commissioners two days later by demanding a full statement of their instructions from the President. Reluctantly Campbell and Meriweather opened negotiations in writing at the request of the Cherokees. "A novel procedure," remarked Campbell, this "correspondence in writing conducted with a government regularly organized, composed of Indians." Cajolery failed and threats followed which failed also. Then the commissioners played the old game. Their tool was William MacIntosh, the Creek chief, who at the time was held in high esteem by the Cherokees. He, together with several other Creek leaders, arrived ostensibly for a courtesy visit. After the formal greetings a note in broken English was secretly handed to John Ross offering him and two other Cherokee councilors two thousand dollars each for a treaty and adding, "no one shall know it." The next day, when the speaker, Major Ridge, opened the Meeting of the General Council, John Ross rose to speak. In scathing terms he denounced the practice of bribery and concluded: "It has now become my duty to inform you that a gross contempt is offered my character, as well as that of the General Council. This letter which I hold in my hand will speak for itself." He handed it to the clerk of the Council. When the clerk had finished reading it, the aged Path Killer arose deeply moved. He expressed his grief and astonishment that a chief whom he had counted a brother had sought to betray the Cherokees for a handful of gold. There could be no condoning the offense; the head man of the Creeks must be dealt with as a traitor. In the angry confusion which followed MacIntosh escaped. A short time later the two discomfited commissioners walked into the office of Secretary Calhoun to report.

ACTS

OF THE

STATE OF GEORGIA

AN ACT

To ratify and confirm certain articles of agreement and cesſion entered into on the 24th day of April 1802, between the Commiſſioners of the State of Georgia on the one part, and the Commiſſioners of the United States on the other part.

WHEREAS the Commiſſioners of the State of Georgia, to wit: James Jackſon, Abraham Baldwin, and John Milledge, duly authorized and appointed by, and on the part and behalf of the ſaid State of Georgia; and the Commiſſioners of the United States, James Madiſon, Albert Gallatin, and Levi Lincoln, duly authorized and appointed by, and on the part and behalf of the ſaid United States, to make an amicable ſettlement of limits, between the two Sovereignties, after a due examination of their reſpective powers, did, on the 24th day of April laſt, enter into a deed of articles, and mutual ceſſion, in the words following, to wit:

ARTICLES of agreement and ceſſion, entered into on the twenty-fourth day of April, one thouſand eight hundred and two, between the Commiſſioners appointed on the part of the United States, by virtue of an act entitled, "An act for an amicable ſettlement of limits

243 First page of the agreement between the United States and Georgia for the removal of the Cherokees, April 24, 1802, from the original in the Department of State, Washington

THE REMOVAL BILL

HEATED protests came from Georgia at the ineffectiveness of the United States. The Georgians charged that the Cherokees were a semi-barbarous people who stood in the way of state progress. What basis there was for such a charge was to be found in the retention by the Cherokees of some of their primitive government customs. In order to meet this attack Indian delegates assembled at New Echota on July 4, 1827, to take up the work of framing a constitution. The document was modeled after the Constitution of the United States, with only such changes as were necessary to meet local needs. The preamble contained bold words. "We, the Cherokee people, constituting one of the sovereign and independent nations of the earth, and having complete jurisdiction over its territory to the exclusion of the authority of any other state, do ordain this constitution." The constitution was formally ratified by the people. The Georgia legislature answered the constitution by reaffirming the old claim that the Indians were tenants at will on state lands and warning the Federal Government that it would be given one more chance to extinguish the Indian titles. If the Government failed again, the jurisdiction of Georgia would be extended to the borders of the state. In the following year Andrew Jackson was elected President of the United States and John Ross became the chief executive of the Cherokee republic. In 1829 a removal bill was introduced into Congress where it precipitated a sharp controversy. Able spokesmen defended the position of the Indians on the grounds of humanity and justice. Advocates of the measure appealed to party solidarity and to sectional prejudice. In May 1830, it became a law over Jackson's signature. Thomas Benton remarked that it was "one of the closest and most earnestly contested questions of the session, and was carried by an inconsiderable majority."

CONSTITUTION

OF THE

CHEROKEE NATION,

MADE AND ESTABLISHED

AT A

GENERAL CONVENTION OF DELEGATES,

DULY AUTHORISED FOR THAT PURPOSE,

AT

NEW ECHOTA,

JULY 26, 1827.

PRINTED FOR THE CHEROKEE NATION,
AT THE OFFICE OF THE STATESMAN AND PATRIOT,
GEORGIA.

244 Title-page of the original in the New York Public Library

THE REMOVAL BILL ATTACKED

THE debate on the Removal Bill had so aroused the country that bitter denunciations began to be directed against both Congress and the President. To add to the embarrassment of the Government the constitutionality of the act was doubtful. The Congress of the Confederation had, unfortunately, explicitly acknowledged the existence of the independent Cherokee nation in the treaty of the Holston. The Constitution made treaties a part of the "supreme law of the land." Georgia, however, began extending its jurisdiction to the Cherokee lands within its boundaries. Acting on the suggestion of Daniel Webster and Frelinghuysen of New Jersey, Ross appealed to the Supreme Court. Before the case was initiated, however, President Jackson had sought by an adroit move to render Ross powerless. Under old treaties providing for land cessions the United States paid each year annuities of considerable size to the Cherokee nation, money which was administered by that nation for the collective benefit of all.

THE CASE

OF

THE CHEROKEE NATION

against

THE STATE OF GEORGIA:

ARGUED AND DETERMINED AT

THE SUPREME COURT OF THE UNITED STATES,

JANUARY TERM 1831.

WITH

AN APPENDIX,

Containing the Opinion of Chancellor Kent on the Case; the Treaties between the United States and the Cherokee Indians; the Act of Congress of 1802, entitled 'An Act to regulate intercourse with the Indian tribes, &c.'; and the Laws of Georgia relative to the country occupied by the Cherokee Indians, within the boundary of that State.

BY RICHARD PETERS,
COUNSELLOR AT LAW.

Philadelphia:
JOHN GRIGG, 9 NORTH FOURTH STREET.
1831.

245 Title-page of the original in the New York Public Library

246 William Wirt, 1772–1834, from an engraving of the portrait by J. B. Longacre, in the possession of the publishers

THE DECISION OF THE SUPREME COURT

In 1830 an executive order forbade the paying of government annuities into the Cherokee treasury and required that it be distributed among the people, some forty-two cents to each person. In this way the Cherokee leaders would be deprived of their ability to hire attorneys and even to finance the *Cherokee Phoenix*. The Cherokees refused to receive the annuity thus. Ross borrowed money and retained no less a lawyer than William Wirt. In 1832 the Supreme Court declared unconstitutional those laws of Georgia extending the jurisdiction of the state over Indian lands. This news, said one of the Cherokees, was like "a shower of rain on thirsty vegetation." In 1829 Jeremiah Evarts concluding a series of essays published in the *National Intelligencer* over the name of "William Penn" had issued a warning to which the decision of the Court seemed to be a reply: "Government has arrived at the bank of the Rubicon. If our rulers now stop, they may save the country from the charge of bad faith." Marshall's action, however, proved of no avail. The decision was in effect ignored by Georgia and never enforced by the President. In another case the court called the Indians "domestic dependent nations," whatever that might mean.

THE TREATY OF REMOVAL

In 1831, before Chief Justice Marshall had handed down his decision, Boudinot had written in despair. "We have hardly known which way to turn. Trouble upon trouble, vexation upon vexation. I allude to the Georgia affair. The war is becoming hotter and hotter every day. . . . Our enemies cannot complete their designs until they get the land — they intend to get it by force, — and that before long too. . . . The enemy is at the door and there is no time to be lost. . . ." When the action of the Supreme Court failed to check the advance of the white aggressor, he gave up hope. Resigning as editor of the *Phoenix* he became one of the leaders of a minority group who believed that the best interests of the Cherokee nation would be served by voluntary removal rather than awaiting the inevitable ejection by force with the demoralization which that could bring. His letter of resignation to John Ross, as he openly espoused the unpopular cause, contained a defense of his patriotism. "I love my country and I love my people . . . and for that reason I should deem it my duty to tell them the whole truth. I cannot tell them that we will be reinstated in our rights, when I have no such hope, and after our . . . friends in Congress, and elsewhere, have signified to us that they can do us no good." In December, 1835, the Washington Government made a treaty with three hundred men, women, and children out of a nation of about fifteen thousand. Major Ridge and John Ridge were numbered among this handful who signed away the ancient Cherokee homeland.

247 Jeremiah Evarts, 1781–1831, from an engraving by J. B. Longacre after a portrait by S. F. B. Morse, in E. C. Tracy, *The Life of Jeremiah Evarts, Esq.*, Boston, 1845

THE ARMY IN THE CHEROKEE COUNTRY

Some of the three hundred present at the signing of the treaty were bribed, some intimidated, and some, like Boudinot, were acting in accordance with their conscience. The Cherokee Council protested to Washington that no official of the nation had signed the treaty and demonstrated that the great majority of the Cherokees supported the Council. The action was of no avail. The treaty was ratified by the Senate with one vote to spare. The list of those who opposed the despoiling of the Indians included Clay of Kentucky, Crockett of Tennessee, Storrs of New York, Frelinghuysen of New Jersey, Sprague of Maine, and Everett and Webster of Massachusetts. Some thirteen thousand of the Cherokees refused to go. In 1838 the army entered their country. Swiftly the troops passed from settlement to settlement, surprising households and driving the Indians into stockades. Many a family, looking back upon the home which they were leaving at the point of the bayonet, beheld the cabin in flames and a rabble of looters, who followed the soldiers, driving off the live stock. One old full-blood called his children and grandchildren to prayer when he discovered the soldiers about his house. The astonished bluecoats waited until the supplications, spoken in their own language, were ended. The cataclysm brought terrible suffering to the Indians. No proper sanitary provisions for prolonged occupancy were made at the stockades. Food was scarce and frequently unfit to eat. Disease broke out and raged widely. Medical arrangements had been almost wholly lacking. Conditions became so bad that the Cherokee Council approached General Scott with the request that they be permitted to manage the exodus. The general consented on the condition that the first contingent be actually on the road on September 1. The people were allowed to scatter to more healthful camp sites and conditions became better. The quack doctors who had gathered like vultures to fatten on the refugees were driven off. Sadly the Indians waited their turn to depart.

Washington April 11th 1838.

Upon your arrival in the Cherokee nation propositions should be made to you by the party opposed to emigration under the Treaty with a copy of which you have been furnished, the acceptance of which you shall have good reason to believe will prevent the shedding of blood, & by which a voluntary emigration of the whole nation can be promptly effected; you are authorized to receive & transmit them to the Department of War for the consideration of the President & Senate: Provided the said propositions do not in any degree impugn the Treaty with the

248 First page of a letter from Martin Van Buren to General Winfield Scott, April 11, 1838, transmitting orders for the removal of the Cherokees, from the original in the Van Buren Papers, Library of Congress, Washington

249 Tah-Chee, a Cherokee Chief, from a lithograph in Thomas L. M'Kenney, *History of the Indian Tribes of North America*, Philadelphia, 1872

THE SPIRIT OF THE CHEROKEES

One party of Scott's soldiers bringing a group of Indians to the stockades was suddenly set upon by their captives and one white man was killed. Tsâli together with several other Indians escaped to the mountains. Efforts to retake them proved unavailing. Finally Scott, through the medium of a trader, persuaded most of the band to surrender. Tsâli with his two eldest sons then gave himself up voluntarily. He was tried by court-martial for murder, convicted, and sentenced to be shot. While bound to a tree just before his execution he asked to speak. Turning to an Indian friend near by he is reported to have said: "Euchela, there is one favor I wish to ask at your hands. You know I have a little boy who was lost among the mountains. I want you to find that boy, if he is not dead, and tell him that the last words of his father were that he must never go beyond the Father of Waters, but die in the land of his birth. It is sweet to die in one's native land and be buried by the margin of one's native streams."

LETTERS

AND OTHER PAPERS RELATING TO

CHEROKEE AFFAIRS;

BEING IN REPLY TO

Sundry Publications Authorized by

JOHN ROSS.

BY E. BOUDINOT,

FORMERLY EDITOR OF THE CHEROKEE PHŒNIX.

ATHENS:

PRINTED AT THE OFFICE OF THE "SOUTHERN BANNER."

1837.

250 From the title-page of the original, in the possession of Dudley L. Vail, New Haven, Conn.

THE "TRAIL OF TEARS"

Several hundred Cherokees eluded the soldiery and hid in the forests of their old home. They were allowed to remain on a reservation and became the "Eastern Band" of the Cherokees. For them and for their migrating kinsmen expulsion was a catastrophe. In spite of their intellectual growth, their material development, and their general acceptance of the Christian religion, the Cherokees, like every other Indian people, found that dangerous evils were born of contact with the whites. With the flaming words of a Hebrew prophet, Boudinot in 1837 reminded John Ross of the evils which beset the people while still at peace in their ancient home. "Look, . . . see the progress that vice and immorality have already made. See the spread of intemperance and the wretchedness and misery it has already occasioned . . . you will find an argument in every tippling shop in the country — you will find its cruel effects in the bloody tragedies that are frequently occurring . . . in the tears and groans, of the widows and fatherless, rendered homeless, naked, and hungry, by this vile curse of our race. . . . Oh, it is heart rending to think of these things, much more to speak of them. . . . In another country, and under other circumstances, there is a better prospect. . . . I would say to my fellow countrymen, you among the rest, fly from the moral pestilence that will finally destroy our nation." Boudinot's hope that removal would cure the ills of the harassed Indians was vain. The forces of evil triumphed when the Cherokees became miserable refugees driven in dejection from the land of their birth. The sanctions of ancient custom and of public opinion relaxed when the nation was in flux, and suffering was everywhere. A third of the people perished in the autumn and winter of 1838 when the Cherokees followed what they called the "trail of tears" which led through Nashville and western Kentucky to the plains beyond the Father of Waters. A dejected, disillusioned nation faced the task of reconstruction in a strange environment.

THE END OF THE SCENE

Of all the Indian tribes within the United States the Cherokees made the greatest progress in their efforts to bridge the chasm which separated the men of the stone age from the conquering whites. Some of the young men of the tribe in school had read hopefully in the Declaration of Independence the words of the white man when he fought for freedom: "We hold these truths to be self-evident, that all men are created equal, that they are endowed by their Creator with certain inalienable Rights, that among these are Life, Liberty, and the Pursuit of Happiness." The very success of the Cherokees, however, hastened their undoing, for it increased the fear of those people who coveted the Cherokee lands that the soil might slip from their grasp. Perhaps John Ross, as he buried his wife with a Christian burial service on the westward trek, remembered cynically that he and his people were dealing with a Christian nation. As for the Cherokees, their sufferings caused a momentary flurry among American citizens and then were forgotten. Oblivion has given an artistic completeness to the tragedy of the red mountaineers of the southern Appalachians.

251 John Ross, 1790–1866, from a portrait in Thomas L. M'Kenney, *History of the Indian Tribes of North America*, Philadelphia, 1872

252 Drawn expressly for *The Pageant of America* by Gregor Noetzel, American Geographical Society, New York

THE FRONTIER OF 1820

FREDERICK J. TURNER has remarked that while "the frontier folk spread north of the Ohio and up the Missouri, a different movement was in progress in the Gulf region of the west. In the beginning precisely the same type of occupation was to be seen: The poorer classes of southern emigrants cut out their clearings along rivers that flowed to the Gulf and to the lower Mississippi. . . . Almost all the most recently occupied area was but thinly settled. It represented the movement of the backwoodsman, with axe and rifle, advancing to the conquest of the forest. . . . But while this population of log-cabin pioneers was entering the Gulf plains, caravans of slave-holding planters were advancing from the seaboard to the occupation of the cotton lands of the same region. As the free farmers of the interior had been reduced in the upland country of the south by the slave-holding planters, so now the frontiersmen of the southwest were pushed back from the more fertile lands into the pine hills and barrens. Not only was the pioneer unable to refuse the higher price which was offered him for his clearing, but, in the competitive bidding of the public land sales, the wealthier planter secured the desirable soils. Social forces worked to the same end. When the pioneer invited his slave-holding neighbor to a 'raising,' it grated on his sense of the fitness of things to have the guest appear with gloves, directing the gang of slaves which he contributed to the function. Little by little, therefore, the old pioneer life tended to retreat to the less desirable lands, leaving the slave-holder in possession of the rich 'buck-shot' soils that spread over central Alabama and Mississippi and the fat alluvium that lined the eastern bank of the Mississippi. Even today the counties of dense negro population reveal the results of this movement of segregation." — *The Rise of the New West*, 90–92. The extension of the cotton-raising plantation carried the principles and practice of aristocracy westward along the Gulf Coast.

CHAPTER VI

IN THE GREAT LAKES COUNTRY

THE sun was dropping toward the irregular line of tree tops which marked the western horizon when, on August 17, 1803, a lieutenant of the United States Army halted a small, travel-stained detachment of regular troops on the bank of the sluggish Chicago River. Lieutenant Swearingen and his men had marched along forest trails from Detroit two hundred and seventy miles away. Their mission was to undertake the establishment of Fort Dearborn. Captain Whistler, the commanding officer of the post, forced by ill health to take the lake route from Detroit to the mouth of the Chicago, arrived in due time and took charge of the building of the fort. Curious Indians came out of the forest to watch the white men and to gaze with some wonder upon the canoe with wings which was anchored off shore. They offered no objection to the activities of the soldiers, who were cutting and shaping logs for blockhouses and posts for the high stockade. Perhaps their minds ran back to that doleful day in the history of their race in 1795 when General Anthony Wayne, victor at Fallen Timbers, had read to one of the greatest councils ever assembled in the Northwest the terms of the treaty that he would accept. Thoroughly informed as to the needs of the frontier, he had included in the arrangement the cession by the Indians of a tract six miles square at the mouth of the Chicago River. After eight years the government of the United States had begun to take advantage of the rights acquired on distant Lake Michigan.

Swiftly the painted braves carried the news of the advent of the whites to the Indian villages which dotted the Wisconsin country. Scores of lodge fires lighted circles of bronze faces discussing with many a savage grunt the meaning of the appearance of the Long Knives at the lower end of Lake Michigan. An occasional white man could have been seen in the council circle. Some of these whites were British, hailing from Scotland, England, or Canada, but more were French. These white traders were as much interested as the Indians themselves at the news from the mouth of the Chicago. Already Mackinac, guarding the junction of Lake Michigan with Lake Huron, flew the American flag. The Americans seemed to be advancing steadily to conquest. Certain treaties drawn up in far-away Europe said that the hunting grounds south of the Great Lakes were a part of the soil of the United States. They were, in reality, Indian property and the redskins of the region were friends and allies of the British. These tribesmen feared the Long Knives. They looked upon them as a greedy, pushing people who chopped down the forest and drove off the red man. Such fears the British traders did not attempt to abate. But they told their Indian friends that one day the Great Father in England would take back his own. The Long Knives should never chop down the forests that fringed the mighty inland seas where floated the canoe fleets of the fur trade. The conviction of the traders that the lake country would remain English was the child of hope. Yet the traders had some justification for their faith. Two decades had passed since the signing of the treaty of 1783 during which Americans had taken no effective measures to drive the foreigner from the Wisconsin country. The feeble young republic seemed scarcely capable of coping with what was, in spite of the American Revolution, the greatest empire in the world.

THE CHIPPEWAS

253 Chippewa Burial Rites, from an engraving by J. C. McRae after a drawing by A. A. Gibson, in H. R. Schoolcraft, *Information Respecting the History, Conditions and Prospect of the Indian Tribes of the United States*, 1851–57

THE eighteenth-century *voyageur* stopping over at Mackinac, where Lakes Huron and Michigan meet, would have found at certain seasons numerous Chippewa Indians lounging about the fort. Perhaps they had paddled down to the stockade from their villages along the north or the south shore of Lake Superior. Visiting one of these on the margin of this majestic inland sea, the trader would have discovered wigwams made of poles set in the ground in a circle, bent together, and tied in the center. Over this semi-spherical framework was laid a covering of birch bark or grass mats. Out through a hole in the roof floated the smoke of the lodge fire. The Chippewas were fishermen and also hunters in the forests that surrounded the Great Lakes. They knew where lay the fields of wild rice in the Lake Superior region and used this cereal for food. Like practically all American Indians their religion played a powerful part in their lives. In the warm months of summer as the Chippewa brave deftly paddled his canoe on lake or river, he was conscious of a mysterious power dwelling in the trees and bushes, the birds and animals, and the rocks and river banks about him. These Manitous were ever wakeful and ever quick to hear in summer, but they were torpid when the snow lay deep upon the ground. The memory of these spirits of the wilderness is kept alive in the name of Manitou Island off Keweenaw Point on the southern shore of Lake Superior. When a Chippewa died, his body was most commonly placed in the grave in a sitting posture facing the setting sun. Thus it rested while the departing spirit took the broad, well-beaten path which led westward to that happy land which abounds in everything which the Indian desires. The Chippewas, even as other folk, mourned the loss of their loved ones. For a full cycle of seasons they honored the dead unless the period was shortened by a special religious ceremony or by the exploits of war. "The Chippewas and the Sioux are hereditary enemies . . . ," wrote Governor Lewis Cass. "I endeavored, when among them, to learn the cause which first excited them to war, and the time when it commenced. But they can give no rational account. An intelligent Chippewa chief informed me that the disputed boundary between them was a subject of little importance, and that the question respecting it could be easily adjusted. He appeared to think that they fought because their fathers fought before them. This war has been waged with various success, and, in its prosecution, instances of courage and self-devotion have occurred, within a few years, which would not have disgraced the pages of Grecian or of Roman history. Some years since, mutually weary of hostilities, the chiefs of both nations met and agreed upon a truce. But the Sioux, disregarding the solemn compact . . . attacked the Chippewas, and murdered a number of them. Babisikundabi, the old Chippewa chief, . . . was present upon this occasion, and his life was saved by the intrepidity and generous self-devotion of a Sioux chief. This man entreated, remonstrated and threatened. He urged his countrymen by every motive, to abstain from any violation of their faith, and, when he found his remonstrances useless, he attached himself to this Chippewa chief, and avowed his determination of saving, or perishing with him. Awed by his intrepidity, the Sioux finally agreed that he should ransom the Chippewa, and he accordingly applied to this object all the property he owned." — Quoted in H. R. SCHOOLCRAFT, *History of the Indian Tribes of the United States*, 1857, part VI, 387–88.

254 The Foxes and Sauks in Battle, from an engraving by C. E. Wagstaff after a drawing by Seth Eastman, in Henry R. Schoolcraft, *Indian Tribes of the United States*, 1851–57

255 Chippewa Indian Lodge, from a lithograph in Thomas L. McKenney, *Sketches of a Tour to the Lakes*, Baltimore, 1827

CONQUESTS OF THE CHIPPEWAS

FROM these white friends from the St. Lawrence they obtained firearms. Then they began a triumphal march westward. Early in the eighteenth century they drove the Foxes from northern Wisconsin. They turned upon the Sioux whom they forced across the Mississippi and into the country south of the Minnesota River. They continued their westward advance until they built their lodges in the valley of the Red River and the smokes of their westernmost band rose amid the uplands of Turtle Mountain. Like the Iroquois, the Chippewas controlled an imperial domain. But this powerful people of the upper Great Lakes finds no such place in history as their enemies south of Lake Ontario. They were too far from the frontier during the wars of the eighteenth century. When in later years the farmer-pioneer at last reached their remote habitat, their stamina had been sapped by contact with the whites and they had learned the futility of war against the invader.

THE FOXES

IN the pine forests about Winnebago Lake and the Fox River in Wisconsin lived in the eighteenth century the "red earth people," believing that they had been created from red clay. They got their historic name from an accident. A Frenchman, falling in with a party of the Fox clan of these Indians, asked them who they were. They answered, "Foxes," using their clan designation, and from that day the "red earth people" were "Foxes" to the white man. Like the Shawnees the Foxes had many enemies. There is a certain bitterness in the description of them by the Frenchman, Charlevoix. They "infested with their robberies and filled with murders not only the neighborhood of the Bay [Green Bay], their natural territory, but almost all the routes communicating with the remote colonial posts, as well as those leading from Canada to Louisiana. Except the Sioux, who often joined them, and the Iroquois, with whom they formed an alliance, . . . all the nations in alliance with us suffered greatly from these hostilities." French *couriers de bois*, paddling their canoes along the shores of Green Bay, would see occasionally a burning torch upon the beach. This was a signal from the Foxes for the trader to land and pay the tribute exacted from all. If the trader refused, the Indians became angry and vented their spleen upon him according to the whim of the moment. Deeply incensed by such practices, a leading *courier de bois*, one Morand, raised a volunteer force of French and Indians, fell upon the Fox villages, and drove them down the Wisconsin River to the country near its mouth. From this region about 1780 the Foxes, in alliance with the Sioux, made their way northward through the wooded country to fight the Chippewas in the valley of the St. Croix River. But the Foxes had struck once too often. After the encounter the wild chant of the scalp dance echoed through the forests about the lodges of the exultant Chippewas, while a miserable handful of defeated and dejected Fox braves merged their nation with that of their close kinsmen, the Sauks.

256 Fox Warrior, from a lithograph after a drawing by Charles Bodmer, in Maximilian, Prince of Wied, *Travels into the Interior of North America, 1832–34*, London, 1838–43

THE MENOMINEES

To the north and east of the Fox River lived a peaceful Algonquin tribe under the shadow of the powerful Chippewas. The Menominees, "people of the beneficent wild rice," lived largely, as their name implies, from the rice fields in their home land. But they were also hunters. Lieutenant Zebulon Pike, exploring the upper Mississippi in 1806, met some of their men and described them as "straight and well made, about middle size; their complexions generally fair for savages, their teeth good, their eyes large and rather languishing; they have a mild but independent expression of countenance that charms at first sight." They were not a conspicuous or powerful people and their culture showed the overwhelming influence of the Chippewas. In their day they were destined to serve well the traders of northern Wisconsin.

257 Indian Wild Rice Fields, from the painting by Seth Eastman in the Room of the House Committee on Indian Affairs, Washington

THE SAUKS

Next to the Chippewas the Sauks were the most powerful Indians dwelling in the Wisconsin woodlands. These "people of the outlet" or, perhaps, "people of the yellow earth" to distinguish them from their kin, the Foxes, were of Algonquin stock. Their original habitat seems to have been in northern Michigan not far from the margin of the picturesque Saginaw Bay. From this country they were driven by the Ottawas and the Neuters. Making their way through the forests south of Lake Superior, they finally came to rest in central Wisconsin. They were a canoe people in a land of lakes and rivers. Their culture was that of the Indians of the eastern woodlands, though their contacts with the Sioux brought them into touch with the culture of the western plains. Like the Chippewas they believed in the Manitous and taught their children early in life to come into close personal relations, through fasting and vigil, with one of these nature spirits. Also, as among the Chippewas, the spirits of their dead journeyed westward to a land where the brother of their culture-god ruled and waited. The culture-god himself dwelt in the icy north preparing one day to return to his people and inaugurate a new epoch in world affairs. This belief in a coming Messiah was one of the most widespread culture traits among the North American Indians. Almost everywhere the redskins were markedly religious and emotional. Their artistic tendencies should be set against this psychological background.

258 Group of Sauk and Fox Indians, from a lithograph after a drawing by Charles Bodmer in Maximilian, Prince of Wied, *Travels in the Interior of North America, 1832–34*, London, 1838–43

259 The Lodge of a Midewin Prophet, from an engraving by Illman after a drawing by J. C. Tidball, in Henry R. Schoolcraft, *Indian Tribes of the United States*, 1851–57

THE MIDEWIN SOCIETY

MOST striking of the institutions of the Sauks was the secret society, the Midewin or Midewiwin, common to many of the Great Lakes tribes (see Vol I, p. 27). Once a year, in the spring, when the forest was clothed with new green, the society met. At such times new members, men and women, were initiated to take the places of those who had died during the previous year. Among the Chippewas there were four lodges, like different Masonic degrees, in this Grand Medicine Society. The fortunate initiate paid well in worldly goods before he was admitted to the first lodge, whence, after the payment of more goods, he passed in succession to the others. A part of the initiation ceremony was public, to impress the people, and a part was secret, in which the initiate, as he passed from lodge to lodge, learned more and more of the medicinal qualities of certain herbs. A phase of the ceremony consisted of simulating the shooting of a sacred shell or pebble into the body of the initiate. This brought spiritual power to the new member. He became more than a man. So equipped he went forth to combat those evil spirits which brought disease, suffering, or defeat to his people.

THE WINNEBAGOS

NEIGHBOR to the Foxes on Green Bay lived a Siouan people, the Winnebagos. They were the easternmost of four kindred tribes, three of whom, the Iowa, the Oto, and the Missouri, roamed the plains country west of the Mississippi. The culture of the Winnebagos was that of the eastern forest Indians influenced slightly by the customs of the bison hunters of the western grasslands. They were a friendly people in whose country the unhappy Ottawas found refuge when they were driven by the Iroquois from their homes about Lake Huron. Practically alone among the Wisconsin tribes the Winnebagos had no serious trouble with the Foxes. Through all the difficult years of the eighteenth century, when inter-tribal war wrought many changes among the Indians of the upper Mississippi Valley, the villages of the Winnebagos remained where the white man had first found them. They were friends of the French and, when New France fell, they became friends of the British. They were slow at first to accept the newcomers, but once the transition had been made they remained faithful to the new friendship. When, however, the shadow of the United States fell across their hunting grounds, they long refused allegiance.

260 A Winnebago Camp, from a drawing by Seth Eastman in the United States National Museum, Washington

THE ILLINOIS AND THE KICKAPOOS

261 Illinois Indians Presenting Pipe of Peace to French Explorers, from an engraving on the border of Nicholas de Fer's Map of America, 1705

THE story of the Illiniweks which name the French changed to Illinois is a wilderness tragedy. They built their lodges on the prairies and in the woodlands of the northern part of the state which bears their name, and on the rolling, bison-covered plains of Iowa and Missouri. Six tribes made up the Illinois confederacy; the Cahokia, Kaskaskia, Michigamea, Moingwena, Peoria, and Tamaroa. Though in the heyday of their prosperity they numbered perhaps nine thousand persons, they were not a powerful people. War parties of the Sioux and Foxes frequently fell upon their towns and returned triumphantly northward with captives and plunder. Under pressure of conflict their scattered bands drew together in the valley of the Illinois. Here La Salle, bent on the exploration of the Mississippi, found them. And here, while the great Frenchman's canoes were still on the river, they felt the heavy hand of the distant Five Nations. Year after year bands of Senecas or Mohawks fought the Illinois braves and fell upon their villages. Their numbers were depleted and their strength ebbed. Already the French trader with his brandy was among them. War and fire water broke them. They declined in stamina and culture. By 1750 they could count less than two thousand persons. The end, swift and terrible, came in 1769. In that year Pontiac, the Ottawa chief who had led one of the most threatening of border wars against the British, was among the Illinois paying a ceremonial visit. He was as great in defeat as he had been in war. Tribesmen in far-away forests, speaking his name with awe, recognized in him a man who had risen above petty tribal loyalties and had become the leader of a race. As he left a feast in an Illinois village where he had been an honored guest, a Kaskaskia Indian struck him from behind with a tomahawk. A keg of whiskey offered by an English trader was the motive for the murder. Then the measure of Pontiac's influence over his people became manifest. Along the forest trails leading southward from the Great Lakes passed war parties of many tribes, breathing vengeance and bent on extermination. When the war whoops died away and the blood-stained tomahawks were dry, a pitiful handful of Illinois turned in supplication to the white man, and the French people at Kaskaskia gave them succor. Four tribes profited by the destruction of the Illinois. To the Sauks and Foxes passed many of their hunting grounds. The Potawatomis, who dwelt along southwestern Lake Michigan, received a share as did their neighbors on the north, the Kickapoos. These last tribesmen lived for a space in the region of the present Peoria. Then one group, known as the Prairie band, moved to the banks of the Sangammon, famous later for its associations with the young Lincoln. The other or Vermillion band made its way east to the Wabash Valley where it settled, despite the protests of the Miamis and the Piankashaws, in a region where already the redskin was pressing hard upon the subsistence offered by the hunting ground.

262 A Full-Blood Kickapoo Warrior, from a photograph in the Bureau of American Ethnology, Washington

263 French Fur Traders on the Great Lakes, from the mural by C. Y. Turner (1850–1918) in the Wisconsin State Capitol, Madison

THE FRENCH IN WISCONSIN

THE Indians west of Lake Michigan and south of Lake Superior had known the white man since that distant day in the seventeenth century when the waters of Green Bay were cut by the canoe of that French *voyageur*, Sieur Nicolet. Skirting the forested shore he had kept a sharp eye out for Indian habitations and had finally brought his journey to an end amid the lodges of the Winnebagos. For more than a hundred years after Nicolet the French tongue was practically the only white man's language heard beside the council fires of the Indians of the Northwest. The ubiquitous French traders in the course of time learned the secrets of that labyrinth of rivers between the Great Lakes and the Mississippi and the fur trade began to flow through three main channels. The most southerly was the Chicago-Illinois River route with an easy portage across flat country. Farther north was the Wisconsin-Fox River route whose eastern terminus was the head of Green Bay. A third route connected the head of Lake Superior with the lake country where lay the headwaters of the Mississippi. At strategic points on Lake Superior and at the mouth of the Fox River appeared the habitations of the traders. From these places in the summer season fleets of fur-laden canoes put off for the long paddle to Fort Mackinac, from whence they made their way to Montreal.

THE FRENCH TRADER

THE French trader of the days when France still dreamed of empire in the New World was never more at home, never more happy and contented than in that region of cold winters and dark forests which lay close to the southern shores of the Great Lakes. He readily adapted himself to Indian ways. He learned to smoke in silent dignity the ceremonial pipe and to address an Indian council with that symbolism drawn from nature which filled the Indian speeches. At certain seasons of the year he could be seen passing noiselessly along ancient forest trails with a band of hunters. Though he made friends with the Indians and married their women, he was not above overreaching the simple forest folk, if occasion offered. At best he paid them a low price for their furs. Nevertheless many a trader became the trusted advisor of some one or other of the most powerful chiefs of the Northwest. And the passing years saw a great increase in the peltries that made their way to Mackinac and thence ultimately to France. Intermarriage with the Indians brought into being an ever increasing mixed-blood population. These children of unions across the race line almost invariably identified themselves with the redskins. Frequently they became tribal chieftains or leaders while at the same time playing the rôle of traders.

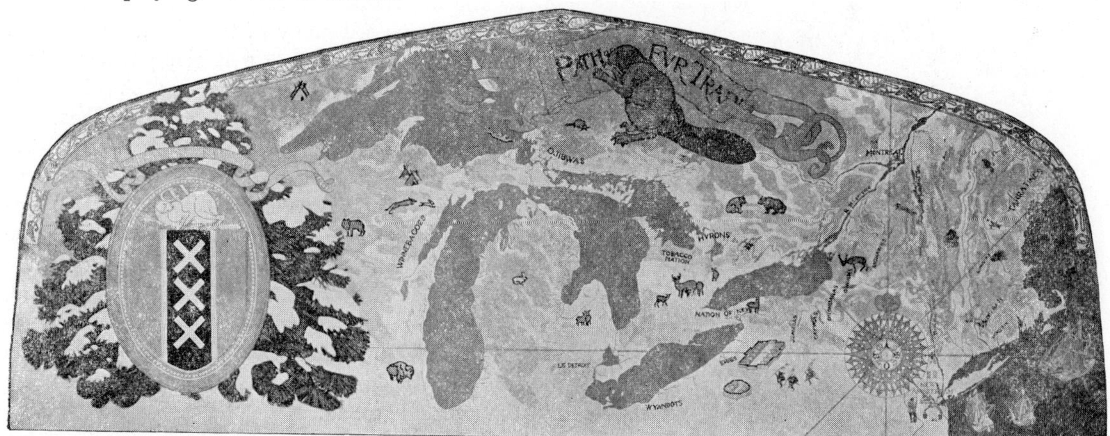

264 Picture Map of the Path of the Fur Trade along the Great Lakes, by Barry Faulkner (1881–) in the Washington Irving High School, New York

265 Herculaneum, where shot was made for the War of 1812, from a lunette by Oscar E. Berninghaus (1874–), in the Missouri State Capitol, St. Louis

LEAD MINING

THE keen eyes of the French explorers and traders in the continental interior did not fail to observe another source of wealth than furs. The Frenchmen were quick to notice that some Indians of the continental interior possessed bits of copper, which they sometimes hammered into ornaments, and that other tribes had lead. In 1719 the exploitation of the ore of the lead district of the upper Mississippi Valley began under the leadership of the local French commander, one Boisbriant. In the next year Philippe François Renault, formerly a Paris banker, began the vigorous mining of lead by the crude methods of the day and searched industriously for evidence of copper and silver. Though Renault disposed of his mineral holdings in 1744, mining did not cease. On the contrary the number of miners increased. The Indian in the bow and arrow stage had little use for lead but the firearms which the traders put into his hands gave the metal a new value for him. The lead district produced practically all the bullets which the Indian hunter needed for gathering pelts. With the fall of New France in 1763, when Spain and England assumed jurisdiction on the opposite banks of the Father of Waters, they divided the ore deposits. As early as 1766 the shipment of ore by boat to New Orleans began. During the last quarter of the eighteenth century lead stood next to peltries as the most important and profitable export from this western country. The metal was dug from shallow holes by individual miners, most of them Indians, though there were many whites. Some of these miners are said to have made "thirty dollars per day, for weeks together," fabulous riches for the frontiersman. The miners, like the Indian hunters, sold their product to the trader. To Julien Dubuque the blue-gray metal and the furs which he obtained from the Indians brought wealth. In 1788 he received a concession from the Sauks and Foxes. At the time of the founding of Chicago his operations were carried on over extensive tracts on both sides of the river.

266 A Primitive Lead Mine at Galena, from a photograph in *Galena's Century Milestone*, Bale's Drug Store, Galena, Ill.

267 An Indian Copper Mine near Lake Superior, from a drawing by J. C. Tidball, in H. R. Schoolcraft, *Indian Tribes of the United States*, 1851–57

268 Festivities of the Early French in the Northwest, from an engraving in Henry Howe, *Historical Collections of the Great West*, Cincinnati, 1851

A SUCCESSION OF RULERS

In 1763 the Indians of the Northwest learned with surprise and regret that their French brothers had surrendered and that the British would be the chief traders of the future. The Englishman, in general, did not treat the redskin with the same easy familiarity as did the Frenchman. He was apt to be contemptuous and domineering, but he paid more for his furs. As the years passed, however, the tribesmen noted with satisfaction that the French trader still lived in their country, frequently in their villages. The Indians cared naught that he was now the employee of some capitalist who was risking his money in the fur trade. They only observed that the tiny French settlement at La Baye on the lower Fox River was little changed. The French military commandant was replaced by a British officer. Some British traders appeared, but the French people stayed. The habitant still cultivated his acres abutting against the river bank. The well-to-do French trader, now perhaps an important subordinate of a British trading enterprise, still lived in the Green Bay country and sent his children to Montreal to be educated. In the course of time, moreover, the Indian came to be on excellent terms with the British who had come to his country. Particularly after 1783 he found these business men anxious to get on well with him and even become his close friends. About that date he heard vague rumors that the control of his hunting grounds had passed to the government of the Long Knives or the Bostonaise, as the French traders contemptuously called them. These reports were disturbing, for many a brave from the Wisconsin country during the Revolution had joined in raids against Kentucky and many chiefs had met the intrepid George Rogers Clark in that famous council of which he was the complete master. But while British soldiers remained at Mackinac there seemed to be little danger.

CHANGING TIMES

In 1794 news of Wayne's crushing victory at Fallen Timbers was carried through the Wisconsin country. Soon afterward came word that British soldiers were to turn over the frontier posts at Detroit and Mackinac to the Americans. British, French, and Indians meeting in the forest, on the rivers, or at the settlements discussed the reports with grave concern. The aggressive Bostonaise were evidently to be reckoned with. In 1795 the defeated Ohio Indians signed a highly unfavorable treaty at Fort Greenville. In October 1796, the American flag was raised above Mackinac. Yet the British traders could not believe that the intruders would long remain. The trader noted with satisfaction that the garrison at Detroit had withdrawn only a little way down the river to a new fort called Malden and the one at Mackinac had occupied a new fortification on St. Joseph's Island some fifty miles northeast of the famous post. The flying of the Stars and Stripes at Fort Mackinac, moreover, made scarcely a ripple in the quiet life of the Green Bay region. To this settlement no Americans came. The people still looked upon themselves as subjects of the British King.

269 The American Flag floating over Mackinac, from an engraving by J. C. McRae after a drawing by Seth Eastman, in H. R. Schoolcraft, *Indian Tribes of the United States*, 1851–57

CHARLES REAUME

In 1803, the same year in which news reached the British and French settlers of the founding of Fort Dearborn, they came into momentary contact with the government of the United States when Governor Harrison of Indiana Territory, of which the Wisconsin country was at the time a part, appointed one of their number, the pompous and elderly Frenchman, Charles Reaume, justice of the peace. For more than a decade Reaume, apparently forgotten by his superiors, married his neighbors, held court, and acted as a general scribe, notary, and civil functionary for the greater part of the country west of Lake Michigan. His counterpart in the valley of the Mississippi was an American trader, Henry Monroe Fisher, who was appointed about the same time, and who lived at the little trading settlement at Prairie du Chien. Fisher was presently succeeded by John Campbell.

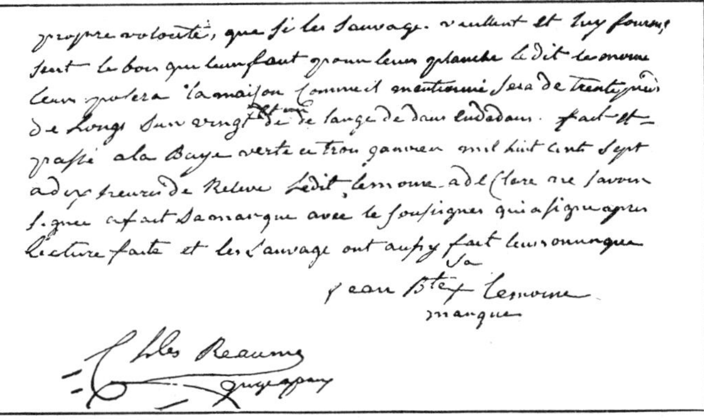
propre volonté, que si les sauvage veulent et luy fournis-
sent le bois qui leur faut pour leur planche le dit Lemoine
leur potera la maison comme il mentionné sera de trente pieds
de longs sur vingt pieds de large de dans en dedans. fait et
passé a la Baye verte ce trois janvier mil huit cent sept
a dix heures de Releve Ledit Lemoine a declare ne savoir
signer a fait sa marque avec le soussignes qui a signé apres
lecture faite et les sauvage ont aussy fait leurs marques

sa
Jean Bte + Lemoine
marque

Chles Reaume
Juge a paix

270 Document signed at La Baye by Charles Reaume, Justice of the Peace, from the original in the State Historical Society of Wisconsin, Madison

RIVAL FUR TRADERS

271 Front View of the American Fur Company's Buildings, Fond du Lac, Wisconsin, from a lithograph in Thomas L. McKenney, *Sketches of a Tour to the Lakes*, Baltimore, 1827

In spite of the Jay Treaty ratified in 1796, British influence remained dominant in the Northwest. The profits of the fur trade still flowed into British coffers. In the winter of 1803–04 many of the traders from Canada who had been operating south of the Great Lakes organized the Northwest Company. The new Northwest Company and the old Hudson's Bay Company, in effect, divided the Canadian fur trade between them. The former, moreover, was active south of the international border. For many years it was practically supreme in most of the Wisconsin region. Its success meant the continued hostility of the Indians of the region to the United States. In 1809 an important rival appeared when the American, John Jacob Astor, who had been operating for some years as an independent trader from Montreal, organized the American Fur Company. He established his headquarters at Mackinac. When the War of 1812 began, three years later, Astor was beginning to threaten the ascendancy of the Northwest Company in the Wisconsin country.

272 Rear View of American Fur Company's Buildings at Fond du Lac, Wisconsin, from a lithograph in Thomas L. McKenney, *Sketches of a Tour to the Lakes*, Baltimore, 1827

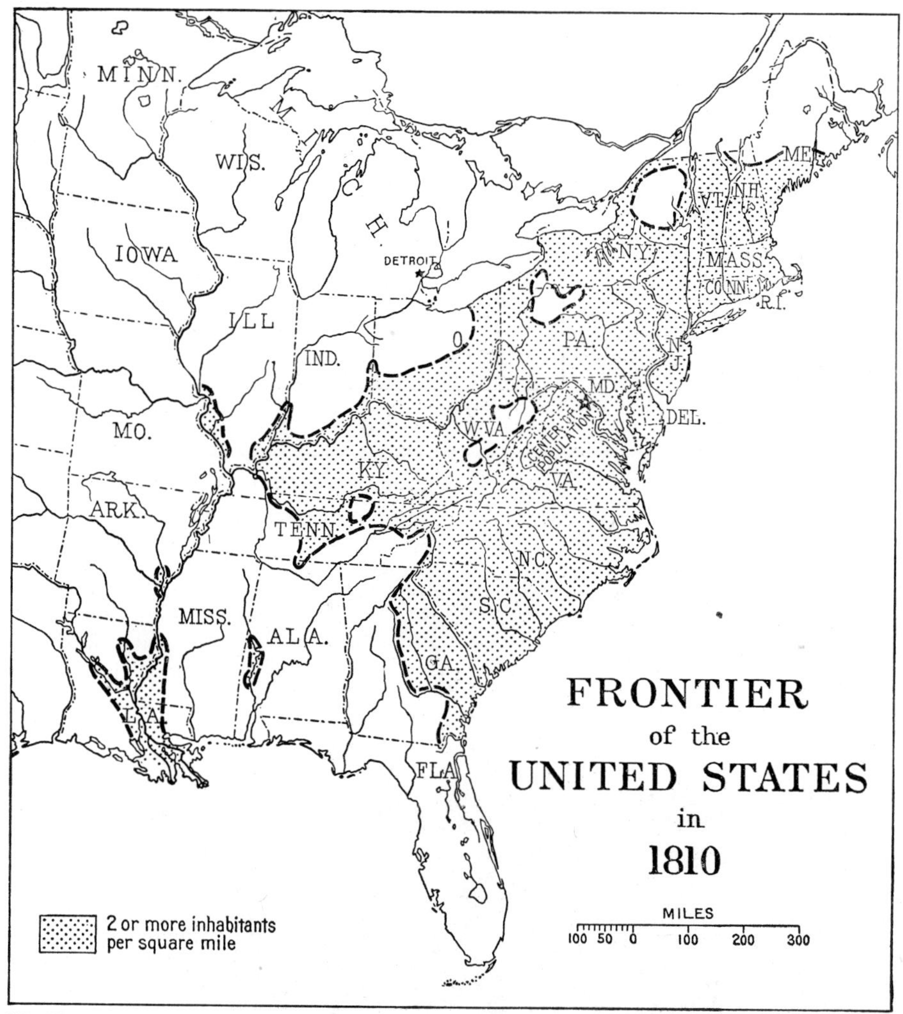

273 Drawn expressly for *The Pageant of America*, by Gregor Noetzel, American Geographical Society, New York

THE WHITE FRONTIER

In the years 1809 and 1810 messengers came to the villages of the Indians living in the valleys of the Illinois and the Wisconsin bearing news of the proposed Tecumseh confederacy. The white frontier which Tecumseh faced lay along an irregular line running roughly northeast and southwest. The right flank of this vanguard of civilization was at Detroit, still a village though its traditions already ran back a century. The people of Michigan had built their habitations in the southeastern part of their present state. They numbered less than five thousand, the great majority of whom were of French-Canadian descent. Michigan was literally an island in the forest, exposed to attack from Canada on the east and from the Indians on the north and west. Miles of wilderness separated the Michigan people from the farms of Ohio or the frontier cabins of Indiana. In the latter territory the settlements were clustered about Vincennes or extended along the north bank of the Ohio in the region across from Louisville. The Hoosiers numbered perhaps thirty thousand persons. As in the old French days the Illinois pioneers lived in the country about Kaskaskia and Cahokia. Illinois could boast but half as many people as Indiana. Far in advance of this frontier and deep in the Indian country stood the blockhouses and the stockade of Fort Dearborn near which clustered a few cabins. Tecumseh, surveying the situation from Detroit to Cahokia, was full of hope. Fort Detroit was a two-company post, garrisoned by ninety-four men. Forts Wayne, Harrison, Mackinac, and Dearborn were each held by a single company. This protection which the National Government offered the frontier of the Northwest reflected its dislike of a standing army in time of peace. The obvious weakness of the United States in this region bred insolence and defiance in the Indian.

274 Ft. Dearborn in 1803, from a lithograph by C. E. Petford, in the Chicago Historical Society

IMPENDING DANGER

The years of 1810 and 1811 brought deep anxiety to that little knot of people living in and about Fort Dearborn. Many of the officers and soldiers of the garrison had brought their wives to share with them the loneliness of the wilderness. In addition to the fort, the settlement consisted of some American traders and a government factory (see No. 281). As the months passed the traders sensed a growing menace as they went about their usual business with the Indians. They feared a war with England and they knew that such an occurrence would bring thousands of yelling hostiles about their cabins. The military men, following instructions from Washington, urged the redskins to remain neutral in the event of a clash between the two English-speaking peoples. Surgeon Van Voorhis wrote to a friend from Fort Dearborn in October 1811: "I cannot but notice the villainy practiced in the Indian country by British agents and traders; you hear of it at a distance, but we near the scene of action are sensible of it. They labor by every unprincipled means to instigate the Savages against the Americans, to inculcate the idea that we intend to drive the Indians beyond the Mississippi, and that in every purchase of land the Government defrauds them; and their united efforts aim too at the destruction of every trading house and the prevention of the extension of our frontier. Never till the prohibition of all foreigners, and especially British subjects, into the Indian Country takes place, will we enjoy a lasting peace with the credulous, deluded, and cannibal savages." The belief that the foreign trader was inciting the Indian to hostilities was universal on the frontier. The westerner demanded war against England. Such a conflict, he believed, would extend American sovereignty to Canada.

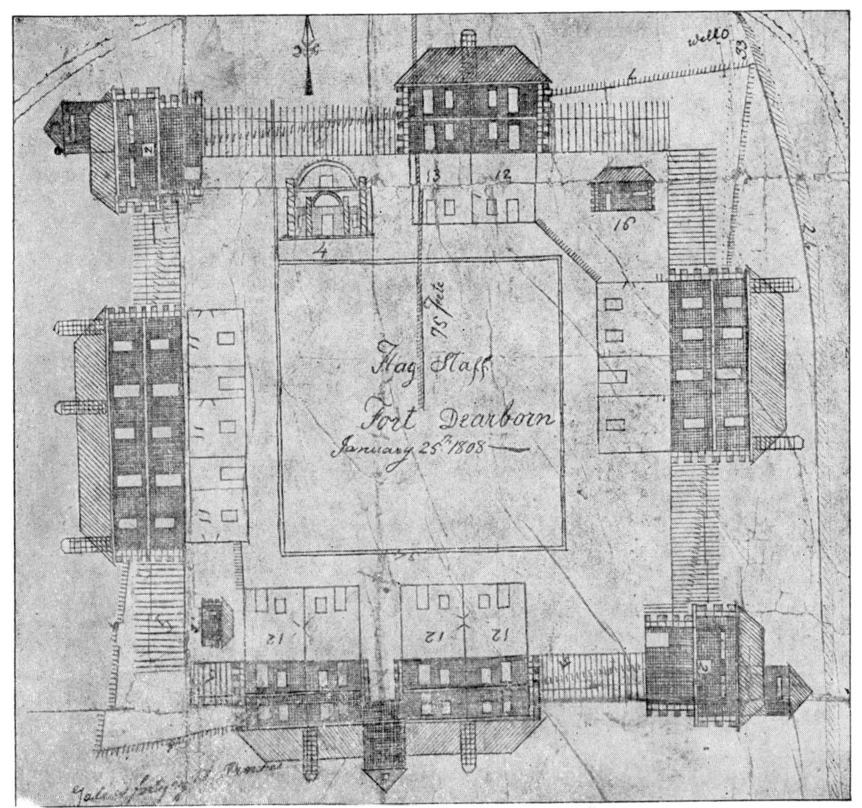

275 Interior of the Stockade at Fort Dearborn, detail from a sketch made in 1808 by Captain Whistler, in the War Department, Washington

276 Model of Fort Dearborn, in the Chicago Historical Society

THE EVACUATION OF FORT DEARBORN

In the middle of July 1812, a courier passed through the gates of Fort Dearborn and handed a dispatch to Captain Heald, its commanding officer. The latter promptly issued orders notifying the post of the outbreak of war. It was not unexpected; for some weeks past the Indians had been visibly restless and news of atrocities had drifted into the settlement on the banks of the Chicago. The fort was in readiness. No war party of braves could storm its stockade with any hope of success. Only a protracted and exhausting siege, of which the redskins were notoriously incapable, could bring down the flag then flapping from its mast. To meet such a contingency there were stores of ammunition and provisions in the warehouse. If the garrison should be reduced to extremity, militia from Illinois, Indiana, and even Kentucky could be counted on to bring aid. The traders brought their families within the stockade and themselves ventured forth only with extreme caution. So the little garrison stood guard and waited during July and early August. Then came, in August, another courier and Captain Heald read an order from General Hull for the "Evacuation of your Post owing to want of Provisions. . . . You will therefore Destroy all arms and ammunition (beyond the needs of the garrison), but the Goods of the Factory you may give to the Friendly Indians who may be desirous of Escorting you on to Fort Wayne and to the Poor and needy of your Post." Hull, soon to surrender Detroit without a blow, knew nothing of the immediate situation at Fort Dearborn. He assumed a grave responsibility when he wrote an order which allowed Heald no discretion. Apparently without fully weighing the possible consequences, he had ordered his subordinate to quit his defenses and to plunge with a handful of men into a forest filled with enemies. The ultimate responsibility for the tragedy which followed rests, however, upon the Government which had failed to train officers prepared to take intelligent charge of military affairs in an emergency like that of the summer of 1812.

THE MASSACRE

On August 14 the smoke curled from the temporary lodges of hundreds of braves who together with their squaws and children had gathered to share in the goods of the government factory and to behold the retreat of the white man. Before night they were rejoicing in the possession of their unexpected wealth. They were also speaking in low tones of the news which a runner sent by Tecumseh had brought. Hull had retreated into Detroit and a detachment of his army had been defeated. The British arms were in the ascendant; the Chicago people could be punished with impunity. About nine o'clock next morning the gates of the fort opened. Out came a vanguard of Miami Indians led by William Wells, a famous frontier scout. These had come over from Fort Wayne to aid in the retreat. The garrison followed, a little company of alert and well-trained regulars. Behind them were the women and the older children walking beside a few wagons loaded with supplies. In one of these were the smaller children of the settlement. A few Chicago militiamen brought up the rear. The Indians watched the little party start bravely on its way. About a mile and a half from the fort they struck. The Miamis fled and Wells spurred back to aid the women and children. In fifteen minutes of terrible fighting half the regulars were killed or wounded. The militia, fighting with the madness of desperation to keep the Indians from the wagons, were struck down to a man. Two women were killed. One warrior crazed with blood made his way through the mêlée to the vehicle which bore the little tots and butchered them without purpose or mercy. His act was typical of the fury of the savage at its worst. Captain Heald had no alternative but surrender.

277 From the Bronze Group on the Site of the Fort Dearborn Massacre, courtesy of the Chicago Historical Society

THE REBUILDING OF FORT DEARBORN

278 Fort Dearborn after Rebuilding, 1816, from a lithograph in the Chicago Historical Society

On July 4, 1816, a detachment of American troops debarked at the mouth of the Chicago River. Their officers hurried to the site of Fort Dearborn where they found that all the public buildings save the magazine had been destroyed. But soon the surrounding forest echoed with the noise of axes and hammers. Fort Dearborn was rising from its ashes; the reoccupation of the frontier had begun. More than a year before, Lewis Cass, Governor of Michigan Territory, had warned the War Department at Washington that British traders were again penetrating the upper Mississippi Valley, smuggling goods across the international boundary, and cultivating the old-time friendship with the Indians. Cass recommended the reëstablishment of Fort Dearborn but he pointed out that the middle trade route, which led through Green Bay, was the most important.

AMERICANS IN WISCONSIN

The end of the War of 1812 found La Baye a prosperous and attractive settlement of forty odd families extending along the banks of the Fox River. The outcome of the war had brought deep resentment to the hearts of these people, all avowedly British subjects. They looked upon the forest country which they knew so well almost as conquered territory and themselves as a conquered people. They could not shake off the conviction that the Americans were intruders who had aspirations different from their own. The traders looked to the forest as the very foundation of their lives and to the Indians who lived in it as friendly allies in the exploitation of the bounties of nature. Before the advance of the Americans the forest vanished and its trails, trod by the moccasined feet of countless generations, became rutted highways. The Americans were agriculturists. In their life the Indian had no place. He was driven westward or confined within the cramped boundaries of a reservation. The traders resented the dawning of the new era. On July 18, 1815, they met with what grace they could muster the first American official to set foot in their village street. They found Colonel John Bowyer a friendly person. To their surprise they soon became fond of this officer whose dash of French blood served both himself and his government well. The lot of Major Matthew Irwin, who started a government factory (Indian trading post), was, through no fault of his own, not so pleasant. After the arrival of these two men the name, La Baye, gradually dropped out of use. The French régime had come to an end. On August 7, 1816, the people living beside the Fox River watched with interest the arrival of four ships and the debarkation of several companies of the Third Infantry. Colonel John Miller, who commanded, promptly set about the building of Fort Howard on the west bank of the river. In the same year Brigadier-General Thomas A. Smith led four companies of the Third Infantry to Prairie du Chien, where he erected Fort Crawford. John W. Johnson of Maryland was placed in charge of the government factory established at the latter post. After thirty-three years during which the region had been within the boundaries of the United States the military power of the government was at last felt in this far corner of the Old Northwest. The mission of the army was to secure peace on the frontier and American ascendancy in the fur trade of the upper Mississippi Valley. Many years, however, were to elapse before the soldiers and the local inhabitants felt the kinship which comes from common citizenship.

279 Bluffs on the Upper Mississippi near Prairie du Chien, Wisconsin, from a print in the New York Public Library

280 A Session of the Second Continental Congress, from The Chronicles of America Photoplay, *The Declaration of Independence*

THE INDIAN POLICY OF THE SECOND CONTINENTAL CONGRESS

BEHIND the government factory which Major Irwin opened was an interesting background. From the earliest English settlements the colonies had sought the best means for conducting the Indian trade. At both Plymouth and Jamestown the trade at the beginning was an affair of the colony. The Massachusetts Bay Company before leaving England reserved to itself the trade in furs. In all the colonies, however, private traders quickly appeared and took over the business. Massachusetts in the first half of the eighteenth century revived the idea of government trading with the Indians and carried on experiments with "truck houses" in the country of the redskins. Benjamin Franklin is believed to have investigated the Massachusetts system and urged the adoption of a similar plan in his own colony. Indian relations were very much in the minds of Americans in the opening years of the Revolution. Less than a month after the Battle of Bunker Hill, Congress voted to establish three Indian departments; in the north, in the middle colonies, and in the south. These were to have power to supervise relations with the forest people. In November of the same year a committee was appointed to work out a plan for trading with the Indians. The Americans recognized that the Indians had become dependent upon trade with the white man and that the Indian was bound to take the side from which he obtained his supplies, notably guns and ammunition for hunting. In January and February 1776, Congress worked out a complete and very able Indian policy. The Indian trade should be carried on by licensed traders operating under bond and guided by instructions laid down by the commissioners. Congress voted forty thousand pounds to procure goods for these traders. The remainder of the policy dealt with the extension of the white man's culture to the red man. The commissioners were to report upon suitable places in their departments for the placing of schoolmasters and ministers of the gospel. These regulations were passed before Congress sensed the magnitude of the task which had been undertaken in fighting England. The plan remained an unfulfilled hope and on every frontier the Americans found the Indians ranged with their enemies. In all probability the American Government could not under any circumstances at this time have shaken the hold of the British trader over the tribesmen.

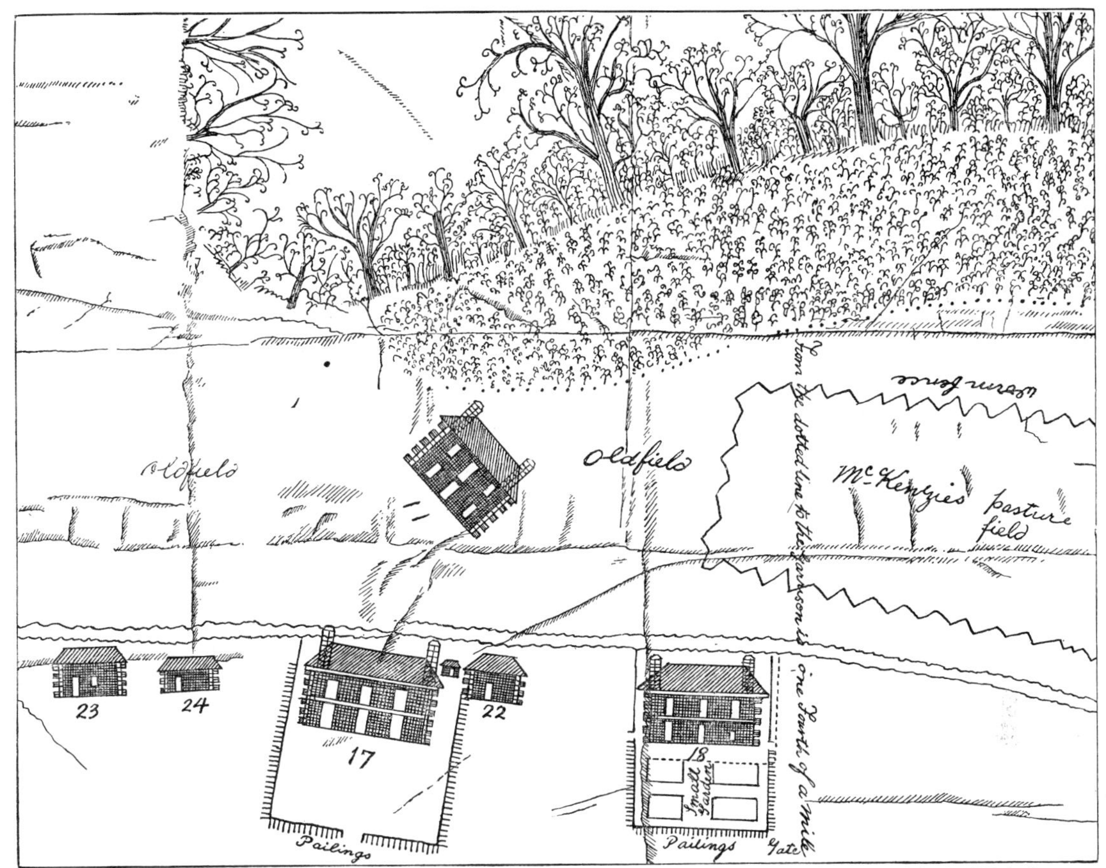

281 Typical Home of a Government Factor and Agent, detail from A Sketch of Fort Dearborn, made by Captain Whistler in 1808, in the War Department, Washington

LEGEND: 11. Officer's Barracks. 17. Agent's House. 18. Factor's House. 22. Bake House. 23. House in Factor's Department. 24. Stables.

THE ESTABLISHMENT OF THE FACTORY SYSTEM

During the years immediately following the Revolution the central government failed to establish an Indian policy. Finally in 1786 the Congress of the Confederation passed for the regulation of the Indian trade an ordinance as well conceived as the famous Ordinance of 1787. The Indian Department was divided into two districts with a superintendent and deputy for each. Only citizens of the United States were to be permitted to engage in the Indian trade within the national boundaries. Before a trader could operate, his moral character must be guaranteed by the Governor of his state, he must pay a fee of fifty dollars, and give bonds to ensure his obedience to the regulations laid down. Unlicensed trading was to be punished by a penalty of five hundred dollars and forfeiture of goods. Could this act have been put into effect, it would have driven the foreign trader from the Northwest and would have done much to stamp out that vicious practice of irresponsible traders of debauching the Indians with whiskey. Enforcement of the ordinance, however, required more political and military strength than the Congress of the Confederation possessed. It seems to have been lost sight of in the confusion incident to the transition from one form of government to another. President Washington, despite the fact that he was extremely desirous of establishing friendly relations with all the tribes within the boundaries of the United States, found himself almost from the beginning of his administration involved in Indian war in the Ohio country. When Wayne's victory gave the Government a breathing space, the President urged upon Congress the consideration of an Indian policy that would guarantee the peace of the frontier. Washington favored the defense of the white frontier with an adequate number of forts and regular troops, the protection of the Indian country from illegal invasion by predatory whites, and the establishment of proper regulation for the fur trade. Congress did none of these things. Its only important action in this connection was to institute in 1795 an experiment in government trading houses or factories. Fifty thousand dollars were voted for initiating the plan and two factories were established among the Cherokees, Creeks, and Chickasaws.

282 Government Factory at Beaubienville, from a drawing in the Chicago Historical Society

GROWTH AND DECLINE OF THE FACTORY SYSTEM

In 1805 a government factory was established at Chicago, where it proved an undoubted success. The Indians received goods at a fair price and could buy with brains unclouded by liquor. Three years later a factory was started at Mackinac. By the outbreak of the War of 1812 twelve government factories were in operation. The success of the system is demonstrated by the fact that the four years ending in 1815, in spite of the disturbance to trade caused by the war, saw these factories make a profit of some sixty thousand dollars. This was largely neutralized by the loss of five factories, including those at Chicago and Mackinac, as a result of the fighting. Despite such profits the factory system did not grow rapidly, primarily because of the attitude of Congress. That body not only permitted the private trader to continue his operations in competition with the government factory, but put the National Government in the curious position of refusing, on the one hand to monopolize the fur trade and, on the other, to turn the trade over entirely to private enterprise under proper and rigorous restrictions. The private fur trading interests of the Northwest were rapidly being monopolized by Astor's American Fur Trading Company, one of whose most important posts was at Mackinac. In 1816 the Government of the United States passed a law to exclude foreigners from trading within its boundaries. When Major Irwin opened the government factory at Green Bay, he faced not only the hostility of the local people because he was an American but the active opposition of the Astor men as well. The year 1816 saw the reëstablishment and extension of the government factory system. It also marked the beginning of the open war between the American Fur Trading Company and the government factory. Because of this hostility neither the factory at Chicago nor the one at Green Bay prospered. The Astor people carried the battle to Washington. In 1821 the admission of Missouri as a state brought Thomas H. Benton to the Senate of the United States. Getting much of his information from Ramsay Crooks, high in the councils of the Astor company, Benton at the very outset of his legislative career assailed the government factory system. He charged fraud and gross incompetence. He spoke with the authority of one who, coming from a frontier state, was supposed to be an expert in the matter of the fur trade. His charges for the most part failed of substantiation, yet his attack upon the government system was successful. In 1822 the government factories were abolished. Benton had been aided by the votes of many men who believed that the business of trading was not a proper function for the Government of the United States. Whether the factory system would have accomplished what its advocate hoped is doubtful. It labored under one great disadvantage: transactions at the factory were practically always on a cash basis. The improvident Indian needed credit. In the autumn the private trader advanced the hunter his equipment and his ammunition for the hunting and trapping season. Frequently the trader followed the redskin on the expedition and was paid back as the furs came in. The private trader could, therefore, adapt himself to the needs and peculiarities of the Indians in a way which was impossible for an institution hampered by a mass of rules and backed by an indifferent Congress. The spectacle of their Government in competition with its citizens was, moreover, peculiarly repugnant to nineteenth-century Americans.

283 Thomas H. Benton, 1782–1858, the Antagonist of the Factory System, from an engraving by J. Rogers, in the Fridenberg Collection, New York

THE LAST PHASE OF THE WISCONSIN FUR TRADE

284 American Fur Company Warehouse at Prairie du Chien, Wisconsin, from a photograph, courtesy of the Wisconsin Historical Society, Madison

In the decades immediately following the close of the War of 1812 the fur trade of the Old Northwest was marked by an autumnal glory. During this period the Chippewas occupied the northern third of the present Wisconsin with about six hundred hunters. Their peltries went out to Mackinac mostly by way of Lake Superior. To the south of them four hundred Menominees worked the country about the Fox River and the northeastern part of Wisconsin. Their pelts came to Green Bay. The Winnebagos hunted about the lake which bears their name, in the upper reaches of the Fox, and in the region of the Madison Lakes. To the east and south of them scattered bands of Potawatomis, about two hundred hunters, ranged the forests along the west shore of Lake Michigan and brought their furs to Milwaukee. The Sauks and Foxes did a little hunting in the lead country and traded at Prairie du Chien. Until about 1830 the fur trade was the dominant commercial interest in the Wisconsin area. There were many independent and semi-independent traders but for the most part the business was controlled by the American Fur Trading Company.

THE FUR TRADE AND THE INDIAN

"The introduction of the fur-trade by Europeans wrought a serious change in the life and manners of the Indians. They were induced to abandon much of their agriculture and most of their useful village arts. Becoming hunters they thus took a backward step in the long and painful road toward civilization. Heretofore they had needed furs only for raiment, sleeping mats, and tepee coverings; now peltries were eagerly sought by the stranger, who exchanged for them weapons, cloth, iron kettles and tools, ornaments and other marvelous objects of European manufacture, generally far better and more efficient than those which they had been wont to fashion for themselves. Thus the Indians soon lost the arts of making clothing out of skins, kettles from clay, weapons from stone and copper, and beads (used both for ornament and currency) from clam-shells. They were not slow to discover that when they hunted, their labor was far more productive than of old. Comparatively slight effort on their part now enabled them to purchase from the white traders whatever they desired. . . . The general result was disastrous to the improvident aborigines, for in considerable measure they ceased to be self-supporting. They soon came to depend on the fur-traders for most of the essentials of life; and so general was the credit system among them, the summer's supplies being bought on the strength of the following winter's hunt, that tribesmen were practically always heavily in debt to the traders, which rendered it advisable for them to stand by their creditors whenever two rival nations were contesting in the field. In the end these conditions materially assisted in the undoing of the Indian." — R. G. Thwaites, *Wisconsin*, 196–97.

285 Indian Hunters, from the mural by Barry Faulkner in the Washington Irving High School, New York

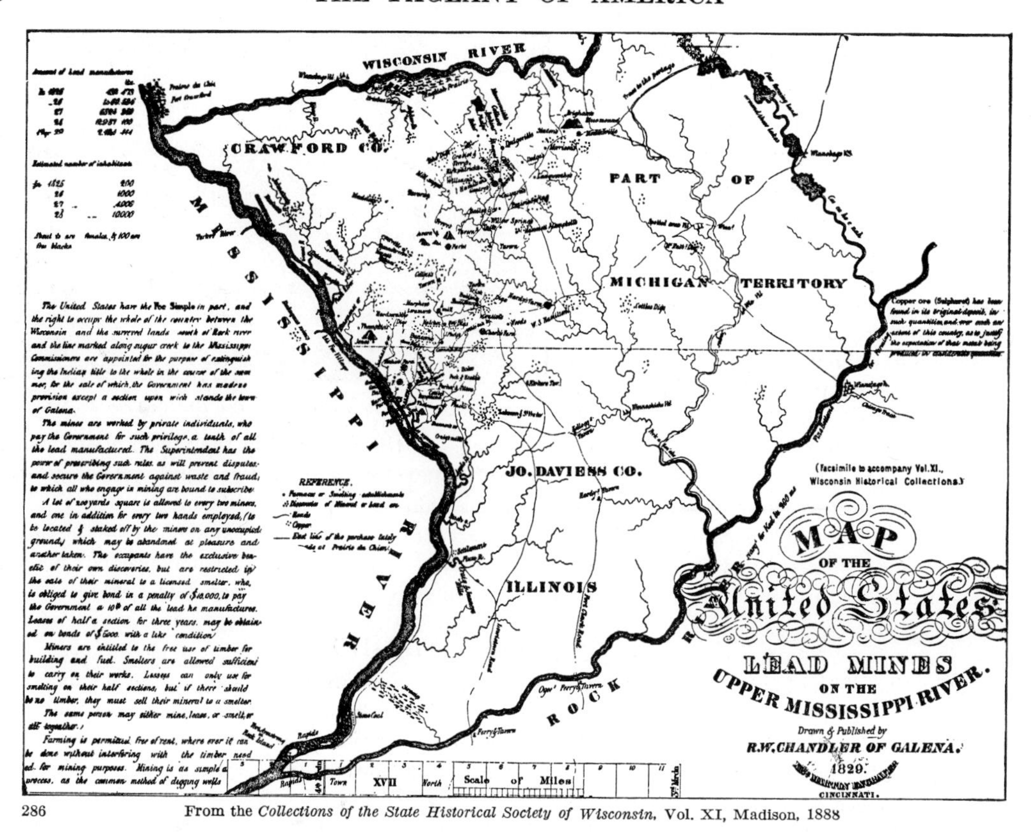

286 From the *Collections of the State Historical Society of Wisconsin,* Vol. XI, Madison, 1888

THE LEAD COUNTRY

From first to last the product of the lead country was of vital importance to the fur trade. Long before that trade failed in the Wisconsin region the lead country had been pock marked with the shallow diggings made by either Indians or the early prospectors. The British who followed the French had derived much wealth from the ore veins east of the Mississippi. Their profits early stirred the Government of the United States to take measures to control the region. In 1804, the year after President Jefferson had purchased Louisiana, the Sauk and Fox Indians were called to St. Louis for a conference. In the middle of that year some Sauks had murdered three Americans settled near the mouth of the Missouri. Demanding reparation for this outrage the Government of the United States forced the Sauks and Foxes in November to cede over fifty million acres of land in the lead country of Missouri, Illinois, and Wisconsin. For this cession the Indians received a trifling consideration. They retained, however, the privilege of occupying the region until such time as the United States should dispose of the lands to actual settlers. Black Hawk later maintained that this treaty was made with a few chiefs who were made drunk and whose action could not bind the tribe. In 1816, however, a second conference with the Sauks and Foxes confirmed the old arrangement in a new treaty, which Black Hawk himself signed. So passed the legal rights of the Indians to one of the richest regions of the frontier. As early as 1809 a shot tower was erected at Herculaneum, Missouri. Two years later the Indian agent at Prairie du Chien reported to his superiors that the Sauk and Fox Indians, east of the Mississippi, and the Iowa tribe on the western bank had "mostly abandoned the chase, except to furnish themselves with meat, and turned their attention to the manufacture of lead." In 1810 they smelted in the crude furnaces which they used some four thousand pounds of metal, turning most of this over to British traders in return for supplies. After the War of 1812 the British quickly disappeared and their profitable business fell into the hands of Americans. In the summer of 1819 Major Thomas Forsyth, Indian Agent for the Sauks and Foxes, journeyed up the Mississippi from St. Louis to the falls of St. Anthony and made it his business to investigate and report on "the number, situation, and quality of all lead mines between Apple Creek and Prairie du Chien." Three years later Colonel James Johnson of Kentucky leased the present site of Galena. Johnson brought efficient tools, trained men, and a military guard. His swift success meant that the day of the large-scale exploitation of the lead district had dawned.

THE RUSH TO THE LEAD COUNTRY

287 Weighing Pig Lead, 1866, from an engraving in *Harper's New Monthly Magazine*, May 1866

In the latter half of the decade of the eighteen-twenties immigration into the lead country took on the proportions of a "rush." From all sections of the East men came on foot, on horseback, by wagon, and by river boat. From the country down the Mississippi came others many of whom pushed past Galena into the country that was one day to be Wisconsin. "Their habits in the early years in the lead country gave rise to nicknames that have stood the test of time. The 'badgers' came up the river, dug in, and stayed as permanent members of a new community; the 'suckers,' like their finny namesakes, came up in the spring, and returned to Illinois before winter." — Paxson, *History of the American Frontier*, 287. The Yankee twang of New Englanders mingled with the drawl of men from the South. Everywhere were prospectors sinking their picks into the slopes of every promising hill. Everywhere were hastily thrown up log shanties, surrounded by stockades through the gates of which white children ran back and forth in their play. In a season Indian trails were broadened into roads along which straining horses pulled coaches and wagons filled with freight. At important lodes, at crossroads, and at shipping points on the rivers mushroom towns sprang up. The country became dotted with smelting furnaces to which the miners brought their ore. Many a Sauk and Fox miner, returning from his winter hunt, found his diggings occupied by armed white men. The Indians were impotent before the rush. Doubtless the minds of many of their old men ran back to the warning of the British traders who had told them that the Americans were aggressive and greedy, that they would drive the Indian out of his country and take it for themselves. The redskin now became aware of the fact that he had few rights which the American frontiersman felt bound to respect. The day of the complete enforcement of the treaties made in 1804 and 1816 was at hand.

288 Hughlett's Smelting Furnace, Galena, Illinois, 1866, from an engraving in *Harper's New Monthly Magazine*, May 1866

HENRY DODGE, 1782–1867

One of the badgers who came up in 1827 was Henry Dodge, who abandoned his home a little below St. Louis and brought his wife and nine children to the wild country of southern Wisconsin. He became a squatter on land which had not yet been opened up for settlement. He was in the Winnebago country and he purchased permission from that tribe to remain. Dodge had located abundant ore which was near the surface. His success was immediate and during the first winter after his arrival it brought men flocking to the region. The Winnebagos became fearful and their councils took on an angry tone. The natural attitude of the tribesmen worried the Indian agent at Prairie du Chien who sent a subordinate to order Dodge to quit the country at once.

289 Henry Dodge, from the portrait by Bowman in the Wisconsin Historical Society, Madison

290 Early Lead Mine Furnaces and Shot Tower in Southern Wisconsin, from an engraving in *The Wisconsin Agriculturist*, Racine, February 18, 1928

A SQUATTER

The messenger reported on his return that "Gen. Dodge resides in a small stockade fort near the principal mine. There are about twenty log houses in the immediate vicinity, besides several more remote. He has a double furnace in constant operation, and a large quantity of lead bars in the crude state. From the best information I have been able to obtain there are about one hundred and thirty men engaged in mining at this place, and completely armed with rifles and pistols. I was also informed that there were about fifteen Winnebagos ten or twelve miles distant, who frequently visit the mines and who have been presented by Gen. Dodge with several hundred dollars worth of provisions and merchandise." Dodge refused to leave. The agent made an abortive attempt to call out militia to drive him off. In 1829 the Winnebagos sold their lands in the mining region to the United States and in the same year the territory of Michigan, which at the time included the region where Dodge had settled, established Iowa county so that these squatters might have some form of government. The activities of Dodge are typical of American penetration of the Indian country.

THE ORIGIN OF THE WINNEBAGO WAR OF 1827

Before Dodge settled in Iowa county in November 1827, he had played a conspicuous part in the so-called Winnebago War, which was brought to a conclusion in the summer of that year. Dodge was not the first trespasser on the Winnebago lands. The brusque treatment accorded the Indians by the lead miners had bred deep resentment. By 1826 the treaty which the Winnebagos had made the year before with the United States was being broken by irresponsible whites. These Indians, together with other tribes from southern Wisconsin, chafed also under the treatment which they had received at the hands of General William Clark, Indian superintendent, and Lewis Cass, with whom they had held a council at Prairie du Chien in the summer of 1825. The purpose of this meeting, at which Sioux and Iowas were also present, was to put an end to the intertribal fighting which kept the region in frequent uproar. Particularly deep was the animosity between the Sioux, the Sauks, and the Foxes. The treaties were agreed to by the various tribes but the popularity of the white peacemakers and the government which they represented was impaired. The braves accused Cass and Clark of cold formality and with failing to supply them liberally with either presents or rum. The attitude of the Americans was in sharp contrast with that of the British traders in the happy days gone by. In 1826 the ill feeling of the Winnebagos was deepened by the imprisonment at Prairie du Chien of two of their warriors, who were charged with small offenses. The atmosphere was tense, the outlook threatening.

291 View of the Great Treaty Held at Prairie du Chien, from a lithograph by Lehman and Duval after the painting on the spot by J. O. Lewis, in the Wisconsin Historical Society, Madison

AN EYE FOR AN EYE

292 A Winnebago Warrior, from an engraving after a drawing in H. R. Schoolcraft, *Indian Tribes of the United States*, 1851–57

During the summer of 1826 the menacing Indian situation at Prairie du Chien caused much uneasy talk among the whites of the possibility of an attack. At this juncture the War Department at Washington made matters worse by requiring the sudden transfer of the whole garrison of Fort Crawford to Fort Snelling, some two hundred miles up the river. News of this event emboldened the Indians, for as the braves discussed it about their lodge fires it seemed to signify retreat and weakness. In the following March 1827, a party of young Winnebago bucks wiped out a half-breed family a dozen miles north of Prairie du Chien. The situation on the frontier became alarming. A few weeks later a party of Sioux, visiting the Winnebagos, gave them, perhaps deliberately, false news of the execution of the two Winnebago prisoners who had been carried to Fort Snelling. The Indian code demanded revenge — two scalps for one. In June Red Bird, a lesser chief, together with three of his warriors paused at the farm of Registre Gagniér. When the Indians departed, Gagniér and a negro slave were dead, Gagniér's wife and a ten-year-old son had fled, while an eighteen-months-old daughter lay scalped but living in the home. The baby girl was later rescued and grew to womanhood. Red Bird with three scalps, one short of the required number, soon joined with a party of Winnebago hunters who had stopped for a space near the bank of the Mississippi at the mouth of the Bad Axe. Two keel boats with white crews passed the Bad Axe. Apparently the bravado of the white rivermen provoked a skirmish with the Indians. Both redskins and whites were killed. The news of the murders and the battle filled the lead country with panic. Henry Dodge, on his way northward, stopped at Galena whither many refugees had fled. Known as an experienced Indian fighter, he was made by common consent the leader of the band of volunteers formed at that place.

MAJOR WHISTLER

In spite of his actions Red Bird does not seem to have wanted war. From first to last he had been impelled by the only code he knew, the primitive law of vengeance. In his own eyes and those of his people he had committed no wrong. Yet he promptly perceived that what he had done was threatening his tribe with annihilation. Brigadier-General Atkinson hurried from St. Louis to Fort Crawford with six hundred infantry and prepared to march into the Winnebago country by way of the Wisconsin River. Dodge, with a hundred mounted volunteers, pushed northeastward from Galena. Major Whistler came up the Fox from Fort Howard and stopped at the Fox-Wisconsin portage to wait for Atkinson. Whistler, knowing the Indians well, had sent runners to the Winnebagos to warn them to give up the murderers if they would avoid extermination.

293 Fort Howard, Wisconsin, from a daguerreotype in the Wisconsin Historical Society, Madison

294 Fort Winnebago, 1831, from a lithograph by Sarony after a drawing by Mrs. J. A. Kinzie, in Mrs. Juliette A. Kinzie, *Wau-bun*, Chicago, 1857

AN INDIAN PATRIOT

On September 2 occurred one of the most striking episodes in the annals of the frontier. Whistler, having been appraised of what would happen, formed his troops on parade. At three in the afternoon Red Bird, clad in the picturesque regalia of a chief, approached, proudly erect, singing his death song. With him was a warrior, one of the murder party whom he had compelled to join him. Whistler received the chieftain with military honors. Red Bird had saved his people. Imprisoned at Prairie du Chien, the chieftain was given much freedom and more than once sympathetic soldiers placed in his way opportunities to escape. But Red Bird remained steadfast to his pledge to stand trial. While waiting he caught the contagion of an epidemic which broke out in the village and was gathered to his fathers. Two others of the murder party were ultimately tried and condemned to death but were saved from the gallows by the pardon of President John Quincy Adams. So ended what has sometimes been called the Winnebago War. In 1828 Fort Winnebago was erected at the Fox-Wisconsin portage to keep that restless tribe under control.

THE ORIGIN OF THE BLACK HAWK WAR

The voluntary surrender of Red Bird had avoided conflict in 1827 but trouble was developing to the southward. If the Battle of Tippecanoe was the prologue of the War of 1812, Black Hawk's War may fittingly be called its epilogue. In the former conflict Black Hawk had fought by the side of Tecumseh. After peace had been concluded, he failed to sense the meaning which the outcome of the conflict had for the Indians of the Old Northwest. The Black Sparrow Hawk was not a chief but the natural leader and head man of a strong band of Sauks who lived near the mouth of the Rock River beside an ancient burying ground of the tribe. As the years passed the Hawk continued to lead his "British Band" from time to time over the old Sauk trail to Malden, where they traded with the British and received presents from them. The greater part of the Sauks and Foxes, under the head chief, Keokuk, had bowed to the inevitable and, in accordance with the treaties of 1804 and 1816, had crossed to the western bank of the Mississippi. But Black Hawk stubbornly remained amid the old surroundings. In the spring of 1830, when Black Hawk's people returned from their winter hunt to the site where for every summer since the oldest man could remember they had built their lodges, they found that white men had preceded them, had seized their cornfields and driven furrows across the graves of their dead. The men were squatters without legal rights, for this land had not yet been included in the governmental surveys. There is something childlike in Black Hawk's reaction to the crisis. He led his people over the familiar trail south of Lake Michigan to Fort Malden to consult there with his British friends. The military agent at Malden, thinking perhaps in terms of the Indian policy of his own province, advised the forlorn Sauk leader that the spirit of the treaty of 1804 had been violated by these frontiersmen, who had pushed beyond the surveyed lands. Let Black Hawk resist this encroachment and the Government of the United States, actuated by a sense of fair play, would doubtless support him. Frontiersmen were inclined to ascribe a malicious intent to the British trader's advice.

295 Black Hawk, 1767–1838, from the portrait by Thomas Sully in the Wisconsin Historical Society, Madison

BLACK HAWK'S INVASION

In the spring of 1831 Black Hawk and his people were again at the old village site, where they found more whites than were there the year before. The Hawk ordered the squatters off and threatened force. His answer was a flaming proclamation by Governor Reynolds calling out the militia to meet this Indian invasion. In a few weeks an overwhelming force of regulars and militia was massed close beside his village. Black Hawk fled beyond the Mississippi after making a formal promise to General Gaines never to return. The winter of 1831–32 in the Iowa country was hard and Black Hawk's people, who for two years had not been able to raise a crop, suffered severely. The Hawk listened to counselors who urged him to return and fight for his rights. White Cloud in particular, the Winnebago medicine man of his band, urged him to take up the hatchet. Despite the events of the intervening years he seems to have been in mind and spirit living still in the days of Tecumseh, when war against the whites offered some possibility of success. In the spring of 1832 he recrossed the Mississippi with a force of about five or six hundred warriors, mostly Sauks, together with their women and children. The frontier was struck with terror. In a short time the village of Chicago was full of refugees and there was wild talk of abandoning the place. Again the militia was called out, together with the regulars under General Atchison. The Hawk retreated up the Rock River but paused long enough to put to inglorious flight a pursuing band of militiamen under Major Stillman. While the whites were concentrating their strength there were Indian depredations along the frontier. Rumor and the blazing headlines of local papers made Black Hawk a name which would cause men to blanch and would send women and children flying to whatever protection chanced to be offered.

296 White Cloud, from a portrait in the Wisconsin Historical Society, Madison

THE END OF THE WAR

June and July 1832, were for Black Hawk months of retreat through the swamps and forests and across the prairies and rivers of southern Wisconsin. On July 21 a battle was fought at Wisconsin Heights with some loss on either side. An outstanding feature of the encounter was the skillful work of Black Hawk in getting his women and children across the Wisconsin. He fled toward the Mississippi while his opponents paused to await reinforcements. Ten days later the Indians, sadly depleted as a result of hardship and starvation, were at the mouth of the Bad Axe trying to get across the Father of Waters. On August 2 the white troops closed in on them and, aided by the guns of the *Warrior*, a government supply steamer in the river, cut them to pieces. The Hawk, who fled inland, was promptly turned over to the army by the Winnebagos. In Black Hawk the once proud spirit of the Indians of the Old Northwest flared up for the last time, only to cause his British Band to be wiped out with that ruthlessness which characterized the frontiersman when he made war upon the redskin. The captive Hawk was paraded like a caged animal through the towns of the East. In 1837, the year before his death, Black Hawk told a group of whites the motives which actuated him. "Rock River was a beautiful country. I liked my town, my cornfields, and the home of my people. I fought for them."

297 Battle of the Bad Axe, from a lithograph after a drawing by Henry Lewis in *Das Illustrirte Mississippi-Thal*, Düsseldorf, 1844

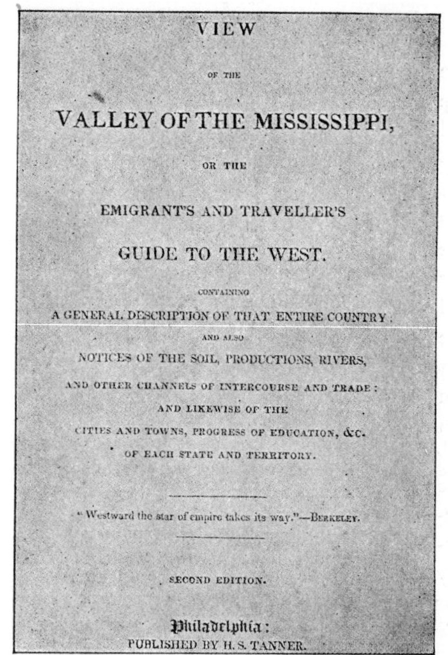
VIEW

OF THE

VALLEY OF THE MISSISSIPPI,

OR THE

EMIGRANT'S AND TRAVELLER'S

GUIDE TO THE WEST.

CONTAINING

A GENERAL DESCRIPTION OF THAT ENTIRE COUNTRY;

AND ALSO

NOTICES OF THE SOIL, PRODUCTIONS, RIVERS,

AND OTHER CHANNELS OF INTERCOURSE AND TRADE:

AND LIKEWISE OF THE

CITIES AND TOWNS, PROGRESS OF EDUCATION, &C.

OF EACH STATE AND TERRITORY.

"Westward the star of empire takes its way."—BERKELEY.

SECOND EDITION.

Philadelphia:
PUBLISHED BY H. S. TANNER.

298 Pamphlet encouraging Immigration to Illinois and Wisconsin, in the New York Public Library

THE AFTERMATH OF THE WAR

BLACK HAWK stands last on that list of able Indian leaders of the Old Northwest which includes the names of Pontiac, Cornstalk, Little Turtle, and Tecumseh. One after another these men had striven unsuccessfully to stop the advance of the whites. Thereafter the Indians of this region ceased to kick against the pricks. In 1856 the last Indian titles, save small reservations, were extinguished in Wisconsin. But the war did more than teach the Indian the futility of further struggle against fate. It gave to the beautiful and fertile region of northern Illinois and southern Wisconsin incomparable advertising. Immigrants in great numbers turned their faces toward this new land of promise. Frederick Paxson has made clear that the advance of the frontier was marked by pulsations rather than by a steady advance. The middle years of the eighteenth century saw one wave; the inauguration of President Jefferson roughly coincided with the crest of another. The "Great Migration" which began after the War of 1812 was followed by another wave in the 'thirties. The period from 1832 to 1836 was a time of general land boom in the West. In 1834 the sale of Wisconsin lands began on a large scale and two years later nearly eleven thousand people were living in the Wisconsin country.

WESTWARD HO

IN 1835 the people of Chicago, now a rapidly growing mushroom village, witnessed the passing of the local Indians, the Potawatomis. Two years before, they had sold the last of their lands to the Government and promised to move westward. As was usual the half-breed traders secured special favors, particularly in land concessions. The Indians got relatively little. In 1835 these latter, about to move, determined to say a brave farewell to the race which had dispossessed them. In August the Potawatomis danced a war dance through the streets of Chicago. From the Saugenash Hotel John D. Caton, later to be Chief Justice of the Supreme Court of Illinois, watched the spectacle. His point of view was that of the frontiersman who saw in the Indian only an obstacle to the advance of civilization. "Their eyes were wild and bloodshot," wrote Caton, "their countenances had assumed an expression of all the worst passions which could find a place in the breast of a savage; fierce anger, terrible hate, dire revenge, remorseless cruelty, all were expressed in their terrible features. Their muscles stood out in great hard knots, as if wrought to a tension that must burst them. Their tomahawks and clubs were thrown and brandished about in every direction with the most terrible ferocity, and with a force and energy which could only result from the highest excitement, and with every step and every gesture they uttered the most frightful yells, in every imaginable key and note, though generally the highest and shrillest possible. The dance, which was ever continued, consisted of leaps and spasmodic steps, now forward and now back or sideways, with the whole body distorted into every imaginable unnatural position, most generally stooping forward with the head and face thrown up, the back arched down, first one foot forward and then withdrawn, and the other similarly thrust out, frequently squatting quite to the ground, and all with a movement as quick as lightning. Their weapons were brandished as if they would slay a thousand enemies at every blow, while the yells and screams they uttered were broken up and multiplied and rendered all the more hideous by a rapid clapping of the mouth with the hand." It was a brave and pathetic show, "a funeral ceremony of old associations and memories," an epoch in Chicago history.

299 A full-blood Potawatomi, from a photograph in the De Lancey Gill Collection, Washington

THE SETTLEMENT OF ILLINOIS

IN 1818, long before Black Hawk was crushed, Illinois became a state. During the previous decade settlers had been making their way into that region which, in the twentieth century, is the heart of the corn belt of the United States. For the most part the newcomers floated to Illinois on the lazy waters of the Ohio River. Some made their homes on the banks of that stream. Others poled their flatboats up its tributaries. Many families followed the Ohio until it joined with the Mississippi and then turned northward on the Father of Waters. Cabins sprang up beside the Big Muddy and the Illinois rivers and along the east bank of the Mississippi itself. Morris Birkbeck and George Flower, both Englishmen, established in 1817 a settlement made up of British immigrants in the southeastern corner of the state in what was later Edwards County. To this settlement came many folk from the British Isles who were suffering from the economic dislocation caused by the termination of the long drawn out Napoleonic wars. Almost without exception the early Illinois settlers clung to the forest country and avoided the prairies. They had no plows with which to turn the tough sod. They knew the woodlands but had little confidence in the fertility of soil that did not produce trees. The forest, moreover, gave them materials for building their cabins and fuel to heat them. Not until the wooded country was largely occupied did pioneers in important numbers venture out upon the wind-swept grasslands.

300 LETTER TO [Part III.

TO

MORRIS BIRKBECK, ESQ.

OF

ENGLISH PRAIRIE, ILLINOIS TERRITORY.

North Hempstead, Long Island,
10 Dec. 1818.

MY DEAR SIR

569. I HAVE read your two little books, namely, the "*Notes on a Journey in America*," "and the *Letters from the Illinois.*" I opened the books, and I proceeded in the perusal, with *fear and trembling;* not because I supposed it possible for you to put forth an *intended* imposition on the world, but, because I had a sincere respect for the character and talents of the writer; and because I knew how enchanting and delusive are the prospects of enthusiastic minds, when bent on grand territorial acquisitions.

570. My apprehensions were, I am sorry to have it to say, but too well founded. Your books, written, I am sure, without any intention to deceive and decoy, and without any, even the smallest, tincture of base self-interest, are, in my opinion, calculated to produce great disappointment, not to say misery and ruin, amongst our own country people (for I will, in spite of your disavowal, still claim the honour of having you for a countryman), and great injury to America by sending back to Europe accounts of that disappointment, misery, and ruin.

571. It is very true, that you decline *advising* any one to go to the ILLINOIS, and it is also true, that your description of the *hardships* you encountered is very candid; but still, there runs throughout the whole of your *Notes* such an account as to the *prospect*, that is to say, the *ultimate effect*, that the book is, without your either wishing or perceiving it, calculated to de-

300 Published letter from William Cobbett to Morris Birkbeck, in the New York Public Library

THE SETTLEMENT OF MICHIGAN

THE settlement of Michigan waited upon the development of transportation facilities. One of the reasons why the timorous Hull in the War of 1812 surrendered Detroit without a blow was that three hundred miles of wilderness, broken only by the road his army had cut through it, separated him from the nearest settlements. The Ohio River, the main artery for westward migration, flows far to the south of Michigan. In 1812 the few thousand whites living in the territory were mostly of French descent or were the English fur traders who replaced the *couriers de bois*. During the second war with England three roads, cut through the forest from the valley of the Ohio, converged upon Detroit. More important was the beginning of steam navigation on Lake Erie when, in 1818, the *Walk in the Water* first churned the waters of this inland sea. In 1825 the completion of the Erie Canal opened a direct water route from southeastern Michigan to the most thickly settled region of the older United States. Immediately thereafter thousands of people began pouring into the southern part of the territory under the lakes. In 1836 the people of swiftly growing Michigan knocked insistently at the doors of Congress and were admitted to the union of the states.

301 Transfer Service in New York City for Emigrants on their way to Michigan and other Western States, from an engraving in E. H. Mott, *The Story of Erie*, New York, 1889

302 Winnebago Indians, from a lithograph by Ferdinand Pettrich, in Ferdinand Pettrich, *Portraits of Distinguished Indians from Several Tribes, who Visited Washington in 1837*, Baltimore, 1842

THE LURE OF THE WISCONSIN FORESTS

THE Potawatomis followed the trail toward the setting sun which the Sauks and Foxes had taken earlier. The Indians farther north, however, were never entirely driven out. The Menominees and the eastern bands of the Chippewas continued to live for the most part on reservations in the region south of Lake Superior. In the Wisconsin country remained also certain immigrant Indians. In the Berkshire Hills of western Massachusetts dwelt in colonial times the Stockbridge Indians among whom Jonathan Edwards preached for a time. Neighbor to these were other Christian Indians, the Brothertown people, made up of remnants of several New England tribes. During and immediately after the Revolutionary War the Stockbridge and the Brothertown Indians, now well advanced toward civilization, moved to western New York where they settled beside the villages of the Oneidas and a branch of the Delawares known as the Munsees. By 1810 the advance of the frontier in New York compelled these four peoples to move. Ten years later Dr. Jedediah Morse, a minister and father of the inventor of the telegraph, was sent by the War Department into Wisconsin to locate lands for the Stockbridges, in whom he was particularly interested. Twelve years passed, however, before the main body of the New York Indians came to Wisconsin. The Stockbridge and Brothertown tribes established themselves east of Lake Winnebago and in course of time became farmers owning and cultivating their separate farms. The Oneidas and the Munsees settled near the mouth of the lower Fox and on the Oneida reservation near Green Bay. They too abandoned their communal ownership of land and began living, in the 'nineties, on their separate farms. Not so tractable were the Winnebagos. From 1848 to 1872 attempts were made at intervals to remove this famous tribe to reservations beyond the Mississippi. Twice the major part of the tribesmen, who offered no resistance, were transported to the grasslands west of the Father of Waters, and each time, after a short space, most of them came trailing back pining for their familiar woods. Nearly half the Winnebagos still live in Wisconsin, while the greater part of the remainder dwell on a reservation in Nebraska.

303 Travel in the Northwest, 1820–30, from an engraving in *Transactions of the Kansas State Historical Society*, Vol. IX, Topeka, 1906

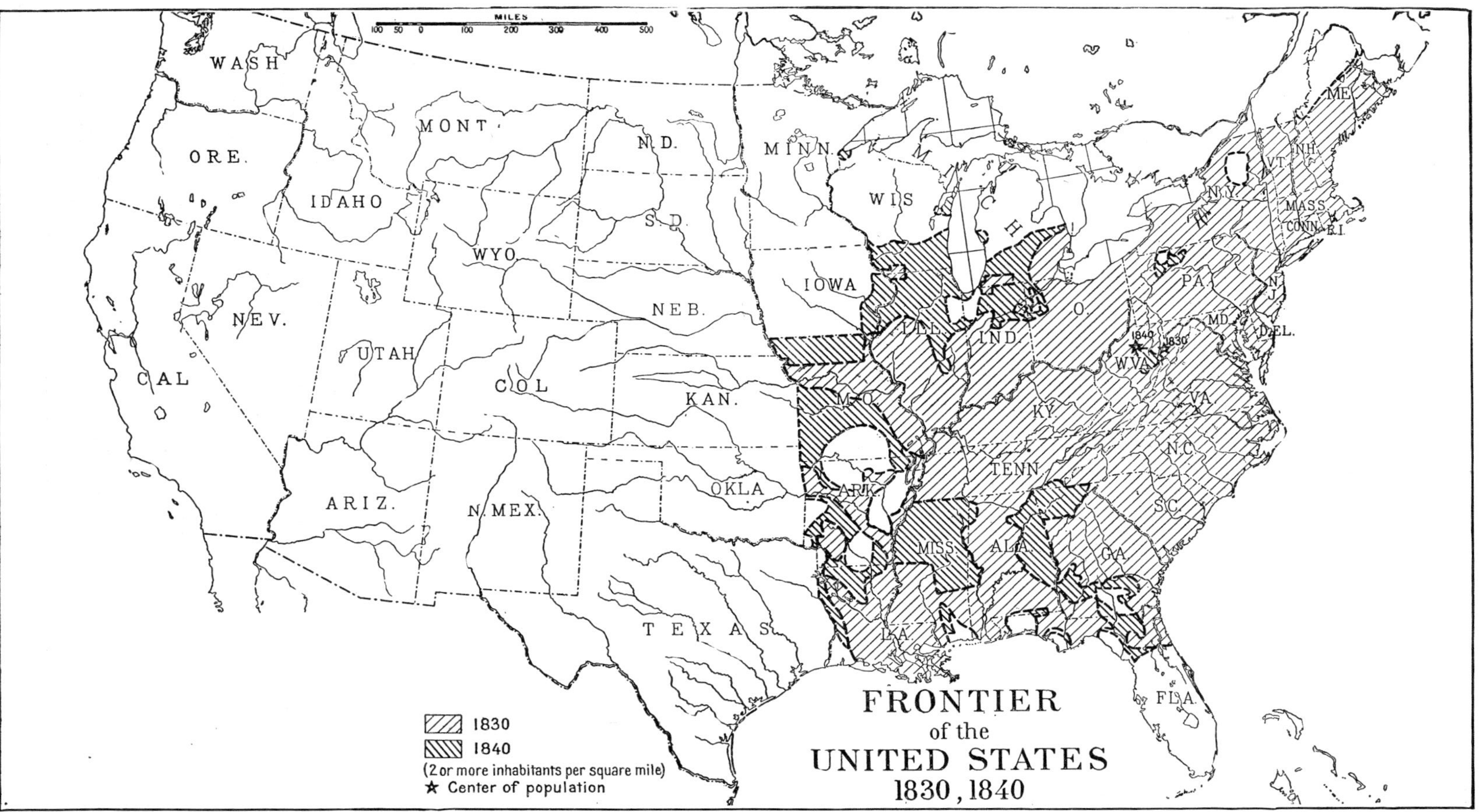

304 Drawn expressly for *The Pageant of America* by Gregor Noetzel, American Geographical Society, New York (Settlements in Texas and west of the Rockies not shown, because these areas in 1840 were not part of the United States)

THE FRONTIER OF 1840

By 1840 the fringe of settlement had passed the Mississippi in its westward advance and was approaching the Great Plains. In Texas, independent after the successful revolution of 1836, settlement had made its deepest penetration of the wilderness. The decade which lay ahead was to see pioneer-farmers begin crossing the grasslands and the western mountains to Oregon. Thirty-four years before the census year of 1840 Lewis and Clark had returned from their successful exploring trip to the Pacific. They were the forerunners of the trapper, the fur trader and the settler. Their report threw a flood of light not only upon the far Northwest but upon that vague territory of Louisiana which Jefferson had recently purchased from France.

CHAPTER VII

EXPANSION AND EXPLORATION

FEW men have ever entered the White House with hopes as high as those of Thomas Jefferson. In the very year of his successful campaign the war between the United States and his beloved France had come to an end. Fighting in Europe had also ceased. The civilized world was at peace and the pacific Democratic-Republican President of the United States rejoiced in the opportunity to carry into effect his purpose to reduce the national expenditures and to enhance the relative importance of the states. From the very day of his inauguration, however, he was troubled by the persistent rumor that Napoleon had negotiated the transfer of Louisiana from Spain to France on the day after making peace with the American republic. No news could be more disturbing than this. Jefferson understood fully the importance of the control of the mouth of the Mississippi over the development of the economic life of the communities west of the Appalachian Mountains. He knew also the turbulent spirit of the Westerners and the weakness of the bond which held them to the Union. They might at almost any time descend the Mississippi and try conclusions with the Spaniards before the Spanish garrison surrendered their authority to representatives from Paris. Ownership of Louisiana by France would be an unmitigated calamity to the United States. Even Jefferson, Francophile that he was, admitted that so long as France controlled the mouth of the Mississippi River that nation must be the enemy of the United States. The President remarked that his Government must marry itself to the British fleet, a recourse extremely distasteful to the man who had sympathized deeply with the French people in the days of their struggle for freedom.

Events were to demonstrate the literal truth of the rumors. Napoleon, freed from European war, turned his dynamic energy to the reëstablishment of the vanished empire in the New World. Haiti and Louisiana were to be its two parts, the former a land of rich sugar plantations, the latter capable of producing a multitude of sub-tropical and temperate zone products. The dream faded because the most terrible insurrection of slaves in the annals of North America drove out of Haiti those French who escaped massacre. The ability of the blacks, the difficulties of the terrain, and yellow fever all combined to balk the military efforts of Napoleon to reëstablish white supremacy in the island. Without Haiti distant Louisiana was of little use. Moreover, war with England was again looming in the opening years of the nineteenth century. New Orleans would be hard to defend against a British naval expedition. Napoleon could derive small comfort from the securing of Louisiana from Spain only to have it fall into the lap of England. Events in the Old World were helping to shape the destinies of the New. For the moment, however, the future seemed to Jefferson clouded with uncertainty.

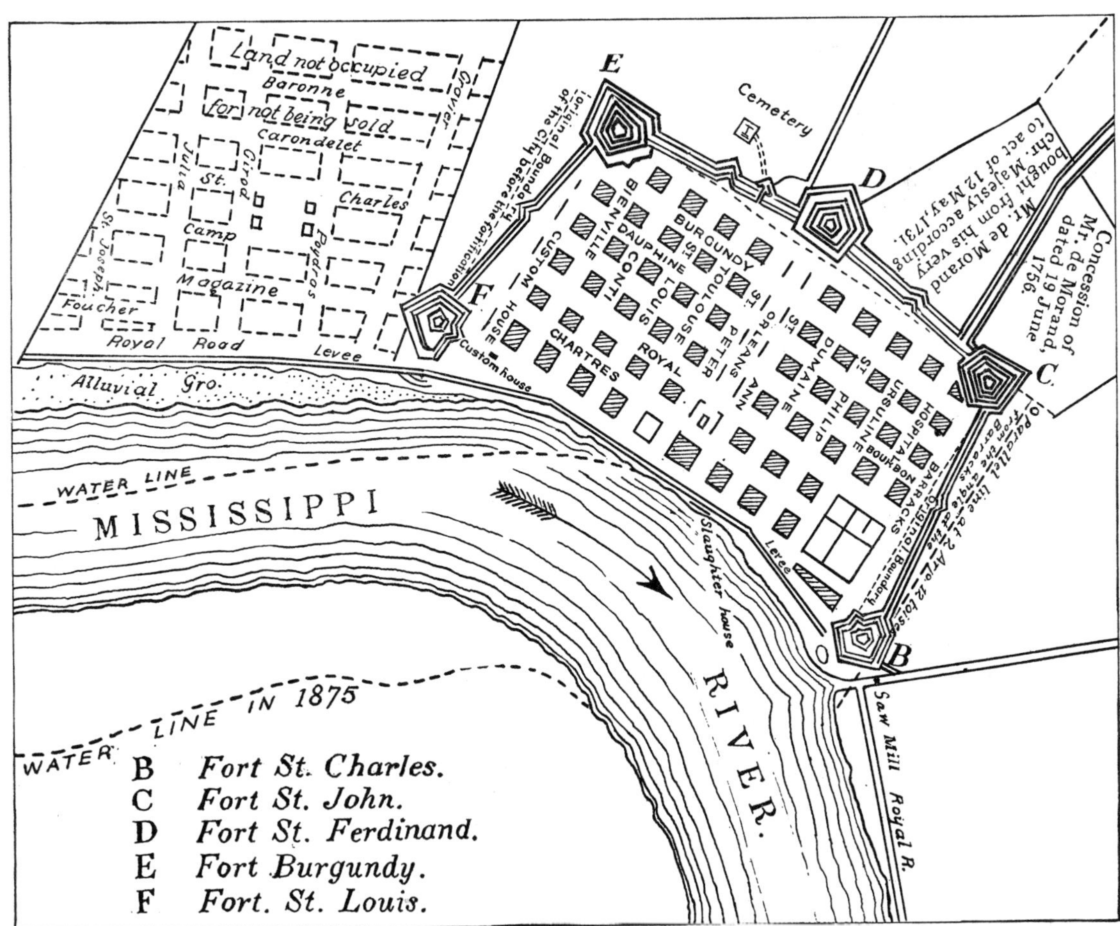

305 Detail redrawn from *A Plan of the City of New Orleans and Adjacent Plantations, compiled in accordance with an ordinance of the Illustrious Ministry and Royal Charter, Dec. 24, 1798, signed Carlos Trudeau.* From a copy, published 1875, in the New York Public Library

PLAN OF NEW ORLEANS

THE old French and Spanish city of New Orleans lay beside the Mississippi, enclosed on three sides by ramparts and on the fourth by the levee which held back the river. Early in the eighteenth century Sieur La Blonde de la Tour had laid out the town with all the regularity of a military camp, the streets running at right angles and the Place d'Armes precisely in the center. At the opening of the nineteenth century the stamp of La Tour could still be seen in the developing population center. The old city, surrounded by ramparts, lay in the midst of an urban area that was sprawling beyond the ancient limits. But the fortifications of the eighteenth century were not abandoned. Five large bastions, each mounting a few rusty cannon, rose one at each corner and one in the rear of the old town. Every day sentries walked before the gates and came to attention with a click when the officer of the day appeared, or when Governor Estevan Miro passed by. At night the portals were carefully closed. Tennesseeans trading down river looked at these fortifications with the eyes of Indian fighters. They felt considerable contempt for the pompous soldiery that upheld the dignity of Spain. A vigorous push, they thought, would demonstrate the hollowness of Spanish power. There were few among them who would not have been glad to participate in an attack.

306 Don Estevan Miro, from a miniature in the Louisiana State Museum, New Orleans

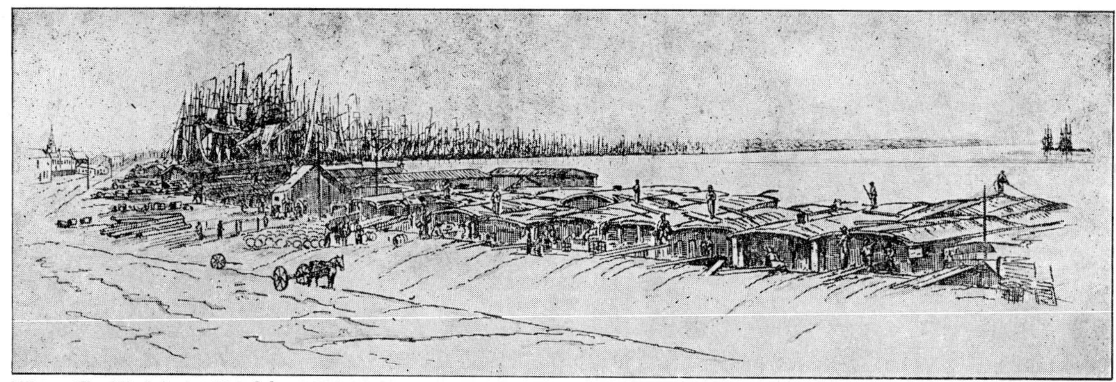

307 The Mississippi at New Orleans, from an etching by W. H. Lizars, in Basil Hall, *Forty Etchings from Sketches Made with the Camera Lucido in North America*, Edinburgh, 1829

COMMERCIAL NEW ORLEANS

DOWN the great Mississippi floated the flatboats and the broadhorns from the Kentucky and Ohio settlements, bearing ham and bacon, wheat, corn, and whiskey. They tied up at the levee beside the sailing ships that put in from the sea. Already New Orleans had become the outlet of the West. In 1802 ships registering some thirty thousand tons had sailed away loaded with products worth two million dollars. The business of the city was done on the levee, piled high with cotton bales, barrels of sugar, produce from up the river and commodities that the merchants had imported from abroad. Here the merchants and traders met and made their deals. From here curious Americans looked upon a city unlike any they had ever seen. Some houses were adobe with half-cylindrical tiled roofs. Others were of brick covered with yellow stucco. Extraordinary wrought-iron work adorned the balconies, gates, and windows. Above the lesser buildings rose the Cabildo and the St. Louis Cathedral. Between them all ran unpaved streets, rough with the mounds of crayfish when the weather was dry, and covered by an inch or two of water by every passing thunder shower. In rainy weather straining teams of mules dragged wagons through a sea of mud. New Orleans was pervaded with the leisurely atmosphere of a town on the edge of the tropics.

308 New Orleans in 1803, from an engraving after the original painting by Boqueta de Woisseri, in the Louisiana State Museum, New Orleans

SOCIAL LIFE

WHEN the cool evening followed the heat of the day, the people of New Orleans laid aside their business, and the social life of the city began to stir. Again the levee was crowded but not by merchants. There were rough dances and carousals on the decks of the ships moored along the river bank. The society which did not fill the coffee houses with chatter came out to walk beside the cool river. Young gallants bowed to the quadroons who with their mothers or chaperons were also at the water's edge. New Orleans society was urbane, at times brilliant. The picturesqueness of the eighteenth century still survived and social intercourse had a Latin flavor. The presence of numbers of negro slaves set it off from the towns of southern France or of Spain and gave it a certain likeness to Mexico City where, at the opening of the nineteenth century, a brilliant white aristocracy ruled lower classes made up of Indians and mixed bloods. Uncouth frontiersmen from up river found in the sprawling city nothing to suggest their own mode of life or thoughts. Riding homeward over the Natchez trail, they gossiped of the strange life they had met on its streets. They commented on the obvious weakness of the Spanish garrison. What an enterprise the conquest of New Orleans would be!

309 The Duplantier Mansion near New Orleans, occupied as Headquarters by General Wilkinson, from an engraving by W. Birch, in his *The Country Seats of the United States of North America*, Springland, Pa., 1808

LOUISIANA PLANTERS

New Orleans was the center of the life of the plantation area which surrounded it. Sugar cane grew on the Louisiana lowlands and fields of cotton could be seen. Not far from the city on the east and north were the villages of the powerful Choctaws, still living in their original habitat and plying a vigorous trade with New Orleans merchants. Pushmataha (No. 227), himself, must have been an occasional visitor at the river port. On Sunday the planters rode into the city to join its people in attendance upon mass. Religious duties over, the town became a scene of frolic and gaiety. Cards and billiards were favorite games and the theater was likely to be well filled. In the spirit and temper of the New Orleans people was little suggestion of the fact that their city was perhaps the chief danger spot of the New World, that with its destiny was linked that of nations. They worked and played and took no heed of the menace from the north. Meanwhile, in 1803, President Jefferson, profoundly worried, sent James Monroe to Paris to coöperate with the American ambassador, Robert R. Livingston, in an effort to buy from the mighty Corsican the island upon which New Orleans rested.

310 Robert R. Livingston, from the portrait by Gilbert Stuart in the possession of Mrs. John Henry Livingston, Clermont, New York, courtesy of the Frick Art Reference Library, New York

ROBERT R. LIVINGSTON, 1746–1813

Just before Monroe arrived in Paris Livingston was astounded by a question of Talleyrand asking what he would give for all of Louisiana. A few days later the American mentioned the matter to Marbois, head of the French treasury. Yes, he knew of it. A midnight conversation followed. Both Frenchman and American haggled over terms. Finally Marbois suggested that America pay just under twelve million dollars and assume the claims of American citizens against France arising out of the informal naval war between the two nations in the last two years of the eighteenth century. Livingston refused to commit himself and went off to confer with Monroe.

311 James Monroe, 1758–1831, from an engraving after a portrait by Gilbert Stuart, in Alcée Fortier, *A History of Louisiana*, Goupil & Co., Paris, 1904

THE PURCHASE OF LOUISIANA

For a few days there was discussion between Marbois and the Americans but the Frenchman stuck to his terms and the Americans yielded. Under the date of April 30, 1803, three treaties were prepared and signed completing the agreement. Tradition has it that when Marbois, Livingston, and Monroe had affixed their signatures, Livingston remarked as they all shook hands: "We have lived long, but this is the noblest work of our whole lives. The treaty which we have just signed has not been obtained by art or dictated by force. From this day the United States take their place among the powers of first rank. The instruments which we have just signed will cause no tears to be shed; they prepare ages of happiness for innumerable generations of human creatures."

312 Marquis de Barbé-Marbois, 1745–1837, from an engraved portrait in Alcée Fortier, *A History of Louisiana*, Goupil & Co., Paris, 1904

THE BOUNDARIES OF THE LOUISIANA PURCHASE

France ceded to the United States the territory of Louisiana — in the words of the treaty — "with the same extent that it now has in the hands of Spain, and that it had when France possessed it, and such as it should be after the treaties subsequently entered into between Spain and other States." What its exact boundaries were no one knew. When pressed by the Americans for a definite statement as to what the territory included Talleyrand with a shrug replied that the United States had made a noble bargain and he supposed that they would make the most of it. The transfer of the Mississippi River to the United States is one of the momentous events in the history of the North American continent. At a single stroke the possibility of sanguinary wars was dissipated. The young republic could look forward to the peaceful development of those immense and fertile plains drained by the Father of Waters.

313 Drawn expressly for *The Pageant of America* by Joseph L. Cain

THE FRENCH OCCUPATION OF NEW ORLEANS

314 Peter Clement Laussat, from a portrait in the Louisiana Historical Society, New Orleans

On Tuesday the twentieth of December 1803, the good people of New Orleans crowded to the gates to watch an American army, drawn up in battle order, march toward their city. Going out to meet it were Spanish troops in the same formation. Twenty-one days before, the Spanish flag had been hauled down and the French tricolor raised. For twenty days New Orleans had been ruled by Peter Clement Laussat, in the name of Napoleon. Now two representatives of the United States, William C. C. Claiborne and General James Wilkinson, were approaching to set up the authority of the American republic. The crowd was little moved by the prospective change. They were accustomed to new rulers. "Ninety-one years before, when scarcely a thousand white men dwelt on her soil, Louis XIV had farmed Louisiana to Antoine Crozat, the merchant monopolist of his day. Crozat, unable to use it, made it over in 1717 to John Law, Director-General of the Mississippi Company, which surrendered it in 1731 to Louis XV, who gave it in 1762 to the King of Spain, who made it over to Napoleon, who sold it to the United States." — John Bach McMaster. Who could tell how long the American possession would last? The wise citizen of New Orleans avoided politics. They were too apt to lead to trouble.

THE TRANSFER OF LOUISIANA

Claiborne and Wilkinson went to the Cabildo where a large crowd of citizens had assembled. The credentials of the Americans were read together with the authority of Laussat to hand over Louisiana to them. The keys of the city were given to Claiborne, and the inhabitants dissolved from their allegiance to Napoleon. Then Claiborne welcomed them as citizens of the United States. A moment later outside the building Frenchmen, Spaniards, and a few Americans watched the tricolor hauled slowly down while the stars and stripes were raised. Midway on the flag staff the two banners met and were saluted. The ceremony was over. Louisiana, including whatever territory that name might designate, was a part of the United States.

AU NOM DE LA RÉPUBLIQUE FRANÇAISE,

LE PREFET COLONIAL,

COMMISSAIRE DU GOUVERNEMENT FRANCAIS,

AUX CITOYENS FRANCAIS,

QUI SE TROUVENT A LA LOUISIANE.

CITOYENS FRANCAIS,

Le Drapeau Français flotte aujourd'hui ſous vos yeux de toutes parts; il vous rappelle, ſur cette terre lointaine, vos combats & vos victoires, votre dévouement & votre valeur.

Il cherche en vain autour de lui le rempart accoutumé de ces formidables baïonnettes, qui l'ont couronné de tant de puiſſance & de gloire.

Mais accueilli par un Allié loyal & fidelle, il ſera gardé par des Louiſianais, ces dignes enfans de nos pères; il le ſera par votre préſence, par votre reſpect, par votre amour.

C'eſt le ſigne chéri de notre ralliement, Citoyens Français, & je le jure devant lui en votre nom & ſur votre honneur: ſon court paſſage dans ces contrées y laiſſera, par votre concours & vos efforts, un long ſouvenir des jours de tranquillité, d'ordre & de concorde, dont il y aura conſtamment offert le ſpectacle & ſignalé la durée.

A la Nouvelle-Orléans, le 8 Frimaire An XII (30 Novembre 1803.)

Signé LAUSSAT.

Par le Préfet Colonial, Commiſſaire du Gouvernement Francais,

Le Secrétaire de la Commiſſion,

Signé DAUGEROT.

315 Proclamation by Laussat to the French Citizens of New Orleans, announcing the transfer of Louisiana to the United States, from the original in the Louisiana Historical Society, New Orleans

316 Ceremonies Attending the Transfer of Louisiana to the United States, from the painting by Thure de Thulstrup (1848–), in the Louisiana Historical Society, New Orleans

317 William C. C. Claiborne, from an engraved portrait by J. B. Longacre after a miniature by A. Duval, in the New York Public Library

WILLIAM C. C. CLAIBORNE, 1775–1817

In the year 1800 when the election of the President was thrown into the House of Representatives, Claiborne was a young representative in Congress from Tennessee. Through the long balloting he had cast the vote of Tennessee steadily for his old friend Jefferson. His reward was the Governorship of Mississippi Territory and then that of Louisiana. Supported by an act of Congress giving him executive, legislative, and judicial powers, Claiborne undertook to govern a people whose languages, French and Spanish, he could neither read nor speak and whose customs and institutions he did not understand. Laussat wrote home that the new Governor was a man of many virtues in private life but weak and awkward, quite unfit to govern a high-spirited people who loved ceremony and polish. Wilkinson, who became military commander, was an adventurer for whom loyalty, either to friend or nation, had no meaning. As Laussat remarked, the new government made a bad beginning.

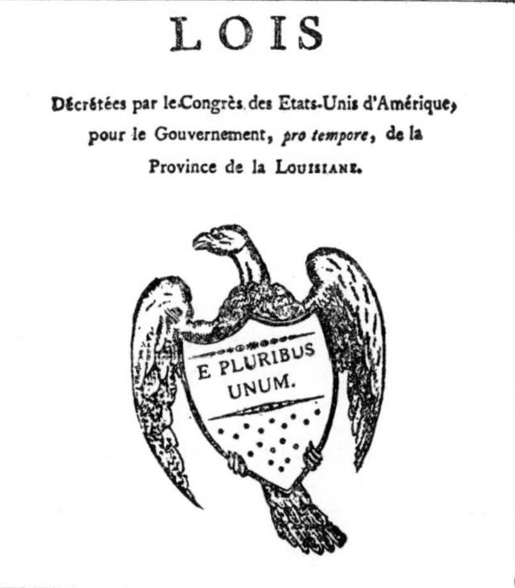

LOIS

Décrétées par le Congrès des Etats-Unis d'Amérique, pour le Gouvernement, *pro tempore*, de la Province de la Louisiane.

318 Title-page of New Decrees of Congress Regulating French Population in the Province of Louisiana, from a photostat in the New York Public Library of the original in the H. H. Bancroft Collection

THE CLAIBORNE ADMINISTRATION

The people of New Orleans resented many of the acts of Claiborne and Wilkinson as studied insults when they were in reality the result of ignorance. The language of the people was abolished in the courts and the citizens compelled to speak to their rulers through interpreters. American judges trained in American and English law set about the administration of Spanish law of which they knew practically nothing. The people had no control over the acts of their Governor nor could they appeal from his decisions. With satisfaction they saw Spanish officers and soldiers remain in the city long after they were supposed to have gone. They believed that this meant that Spain was still trying to recover her colony. When Jefferson appointed a legislative council, five of its members refused to serve.

THOMAS JEFFERSON, 1743–1826

Jefferson had remarked, when the Louisiana Purchase was consummated, that he had stretched his power until it cracked. In 1776 he had written the first draft of the Declaration of Independence. In 1800 he had led the party of democracy to victory. A strange fate now made him the President who set up in Louisiana a colonial government more powerful and more arbitrary than any that England had ever established in America. With curious feelings he must have read the remonstrance signed by some two thousand families and brought to Washington just a year from the month in which the tricolor came down. The folk of Louisiana declared that grievances which the colonies had given as justification for the separation from England had been inflicted on them. The result was the organization of the greater part of the vast area covered by the name Louisiana as the territory of Louisiana, and the southern portion about New Orleans as the territory of Orleans. The people of the southern portion were allowed to elect an assembly and were promised that, when their free population should reach sixty thousand, they should be admitted to the Union.

319 Thomas Jefferson, from the engraving by St. Memin in the Corcoran Gallery of Art, Washington

CAPTAIN MERIWETHER LEWIS

One of the official witnesses at the transfer of Upper Louisiana to the United States was Captain Meriwether Lewis, late private secretary to President Thomas Jefferson, now busy in the frontier village of St. Louis finishing his preparations for an exploring expedition up the Missouri and across the Rocky Mountains to the Pacific. Jefferson had long wanted to know more of that vast unknown land which lay beyond the Mississippi. Lewis had served with distinction under General Wayne at Fallen Timbers, and the President had later found his secretary "brave, prudent, habituated to the Woods, and familiar with Indian manners and character." So he was picked to command an expedition that, under his leadership, became one of the most important exploring ventures of the nineteenth century within the United States. Jefferson wrote of the young commander: "I had now had opportunities of knowing him intimately. Of courage undaunted; possessing a firmness and perserverance of purpose which nothing but impossibilities could divert from its direction; careful as a father of those committed to his charge, yet steady in the maintainance of order and discipline; intimate with the Indian character, customs and principles; habituated to the hunting life; with all these qualifications, as if selected and implanted by nature in one body for this express purpose, I could have no hesitation in confiding the enterprise to him." With Lewis was a young man of his own choice, his good friend William Clark. William was a younger brother of the Revolutionary colonel who had captured Hamilton at Vincennes. He had grown to manhood in Louisville, a Kentucky outpost across the river from the hunting grounds of the Ohio Indians. His education was in frontier life rather than in books. When Lewis wrote him inviting him to share the great adventure on terms of equality and command and honor, he joyfully accepted. So Clark began a long and distinguished career of public service on the frontier. On May 14, 1804, he together with Lewis crossed the Mississippi with forty-three men; and, to quote Clark, "proceeded on under a Jentle brease up the Missourie."

320 Meriwether Lewis, 1774–1809, from an engraving by St. Memin in the Corcoran Gallery of Art, Washington

321 Transfer of Upper Louisiana to the United States, St. Louis, March 9, 1804, from an engraving after the painting by Alfred Russell, in James W. Buel, *Louisiana and the Fair*, World's Progress Co., St. Louis, 1904–05

UP THE MISSOURI

Day after day during the summer months the explorers made their way up the Missouri. They looked out over a rolling, treeless country where herds of bison grazed and where parties of mounted Indians trotted here and there. The President had instructed Lewis to establish trade relations with these red men of the plains and had provided him with presents, uniforms with gold braid, certificates of honor, trinkets, and medals. On the face of the latter was a representation of Jefferson and on its back clasped hands. On August 3 Lewis held a council with some chiefs of the Otoes, a branch of the Pawnees, on a cliff about twenty miles from the present city of Omaha and named the highland Council Bluff. Medals and presents were distributed. The journey up the Missouri was a long, hard grind. Sand bars and innumerable snags were encountered. The boats were poled ahead or towed by men on the bank. Hunters were always out to keep the party supplied with game. At night the weary men were so harassed by "ticks and musquiters" that smudge fires were often necessary. The average progress was nine miles per day.

322 Lewis and Clark Monument, Charles Keck, sculptor, Charlottesville, Virginia, photo by Louis H. Dreyer, New York

WITH THE INDIANS

North of Council Bluff Lewis and Clark came into the country of the Sioux, dangerous Indians who were among the best fighters on the plains. The explorers held councils with them but they were often intractable. Clark, experienced in the ways of the redskins, went ashore in a pirogue at one place to make peace with a party that seemed hostile. The Indians seized the boat and were insolent. Clark whipped out his sword and motioned his crew to prepare for defense. Bows and arrows rattled as the Indians got themselves into a good position to fight. The little swivel cannon on the pirogue was swung to face them. There were loud words on both sides as the Indians cautiously drew back a space. Then Clark held out his hand; but the chiefs refused it. Turning to his boat he started to push off when the leading redskins, having changed their minds, hurried into the water offering their hands. Such were Clark's methods. His courage avoided a battle and paved the way for a friendly powwow. The party rowed on through the country of the Sioux and, when heavy frosts warned of approaching winter, reached the villages of the Mandans. Here they built, in what is now North Dakota, a fort among a people less warlike and more sedentary than the Sioux. The winter with the Mandans brought into sharp relief some serious defects in the organization of the expedition. Practically all of the men, including the leaders, had been picked for their ability to get on in the wilderness. The captains knew Indian ways after the manner of the frontiersman rather than the ethnologist. There was no scientist among them, though Lewis had an amateur interest in botany. Before starting he had learned the rudiments of determining latitude and longitude. The lack of trained observers to bring back exact information concerning the region traversed could not, however, be charged entirely to neglect. President Jefferson complained of the complete lack of trained men available for such a task. Science was still young and America as yet far from European centers of learning. The primary object of the expedition, however, was to discover fur trading possibilities. A most surprising omission in organizing the expedition was the absence of a physician.

323 Mandan Village on the Missouri, from a lithograph after a drawing by Charles Bodmer, in Maximilian, *Travels in North America, 1832–34*, London, 1838–43

CHARBONEAU

AMONG the Mandans Lewis and Clark employed a Frenchman, one Charboneau, as guide for the coming summer. He had married a young squaw, Sacajawea, who had been born among the Shoshones in the mountains to the west. As a girl she had been captured by the Minatarees, neighbors to the Mandans on the north, and sold to Charboneau. When Lewis paid visits to the villages near the Mandans, this "Bird Woman" sometimes proved of great help. Clark's negro slave knew a little French. Through him Lewis could communicate with Charboneau. Charboneau translated to his wife who talked with the Indians. With such faulty means of communication it was impossible for Lewis to take full advantage of his opportunity to study the culture of the Mandans and their neighbors. In fact for the early part of the winter stay he was absorbed in the task of counteracting the influence of some traders of the British Northwest Company who told the Indians that these strange white men who had come among them were but the vanguard of an army of settlers who would overrun their country and destroy their game. Some Mandans lived to verify this evil prophecy. For the time being, however, Lewis quieted their fears and aroused their interest by telling them that traders from the United States would speedily come among them with better and cheaper goods than they had ever known before. When the spring floods had washed the ice out of the river, Lewis and Clark again turned their faces toward the west. With them were Charboneau and the Bird Woman. During the winter she had borne a son whom that summer she carried over the mountains to the Pacific.

324 An Indian Warrior of the Upper Missouri, from a lithograph after a drawing, *Minataree Warrior*, by Charles Bodmer in Maximilian, *Travels in the United States, 1832–34*, London, 1838–43

THE GREAT FALLS

THE country grew rougher as the party pushed westward. Moreover, the leaders of the expedition, instructed to be on the lookout for new and unfamiliar forms of animal and plant life, had no difficulty in discovering the presence of brown-gray bears larger and fiercer than any in the eastern woods. The grizzly had entered the annals of civilized America. These creatures had not learned to be wary of the white man. With a terrifying ferocity they rushed more than one member of the exploring party. Day after day the boats continued westward. The hunters, working along the shore, met bighorns, monster elk, antelope, and great herds of bison. They noted the coyote and the fact that wolves were increasing in number. The party made a feast on beaver, Lewis finding "the tale a most delicious morsel." The country was full of rattlesnakes. And Lewis did not fail to record: "Our trio of pests still invade and obstruct us on all occasions, these are the Musquetoes eye knats and prickly pears, equal to any three curses that ever poor Egypt laboured under, except the Mahometant yoke." In June the party reached the great fork and the leaders rightly decided that the southern branch was the Missouri. At the fork they hid their largest boat and made a cache of provisions, salt, tools, and ammunition. Up the river they went with their lightened load. Leaving Clark in charge of the boats, Lewis pushed on ahead until spray hanging above the river and the roar of falling water led him to the Great Falls of the Missouri. For a time he sat enjoying "this truly magnificent and sublimely grand object which has from the commencement of time been concealed from civilized man."

325 The Great Falls of the Missouri River, from a lithograph by Sarony after a drawing by G. Sohon, in *Reports of Explorations and Surveys . . . for a railroad*, Washington, 1855

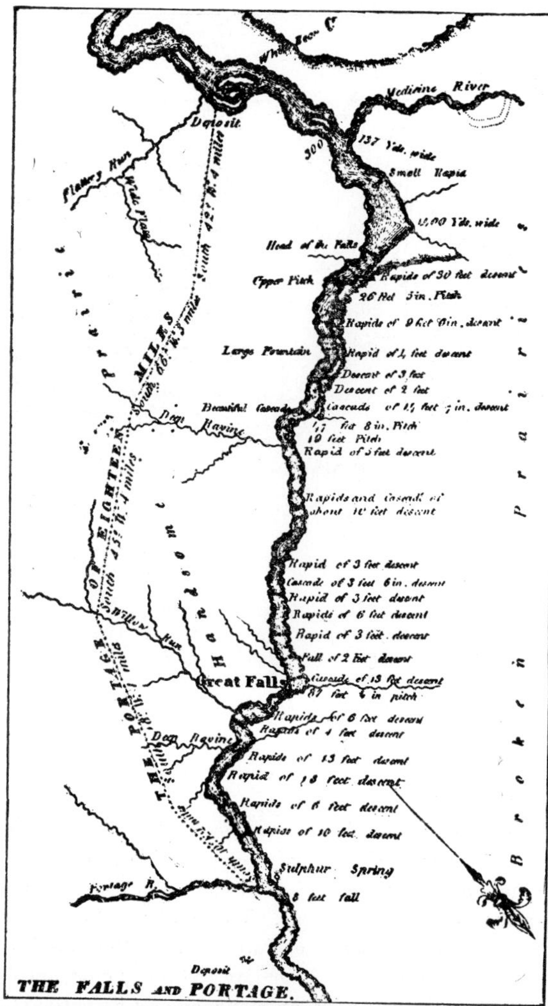

326 Survey by William Clark of the Vicinity of the Great Falls of Missouri, from an engraving in *History of the Expedition under the Command of Captains Lewis and Clarke*, Philadelphia, 1814

THE PORTAGE

THE Great Falls made a portage necessary. Drawing the boats on shore, the voyagers mounted them on wheels roughly shaped from a lone cottonwood on the bank. For thirteen days the party dragged the boats across dry plains trenched with the trails of bison. More than once the willow axles broke and had to be repaired. At last they reached safe water above the falls and again turned the prows of their boats west with the Rockies in sight. The map is a good example of the type of information that the expedition brought to the Government of the United States.

AT THE THREE FORKS

ON July 25, after days of weary poling, the exploring party reached the spot where three rivers unite to make the Missouri. Jefferson, Madison, and Gallatin were the names given to the streams. They paused to discover the possibilities of the various branches. They were now in the country of the Bird Woman. She told them that near this very confluence she had been taken prisoner five years before. Anxiously she scanned the horizon for the smokes of her people. For the party the finding of a Shoshone village had become a matter of vital importance. The towering Rockies loomed just to the west, their snowcapped peaks in full view. Horses and guides were needed for the crossing of this great divide. Lewis and Clark pushed westward up the Jefferson. Rough mountains, scantily clad with pitch pine, rose on either side of the river. The shallows and rapids increased, until the men were worn out with pushing and hauling the boats.

327 The Lewis and Clark Party at the Three Forks, from the painting by E. S. Paxson, in the State Capitol, Helena, Mont., courtesy of the Historical Society of Montana

MEETING THE SHOSHONES

328 The Lewis and Clark Party Meeting the Shoshones, from the painting by Charles M. Russell in the State Capitol, Helena, Mont., courtesy of the Montana Historical Society

FOR the hunters the going on land became harder because the prickly pear on the uplands filled their moccasins with thorns, and other thorn bushes covered the river bottoms with dense brush. Anxiously the captains looked for signs of Indians. The river valley became a virtual canyon. On August 12 the party reached the source of the Missouri, a cold spring "issuing from the base of a low mountain or hill." The next day Lewis, traveling with a few followers in advance of the main party, came upon a group of Shoshone squaws to whom he made presents of beads, moccasin awls, pewter looking-glasses, and paint. The women took them into camp where the warriors, hearing the story of the squaws, embraced the strangers until "we were all caressed and besmeared with their grease and paint till I was heartily tired of their national hug." For three days Lewis and his small band were alone with the Shoshones, able to communicate with them only in the sign language of the plains. The Indians suspected treachery when Clark did not appear. The leader of the overland exploring expedition was in grave danger of his life.

THE BIRD WOMAN

THESE Shoshones were a weak people driven about by their more powerful neighbors, the Blackfeet. The band that Lewis had encountered was making, half starved, for the bison country down the Missouri. At last Clark with Charboneau and the Bird Woman arrived in camp. With a cry Sacajawea recognized a young woman who had been her playmate as a girl and who, captured at the same time as the Bird Woman, had managed to escape. "The meeting of those people was really affecting," wrote Lewis. Meanwhile the Shoshone chief held a council with Lewis and Clark in his lodge. The peace pipe was passed and smoked. The white men needed horses and the Shoshones had many. They hoped also that the chief himself, who seemed an intelligent and sensible man, would guide them through that bewildering maze of gulches and canyons that lay immediately to the west of them. They sent for the Bird Woman to act as interpreter. She listened to the name of the chieftain, rose quickly, stepped to his side, and put her blanket around him. In Cameahwait she had recognized her brother. The tribe was filled with joy at this recovery of the long-lost sister of the chief. Council followed council. The Indians proved shrewd bargainers and greatly diminished the white man's trading goods in selling them twenty-nine horses. The contract, however, was finally made. Then Cameahwait led the white men to the northern Nez Percé trail followed from time immemorial by Indians traveling across the confusion of ridges between the upper waters of the Missouri and those of the Columbia.

329 Statue of Sacajawea, the Bird Woman, by Alice Cooper, in City Park, Portland, Oregon

our rout lay along the ridge of a high mountain
course S 20. W. - 18. ms. used the snow for cooking. -
Thursday September 19th 1805.
Set out this morning a little after sunrise and
continued our rout about the same course of yesterday
or S. 20. W. for 6 miles when the ridge terminated and
we to our inexpressable joy discovered a large
tract of Prairie country lying to the S.W. and widening as it appeared to extend to the W. through that
plain the Indian informed us that the Columbia
river, (in which we were in surch) run. this plain
appeared to be about 60 Miles distant, but our guide
assured us that we should reach it's borders tomorrow
the appearance of this country, our only hope for
subsistance greately revived the spirits of the party
already reduced and much weakend for the want of
food. - the country is thickly covered with a very

330 Entry in the Diary of Meriwether Lewis, recording the Crossing of the Continental Divide, from the original in the American Philosophical Society, Philadelphia

CROSSING THE CONTINENTAL DIVIDE

THE trail was difficult and dangerous. Many times it led along the brink of a precipitous cliff. The air was cold and the party pushed ahead in the teeth of roaring mid-September blizzards. Game was scarce and, as a consequence, rations scanty. The horse that fell beneath its load, worn out by the climb, was promptly killed and eaten. The men became thin and often ill. The leaders were discouraged. Such was the background for the emotion which went into the writing of this page. "Thursday September 19th 1805. Set out this morning a little after sunrise and continued our rout about the same course of yesterday or S. 20 W. for 6 miles when the ridge terminated and we to our inexpresable joy discovered a large tract of Prairie country lying to the S.W. and widening as it appeared to extend to the W. Through that plain the Indian informed us that the Columbia river, (in which we were in surch) run. This plain appeared to be about sixty miles distant, but our guide assured us that we should reach its border tomorrow. The appearance of this country our only hope for subsistance greately revived the spirits of the party already reduced and much weakened for the want of food. . . . " This is in the hand of Lewis.

THE COLUMBIA RAPIDS

THE explorers finally reached the Columbia where they found friendly Indians drying salmon. Save for the rapids in the gorge of the upper river the path to the ocean was easy. Long before they reached the rapids they had built boats by burning out logs after the Indian fashion. Of this adventure Clark wrote: "As the portage of our canoes over this high rock would be impossible with our strength, and the only danger in passing thro those narrows was the whorls and swills arriseing from the compression of the water, and which I thought (as also our principal waterman Peter Crusat) by good stearing we could pass down safe, accordingly I determined to pass through this place, not with standing the horred appearance of this agitated gut swelling, boiling and whorling in every direction from which the top of the rock did not appear as bad as when I was in it; however we passed safe to the astonishment of the Inds." These "Inds" were an inferior lot, dirty and flea-bitten. In their clothing and utensils they showed the results of contact with white traders from the coast. They also were hard bargainers, and Lewis and Clark paid well for the dogs they bought to vary the steady diet of fish which was proving harmful to some of the men.

331 The Dalles of the Upper Columbia River, from a photograph. © Weister Co., Portland, Oregon

332 Columbia River Landscape, from a photograph. © Weister Co., Portland, Oregon

333 Mount Hood from the Columbia River, from an engraving by R. Hinshelwood after a drawing by R. S. Gifford, in *Picturesque America*, New York, 1847

DOWN THE COLUMBIA

Down the broad Columbia the voyageurs floated to the sea. As they passed Mount Hood, they began to notice the tide. Finally, on November 7, there was "Great joy in camp, we are in *view* of the *Ocian*. . . . This great Pacific Ocean which we have been so long anxious to See, and the roring or noise made by the waves brakcing on the rockey shores may be heard distinctly." Eight days later, after passing through a pelting rainstorm of many days' duration, they rounded a blustery point and found a "butiful Sand beech thro which runs a Small river from the Hills." They had achieved their objective; the continent had been crossed by an American exploring party. Long since, they had left behind American soil. The land through which ran the course of the beautiful Columbia was a region of vague and conflicting claims. Over its rich valley bottoms and forested mountain slopes lay the shadows of Spain, Great Britain, and the United States which had just purchased Louisiana. An American sea captain, Gray, had discovered the mouth of the Columbia. The journey of Lewis and Clark vastly strengthened the claim of the young nation whose frontier was pushing steadily westward.

THE WINTER ON THE PACIFIC

Lewis and Clark wintered close to the Pacific among the Clatsop Indians. The men were busy with preparations for the return across the mountains while the leaders filled their journals with accounts of the customs and language of their neighbors. The mosquitoes and gnats of the summer had passed but their unhappy memory was kept fresh by the fleas which migrated in vast numbers from the Indian huts to the camp of the white men. The first task of the morning was to rid the blankets of these unwelcome visitors. Skins were dressed and leather clothing prepared for the summer trip through the forest. A detail spent two months in boiling twenty gallons of salt from sea water. In March Lewis prepared a list of the names of the men in the party with a record of their feat in crossing the continent and handed it to a native chief with instructions to give it to the first white trader who visited their country. Then, with many men half sick from improper food, Lewis and Clark turned their faces eastward and, on March 23, began the long journey toward home. With them still were Charboneau and Sacajawea.

334 Lewis and Clark on the Columbia, from the painting by Frederic Remington. © P. F. Collier & Son Co.; reproduced by permission

335 The Headwaters of the Yellowstone River, from an engraving in the New York Public Library

THE RETURN

Coming home the explorers crossed the continental divide through Lo Lo Pass on June 20. Again in the country where the streams flowed into the Mississippi the party separated for exploring trips. Lewis struck north into the country of the Blackfeet to look for a better pass over the mountains. He found no pass and encountered hostile braves. But he led his party safely back. Clark, meanwhile, took his band overland to the Yellowstone. Here he built a boat and floated down this river, mapping and describing many of its famous features and finally joined Lewis where it debouches into the Missouri. On August 14 they were back among the Mandans. Here they left Sacajawea and her family, for her French husband wished to stay among the Indians. Clark expressed his regard for the Bird Woman by offering to take and educate her nineteen months old babe. The party put off in their boats, passed again the country of the dangerous Sioux, and on September 23 fired a small cannon to announce their arrival to the villagers of St. Louis. That day Clark wrote a letter to his brother and Lewis sent one off to Jefferson.

THE DEATH OF LEWIS

On August 18, 1805, while with the Shoshone kinsfolk of the Bird Woman Meriwether Lewis wrote in his journal: "This day I completed my thirty-first year, and conceived that I had in all human probability now existed about half the period which I am to remain. . . . I had as yet done but little . . . to further the happiness of the human race, or to advance the information of the succeeding generation. . . . I resolved, in future, to redouble my exertions and at least indeavor to promote those two primary objects of human existence, by giving them the aid of that portion of talents which nature and fortune have bestowed on me; or in future, to live *for mankind,* as I have heretofore lived *for myself.*" For two years after the return from the expedition he was Governor of Louisiana Territory. In 1809 when riding with only a servant along the Natchez trace on his way to Washington, he stopped for the night at a lonely inn some seventy miles below Nashville. Here he was murdered probably for the money and for certain documents on his person. In later years Tennessee raised a marble column above his grave.

336 Monument over the Grave of Captain Lewis, Lewis County, Tennessee, from an engraving in O. D. Wheeler, *The Trail of Lewis and Clark,* G. P. Putnam's Sons, New York, 1904

ROBERT GRAY, 1755–1806

337 Captain Robert Gray, from an engraving by Theodore Gegaux (1916), after an old sketch, courtesy of the Oregon Historical Society, Portland

THE death of Lewis was nearly contemporaneous with that of another explorer, Robert Gray. In October 1787, this promising Boston mariner had put out to sea from his home port in a ninety-ton sloop, the *Lady Washington.* With him in command of the *Columbia,* a much larger vessel, was Captain John Kendrick. In September of the following year Gray reached Nootka Sound on the Alaskan coast bent on prosecuting the fur trade with the Indians. Russians were already active in the Aleutian Islands to the north. Gray discovered, moreover, that the ubiquitous British had preceded him. Kendrick put in his appearance some weeks later and the two American vessels cruised among the islands from the Strait of Juan de Fuca to Nootka Sound. A rich load of furs was accumulated and the two American vessels, following the example of the British, crossed the Pacific to China where the cargoes were disposed of. Kendrick in the *Lady Washington* returned to Nootka Sound. Gray took the *Columbia* around the world, reaching an excited and enthusiastic Boston in August 1790. In the early summer, 1791, Gray with the *Columbia* was again in the northwest Pacific. On this trip his boldness and skill made him the discoverer of that great river to which he gave the name of the ship he commanded. Fourteen years elapsed between that time when Gray had sailed up the broad Columbia and the day when Lewis and Clark looked for the first time on the Pacific. During the interval many traders, Englishmen, Russians, and Americans, had come by sea to prosecute the fur trade with the Indians of the northwest coast. Lewis and Clark demonstrated that this far-away country could be reached by land.

JOHN JACOB ASTOR, 1763–1848

OF all Americans John Jacob Astor was probably the one most interested in the story of the adventures of Lewis and Clark. Immediately he began the formulation of plans for a continent-wide undertaking. New York should be the center of his vast enterprise. Mackinac should control the fur trade of the Great Lakes, St. Louis that of the western plains, and at the mouth of the Columbia a fort should be built which should dominate the fur trade of the far Northwest and should deal directly with China. In 1808, two years after the return of Lewis and Clark, the American Fur Company was incorporated. The organization of a subsidiary company, the Pacific Fur Company, followed, Astor furnishing the entire capital. Personal risks, however, were to be borne by ten partners. Astor recruited his associates in the Pacific enterprise for the most part from experienced traders from the British Northwest Company, men who knew the plains and the Rocky Mountains and who knew also the difficulties and the tricks of the fur trade. In July 1810, a party of Astor men filed down the streets of Montreal to their boats and turned their faces toward Mackinac and the mouth of the Columbia. In September a small ship, the *Tonquin,* dropped down New York Bay and pointed her prow toward Cape Horn. Astor expected that the two expeditions would arrive on the Columbia the following year at about the same time. His hopes were high; he did not realize that he had chosen ill when he picked an American with no western experience to lead the overland expedition and when he put a petty tyrant and martinet in command of the *Tonquin.*

338 John Jacob Astor, from the portrait, artist unknown, in the possession of Vincent Astor, Rhinebeck, N. Y.

339 Map of the Astoria Region, from Grace Flandrau, *Astor and the Oregon Country*, published for the Great Northern Railroad Co.

THE FOUNDING OF ASTORIA

ON May 25, 1811, the *Tonquin* came to anchor in the quiet waters of the Columbia. Land was a welcome sight to the Astor partners on board who more than once had been driven to the verge of mutiny by Captain Thorn. He hurried the Astor men in their selection of a site for their fort and in the unloading of tools and a part of the supplies. He was anxious to be off up the coast to the north to anticipate the British in trade with the Indians. In June the *Tonquin* was in Nootka Sound and her decks were covered with Indians plying an eager trade. Thorn had no experience with redskins and had never visited the region before. He refused, moreover, to heed the advice of men who understood the Indian character. Among these was Alexander McKay, formerly of the Northwest Company, the ablest of the Astor partners who had rounded the Horn. McKay, who had gone up the coast with Thorn as supercargo, warned the irascible sea captain of the risk he ran in letting too many Indians on board. These natives were no innocent barbarians but a fierce tribe of traders and warriors who knew the ways of the white man from long and bitter experience with the ships that had come to their shores. When Thorn lost control of himself and struck one of the redskin chieftains, the *Tonquin* was in danger. Nevertheless with singular lack of judgment Thorn permitted the Alaskans on the following day to swarm over the decks of the ship and, at first, perceived no significance in the fact that they would trade only for knives. Too late he ordered up the sails. He and McKay were among the first to fall. A handful of unarmed survivors who had escaped the murderous onslaught waited out the day below. Their plight was desperate. They were too few to take the ship back up the Columbia; to put off in an open boat meant certain death at the hands of the natives. On the morning after the disaster the Indians flocked again to the *Tonquin* to plunder. Suddenly an explosion split the air and the sea was covered with fragments of the ship and of human bodies, both white and red. The white men had sold their lives for a dear price.

AT THE MOUTH OF THE COLUMBIA

THE loss of the *Tonquin*, below whose decks on her last voyage was the greater part of the trading supplies and the ammunition intended for the Astoria trading post, was an irreparable blow. The men on shore, however, had no choice but to persist and to await the coming of the overland expedition. The summer was used up in clearing away the mammoth firs from a small space and in erecting a fort. In July, in the midst of the activities of the Astor men, David Thompson, a partner of the Northwest Company, beached his boat before Astoria and hailed his old friends who had cast their lot with Astor. He was given a royal welcome, one that surprised a little some of the Americans in the Astor party. His visit, which marked the climax of a difficult journey through Canada across the continent, was evidence that the American undertaking on the Columbia was not to go unchallenged. Autumn brought no news of Astor's overland expedition.

340 The *Tonquin* in the Mouth of the Columbia, from an engraving by Avery after a drawing by Parsons, in Gabriel Franchère, *A Narrative of a Voyage to the Northwest Coast of America in the Years 1811, 12, 13 and 14*, New York, 1854

THE OVERLAND EXPEDITION

BAD leadership brought the overland expedition to ruin. Yet Wilson Price Hunt, the commander, had associated with him men of experience and ability like Donald Mackenzie, formerly of the Northwest Company, and Ramsay Crooks. The latter had traded on his own for a time at Council Bluffs and had later joined the Missouri Fur Company. He finally cast his lot with Astor. Hunt wintered four hundred and fifty miles up the Missouri from St. Louis in order to avoid the expense of staying in the town. He was compelled to return in the spring, however, to replace the American hunters and trappers who had deserted him because of the poor fare he gave them. In the early months of 1811 Manuel Lisa, a St. Louis trader, raced past Hunt and preceded him to the Indian villages of the upper Missouri. Lisa, however, assisted the Astor men to provide themselves with horses from the Arikaras for their journey across the plains through the country of the Crows. Hunt had decided to abandon the route of Lewis and Clark because of the menace of the Blackfeet and to pass to the southward of the hunting grounds of that fierce tribe. In the middle of October the party was across the continental divide and camped on the banks of the Snake. Making no effort to explore the stream Hunt abandoned his horses and entrusted his baggage and men to fifteen "crazy and frail" canoes. Eight days later he discovered his mistake when he saw the Snake enter its canyon and tumble over endless rapids toward the Pacific. Leaving behind most of their supplies, the party divided and continued on foot. Some reached Astoria in January, others in February. In April Stuart's brigade returning to Astoria from its winter trading in the interior picked up along the banks of the Columbia Ramsay Crooks and a companion "so changed and emaciated . . . that our people for some time could scarcely recognize them to be white men."

341 Wilson Price Hunt, from a portrait, artist unknown, in the Missouri Historical Society, St. Louis

THE FALL OF ASTORIA

IN the summer of 1812 England and the United States entered upon war. The news reached Astoria via the Northwesters in the following December. Meanwhile Astor had besought President Madison in vain to send a warship to protect the distant outpost of American commerce on the banks of the Columbia. In 1813 the partners of the Pacific Fur Company in Astoria sold the property to the Northwest Company at a heavy sacrifice. Astor's men were mostly British subjects. Some of the leaders made good terms for themselves with the Canadian company to which they had once belonged. The Astor enterprise on the Pacific was at an end. Its failure was due only in part to the inability of the United States to defend it in time of war. Astoria, to be sure, could be attacked from the sea, but removal of the stores and personnel inland beyond the reach of a naval expedition was both easy and feasible. In some well-defended spot the Astorians could have maintained themselves and awaited the end of the war. The Northwest Company would have been quite incapable of dislodging them. The ultimate responsibility for the failure of the enterprise rests, therefore, on Astor himself, who entrusted the carrying out of the undertaking to a group of men almost all of whom were British subjects and who abandoned him when confronted with the crisis of war.

342 Astoria in 1813, from an engraving by Avery after a drawing by Parsons, in Franchère, *Narrative of a Voyage to the Northwest Coast*, New York, 1854

343 General William Clark, from the painting by Charles Willson Peale, in Independence Hall, Philadelphia

GENERAL WILLIAM CLARK, 1770–1838

Clark impressed his name deeply on the country which he had helped to explore. He was Governor of the territory of Missouri from 1813 to 1820 when Missouri became a state. He later became Superintendent of Indian Affairs and wielded a wide and beneficent influence among the red men. He did not forget the family of the Bird Woman, whose son he had offered to adopt; for, doubtless through his influence, the old Frenchman, Charboneau, was appointed official interpreter at the Missouri sub-agency in 1837. The troubles of his older brother, George Rogers Clark, weighed upon his mind. He sought unsuccessfully to get the Virginia legislature to pay the debts which Clark had contracted to outfit his Illinois campaign. When the elder Clark could not pay them, the younger brother did. The death of William Clark marked the passing of one of the great figures of the frontier.

THE SOURCE OF THE MISSISSIPPI

While Lewis and Clark, westward bound, were approaching the confluence of the Jefferson, Madison, and Gallatin rivers, where the Bird Woman had been captured, a young first lieutenant of the First Infantry (in which Lewis was a captain) saluted his chief, General James Wilkinson, and received orders to explore the source of the Mississippi. Lieutenant Zebulon Pike manifested, when thrown on his own, unusual courage and executive ability. Mere exploration was but a part of the objective assigned him. He was to report on sites for military posts, to enter into treaties with the Indians, to bring about peace, if possible, between the Sioux and the Chippewas, and to discover everything he could concerning the trading activities of the Northwest Company south of the international border and the extent of their influence with the northern tribes. Building a stockade at Little Falls which was the limit of navigation for his boats, Pike struck northward with a small force. The rigorous winter of a continental interior froze the streams and covered the land with a mantle of snow. Under this handicap Pike erred in his location of the source of the Mississippi. But the inclemency of the season did not prevent his returning with an excellent map of the region. Pike reported that the party returning "reached the lower Sac [Sauk] village on the evening of the 27th [April]. . . . They stopped at some islands about ten miles above Salt river, where there were pigeon roosts. The men, in fifteen minutes, brought two hundred and ninety-eight on board the boats. The imagination can scarcely conceive the numbers of these birds here found." — *An Account of a Voyage up the Mississippi, etc.*, 66. Pike reported to his commanding officer in April 1806, bringing valuable information and treaties of peace.

344 Itasca Lake, the Source of the Mississippi, from a lithograph after a drawing by Seth Eastman, after a sketch by H. R. Schoolcraft, in the possession of the publishers

PIKE'S SECOND EXPEDITION

In the summer of 1806, that summer in which the West was filled with speculation regarding the mysterious designs of Aaron Burr, who the year before had made a journey through the region, the shifty General Wilkinson sent Captain Pike upon an expedition toward the ancient Spanish settlements in New Mexico. The young commander was to bring about a peace between the Kansas and the Osages, to "establish a good understanding" with the Yanktons and the Comanches, and to "ascertain the direction, extent, and navigation of the Arkansaw and Red rivers." The boundary line between Spanish Mexico and the Louisiana territory had never been determined. Accurate information concerning this region might be of great diplomatic importance. For the same reason the importance of the friendship of the Indians in the region was not to be ignored. Talk of a war with Spain still persisted in the western settlements even after the Louisiana Purchase. Pike, so far as is known, had no knowledge of the fact that his commanding officer was a Spanish pensioner as well as an officer in the army of the United States. After a spirited dialogue with a dangerous party of Pawnees in which he showed the greatest bravery, Pike pushed up the Arkansas River nearly to the present site of Leadville in Colorado. He paused en route to essay a mountain which towered above him on the north and so gave his name to Pike's Peak. This adventure was in the middle of November.

345 General James Wilkinson, 1757–1825, from the portrait by James Sharpless (1751–1811), in Independence Hall, Philadelphia

346 General Zebulon M. Pike, from the portrait by Charles Willson Peale, in Independence Hall, Philadelphia

347 Pike's Capture by the Spaniards, from the painting by Frederic Remington. © P. F. Collier & Son Co.; reproduced by their permission

CAPTURE BY THE SPANIARDS

December and early January found Pike and his party floundering in deep snow in the foothills of the Rockies, searching for the headwaters of the Red River. Finally Pike crossed the Sangre de Christo Range and reached, on January 30, 1807, the Rio Grande del Norte. On the west bank of the river he built a stockade. From here one Dr. Robinson, a volunteer physician who had accompanied the expedition, made his way to Santa Fé — ostensibly to collect a debt, actually to spy out this ancient Spanish stronghold. In February Pike was made a prisoner by a Spanish military detachment too strong for him to fight. His expedition was at an end and his notes and papers were taken from him to find a resting place in the archives at Mexico City. Here they were discovered by Herbert E. Bolton. Later they were courteously transferred by Mexico to the archives of the War Department at Washington. In the summer of 1807 Pike, after having received nothing but courteous treatment at the hands of his captors, was delivered to Wilkinson at Nacogdoches. His sudden emergence came at a most unhappy time, for the settlements of the Mississippi Valley were aflame with excitement regarding the Burr conspiracy in which affair Pike's commanding officer was deeply involved. Pike's disclaimer of connection with the conspiracy seems to have been accepted. Six years later the young explorer, now a brigadier general, was killed at York (Toronto) in the second year of the War of 1812.

348 Aaron Burr, 1756–1836, from a miniature, artst unknown, in the Louisiana Historical Society, New Orleans

THE BURR CONSPIRACY

Aaron Burr of New York concluded his public life by taking position in the public mind of his day as the arch conspirator, next to Benedict Arnold, in the history of the United States. The mystery of the Burr intrigue, which remains as yet unsolved, and the important personages involved in one way or another in the episode made it in its time an affair of transcendent public interest. Burr intrigued with the British and Spanish ministers at Washington, with General Wilkinson at New Orleans, and with Blennerhasset, a wealthy and gullible Irishman who owned a large estate on the Ohio. At the island home of the latter a small force of armed men were assembled in the autumn of 1806 and made their way under Burr in December and January down the Mississippi in a flotilla of boats. President Jefferson issued a proclamation calling upon the group to disband. General Wilkinson at New Orleans proclaimed martial law and made some bombastic pronouncements. Burr abandoned his men, took flight, was apprehended, and arrested for treason. Brought before Judge John Marshall, sitting in the circuit court of the United States, Burr was acquitted of treason for lack of evidence. But the episode forced him to flee the country. The Spanish minister, Yrujo, remarked of Wilkinson who played a prominent, though somewhat unhappy, rôle in the Burr trial, that "he has sacrificed Burr in order to obtain advantages." Yrujo prophesied that the general would apply to the Spanish Government for special compensation for extraordinary service. The Burr-Wilkinson episode is the final manifestation of the separatist tendencies that for more than two decades had marked the spirit of the West.

349 Marquis De Casa Yrujo, from the portrait by Gilbert Stuart, in the possession of Thomas McKean, Philadelphia

CONSTITUTION

OR

FORM OF GOVERNMENT

OF THE

STATE OF LOUISIANA

BY AUTHORITY

NEW-ORLEANS:

PRINTED BY Jo BAR BAIRD, PRINTER TO THE CONVENTION

1812.

350 Title-page of the pamphlet in the New York Public Library

THE STATEHOOD OF LOUISIANA

In 1812 Louisiana became a state. The old French settlement at the mouth of the Mississippi was thereby incorporated in the nation on an equal footing with each of the thirteen original commonwealths. In that year, which marked the outbreak of the second war with England, most Westerners believed that but a short time would elapse before Canada would be severed from the British Empire and become a part of the growing United States. This dream was destined never to come true. Two years after the war was over the territory on the east bank of the Mississippi was erected, in 1817, into the state of Mississippi. Another two years found Alabama in the Union. The frontier had crossed the Mississippi and was well advanced up the slope of the Great Plains toward the snow-capped Rockies.

CHAPTER VIII

TRADERS AND TRAPPERS ON THE GREAT PLAINS

ON that vast grassland which, west of the Mississippi, slopes gradually up to the Rockies, a spectacular and picturesque drama was played out in the eighteenth and nineteenth centuries. When, in the sixteenth and seventeenth centuries, an occasional Spaniard or Frenchman lifted a corner of the curtain, seemingly limitless plains could be seen, dotted here and there by masses of trees, huddled close to the river banks. Herds of bison of incredible size grazed over the summer bunch grass, or trampled wide tracks in the winter snow, always, whatever the season, alert for their untiring enemies, the wolves and the Indians. The red men seem to have been relatively few in those distant decades when Europeans first saw the Great Plains. This country just east of the Rocky Mountains was not, in all respects, a friendly environment. The scarcity of wood was a serious drawback. In places the rainfall was deficient. The plains, however, abounded in game. But the bison was both fleet and fierce, and the Indian, without a horse, must solve a difficult problem in his capture. Even so, here and there on the plains, smoke could be seen rising from the simple, primitive habitations of the redskins. Perhaps a tribe might be encountered traveling, as it followed a bison herd. Half-tamed, wolfish dogs were the only beasts of burden, and the travois the only means of conveyance save the strong backs of the women who helped to transport the few possessions of the nomads.

As the years passed, herds of wild horses began to appear in the bison country, originating probably in Mexico. Not until the horse was available did the Indian venture, in large numbers, out upon the grasslands. At some time in the past, whether before or after the advent of the horse must remain a mystery, some Athapascan peoples left their kinsmen in northwestern Canada and made their way southward until they came to rest beside the banks of the streams that flow into the Gulf of Mexico. Perhaps some of these wanderers, during their progress southward, fell in with tribes of Caddoans, making their way into the grasslands from the southwestern deserts. The urge that drove forward these two Indian stocks will doubtless never be known. They were not, however, the only peoples who came into the bison country. When the Europeans had firmly established themselves on the eastern seaboard, white influence spread rapidly westward into the continental interior. The eastern Indians received, through trade with the white man, new and more efficient weapons which the red men frequently turned against the neighboring tribes of the West. As a result, the very advent of the whites, even before the frontier of his settlements began sweeping swiftly westward across the continent, unsettled the lives of many tribes far in the interior and caused readjustments among the Indian peoples living deep in the forest. For the Indians in that border zone, where the wooded country merged into the prairies, the readjustments were far-reaching. These people were either pushed out into the grasslands or chose deliberately to hazard their lives and fortunes in the bison country. The Cheyennes, of Algonquian stock, and the Sioux left their ancient hunting grounds in the forest around the Great Lakes and the Lake of the Woods, abandoned the old method of life, and adapted themselves to the novel conditions of the Great Plains.

351 Sioux Village, from an engraving by S. V. Hunt after a painting by A. Bierstadt, in *The Ladies Repository*, New York, 1860

THE DAKOTAS OR "SIOUX"

On those northern plains, covered in the summers of the twentieth century with wheat fields, once lived the largest division of the great Siouan family of Indians. The Dakotas, commonly called Sioux, had formerly dwelt in the forest to the eastward and a tradition lingered long among the Chippewas that they had first met the Dakotas in the region of the present Soo Canal. From that first meeting until the time when the white man put an end to all inter-tribal wars, the Dakotas and the Chippewas were deadly rivals. No village of either people was ever safe from prowling bands of the other. The history of the two tribes is a tale of a prolonged and bloody conflict. In the middle years of the eighteenth century, the Dakotas lived about the headwaters of the Mississippi, a forest people, practicing the arts of woodland tribes. Half a century later, Lewis and Clark found many Dakota villages far out on the plains, beside the banks of the Missouri. To say that these people had been driven on to the plains because of their constant warfare with the Chippewas would hardly be true; yet that perennial conflict no doubt played a part in their decision to change their habitat. They adjusted themselves quickly to the necessities of their new life and Lewis and Clark found them among the best of the Indians in the grasslands.

352 Scalp Dance of the Dakotas, from an engraving after a drawing by Captain Seth Eastman, U. S. A., in the possession of the publishers

THE FIGHTING DAKOTAS

From boyhood the braves of the Dakotas were reared to war. In the lives of no Indians was the martial code of greater importance. Physically and mentally they were among the ablest Indians the race has produced. They were brave and aggressive. From time to time their young men formed associations, the members of which pledged themselves to face their enemies unarmed and never to retreat. Such societies subjected their members to the severest of tests. Against men who could take such vows and carry them through, few Indians could stand. The Chippewas fought the Dakotas on even terms but other neighbors suffered heavily under their attacks. Again and again the braves of the Dakotas returned to their villages to exhibit proudly the scalps which they had secured. The women took these and intoned the wild chants of the Scalp Dance. In the midst of the ceremony the dancers called to their vanquished foes in derision; asked them where was their courage and the fighting power of their warriors, and likened their braves unto women. Far into the night the exultations of the victors resounded over the plains.

353 A Dakota Horse Race, from a lithograph after a drawing by Charles Bodmer, in Maximilian, *Travels in the Interior of North America, 1832–34*, London, 1838–43

WANETA

WANETA was one of the greatest of the Sioux chieftains. The War of 1812 had found this warrior still in his teens; yet he enlisted eagerly in the conflict on the side of the British. He fought at Fort Meigs and Sandusky, where he won a great reputation among the whites for his courage and aggressiveness. After the war he remained a friend of the British and a hater of the Americans until 1820, when Colonel Snelling thwarted his attempt to destroy Fort Snelling on the Mississippi. Then Waneta made peace with the Americans and remained their friend until his death. Major Long met him in 1820 and was deeply impressed by this wild son of the plains. "We have never seen a nobler face, or a more impressive character, than that of the Dacota chief, as he stood that afternoon in this manly and characteristic dress, contemplating a dance performed by the men of his own nation." Waneta was at this time a man who had passed through the severest test of his race. In the fulfillment of a vow he had danced the Sun Dance. A pole had been erected near his lodge and thongs, attached to the top of this, had been tied to loops of skin and flesh, cut in his arms and breast. For three days he had fasted and danced, to be cut down, exhausted, at the end of the third after two of the loops had given way. Waneta signed two treaties with the Americans in 1825 which helped materially to further the good relations between the Indians and the white men.

354 Wanotan (Waneta) and his Son, from an engraving by R. Fenner in *A Narrative of an Expedition to the Source of the St. Peter's River, compiled by William H. Keating, from the Notes of Major Stephen H. Long*, London, 1825

THE MANDANS

ON the banks of the Missouri, to the north and west of the Dakotas, lived a Siouan people, the Mandans, who were closely related to the Winnebagos. Perhaps in the hazy and forgotten past the Mandans had lived in the forest about the shores of the Great Lakes; their traditions narrated a migration from the east. All that is known of them is that from time to time they moved up the Missouri, driven perhaps by the puissant blows of the neighboring Dakotas. The Mandans were a numerous people when white men first left records of visits to their villages. There were nine of these in the middle years of the eighteenth century, situated on both banks of the Missouri, near the mouth of the Heart. About their habitations were gardens where grew beans, gourds, maize, and sunflowers, for the Mandans were agricultural people. The women cultivated the soil and the men hunted bison. In spite of the gardens, however, there was want in the Mandan villages when the grazing herds drifted far to the southward, for the Mandans, unlike the Dakotas, did not pick up their tents and follow the animals. They were rooted to the soil and lived in permanent habitations, instead of skin tipis. The Mandan house was a round hut, with sturdy posts and cross beams supporting a roof made of osiers, over which was laid dried grass and earth. With a brisk fire burning on the hearth such habitations were warm and comfortable, even when biting winter blizzards swept across the unprotected northern plains.

355 Dance of the Mandan Indians, from a lithograph after a drawing by Charles Bodmer, in Maximilian *Travels in the Interior of North America, 1832–34*, London, 1838–43

356 Dog-Sledge Transportation of the Mandans, from a lithograph after a drawing by Charles Bodmer, in Maximilian, *Travels in the Interior of North America, 1832–34*, London, 1838–43

THE DECLINE OF THE MANDANS

LEWIS and Clark, seeking a way to the Pacific, found the Mandans a physically vigorous people, well-formed, strong, and a little above medium stature. Their women were usually short and broad-shouldered, the latter a desirable trait for burden-bearers such as they were. The Mandans were friendly to the whites and no war may be found in the record of the intercourse of the races. Yet the white man was the unwitting cause of the passing of the tribe's greatness even before he had scarcely come to know them. In the latter years of the eighteenth century the scourge of smallpox, added to the attacks of the Dakotas and the Assiniboins, sadly depleted the numbers of these farmers and hunters of the plains. They fled from their death-swept villages and a dejected remnant established farther north the two towns in which Lewis and Clark wintered in 1804–05.

THE HIDATSAS, OR GROS-VENTRES

THE Mandans and the Hidatsas must be linked together so long as the memory of these peoples lasts. Many names have been applied to this Siouan tribe, whose language is closely related to that of the Crows. The Hidatsas are also called Minatarees, and their official designation is Gros-Ventres. Their villages were once joined with those of the Crows and the two peoples lived in close association. Before the time of recorded history, however, the two tribes had separated, the Hidatsas clinging to the upper Missouri and the Crows moving farther to the west. Fortune brought the Mandans, migrating up the Missouri in the eighteenth century, into the country of the Hidatsas. The two peoples became allied and Lewis and Clark found their villages built close together. The culture of the two distantly related peoples became virtually identical. The union of these two tribes, speaking quite different languages, is evidence of the dangers of the plains in the early nineteenth century. Before joining with the Mandans, the Hidatsas had absorbed another small tribe, driven to desperation by the blows of their enemies. After the coming of the horse, the bison country was no refuge for weak peoples. Perhaps nowhere north of the Rio Grande was the competition for life keener than among the Indians of the grasslands.

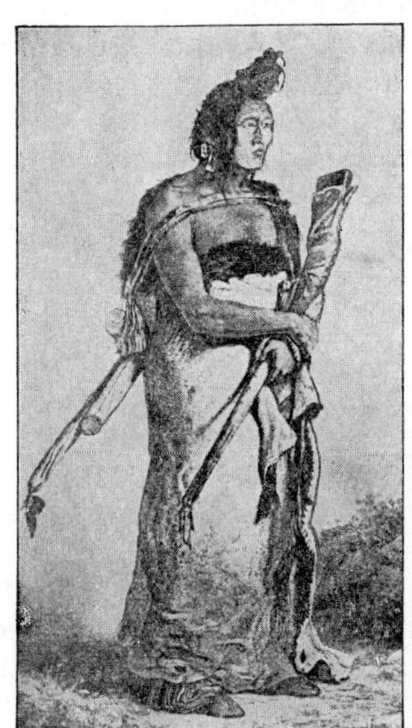

357 Menkemanastan, A Chief of the Gros-Ventres, from a lithograph after a drawing by Charles Bodmer, in Maximilian, *Travels in the Interior of North America, 1832–34*, London, 1838–43

THE CROWS

COUSINS to the Gros-Ventres were a Siouan people, commonly known as the Crows, one of the proudest and most haughty of the plains tribes. They were hunters and warriors, in search of game along the eastern edge of the Rocky Mountains, in what is now Wyoming and Montana. Two bands developed, one living in the mountains and the other near the banks of the Yellowstone. Trappers and traders who came among them in the early nineteenth century found them living in skin tipis, almost identical with those of the Dakotas. Maximilian described these as decorated near the top with pieces of brightly colored cloth, which flapped in the wind, contrasting with the scalps dangling from the poles of the Dakota lodges. The Crows did not cultivate the soil, except to raise tiny patches of tobacco. They were primarily a hunter people and were said to have possessed, at one time, between nine and ten thousand horses.

358 Crow Indians at Fort Clarke, from a lithograph after a drawing by Charles Bodmer, in Maximilian, *Travels in the Interior of North America, 1832–34*, London, 1838–43

THE BLACKFEET

359 Blackfeet Indians, from a lithograph after a drawing by Charles Bodmer, in Maximilian, *Travels in the Interior of North America, 1832–34*, London, 1838–43

North of the Crow country lived one of the most remarkable tribes of the Plains Indians. The Blackfeet, or Siksiksas, were in reality a confederacy of three Algonquian peoples, the Siksiksas proper, the Bloods, and the Piegans. They ranged over the broad area stretching from the Saskatchewan River, on the north, to Montana, on the south. They had no permanent habitations but erected their skin tipis when night overtook them on their wanderings in pursuit of prey. They had no pottery and planted no crops. In their culture might be found faint suggestions that they had been once a forest people, but that time had evidently long since passed. Their lives were completely adjusted to the peculiar characteristics of the bison country. The climate of their habitat, lying far to the north, severely tested the strength of this people. They had to face cold winters when dangerous blizzards swept across the plains. They lived in dread of starvation in the cold months, when storms sent the bison trekking southward. Hunting over the snow was a desperate adventure. Many a man, searching on snowshoes for the herds which would sustain the life of his family, failed to return because of a sudden storm. Perhaps, in the spring when the snow had gone, his bones would be found where he had fallen. The Blackfeet, therefore, were a people among whom only the vigorous and strong could survive. Skillful riders and fierce warriors, they were a predatory tribe, at war almost constantly with their neighbors, the Crees, the Assiniboins, the Dakotas, the Crows, the Flatheads and the Kutenais. Americans, coming in the early nineteenth century to the southern part of their domain, suffered more than once from their animosity. They were destined to play an important part in the development of the fur trade.

THE PAWNEES

The Pawnees belonged to the Caddoan family which had migrated from the desert country of the southwest. Leaving behind them the rugged mountain country, the Caddoan tribes had cast their lot upon the sub-arid plains which lie within the rain shadow of the Rockies. One small tribe, the Arikaras, went north and, far separated from their kinsmen, built their lodges in the country of the upper Missouri, where lived also the Mandans and the Gros-Ventres. Three other tribes, the Caddo, the Kichai, and the Wichita, followed a southern course and established their villages in the warm river bottoms of the Red River in Louisiana, and its tributary in Arkansas and southern Oklahoma. The powerful Pawnee confederation followed a middle course. The white men found them in the valley of the Platte, in western Nebraska. The Pawnees ranked, with the Dakotas and the Blackfeet, among the most powerful of the Plains Indians. In 1838 they were estimated to number about ten thousand souls.

360 Pawnees Looking for Enemies, from an engraving in the Print Room, New York Public Library

361 From the painting *The Pony Boy*, by Maynard Dixon (1875–), courtesy of the artist

THE GENTLE ART OF HORSE STEALING

Most valued among the possessions of the Plains Indian was the horse. Without it he was virtually impotent alike in the chase and in war. The horses of a village must be guarded vigilantly during the hours of darkness if the owners expected in the morning to find their grazing herds undepleted. In adjustment to this constant danger the wary Pawnees had outguards, after the manner of an army, both on the march and during the night encampment. "Besides this precaution, a great many of the young men lie in their blankets, at a little distance from it [the camp] chanting their war and hunting songs; and they prefer sleeping in that manner to the confinement of their tents. . . . The manner in which . . . enemies of the Pawnee steal horses is as follows: Two or three approach the encampment, cautiously, soon after nightfall, and take advantage of any creek, dell, or brushwood, that may serve to conceal them from the observation of the out-piquets; if they succeed in reaching the extremity of the village undiscovered, they stand up and walk deliberately through it, wrapped in their buffalo robe. Of course they can no longer be distinguished from the Pawnees by the faint light of the half extinguished fires; and as they pass the groups of horses collected before their respective owners' lodges, they cut, with a sharp knife, the laryettes which fasten those that they purpose to carry off. As soon as they have loosened the required number, each man jumps upon one, and they drive off the rest at full speed, shaking their blankets, and urging the alarmed animals to their utmost exertions. Of course they obtain a considerable start of any pursuit; and if the night is dark, run but little risk of being overtaken. . . ." — Murray, *Travels in North America*, I, 209–11.

"GENEROUS, YET SAVAGE MEN"

In 1834 John T. Irving, Jr., was a member of a United States expedition to the Pawnees, the purpose of which was to call an Indian council which would bring about an end to the inter-tribal wars of the Plains Indians. After two months among the Pawnee tribes Irving summed up his impression of the wild sons of the plains, and in so doing unconsciously colored his statement with the sentiments and point of view of cultivated eastern Americans of the early nineteenth century. The idealization of the Indian had already begun. "We had seen him in his moments of joy, and pain; in his moments of pride and humility; in his paroxysms of excitement, when urged on by his impetuous nature; and in his hours of relaxation, when a calm was upon his burning bosom, and his passions were asleep. We had seen him, in his home, in the midst of his family, where the gushes of his heart were unrestrained; when the feelings of the husband, and father, and all the kind impulses of nature had burst the iron fetters of habit, and resumed their empire. The illusions thrown around him by the exaggerated reports of travelers, and the fictions of poets, had been removed; and we had beheld him, as he really was; an untutored, generous, yet savage man. He had lost much of the romance with which imagination had clothed him. His faults, his vices, his crimes, now stood out in glaring colours, and threw into the shade many of his higher qualities. Still with all his imperfections, we had learned to admire his chivalrous nature; and to look upon him while uncontaminated by communion with the whites, as among the noblest works of his Maker." — *Indian Sketches*, II, 162.

362 A Blood Indian, from a pastel by Edmund Montague Morris in the Alberta Government Collection, reproduced by permission of the artist

THE CHEYENNES

NEIGHBOR to the Pawnees on the west was a tribe of Algonquian Indians, far separated from their kin living to the east and the north. They are known to history by the name "Cheyenne," given to them by the Sioux and meaning "those who speak a strange language." When first found by the white men the Cheyennes were living in the north country, not far from the Lake of the Woods, and their neighbors were the Assiniboins and the Crees. The Crees first, then the Assiniboins, secured arms from the white men and the Cheyennes moved west to the upper Missouri. Here they were neighbors to the Arikaras, the Mandans, and the Gros-Ventres. To the east lived the powerful Dakotas, significantly referred to in the sign language of the plains by drawing the hand, like a knife, across the throat. The Cheyennes planted corn on the banks of the Missouri. But many of their young men were restless. The wild freedom of the plains covered with bison herds lured them from their settled villages. They became a wandering people, their villages widely scattered, and they gave up the building of permanent houses like those of the Mandans and the Pawnees. But they still planted corn. During the eighteenth and nineteenth centuries their general drift was west and south.

363 Cheyenne Chiefs, members of the Southern Cheyenne Delegation of 1909, from a photograph, courtesy of the Bureau of American Ethnology, United States National Museum, Washington

THE CHEYENNE WOMEN

AMONG the Cheyennes, as in every tribe of Plains Indians, travelers noted that the women were the burden-bearers. "It is true that the women performed many laborious tasks — tasks that the civilized man regards as toil — and that the work done by the men — hunting and going to war — are occupations that the civilized man is disposed to regard as sport or recreation; but for this division of labor there were good reasons. The work of providing food and defense against enemies was hard and dangerous; while fighting and the use of arms were no part of women's work. As almost everywhere in the world, her share in the life of the community was the care of the household — the welfare of the family. The man's duty was to defend his wife and children, and the tribe at large, in case of attack, and if the enemies were too strong to be defeated and driven away, at least to fight them off, to hold them in check, so that the women and children might escape by flight. To fight to advantage, to be in a position to repel enemies that might try to kill his people, a fighting man must be unhampered by a load. . . . Among the Cheyennes, the women are the rulers of the camp. They act as a spur to the men, if they are slow in performing their duties. They are far more conservative than the men, and often hold them back from hasty, ill-advised action. If the sentiment of the women of the camp clearly points to a certain course as desirable, the men are quite sure to act as the women wish. . . . Family rank, which existed among the Cheyennes as among other Indians, depended upon the estimation in which the family was held by the best people. A good family was one that produced brave men and good sensible women, and that possessed more or less property." — GEORGE BIRD GRINNELL, *The Cheyenne Indians*, I, 127–29.

364 Cheyenne Women Returning to Camp with Firewood, from a photograph, courtesy of George Bird Grinnell, New York

365 War Dance of the Kiowas, from a lithograph after a drawing in color by a Comanche Boy, September 1890, in *The Eleventh Census of the United States*, Washington, 1890

THE KIOWAS AND COMANCHES

SOUTH of the villages of the Pawnees and the Cheyennes were the camps of a peculiar people, the Kiowas. Though they were few in number they formed a group apart, with no known kin among the tribes of the Indian race. They were dark-skinned and heavily built, contrasting sharply with the slender, lithe, and lighter-colored peoples about them. Inferior to their nearest neighbors, the Comanches, they had, however, the distinction of fighting the white men longer than practically any other Indian tribe. Before they were finally settled on reservations, they had, in all probability, killed more white men in proportion to the numbers of the tribe than any other Indian people. Associated with them, though speaking a different language, was an Athapascan tribe known as the Kiowa-Apaches. These two allied peoples, through the passing years, kept the frontier of Texas and Mexico aflame with war. Partners with the Kiowas on many a raiding expedition were the Comanches, closely federated with them during all the nineteenth century. These nomad bison hunters were esteemed the finest horsemen of the plains. They made only the feeblest attempts to cultivate the soil and depended almost solely upon the herds for the things they required. They were members of the great Shoshonean family, the tribes of which lived in the Rocky Mountains and in the Central Basin which lies between the Rockies and the Sierras. The Comanches, alone of their kin, abandoned the ancient mountain habitat and cast their lot upon the grasslands.

ON THE TRAIL OF LEWIS AND CLARK

THE banks of the Missouri River were beginning to green with the herbage of spring when in 1807 the members of a small expedition bade good-bye to friends at the village of St. Louis and turned their faces toward the Indian country. A Spaniard, Manuel Lisa, was in command. He was inspired by the news he had heard from the lips of Lewis and Clark as he had conversed with those returned explorers in St. Louis the year before. His destination was that far distant northwestern region where the Missouri flows close to the Rocky Mountains. Slowly he toiled upstream. At the mouth of the Platte good fortune awaited him, for here he met John Colter floating alone down the broad river with some furs he had taken the previous winter about the headwaters of the Missouri. He had been a member of the Lewis and Clark expedition and had crossed the continent with them. He had left them on their return, however, to hunt and trap. For Lisa he now became an invaluable guide and councilor. The expedition passed through the dangerous Dakota country without molestation. Farther upstream Lisa's party beheld gathered on the bank a crowd of Arikaras, painted and bedecked with feathers. Shots across their bow warned the white men to stop. The Indians evidently meditated trouble. But in the tense meeting which followed they failed to catch Lisa off his guard and a little later the expedition was again proceeding. Difficulties awaited among the Mandans, a short distance upstream, but the skill of the white leader prevented serious consequences. Farther on, a large and menacing group of Assiniboins were overawed by a show of force. The Lisa party then spent a busy winter on the Yellowstone, hunting, trapping, and trading with the Crows, ignorant that in so doing they were arousing against themselves and their successors the bitter and lasting enmity of those dearest enemies of the Crows, the Blackfeet. The following summer found Manuel Lisa back in St. Louis, flushed with the success of this pioneering venture and dreaming of greater things to come.

366 Indians Crossing the Missouri River in Bull Boats, from the painting by William de la Montagne Cary, courtesy of the American Museum of Natural History, New York

THE FOUNDING OF THE MISSOURI FUR COMPANY

367 Pierre Chouteau, 1749–1849, from a portrait, artist unknown, in the Missouri Historical Society, St. Louis

Long talks followed the return of the Lisa party to St. Louis in 1808. Excitement ran high among the principal men of that frontier town. Listening to Lisa, one after another decided to join the enterprise which was duly incorporated under the name of the St. Louis Missouri Fur Company. On the records appear most of the leading citizens of St. Louis: Manuel Lisa, William Clark, who had helped to blaze the trail across the continent, Pierre Chouteau, Sr., Auguste P. Chouteau, Reuben Lewis, and Sylvester Labadie. To this list other names were added: Pierre Menard and William Morrison of Kaskaskia in Illinois, Andrew Henry of Louisiana, and Dennis Fitz-Hugh of Louisville, Kentucky. The Spaniard, Frenchman, and Englishman, reflecting in their very names the history of the Louisiana country, united to exploit the rich fur country of the Upper Missouri. Frequently in the conferences which brought about the company John Jacob Astor was mentioned, and the St. Louis and Kaskaskia promoters determined that this rising financial giant of the East should not be given an opportunity to buy even a single share in their company. They agreed that no new man should be admitted to their enterprise without the consent of all. So organized, the company made a contract with the Government of the United States to convey to his people a Mandan chief who had visited Washington. An attempt to return him the year before had failed because of the hostility of the Dakotas. In the spring of 1809 the first expedition of the Missouri Fur Company, as it was commonly known, pointed its boats up the river. It comprised some hundred and fifty men and carried a great quantity of merchandise to be used in the establishment of several posts. With it also was the Mandan chief.

THE WHEEL OF FORTUNE

The year 1809 opened under auspicious skies for the Missouri Company. By the end of the summer the Mandan villages had been passed and parties had been left behind at various points to establish trading posts. In late October the main body went into winter quarters in the Crow country. The autumn, winter, and succeeding spring saw the members of the main body carrying on a brisk and profitable trade in the Crow villages and also securing many pelts through trapping. Early in the spring of 1810 a considerable party pushed on to the final objective, Three Forks, where they planned to establish a post in the Blackfoot country. Beaver abounded and excitement grew as day after day added prodigious catches to the packs already in hand. Then without warning on the morning of April 12 a band of Blackfeet fell suddenly upon the camp whence most of the trappers had put forth to make their routine rounds. These returned to find death and desolation. Their horses, guns, ammunition, and the packs of furs they had labored so hard to gather were gone and five of their comrades lay dead. The blow was stunning. They tried to remain and to negotiate with the Blackfeet but these hostiles harassed the white men until all thought of trapping in the region had to be abandoned. The discouraged party left the country. They did not, however, give up trapping but moved southward across the continental divide and established a post on the north fork of the Snake River. But they found the country bare of game and nearly perished in the terrible winter which followed. In the spring of 1811 the band of trappers, thoroughly discouraged, broke up, different parties going in different directions. The leader, Henry, brought back the small catch to Lisa. Meanwhile in the summer of 1810 the post at Cedar Island had burned, destroying some fifteen thousand dollars' worth of furs. The climax of adversity was reached when the price of furs dropped. In spite of the manifold misfortunes which beset it in these distressing years the Missouri Fur Company saved its capital and even made a small profit. Its experiences demonstrate the peculiar hazards of the fur trade.

368 Auguste P. Chouteau, 1786–1838, son of Pierre Chouteau, from a print in the Missouri Historical Society, St. Louis

369 Manuel Lisa, *ca.* 1776–1820, from a portrait, artist unknown, in the Missouri Historical Society, St. Louis

MANUEL LISA, TRADER AND INDIAN AGENT

A LETTER from Lisa to Governor William Clark, dated July 1, 1817, gives a glimpse of the methods of the leading figure in the Missouri Fur Company. ". . . I received this appointment as sub-agent to the Indians when War was raging between the United States and Great Britain, and when the activity of British emissaries had armed against the Republic all the tribes of the Upper Mississippi and of the northern lakes. . . . The Indians of the Missouri are to those of the Upper Mississippi as four to one. . . . They did not arm against the Republic; on the contrary they armed against Great Britain and struck the Iowas, the allies of that power. . . . Before I ascended the Missouri as sub-agent, your excellency remembers what was accustomed to take place. The Indians of that river killed, robbed and pillaged the traders; these practices are no more. . . . But I have had success as a trader; and this gives rise to many reports. . . . Well, I will explain how I get it. First, I put into my operations great activity; I go a great distance, while some are considering whether they will start today or tomorrow. I impose upon myself great privations; ten months in a year I am buried in the forest, at a vast distance from my own house. I appear as the benefactor, and not as the pillager of the Indians. I carried among them the seed of the large pompion, from which I have seen in their possession the fruit weighing one hundred and sixty pounds. Also the large bean, the potato, the turnip; and these vegetables now make a comfortable part of their subsistence, and this year I promised to carry the plough. Besides, my blacksmiths work incessantly for them, charging nothing. I lend them traps, only demanding preference in their trade. My establishments are the refuge of the weak and of the old men no longer able to follow their lodges; and by these means I have acquired the confidence and friendship of these nations, and the consequent choice of their trade." — Quoted in CHITTENDEN, *History of the Fur Trade in the Far West*, III, 899–901. Purely as a matter of policy Manuel Lisa sought the hand of one of the most beautiful daughters of the Omaha nation. Bringing the customary presents to the parents he told them frankly that he was already married, a circumstance of no consequence in their eyes. Lisa's Indian bride, at first indifferent, became deeply attached to this indefatigable trader who traveled so much up and down the Missouri. Two children came to share her lodge. Then one day in 1817, three years after her marriage, she stood on the bank of the great river and watched Manuel's boat drift out of sight, carrying her eldest, a daughter, to St. Louis. She vaguely realized that the baby girl would grow up in a different and better life than hers. But when the boat had passed from view and she knew that her child was forever lost to her, she gave way to frantic demonstrations of grief. Many months passed. Lisa's first wife died and he married again among his own people. In the winter of 1819–20 he brought this second white wife to Fort Lisa in the Omaha country after the Indian spouse had been sent some distance away from the post. The latter returned to the neighborhood, however, and sent her son to Lisa who received him with affection. Giving the mother presents, Lisa told her to return to her people. When the spring floods of 1820 had washed the ice from the Missouri and Manuel was preparing to descend to St. Louis, he told the Omaha woman that he planned to take their son to the city to have him educated. The squaw in a frenzy of fear seized her only remaining child and fled by boat across the river. After a night in the open she returned and turned over the boy to his father, saying that it would be the best for him. Then, with all the persuasiveness which she possessed, she begged to go also. Lisa was adamant regarding the latter point. He would, however, have taken the child from the despairing mother had not the local Indian agent forbidden him.

370 A full-blood Omaha Woman, from a photograph in the Bureau of American Ethnology, Washington

371 Fur Traders on the Missouri River, from the painting by George Caleb Bingham (1811–79), owned by Colonel Robert B. Dumont, Mobile, Ala.

HISTORY OF THE MISSOURI FUR COMPANY

THE Missouri Fur Company persisted in one form and another until 1830. It passed through and survived the War of 1812. But reorganization followed reorganization. As the years passed, one by one the names of its original founders disappeared. But that of Manuel Lisa remained and this aggressive trader dominated the company from the close of the war until his death in 1820. His mantle fell on a worthy subordinate, Joshua Pilcher. Under his leadership the activities of the company penetrated again to the upper waters of the Missouri. In the summer of 1822 some twenty-five thousand dollars' worth of furs were sent down the river to St. Louis. But again the enterprise ended in tragedy. On May 30, 1823, a party of twenty-nine men were ambushed on the Yellowstone by an overwhelming war party of Blackfoot braves. The Indians had few guns and rushed the white men armed with flint weapons they knew so well. The trappers lost most of their property and five of their number. The news of this disaster was a heavy blow to Pilcher. "The flower of my business is gone," he wrote, "my mountaineers have been defeated, and the chiefs of the party both slain." Bitterly he assigned the cause of this continued hostility of the northern Indians to the influence of British fur traders operating from the valley of the Red River. When seven years later Pilcher gave up the business the career of the Missouri Fur Trading Company came to an end.

THE YELLOWSTONE EXPEDITION

THE year of Manuel Lisa's death saw great activity along the lower Missouri. The people of the trans-Mississippi settlements were filled with buoyant hope and the gossip of the frontier villages was of great things to come. The Government of the United States was equipping such an expedition as the Missouri River had never seen. An army capable of overwhelming any force of Indians likely to come in its way was to advance into the Upper Missouri country. "The expedition," wrote Secretary of War, Calhoun, "ordered to the mouth of the Yellowstone, or rather to the Mandan village, is a part of a system of measures which has for its objects the protection of our northwestern frontier and the greater extension of our fur trade." In addition to the trading benefits that were to flow from the establishment of a military post in the heart of the fur country the expedition planned to add to the scientific knowledge of the West. For this latter purpose Major Long of the Engineer Corps had gathered about himself a group of scientists who were to report on the various phases of nature in this western country. The expedition turned out to be the worst military fiasco since the War of 1812. The Government was betrayed by a rascally contractor. The army never reached its objective and consequently could not accomplish its mission.

372 Major Long Holding a Council with the Pawnees, from an engraving by I. Clark after a drawing by S. Seymour, in *An Account of an Expedition from Pittsburgh to the Rocky Mountains in the Years 1819, 1820 . . .*, London, 1823

373 The Platte River issuing from the Rocky Mountains, from an engraving by I. Clark after a drawing by S. Seymour, in *An Account of an Expedition from Pittsburgh to the Rocky Mountains in the Years 1819, 1820 . . .*, London, 1823

MAJOR LONG

After the failure of the military part of the enterprise, Major Long, with a small and inadequately supplied expedition, crossed the plains to the base of the mountains. He saw in the distance the towering pinnacle of the peak which bears his name and returned to make his report, destined to become famous for the inaccuracies it contained. "In regard to this extensive section of country," wrote the Major, "we do not hesitate in giving our opinion, that it is almost wholly unfit for cultivation, and of course uninhabitable by a people depending upon agriculture for their subsistence. . . . The whole of this region seems peculiarly adapted as a range for buffaloes, wild goats, and other wild game, incalculable multitudes of which find ample pasturage and subsistence upon it." With such words the commander of the expedition, to which western people had looked with such confidence to inflame the minds of men in the East with the possibilities of the West, actually retarded the development of the trans-Mississippi country and aided in fixing on the contemporary maps of the United States in the region west of the Mississippi the words, "The Great American Desert."

THE ARIKARA CAMPAIGN OF 1823

Two years after the return of Long, keel boats loaded with military supplies started on a hurried trip up the Missouri. Colonel Leavenworth with a detachment of the Regular Army was moving to punish the Arikaras who had committed depredations against the greatest of Rocky Mountain fur traders, General Ashley. Leavenworth who had served with distinction in the War of 1812, had been since 1816 Indian agent for what was called the "Northwest Territory." He had established Fort Snelling in Minnesota and the fort in Kansas which bears his name. Joshua Pilcher with a company of men from the Missouri Fur Company joined the expedition of 1823 against the Arikaras. A band of Dakotas also coöperated with Leavenworth and boldly sallied forth to give battle to the Arikara braves. Leavenworth laid siege to the Arikara village of domed earthen huts about each of which was a slight palisade. When the Arikaras sued for peace, Leavenworth chose to take them at their word rather than to begin a battle which would inevitably have resulted in a general massacre of men, women, and children. Pilcher sharply criticized Leavenworth's humanity on the ground that the Arikaras, who escaped with what seemed to him a light punishment for their depredations, were emboldened to continue their attacks. The administration at Washington, however, strongly supported Leavenworth. John C. Calhoun, Secretary of War and Leavenworth's immediate superior, expressed approval: "I am decidedly of the opinion that the conduct of the Colonel with that of his officers and men was such as to merit marked applause." The Arikara episode illustrates the difference in concept of a proper Indian policy between responsible officials at Washington and frontiersmen who were pushing ruthlessly into the Indian country.

374 Pashtuwa-Chta, an Arikara Indian, from a lithograph after a drawing by Charles Bodmer, in Maximilian, *Travels in the Interior of North America, 1832–34*, London, 1838–43

THE WESTERN DEPARTMENT OF THE AMERICAN FUR COMPANY

UNDER the date of April 23, 1822, Ramsay Crooks wrote to his chief, John Jacob Astor: "I regret beyond measure that our fastidiousness about interfering with our St. Louis friends induced us to postpone until the present time any attempt to participate in the Missouri trade." At last the powerful Astor interests were to extend their trading operations to the rich fur country of the Upper Missouri. The decision marked the opening of a new epoch in the history of the fur trade out of St. Louis. The fur traders of that frontier city must now face one of the most powerful financial combinations of the time in the United States. They could either make peace with the new competitor or look forward to a war whose object would be their complete elimination from the business. Competition on the Indian frontier beyond the reach of the law had already developed practices which involved personal as well as financial danger. For years stories had drifted into St. Louis of the unethical methods used by the British traders in seeking to outdo their American competitors or to drive them from desirable regions. After the American Fur Company began its operations, ugly rumors were carried eastward from the plains which always told of brusque methods used in getting rid of small traders and sometimes even hinted at the murder of persons whose disappearance would serve the interests of the great corporation. Doubtless most of these tales were without foundation and were born of the general animosity of a frontier people, imbued with a spirit of independence and democracy, toward a powerful combination of capitalists. Most of the small rivals, nevertheless, were eliminated and, though they continued to spring up, they were of relatively little consequence in the trade. Certain companies, however, challenged successfully the monopoly which the American Fur Company sought to establish. When these could not be driven from the field, negotiations were opened and in most cases they were bought out or merged with the larger concern. In this manner came into the American Fur Company one of the most remarkable men associated with it in the Missouri country.

375 Ramsay Crooks, 1787–1859, from a portrait by E. Saintain in the Wisconsin Historical Museum, Madison

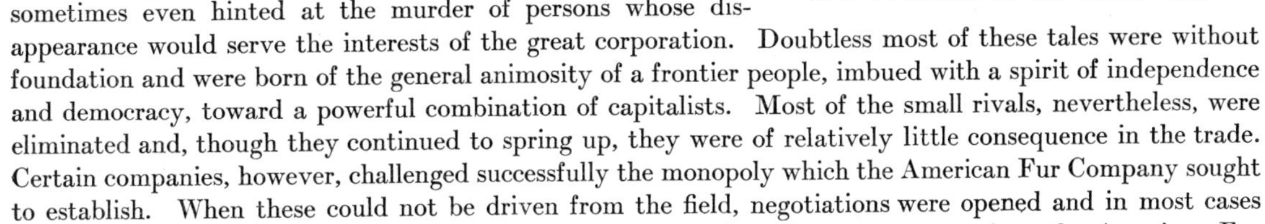

KENNETH MACKENZIE, 1797–1861

MACKENZIE was thirty-one years of age when, in 1827, he was put in charge of the "Upper Missouri Outfit" of the American Fur Company and became "King" of the country. He was a Scotchman of distinguished birth and he had been an officer in the British Army in the War of 1812. After the close of that conflict he had been a leading spirit in the building up of an enterprise, popularly known as the Columbia Fur Company, whose success with the Indians of the northern plains forced the Astor concern to effect an amalgamation. Mackenzie governed as one who had been born to rule. He assumed a pomp reminiscent of the days of feudalism which aided materially in the management of the rough men whom he must of necessity employ. He was an executive of rare ability. The task allotted to him was nothing less than the development of the fur trade in a region which the St. Louis traders, after efforts lasting through two decades, had failed to exploit completely. More than once that rich beaver country which lay within the range of the Blackfeet had lured the St. Louis men to financial disaster and to death.

376 Kenneth Mackenzie, from a portrait, artist unknown, in the Missouri Historical Society, St. Louis

377 Calf Child, a War Chief of the Blackfeet, from a pastel by Edmund Montagne Morris in the Alberta Government Collection, reproduced by permission of the artist

MACKENZIE AND THE BLACKFEET

MACKENZIE determined to open trade relations with the hostile Blackfeet. He consolidated his position among the Mandans, the Arikaras, and the Crows by the building of forts. Within four years after assuming control of the Upper Missouri outfit the Scotch trader was ready to advance into the Blackfoot country. These Indians had traded for some time in a small way with the Hudson's Bay Company. Mackenzie had the luck to find a former H. B. C. employee at one of his forts, a man who knew a little of the Blackfoot tongue. He consented to lead a small expedition into the country of the hostiles. This venture, fraught with the gravest danger, proved a complete success. The party was received by a Blackfoot village and chiefs of the tribe were persuaded to return for the purpose of opening trading relations. This success paved the way for a dramatic episode which displayed the quality of the Upper Missouri outfit.

PEACE WITH THE BLACKFEET

IN 1831 Mackenzie concluded at Fort Union one of the most interesting treaties in the annals of the relations between the Indians and the whites. It was a tripartite covenant between the Blackfeet, their ancient enemies the Assiniboins, and Mackenzie's company. Its wording shows clearly Mackenzie's methods of dealing with the haughty and belligerent northern tribes. The treaty contains a blend of ideas derived from Indian and white sources which illuminates certain aspects of the contact between the races. "We send greetings to all mankind. Be it known unto all nations that the most ancient, most illustrious, and most numerous tribes of redskins, lords of the soil from the banks of the great waters unto the tops of the mountains on which the heavens rest, have entered into a solemn league and covenant to make, preserve and cherish a firm and lasting peace, that so long as the water runs, or the grass grows, they may hail each other as brethren, and smoke the calumet in friendship and security. On the vigil of St. Andrew in the year 1831, the powerful and distinguished nation of the Blackfeet, Piegan, and Blood Indians by their ambassadors appeared at Fort Union near the spot where the Yellowstone River unites its current with the Missouri, and in the council chamber of the Governor, Kenneth Mackenzie, and the principal chiefs of the Assiniboin nation . . . when, conforming to all ancient customs and ceremonies, and observing the due mystical signs enjoined by the great medicine lodges, a treaty of peace and friendship was entered into by the high contracting parties, and is testified by their hands and seals hereunto annexed, hereafter and forever to live as brethren of one large, united, and happy family; and may the Great Spirit who watcheth over us all approve our conduct and teach us to love one another. . . ."

378 Blackfeet Going to a Winter Camp, from a painting by William de la Montagne Cary, courtesy of the American Museum of Natural History, New York

379 A Whiskey Trader, from the painting by William de la Montagne Cary, courtesy of the American Museum of Natural History, New York

THE LIQUOR TRADE

THE Great Spirit would doubtless approve the peace that the Mackenzie covenant aimed at, while perhaps looking somewhat doubtfully upon some of the Scotch trader's practices. Mackenzie's method of displaying his love for his new redskin friends was one as ancient as the fur trade itself. The magic formula which brought the riches of the fur country pouring into the coffers of the traders was firewater, the one indispensable trading commodity. The Indians clamored for the white man's drink and their pelts went to him who supplied them most liberally.

MACKENZIE'S FALL

If Mackenzie freely dispensed rum and whiskey, he was doing no different than traders from time immemorial. Under the circumstances, the head of the Upper Missouri Outfit was stunned by the news which sped swiftly up the Missouri that by an Act of July 9, 1832, the United States had prohibited the introduction of liquor into the Indian country. Mackenzie estimated the situation swiftly and correctly. Smuggling would be easy for small and little-known traders, but practically impossible for the great American Fur Company whose enemies were everywhere. The result of the law would be to raise up a host of individual competitors, armed with liquor illegally brought to the Indian villages. Ramsay Crooks, excited and desperate, besought the War Department to be lenient in the application of the law. He sought to make the British trader serve his purpose by arguing that, if Americans were forbidden to take liquor to the Indians, the peltries of the northwest would go to their English competitors across the border. But his efforts availed nothing. After Mackenzie had had a cargo of fire water confiscated at Fort Leavenworth, the enterprise which he headed seemed to be in a dangerous predicament. The resourceful Scotchman then fell back upon the expedient of establishing a distillery at Fort Union and for some months the Upper Missouri outfit enjoyed an overwhelming advantage over all its rivals. Mackenzie, with a lawyer's subtlety, pointed out that the federal law forbade the importation but not the manufacture of liquor. The palmy days of the distillery, however, were short-lived. News of its existence reached the Indian Agent, General William Clark, who promptly called upon the Company for an explanation. The question was quickly referred from Clark's office at St. Louis to Washington. The year 1833 found the American Fur Company faced with the imminent danger of the loss of its license, a disaster which its old-time friend, Senator Benton of Missouri, aided in averting. The episode marked, however, the end of Mackenzie's usefulness in Upper Missouri.

380 Upper Missouri Terrain, from a lithograph after a drawing by Charles Bodmer, in Maximilian, *Travels in the Interior of North America, 1832–34*, London, 1838–43

381 Fight Between the Assiniboins and Blackfeet Before Fort Mackenzie, detail from a lithograph after a drawing by Charles Bodmer, in Maximilian, *Travels in the Interior of North America, 1832–34*, London, 1838–43

LATER EPISODES

In 1832, at the zenith of his career, Mackenzie had established Fort Mackenzie in the Blackfoot country. Within the palisade of this post, in August 1833, tarried the explorer Maximilian with his artist Bodmer. Outside the paling were lodges of Assiniboins and Blackfeet who had come to trade. On the morning of the 28th the ties of brotherly love, established two years before, were rudely snapped asunder. Armed with knives, tomahawks, and firearms, the Assiniboins fell suddenly upon the Blackfeet. Blood flowed freely. The Blackfeet were received within the fort, whence their braves sallied forth and, after a day's fighting, drove off the Assiniboins. From the fort Bodmer watched the fray. His picture, depicting with a brutal realism the savageness of Indian warfare, is one of the most illuminating of the records which have come down from the frontier.

382 Fur Traders on the Upper Missouri, from an engraving in George Bird Grinnell, *Trails of the Pathfinders*, New York, 1911, courtesy of Charles Scribner's Sons, New York

THE DECLINE OF THE FUR TRADE

Ten years later mismanagement on the part of the man in charge of Fort Mackenzie, which culminated in an unsuccessful attempt of a few whites to massacre a village of Bloods, caused the violent expulsion of the Upper Missouri Outfit from the Blackfoot country. Already the heyday of the fur trade had passed and the American Fur Company was suffering from the decline. Chastened by Mackenzie's experience, the company had scrupulously obeyed the liquor law and had seen its rivals cut into its trade by smuggling fire water into the Indian country. Harassed by such competition, the company secured the appointment of one of the most able of its former traders to the resurrected post of Indian Agent of the Upper Missouri. Following this maneuver the Upper Missouri Outfit in the latter phase of its existence busied itself in giving every possible aid to the efforts of the new agent to stop the wholesale illegal importation of liquor. The outfit had persisted into an age when, for it at least, righteousness and profit went hand in hand.

THE STEAMBOAT

The year 1832 marked an epoch in the transportation methods on the Missouri. In that year the *Yellowstone* churned its way up the river as far as Fort Union, demonstrating the navigability of this route of the fur trade. Indian hunting parties in search of bison stopped to view in amazement the great white boat riding high out of the water, gliding smoothly, irresistibly through their country, its tall stacks belching clouds of black smoke. To a later generation a glamour of romance clings to the stories of these early steamboats, threading their way among the sand bars and the snags of the swift-flowing Missouri. To the men who labored on them, however, the river life offered little romance. Handling cargo and stoking boilers was hard work and the flat plains stretching to the horizon became monotonous. At the end of the journey the last of the cargo was put quickly ashore and the last of the furs hurried aboard. Then the steamer slipped swiftly down the river, lest the abating of the spring floods leave her stranded in the interior.

383 The Steamer *Yellowstone* on the Missouri River, 1832, from a lithograph after a drawing by Charles Bodmer, in Maximilian, *Travels in the Interior of North America, 1832–34*, London, 1838–43

FORT PIERRE

384 Fort Pierre, 1834, from a lithograph after a drawing by Charles Bodmer, in Maximilian, *Travels in the Interior of North America, 1832–34*, London, 1838–43

ON May 31, 1832, the *Yellowstone* stopped at old Fort Tecumseh, three miles above the mouth of the Teton, in the heart of the Dakota country. Fort Tecumseh had been established probably ten years earlier, by the Columbia Fur Company. In 1827, when the amalgamation took place, it was turned over to the American Fur Company with an inventory amounting to something more than fourteen thousand dollars. Then the Missouri River had begun undermining the bank on which the fort rested. In 1831 a new and greater fort was undertaken, a little distance from the old one and farther back from the river. When the *Yellowstone* tied up before it on that May day, the new structure was practically completed. For six days the steamer paused while, with due ceremony, the post was christened Fort Pierre, for Pierre Chouteau, who had come up the river to represent the company. Chouteau's name ranks also among those of the ablest servants of the American Fur Company. The fort was three hundred and forty feet in length by three hundred and twenty-five in width. It was the largest and most important on the Missouri.

FORT CLARK

FARTHER up the Missouri, some fifty-five miles above the present town of Bismarck, stood Fort Clark, perched on a bluff overlooking the river. This post was in the Mandan country and a village of their rounded huts lay not far from its walls. Fort Clark was typical of the fur-trading posts owned by private companies. From its gates parties of trappers were sent into the mountains and traders were dispatched to neighboring tribes of Indians. Within the walls skins were prepared and packed, accounts were kept, and a constant guard maintained against attack. There was little adventure and much dull routine in these outposts beyond the line of the frontier. The great event of the year was the coming of the steamboat. Letters and a bundle of newspapers brought word of the outside world. The arrival of the steamboat marked the end of the old and the beginning of the new year. Employees who were returning to civilization said good-bye and their places were taken by newcomers from St. Louis. When the boat passed out of sight down the river the fort relapsed into the humdrum of the daily routine.

385 Fort Clark, from a lithograph after a drawing by Charles Bodmer, in Maximilian, *Travels in the Interior of North America, 1832–34*, London, 1838–43

386 Fort Laramie, from a lithograph in Howard Stansbury, *Exploration of the Valley of the Great Salt Lake of Utah*, Philadelphia, 1852

FORT LARAMIE

Fort Laramie was on the Platte, southwest of Fort Pierre which controlled its trade. This differed from the typical plains fort in being of adobe rather than of wood, but its plan of construction was the same as its neighbors. A rectangular enclosure contained the warehouses, the office, and the dwellings of the post. At opposite corners jutted two-story blockhouses, so placed as to make possible an enfilade fire along all four walls of the fort. The first floor of the blockhouse was the artillery room and was equipped with loopholes for rifles. Frequently an elevated walk was bracketed on the inside of the palisade, making it possible for defenders to fire over the top. The gate in the larger forts was double, with trading counters between the outer and inner doors. So constructed, the trading posts, though isolated in the midst of tribes that were sometimes fiercely hostile, were practically impregnable. There is no record of one succumbing to a siege.

BENT'S FORT

A traveler through the West has left a vivid account of one of the most interesting of the trading posts, Bent's Fort, which stood on the bank of the Arkansas River within the limits of the present boundaries of Colorado. "Bent's Fort is situated on the left or northern bank of the river Arkansas, about one hundred miles from the foot of the Rocky Mountains — on a low and level bluff of the prairie which here slopes gradually to the water's-edge. The walls are built entirely of adobes — or sun-burned bricks — in the form of a hollow square, at two corners of which are circular flanking towers of the same material. The entrance is by a large gateway into the square, round which are the rooms occupied by the traders and employees of the post. These are small in size, with walls colored by a whitewash made of clay found in the prairies. Their flat roofs are defended along the exterior by parapets of adobe, to serve as a cover to marksmen firing from the top and along the coping grow plants of cactus of all the varieties common in the plains. In the center of the square is the press for packing the furs; and there are three large rooms, one used as a store and magazine, another as council-room, where the Indians assemble for their 'talks,' while the third is the common dining-hall where the traders, trappers, and hunters, and all employees, feast upon the best provender the game-covered country affords. . . . Here congregate at certain seasons the merchants of the plains and mountains with their stocks of peltry. Chiefs of the Shian, the Kioway, and Arapaho sit in solemn conclave with the head traders, and smoke the 'calumet' over their real or imaginary grievances. . . . In the corral, groups of leather-clad mountaineers, with 'decks' of 'euker' and 'seven up,' gamble away their hard-earned peltries. The employees — mostly St. Louis Frenchmen and Canadian *voyageurs* — are pressing packs of buffalo skins, beating robes, or engaged in other duties of a trading fort. Indian squaws, the wives of mountaineers, strut about in all the pride of beads and fofarrow, jingling with bells and bugles, and happy as paint can make them. . . . The appearance of the fort is very striking, standing as it does hundreds of miles from any settlement, on a vast and lifeless prairie, surrounded by hordes of hostile Indians, and far out of the reach of intercourse with civilized man; its mud-built walls inclosing a little garrison of a dozen hardy men, sufficient to hold in check the numerous tribes of savages ever thirsting for their blood. . . ." — Ruxton, *Life in the Far West*, 189–91.

387 Bent's Fort, 1845, from a lithograph in J. W. Abert, *The Upper Arkansas and the Country of the Comanche Indians*, 1846

THE TRAPPING FRATERNITY

THE American frontier has never produced a more picturesque figure than that of the independent trapper of the first half of the nineteenth century. He was free — free to wander whither he would over the plains and through the mountain, free to build his campfire and throw up his rude shelter where it would serve his purpose best, free to catch what prey he could, free to work when he chose or to loaf when the mood was on him, free to starve. He was beyond the pale of civilization and beyond the law. From time to time he brought his peltries to the nearest fort, where he sold them for what he could get. With money in his pocket he replenished his stock of necessities. This business over, he tarried for a few days of gambling and drinking until his money was gone, then he set out to work again. As he turned his horse's nose toward the setting sun he had no regrets that he had no money jingling in his pockets or put away in some place of safekeeping. Improvidence and poverty were parts of the code of the trapper fraternity.

388 Hunters and Trappers in the West, from an engraving after a drawing by Felix O. C. Darley, in the possession of the publishers

BILL WILLIAMS, A TRAPPER TYPE

"WILLIAMS always rode ahead, his body bent over his saddle-horn, across which rested a long heavy rifle, his keen gray eyes peering from under the slouched brim of a flexible felt-hat, black and shining with grease. His buckskin hunting shirt, bedaubed until it had the appearance of polished leather, hung in folds over his bony carcass; his nether extremities being clothed in pantaloons of the same material. . . . His feet were thrust into a pair of Mexican stirrups made of wood. . . . In the shoulder-belt, which sustained his powder-horn and bullet-pouch, were fastened the various instruments essential to one pursuing his mode of life. An awl, with deer-horn handle, and the point defended by a case of cherry-wood carved by his own hand, hung at the back of the belt, side by side with a worm for cleaning the rifle; and under this was a squat and quaint-looking bullet-mold, the handles guarded by strips of buckskin to save his fingers from burning when running balls, having for its companion a little bottle made from the point of an antelope's horn scraped transparent, which contained the 'medicine' used for baiting the traps. The old coon's face was sharp and thin, a long nose and chin hob-nobbing each other; and his head was always bent forward giving him the appearance of being hump-backed. He *appeared* to look neither to the right nor left, but, in fact, his little twinkling eye was everywhere. He looked at no one he was addressing, always seeming to be thinking of something else than the subject of his discourse, speaking in a whining, thin, cracked voice. . . . On the present occasion he had joined this band, and naturally assumed the leadership (for Bill ever refused to go in harness), in opposition to his usual practice, which was to hunt alone. His character was well known. Acquainted with every inch of the Far West, and with all the Indian tribes who inhabited it, he never failed to outwit his Red enemies, and generally made his appearance at the rendezvous, from his solitary expeditions, with galore of beaver when numerous bands of trappers dropped in on foot, having been despoiled of their packs and animals by the very Indians through the midst of whom old Williams had contrived to pass unseen and unmolested. On occasions when he had been in company with others, and attacked by Indians, Bill invariably fought manfully . . . but always 'on his own hook.'" — RUXTON, *In the Old West*, 123–25.

389 A Trapper Fording a Stream, from a drawing by Frederic Remington, in Theodore A. Dodge, *Riders of Many Lands*, Houghton, Mifflin Co., New York, 1901

390 A Fur Trader in the Council Tipi, from a drawing by Frederic Remington for Julian Ralph, "A Skin for a Skin," in *Harper's New Monthly Magazine*, February 1892

THE FRENCH AND THE AMERICAN

French and Americans mingled among the white men of the plains. They differed much from one another and their virtues were complementary. Perhaps four-fifths of the lower grade employees were French *voyageurs*, hailing originally from Canada or New Orleans. The *voyageur* had a volatile temperament, always singing at his work, laughing and joking. Some of the most precious of the fragments of that life of the plains that have been preserved after the culture has long since disappeared are the boat songs of the *voyageurs*, songs which helped to ease many a weary hour when a long line of men with a cable over their shoulders trudged for endless days along the banks of the Missouri, dragging a great keel boat against its current, to some fort far in the interior.

Dans mon chêmin j'ai rencontré
Trois cavalières bien montées,
L'on, ton, laridon danée
L'on, ton, laridon, dai.

Trois cavalières bien montées
L'une à cheval, l'autre à pied,
L'on, ton etc.

They worked with little complaint, for scant pay and sometimes with little food and shelter. The great rivers of the continental interior were their natural element and the canoe their conveyance. In these they performed at times prodigious feats of endurance. They were illiterate, superstitious, and timid. The *voyageur* could be trusted to perform the most arduous tasks but he was not dependable in a fight. The American would not work so hard nor submit so completely to authority. He was more independent, more inclined to desert, less gay and happy. But he feared no man, either red or white. John Jacob Astor once remarked that on the plains a Frenchman was worth three Americans. In mountain or Indian country, however, the American was vastly superior.

GEORGE CATLIN

The *Yellowstone*, on its pioneer trip up the Missouri, bore among its passengers one of the most interesting figures to visit the Indian country. George Catlin, born in eastern Pennsylvania near the spot of the famous Wyoming massacre of the American Revolution, had early in life developed a deep interest in the American Indian. In 1829 he plunged into the Indian country, where he remained for eight years. Catlin felt almost the call of a religious zealot to preserve for posterity the life and features of the Indians, so soon to lose their ancient culture. He devoted himself to studying their ways and to drawing pictures of all their doings. He idealized the Indians and this bias makes his work somewhat untrustworthy. Nevertheless, there is much of value in what he has left and his pictures are among the best that have come down from these early decades. Bringing with him his drawings and a collection of specimens of Indian arts and crafts, Catlin returned east where he attracted the attention of many notable men. In 1839 he took his collection to London and on the strength of it became a lion of the hour. The contrast between the English and American conception of Catlin's Indian work is significant of the attitude of the two peoples. To the British the Indian had not only been an ally in the American Revolution and the War of 1812, but an ally who was picturesque and romantic. To few Americans was the Indian romantic, although Fenimore Cooper's Leatherstocking Tales were widely read. The people of the United States still considered the redskin an obstacle in the way of their western progress and their memories of contact with him in the past called to mind deeds of treachery and blood.

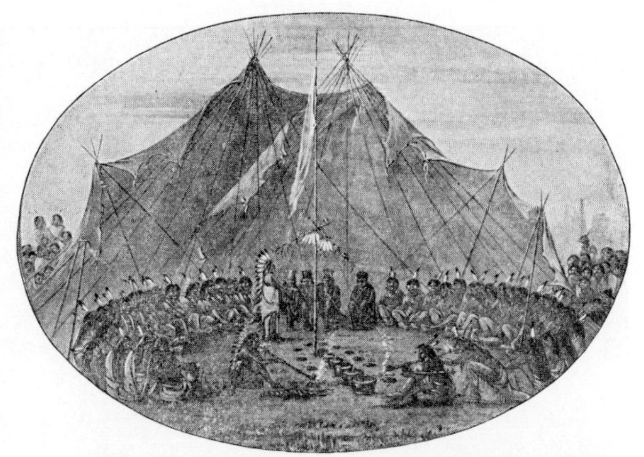

391 A Feast Given by the Sioux to Catlin and Major Sanford, from the painting by George Catlin in the American Museum of Natural History, New York

PRINCE MAXIMILIAN

Two years after Catlin had ascended the Missouri, the *Yellowstone* bore upstream on its annual trip a German Prince with his entourage, making his way into the Indian country to study the life of the red men. Maximilian was a German savant, Prince of a small House in Rhenish Prussia. The North American Indian had intrigued his imagination and he determined to see at first hand this little-known race. He came to the Indian country after some exploring experience in South America. He brought with him Charles Bodmer, a Swiss artist later to win considerable fame for his landscapes and to receive the ribbon of the Legion of Honor. In the spring of 1833 Maximilian and his party were at St. Louis, planning to strike west into the Rockies. General William Clark advised against a trip into the mountain country, which would be fraught with much danger and would be unlikely to produce scientific results of great value, because the fur traders in the mountains tried to avoid the Indians rather than to cultivate their friendship. Upon Clark's suggestion, Maximilian took passage on the American Fur Company's steamer and made his way finally into the country of the Blackfeet. Bodmer was as deeply interested in the work as was his chief. With great ingenuity and with unwearied patience the Swiss artist secured sittings from well-known Indian chiefs and has left a permanent and accurate record of their features and costumes. To Maximilian and to Bodmer posterity owes a great debt for their work in the preservation of the wild life of the Plains Indians and also of the incidents and tales of the fur trade itself.

392 A Maximilian Bivouac in the Forest, from a lithograph after a drawing by Charles Bodmer, in Maximilian, *Travels in the Interior of North America, 1832–34*, London, 1838–43

393 Prince Maximilian (second from right; with Charles Bodmer, extreme right) Meeting the Minatarees at Fort Clark, from a lithograph after a drawing by Charles Bodmer, in Maximilian, *Travels in the Interior of North America, 1832–34*, London, 1838–43

394 Drawn expressly for *The Pageant of America* by Joseph L. Cain

SANTA FÉ

THE year before Ramsay Crooks wrote to Astor regarding the extension of the company's business to the western plains, the people of St. Louis had listened eagerly to news which came in from the southwest. Mexico had revolted, thrown off the yoke of Spain, and was now an independent nation. This meant that the ancient Spanish law forbidding foreigners to trade within the Mexican country had passed away. Merchants in the counting houses of St. Louis argued that the guard at Santa Fé would be gone. They recalled the report of that isolated community which Pike had brought back in 1807. They recalled also later unsuccessful efforts of traders to get past the Spanish guards. They discussed with growing animation the need of the Santa Fé people for American goods. From the beginning of its settlement Santa Fé's only connection with the outside world had lain through Vera Cruz, a port far distant from this Spanish frontier town. The road to it led through a semi-desert country. Santa Fé had, as a consequence, stagnated through the years. Contact with American trading centers should now bring new life to its streets, bordered by shops and houses of adobe. New Mexico offered prospects for rich profits.

CAPTAIN BECKNELL

THE route from the American frontier to Santa Fé passed through a difficult country. For part of the distance water is scarce, and more than one trader was destined to lose his life on this account. Dangerous Indian tribes, moreover, lived along the trail. The Comanches and the Kiowas were enemies whom white men must avoid if possible. In spite of the difficulties Becknell, a citizen of Missouri, acted swiftly in 1821 when he learned of the Mexican revolution. "During the same year, Captain Becknell, of Missouri, with four trusty companions, went out to Santa Fé by the far western prairie route. This intrepid little band started from the vicinity of Franklin, with the original purpose of trading with the Iatan or Comanche Indians; but having fallen in accidentally with a party of Mexican rangers, when near the Mountains, they were easily prevailed upon to accompany them to the new emporium, where, notwithstanding the trifling amount of merchandise they were possessed of, they realized a very handsome profit. . . . The favorable reports brought by the enterprising Captain, stimulated others to embark in the trade; and early in the following May, Colonel Cooper and sons, from the same neighborhood, accompanied by several others (their whole number about fifteen), set out with four or five thousand dollars' worth of goods, which they transported upon pack-horses." — GREGG, *Commerce of the Prairies*, edition of 1926, 6–7.

395 A Pack Train on the Santa Fé Trail, from the mural painting by Edward Holslag, in the First National Bank, Pueblo, Col.

396 A Caravan Encamped, from the mural painting *Commerce of the Prairies* by Allen True, in the Warren Library, Denver, Col.

THE SANTA FÉ TRADE

ONCE begun, the Santa Fé trade sprang into vigorous life. From first to last it remained a typically frontier trade. No great companies like the American Fur Company participated. The traders were small individual proprietors, many of whom risked their entire capital on a single expedition. Pack horses and great canvas-covered wagons carried the commodities which the American had to sell and which the Spaniard in this Santa Fé country was eager to buy. Stowed away in the lumbering vehicles were bolts of cloth, sometimes silk but more often cotton. Side by side with these was a miscellaneous variety of other manufactured articles. Coming back the loads were of fur, the result of the activities of traders and trappers in the Colorado country. Bags of specie were also to be found and occasionally droves of horses and mules from distant California. The trade did not stop at Santa Fé but spread into Chihuahua and on across the desert and the mountains to California. It lasted from the 'twenties to the 'forties when, on the eve of the outbreak of the war with the United States, the Mexican Government finally stopped it. As sixteenth-century Spaniards, passing through the waters of the Spanish Main infested by Dutch and English buccaneers, collected their merchant ships together into great fleets which could be protected by escorts, so the American traders into Santa Fé united their wagons into caravans when they passed through the dangerous Indian country. Competition was keen among them and their intercourse was marked by the spirit of individualism that ever characterized the American frontiersman. They were not willing to organize their caravan at the eastern end of the route but each man pushed on to the very edge of the dangerous zone and the caravans were made up at Council Grove. Captains and subordinate officers were elected, after the vigorous electioneering which has ever characterized American political methods. But the authority of these officers was slight. A caravan was frequently split up into four divisions, each in the charge of a lieutenant. "Upon encamping, the wagons are formed into a 'hollow square' (each division on a side), constituting at once an enclosure (or corral) for the animals when needed, and a fortification against the Indians. Not to embarrass the cattle-pen, the camp fires are all layed outside of the wagons. Outside of the wagons also the travelers spread their beds which consist for the most part of buffalo rugs and blankets. Many content themselves with a single mackinaw; but a pair constitutes the most regular pallett. . . ." — GREGG, *Commerce of the Prairies*, 1845, I, 50.

397 Arrival of a caravan at Santa Fé, from an engraving by A. L. Dick after a drawing by E. Didier, in Josiah Gregg, *Commerce of the Prairies*, 1845

THE INDIAN MENACE

THE Santa Fé trail passed through a country where ranged hunting or war parties of many tribes. On one occasion a caravan came into contact with a band of Blackfeet seeking prey and profit far from their northern plains. Gregg has left many vivid descriptions of meetings between the redskins and the traders. "The hour of midnight had passed away, and nothing had been heard except the tramping of the men on guard, and the peculiar grating of the mules' teeth, nibbling the short grass of the valley. Ere long, however, one of our sentinels got a glimpse of some object moving stealthily along, and as he was straining his eyes to ascertain what sort of apparition it could be, a loud Indian yell suddenly revealed the mystery. This was quickly followed by a discharge of firearms, and the shrill note of the Pawnee whistle, which at once made known the character of our visitors. As usual, the utmost confusion prevailed in our camp: some, who had been snatched from the land of dreams, ran their heads against the wagons — others called out for their guns while they had them in their hands. During the height of the bustle and uproar, a Mexican servant was observed leaning with his back against a wagon and his fusil elevated at an angle of forty-five degrees, cocking and pulling the trigger without ceasing. . . . The firing still continued — the yells grew fiercer and more frequent; and everything betokened the approach of a terrible conflict. Meanwhile a number of persons were engaged in securing the mules and horses which were staked around the encampment; and in a few minutes they were all shut up in the *corral* — a hundred head or more in a pen formed by seven wagons. The enemy failing in their principal object — to frighten off our stock — they soon began a retreat; and in a few minutes nothing more was to be heard of them. All that we could discover the next morning was, that none of our party had sustained any injury, and that we had not lost a single animal."

As Santa Fé was approached the organization that had been preserved in crossing the prairies broke up and each "proprietor" rushed his wagons forward in his own way to be first in the market. He first had to get his goods through the Mexican customs house and then they would be ready for distribution to the merchants of Santa Fé and to traders from outlying districts who came in for the great occasion of the year. Gregg had ridden on ahead into the little adobe city of Santa Fé. "Five or six days after our arrival, the caravan at last hove in sight, and wagon after wagon was seen pouring down the last declivity at about a mile's distance from the city. To judge from the clamorous rejoicings of the men, and the state of agreeable excitement which the muleteers seemed to be laboring under, the spectacle must have been as new to them as it had been to me. . . . The arrival at Santa Fé produced a great bustle and excitement among the natives. 'Los Americanos! — Los Carros! — La entrada de la caravana!' were to be heard in every direction; and crowds of *leperos* hung about as usual to see what they could pilfer. The wagoners were by no means free from excitement on this occasion. Informed of the 'ordeal' they had to pass, they had spent the previous morning in 'rubbing up'; now they were prepared, with clean faces, sleek combed hair, and their choicest Sunday suit, to meet the 'fair eyes' of glistening black that were sure to stare at them as they passed. There was yet another preparation to be made in order to 'show off' to advantage. Each wagoner must tie a brand new 'cracker' to his whip; for, on driving through the streets and the plaza pública, every one strives to outvie his comrades in the dexterity with which he flourishes this favourite badge of his authority." — GREGG, 101–03.

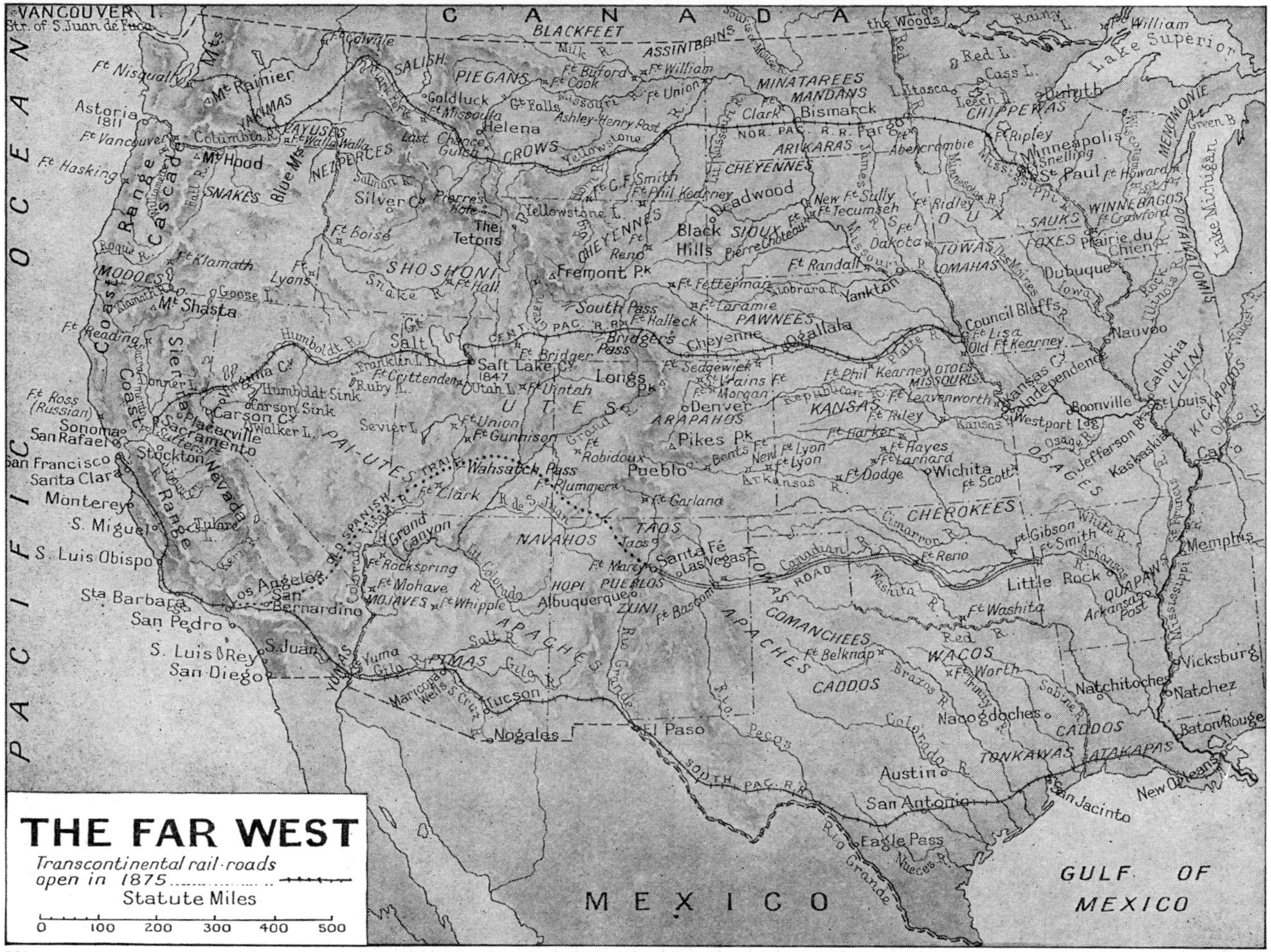

THE FAR WEST

Transcontinental rail-roads open in 1875

Statute Miles

0 100 200 300 400 500

398 Drawn expressly for *The Pageant of America* by John L. Philip, American Geographical Society, New York

A PERMANENT INDIAN POLICY

WHILE western merchant adventurers were following the dusty trail to Santa Fé and the American Fur Company was laying the foundation for its business in the Valley of the Missouri, the Government of the United States was turning its attention to the formulation of a definite and permanent Indian policy. In a sense the War of 1812 had marked a turning point in the relations of the Indians to the United States. During that conflict the Tecumseh confederacy had been completely destroyed and Tecumseh himself killed. General Andrew Jackson, moreover, had crushed the Creeks on the southwestern frontier. The war, therefore, had left the Government in a much stronger position in its dealings with the tribes. The conflict had increased the national consciousness of the American people, who began more and more to turn to the central government to carry out projects in which the people of different states were interested. Naturally, the people looked to the United States to eradicate the Indians from the regions where the whites had settled, or desired to settle. The Americans in the first third of the nineteenth century could not brook the possession by redskins of areas of fertile land, nor were they usually willing to live side by side with the Indians confined on reservations. As the years passed the whites protested more and more vigorously to the Government that the Indians were not moved off rapidly enough from the lands which the Americans demanded.

399 John C. Calhoun, 1782–1850, from a photograph in the collection of L. C. Handy, Washington

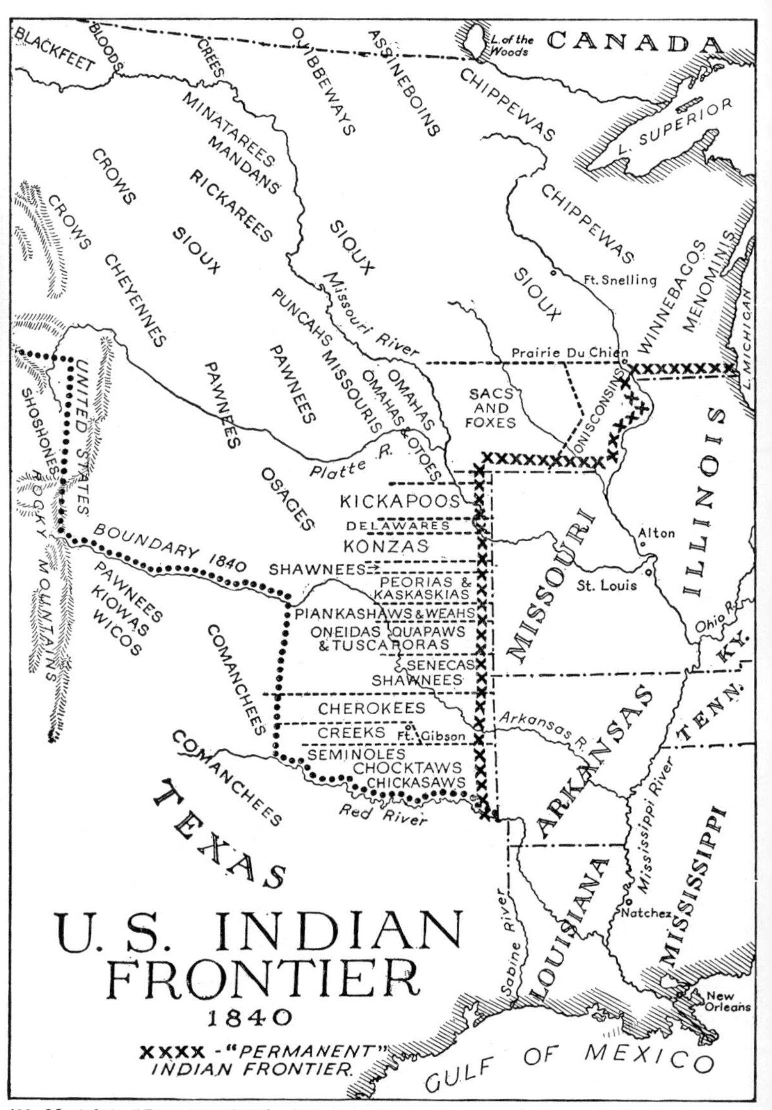

400 Map of the "Permanent" Indian Frontier, 1840, based on a map in George Catlin, *North American Indians*, drawn expressly for *The Pageant of America* by Joseph L. Cain. Catlin's spelling of Indian tribe names has been followed

THE FORMULATION OF THE POLICY

In January 1825, President Monroe submitted to Congress a proposed solution for the Indian question. The data on which the plan rested and the details of the plan itself had been the result of the labors of Monroe's Secretary of War, John C. Calhoun. Behind Calhoun, with an influence on the formulation of the plan probably equaled by no one, was a man soon to become Calhoun's bitter personal enemy, the popular Indian fighter and hero of New Orleans, Andrew Jackson. Jackson had no love for the redskins, though he had personal friends among them. The plan formulated under such auspices was to secure the removal to the bison country of virtually all the Indians east of the Mississippi River. Some tribes were to be permitted to remain in the isolated country about the southern shores of Lake Superior. But for the most part, they were to go to a land which more than one observer of standing had pronounced to be unsuitable for habitation by the whites. The Indians were, in fact, to be moved to the westernmost border of the nation. From many Indian villages it would be possible to look out upon the mountains, then under the sovereignty of Mexico. An Indian zone was to separate the two nations. The redskins were to exchange the fertile lands which they held in the region east of the Mississippi for some semi-arid tracts beyond the western boundary of Missouri and the territory of Arkansas. For them it was argued that the change would be beneficial because under shadow of the mountains they would find a permanent home. They would no longer be harried from place to place, suffering the demoralization incident upon such disruptions in the life of the tribes. Calhoun, in advocating the removal policy, seems to have been entirely sincere in the belief that it would ultimately benefit the Indians. The result was the establishment of a permanent Indian frontier beyond which the white man would not go. In 1825 General William Clark carried through negotiations with the Osage and Kaw tribes which resulted in the freeing of a considerable area immediately west of Missouri and Arkansas, in which the tribes from the east could be settled.

THE DEFENSE OF THE FRONTIER

401 A Cavalry Charge on the Southern Plains, from a painting by Frederic Remington in the Metropolitan Museum of Art, New York

THE Indian frontier, established in the 'twenties and 'thirties, presented military problems of a complicated nature. The new tribes must be protected against the Plains Indians. The white settlements lying east of the frontier lines must also be defended against all the peoples beyond it. To the army of the United States was entrusted this duty, at a time when the officers and men in the regular military establishment of the United States numbered a little less than six thousand men. For purposes of national defense the War Department divided the nation into two zones, northeast and southwest of a line drawn diagonally from Florida to the northwestern extremity of Lake Superior. These were the Eastern and Western Departments. Control of the Indians south of Lake Superior, therefore, fell for the most part to the Eastern Department. The army, in adjusting itself to the task of defending the frontier, depended heavily on cavalry and developed, for a time, a new mounted branch of special Indian fighters, known as "Dragoons" or "Rangers." It was expected that these Rangers, specially recruited for Indian service, would be of a higher type and more efficient than the regular units of the army. This anticipation, however, did not prove to be well founded, for the regular cavalry was found to be best suited for the task in hand. Mounted troops were obviously needed, if marauding bands of Indians were to be apprehended and punished, for the Indians were well mounted and were excellent horsemen. There were not, however, enough mounted troops for the service and detachments of infantry had to be used all along the frontier. The army was, in fact, too small for the task imposed upon it.

THE LINE OF FORTS

THE building of forts was an obvious part of the defense of the frontier and before 1835 a line of fortifications had been established from Fort Howard on Green Bay and Fort Snelling on the Upper Mississippi to Fort Smith on the Arkansas. In addition to these were some cantonments in Louisiana. Jefferson Barracks, near St. Louis, established in 1826, was the center of the defense organization; and the line of forts from Louisiana to Lake Michigan formed an arc of a great circle, passing through Fort Leavenworth, established in 1827 on the right bank of the Missouri near the Little Platte for the protection of the Santa Fé trade. At Jefferson Barracks was located a reserve force, considerably larger than that at any of the outlying posts, and from this central point reinforcements could be rushed by water up or down the Mississippi and up the Missouri, the Arkansas or the Red Rivers. In all these western forts, including Jefferson Barracks, there were, in 1833, two thousand, four hundred and twenty-one men and one hundred and fifty-one officers, and other years about this time show but little variation. The army guarding the West and maintaining peace among the Indians was, therefore, little more than a tiny and widely scattered police force. (See map No. 398.)

402 Fort Snelling, from a lithograph after a drawing by Henry Lewis, in *Das Illustrirte Mississippi-Thal*, Düsseldorf, 1844–45

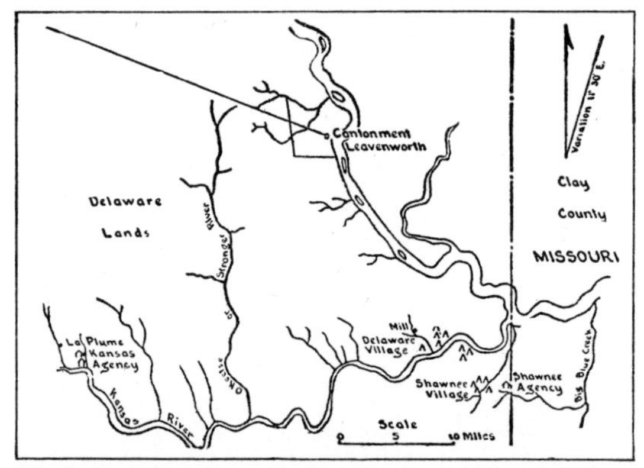

403 Isaac McCoy's Survey Showing Delaware and Shawnee Villages, in 1830, from Major Elvid Hunt, *History of Fort Leavenworth*, Fort Leavenworth, Kansas, 1926

THE PLAINS INDIANS AND THE NEWCOMERS

THE Plains Indians viewed with deep dislike the coming of the tribes that had once lived in the eastern forests. They were so many more hunters to pursue and decimate the herds of antelope and bison, so many more braves who might have to be fought. They were moreover, in the main, peoples who had accepted many of the white man's ways and who had suffered degeneration as a result of prolonged contact with the frontier. An Englishman, C. A. Murray, visiting the Pawnees in the eighteenth-thirties, chanced to observe an instance of the hatred of the old Plains Indians for the newcomers. One summer day, when the tribe was moving, their scouts noticed a hunting party of Shawnees and Delawares who, after being observed, made boldly for the Pawnee camp. An excited tribal council of the Pawnees decided on peace, perhaps through fear of punishment by the United States Government. "The dislike of the Pawnees for their new guests was but ill-concealed, . . . The Pawnees consider these corn-growing settled tribes as half-white men, and deny their right to hunt in the buffalo plains and mountains; and the party now present had passed through the very range which the Pawnees were about to travel and had probably driven off many of the buffalo. . . . They wished to pass the Pawnee without being observed by them; but finding that they had been observed by the distant scouts, they at once adopted the safest, though apparently the rashest, course, by presenting themselves peacefully and fearlessly to the whole nation. . . . The Delawares, degraded in spirit and diminished in numbers as they are, have yet some lingering pride, some remains of that haughty assumption which led their ancestors to call themselves the 'Lenni Lenape' ('Fathers of Men')." — MURRAY, I, 286–87. In 1833 was held at Fort Leavenworth a great Indian council in which the wild tribes of the plains were brought face to face with their new neighbors from the east. John T. Irving, who was present, has left a vivid account of the proceedings. "First came the Delawares, gay with silver ornaments and ribands. They were not very warlike in their appearance, but the Pawnees had discovered that their looks belied them and regarded them, few as they were, as their most formidable foe. . . . After the Delawares, came the Shawnees, reeking with paint and gaudy with ribands. . . . Then came the rest of the migratory tribes: the Peorias, Piankashaws, Pottowatomies, and Kickapoos, who all as they arrived, took their places among their civilized brethren. After they were seated, the Otoes made their appearance, coming across the green in single file, . . . They seated themselves a short distance apart from the civilized Indians. Last of all came the wild band of Pawnees. In front of them strode the Wild Horse, his savage features not rendered any the less hideous by a drunken frolic in which he had been engaged on the previous day. His hair hung in tangled masses about his head and shoulders, and his body as usual was smeared with red ochre. . . . [The Indian commissioner opened the council and explained the terms of the proposed treaty of peace. After much speaking by many Indians, Sou-wah-nock, chief of the Delawares, arose.] 'The Pawnees,' he said, 'met my young men upon the hunt and slew them. I have had my revenge. Let them look at their town. I found it filled with lodges, I left it a heap of ashes. . . . I am satisfied. . . . I am not afraid to avow the deeds that I have done, for I am Sou-wah-nock, a Delaware warrior; but I am willing to bury the tomahawk and smoke the pipe of peace with my enemies. They are brave men and fight well. . . . [Wild Horse replied.] His speech abounded with one of those wild bursts of eloquence which peculiarly mark the savages of North America, and concluded in a manner which spoke highly of his opinion of what a warrior should be. 'I have promised to the Delawares,' he said, 'the friendship of my tribe. I respect my promise and I cannot lie, for I am a Pawnee chief.'" — *Indian Sketches*, II.

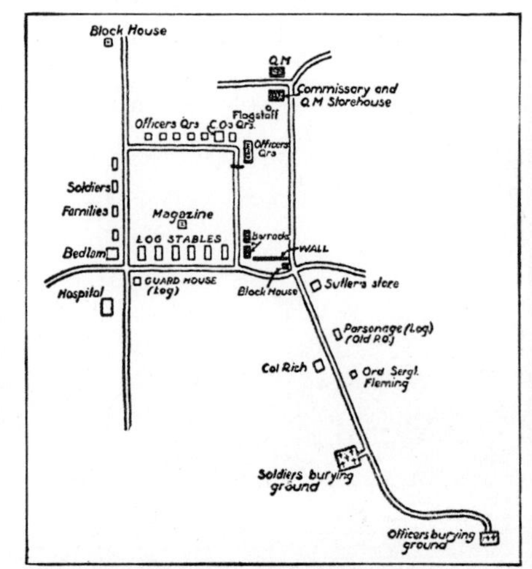

404 Location of Fort Leavenworth Buildings About 1849, from a diagram in Major Elvid Hunt, *History of Fort Leavenworth*, Fort Leavenworth, Kansas, 1926

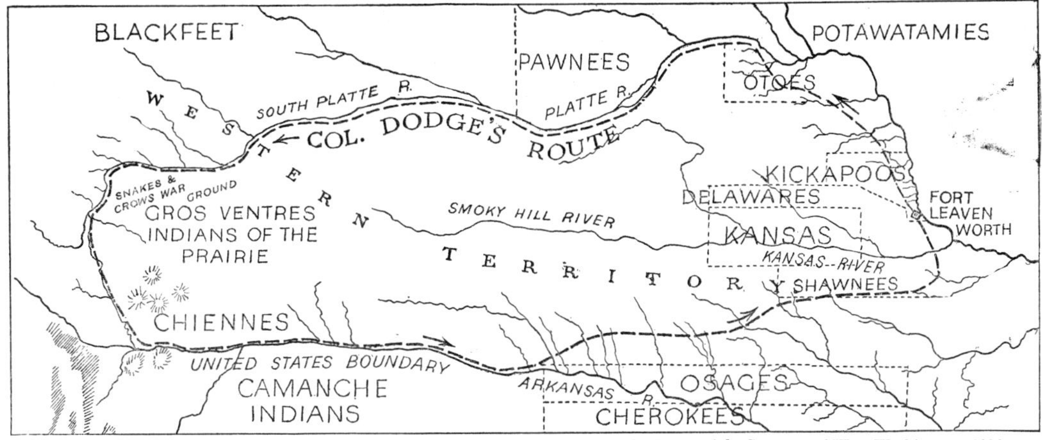

405 Route of the Dragoons Under Colonel Dodge in 1835, redrawn from a map in *The Report of the Secretary of War*, Washington, 1836

IMPRESSING THE INDIANS

In 1834, the year following the Great Council at Fort Leavenworth, Colonel Henry Dodge, who was stationed at Fort Gibson on the Arkansas River, was ordered to proceed to Fort Leavenworth. At the latter post he left nearly two hundred men and with a force of three hundred turned his face toward the Pawnee country. Across the treeless plains, through the hottest days of midsummer, the weary force plodded on and on until they reached the village of the Pawnees. Here they rested, conferred with the chiefs of this fierce and proud people, and then returned to Fort Gibson. They were gone two months. The next year, 1835, Colonel Dodge was again in the Indian country, this time with three companies of dragoons. The Arikaras had been driven out of their villages by the Dakotas and sent fleeing into the domain of the Pawnees. There was danger of the spread of inter-tribal wars. Since the mission of the army on the frontier was to prevent such conflicts, which spread confusion and destruction, Colonel Dodge was sent to impress the Arikaras and the Pawnees with the power of the government. He marched northwest near the west bank of the Missouri River as far as the Platte. Then he followed the south bank of that stream almost to the mountains. He accomplished his purpose among the Indians but he passed beyond their country. As the party turned south to strike the Santa Fé trail its members could look up and see Pike's Peak rising on the western horizon. After nearly four months Dodge returned to Leavenworth along the route which took the traders to Santa Fé. His animals and men were exhausted but he had accomplished his mission. He had impressed the Indians and, what was even more important, he had added much to the white man's knowledge of the characteristics of the Indian country.

BUILDING ROADS

The army did more than march — more even than establish cantonments and build forts. The troops and the white population alike needed roads and the army undertook to build many of them. One of the most important was a highway connecting Madisonville, Louisiana, with the Tennessee River at a point some twenty-one miles north of Mussel Shoals. This was completed between 1817 and 1820. In 1820 General Atkinson ordered and carried out the building of a road from Council Bluffs to the Grand River in Missouri, a stretch of highway three hundred miles in length. Seven years later the army constructed more than a third of the two hundred and eight miles of road that was laid out between Little Rock, Arkansas, and Fort Gibson, which stood in the country allotted to the Cherokees. Other roads were built, particularly in the Louisiana country.

406 The Missouri River and Council Bluffs, from a steel engraving after a sketch by Frederick Pieray, in James Linforth, *Route from Liverpool to Great Salt Lake Valley*, London, 1855

407 Offerings of the Mandans, from a lithograph after a drawing by Charles Bodmer, in Maximilian, *Travels in the Interior of North America, 1832–34*, London, 1838–43

THE PASSING OF THE MANDANS

ONE result of the advent of the white men in the Indian country became clear in 1837. In the spring of that year the *St. Peters*, the annual steamboat of the American Fur Company, churned up the Missouri on its customary business. After it had left St. Louis the dreaded smallpox broke out among its crew. The boat kept on, however, knowing that the Indians and the forts along the Upper Missouri would be anxiously awaiting its arrival. At Fort Clarke, as the *St. Peters* lay along the bank, the whites strove desperately to keep the Indians from coming on board, but they, childlike people that they were, could not understand the warnings of the traders. A Mandan chief stole a blanket from a white man ill with the disease. A few days later smallpox began to rage in the Mandan villages. Never had an epidemic of such virulence been known to these western traders. A brave, vigorous and healthy in the morning, would be stricken as if by an unseen hand and in the midst of terrible sufferings die before the sun went down. Nearly all those who were attacked succumbed. There were many men who, beholding the agonies of the sick, killed themselves with their knives rather than await the disease. The lodges and the streets of the villages were strewn with unburied dead. Some fled to the open plains where they contracted the disease and died uncared for and alone. When the epidemic had burned itself out, something less than fifty terror-stricken and despairing Mandans, a tiny remnant of a once important people, remained. These went to live with the Hidatsas and the independent history of the Mandans came to an end.

SPREADING OF THE PLAGUE

THE plague did not end in the Mandan villages, for the *St. Peters* went on up the river, stopping at forts and carrying the smallpox to tribe after tribe. The pestilence raged among the Assiniboins; it reached the Blackfeet. Wherever it went it took a heavy toll of death. The Assiniboins accused the white men of bringing desolation to their villages and urged war against them. The Blackfeet looked upon the scourge as a punishment from their gods for the war they had undertaken against the white men. Yet the white man was responsible. The American Fur Company, which could have prevented the spread of the disease among the Indians, allowed the *St. Peters* to continue on its course. Cupidity, and the desire for gain, outweighed whatever humanitarian feelings the traders may have had. Yet they also were among the sufferers, for the epidemic raged in the forts where there were many who had not been vaccinated. They suffered also in the decline of the amount of furs and robes brought in by the decimated tribes. This plague, more terrible than any war between hostile tribes, far surpassed any disaster known to the Great Plains in the Indian days.

408 Tent of an Assiniboin Chief, from a lithograph after a drawing by Charles Bodmer, in Maximilian, *Travels in the Interior of North America, 1832–34*, London, 1838–43

REFUGEES FROM THE APPALACHIANS

Two years after the despairing remnant of the Mandans had thrown in their lot with the Gros-Ventres, another group of discouraged Indians camped for the winter of 1839 on a small river called the Illinois in what is now eastern Oklahoma. (See Chapter V.) They were the Cherokee nation, driven from their ancient hills and valleys. With them they brought their constitution and their organization as a nation. They were filled with bitterness when, here on the western plains, they were brought face to face with that handful of their own number who had signed the treaty of New Echota. This group, in the opinion of the bulk of the refugees, had betrayed their people. They had broken the law which forbade any individual to sign a treaty ceding away the Indian lands. Three hundred Cherokee full-bloods, every one of whom had suffered some peculiar misfortune in the transfer from the old land to the new, banded themselves together to punish the treaty men. In June of 1840, John Ridge, Major Ridge, and Elias Boudinot fell by the hands of assassins. Their alleged treachery was repaid in blood. The treaty men, however, were not the chief problem which confronted the migrating Cherokees. For many years a part of the nation had lived along the banks of the Arkansas. These were now known as the Old Settlers. They had long had their own government and now they looked somewhat askance upon their kinsmen from the East who claimed to represent and to exercise the authority of the Cherokee nation. The Old Settlers, as individuals, met the refugees with hospitality and friendship, but between the two groups a sharp party fight developed, arousing the passions of both sides. For more than a decade political division disturbed the harmony of the Cherokee nation. In the end, however, the difficulties were settled and the government which had been brought from the mountains extended its control to all the Cherokees. But the contest for power between the Emigrants and the Old Settlers prevented the settlement of the financial arrangements between the tribe and the United States. For a decade, therefore, the Indians struggled against great adversity to establish themselves in their new country.

28th Congress, *1st Session.* — Doc. No. 235. — Ho. of Reps.

CHEROKEE INDIANS.

MEMORIAL

of

JOHN ROGERS, *Principal Chief*,

and

JAMES CAREY *and* THOMAS L. RODGERS,

Chiefs and head men, being members of a Committee on behalf of the Cherokee old settlers west of the Mississippi, for themselves and their people.

April 13, 1844.
Referred to the Committee on Indian Affairs.
April 17, 1844.
Ordered to be printed.

To the Senate and House of Representatives of the United States of America:

An oppressed and ruined people, stripped of the property and deprived of the protection which were repeatedly promised and solemnly guarantied to them by the Government of the United States, appeal to the Congress of those United States for reparation. Pennyless and in exile, we are able to bring no influence to bear on the Government or people of this Republic, but the power of truth and the sympathy which wrong and oppression, when made manifest, never fail to excite. If these be not sufficient to procure your interposition in our behalf, nothing will be left to us and our people but oppression, dispersion, despair, and death.

Do not, we beseech you, turn a deaf ear to our complaints because other portions of the red men have been troublesome to your Government. If your policy has at times been thwarted, it was not by the Western Cherokees; if frauds have been committed, it was not by them; if your treasury has been plundered, they have shared no part of the spoil. In all their dealings with the United States, they have been open and fair and honest; always ready to accede to every reasonable wish expressed by your Government, committing encroachments upon none, and asking only to be allowed the enjoyment of their country and their homes in

409 Protest of the "Old Settlers" against their Treatment by the United States, from a pamphlet in the New York Public Library

ON THE BANKS OF THE ARKANSAS

The Cherokees, after their first winter, promptly set to work to cultivate the land which had been allotted to them. The nation owned it in common and any Cherokee might lay out his farm where he chose. His improvements, however, were his personal property. The soil proved to be fertile and the Cherokees, in spite of their difficulties, began again to prosper. Two decades passed. The first rude shacks gave way to log cabins and these in turn to occasional houses of brick. Two years after reaching the Arkansas, the Council provided for the establishment of eleven primary schools for the education of their children. Five years later there were eighteen such schools, with an enrollment of more than six hundred and fifty pupils. The teachers were Cherokees who had proved themselves qualified for their tasks. In 1846 a law was passed by the Council establishing two seminaries of high-school rank, one for boys and one for girls. There was little money in the public treasury; yet the Cherokees built two brick buildings and to these seminaries came many students. Finally, a selected few of the young men and women of the tribe went to eastern colleges, particularly Mount Holyoke and Princeton, to complete their education. After their four years of academic life they returned to their own people to further the development of their nation and to help improve the lot of their kinsmen. The printing press which the United States had seized at New Echota had not been paid for. So the nation itself was compelled to buy a new one. In 1843 began the publication in Cherokee and English of *The Cherokee Advocate*, intended to disseminate information and to encourage agriculture, education, and religion.

CHEROKEE PRIMER.

PARK HILL:
Mission Press. John Candy, Printer.
1845.

410 Cherokee Primer in the New York Public Library

411 The Cherokee Capitol Building at Tahlequah, from an engraving after a photograph in *Harper's New Monthly Magazine*, November 1893

A GREAT COUNCIL

The Cherokees as well as the other emigrant tribes had trouble with the wild Indians of the plains. In particular, a dispute developed with the Osages regarding land titles in the western part of the Cherokee country. The Plains Indians looked with suspicion and fear upon these slave-holding, agricultural Indians from the eastern mountains. The Cherokee nation became aware of the situation and the Council invited the roving tribes of bison hunters to send representatives to a great conclave. In June 1843, at Tahlequah the Cherokee capital (named for Tellico, the ancient capital in the valley of the Tennessee), representatives from the villages of the plains came gathering in: Pawnees, Cheyennes, Kansas, Osages, Kiowas, Comanches, and many others. For ten days the guests enjoyed the hospitality of the Cherokees and conferred together on matters of mutual interest. Poor as they were, the Cherokees dealt liberally with these members of their race, with whom they sought to enter into lasting friendship. There were barbecues at which were served all the delicacies that pleased the Indian tongue. There were many speeches and much playing of games. The peace pipe was smoked in solemn ceremony and the significance of the symbols on the wampum belts was explained by the old men of the tribes. Then the guests went home fast friends with the Cherokees. The danger of conflict and war had been permanently allayed.

THE SECOND TRAGEDY

In 1860 the Cherokees took a profound interest in the election which resulted in the elevation of Abraham Lincoln to the presidency. When war broke out between the North and the South, many impulsive Cherokee slaveholders joined the Confederacy and the Cherokee Regiment was organized to coöperate with the Confederate armies. The majority of the nation, in spite of their vivid memories of the treatment they had received at the hands of the United States, were loyal to the Union. And among these a regiment was organized to fight beside the blue-uniformed soldiers from the North. The Cherokee government, under the somewhat autocratic leadership of John Ross, sought at first to remain neutral, and then attempted to direct its policy in such a way as to further the best interests of the Cherokees. Ross was first of all a Cherokee. As a result, the Cherokee nation allied itself with the Southern Confederacy but, before the end of the war, discontinued the alliance. The strength of the Cherokees was too slight to play any important part in determining the outcome of the conflict. The war, however, brought these Indians face to face with ruin and starvation. Bands of Confederates swept through their country, carrying off horses and mules and such other things as suited their desires. A force of Germans, fighting on the northern side, made an incursion through the same region, inflicting barbarities that a misinformed northern public charged to the Indians themselves. When the war was over, the Cherokee country, which in 1860 had been a land of growing crops and prosperous communities, was a desolation. The fences were tumbled down, weeds grew in the cultivated fields, and where houses had once stood only gaunt, blackened chimneys remained. Within less than a quarter century after the tragedy of emigration the Cherokee people had a second time met with disaster.

412 Wounded Indians at the Battle of Fredericksburg, from a photograph, courtesy of *Review of Reviews*, New York

CHAPTER IX

THE MOUNTAIN WILDERNESS

WEST of the Great Plains rise the snow-capped Rockies whose irregular peaks once marked an international boundary. Americans of the early nineteenth century looked upon the southernmost of these mountains as a natural and fortunate barrier separating their country from Spanish-speaking Mexico. They moved the Indians of the eastern forests to that sub-arid country just east of the cordilleras which Major Long had pronounced unfit for white habitation. To the west of the mountains lay a land of mystery. Lewis and Clark had crossed it far to the north in an adventure which thrilled the nation. Astor's Overlanders had also crossed it but only at the price of terrible suffering. The country south of the routes of these pioneers was unknown. The greater part of it bore the name of Mexico. Sante Fé was an old center for Spanish settlements. Other Spanish settlements dotted the coast of California southward from San Francisco Bay. But the vast region bounded by the Sierras, the Colorado River, the Rockies, and the Snake River was Indian country where few if any white men had ever set foot.

In the 'twenties the American frontier was only beginning to cross the Mississippi River. The soil of neither Illinois nor Alabama was completely occupied. The settlement of Michigan and Wisconsin was yet to come. To Americans who shuddered at the newspaper accounts of Black Hawk's atrocities the Rocky Mountain country was so distant as to be given but scant attention. Yet ten years before the Hawk broke his pledge and crossed to the east bank of the Mississippi American trappers had begun the penetration of the cordilleras. They cared nought for the niceties of questions of sovereignty. They sought furs and the wealth that furs would bring. Though they did not realize it, they were the precursors of empire.

So the American people began the task of adjusting themselves to the western cordilleras. As a people they had never faced such an environment, for the Appalachians are an old and worn-down system, covered in the days of the pioneers with a mantle of forest. The cordilleras are young mountains piercing the sky with jagged peaks so high as to rise above the limit of tree growth. The pioneer who ventured beyond the Rockies found mountain ridges, plateaus, canyons, deserts, salt lakes, and forests thrown together in bewildering confusion. To make matters worse the region was one of vast distances. Strange animals unknown to the eastern forests or the Great Plains lived in the mountain country. Hulking grizzlies padded through the defiles, while mountain sheep and goats scaled the difficult uplands. Thin blue smoke rising from the banks of mountain streams warned the white man that the redskin already occupied the region. In the first quarter of the nineteenth century traders and trappers led the way into the mountains.

413 Nez-Percé Encampment on the Yellowstone River, Montana, from a photograph in the De Lancey Gill Collection, Bureau of American Ethnology, Washington

THE NEZ-PERCÉS

West of the country of the Crows and the Blackfeet and beyond the jagged peaks of the Bitter Root Mountains stretches a broad plateau, cut by the deep canyon of the Snake River. On the south it merges into the arid country of the Central Basin. On the west it is bordered by the domed peaks of the Blue Mountains. In this region lived the Nez-Percés in villages built in the narrow valley bottoms. They erected long communal houses in each of which dwelt many families. Because the food supply varied the Nez-Percés at certain seasons of the year abandoned their valley-bottom villages where they lived purely on fish and climbed the rugged upland slopes to hunt. On such trips they lived in the conical tipi of the Plains Indian. This habitation of the hunting season typifies an outstanding trait of this mid-mountain people. Though they were isolated, their culture bore the unmistakable stamp of the influence of the Plains Indians to the east, and of the Pacific Coast tribes to the west. In fact, their culture showed an even balance of traits derived from their neighbors on either side and but few elements that were distinctively their own. Ambitious to make the most of the opportunities presented to them and to progress in the arts of civilization, they deliberately borrowed from the tribes about them. Some Nez-Percé braves, at the risk of their lives, entered the Crow country and surreptitiously learned the music and the steps of the war dance of that people. Taking it back to the villages in the canyon of the Snake, the Nez-Percés then abandoned their own war dance for that of the Crows. A more famous story is that which recounts the sending of a Nez-Percé delegation of chiefs to St. Louis to ask that the wonderful Book of the white man be sent to their mountain country. (See Vol. X.) In time the white man's religion modified their own. They gave up many of their ancient beliefs; they ceased to bring sacrifices to the celebrated ram's skull, miraculously embedded in a large pine tree.

THE CHINOOK INDIANS

West of the country of the Nez-Percés were the villages of the Chinook tribes, stretching along the Columbia River from the Dalles to its mouth. This Indian family extended along the coast for a short distance north and south of the mouth of the river which Gray discovered. They lived in communal houses and from them the Nez-Percés seem to have taken this culture trait. Their villages were fairly permanent and clung to the edge of the great river. They were a canoe people, skillful in handling the craft which they made from logs. Of all the Indians in the northwest of what is now the United States the Chinooks were the greatest traders. Not only did one of their own villages trade with another but they reached out to establish contact with the tribes to the north and east and south. As a consequence their tongue became the basis of a common trading language which, though modified somewhat with the passing years, still exists among the Indians of the Pacific Coast from the mouth of the Columbia north to Alaska. The "Chinook jargon," like the sign language of the plains, was the outgrowth of continuous and frequent inter-tribal contact. Both played a vital part in the lives of the peoples who used them. Had it not been for Lewis and Clark very little would be known about these early traders of the Columbia Valley who kept slaves. In 1829 a mysterious plague, known as "ague fever," swept through the Chinook villages. When this dread disease had spent its force the Chinooks had practically ceased to exist. The Chinooks, therefore, were never able to dispute the occupation of their country by the whites.

414 A Chinook Man, from a photograph, courtesy of the American Museum of Natural History, New York

415 An Encampment of the Shoshones in the Wind River Mountains, Wyoming, from a photograph in the De Lancey Gill Collection, Bureau of American Ethnology, Washington

THE SHOSHONES

South of the country of the Nez-Percés lived many tribes of the Shoshonean family. Like the Cherokees in the east they were true mountain Indians. Only occasional groups, like the Comanches of the plains or the Hopis of the southwestern desert, abandoned the upland habitat. They ranged from southern Montana and Idaho, over Utah, Nevada, and Colorado, extending their influence even west of the Sierra Nevada Mountains into California. In the main, the Shoshone tribes were hunter peoples and, wherever the environment permitted, they subsisted on large game. Not everywhere, however, did their habitat offer the deer, antelope, and bear which were their favorite foods. Much of the country which is now Utah and Nevada is arid, a region whose waters never reach the sea, a country of alkaline streams and salt lakes. In this impoverished environment wandering trappers found many villages of Indians, struggling hard to maintain the spark of life by digging roots, catching fish and rabbits, and gathering nuts and seeds. The white men conceived a peculiar contempt for these Indians whose fortune had placed them in a region so ungrateful. They called them "Digger Indians" and the name has persisted. The culture of these peoples was perhaps the lowest among any tribes on the North American continent with the possible exception of certain Californian peoples. None of the Shoshone tribes, except the Hopis, were farmers; all were wandering hunters. Like the Nez-Percés, many of them had borrowed the tipi from the Plains Indians. Others in the north lived in rude shelters whose walls were of sagebrush, built in a half-circle without roofs, offering but little protection against the storms and cold of the winter months. The half-starved band of Shoshones which Lewis and Clark met risking their lives by migrating into the buffalo country in search of food, typified the lot of this wretched upland people.

416 Full-Blood Yuman Warrior, from a photograph in the Bureau of American Ethnology, Washington

THE YUMAN TRIBES

South of the Digger Indians the nineteenth-century traveler found the villages of the Yuman tribes scattered along both banks of the Colorado and the Gila rivers. Other members of the family lived in southern California. The more northern Yuman tribes, of which the Mohaves and the Yumas were the most important, were agricultural peoples, dwelling on the alluvial plains beside the banks of streams. Beans, nuts, tortillas, and various seeds and roots were the main food of these Indians. Tribes like the Mohaves, dwelling near the Colorado, hunted but little, deriving their subsistence primarily from their gardens. Since rainfall was deficient they depended, like the early Egyptians, upon floods to water their crops. Trappers making their way along the banks of the Colorado found the houses of the Mohaves low, square structures with roofs nearly flat. Neither the Mohaves nor the other Yuman tribes were warlike in the sense of the Sioux or the Iroquois; yet, upon occasion, they could fight effectively as many a white man learned to his sorrow.

417 California Indian, from a lithograph after a sketch by Captain W. Smyth, R.N., in Alexander Forbes, *California, A History*, 1839

CALIFORNIA INDIANS

South of the country of the Chinooks lived a confusion of Indian peoples presenting an anthropological problem which has only partly been solved. The first whites, making their way into what is now central and northern California, found there villages of aborigines living in abject poverty. They were not all of one linguistic stock, like the Algonquian or the Siouan peoples, but among them have been discovered more than a score of linguistic families. Whence came they? Their traditions offer no explanation, for their own tales suggest their origin in the place where they were found. Perhaps one day they will be proved to be, as has been suggested, fragments of those earliest Indian peoples who came to North America from Asia. The cordillera region and the plains which lie immediately to the east seem to have been the zone through which the Indians passed southward, attracted perhaps by more favorable habitats in the warmer regions, or driven, it may be, by incoming groups from the north. The complex California group may be the remnants of tribes who once lived in the mountain region, who were brusquely pushed out by the migrating hordes, and were left, like an eddy beside the current of the main stream, in the locality where the whites found them. They practiced no agriculture; they hunted and fished a little but their weapons were crude and ineffective. They depended in the main for subsistence upon varieties of acorns and on the seeds from grasses and herbs. In a cultural sense they were as simple and crude as any Indians to be found on the continent of North America, rivaling the miserable Digger Indians of the Central Basin. Pottery was only slightly known and working with wood or stone was but little practiced. Their habitations were almost as primitive as the unroofed wickiups of the Shoshones of the mountains. In basket making they reached the apex of their cultural development. These tribes, if such a word be warranted by their loose organization, never offered a serious obstacle to the advance of the white frontier. They still persist, diminished in number, living in poverty like that of a century and more ago.

THE HUDSON'S BAY COMPANY

North of the habitat of the California Indians the Northwest Company at Astoria continued the work of the Americans whom they dispossessed during the War of 1812. The three hundred odd engagés of the company in the valley of the Columbia did not prosper. They were a mixed lot, Iroquois hunters, Hawaiian sailors, and some whites of poor quality. They incurred the enmity of the Indians to the south by unprovoked murders. Their principal accomplishment was the building of Fort Walla Walla on the Snake River. In 1821 the Northwest Company merged with the Hudson's Bay Company. In 1824, with the appointment of Dr. John McLoughlin as chief factor of the Columbia district, the Oregon country entered upon a new era. McLoughlin virtually abandoned Astoria and built Fort Vancouver farther up the river. He promptly undertook the task of exploiting the agricultural resources of the region in order to make his district self-sufficient. He ruled not only his followers but the Indians about him with firmness and justice. More than one forlorn American fur trader, the victim of ill fortune, found the Scotch doctor a generous and considerate host. In the 'thirties, before the trade began to decline, the annual cargo of furs which McLoughlin sent to London sometimes brought a million dollars. In 1839 McLoughlin was not only able to supply food to his own posts in the northwest but to enter into a contract to provide wheat flour and other provisions to the Russian-American Fur Company whose headquarters were in Alaska. (See p. 305.)

418 John McLoughlin, 1784–1857, from a daguerreotype in the Library of Leland Stanford, Jr., University, Palo Alto, California

419 Old Fort Walla Walla, from an engraving in *Reports of Explorations and Surveys . . . for a railroad*, Washington, 1855

FORT WALLA WALLA

An American missionary, Parker, has left a description of Fort Walla Walla which throws much light on the methods of the Hudson's Bay Company and its chief factor. "This establishment is not only supplied with the necessaries of life, but also with many of the conveniences. They have cows, horses, hogs, fowls, &c. and cultivate corn, potatoes, and a variety of garden vegetables; and might enlarge these and other productions to a great extent. They also keep on hand dry goods and hardware, not only for their own convenience, but also for Indian trade. Most of the year they have a good supply of fish; of which there are abundance of salmon of the first quality. There is a great deficiency in religious privileges. . . . The gentlemen belonging to the Hudson's Bay Company are worthy of commendation for their good treatment of the Indians, by which they have obtained their friendship and confidence, and also for the efforts which some few of them have made to instruct those about them in the first principles of our holy religion; especially in regard to equity, humanity, and morality. This company is of long standing, has become rich in the fur trade, and they intend to perpetuate the business; therefore they consult the prosperity of the Indians as intimately connected with their own. I have not heard as yet of a single instance of any Indians being wantonly killed by any of the men belonging to this company. Nor have I heard any boasting among them of the satisfaction taken in killing or abusing Indians, as I have elsewhere heard." — Parker, *Journal*, 123–24.

THE ROCKY MOUNTAIN FUR COMPANY

In 1822, two years before McLoughlin became chief factor on the Columbia, a fur trader of St. Louis, William H. Ashley, sent an expedition far up the Missouri. A river accident, thefts by the Assiniboins, and hostilities on the part of the Blackfeet combined to destroy the profits of the enterprise, which was under the command of Ashley's second, Andrew Henry. Henry remained, however, in the Upper Missouri country and Ashley planned to join him in 1823 with a larger expedition. The plans of the fur trader, however, were balked by the treacherous Arikaras, who suddenly fell upon the Ashley party in 1823 and prevented its ascent of the river. The aftermath of this episode has already been recounted (see page 190). After the partial success of the Leavenworth campaign the Ashley Company vigorously pushed forward its enterprise. The very year which brought defeat at the hands of the Arikaras saw the turning point in the history of the Rocky Mountain Fur Company. Henry, accompanied by two other Ashley leaders, James Bridger and Etienne Provost, made his way upstream along the banks of the North Platte River. They entered the mountain country through South Pass, which is the easiest of all the passes through the Rockies and which was later made famous by the Oregon Trail. They penetrated to the Great Central Basin. As they explored the streams of this country they found that they had stumbled upon a veritable El Dorado.

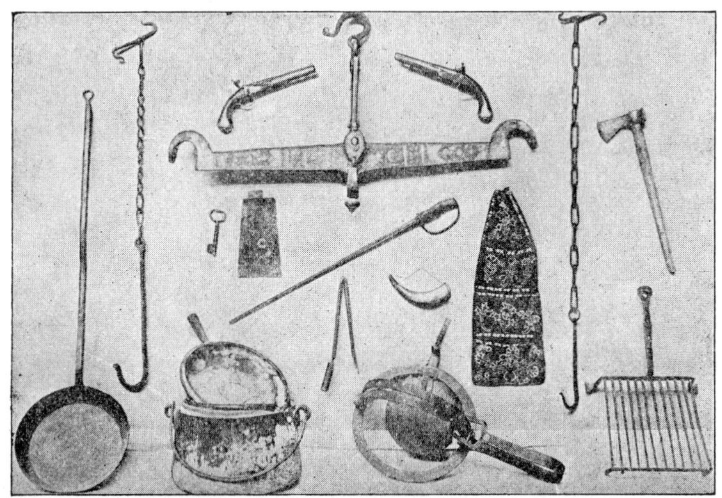

420 Implements Used in the Fur Trade, from the collection of the Wisconsin Historical Society, Madison

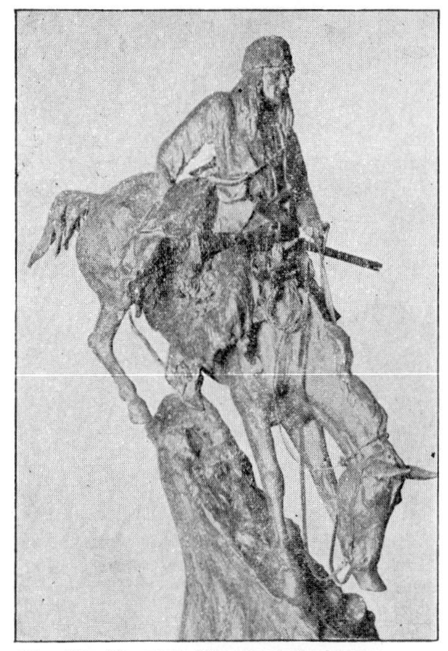

421 The Mountain Man, from the bronze statue by Frederic Remington

THE SUCCESS OF ASHLEY

THE knowledge which Henry's expedition brought to Ashley inspired that genius of the fur trade to the greatest efforts of his life. The year 1824 found him with a well-equipped expedition beyond the Rocky Mountains. But free trappers already were exploiting the rich fur resources of the mountains. St. Louis was far away, and Ashley organized his business in such a way that his own employees and the free trappers need never leave the mountains. Once a year in the summer, when the furs were not good, he gathered the trappers together at a great rendezvous. In this picturesque assemblage the furs which had been caught during the previous season were exchanged for the commodities which the trapper needed — food, clothing, ammunition, and liquor. By the end of the year 1827 Ashley and his company had brought out of the mountains furs of a value aggregating approximately a quarter of a million dollars. Ashley had won for himself a fortune and a fame second only to that of Astor among the American fur traders. Genius though he was, Ashley disliked the wild, rough life of the fur business and in the latter part of 1827 sold out his interest in the Rocky Mountain Fur Company to Jedediah Smith, Sublett, and others. In the eleven years which remained to him, Ashley continued to win an indirect profit from the fur trade by maintaining at St. Louis a commercial house which handled traders' supplies. Ashley, moreover, had political ambitions and in 1831 was elected to Congress, where he served until March 4, 1837. Washington Irving has described a mountain rendezvous: "From the middle of June to the middle of September . . . is the trapper's holiday. . . . The leaders of the different companies, therefore, mingled on terms of perfect good fellowship; interchanging visits, and regaling each other in the best style their respective camps afforded. But the rich treat for the worthy captain was to see the 'chivalry' of the various encampments, engaged in contests of skill at running, jumping, wrestling, shooting with the rifle, and running horses. And then their rough hunters' feastings and carousals. They drank together, they sang, they laughed, they whooped; they tried to outbrag and outlie each other in stories of their adventures and achievements. Here the free trappers were in all their glory; they considered themselves the 'cocks of the walk,' and always carried the highest crests. Now and then familiarity was pushed too far, and would effervesce into a brawl, and a 'rough and tumble' fight; but it all ended in cordial reconciliation and maudlin endearment. The presence of the Shoshone tribe contributed occasionally to cause temporary jealousies and feuds. The Shoshone beauties became objects of rivalry among some of the amorous mountaineers. Happy was the trapper who could muster up a red blanket, a string of gay beads, or a paper of precious vermilion with which to win the smiles of a Shoshone fair one. The caravans of supplies arrived at the valley just at this period of gallantry and good-fellowship. Now commenced a scene of eager competition and wild prodigality at the different encampments. Bales were hastily ripped open and their motley contents poured forth. A mania for purchasing spread itself throughout the several bands, — munitions for war, for hunting, for gallantry were seized upon with equal avidity — rifles, hunting knives, traps, scarlet cloth, red blankets, garish beads, and glittering trinkets were bought at any price, and scores run up without any thought how they were ever to be rubbed off." — WASHINGTON IRVING, *The Adventures of Captain Bonneville,* 180–82.

422 Trappers, from the painting by Allen True, in the Wyoming State Capitol, Cheyenne

THE RENDEZVOUS OF 1834

423 Fur Traders' Camp at Pierre's Hole, from an engraving in A. L. Van Osdel, *Historic Landmarks*, Yankton, S. D., 1922

PARKER, the missionary, has left a vivid account of the rendezvous of 1834. "These days are the climax of the hunter's happiness. I will relate an occurrence which took place near evening, as a specimen of mountain life. A hunter, who goes technically by the name of the great bully of the mountains, mounted his horse with a loaded rifle, and challenged any Frenchman, American, Spaniard, or Dutchman, to fight him in a single combat. Kit Carson, an American, told him if he wished to die, he would accept the challenge. Shunar defied him — C. mounted his horse, and with a loaded pistol rushed into close contact, and both almost at the same instant fired. C.'s ball entered S.'s hand, came out at the wrist, and passed through the arm above the elbow. S.'s ball passed over the head of C. and while he went for another pistol, Shunar begged that his life might be spared. Such scenes, some times from passion, and some times for amusement, make the pastime of their wild and wandering life. They appear to have sought for a place where, as they would say, human nature is not oppressed by the tyranny of religion, and pleasure is not awed by the frown of virtue. . . . Their demoralizing influence with the Indians has been lamentable, and they have imposed upon them, in all the ways that sinful propensities dictate." — SAMUEL PARKER, *Journal of an Exploring Tour*, 79–81. The killing of Shunar was one of the high points of Kit Carson's mountain life. Rivalry for the favor of an Indian beauty seems to have been the cause of the duel. Carson married the daughter of the mountains, a happy and successful union, broken after several years by the death of the girl.

THE MOUNTAIN TRAPPER AT WORK

"THE outfit of a trapper is generally a rifle, a pound of powder, and four pounds of lead, with a bullet mould, seven traps, an axe, a hatchet, a knife, an awl, a camp kettle, two blankets, and, where supplies are plenty, seven pounds of flour. He has, generally, two or three horses, to carry himself, and his baggage and peltries. It is a service of peril, and even more so at present than formerly, for the Indians, since they have got into the habit of trafficking peltries with the traders, have learnt the value of the beaver, and look upon the trappers as poachers, who are filching the riches from their streams, and interfering with their market. They make no hesitation, therefore, to murder the solitary trapper, and thus destroy a competitor, while they possess themselves of his spoils. It is with regret we add, too, that this hostility has in many cases been instigated by traders, desirous of injuring their rivals, but who have themselves often reaped the fruits of the mischief they have sown. When two trappers undertake any considerable stream, their mode of proceeding is, to hide their horses in some lonely glen, where they can graze unobserved. They then build a small hut, dig out a canoe from a cotton-wood tree, and in this, poke along shore silently, in the evening, and set their traps. These, they revisit in the same silent way at daybreak. When they take any beaver, they bring it home, skin it, stretch the skin on sticks to dry, and feast upon the flesh. The body, hung up before the fire, turns by its own weight, and is roasted in a superior style; the tail is the trapper's titbit; it is cut off, put on the end of a stick, and toasted, and is considered even a greater dainty than the tongue or the marrow-bone of a buffalo. With all their silence and caution, however, the poor trappers cannot always escape their hawk-eyed enemies. . . . Sometimes they are pounced upon when in the act of setting their traps; at other times they are roused from their sleep by the horrid war-whoop; or, perhaps, have a bullet or an arrow whistling about their ears, in the midst of one of their beaver banquets." — WASHINGTON IRVING, *The Adventures of Captain Bonneville*, 382–84.

424 The Trapper at Work, from the sketch by E. Willard Deming, in the New York Public Library

425 Typical Trapper, from an engraving after a drawing by Frederic Remington, in Francis Parkman, *The Oregon Trail*, Little, Brown & Co., Boston, 1892

DEATH OF BILL WILLIAMS

Ruxton picked up and narrated a story concerning the death of old Bill Williams. It may not be true but it is typical of many a trapper's end. "During the past winter, a party of mountaineers, flying from overpowering numbers of hostile Sioux, found themselves, one stormy evening, in a wild and dismal cañon near the elevated mountain valley called the 'New Park.' . . . What, however, was their astonishment, on breaking through the cedar-covered entrance, to perceive a solitary horse standing motionless in the center of the prairie. Drawing near, they found it to be an old grizzled mustang, or Indian pony, with cropped ears and ragged tail. . . . Its bones were nearly through the stiffened skin, the legs of the animal were gathered under it; while its forlorn-looking head and stretched-out neck hung listlessly downward, almost overbalancing its tottering body. The blazed and sunken eye — the protruding and froth-covered tongue — the heaving flank and quivering tail — declared its race was run; and the driving sleet and snow, and penetrating winter blast, scarce made impression upon its callous and worn-out frame. One of the band of mountaineers was Marcellin, and a single look at the miserable beast was sufficient for him to recognize the once renowned Nez-percé steed of old Bill Williams. That the owner himself was not far distant he felt certain; and, searching carefully around, the hunters presently came upon an old camp, before which lay, protruding from the snow, the blackened remains of pine logs. Before these, which had been the fire, and leaning with his back against a pine trunk, and his legs crossed under him, half covered with snow, reclined the figure of the old mountaineer, his snow-capped head bent over his breast. His well-known hunting-coat of fringed elk-skin hung stiff and weather-stained about him; and his rifle, packs, and traps, were strewed around. Awe-struck, the trappers approached the body, and found it frozen hard as stone, in which state it had probably lain there for many days or weeks. A jagged rent in the breast of his leather coat, and dark stains about it, showed he had received a wound before his death; but it was impossible to say, whether to his hurt, or to sickness, or to the natural decay of age, was to be attributed the wretched and solitary end of poor Bill Williams." — *Life in the Far West*, 233–34.

EXPLORERS

As the British fur-trading enterprise at Astoria extended its activity into the valley of the Columbia, its members sought to unravel the tangle of rivers and canyons of the mountain country. Finally, after 1824 Ashley's men took the lead in discovering the secrets of the vast but little-known mountain area. Wherever a river seemed to give promise of fur-bearing animals there went the trapper. So John Colter in 1809 passed through and discovered what is now Yellowstone Park. As the years passed, the most remote recesses of the mountain country were entered and explored and the desert which lies between the mountains crossed and re-crossed. The turbulent and uncharted rivers of the cordillera took a heavy toll of lives when the boats of fur-trapping expeditions became unmanageable in raging floods. The bones of many a solitary trapper who met death by an Indian arrow, by accident, or by disease were left to whiten in remote valleys, the existence of which he never lived to make known. A by-product of the hunt for furs, therefore, was a vast accumulation of accurate knowledge of the mountain country and of the Central Basin. The trappers cared little that much of the country they were traversing belonged to a foreign nation. The arm of Mexico was rarely felt north of the Colorado River and in the 'twenties and 'thirties Americans came to know more of this region than did the Mexicans themselves.

426 Explorers in the Shadow of the Rockies, from an engraving in H. J. Warre, *Sketches in North America*, London, 1849

THE DISCOVERY OF GREAT SALT LAKE

ONE of the most important of these trapper-explorers was Ashley himself, who mastered and made known to the world the topography of the North Platte, the South Pass, and the land which stretched between this and the Great Salt Lake. The Great Salt Lake was supposed to have been discovered by Jim Bridger, who was with Ashley's expedition of 1825. The story is told that Bridger, as a result of a wager, was selected to discover the outlet of the Bear River, near which the main body of Ashley's men were camped, and that this quest took him to the region of that great inland saline sea. Etienne Provost next saw the lake and, if the Bridger story is untrue, was its discoverer. The greatest explorer among Ashley's men, however, was Jedediah S. Smith.

427 Jim Bridger on the Shores of Great Salt Lake, from the mural by A. E. Foringer (1878–) in the Utah State Capitol, Salt Lake City

JEDEDIAH S. SMITH

SMITH was one of the striking figures of the mountain country in the first half of the nineteenth century. He had been born in the Susquehanna Valley in New York state when that region was itself on the frontier. His childhood training fixed in his life strong religious beliefs which continued to the end. Fortune took him westward, until finally he became associated with Ashley. In 1827, when the latter retired from the fur trade, Smith became one of the leaders in the affairs of the Rocky Mountain Fur Company. Ashley had opened up the region along the western slope of the Rockies and had pushed his expeditions to Great Salt Lake. He planned to keep on advancing westward, and, like Astor before him, dreamed of a possible outlet for the furs of the mountain region through a port on the Pacific Coast. Smith went into the unknown region west of Great Salt Lake to explore the terrain and to discover its fur resources. In the summer of 1826, with a party of fifteen men he turned his face to the southwest passing through the country of the Digger Indians. The party followed the Virgin River to the Colorado, where it came upon the villages of the Mohaves. Smith was now in the arid region of the southwest. Securing fresh horses he turned westward, and after a desperate march of three weeks across the desert reached the San Gabriel Mission in California. The coming of the Americans from the mountains brought consternation to the Mexican leaders of southern California. Smith had gone as pioneer over the route which was in later time approximately followed by the San Pedro, Los Angeles, and Salt Lake Railroad.

428 Jedediah Smith Crossing the Mohave Desert, from the painting by Frederic Remington. © P. F. Collier & Son Co., reproduced by their permission

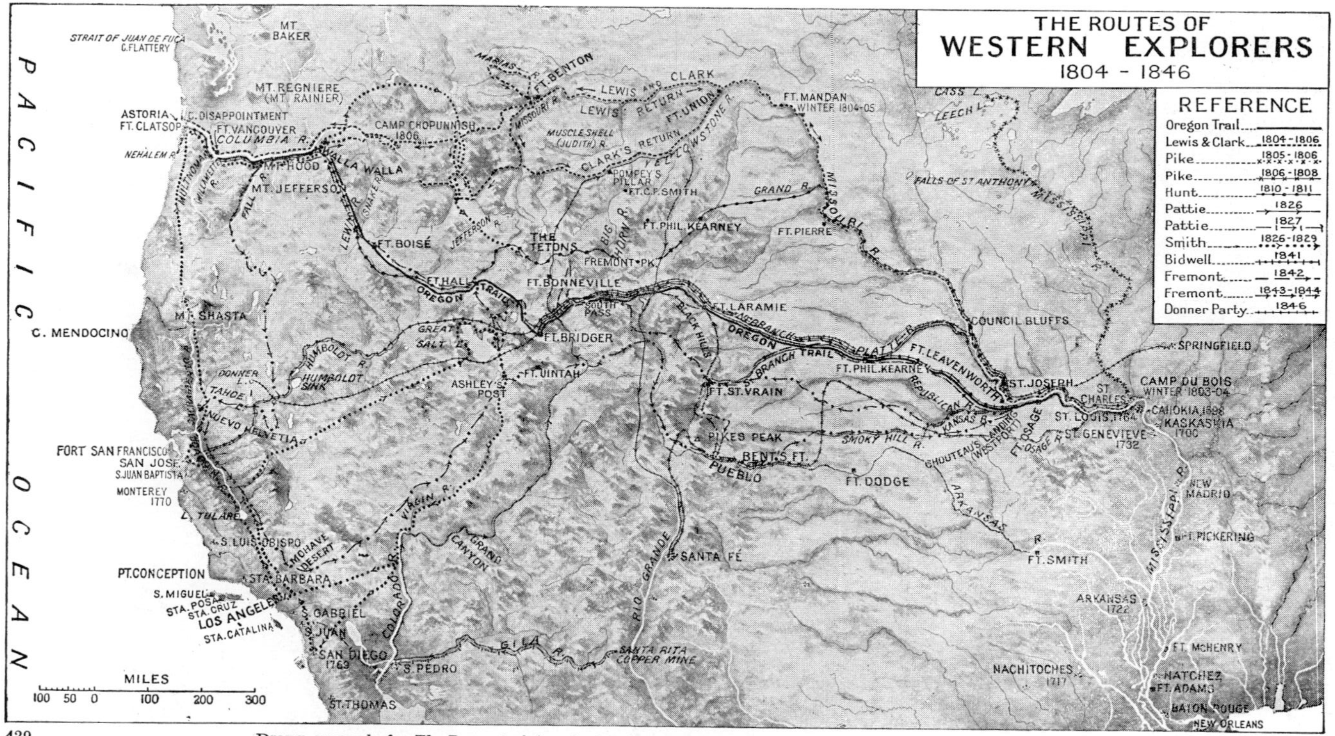

THE ROUTES OF WESTERN EXPLORERS 1804 - 1846

429 Drawn expressly for *The Pageant of America* by Gregor Noetzel, American Geographical Society, New York

THE EXPLORATIONS OF SMITH

The timorous Mexicans ordered Smith out of their country. The American party, therefore, pushed due north and entered San Joaquin Valley. Here they found beaver in plenty and here they trapped during the winter of 1826–27. In the spring Jedediah Smith leaving the main valley, started eastward for Salt Lake with two companions, seven horses, and two pack mules. His objective was the summer rendezvous of the mountain men, where he sought to obtain fresh supplies. He crossed the Sierras by the Merced River and the Sonora Pass, naming Mount Joseph on the way. The snow was deep in the elevated country but, though the suffering was great, the men and animals got through in eight days. Between Smith and his objective there stretched the desert of the Central Basin. "When we arrived at the Salt Lake," the leader reported, "we had but one horse and one mule remaining, which were so feeble and poor that they could scarce carry the little camp equipage which I had along; the balance of my horses I was compelled to eat as they gave out." On the return trip, Smith had approximated the route of the Central Pacific Railroad. Smith remained at Salt Lake only long enough to secure a new outfit, when he set out again for California to recover the party he had left and to bring back their catch of furs. This expedition met disaster on the banks of the Virgin River when it was attacked by Indians. Ten men were killed and all the supplies were lost. Smith, with the remnant, made his way across the desert to San Gabriel Mission, where he left two wounded men. A second time he was ordered out of California. He rejoined the men left in the valley of the San Joaquin. In the spring of 1828 the party crossed the mountains by following an Indian trail over the Siskyou Pass and down the Rogue River to the Umpqua. Smith was seeking to avoid the desert of the Central Basin by going round its northern edge. Again, however, he suffered tragedy. One morning, while the leader was away from the camp searching for a better trail, a band of Indians who had misled the whites by their friendly bearing fell suddenly upon the trappers. Two men only escaped. One of these joined Smith, and together they made their way down the Willamette to Fort Vancouver. Smith was the first white man to make the journey from southern California to the Columbia Valley.

DISTANT OREGON

430 Hall Jackson Kelley, from the portrait, artist unknown, in the Oregon Historical Society, Portland

DURING those busy years after the fall of Astoria, when the British fur-trading interests were strengthening their hold on the Columbia Valley, the North Atlantic states were adjusting themselves to the new era which followed the War of 1812. New England seaports bustled as trading ships and whalers once more put to sea. Managers of the factories that had sprung up during the abnormal years of war looked anxiously to the future and wondered whether they could continue their enterprises in the face of British competition. At this time, when Americans gladly forgot the war and turned to the tasks of peace, the word "Oregon" was sometimes heard in the gossip of the day. In 1811 Nicholas Biddle of Philadelphia had brought out a popular edition of the journals of Lewis and Clark and this great adventure story had been widely read. Two years after the close of the war Americans hailed with enthusiasm the advent of a new poet. In William Cullen Bryant's "Thanatopsis" the cultivated folk of the period found a moving reference to

> "The continuous woods
> Where rolls the Oregon and hears no sound
> Save his own dashing."

The word Oregon was echoing through the East. The journals of Lewis and Clark stirred the imagination of an eccentric schoolmaster of Boston, one Hall J. Kelley. Oregon became with him an *idée fixe*. He saw this distant country as a land of wonderful opportunity where, if men would but go thither, they must be prosperous and happy. His enthusiasm outran his judgment. As in his own small way he spread the glad tidings from the shores of the Pacific, he seemed to have no conception of the difficulties to be encountered in getting there. The hard-working folk of the 'twenties had little time to heed the vaporings of Kelley. Yet Kelley persisted.

THE OREGON QUESTION

OTHER Americans besides Kelley began to think of Oregon, particularly as the year 1828 approached. At that time the ten-year agreement with England with respect to Oregon was to terminate. In 1818, though the governments of both Great Britain and the United States had been mildly interested in the far Northwest, neither party had had a clearly defined policy with regard to the region. The treaty of that year had provided for the joint occupation of Oregon by the two nations for ten years. During the 'twenties Congress listened to suggestions to establish a fort in the far-away valley of the Columbia, which would strengthen American claims and perhaps facilitate American settlement. One ardent advocate of the measure, filled with an enthusiasm for canals that was typical of the decade, prophesied ere long a transcontinental canal. The fort, however, was not established and the arrangement for the joint occupation of the region was continued indefinitely. Practical Americans of the 'twenties, when they gave thought to the matter, did not see how Oregon could ever become a part of the United States. The distance across the continent and the difficulties of traveling in the mountain country were so great as to make proper representation at Washington of a state on the Pacific Coast even more difficult than would have been the representation of eighteenth-century Virginia in the House of Commons. This conviction was destined to continue until the development of the railroad began the solution of the American problem of great distances.

RIDICULOUS EXHIBITION; OR, YANKEE-NOODLE PUTTING HIS HEAD INTO THE BRITISH LION'S MOUTH.

431 Cartoon Satirizing America's Attitude on the Oregon Question, in *Punch*, Volume X, London, 1846

432 Nathaniel J. Wyeth, from an engraved portrait in *Harper's New Monthly Magazine*, November 1892

NATHANIEL J. WYETH

PERHAPS the most important of the occasional Easterners who, in spite of the general apathy, fell under the spell of Oregon was an enterprising Boston merchant who had won a signal success in the ice business, Nathaniel J. Wyeth. In the spring of 1831 Boston people were interested and somewhat amused at a camp which had been established on one of the islands in the harbor. Wyeth had organized a trading expedition which he planned to lead to the Columbia Valley. He was training his men in their island camp for the wild life of the West. He had borrowed an idea from the Gloucester fishermen and had put the expedition on a profit-sharing basis. Thinking to make a great improvement in the methods of communication in the Far West, with that ingenuity which characterized the Yankee of the first half of the nineteenth century, he had devised an amphibious wagon which would travel equally well on land and water. In the autumn of 1831 he abandoned this curiosity at St. Louis, amid the jeers of men who knew the western country. By the end of October of the following year he had reached his goal, though abandoned by the greater part of his company, who had quailed before the difficulties and dangers of the journey through the wilderness. A ship, moreover, which he had prevailed upon a Boston house to send around Cape Horn to coöperate with him in the trade had been wrecked. The discouraged Wyeth went east, organized a second expedition, made his way again to the Columbia Valley, and again failed. Then, on the eve of the Panic of 1837, he gave up his dreams of profit in Oregon and returned to the ice business. On each of his two trips, however, he had left behind some men who stayed in Oregon to farm, with the assistance of the Hudson's Bay Company. They formed a nucleus for later settlements.

MISSIONS AND THE SETTLEMENT OF OREGON

THE first whites who, after the fur traders, turned their attention to the Oregon country were missionaries solicitous of the spiritual welfare of the Indians. In 1831, the year in which Wyeth first came to St. Louis from Boston, some representatives of the Nez-Percés and other Flathead Indians journeyed to the frontier city at the mouth of the Missouri seeking to learn the secret of the white man's success, convinced that the white man's God was more potent than the spirits whose aid the Indian sought. (See Vol. X.) They went to the home of General William Clark and asked that missionaries be sent among them. This request was played up by religious bodies of the East as a call from Macedonia. Enthusiasm for missions in distant Oregon grew apace. In 1834 Jason and Daniel Lee together with Cyrus Shepard and P. L. Edwards crossed the mountain country with Wyeth's second expedition. Strange to say they passed the Nez-Percé villages nestling in the bottoms of steep-sided mountain valleys and passed on to the fertile flood plains of the Willamette. Their excuse for their failure to heed the call from the most promising Indian people in the northern mountains was that "a larger field of usefulness was contemplated as the object of the mission than the benefiting of a single tribe." Before many years passed, however, they discovered that their efforts availed little with the Chinooks, debauched and diseased as a result of contact with white traders extending over more than a third of a century. The Lee mission then turned its attention to ministering to the whites of the Willamette Valley and to solving the problems of frontier settlement.

433 Hi-Youts-To-Han, one of the Nez-Percé Delegation to St. Louis, 1831, from a drawing by George Catlin, *North American Indian Portfolio*, London, 1844

THE MISSIONS

434 Dr. Whitman Starting for the East, from an engraving in Oliver W. Nixon, *How Marcus Whitman Saved Oregon*, Chicago, 1895

IN 1834, the year in which the Lees started across the continent, the American Board of Commissioners for Foreign Missions sent the Reverend Samuel Parker, accompanied by a young doctor named Marcus Whitman, to explore the missionary opportunities offered by the Nez-Percés and the Flathead Indians. In August these two missionary explorers were present at the rendezvous of the mountain trappers. "While we continued in this place, Doctor Whitman was called to perform some very important surgical operations. He extracted an iron arrow, three inches long, from the back of Captain Bridger, which he had received in a skirmish three years before, with the Blackfeet Indians. It was a difficult operation in consequence of the arrow being hooked at the point by striking a large bone, and a cartilaginous substance had grown around it. The doctor pursued the operation with great self-possession and perseverance; and Captain Bridger manifested equal firmness. The Indians looked on while the operation was proceeding with countenances indicating wonder, and when they saw the arrow, expressed their astonishment in a manner peculiar to themselves. The skill of Doctor Whitman undoubtedly made upon them a favorable impression. He also took another arrow from under the shoulder of one of the hunters, which had been there two years and a half. After these operations, calls for surgical and medical aid were constant every hour in the day." — SAMUEL PARKER, *Journal*, 76. Whitman, after conferences with the Nez-Percés and the Flatheads, became so enthusiastic regarding the missionary possibilities that he hastened east to make arrangements for the forwarding of workers to the mission.

THE MISSIONS OF THE INTERIOR

THE upshot of the Whitman-Parker expedition was the building of missions in the villages of the Indians of the interior. Mr. and Mrs. Spalding and Dr. and Mrs. Marcus Whitman were the religious pioneers in these enterprises. Like the Methodists in the Willamette Valley, the missionaries of the interior established farms and built substantial habitations. They sought to teach the Indians the arts of the white man as well as the Christian religion. Lonely indeed was the life of these missionary families, living in Indian villages, isolated from one another and from the outside world. Other missionaries came to aid in the work. The gospel was preached to the natives, portions of the Bible were translated into their languages, and the Indians were helped to build houses for themselves. As the decade of the 'thirties came to an end the Whitmans saw occasional trappers with their Indian wives and halfbreed children going westward. The fur trade was declining and these men were abandoning it to try their hand at farming in the valley of the Lower Columbia. Whitman saw clearly that the day of the coming of the agricultural immigrant was not far distant. With a sound estimate of the situation he wrote: "Although the Indians have made and are making rapid advance in religious knowledge and civilization, yet it cannot be hoped that time will be allowed to mature either the work of Christianization or civilization before the white settlers will demand the soil and seek the removal of both the Indians and the mission. What Americans desire they always effect and it is equally useless to oppose or desire it otherwise. To guide as far as can be done, and direct these tendencies for the best is evidently the part of wisdom." Whitman went east to encourage the emigration to Oregon of Christian whites who would counteract the influence of the unrestrained frontiersmen. (For the story of the Oregon missionaries, see Vol. X, 247–51.)

435 First Methodist Mission on the Willamette, from an engraving in Charles Henry Carey, *History of Oregon*, Portland, 1922, courtesy of Pioneer Historical Publications

436 A Catholic Mission among the Oregon Indians, from a lithograph by Van der Schelden after a drawing by P. Van de Steene, in Peter John de Smet, *Oregon Missions and Travels over the Rocky Mountains*, New York, 1847

THE CHRISTMAS OF 1844 AMONG THE FLATHEADS

Father de Smet has left a moving account of a Catholic missionary's devotion to his work in Oregon: "The great festival of Christmas, the day on which the little band was to be added to the number of the true children of God, will never be effaced from the memory of our good Indians. The manner in which we celebrated midnight Mass, may give you an idea of our festival. The signal for rising, which was to be given a few minutes before midnight, was the firing of a pistol, announcing to the Indians that the house of prayer would soon be open. This was followed by a general discharge of guns, in honor of the birth of the Infant Saviour, and three hundred voices rose spontaneously from the midst of the forest and intoned in the language of the Pends d'Oreilles, the beautiful canticle: '*Du Dieu puissant tout annonce la gloire.*' 'The Almighty's glory all things proclaim.' In a moment a multitude of adorers were seen wending their way to the humble temple of the Lord — resembling, indeed, the manger in which the Messiah was born. . . . A grand banquet, according to Indian custom, followed the first Mass. Some choice pieces of the animals slain in the chase had been set apart for the occasion. I ordered half a sack of flour, and a large boiler of sweetened coffee to be added. The union, the contentment, the joy, and charity, which pervaded the whole assembly, might well be compared to the *agape* of the primitive Christians. . . . Here, indeed, the Indian missionary enjoys his greatest consolations: here he obtains his strength, his courage, his zeal to labor to bring men to the knowledge of the true God, in spite of the poverty, the privations of every description, and the dangers with which he has to contend. Yes, surely, even in this life is the promise of the Saviour fulfilled with regard to him, 'Ye shall receive a hundred fold.' The trifling things of the world he abandons, are nothing to be compared with the blessings he finds in the wilderness." — Thwaites, *Early Western Travels*, XXIX, part 2, 297–99.

THE MOVEMENT TO OREGON

In the 'thirties the characteristics of Oregon were becoming steadily better known to the American people. Missionaries wrote many letters which were published in widely read religious journals. The tales of travelers and fur traders returning to St. Louis from the distant West made the people of that city familiar with the valley of the Columbia. Both on the Atlantic Coast and in the Mississippi Valley, therefore, the existence of Oregon with its remarkable forests, its fertile soil, its rivers abounding in salmon and offering abundant opportunities for the development of water power, became the common knowledge of the people. It became known, moreover, that this land could be reached by a route which led through passes in the mountain country. The native wealth of Oregon was of the kind which was most likely to draw the farmer-pioneer. Fertile soil abounded and heavy forests offered wood for habitations and fuel. A curious combination of circumstances at the end of the 'thirties and the opening of the 'forties brought about a great migration to the far distant region.

437 An American Village in Oregon, from a lithograph by Dickinson & Co. after a drawing by H. J. Warre, in H. J. Warre, *Sketches in North America*, London, 1849

THE BEGINNING OF THE MIGRATION

438 On the Way to Oregon, from an engraving, courtesy of the Oregon Historical Society, Portland

THE Panic of 1837 plunged the American people into want and suffering unlike any they had ever experienced outside of war. Recovery from the financial disaster was not immediate; hard times continued for some five years after the initial crash. The result was discontent and restlessness among Americans all over the nation. Men of all kinds were casting about desperately for ways of bettering their lot. In the Southwest, moreover, the rapid expansion of the plantation system was tending to drive the small farmers out of Mississippi and Alabama. All along the frontier in the Mississippi Valley the normal frontier restlessness was increased and accentuated by the financial difficulties of the times. Under such circumstances the rich lands in Oregon beckoned with a peculiar persuasiveness. Suddenly, in 1842 and 1843 the flood of pioneers over the Oregon Trail began.

439 The End of the Oregon Trail, from an engraving, courtesy of the Oregon Historical Society, Portland

THE "PATHFINDER"

THE United States Government sensed the importance of Oregon to the American people. In 1841 Lieutenant Charles Wilkes, Commander of the Pacific Exploring Squadron, visited Oregon and made a careful study of its settlements and resources. His report was available to the emigrants of 1843. In 1842, John C. Frémont was commissioned to survey the overland route to Oregon and California. Because of the general popularity of Frémont's well-written reports of his various expeditions his name became widely known throughout the East. More than any single explorer he awakened a public interest in the mountain country, much of which, when he first began his explorations, lay within the sovereignty of Mexico. He was given the name of "pathfinder" but not with entire justice, for he blazed no new trails in the sense in which Lewis and Clark did. From first to last his service — and it was a great one — consisted in making available for the general public information that was locked up in the minds of the hunters and trappers of the mountain country. His expedition made accurate maps, gathered scientific information, and, in the days before photography, produced pictures of a vividness like that of the *View of the Wind River Mountains*. In these very mountains stands the highest peak in the Rockies. Frémont's description of scaling this eminence is typical of the quality of his published work. He brought imagination to his task and made his readers share in his adventures.

440 John C. Frémont, 1813–90, from an engraving by Burt, in Walter Colton, *Three Years in California*, New York, 1859

441 Frémont's Party Ascending the Highest Peak in the American Rockies, from an engraving in the possession of the publishers

ASCENDING THE HIGHEST PEAK IN THE AMERICAN ROCKIES

"PUTTING hands and feet in the crevices between the blocks, I succeeded in getting over it, and, when I reached the top, found my companions in a small valley below. Descending to them, we continued climbing, and in a short time reached the crest. I sprang upon the summit, and another step would have precipitated me into an immense snow field five hundred feet below. . . . As soon as I had gratified the first feelings of curiosity, I descended and each man ascended in his turn; for I would allow only one at a time to mount the unstable and precarious slab, which it seemed a breath would hurl into the abyss below. We mounted the barometer in the snow of the summit, and, fixing a ramrod in a crevice unfurled the national flag to wave in the breeze where never flag waved before. During our morning's ascent we had met no sign of animal life except the small, sparrow-like bird already mentioned. A stillness the most profound and a terrible solitude forced themselves constantly on the mind as the great features of the place. Here on the summit where the stillness was absolute, unbroken by any sound, and the solitude complete, we thought ourselves beyond the region of animated life; but, while we were sitting on the rock, a solitary bee (bromus, the humble-bee) came winging his flight from the eastern valley, and lit upon the knee of one of the men. It was a strange place — the icy rock and the highest peak of the Rocky Mountains — for a lover of warm sunshine and flowers; and we pleased ourselves with the idea that he was the first of his species to cross the mountain barrier, a solitary pioneer to foretell the advance of civilization." — FRÉMONT, *Report*, 1845, 69–70.

FRÉMONT'S SECOND EXPEDITION

PERHAPS the most difficult of Frémont's achievements came in his second expedition, 1843–44, which followed the Santa Fé Trail to Fort Bent and then turned northward through the mountain country across Mexican soil to the Columbia River. In November 1843 Frémont was in Oregon. Here he decided to turn south to Sutter's Fort in California, where he hoped to gather the supplies that would take the expedition home. He made a winter trip through the little known Sierra Nevada Mountains. The purpose of this expedition was to test the truth of reports relating to a river flowing from the Central Basin to the Pacific. Frémont demonstrated that no such stream existed, his work proving conclusively the existence of an intermontane drainage area, whose waters never reach the ocean. His report increased, as it was intended to do, American interest in the acquisition of California. The character of Frémont showed to advantage particularly when this expedition confronted great natural difficulties. The trail which the explorers followed was fraught with all the dangers attendant to traveling in unknown mountains. "But throughout these half thousand painful miles," in the words of Thwaites, "the leader was undaunted; his wonderful endurance, unconquerable determination, and masterly management have never been surpassed by any explorer."

442 Frémont's Exploring Party on the Edge of Pyramid Lake, from a lithograph in John C. Frémont, *Report of the Exploring Expedition to the Rocky Mountains*, Washington, 1845

KIT CARSON, 1809–1868

443 Kit Carson, from an engraving after a daguerreotype now destroyed (formerly in the California Hall of Pioneers, San Francisco), in the possession of the publishers

CARSON was Frémont's guide on his first two expeditions. He knew the mountain country as thoroughly as Bridger. When the second expedition had penetrated far into California, an incident occurred which made Kit a national hero. A band of Indians made off with a herd of some sixty horses belonging to some Mexicans who had recently fallen in with Frémont's party. Carson and a Frenchman, named Godey, followed the trail. Frémont described their return with most of the horses, " 'two bloody scalps dangling from the end of Godey's gun. . . . The time, place, object, and numbers considered, this expedition of Carson and Godey may be considered among the boldest and most disinterested which the annals of western adventure, so full of daring deeds, can present. Two men, in a savage desert, pursue day and night an unknown body of Indians into the defiles of an unknown mountain — attack them on sight, without counting numbers — and defeat them in an instant.' . . . Kit used to say that he owed more to Frémont than to any living man. Unquestionably, he did. Frémont was just the person to advertise him to the reading public and thereby serve his own and Senator Benton's aims. . . . Kit was to be the hero who personified American enterprise in the Far West — the banner which was to wave the pioneers forward into the Great American Desert. Senator Benton and his party would never rest until the United States extended to the waters of the Pacific." — STANLEY VESTAL, *Kit Carson*, 188.

THE GREAT MIGRATION

IN the year of Frémont's first exploration, Doctor Elijah White took one hundred and twenty settlers to Oregon. In the next year the flood across the mountains began and was destined to continue until the Columbia Valley was reclaimed from the wilderness. Scarcely had the permanent Indian frontier been established when the whites broke through this Indian zone and made their way by thousands across the bison country. Francis Parkman has left a picture of some pioneer types. "But a few moments elapsed before the heavy caravans of the emigrant wagons could be seen steadily advancing from the hills. They gained the river, and, without turning or pausing, plunged in, passed through, and slowly ascending the opposing bank, kept directly on their way by the fort and the Indian village, until, gaining a spot a quarter of a mile distant, they wheeled into a circle. . . . The emigrants were preparing their encampment; but no sooner was this accomplished than Fort Laramie was taken by storm. A crowd of broad-brimmed hats, thin visages, and staring eyes appeared suddenly at the gate. Tall, awkward men, in brown homespun, women with cadaverous faces and long lank figures, came thronging in together, and, as if inspired by the very demon of curiosity, ransacked every nook and corner of the fort. . . . On visiting the encampment we were at once struck with the extraordinary perplexity and indecision that prevailed among them. They seemed like men totally out of their element, bewildered and amazed, like a troop of schoolboys lost in the woods. It was impossible to be long among them without being conscious of the bold spirit with which most of them were animated. But the *forest* is the home of the backwoodsmen. On the remote prairie he is totally at a loss."

444 Westward Ho!, from the painting by Allen True, courtesy of H. A. True, Jr., Cheyenne, Wyoming

445 Emigrants to the West, from an engraving after a drawing by William de la Montagne Cary, in Bryant and Gay, *A Popular History of the United States*, New York, 1883

A CARAVAN IN CAMP

"AN unoccupied spectator, who could have beheld our camp today, would think it a singular spectacle. The hunters returning with the spoil; some erecting scaffolds, and others drying the meat. Of the women some were washing, some ironing, some baking. At two of the tents the fiddle was employed in uttering its unaccustomed voice among the solitudes of the Platte; at one tent I heard singing; at others the occupants were engaged in reading, some the Bible, others poring over novels. While all this was going on, that nothing might be wanting to complete the harmony of the scene, a Campbellite preacher, named Foster, was reading a hymn, preparatory to religious worship. The fiddles were silenced, and those who had been occupied with that amusement betook themselves to cards. Such is but a miniature of the great world we had left behind us, when we crossed the line that separates civilized man from the wilderness." — JOEL PALMER, *Journal of Travels Over the Rocky Mountains*, 1847, 23. Palmer journeyed to Oregon in 1845.

FORT HALL

"WE traveled but five miles which brought us to Fort Hall. This is a trading post in the possession of the *Hudson's Bay Company*. Like the forts on the east side of the mountains, it is built of mud or adobe. . . . Captain Grant is now the officer in command; he has the bearing of a gentleman. The garrison was supplied with flour, which had been procured from the settlements in Oregon and brought here on pack horses. They sold it to the emigrants for twenty dollars per cwt., taking cattle in exchange; and as many of the emigrants were nearly out of flour, and had a few lame cattle, a brisk trade was carried on between them and the inhabitants of the fort. . . . Our camp was located one mile to the south-west of the fort; and as at all the other forts, the Indians swarmed about us. . . . While we remained in this place [Fort Hall] great efforts were made to induce the emigrants to pursue the route to California. The most extravagant tales were related respecting the dangers that awaited a trip to Oregon, and of the difficulties and trials to be surmounted. The perils of the way were so magnified as to make us suppose the journey to Oregon almost impossible. . . . In addition . . . it was asserted that three or four tribes of Indians, in the middle region, had combined for the purpose of preventing our passage through their country, and should we attempt it, we would be compelled to contend with these hostile tribes. In case we escaped destruction at the hands of the savages, a more fearful enemy, that of famine, would attend our march; as the distance was so great that winter would overtake us before making the passage of the Cascade Mountains. . . . Mr. Greenwood, an old mountaineer, well stocked with falsehoods, had been dispatched from California to pilot the emigrants through." — PALMER, *Journal of Travels Over the Rocky Mountains*, 42–44. This attempt to deflect Oregon emigrants to California arose from the unsettled conditions in that Mexican province and the determination of American settlers in the region to secure California for the United States.

446 Interior of Fort Hall, from a lithograph in the possession of the publishers

THE INDIANS AND THE CARAVANS

447 A Caravan Attacked by Indians, from the painting *The Emigrants*, by Frederic Remington. © P. F. Collier & Son Co., reproduced by their permission

THE Indians naturally resented the ever-increasing flood of wagons crossing their hunting grounds. The whites killed much game and drove the bison herds from the region near the Oregon Trail. Perhaps of equal importance in determining the attitude of the plains tribes toward the transcontinental emigrants was the fact that the latter transported through the Indian country wealth in flocks and herds and in other things, highly desirable in the eyes of the red man. From time immemorial, thievery on the part of one tribe against another had been a fundamental part of the code of the grasslands and the redskins now sought to make the most of their opportunities. Parkman in 1846 watched the development of a dangerous spirit among the Sioux. While at Fort Laramie he saw a Dakota village, under a chief by the name of Smoke, come from some distant region and camp outside the walls of the fort. They were awaiting the arrival of a caravan. When this arrived its members, unaccustomed to the ways of the redskins, were afraid of them. Parkman observed that if "you betray timidity or indecision, you convert them from that moment into insidious and dangerous enemies. The Dakotas saw clearly enough the perturbation of the emigrants, and instantly availed themselves of it. They became extremely insolent and exacting in their demands. It has become an established custom with them to go to the camp of every party, as it arrives in succession at the fort, and demand a feast. Smoke's village had come with this express design, having made several days' journey with no other object than that of enjoying a cup of coffee and two or three biscuits. So the 'feast' was demanded, and the emigrants dared not refuse it. . . . Before we left this country this dangerous spirit on the part of the Dakotas had mounted to a yet higher pitch. They began openly to threaten the emigrants with destruction, and actually fired on one or two parties of them."

FORT BRIDGER

ELIJAH WHITE'S expedition in 1842 seems to have convinced that canny hunter, trapper, and guide, James Bridger, that a new era had dawned in the history of the West. In the winter of 1842–43 Bridger, in partnership with one Louis Vasquez, provided himself with a novel outfit of supplies. They were not the trinkets and materials needed for the Indian trade but were intended to be sold to emigrants. On December 10, 1843, the ex-trapper, who had never learned to write, caused a letter to be indited to Pierre Choteau, Jr. — "I have established a small fort, with a black-smith's shop and a supply of iron in the road of the emigrants on Black Fork on Green River which promises fairly. In coming out here they are generally well supplied with money, but by the time they get here they are in need of all kinds of supplies, horses, provisions, smith-work, etc. They bring ready cash from the states, and should I receive the goods ordered, will have considerable business in that way with them, and establish trade with the Indians in the neighborhood. . . . The fort is a beautiful location on Black's Fork of Green River, receiving fine, fresh water from the snow on the Uintah Range. The streams are alive with mountain trout. It passes the fork in several channels, each lined with trees, . . ." If the return of Lewis and Clark marked the opening of the fur trade west of the Mississippi, the building of Fort Bridger symbolized the passing of its importance. The day of the settler had dawned. The region was emerging from the hunting into the agricultural stage of the arts.

448 Fort Bridger, from a lithograph by Ackerman, in Howard Stansbury, *Exploration and Survey of the Valley of the Great Salt Lake of Utah*, Philadelphia, 1852

449 Jim Bridger, from a photograph in the Montana State Historical and Miscellaneous Library, Helena

JIM BRIDGER, 1804–1881

PERHAPS the greatest of the free traders was Jim Bridger, born in 1804 in Richmond, Virginia, the son of a tavern keeper. He was apprenticed in youth to a blacksmith. When he was eighteen he went into the Indian country. He was a member of the party that discovered the South Pass, through which later ran the Oregon Trail. Bridger's restless genius took him to practically every accessible region of the mountains. He entered the employ of two different fur companies and led trapping expeditions of his own. As already mentioned, he became a partner of the Rocky Mountain Fur Company. In 1862 Lieutenant Casper W. Collins, on an expedition with his father into the Rocky Mountain country, described the hunter. "We had Major Bridger with us as a guide. He knows more of the Rocky Mountains than any living man. . . . He is totally uneducated but speaks English, Spanish, and French equally well besides nearly a dozen Indian languages. . . . He has been in many Indian battles and has several arrow wounds, besides being hit so as almost to break his neck. Under him Kit Carson made his first acquaintance with the Rocky Mountain region, and he traveled through them while Frémont was a child." Captain Stansbury, who employed Bridger as a guide in 1850, has also left his picture of the man. The scene was an evening about the camp fire when Indians had come in to make a friendly visit. "Our esteemed friend and experienced mountaineer, Major Bridger, who was personally known to many of our [Indian] visitors, and to all of them by the repute of his numerous exploits, was seated among us. Although intimately acquainted with the languages of the Crows, Blackfeet, and most of the tribes west and northwest of the Rocky Mountain chain, he was unable to speak to either the Sioux or Cheyenne in their own tongue, or that of any tribe which they could understand. Notwithstanding this he held the whole circle for more than an hour perfectly enchained and evidently most deeply interested in a conversation and narrative, the whole of which was carried on without the utterance of a single word. The simultaneous exclamations of surprise or interest, and the occasional bursts of hearty laughter, showed that the whole party perfectly understood not only the theme, but the minutiae of the pantomime exhibited before them. . . ." — Quoted in J. C. ALTER, *James Bridger*, 226–27.

THE ACQUISITION OF OREGON

IN the same year that Bridger established what became one of the most famous posts on the Oregon Trail, the settlers in Oregon itself decided that the time had come to declare their independence of the Hudson's Bay Company. They met in convention and organized a government. Neither convention nor government had, however, any legal authority behind it. Sovereignty over the soil on which stood the cabins of these American pioneers was divided between the United States and Great Britain. In spite of this, these isolated adventurers, a thousand miles beyond the American frontier, followed the example set by the Watauga people (see No. 206). Such spontaneous extra-legal governments were significant of the character not only of American frontiersmen, but of Americans themselves. The year following the establishment of this impromptu state, the acquisition of Oregon became one of the leading issues in the Presidential campaign of 1844. In this political struggle the expansionists won. President Polk promptly took up the settlement of the Oregon question. On June 15, 1846, by treaty between Great Britain and the United States, the forty-ninth parallel of latitude became the international boundary as far west as the Pacific.

450 British Cartoon Satirizing America's Aggressive Attitude on the Oregon Question, in *Punch*, Vol. X, London, 1846

LATTER-DAY SAINTS

451 Brigham Young, 1801–77, from a photograph by Carter, Salt Lake City, in the Albert Davis Collection, Brooklyn, N. Y.

FOURTEEN months after the signing of the treaty which settled the Oregon question, Brigham Young, with an advance party of Mormons, halted near the banks of the Great Salt Lake and began to plant crops. Back of this expedition lay one of the most extraordinary stories in American history. Out of the frontier of western New York in the opening years of the second quarter of the nineteenth century came a prophet, Joseph Smith, Jr., preaching a new religion, a modified form of Christianity. Reacting against the excessive democracy of Protestantism on the frontier, Smith organized a church and a religious hierarchy with pretensions to power surpassing anything ever known within the limits of the United States. Many converts gave their allegiance to the new faith and listened with reverence while the Mormon teachers read passages from the new scriptures, the Book of Mormon, the Book of Abraham, or the Book of Commandments. There is no space here in which to recount the wanderings of the Morman Church, from Kirtland, Ohio, to Independence, Missouri, and thence to Nauvoo, Illinois. Wherever they went the Latter-Day Saints were persecuted because their religion, based on the revelations to be found in new and strange scriptures, jarred with the doctrines held by the frontier folk and because the pretensions of the Mormon Church to both social and spiritual power conflicted with the frontier spirit of democracy. The final outbreak of Gentiles against the Church came at Nauvoo, when rumor, based on good evidence, charged the Mormon leaders with the practice of polygamy. Mormonism had outraged the moral sense of the American people. Yet polygamy was the logical and inevitable result of the rather complicated Mormon theology. In 1844 the unruly folk of the Illinois frontier rose against the Mormons and finally martyred Joseph Smith. In the fall of the next year the Mormons were ordered from the state. In February 1846, the van of the Mormons turned their faces to the west, crossed the Mississippi, and prepared to seek new homes. The early summer of 1846 saw the Mormon refugees making their way across southern Iowa to the "Camp of Israel" near Council Bluffs. Several thousand left Nauvoo and set forth to follow whither their inspired leaders should guide them. They endured persecution and faced the hardships and uncertainties of their lot rather than give up the religion which Joseph Smith had taught them. They believed themselves to be chosen people, who had learned the will of the Lord and had elected to keep his commandments. The end of the world according to their faith was not far off, when unbelievers would be damned to eternal punishment and the faithful would inherit Paradise, when on the last great Judgment Day the shining walls of Zion would rise and the Lord would come in person to rule his people. In the winter months of 1846–47, as the Mormons gathered for worship in the rude shelters scarcely capable of warding off the icy blasts of the prairies, they spoke of that refuge in the western mountains where, faithful to the heavenly vision, they would await the last great day. They listened eagerly as their elders read comforting words from the Book of Commandments: "Lift up your hearts and be glad; your redemption draweth nigh. Fear not, little flock; the Kingdom is yours until I come. Behold, I come quickly; Even so: Amen."

452 Drawn expressly for *The Pageant of America*, by Joseph L. Cain

453 Street in Salt Lake City, from a lithograph by Ackerman, in Howard Stansbury, *Exploration and Survey of the Great Salt Lake of Utah*, Philadelphia, 1852

THE ESTABLISHMENT OF SALT LAKE CITY

In April 1847, Brigham Young, who had become Joseph Smith's successor as head of the Church, had gone west with a chosen band to the banks of the Great Salt Lake. He planned to establish the home of his people on soil to which the sovereignty of the United States would not extend. Yet even as he went California slipped from the weak hands of Mexico, and before another year had passed that nation lay prostrate before the military power of the United States. The first wave of migration reached the new home in September. High, indeed, were the hopes of these people as they faced the great adventure under the eastern rim of the Central Basin. Doubtless more than once, as the wagon train plodded westward, a favorite hymn of the Mormons echoed through the mountain defiles.

"Let Zion in her beauty rise;
Her light begins to shine,
Ere long her King will rend the skies,
Majestic and divine.
The gospel, spreading through the land,
A people to prepare,
To meet the Lord and Enoch's band
Triumphant in the air."

TRANSFORMING THE DESERT

The American frontier never beheld a movement quite like that of the Mormons. The authority of the Church was absolute. This discipline, when coupled with the wise leadership of Young, made the Mormon experiment a success. More than fifteen thousand people made their way to Utah from Nauvoo. The numbers in the mountain settlement steadily increased as converts poured in, coming particularly from England. The opportunity for material success and for independence on the American frontier was a powerful aid to the Mormon missionaries preaching to impoverished and despairing folk of the British Isles. Nor did the control of the Church end with the completion of the trek from Illinois. In Utah Church and State were practically one and through its political as well as spiritual power the Church controlled the economic and social life of the community. Natural leaders who arose among the people were rewarded by ecclesiastical office. Dissension was negligible. Only a community so disciplined and so forgetful of the individualistic characteristics of the American frontier could have established itself in the sub-arid edge of the Central Basin. Irrigation was fundamental to Mormon success, and irrigation was made possible by the close organization of the group. The Mormon settlement is an illustration of the power of religion in molding society.

454 The Deseret Store at Salt Lake City, from an engraving after a photograph, in *Harper's Weekly*, September 4, 1858

THE MORMONS AND THE UNITED STATES

455 Bowery, Mint, and President's House, Salt Lake City, from a lithograph by Ackerman in Stansbury, *Exploration and Survey of the Great Salt Lake of Utah*, Philadelphia, 1852

CAPTAIN HOWARD STANSBURY was sent in 1850 to survey the region about Great Salt Lake. The captain has left an account of their infant settlement. "The city was estimated to contain about eight thousand inhabitants and was divided into numerous wards, each, at the time of our visit, enclosed by a substantial fence, for the protection of the young crops; as time and leisure will permit, these will be removed, and each lot enclosed by itself, as with us. The houses are built, principally of adobe or sun-dried brick, which, when well covered with a tight projecting roof, make a warm, comfortable dwelling, presenting a very neat appearance. Buildings of a better description are being introduced, although slowly, owing to the difficulty of procuring the requisite lumber, which must always be scarce and dear in a country so destitute of timber. Upon a square appropriated to the public buildings, an immense shed had been erected upon posts, which was capable of containing three thousand persons. It was called 'The Bowery' and served as a temporary place of worship, until the construction of the Great Temple. This latter is to surpass in grandeur of design and gorgeousness of decoration all edifices the world has yet seen; and is to be eclipsed only by that contemplated in Jackson county, Missouri, — to be erected when 'the fulness of time shall come,' and which will constitute the head-quarters or central point, whence light, truth, and the only true religion shall radiate to the uttermost parts of the earth. A mint was already in operation, from which was issued gold coins of the Federal denominations, stamped, without assay, from the dust brought from California." — *Exploration and Survey of the Great Salt Lake of Utah*, 129–30. During the 'fifties misunderstandings between the Mormons and the American people increased. Ugly rumors, many of them exaggerated or without foundation in fact, came out of Utah regarding the treatment by the Mormons of the emigrants en route to California. In 1856 the people of the East were incensed by the story of the sufferings of the "Push-Cart Brigade." Following the policy of recruiting the Utah settlement by converts from the British Isles, Mormon representatives sent from Liverpool more than a thousand impoverished emigrants. The funds of the church were not adequate to provide them with suitable transportation across the plains to the mountain refuge. They were to walk, men, women and even children, carrying their personal belongings in specially constructed push carts. The vanguard of this migration got through to Utah without disaster, but the main body, delayed by circumstances over which they had no control, were caught in the winter snows and the loss of life was heavy. In the following year, President James Buchanan became convinced that the Mormon Church was flouting the authority of the United States in the territory of Utah. To reëstablish the prestige of the Government among the Mormons, Buchanan in the summer of 1857 sent Albert Sidney Johnston with a considerable military force to bring the Mormons to terms. The army got as far as Fort Bridger, which they found burned and the old trapper driven off. Operating far from its base, Johnston's detachment was practically at the mercy of the Mormon militia, who cut out and drove off its supply trains and cattle. In the spring of 1858 a truce was agreed upon. The whole affair gave little satisfaction to the Federal Government and left the power of the Mormon Church unbroken. In the latter part of the nineteenth century the Mormons made peace with the United States. The practice of polygamy was abandoned, although the theological foundation for it remained unimpaired.

456 The Hand-Cart Emigrants in a Storm, from an engraving in Thomas B. N. Stenhouse. *Rocky Mountain Saints*, New York, 1873

CHAPTER X

TEXAS AND CALIFORNIA

IN 1821, two years before the vision in western New York of the prophet Joseph Smith, Jr., a strange event occurred in that land of mystery which lay to the south of the Rio Grande. For a brief space the streets of Mexico City seethed with political excitement. A revolution was in progress, but unexpectedly there was no bloodshed. Spanish domination, which in that very year completed its third century, came to an end. The streets, where the Latin and the Indian rubbed shoulders, echoed with shouts of *Viva Mexico*. The news spread swiftly to the United States, whose citizens in the early years of the nineteenth century looked with peculiar sympathy upon the efforts of all oppressed peoples to throw off the yoke of monarchy. Yet scarcely a person in the English-speaking republic understood the true import of the Mexican revolution. For ten years one or another self-constituted leader of the oppressed masses in Mexico had sought without success to throw off the yoke of the Spanish overlord. During the decade before 1820 there had been considerable fighting and some loss of life. Affairs had quieted down when suddenly in 1821 the Spanish Viceroy gave up. The reason for the swift and bloodless consummation of the revolution was to be found not in Mexico but in old Spain, where a liberal government critical of the Catholic Church had, for the moment, established itself in power.

The great *hacendados* of Mexico and others of the small white ruling aristocracy, both temporal and ecclesiastical, looked with grave apprehension upon this political overturn in the mother country. They feared that their ancient rights and privileges might be curtailed. They chose to make Mexico independent rather than to risk unfriendly treatment at the hands of the new rulers in Madrid. So Mexico became free and sought to make king a scion of the ruling Bourbon House in Spain. This project failed and out of the confusion which the revolution had wrought a mixed-blood adventurer, one Iturbide, became emperor. Far from being the strong man which independent Mexico needed, Iturbide was but a mediocrity. His empire crumbled and he found himself an exile. In 1824 Mexico became a republic.

Few national groups have ever faced greater obstacles in the way of establishing a nation politically stable and economically healthy than did the people of Mexico. Even the aristocracy had little training in the government of either Church or State. During three centuries the highest offices in both had been held by Castilians. The masses knew nothing of self-government. Influenced, however, by the ideas which grew out of the French Republic and by the republican practices of the United States, the Mexican leaders established what was in form a republic, modeled somewhat on the government of its northern neighbor. Mexico was far from ready to put the principles of democracy into operation. The revolution, as has been well said, plunged that nation into a witch's cauldron. For a generation the politics of Mexico were in chaos. The aristocracy sought desperately to maintain itself in the midst of the new conditions; military adventurers rose to grasp power whenever opportunity offered; occasional idealists strove earnestly to better the sad lot of the masses of the people. Chaos in politics made the new nation virtually impotent. Much of its vast territory was but thinly populated.

FLORIDA AND TEXAS

Two years before the Spanish viceroy handed over the reins of government to the Mexican revolutionists, the United States had purchased Florida from Spain. In the treaty which consummated the transfer of sovereignty was written a clause establishing the western boundary of the North American Republic at the Sabine River. So was settled, for the moment, the fate of Texas. Some Americans expressed dissatisfaction with an administration which so lightly tossed away all claim to one of the richest areas of the North American continent. They were, however, few in number, for Texas was but little known. The year which saw the formulation of the Florida Treaty found the American people plunged in financial disaster. Times had been uncertain since the close of the War of 1812. A false prosperity, which had reached a climax in the year which brought the panic, had manifested itself in a wave of land speculation, stimulated in part by wildcat banking. The policy of the National Government of selling public land on credit had augmented the speculative craze. As the year 1819 drew to a close, many Americans were bankrupt and many more found themselves in unexpectedly straightened circumstances. In 1820 the United States abolished the credit system and reduced the price of the unoccupied lands which were offered for sale from two dollars to one dollar and twenty-five cents per acre. To Americans suffering from the ravages of the panic, migration to the frontier seemed to offer a last promising way out of their troubles, when suddenly they found themselves confronted with the necessity of paying cash for the land they bought. The most striking manifestation of dissatisfaction with the policy of the United States in giving up its claim to Texas took the form of a filibustering expedition led by James Long across the Mexican line in the panic year. With a handful of followers, some of whom were American frontiersmen and others Mexican adventurers, Long fell upon and captured the old Spanish town of Nacogdoches. With complete effrontery he proclaimed the Republic of Texas. The Spanish rulers of Mexico were, however, not yet impotent. Long's followers were soon sent flying across the international boundary. The chief significance of the episode is its revelation of the turbulent and unruly character of certain elements among the frontier folk of the United States and the possibilities of creating unpleasant international complications which lay within their power.

Declaration of the independence of Texas.

The Louisiana Herald, contains a copy of a declaration, issued on the 23d of June, by the supreme council of the republic of Texas. The following extracts contain all that would be interesting to the American reader.

The citizens of Texas would have proved themselves unworthy of the age in which they live—unworthy of their ancestry—of the kindred republics of the American continent—could they have hesitated in this emergency, what course to pursue. Spurning the fetters of colonial vassalage, disdaining to submit to the most atrocious despotism that ever disgraced the annals of Europe—they have resolved, under the blessing of God, to be FREE. By this magnanimous resolution, to the maintainance of which their lives and fortunes are pledged, they secure to themselves an elective and representative government, equal laws and the faithful administration of justice, the rights of conscience and religious liberty, the freedom of the press, the advantages of liberal education, and unrestricted commercial intercourse with all the world.

"Animated by a just confidence in the goodness of their cause, and stimulated by the high object to be obtained by the contest, they have prepared themselves unshrinkingly to meet, and firmly to sustain, any conflict in which this declaration may involve them.

"Done at Nacogdoches this twenty-third day of June, in the year of our Lord 1819.

JAMES LONG,
President of the Supreme Council.
BIS'TE TARIN, sec'ry.

457 Extract from a Notice of the Declaration of Independence of Texas, from *Niles' Register*, September 11, 1819

MOSES AUSTIN, 1767–1821

THE Florida purchase treaty convinced Moses Austin, a Connecticut Yankee who had spent many years in the Louisiana territory, that the opportunity for speculation in Texas lands was ripe. Hardly had Long's filibustering attempt failed, when it became known that this astute and far-seeing American frontiersman had obtained a grant of land in Texas and colonization rights from the Spanish viceroy, so soon to be driven from power. Austin's concession enabled him to offer rich Texas land to American emigrants at a nominal figure. The *Missouri Advocate* of St. Louis remarked a little later: "Mexico does not think of getting rich by *land speculations*, digging for lead, or boiling salt water, but by increasing the number and wealth of her citizens." Many Americans after the Panic of 1819 read eagerly the reports of Austin's activity and turned their thoughts to Texas as a place where their fortunes might be recouped.

458 Moses Austin, from a portrait (artist unknown), in the Missouri Historical Society, St. Louis

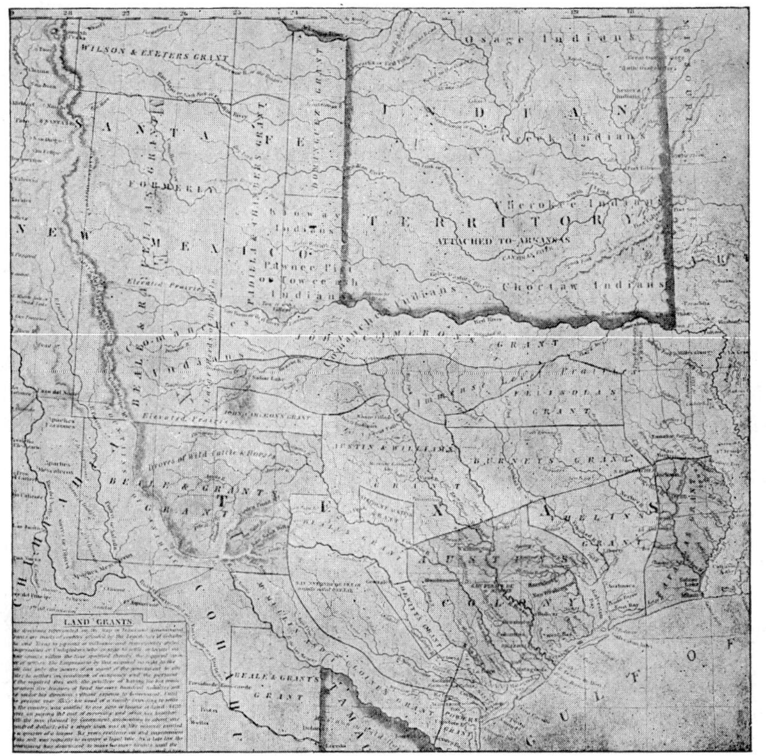

459 Map of the Texas Land Grants, published by S. Augustus Mitchell, Philadelphia, 1836, from the original in the Map Room, New York Public Library

THE EMPRESSARIOS

Moses Austin died before the plan which he had initiated could be put into operation. His mantle fell upon the shoulders of his son, who through character and ability became one of the most significant personages that the American frontier produced. "He was a successful leader with none of the tricks of the demagogue. His influence, it is true, may be attributed in part to his great authority and large power; but at bottom it rested on the solid basis of recognized knowledge, wisdom, and character. He was judicial and honest and fair, and the colonists knew that he was. Though he labored doggedly . . . overcoming one mountain of difficulties only to find himself at the base of another, he sometimes dropped the habit of seriousness in sheer self-defense and joined in the mild pleasures of the time. He appreciated music, liked dancing, and enjoyed social intercourse. In the manner of lonely men, he was given to self-analysis; he thought himself reserved, but he does not appear so in his letters. He was singularly clean in thought and speech, and the language of his writings is uniformly dignified and chaste. In physique he was small of stature, lean and wiry, with fine features and the head of a scholar." — Barker, *The Life of Stephen Austin*, 523. The securing of Mexico's independence cast doubt upon the land title which Moses Austin had obtained from the Spanish Government. The confusion of the first few years after the passing of Spanish power delayed Stephen Austin in carrying the project forward. Just before Iturbide fell, however, Austin secured the desired confirmation of the title and also a colonization law which would make it possible for him to bring immigrants from the United States into Texas. The collapse of the Iturbide government and the establishment of a republic again cast doubt upon the titles. Austin remained yet more months in Mexico City negotiating with those who, for the moment, were in power. In the end he was successful and, in 1824, made his way northward to Texas. His long absence and the convulsions of Mexican politics had served to warn prospective immigrants of the risks they ran if they abandoned the United States and hazarded their fortunes in an unstable country. Immigration into Texas continued, however, in spite of uncertainty in Mexico. Other colonizers besides Stephen Austin appeared. Colonel Henderson's Transylvania scheme in Kentucky suggests the colonization plan adopted by the Mexican Government. Mexico was a nation of great estates, *haciendas*, the proprietors of which, the *hacendados*, made up a large part of the Mexican aristocracy. Quite naturally, therefore, the Mexican Government granted to Stephen Austin, *empressario* (proprietor), a considerable tract of land, part of it arable, but for the most part grazing country. As the habitations of the Indians and mestizos clustered about the great mansion where dwelt the *hacendado*, so the Mexican Government visualized the empressario establishing his immigrants in a sort of village about his own headquarters. For bringing in two hundred the empressario was to receive a bonus of arable and grazing land. Twelve and a half cents per acre was the price set by Austin for his land. The immigrants, according to Mexican law, were to be of responsible character and of the Roman Catholic faith. If they chanced to be slaveholders, no obstacle prevented their bringing their negro property with them. Many Americans sought and obtained the rights of empressarios from the Mexican Government. During the decade of the 'twenties, Americans, practically none of them Catholics, came flooding into Texas until they greatly outnumbered the three thousand odd Mexicans who occupied that vast region.

A QUESTION OF GEOGRAPHY

460 On the Texas Frontier, from an engraving in John Wien Forney, *What I Saw in Texas*, Ringwast and Brown, Philadelphia, 1873

In permitting the westward-moving tide of Americans to cross the international frontier and to obtain a foothold in the rich lands of Texas, the Mexican Government had committed a grave blunder. Mexico is a nation of many distinct geographic areas, separated by climatic and by mountain barriers. There were vast differences in the character and occupations between the people living in the tropical lowlands of Tobasco, in the dry fringes of the Sonora desert, or high up on the temperate Mexican plateau. In the last named region dwelt then, as now, the greater part of the Mexican population. The mixture of the Mexican people, composed of Spaniard, mestizo, and many different tribes of Indians, when added to the geographical complexities of the area, should have warned the Mexican leaders against increasing the ethnic confusion by the establishment of an American colony on the northern frontier. The difficulty of controlling these Americans was augmented by the fact that between Austin's colony and Mexico City stretched a broad semi-desert country, where occasional *hacendados* engaged in the cattle business, and where tribes of wild Indians still roamed at large. The difficulties of compelling the Texans to respect the Mexican law and government were almost insuperable, because of their isolation from the national capital.

THE ATTITUDE OF THE AMERICANS

461 Stephen F. Austin, 1790–1836, from an engraving after the portrait from life, 1836, in the State Capitol, Austin, Texas

No single point of view was common to all the Americans who established their homes in Texas. Austin was sincerely loyal to the Mexican connection and a majority of his colonists followed him in this. There were many Americans, however, who looked upon the Mexicans as intruders north of the Rio Grande and who considered that they were settling upon land which rightfully should be American. The Texans brought with them the industry and thrift that characterized the frontier American of the nineteenth century, together with the frontiersman's spirit of independence and capacity for self-government. They carried also across the international border the American prejudice against the Indian and dislike and contempt for the Spaniard. From the outset the Texan tended to assume an attitude of a racial superiority over the Mexican, an assumption which galled the proud citizen living in what was once the great empire of the Aztecs. Mexican observers, traveling in Texas in the latter years of the 'twenties, were impressed by the prosperity of the American communities, which contrasted sharply with the poverty so prevalent in Mexico. Even they, however, seemed not to have realized the danger for their nation that lurked in these American communities, until Hayden Edwards led the Fredonian Revolt.

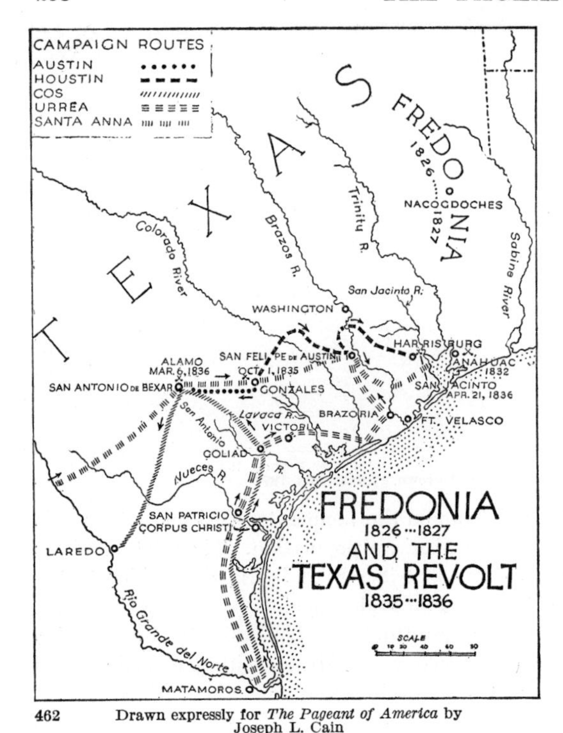

462 Drawn expressly for *The Pageant of America* by Joseph L. Cain

THE FREDONIAN REVOLT

Edwards was an *empressario* who chose the region on the very edge of the international border as the site for his holding. After a series of blunders with the Mexican Government and with American squatters Edwards in 1826 found his contract canceled and himself ordered out of Mexico for the good of the country. He appealed to Austin for aid and was met with a prompt refusal. He then defied the Mexican Government. Gathering some two hundred followers, he raised the flag of revolt and, following in the footsteps of Long, seized the border town of Nacogdoches, and proclaimed the independent Republic of Fredonia. On December 21, 1826, Fredonia adopted a constitution. Before the end of January 1827, however, the revolt was put down and Edwards disappeared from Mexican history. The meaning of the Edwards revolt was not lost upon the politicians in Mexico City. The Americans who had been permitted to enter the country had become a menace to the integrity of the state. The overwhelming majority of these foreigners, to be sure, had remained loyal to the Mexican Government; Edwards' band at best was but a discontented handful. But his revolt had thrown a flood of light upon the possibilities which lurked in Texas. When the Mexican leaders learned from their nation's representatives at Washington of the sentimental sympathy expressed by many American newspapers for this band of two hundred men said to be fighting a battle for democracy against a whole nation, they sensed the danger to Mexico which existed in the temper of the American people. Two years after the collapse of the Fredonian Revolt the Mexican President, Guerrero, on September 15, 1829, promulgated a decree abolishing slavery in Mexico. The Mexican Government, however, was at the moment powerless to enforce this measure in Texas and that region was exempted, for the time being, from its provisions. At the same time the policy of permitting American immigrants to come freely into Texas was discontinued.

MILITARY GOVERNMENT

In 1830 the Mexican Government sought to make its power felt in Texas by the method of military occupation. A ragged, ill-trained, undisciplined army, many of whom were ex-convicts, made its appearance in the prosperous American communities and was scattered over the area in small garrisons. The Texans became excited and talked much of their rights. To their dislike of the Mexican was added an inherited Anglo-Saxon aversion to military control. Yet they did not rise to throw out the army, and eighteen months passed with no serious clash between the troops and the civilian population. The army, to be sure, had little practical significance for the course of events in Texas. Slavery persisted in that region and Americans continued to enter the country. Then one of the revolutions which were so common in Mexico from the winning of independence to the time of Diaz offered the Texans an opportunity. That greatest of all Mexican military adventurers, Santa Anna, was seeking to gain control of the government, calling his followers "Liberals." The Texans became "Liberals," rallied ostensibly to the banner of Santa Anna, and drove from their midst the Mexican army which represented the party in power. They had the luck to side with the victor.

463 A Mexican Military Center, Nacogdoches, Texas, from a photograph, courtesy of the Texas State Library, Austin, Texas

CAUSES OF THE REVOLT OF THE TEXANS

THE years between 1832 and 1835 found Mexican politics in more than their normal state of chaos. Santa Anna was in and out of office several times. In May 1834, he approached his apogee when he succeeded in dissolving the National Congress and in making himself dictator. His policy was to centralize power in his own hands at the National Capital and to destroy or to reduce greatly such local autonomy as the various states possessed. He was successful in dissolving in the same year several state legislatures. Distant Texas, however, stood foursquare against his centralizing tendencies. Since 1830 the Texans had chafed under the act which joined them to the state of Coahuila, an arrangement which gave Mexicans a control over the affairs of the combined territory. The Texans also were restive as a result of the application of the Mexican tariff to products which they were in the habit of importing from the United States, particularly from New Orleans. To encourage settlement, the Mexican Government had promised that the tariff should not apply to the Texan communities for seven years. As Santa Anna waxed in power, the fears of the people of Texas increased. More and more the gossip of the streets of the Texan villages turned to the subject of independence. Two groups appeared among the Americans: one which sought to secure statehood and a greater measure of local autonomy under the Mexican Government for Texas; the other which aimed at nothing short of separation. The success of the Texans in balking in their own community the centralizing policy of Santa Anna drew them inevitably into the maelstrom of Mexican politics. Under the leadership of Stephen Austin a majority of the people of Texas supported the reëstablishment of the republican constitution of 1824, which had been set aside by the wily dictator. Austin hoped that such a move would bring to the aid of his hard-pressed compatriots Mexican liberals who were opposed to the Santa Anna régime. In this he was disappointed. The Texans were left to fight their own battles as best they could. The fighting of battles, however, was what the peaceful Austin sought to avoid. Nevertheless in the year 1835 the clouds of revolution gathered rapidly over Texas. In November a General Consultation of Texans charged that militarism under Santa Anna had destroyed the constitution of the government and declared that the duty and right of Texans was to maintain their government independent of centralized military control. In the spring of 1836 the Napoleon of the West, as Santa Anna was called, set out to chastise his refractory fellow citizens in the north.

464 General Antonio Lopez de Santa Anna, 1795–1876, from the portrait from life, *ca.* 1858, by Paul L'Ouvrier, in the New York Historical Society

465 Sam Houston, 1793–1863, from an engraving after a daguerreotype, in *Texas and the Mexican War* in *The Chronicles of America* Series, Yale University Press, New Haven, 1921

THE FIRST PHASE OF THE REVOLUTION

WHILE Santa Anna, with an army of considerable size, was marching on Texas, the Americans of that region were organizing for defense. Sam Houston had been appointed commander-in-chief of the Texan forces but the volunteer army which he led had virtually neither discipline nor organization. Individually American frontiersmen were good fighters but they had difficulty in submitting to the limitations on personal liberty required by military discipline. As a result, Houston in the early months of 1836 was only nominally commander of the armed bands of Texans which sought to parry the blow from the National Capital.

466 The Alamo, from a drawing after a photograph, in the possession of the publishers

SOUTHWARD MOVEMENTS

DECIDING for themselves what should be done, two detachments struck southward with the intention of falling upon Matamoras, a Mexican town on the south bank of the Rio Grande. To these amateur strategists, such an expedition seemed to offer possibilities of turning the flank of Santa Anna's advancing army. Little heed was given to the fact that such a movement left the Texas settlements uncovered and unprotected from attack from the southwest. While the Texan forces were still advancing, the Alamo tragedy occurred.

THE FALL OF THE ALAMO

IN February 1836, Lieutenant-Colonel William B. Travis commanded a small detachment of some one hundred and fifty men stationed at the Alamo, a fort near San Antonio. On the twenty-fourth the van of Santa Anna's army occupied the city and quickly surrounded the fort. Then began a brief but terrible siege. Travis sent out a call for aid, which breathed determination to fight to the last. He understood the character of his opponents as well as if he had known that Santa Anna had ordered that no prisoners be taken in this war. Outnumbering the Texans sixteen to one, the Mexicans drew their circle of rifles closer and closer to the beleaguered garrison. They paid a price, for the Americans fought with the desperation of men determined to sell their lives dearly. On March 6 the end came. When the sun went down on that day, no defender remained alive. Among the dead were found the bodies of James Bowie and Davy Crockett. The defense of the Alamo has become a classic manifestation of the fighting capacity of the Americans. When the news of the tragedy spread over Texas, the revolution entered its second phase and became avowedly a war for independence. The disaster brought home to the Texans the desperate character of the fight before them and taught them the need of centralized control of their forces.

467 The Battle of the Alamo, from the painting by Percy Moran (1862–). © Gerlach Barlow Co., Joliet, Ill.

THE RETREAT OF THE TEXANS

The crisis which confronted the Texans following the fall of the Alamo served to increase the authority of Houston. He ordered a retreat. One of the detachments which had started for Matamoras under the command of Captain Fannin was attacked by Mexican troops, and some five hundred defeated Texans slaughtered. The war between the Americans and the Mexicans was as bloody as any frontier Indian conflict. The defeat of Fannin, coming close on the heels of the Alamo disaster, was staggering. The Texan people, abandoning their villages and outlying homes, fled eastward toward the Sabine River. The troops of Houston fell back also, in isolated detachments which the commander strove to concentrate near the eastern border. Santa Anna, as he passed through the charred ruins of the towns burned by the hands of the Texans themselves, believed that this northern colony of refractory Americans was at his feet. He hurried after Houston in an effort to cut him off and destroy what remaining strength he had. Houston continued to retreat, perhaps aiming, as some have thought, to fall back across the Sabine where he might receive the assistance of soldiers of the United States, concentrated to protect the interests of the American frontier.

468 General Sam Houston at the Battle of San Jacinto, from the painting by S. Seymour Thomas (1868–), in possession of the City of Houston, Texas, photograph from Wide World Photos

THE BATTLE OF SAN JACINTO

Houston, however, never reached the Sabine but concentrated his troops on the banks of the San Jacinto River. On April 20 the two armies came into contact, but the Mexicans avoided a fight. They took up a position on a low hill and threw up light breastworks. On the following day Santa Anna's troops remained inactive, failing to take even the most elementary security precautions and making apparently no effort to discover the intentions of Houston. They were, therefore, completely surprised when, late in the afternoon, a battle line of armed Texans charged their earthworks from the edge of a nearby wood. The Mexicans, caught unprepared, were thrown into confusion. They became unmanageable and their camp became a shambles. Some three dozen only of Santa Anna's army escaped. The bodies of six hundred odd dead, scarred with bullet or knife wounds, were found on the field. Terrible, indeed, was the revenge of the Americans for the Alamo and the massacre of Fannin's men. A few Mexicans were made prisoners. The victory was complete. On the following day, when the Texans were busy cleaning up the battle field, Santa Anna, a miserable fugitive, was brought to Houston's tent. For nine years Texas was an independent nation. Sam Houston became its president. In 1845 Texas was annexed to the United States.

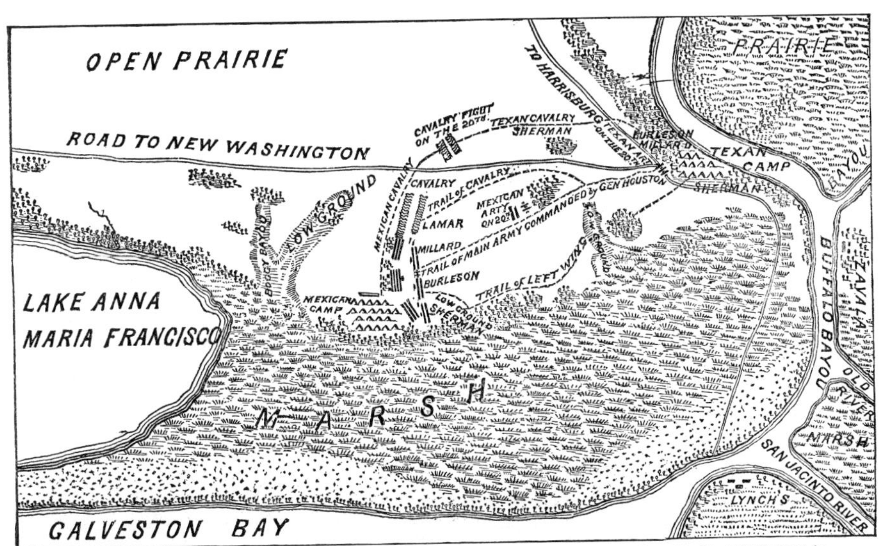

469 Plan of the Battle of San Jacinto, from Henderson Yoakum, *History of Texas, from its First Settlement in 1685, to its Annexation to the United States in 1846*, New York, 1856

THE

PERSONAL NARRATIVE

OF

JAMES O. PATTIE,

OF KENTUCKY,

DURING AN EXPEDITION FROM ST. LOUIS, THROUGH THE VAST REGIONS BETWEEN THAT PLACE AND THE PACIFIC OCEAN, AND THENCE BACK THROUGH THE CITY OF MEXICO TO VERA CRUZ, DURING JOURNEYINGS OF SIX YEARS; IN WHICH HE AND HIS FATHER, WHO ACCOMPANIED HIM, SUFFERED UNHEARD OF HARDSHIPS AND DANGERS, HAD VARIOUS CONFLICTS WITH THE INDIANS, AND WERE MADE CAPTIVES, IN WHICH CAPTIVITY HIS FATHER DIED;

TOGETHER WITH A DESCRIPTION OF THE COUNTRY, AND THE VARIOUS NATIONS THROUGH WHICH THEY PASSED.

EDITED BY
TIMOTHY FLINT

CINCINNATI:
PUBLISHED BY E. H. FLINT.
1833.

470 From the title-page of the original

NEWS OF CALIFORNIA

WHILE events in Texas in the 'thirties centered the attention of the American people on that troubled province, scraps of news relating to distant and mysterious California made their way to the people of the East. Occasional travelers reached that little-known country and published their descriptions. James Ohio Pattie, discouraged by his failure to make his fortune in the West, returned to Kentucky, where he wrote and published an account of his adventures. Kelley, the Oregon enthusiast, was impressed with the opportunities of "High California" and mentioned the region with his usual extravagant enthusiasm. Thomas Jefferson Farnham, whose *Life and Adventures in California* was widely read in the 'thirties and 'forties, described the region with little restraint. "It may be confidently asserted that no country in the world possesses so fine a climate complemented with so productive a soil, as the sea-board portion of the Californias, including the territories on the Bay of San Francisco and the Rivers San Joaquin and Sacramento, but its miserable people live unconscious of these things. In their gardens grow the apple, the pear, the olive, fig, and orange, the Irish and sweet potato, yam and the plantain most luxuriously, side by side; and yet they sleep, and smoke and hum some tune of Castilian laziness, while surrounding nature is thus inviting them to the noblest and richest rewards of honorable toil." In 1840 was first published Richard Henry Dana Jr.'s classic, *Two Years Before the Mast*. Reading this, the people of the United States got a picture of the life of this lightly held Spanish province beyond the mountains. ". . . No sooner was the importance of the country known to the early Spaniards, than the Jesuits obtained leave to establish themselves in it, to Christianize and enlighten the Indians. They established missions in various parts of the country toward the close of the seventeenth century, and collected the natives about them, baptizing them into the Church, and teaching them the arts of civilized life. To protect the Jesuits in their missions, and at the same time to support the power of the crown over the civilized Indians, two forts were erected and garrisoned, — one at San Diego, and the other at Monterey. These were called presidios, and divided the command of the whole country between them. Presidios have since been established at Santa Barbara, San Francisco, and other places, dividing the country into large districts, each with its presidio, and governed by a commandante. The soldiers, for the most part, married civilized Indians; and thus, in the vicinity of each presidio, sprung up, gradually, small towns. In the course of time, vessels began to come into the ports to trade with the missions and receive hides in return; and thus began the great trade of California. Nearly all the cattle in the country belonged to the missions, and they employed their Indians, who became, in fact, their serfs, in tending their vast herds. In the year 1793, when Vancouver visited San Diego, the missions had obtained great wealth and power, and are accused of having depreciated the country with the sovereign, that they might be allowed to retain their possessions . . . ever since the independence of Mexico, the missions have been going down. . . . The priests have no power, except in their religious character. . . . The change had been made but a few years before our arrival upon the coast. . . ." — DANA, 1873, 193–94.

471 From the painting *The Fandango* by Charles C. Nahl, in the G. B. Crocker Art Gallery, Sacramento, California

SECULARIZATION OF THE MISSIONS

472 From the painting *Pilgrims of Old California*, by Lester D. Boronda (1886–), owned by Frank A. Miller, Master of the Mission Inn, Riverside, California

"On the expulsion of the Jesuits from the Spanish dominions, the missions passed into the hands of the Franciscans, though without any essential change in their management. Ever since the independence of Mexico, the missions had been going down; until, at last, a law was passed, stripping them of all their possessions, and confining the priests to their spiritual duties, at the same time declaring all the Indians free and independent *Rancheros*. The change in the condition of the Indians was, as may be supposed, only nominal; they are virtually serfs, as much as they ever were. But in the missions the change was complete. The priests have now no power, except in their religious character and the great possessions of the missions are given over to be preyed upon by the harpies of the civil power, who are sent there in the capacity of *administradores*, to settle up the concern; and who usually end, in a few years, by making themselves fortunes, and leaving their stewardships worse than they found them. The dynasty of the priests was much more acceptable to the people of the country, and, indeed, to everyone concerned with the country, by trade or otherwise, than that of the *administradores*. The priests were connected permanently to one mission, and felt the necessity of keeping up its credit. Accordingly the debts of the missions were regularly paid, and the people were, in the main, well treated, and attached to those who had spent their whole lives among them. But the *administradores* are strangers sent from Mexico, having no interest in the country; not indentified in any way with their charge, and, for the most part, men of desperate fortunes, — broken-down politicians and soldiers, — whose only object is to retrieve their condition in as short a time as possible. The change had been made but a few years before our arrival upon the coast, yet, in that short time, the trade was diminished, credit impaired, and the venerable missions were going rapidly to decay." —Dana, 1873, 194–95.

JAMES OHIO PATTIE, TRADER-EXPLORER

In 1824 two fur traders entered the Rocky Mountains who were destined to play a rôle of some importance in the advance of the frontier across the continent. Sylvester Pattie, the elder, was a man like Daniel Boone. Born in frontier Kentucky, he had moved steadily westward with the fringe of settlement and now, in later life, was striking into the cordilleras. His son, James Ohio, inherited the instincts of the older man. There is no space here to take up in detail the career and adventures of these traders. Accounts of two expeditions will suffice. James Ohio Pattie, on January 2, 1826, set out from the Santa Rita copper mines in New Mexico on a trapping expedition into the unknown West. Within a few weeks the company was nearly destroyed by the Papago Indians near the Gila River. Pattie, however, escaped. He soon fell in with some American trappers and the new organization made its way down the Gila to its junction with the Colorado. Their trapping prospered. After pausing for a space with the Yuma Indians at the mouth of the Gila the trappers made their way up the Colorado. On March 1, 1826, they reached the villages of the Mohaves, about six months before Jedediah Smith paused there on his first expedition to California. The Mohaves resented the intrusion of the Pattie party. Several fights took place in which Indians were killed. Finally, the redskins, taking advantage of night, crept into the white man's camp, surprised the sleeping trappers, and killed two men. Pattie again escaped.

473 View on the Gila River, from a lithograph in Lieutenant-Colonel W. H. Emory, *Notes of a Military Reconnaissance from Fort Leavenworth, in Missouri, to San Diego, in California*, Washington, 1848

474 The Canyon of the Colorado, from a photograph, courtesy of the New York Public Library

UP THE COLORADO

A FEW days later, as the party proceeded up the Colorado, three men who had been sent to explore a tributary stream were found dead, "their bodies cut in pieces and spitted before a great fire, after the same fashion which is used in roasting beaver." So far the expedition had followed the banks of the Colorado. Soon after the last tragedy, however, it reached the Grand Canyon and could proceed no further along the river bank. Painfully climbing to the plateau, the trappers made their weary way along the edge of the gorge, through a country where game was scarce and travel difficult. Ultimately they passed beyond the canyon, and struck northward to the Yellowstone, trapping along that stream. They then turned southward until finally striking the headwaters of the Rio Grande, they followed the course of that river to Santa Fé. The wanderings of these trappers constituted one of the most remarkable exploring ventures in Rocky Mountain history.

THE PATTIES IN CALIFORNIA

SYLVESTER PATTIE had undertaken to exploit the Santa Rita mines, but found himself faced with bankruptcy when a trusted employee disappeared with some thirty thousand dollars. The elder and the younger Patties then took again to trapping, securing a license from the Governor of New Mexico. Again they made their way down the Gila River and paused in the country of the Yuma Indians. Here disaster overtook them, for the redskins, taking advantage of a stormy night, drove off the horses of the expedition. Their only recourse was to make dugouts as hastily as possible. In these the party floated down the Colorado. They trapped as they went, meeting with great success, for the region had hitherto not been exploited. Their progress was checked near the mouth of the great river by the tides which came up from the Gulf of Lower California and which inundated the river banks at night. The waters became too rough for their primitive boats. They turned back and toiled for a time against the current. The month was February and the river was already beginning to rise from the spring flood. The current became too swift to combat. The boats were accordingly abandoned. The furs were cached along the river bank and the party struck westward across the desert of Lower California for the coast. A journey of terrible hardship followed. Once the elder Pattie and another man were left to perish on the sand. Water, discovered soon after, made it possible, however, for all to get through the dry country. With the aid of Indian guides, the Patties reached the mission of Santa Catalina, from whence they were taken under guard to the Governor of California at San Diego. The significance of the journey lay in the fact that the Patties had explored the Lower Colorado and had shown that its lower reaches afforded an approach to California.

475 Pattie and Solver Rescued from Famine, from an engraving in James Ohio Pattie, *A Personal Narrative*, Cincinnati, 1833

JOHN BIDWELL, 1819–1900, PIONEER SETTLER

476 John Bidwell, from an engraving in *The Century Magazine*, November 1890. © The Century Co.; reproduced by permission

Lured by the reports of the richness of California, a band of men and their families among whom was John Bidwell, met at Sapling Grove in Missouri in May 1841. Vague indeed was their knowledge of the country which they must cross to reach the land of promise. They were advised to take with them tools with which to construct canoes. By means of these they could make their way down one of the rivers which was supposed to lead from Great Salt Lake to the Pacific Ocean. Doubtless the expedition would speedily have ended in disaster had it not for the first half of its mountain journey been guided by two experienced mountain men, the trapper, Thomas Fitzpatrick, and the missionary, Father De Smet. West of the South Pass the party turned off from the trail which led to Oregon. A few men who went north to Fort Hall for information could get only the vague warning to avoid the desert of the Central Basin on the south, and also the mountain country on the north, into which many a trapper had gone, never to return. The Bidwell party, with such uncertain directions, made their way westward. They were bewildered by the unfamiliar salt plains, where almost no food was to be had and where the cruel mirage beckoned them to disappointment. They finally reached the Humboldt River, which they followed to the Humboldt Sink. Turning southward they made the Carson River and beyond reached the Walker River. At this place they killed the last of their oxen and jerked the meat, preparatory to the difficult trip over the Sierras. Time pressed; September was on them. They knew that they could neither cross the great mountains during the winter, nor remain on the eastern side. By way of the Walker and the Stanislaus rivers, they made their difficult way over the towering range. In a tangle of gorges and canyons on the western slope they were forced to leave behind many of their animals. Food was scarce and they ate whatever came to hand. At last they reached the rich valley of the San Joaquin. An Indian guided them to the ranch of one Doctor John Marsh. Here the party broke up. "After six months," wrote Bidwell, "we had now arrived at the first settlement in California, November 4, 1841." Bidwell's exploit pointed clearly to the destiny of California.

477 John A. Sutter, from a wood engraving after a photograph by C. M. Bell, Washington, in the Ford Collection, New York Public Library

JOHN A. SUTTER, 1803–1880

Some of Bidwell's men made their way to Sutter's Fort or, as its owner called it, New Helvetia, in the Sacramento Valley, near the confluence of the Sacramento and American rivers. Sutter was one of the strangest figures of the American frontier, a man to be compared with Blennerhassett who was associated with the Burr conspiracy. Born in the Duchy of Baden, of Swiss parents, Sutter as a young man emigrated to the United States. He lived for a time in Indiana, then went to St. Louis. Finally he joined a trapping expedition which took him to Oregon. Taking passage on one of the trading ships that frequented the Oregon coast, he sailed to the Hawaiian Islands. Already his dream had begun to take shape in his mind. He planned nothing less than a great feudal barony in the unsettled part of northern California, and looked forward to the day when the colony which he should plant would become an independent nation. He gained some assistance from American residents in the Hawaiian Islands, and engaged some of the native islanders to help him. In 1840 he was in California. He purchased the property and the land claims of the Russian-American Fur Company at Bodega. He secured permission from the Spanish Governor of California to establish his fort in the Sacramento Valley.

478 Sutter's Fort, 1846, from a drawing by C. W. Jefferys after an old print, in the possession of the publishers

SUTTER'S FORT

TRAVELERS who came to Sutter's Fort in the early 'forties found it a large, rectangular structure of adobe brick, mounting a dozen guns which had been obtained as a result of the Russian purchase, and capable of holding a thousand men. Sutter was not only on friendly terms with the Spanish authorities of California and Mexico, but controlled the Indian tribes which lived about his post. Military discipline prevailed at New Helvetia, where sentries stood guard and the drilling of soldiers was seen each day. Sutter added agricultural and commercial development to military strength. He planted wheat, grazed cattle, built a mill, sent out trapping expeditions, and ran the launch, which he had purchased as part of the Bodega property, on regular trips from San Francisco to New Helvetia. He was a visionary, impractical, generous man, most of whose ventures involved him in loss rather than profit. His significance in the history of the frontier is not, however, to be found in the great dream which never came true, but in the aid which he offered to early American immigrants into California.

EARLY IMMIGRATION

AFTER the success of the Bidwell expedition of 1841, the passing years saw the trickle of immigrants into California increase in volume. The later 'forties were the great years of the Oregon Trail. More and more parties turned off from the Trail and made their way to California. To such persons Sutter's Fort was of vast importance. It was strategically located in northern California and Sutter's control of the Indians kept down their depredations. Unnumbered strangers, exhausted by the journey across the mountains and half starved, found refuge for a time at New Helvetia. Here they were able to rest and recuperate. From the Fort went out many a rescue party to save immigrant expeditions caught in the mountain snows. Finally, so long as Sutter's cannon glowered from the battlements of his fort, the Spanish authorities, whose headquarters lay to the south, could not check the streams of Americans that poured across the northern passes of the Sierras, or overflowed from Oregon into northern California. The winter following that which Frémont spent in the Sierras saw a party of some eighty-seven people come to a halt at what is now called Donner Lake, California, under the eastern edge of the Sierras. They were a part of a great movement of people from the Mississippi Valley across the mountains to California. The Donner party had separated from the main caravan to take what they thought was a better route. During the summer of 1846 they had made their way slowly through the broken country of the Central Basin and had been stopped in the edge of the Sierra Nevada Mountains by winter. Here they built rough shanties to brave the cold months. The snow piled up until, as the rescue party which came in the spring found, they had to cut wood from the topmost branches of trees of considerable size. Thirty-nine of the party had been laid to rest when camp was broken and the journey to California resumed.

479 Donner Lake, California, from an engraving after a drawing by Thomas Moran (1837–1926), in *Picturesque America*, New York, 1872

POLK'S POLICY REGARDING CALIFORNIA

On March 4, 1845, James K. Polk of Tennessee took the oath of office as President of the United States. He appointed James Buchanan as his Secretary of State. Polk, a sincere and thoroughgoing expansionist, turned his attention promptly to the acquisition of Oregon and California. Buchanan dispatched a messenger to Thomas O. Larkin, consular agent for the United States at Monterey. The communication which Larkin received is one of the most remarkable documents in American foreign relations. Larkin, a duly accredited agent to a friendly government, was instructed to engineer, if possible, an independence movement on the part of California and was pointedly informed that the United States would prevent the transfer of California to a European power. The United States, according to the communication, would not foment a revolution in the region, but would assure the Californians of protection if they should throw off the yoke of Mexico. Larkin, with energy and tact, proceeded promptly to the carrying out of his mission. The situation, at the time he received the message, was such as to offer prospects of success.

480 James K. Polk, 1795–1849, from an engraving in the possession of the publishers

WAR WITH MEXICO

A few days before the opening of Polk's administration, Texas had been annexed. The new administration faced the problem of an irate Mexico. Knowing well that the Mexican Government was hard pressed for money, Polk, following the reasoning of an American business man, hoped that he could purchase California. His expectation of a successful deal would doubtless have been increased had he realized that in 1846 California was virtually independent of Mexican control. Polk, however, like most Americans of his day, failed to estimate accurately the temper of the people who lived south of the Rio Grande. They might be poor; their government might be in chronic chaos; but they were proud and extremely sensitive. The American offer was an insult to the Mexicans. Polk's negotiator, Slidell, was not even received by the Mexican authorities. The result was serious. Many Americans, due to the confused conditions in the southern Republic, had suffered in both property and persons at the hands of the Mexicans, with the result that the United States was urging many claims against Mexico. That nation had undertaken to pay some of these. Payment had begun, only to be stopped by the annexation of Texas. Polk's plan had been that these claims should be assumed by the United States as part of the purchase price of California. When the negotiations failed in a manner which increased irritation on both sides, and when in 1846 a skirmish between Mexican and American troops took place on the Rio Grande, the American administration decided on war. The story of this conflict between unequal antagonists has been told in Volume VI, Chapter XV.

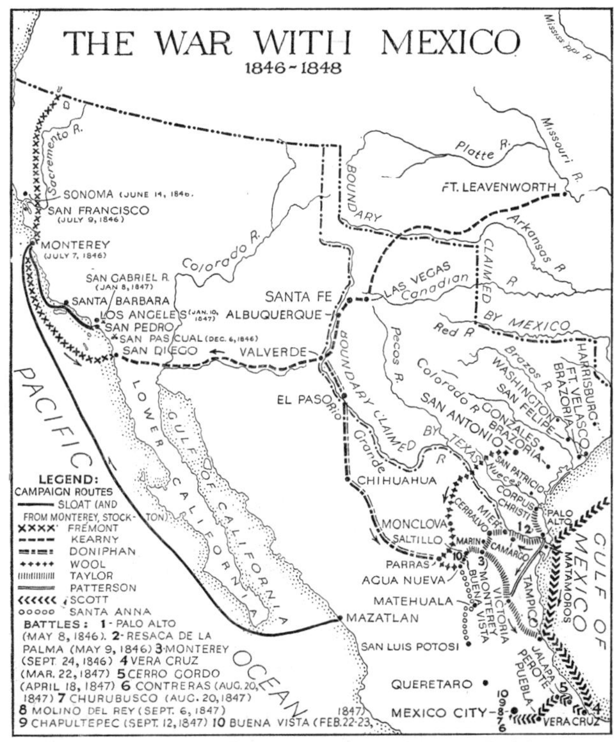

481 Drawn expressly for *The Pageant of America* by Joseph L. Cain

482 The Original Bear Flag, courtesy of the California State Library, Sacramento

THE BEAR FLAG REVOLT

Larkin, meanwhile, had begun dealing with Americans who lived in the Spanish settlements of California. Some of these had allied themselves to Spanish families by marriage and become naturalized Mexican citizens. The effort to bring about a quiet and bloodless separation from the mother state was progressing favorably when suddenly a storm broke from an unexpected quarter. For the previous few years American farmer and trapper immigrants had been coming into the Sacramento Valley, bringing with them a traditional distrust and dislike of the Spaniard. Their antipathy to the Mexican was intensified by the memories of the blood spilled at the Alamo and in the other encounters of the Texan war. In the spring of 1846 this frontier group was disturbed by rumors that the Californians were going to move against them. They saw some significance, moreover, in the fact that Frémont, who had been a short time before in California on a third exploring expedition and who had retired to Oregon as a result of orders from the Californian authorities, now returned. The messenger who had reported to Larkin had also brought word to Frémont. With something more than the moral support of the explorer, a band of frontiersmen, apparently trappers for the most part, rose in revolt, captured the town of Sonoma, had a brush with the Californians, and proclaimed the Republic of California. Their banner bore a star and the image of a grizzly bear. The Bear Flag Revolt nullified the efforts of the suave Larkin.

THE CONQUEST OF CALIFORNIA

Neither Larkin nor the supporters of the Bear Flag movement were destined, however, to win California for the United States. The Mexican War began before either enterprise could accomplish its purpose. Commodore Sloat, replaced after a short time by Commodore Stockton, using the armed forces of the United States, quickly took possession of the much desired province. By August 15, 1846, all of California had fallen into American hands without the shedding of blood. The troops at the disposal of Stockton and of Frémont, whom the former had commissioned a major, were inadequate, however, to hold the region. In the latter part of September, Lieutenant Gillespie, who commanded the small garrison at Los Angeles, found himself unexpectedly confronted by a revolt which he could not put down. He was forced to abandon the city. The uprising spread throughout the whole of the old Spanish settlements. Stockton attempted unsuccessfully to retake Los Angeles. He managed, however, to keep his flag flying at San Diego. The crisis lasted until the arrival of Colonel Stephen W. Kearny who in December reached California from Santa Fé to accomplish the conquest of California. (See Vol. VI, p. 333.) Though Kearny's little band was exhausted by the difficult trip across the southern desert, the combined forces were able to break the resistance of the Californians. On January 10 Kearny entered Los Angeles. Three days later the Californians signed the "Cahuenga Capitulation."

483 From the painting *Hoisting the Flag at Monterey*, by Carlton T. Chapman (1860–), courtesy of the artist

THE DISCOVERY OF GOLD

SLIGHTLY more than a year after the completion of the conquest of California and two weeks before the signing of the Treaty of Guadalupe-Hidalgo, which brought the Mexian War to an end, James W. Marshall, one of Sutter's men, picked some yellow particles out of the tail-race of a sawmill belonging to his employer. Seven years before, grains of gold had been discovered by a Californian in the San Ferdinand Hills, near Los Angeles, and a local flurry of excitement had occurred. Sutter and Marshall, fearing that the news of gold might disrupt the farming operations of New Helvetia, sought to keep the findings of the grains of gold a secret. They succeeded fairly well for about six weeks; then the news spread to the coast settlements and the gold rush began. Most Californians who could dropped their regular tasks and hastened to the creek-bottom gravels glinting with yellow metal.

484 James W. Marshall, discoverer of gold in California, from a photograph in the United States National Museum, Washington

A REGULAR GOLD DUSTMAN.

"HOLLO! WHERE ARE YOU OFF TO NOW?"
"OH! I AINT A GOING TO STOP HERE, LOOKING FOR TEASPOONS IN CINDERS. I'M OFF TO KALLIFORNIER, VERE THERE'S HEAPS O' GOLD DUST TO BE HAD FOR THE SWEEPIN'."

485 From a cartoon in *Punch*, Vol. 16, London, 1849

THE GOLD RUSH OF 1849

THE excitement in California caused by the discovery of gold depicted in miniature the craze which seized the people of the United States in the winter and spring of 1849. The world has never seen a better illustration of the power of gold to affect the lives and destinies of individuals than the rush of 1849. Americans were caught in a craze the like of which the nation had never known. The drawing power of the fur-bearing animals of the forest and of rich soil, which had been responsible for the swift westward advance of the frontier, was as nothing compared to the lure of yellow nuggets. In North and South, in East and West, Americans dreamed of riches acquired over night. In the spring of 1849 a multitude of people, men in large part, but among whom were many women and children, turned their faces westward. Risking everything including life itself, they responded to the beckoning of the kettle of gold that lay beneath the setting sun.

486 From a drawing, *California Gold Diggers — A Scene from Actual Life at the Mines*, in *Ballou's Pictorial Drawing-Room Companion*, May 3, 1856

487 San Francisco in November 1849, from a lithograph after a drawing by Bayard Taylor (1825–78), in his *El Dorado; or Adventures in the Path of Empire*, George P. Putnam, New York, 1850

SAN FRANCISCO IN THE GOLD RUSH

In April 1850, Richard L. Hale of Newbury, Massachusetts, ended an ocean voyage in San Francisco Bay by way of Cape Horn. "This afternoon all went ashore, looking over the city (?) and its surroundings. It was the general opinion that the place had few attractions — a mass of wooden hovels and cloth tents, pitched without order. . . . People from all parts of the world are here, and every language seems to be spoken, but the babel resolves itself into one great motive "Gold, Gold!" and still "Gold!" whatever may be the cost to get it. . . ." After landing, Hale built a rude shack on the hill above the city. He was standing before this one day some time after his landing, looking out over the city. "Suddenly from the direction of the bay, between the hill and shore, came a puff of smoke. I did not pay much attention to it at first, but even as I looked the smoke grew in volume, until without warning, tongues of flame shot out in several directions, and in less time than it takes to write of it, a raging, rolling, whirlwind of fire was tearing through the tent city, gathering terrific impetus from the strong wind urging it onward. Bells rang! Men went rushing down the hillside, and joining the excited crowd. I, too, ran on in the direction of the fire with the hope that I might be of some help, together with the others, in extinguishing it! The flames were utterly beyond control! The dry cloth of the tents, the flimsy wooden shacks, caught and burned like tinder, while the strong wind lashed the flames before it, until there was nothing more for it to gorge its all consuming appetite upon. In a very short time the crude mining town was a thing of the past! Only smoking heaps of ashes, and charred debris told where San Francisco had stood, for the town had burned to the very sand on which the mushroom miners' structures had pushed forward." — Carolyn Hall Russ, *The Log of a Forty-Niner*, 1923, 64, 66.

488 From the painting *Sunday Morning in the Mines*, by Charles C. Nahl, in the G. B. Crocker Art Gallery, Sacramento, California

489 From an engraving, after the painting *Judge Lynch*, by Stanley Berkeley, in the possession of the publishers

A MINING COUNTRY

In 1850, Alfred T. Jackson of Norfolk, Connecticut, was working in the gold fields of what was called Nevada county of California. An excerpt from his diary gives a glimpse of the life and problems of the mining camps. "September 20, 1850. — We finished up the claim last week. It about petered out. We got only five ounces. We are going to try the flat and if that don't pay we will go off prospecting. There was a fight on the creek last week. Donovan, an Irishman, jumped a claim, and when the rightful owner warned him off he drew an Allen's pepper box and shot Tracy, to whom the claim belonged, in the leg. Tracy beat the Irishman over the head with a shovel and left him for dead, although he did not die until yesterday. Tracy was taken over to town and tried before a fellow who sets himself up for an alcalde and was then turned loose, as it was a clear case of self-defense. This is the first death on Rock Creek. The miners are indignant over Tracy being taken to Nevada. There is no more law there than on Rock Creek. Some fellow claims to be a sort of judge, but he's got no legal authority and a miners' court is just as binding here as in town. We held a meeting of all the miners along the creek, and Anderson made a speech. Said it was an unwarranted usurpation and an invasion of our rights, and we resolved that we would not permit it to happen again. We buried Donovan on the hill, and sold his tools and traps at auction, including his cabin, for one hundred and forty dollars. Nobody knows what to do with the money, as it is not known where he came from. Anderson was made custodian of the proceeds in case any claimant should turn up." — C. L. Canfield, *The Diary of a Forty-Niner*, 1906, 26.

NEVADA

In 1858, nine years after the fateful summer which saw the rush of gold seekers to California, some prospectors discovered silver on the side of Mount Davison, just east of the California border. Thousands of men and women had passed near the spot in search of fortunes in California and had not observed the wealth which lay beside the beaten trail. To this region came many people from California and some from the Great Plains, east of the mountains. Carson City sprang into being. The next spring, adventurers, searching eagerly over the region, stumbled upon the deposit that came to be known as the Comstock Lode. These discoveries brought about the founding of Nevada. Eighteen hundred and fifty-nine was a boom year as the fame of the Comstock Lode spread to the borders of the nation. The tide of adventurers sweeping into Nevada in 1859 receded, however, in the following years, leaving a few thousand who remained to set up in 1864 a state government.

490 Sunday Amusement in a Nevada Mining Camp, from a drawing in *Harper's Weekly*, April 24, 1869

491 Miners at the Bar in a Nevada Mining Camp, from a drawing in *Harper's Weekly*, April 24, 1869

VIRGINIA CITY, NEVADA, 1860

"As I passed through the Devil's Gate it struck no indecorous sense, I was simply about to ask where he lived, when, looking up the road, I saw amidst the smoke and din of shivered rocks, where grimy imps were at work blasting for ore, a string of adventurers laden with picks, shovels, and crowbars; kegs of powder, frying-pans, pitchforks, and other instruments of torture — all wearily toiling in the same direction; decrepit old men, with avarice imprinted upon their furrowed brows; Jews and Gentiles footweary and haggard; the young and the old, the strong and the weak, all alike burning with an unhallowed lust for lucre; and then I shuddered as the truth flashed upon me that they were going straight to — Virginia City. . . . On a slope of mountains speckled with snow, sagebushes, and mounds of upturned earth, without any apparent beginning or end, congruity or regard for the eternal fitness of things, lay outspread the wondrous city of Virginia. Frame shanties, pitched together as if by accident; tents of canvas, of blankets, of brush, of potato-sacks and old shirts, with empty whiskey barrels for chimneys; smoky hovels of mud and stone; coyote holes in the mountain-side forcibly seized and held by men; pits and shafts with smoke issuing from every crevice; piles of goods and rubbish on craggy points, in the hollows, on the rocks, in the mud, in the snow, everywhere, scattered broadcast in pell-mell confusion, as if the clouds had suddenly burst overhead and rained down the dregs of all the flimsy, rickety, filthy little hovels and rubbish of merchandise that had ever undergone the process of evaporation from the earth since the days of Noah. The intervals of space, which may or may not have been streets, were dotted over with human beings of such sort, variety, and numbers that the famous ant-hills of Africa were as nothing in the comparison. . . . Upon fairly reaching what might be considered the centre of the town, it was interesting to observe the manners and customs of the place. Groups of keen speculators were huddled around the corners, in earnest consultation about the rise and fall of stocks; rough customers, with red and blue flannel shirts, were straggling in from the Flowery Diggings, the Desert, and other rich points, with specimens of croppings in their hands, or offering bargains in the 'Rogers,' the 'Lady Bryant,' the 'Mammoth,' the 'Wooly Horse,' and Heaven knows how many other valuable *leads*, at prices varying from ten to seventy-five dollars a foot. . . . Jew clothing-men were setting out their goods and chattels in front of wretched-looking tenements; monte-dealers, gamblers, thieves, cut-throats, and murderers were mingling miscellaneously in the dense crowds gathered around the bars of the drinking saloons. Now and then a half-starved Pah-Ute or Washoe Indian came tottering along under a heavy press of fagots and whiskey." — J. Ross Browne, *Harper's New Monthly Magazine*, Vol. XXI, No. 181 and Vol. XXII, No. 123.

COLORADO

In June, 1858, the same year which saw the beginning of interest in Nevada, a group of men known as the Russell Company busied themselves with picks and shovels in the region about the present Denver. Part of them were Georgians and part were Kansans and Missourians. A majority were Cherokee Indians. Days of anxious search and arduous labor yielded only a few particles of gold. In July the disillusioned party began breaking up as many of its members turned their faces to the east. Thirteen only were left, the persistence of whom was rewarded by the discovery of the precious yellow metal in paying quantities in Cherry Creek. Another party prospected in the Pike's Peak region during July and August.

492 Colorado Miners, from the mural painting *Miners* by Allen True in the Dickinson Library, Denver, Col.

493 Denver about 1863, from a lithograph by J. Bien, after a painting by A. E. Matthews, in the possession of the publishers

THE FIFTY-NINERS

NEWS of gold in the Colorado country sped through the Mississippi Valley with incredible swiftness considering the undeveloped methods of communication. All sorts of persons turned eager ears to the reports and wild rumors which issued from the mountain country. The Panic of 1857 had been a sad blow to the folk of the frontier. Hard times continued in 1858 and 1859. Suffering from financial loss and facing gloomy prospects in the immediate future, men turned with more than their wonted eagerness toward the golden sands of the mountains. Eighteen hundred and fifty-nine saw a rush of gold seekers across the plains like that ten years before. But Colorado gold was for the most part locked up in a matrix of quartz. Prospectors' cradles quickly washed from the mountain gravels such free particles as were to be had. Before the end of the year the gold rush was over and thousands of disappointed men were returning to the homes they had so hastily left. Gold mining in Colorado was destined to be the work of companies which controlled sufficient capital to acquire the machinery necessary to excavate the metal from its native rock. The rush, however, had brought about the founding of the principal cities of Colorado and had started the region on its way to statehood. Though thousands left the country, other thousands remained to exploit not only gold but the other natural wealth of the state. The sudden advent of the whites disturbed the Indians and led to serious difficulties between the two races.

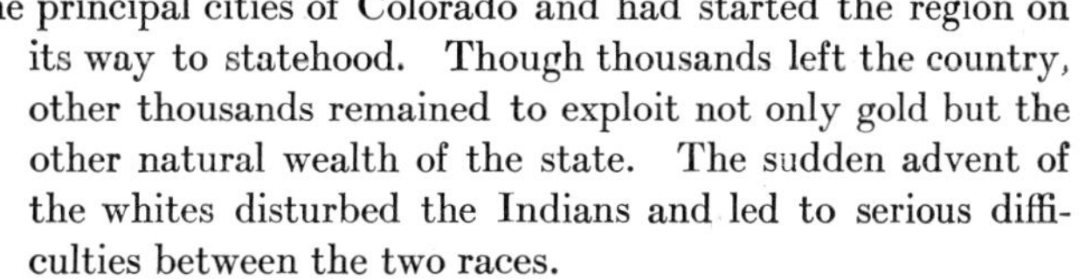

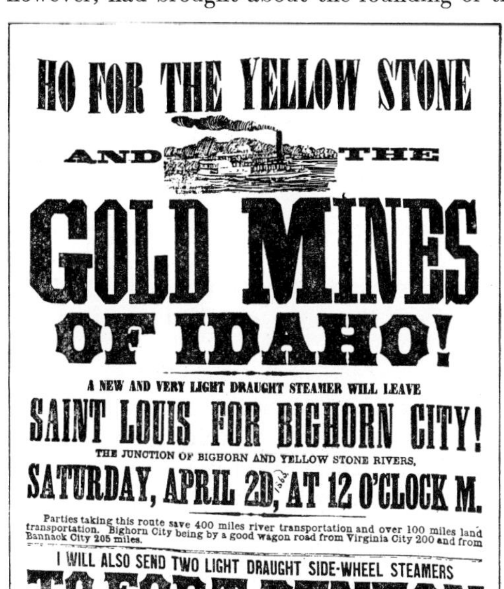

494 Advertisement of Steamboat Transportation to the Gold Mines of Idaho, St. Louis, 1863, from the original in the State Historical and Miscellaneous Library, Helena, Montana

IDAHO

THE discoveries in Nevada and Colorado sent an army of prospectors into every part of the mountain country. These men followed the trails which had been blazed by their predecessors, the trappers. Like the trappers, they frequently stumbled upon wealth in unexpected and isolated places. In the summer which saw Abraham Lincoln nominated for the presidency, gold was found in the valley of the Clearwater, one of the eastern tributaries of the Snake, in the present state of Idaho. During the months of that fateful spring of 1861, when North and South were arming themselves for fratricidal war, a small rush of men from Oregon and Washington territories entered the region of the Clearwater. Prospectors quickly pushed southward up the Snake, finding here and there the gold they sought. Among other towns Boise started on its road to prominence. In 1862 Congress organized the vast region which now includes Idaho, Wyoming, and Montana as a territory. But the end of the gold "strikes" was not yet.

495 Wagon Trains in Helena, Montana, from a drawing by W. M. Cary in *Harper's Weekly*, February 2, 1878

MONTANA

The Bitter Root Mountains separated the diggings in the valley of the Snake from those opened a few months later, which led to the founding of Bannack and Virginia City. In 1864 occurred one of the most headlong of the gold rushes, as men poured into Last Chance Gulch and founded the present city of Helena.

THE PROSPECTOR TYPE

For many years before the discovery of gold that part of the cordilleras which lies within the United States had been the abode of men accustomed to a life of wild freedom. The necessities of the fur trade and dangers from hostile Indians had exercised the chief restraints which had played a part in the creation of the trapper type. The gold rushes which were contemporaneous with the Civil War developed an even wilder and rougher class than the fur trade. In the days of Ashley, Bridger, and Doctor McLaughlin, there had been a distinct code of the mountains. In the early mining days, social conditions were marked by almost complete chaos. Rumors of gold in some distant gulch would speed through the mountain country and almost over night a village of shanties would spring into being. Perhaps, if the rumors chanced to be, as they so often were, grossly exaggerated, the region would quickly return to its former desolation. There was no time in such shifting communities to develop even the most primitive restraints which characterize organized society. The situation was aggravated by the fact that on the streets of such mining towns mingled "tenderfeet" from the East, seasoned mountain men, and desperados. The last class took advantage of the chaos to murder and rob almost at will. They were, in fact, the first to organize themselves. The activities of these wild and depraved men is one of the most revolting parts of the annals of the frontier. The stories of the breaking of the power of the robber bands by vigilante organizations has become the familiar theme of the "wild west" tale.

496 A Prospector Panning for Gold, from a mural painting by Allen True in the Outdoor Theater, Civic Center, Denver, Col.

THE NEW STATE OF NEVADA.

By the President of the United States.

A PROCLAMATION.

Whereas, The Congress of the United States passed an act, which was approved on the 21st day of March last, entitled "An act to enable the peopl of Nevada to form a constitution and State govern ment," and for the admission of such State into the Union on an equal footing with the original States.

Whereas, The said Constitution and State Government have been formed pursuant to the conditions prescribed by the fifth section of the act of Congress aforesaid, and the certificate required by the said act, and also, a copy of the Constitution and ordinances have been submitted to the President of the United States:

Now, therefore, be it known that I, Abraham Lincoln, President of the United States, in accordance

497 Lincoln's Proclamation Admitting Nevada to the Union, from *The New York Times*, October 31, 1864

GOVERNMENT IN THE MOUNTAIN COUNTRY

The deadlock in Congress over the question of slavery, which characterized the decade of the 'fifties, retarded the organization of territorial government in Colorado. The Civil War, absorbing completely the energies of the Federal Government, made it necessary to leave the people of the mountain country almost wholly to their own devices. Yet, during the war, many territories were established. There was strong pressure, moreover, as the civil conflict dragged through weary years, to hasten these mountain territories into statehood before their time. So Nevada became a state in 1864 because the political leaders at Washington feared the potential political power even of a conquered South. Opportunity was also given to Colorado to become a state, but the people of the territory declined to assume the responsibility. In 1868, when the Territory of Wyoming was created, the political map of the mineral empire of the mountains assumed its permanent form.

CHAPTER XI

THE NEW INDIAN POLICY

THE summers of 1849 and 1850 had seen the trails which crossed the plains from the Mississippi River to the mountains crowded with eager parties hurrying toward the California gold fields. The treaty rights of the redskins were little heeded. Vast quantities of game were slaughtered to feed the migrating whites. The Indians became apprehensive, restless. In 1851 the Government of the United States took steps to secure the right of peaceful transit through the Indian country. A council was convened at Fort Laramie in September at which were present Cheyennes, Arapahos, Crows, Assiniboins, Hidatsas, Mandans, and Arikaras. As a result of the deliberations of the assemblage, boundaries were assigned to each of the tribes. Of special significance in the light of later events was the allocation of the Cheyennes and Arapahos to a region which included most of the present Colorado and western Kansas. The Indians retained the "privilege of hunting, fishing, or passing over any of the tracts of country hereinbefore described." They granted to the Government the right to establish roads and military and other posts within their respective territories, in consideration of which the United States agreed to pay the Indians fifty thousand dollars per annum for fifty years, to be distributed among them in proportion to the population of the different tribes. Characteristic of governmental dealings with the Indians was the fate of this treaty when it reached the Senate. Without the knowledge of the Indians the provision "fifty years" was stricken out and "ten years" substituted. The treaty and the annuities which followed its proclamation served to quiet the growing hostility of the Indians. The summer of 1859 saw a new gold rush across the plains and the invasion of the Cheyenne country in Colorado by thousands of fortune seekers. These men, though possessing only the treaty right of transit, took possession of the Indian lands, founded cities, established farms, and opened roads. "Before 1861 the Cheyennes and Arapahos had been driven from the mountain regions down upon the waters of the Arkansas and were becoming sullen and discontented because of this violation of their rights." So wrote, seven years later, an investigating commission sent to examine into the causes of the Indian troubles in Colorado. The Taylor Commission, which included among its members no less a personage than General Sherman, added: "If the lands of the white man are taken, civilization justifies him in resisting the invader. Civilization does more than this: it brands him as a coward and a slave if he submits to the wrong. Here civilization made its contract and guaranteed the rights of the weaker party. It did not stand by the guarantee. The treaty was broken, but not by the savage. If the savage resists, civilization, with the Ten Commandments in one hand and the sword in the other, demands his immediate extermination. . . . These Indians saw their former homes and hunting grounds overrun by a greedy population, thirsting for gold. They saw their game driven east to the plains, and soon found themselves the object of jealousy and hatred. They must go." On February 18, 1861, a new treaty was drawn up at Fort Wise by which the Cheyennes and Arapahos agreed to live in a restricted country lying on both sides of the Arkansas River. The United States agreed to pay each tribe thirty thousand dollars per annum for fifteen years, and further agreed that "houses should be built, lands broken up and fenced and stock animals and agricultural implements furnished."

498 Arapaho Indian, Scabby Bull, from a photograph in the De Lancey Gill Collection, United States National Museum, Washington

THE PLIGHT OF THE ARAPAHOS

IN January 1864, H. B. Bennett, delegate to Congress from Colorado Territory, wrote to the Commission of Indian Affairs — "In 1861 a treaty was made with the Upper Arkansas band of Arapaho Indians by which they relinquished all their right and title to a large tract of valuable land for certain considerations, among which was one that they should be protected in the peaceful possession of their homes — on a reservation upon the Arkansas River. Three years have elapsed and they are still wanderers from their lands; the buffalo on which their forefathers depended for subsistence are passing rapidly away by the encroachment of the whites upon their hunting grounds, and already the Red Man finds hunger and starvation staring him and his in the face; for this and many other reasons this band of Indians are anxious to commence the cultivation of their lands, but this they cannot do, as a military reservation has been made by the War Department within a few months and so located as to deprive them of the very lands they wish to occupy. Therefore, they ask that the troops stationed at Fort Lyon, C. T., may be removed from their reservation to some other point where they will be of more service in preserving the peace and preventing any outbreak between them and the whites." The plight of the Arapahos was the result of the confusion inevitable during the Civil War.

HARRYING THE INDIANS

IN the spring of 1864 trouble broke out. A Colorado ranchman claimed to have had cattle stolen by the Indians. The facts were never proved. Nevertheless a small military expedition penetrated the Indian country on an aggressive mission and brought about a fight. The affair went against the whites. A second punitive expedition, under Major Downing, had better luck. Downing reported: "We started about eleven o'clock in the day, traveled all day and all that night; about daylight I succeeded in surprising the Cheyenne village of Cedar Bluffs, a small cañon about sixty miles north of the South Platte River. We commenced shooting. I ordered the men to commence killing them. They lost, as I am informed, some twenty-six killed and sixty wounded. My own loss was one killed and one wounded. I burnt up their lodges and everything I could get hold of. I took no prisoners. We got out of ammunition and could not pursue them." The affair illustrates the pitiless aggressiveness of the whites.

499 Volunteers and Militia Defeated by Well-Armed Indians, from a sketch in *Frank Leslie's Illustrated Weekly*, September 24, 1864

BLACK KETTLE

500 Members of Black Kettle's Tribe coming into Fort Lyon, from a drawing in Edward S. Ellis, *The Indian Wars of the United States*, Cassell Publishing Company, New York, 1892

THE Indians, already desperate as a result of the inrush of whites into their country, were dazed at the attacks of the spring of 1864. They met hostility with hostility; yet they did not want war. Black Kettle and White Antelope, two of the principal chiefs of the Cheyennes, sought peace. In the autumn Black Kettle sent word to Major Wyncoop, who commanded at Fort Lyon, that war had been forced upon them and that they desired peace. The Major did not feel that he had sufficient authority to make a treaty with the redskins. He was anxious for peace, however, and told Black Kettle to bring his people near to Fort Lyon, where they would be granted military protection. Because of this friendly act Major Wyncoop was relieved of his command, apparently as a result of the influence of his immediate superior, Colonel Chivington, who commanded the military forces in Colorado Territory. Black Kettle did as he was bidden and at Sand Creek, not far from Fort Lyon, established his village, which numbered about five hundred men, women, and children. He felt doubly secure when Major Wyncoop's successor renewed the pledge of protection.

THE SAND CREEK MASSACRE

COLONEL CHIVINGTON did not want to make peace until the Indians had been properly punished. Late in November he marched from Denver to Fort Lyon. About daylight on the morning of the 29th he surrounded Black Kettle's camp and commenced indiscriminate slaughter. George Bent, who was present in Black Kettle's camp on the terrible day of the fight, has left an account of what occurred. "When I looked toward the chief's lodge I saw that Black Kettle had a large American flag up on a long lodgepole as a signal to the troops that the camp was friendly. Part of the warriors were running out toward the pony herds and the rest of the people were rushing about the camp in great fear. All the time Black Kettle kept calling out not to be frightened; that the camp was under protection and there was no danger. Then suddenly the troops opened fire on this mass of men, women and children, and all began to scatter and run. . . . The soldiers concentrated their fire on the people in the pits [dug by the main body of Indians for protection] and we fought back as well as we could with guns and bows, but we had only a few guns. The troops did not rush in and fight hand to hand, but once or twice after they had killed many of the men in a certain pit they rushed in and finished up the work, killing the wounded and the women and children that had not been hurt. The fight here was kept up until nearly sundown, when at last the commanding officer called off his men. . . . As they went back, the soldiers scalped the dead lying in the bed of the stream. . . . At the beginning of the attack Black Kettle, with his wife and White Antelope, took their position before Black Kettle's lodge and remained there after all others had left the camp. At last Black Kettle, seeing that it was useless to stay longer, started to run, calling out to White Antelope to follow him, but White Antelope refused and stood there ready to die, with arms folded, singing his death song:

'Nothing lives long,
Except the earth and the mountains.'

until he was shot down by the soldiers." — GRINNELL, *The Fighting Cheyennes*, 170–71.

501 The Advance Guard, from a painting by Frederic Remington. © Curtis & Cameron, Boston

502 Massacre of United States Troops by the Sioux and Cheyennes near Fort Philip Kearny, December 22, 1866, from a drawing in *Frank Leslie's Illustrated Weekly*, January 19, 1867

THE AFTERMATH OF SAND CREEK

BENT'S account of the fight is confirmed by the report of the Taylor Commission. "The particulars of this massacre are too well known to be repeated here with all its heartrendering scenes. It is enough to say that it scarcely has its parallel in the records of Indian barbarity. Fleeing women, holding up their hands and praying for mercy, were brutally shot down; infants were killed and scalped in derision; men were tortured and mutilated in a manner that would put to shame the savage ingenuity of interior Africa. No one will be astonished that a war ensued which cost the government thirty million dollars, and carried conflagration and death to the border settlements. During the spring and summer of 1865 no less then eight thousand troops were withdrawn from the effective force engaged in suppressing the rebellion to meet this Indian war. The result of the year's campaign satisfied all reasonable men that war with Indians was useless and expensive. Fifteen or twenty Indians had been killed, at an expense of more than a million dollars apiece, while hundreds of our soldiers had lost their lives, many of our border settlers had been butchered, and much property destroyed. To those who reflected on the subject, knowing the facts, the war was something more than useless and expensive; it was dishonorable to the nation, and disgraceful to those who had originated it." — Report of the Secretary of the Interior, 495.

THE HANCOCK EXPEDITION

GRADUALLY, as the months passed, the Cheyenne War waned. Eighteen hundred and sixty-six was a relatively quiet year on the Kansas frontier. During the winter of 1866–67, however, talk of raids in the Kansas country induced Congress to appropriate money for another large military expedition into the Cheyenne country. Meanwhile, Major Wynkoop, who was now agent for the Cheyennes and Arapahos, had been busy with efforts to persuade the Indians to settle down. In the spring of 1867 he reported that they were all off hunting quietly. Wynkoop was naturally very much opposed to the Hancock expedition and his fears were not lessened when he discovered from personal conversation that the efficient and brave general who was Meade's second in command at Gettysburg had no conception of the problems presented by the Indian country. Hancock, at the head of a powerful military force, met the Cheyennes at Fort Zarah. He informed their chiefs that he would continue the negotiations with them in their village, which was situated on Pawnee Fork, about thirty-five miles west of Fort Larned. The Indians, with memories of the Sand Creek massacre fresh in their minds, became frightened as the white chief with his army approached their lodges. They fled, leaving Hancock the empty shell of their camp. He burned the lodges and sent General Custer on a fruitless pursuit. The chief result of the Hancock campaign was to increase the depredations of the Indians, which culminated in the latter part of the summer of 1867 in the wrecking of a train on the Union Pacific.

503 Sioux Indians after capturing a Union Pacific Freight Train, from a drawing in *Frank Leslie's Illustrated Weekly*, September 12, 1868

THE BATTLE OF THE WASHITA

504 Custer Surprising an Indian Camp on the Washita River, from a drawing by J. E. Taylor in Col. Richard I. Dodge, *Our Wild Indians*, 1882

In the autumn of 1867 the Taylor Commission investigated the disorders of the last few years and finally, in October, met the Comanches, the Kiowas, the Arapahos, and the Cheyennes at Medicine Creek Lodge. They entered into a treaty of peace with the tribes and distributed presents. The treaty did not, however, bring the expected peace. The governmental powers of the Indian chiefs were too slight to control the activities of their young men, inflamed by four years of desultory fighting. Eighteen hundred and sixty-eight was a year of Indian raids. General Sheridan, who had replaced General Hancock, determined to punish the hostiles. In the autumn of 1868 a number of peaceful Indians were camped on the Washita River, among them the village of Black Kettle, composed of about seventy-five lodges. Against these redskins who had settled down for the winter Sheridan directed his blow. On the morning of November 23, the commanding general ordered Custer with a force of cavalry to take up the trail which led to the Washita. With admirable stealth the brilliant cavalryman crept up on his unsuspecting prey. As dawn was breaking, his troopers swept down upon the surprised and terrified Indians, shooting as they came. Black Kettle was killed. Many women and children were killed as they sought safety in every possible place of concealment. Swift and terrible as was the blow, the majority of the village escaped. The vicissitudes of life on the plains had trained them to meet such an emergency. They even turned on Custer and annihilated an isolated detachment of his troops. The general destroyed the camp and the food stored up for the winter months, but he wisely made no effort to attack the other villages farther down the Washita. With this episode, which at best was a very doubtful victory for the whites, the Cheyenne War in the south came to an end.

THREE CHEYENNE LEADERS

"In Black Kettle, White Antelope, and Yellow Wolf, all old men, who were killed by the whites, we have three examples of high patriotism. These men were constant workers among the Indians in behalf of peace with the white people. They did this not because they loved the white people, from whom they had received nothing good, but because they loved their own tribe, and wished to guide it in paths that would be for the tribe's greatest advantage. . . . Black Kettle was a frank, good man, who did not hesitate to expose himself to any danger if he thought that his tribe might be benefited thereby. Notwithstanding the attacks made on different parties of Cheyennes by troops in Colorado, Black Kettle was quite willing to visit Governor Evans in Denver. Before and after Sand Creek he consistently talked and acted for peace, and his last words in this behalf were spoken to General Hazen only a few days before he was killed in the village on the Washita. He was the first of the Cheyenne chiefs to dare to attend the meetings of the peace commission at the treaty of Medicine Creek Lodge, in 1867. Taught by past experience — at Sand Creek and on Pawnee Fork — the other Cheyennes feared to present themselves at a place where there was a large number of troops and where they might be attacked without warning. Black Kettle was a striking example of a consistently friendly Indian, who because he was friendly and so because his whereabouts was usually known, was punished for the acts of people whom it was supposed he could control." — Grinnell, *The Fighting Cheyennes*, 298.

505 Council at Medicine Creek Lodge with the Kiowas and Comanches, from a drawing in *Harper's Weekly*, November 16, 1867

506 Red Cloud, from a photograph. © D. F. Barry, Superior, Wis.

RED CLOUD, 1822–1909

The Indian wars in Colorado and Kansas during the 'sixties had a counterpart in the north. The Black Hills country was the hunting ground of the Sioux, the northern Cheyennes, and other tribes. In 1865 the Government planned to build a road across Montana to improve the communications of the Montana gold miners. Opposing the effort was Red Cloud, a principal chief of the Sioux. Red Cloud was the greatest figure that his nation produced and perhaps the greatest of all the Plains Indians. His qualities of mind and heart had brought about his rise to the dominant position among his people. Before his days of fighting were over he had counted eighty coups upon his enemies. In 1865 he captured the small detachment of troops sent into the Sioux country to begin road construction. He held them for some two weeks until he began to fear that his young men would massacre the captives. Then he released them.

RED CLOUD IN 1866

June 30, 1866, saw Red Cloud at Fort Laramie repeating his refusal to permit the whites to build a road across the country of his people. The Indian chieftain realized that such a road would hasten the destruction of the fast dwindling game on which the northwestern Indians depended, and would bring them face to face with starvation. When General Carrington, with a large force, arrived in the midst of the conference and informed the Indians that the road would be built, Red Cloud withdrew. The story goes that, as he left, he placed his hand upon his rifle and declared, "In this and the Great Spirit I trust for the right." The white men made good their threat and began the construction of Fort Phil Kearny and Fort C. F. Smith, the latter being on the Big Horn River in Montana. Red Cloud again protested to Carrington, in vain. Then he surrounded the construction gang at Fort Kearny and brought the work to a halt. In December he cut off a detachment of thirty-one troops from the same fort and killed them all, a terrible disaster known as the Fetterman Massacre. In spite of his efforts, however, the two forts were built. In the autumn of 1867 the Taylor Commission, on its way to the Cheyenne front, made its way into the country of the Sioux and sought to negotiate a treaty. Red Cloud refused to come to the Council, sending in word that he would not appear until the forts had been evacuated. The negotiations broke down. They were continued during the summer of 1868. Finally, on November 6 of that year, Red Cloud came to Fort Laramie and affixed his signature to the treaty which the whites proposed. He came, however, as a man who had won a great victory. His conditions had been completely met. Forts Phil Kearny and C. F. Smith had been abandoned.

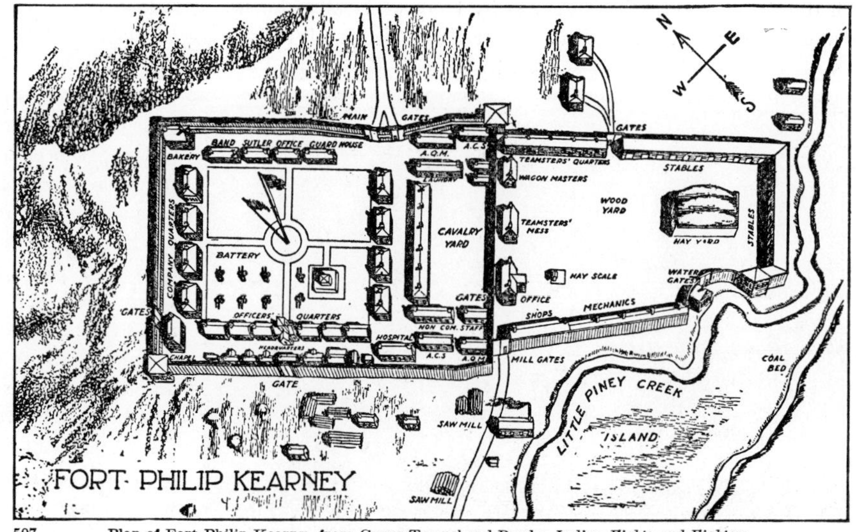

507 Plan of Fort Philip Kearny, from Cyrus Townshend Brady, *Indian Fights and Fighters*, McClure, Phillips & Co., New York, 1904

THE TREATY OF FORT LARAMIE, 1868

By the treaty of Fort Laramie of 1868 the Sioux accepted a reservation in the northwestern country. They reserved, however, the right to hunt in certain areas outside the reservation boundaries, "as long as the buffalo may range thereon in such number as to justify the chase." The Government guaranteed the Indians against white intrusion into their reservation. The signing of the treaty was perhaps the greatest act of Red Cloud's career. He knew that his people must bow to the superior will of the white man. He made the best terms possible, believing that in so doing he served best the interests of the Indians. His decision to make peace with the whites cost him his military leadership, for there were many irreconcilables who would not give up their wild freedom even on the advice of Red Cloud. From that day to the end of his life in 1909 he remained at peace with the white man.

508 United States Commissioners and Indian Chiefs in Council at Fort Laramie, 1868, from a photograph in the United States Signal Corps, War Department, Washington

OUTBREAK OF THE SIOUX WAR OF 1876

One of the most surprising aspects of the history of the exploitation of what Paxson calls the "Mineral Empire" is the lateness of the discovery of gold in the Black Hills region. In spite of the fact that official government reports referred to the possibility of the existence of the precious metal in the Hills, the gold hunters of the late 'sixties and early 'seventies gave virtually no heed to the area. In 1874, the year following a disastrous panic which had prostrated the industrial life of the nation, General Custer, with a small military expedition, made a reconnaissance of the Black Hills and reported definite information of gold. The Indians, suspicious of the intrusion of Custer into their domain, were appalled at what followed his visit. So also were the military authorities responsible for the maintenance of peace on the plains. Eighteen hundred and seventy-five saw a gold rush to the Hills. Men who were clearly trespassers entered the Indian country to dig mines and build towns. The army, though it sought to uphold the rights of the redskins, was utterly incapable of coping with the situation. To certain Indian leaders the advent of the whites meant that the time of the last desperate struggle between the races was at hand. As soon as Red Cloud had signed the treaty between the Sioux and the United States, several bands of his people had refused to recognize the arrangement and had declined to enter the reservation. A medicine man or shaman, Sitting Bull, was the principal leader of this recalcitrant group. He was an Indian who achieved prominence and influence more for his wisdom and organizing abilities than because of prowess in war. As a leader in battle, he was markedly inferior either to Crazy Horse or Gall. The bands led by these irreconcilable chiefs persisted in clinging to the old wild life of the plains. They fought, as in former days, their Indian neighbors like the Mandans or Crows, they stole horses, and they struck at the whites whenever a favorable opportunity offered. The Gold Rush of '75 brought disillusionment to great numbers of the Sioux who had followed the lead of Red Cloud in making peace with the whites. Sitting Bull found that events had made him, for the moment, the most important Sioux chief and the number of his followers was rapidly augmented.

509 Sitting Bull, 1834–90, from a photograph. © D. F. Barry, Superior, Wis.

510 General George Crook, 1828–90, from a photograph in the United States Signal Corps, War Department, Washington

THE ULTIMATUM OF DECEMBER 1875

The Indian Commissioner at Washington watched with growing apprehension the developments of the year 1875. In December he determined on drastic measures. On the sixth of the month he sent word to the different agents to notify all bands of Sioux which, like that of Sitting Bull, were outside the reservation to return by January 31. The order was obviously impossible of fulfillment. At least one messenger from an agent to the outlying tribes did not get back after the delivery of his message until the first week in February. The winter of 1875–76 was severe. Many bands were abroad with permission, seeking game. Yet on January 31 the Commissioner of Indian Affairs turned the solution of the Sioux problem over to the War Department. On March 1 General Crook, one of the most successful and famous Indian fighters of the plains, with a large and well-equipped expedition moved northward from Fort Fetterman in Wyoming to strike the winter villages of the hostiles.

CROOK AND CRAZY HORSE — MARCH 1876

Over the wind-swept plains, through sixteen difficult days, Crook with ten troops of cavalry and two companies of infantry hastened northward. His expedition was one of the most formidable in the plains wars up to that time. On March 16 two Indian hunters were sighted. By a clever ruse Crook misled them as to the destination of the expedition. When they disappeared, the General divided his command, sending Reynolds with six troops of cavalry to follow the trail of the hunters and to attack a village if he found one. Through a bitterly cold night Reynolds' force advanced. Toward morning scouts reported a camp just ahead. As dawn was breaking Reynolds, dividing his troops into three battalions, surprised the village. The redskins, however, had sufficient warning to flee to a nearby stand of timber. The whites seized the camp, which, according to Indian standards, was comfortably supplied with the needs of life. Flames quickly shot up and the redskins saw their tipis, their blankets, and all their other property destroyed. They found themselves homeless, without food and with very little equipment, on the bleak winter plains. Even their ponies had been captured. The blow was crushing. The village was that of Crazy Horse, a chieftain who, in this crisis, rose to great heights. Using fighting methods with which the Sioux were so familiar, inspiring his followers with almost reckless courage by personal example, he fought the victor. Reynolds, whose numbers were slightly greater than those of his adversary, soon found himself involved in a general engagement in which his losses were heavy. He saw, moreover, that he could not defeat his enemy. He began a precipitate retreat. Crazy Horse followed him and recaptured the Indian ponies. Reynolds rejoined Crook. Then the Indian leader, with supreme audacity, cut out and made off with a large drove of cattle upon which the white army depended for its meat. Crook, crippled by his losses, retreated to Fort Fetterman, his campaign a failure. Crazy Horse, though he had received an unexpected and stunning blow, had won a signal victory. By capturing the cattle, moreover, he had saved his people.

511 Crook's Fight with Crazy Horse, from a painting by Frederic Remington in Nelson A. Miles, *Personal Recollections*, The Werner Co., Chicago, 1896

512 Indian Skirmish, from the painting *A Dash for Timber*, by Frederic Remington (1861–1909), in the City Art Museum of St. Louis, Mo.

THE CONVERGING ATTACK ON THE SIOUX

After the repulse of Crook, the military authorities made preparations for a much more formidable advance into the Sioux country, to be carried out in the early summer of 1876. Crook was to move northward to the valley of the Rosebud. Gibbon was to come eastward from the Montana mountains and was to put himself under the command of General Terry, who was to advance westward up the Missouri from his base at Fort Abraham Lincoln in Dakota, near the present Bismarck. Terry started on May 17 and on June 9 his column reached the Yellowstone, at the mouth of Powder River. Crook, meanwhile, had been carrying out his part of the plan. On June 17, near the banks of the Rosebud, he again met the warriors of Crazy Horse. With fifteen troops of cavalry and five companies of infantry he fought a force of Indians equal to his own in number through a long summer day. When night came down the conqueror of the Apaches had been defeated. The following day saw Crook's detachment making its way back to its base for refitting. Crazy Horse had won his second victory.

TERRY'S PLAN OF CAMPAIGN

The defeat of Crook, however, did not mean the inevitable failure of the campaign against the Sioux. Terry had a powerful and well-trained force at his disposal and as second in command he had no other than that redoubtable fighter, General Custer. At the mouth of the Rosebud, on June 22, Terry formulated his plan of attack against the Indian camp, which he believed to be somewhere in the valley of the Little Big Horn. He completed his scheme of maneuver, however, without adequate knowledge either of the strength or the fighting capacity of his adversaries. His principal object seems to have been to catch his enemies before they could run away. With this in mind, he sent Custer with about half the command up the Rosebud, with orders to proceed to the headwaters of the Little Big Horn. Custer was then to sweep down the valley of that stream and meet Terry, who would be advancing up the same river. An Indian village in the valley, therefore, would be caught between the two jaws of a trap. The order which Custer received, however, was discretionary and permitted the general to follow a different course if unforeseen conditions seemed to warrant. On the following day Custer, in high spirits, hurried up the Rosebud.

513 Indian Fighting, from the bronze, *Old Dragoons, 1876*, by Frederic Remington in the Metropolitan Museum of Art, New York

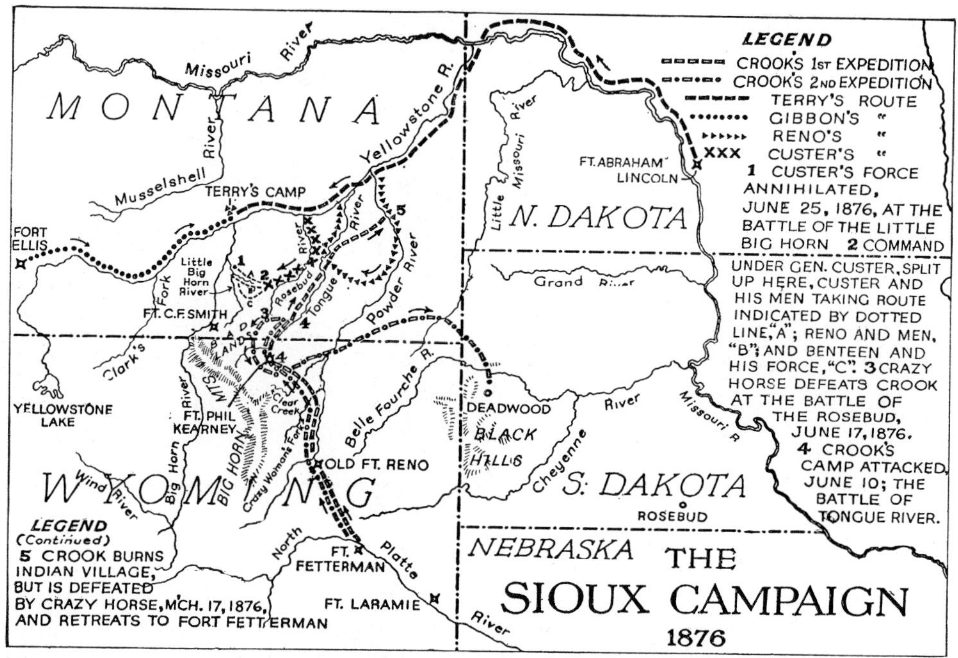

514 Drawn expressly for *The Pageant of America* by Joseph L. Cain

BATTLE OF THE LITTLE BIG HORN
JUNE 25, 1876.

515 Drawn expressly for *The Pageant of America* by Joseph L. Cain

A FATAL DECISION

CUSTER, hoping to achieve a spectacular victory, swiftly followed an Indian trail which had been reported to Terry by scouts some days before. Roughly, half way up the valley the trail turned off toward the Little Big Horn. This, too, had been known to Terry. In the evening of June 24, when the impetuous Custer reached the bend, he decided to disregard his instructions to proceed to the headwaters of the Little Big Horn and, following the trail, to strike overland. Such a move would inevitably bring him to the Indian camp before Terry's coöperating column could reach the place. Custer, smarting at the time under a punishment awarded by a court-martial, has been charged with a desire to retrieve his fortunes by a spectacular individual victory. He was at fault in failing to inform his commanding officer that he was taking the shorter rather than the designated longer route toward the supposed location of the Indian camp.

516 Custer, his officers, and their families, in camp, from a photograph in the United States Signal Corps, War Department, Washington

THE BATTLE OF THE LITTLE BIG HORN

517 Custer's Last Charge, from the painting by Frederic Remington in A. R. Spofford, *A Library of Historic Characters*, W. Finley & Co., Philadelphia, 1894–95

THE morning of June 25 found Custer on the divide between the valleys of the Little Big Horn and the Rosebud. His movements had been observed by the Indians. Even yet, however, he did not know the exact location of the hostile camp. During the forenoon he pushed ahead. He divided his command into three battalions, Major Reno commanding one and Captain Benteen another. In the afternoon, as Custer and Reno, operating close together, approached the Little Big Horn, the camp was discovered on the banks of the river. Custer sent Reno into the valley, with orders to attack the camp and with the understanding that Custer's battalion would support him. Soon after Reno was on his way Custer changed his plan and, avoiding the valley, seems to have started on a circuitous route to put his battalion in the rear of the camp. Meanwhile, Benteen, who had been searching through the Bad Lands to the south of the other two units, had reached the conclusion that the Indians were not there, and of his own volition turned to rejoin the other commanders. He arrived at the valley of Little Big Horn in time to save Reno's battalion from annihilation. That officer, in approaching the hostiles, had found himself confronting overwhelming numbers of armed braves. His battalion was defeated with heavy lossess, and driven across the river to the high banks on the eastern side. Here Benteen came to their rescue and here the combined commands were beseiged throughout the night and for a part of the following day. On the afternoon of the 26th the Indians suddenly abandoned the fight and, breaking camp, moved westward into the unknown. The reason for their change of plan was the approach of Terry up the Little Big Horn. Meanwhile Reno and Benteen were amazed at the failure of Custer to do anything effective or to send word to his subordinates of the progress of his operations. The mystery was explained when, on the 27th, the bodies of Custer and more than two hundred of his battalion were found where they had fallen, on the field of battle. What is known of the fight has come from the Indians. Gall, aided by Crazy Horse, led the attack and won the greatest victory in the annals of the Indian wars. The revenge of the redskins was complete. The annihilation of Custer's battalion meant the failure of the campaign of 1876. The Indian chieftains had out-maneuvered and out-generaled all their opponents.

CUSTER KILLED.

DISASTROUS DEFEAT OF THE AMERICAN TROOPS BY THE INDIANS.

SLAUGHTER OF OUR BEST AND BRAVEST.

GRANT'S INDIAN POLICY COME TO FRUIT.

A WHOLE FAMILY OF HEROES SWEPT AWAY.

THREE HUNDRED AND FIFTEEN AMERICAN SOLDIERS KILLED AND THIRTY-ONE WOUNDED.

SALT LAKE, U. T., July 5.—The correspondent of the Helena (Mon.) *Herald* writes from Still water, Mon., under date of July 2, as follows:

Muggins Taylor, a scout for General Gibbon, arrived here last night direct from Little Horn River and reports that General Custer found the Indian camp of 2,000 lodges on the Little Horn and immediately attacked it.

He charged the thickest portion of the camp with five companies. Nothing is k[illegible]n of the operations of this detachment, except their course as traced by the dead. Major Reno commanded the other seven companies and attacked the lower portion of the camp.

518 Account of Custer's Defeat, from the *New York World*, July 6, 1876

THE AFTERMATH OF THE LITTLE BIG HORN

"THE rejoicing of the centennial celebration was followed by a period of national gloom. The news of this massacre, as it was called, created intense excitement and sympathy. In fact, there had been no such demonstration of sorrow since the appalling tragedy of April 12, 1865. Buildings were draped in mourning. Telegrams were flying between military authorities, and a command was ordered from Fort Leavenworth to move to Montana and take part in the campaign. A part of my regiment, the Fifth United States Infantry, was ordered for this service, and I requested permission to go in command; the request was approved, and within a few days the command was equipped for war and marched away as light-hearted as ever troops proceeded to the field of arduous and hazardous service. We carried with us the confidence and sympathy of those left behind; they bade us adieu with tears and many misgivings for our future. Taking the train at Leavenworth, we moved to Yankton, South Dakota, thence by steamer up the Missouri River. As we passed the military stations along the upper Missouri the small garrisons frequently gathered on the banks, waving their salutations, and signaling 'success' to those who were going to take the places of the ones who had fallen." — MILES, *Serving the Republic*, 137–38.

519 General Nelson A. Miles, from an engraving after a photograph, in the Fridenberg Collection, New York

THE END OF THE SIOUX WAR

GENERAL MILES' commanding officer, Lieutenant-General P. H. Sheridan, submitted the following report to Washington on October 25, 1877, ". . . During the months of December and January the hostile Indians were constantly harassed by the troops under Colonel Nelson A. Miles, Fifth Infantry, whose headquarters were at the mouth of the Tongue River, and who had two sharp engagements with them, one at Red Water and the other near Hanging Woman's Fort, inflicting heavy losses in men, supplies, and animals. . . . This constant pounding and ceaseless activity upon the part of our troops (Colonel Miles in particular) in midwinter began to tell, and early in February 1877, information was communicated which led me to believe that the Indians in general were tired of the war, and that the large bodies heretofore in the field were beginning to break up. On the 25th of that month 229 lodges of Minneconjoux and San Arcs came and surrendered to the troops at Cheyenne Agency, Dakota. They were completely disarmed, their horses taken from them and they were put under guard. This system was also carried out with all who came in afterward to surrender within the departments of Dakota and the Platte. From the 1st of March to the 21st of the same month over 2,200 Indians, in detachments of from 30 to 900, came in and surrendered at camps Sheridan and Robinson, in the department of the Platte, and on the 22d of April 303 Cheyennes came in and surrendered to Colonel Miles at the cantonment on Tongue River, in the department of the Dakota, and more were reported on the way to give themselves up. Finally, on the 6th of May, Crazy Horse, with 889 of his people and 2,000 ponies, came into Camp Robinson and surrendered to General Crook in person. In the meantime Colonel Miles, having had information of the whereabouts of Lame Deer's band of hostile Sioux, surprised his camp, killing 14 warriors, including Lame Deer and Iron Star, the two principal chiefs, capturing 450 ponies, and destroying 51 lodges and their contents. I may mention here that this band commenced to surrender, in small squads of from two to twenty, immediately thereafter, until at length, on the 10th of September, the last of the band, numbering 224, constantly followed and pressed by troops from the command of Colonel Miles, surrendered at Camp Sheridan." — Quoted in MILES, *Serving the Republic*, 164–65. The Sioux war was now over.

CHIEF JOSEPH, 1832–1904

THE year which followed Custer's death witnessed another brilliant Indian military exploit. In 1863 the Nez-Percés had been called upon by the United States to give up their homes in the Wallowa Valley in eastern Oregon. The relations between the Nez-Percés and the whites had been happy and a proud boast of these red mountaineers was that they had never killed a white man. A part of the tribe covenanted to remove to a reservation in Idaho. The band of which Chief Joseph was the principal figure refused, however, to recognize the treaty of 1863 or to leave the valley where lay the ashes of Joseph's father. In 1877 before the difficulty was settled, whites ruthlessly crowded into the disputed country. Sharp fighting developed. Between June 17 and July 12 Chief Joseph with a force which did not exceed four hundred warriors fought three pitched battles with American regular troops. Both sides suffered heavy losses. Joseph, finding that he could not hold off the whites much longer, decided that his wisest course was to flee to Canada. When on July 17 the women struck their tipis, Chief Joseph initiated one of the most extraordinary retreats in American military annals.

520 Chief Joseph, from a photograph in the Historical Section, Army War College, Washington

THE RETREAT OF CHIEF JOSEPH

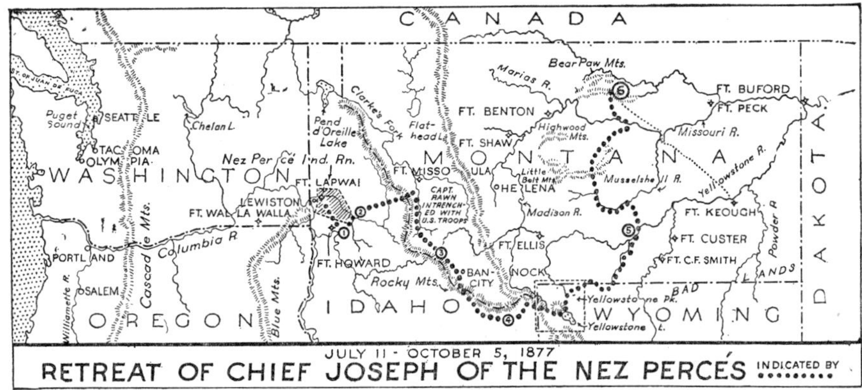

521 Drawn expressly for *The Pageant of America* by Joseph L. Cain

LEGEND: 1. Battle at White Bird Canyon, June 15, 1877. 2. Battle of Clearwater River, July 11. 3. Battle with troops under General Gibbon, Aug. 9. 4. Chief Joseph drives off General Howard's horses in night, Aug. 19–20. 5. Chief Joseph eludes Colonel Sturgis, Sept. 13. 6. General Miles attacks Indians under Chief Joseph Sept. 30 and is repulsed. Chief Joseph surrenders to General O. O. Howard, Oct. 5

CHIEF JOSEPH, taking the Lolo trail in Northwestern Idaho, turned the noses of his ponies toward the east. General Howard was some distance behind in hot pursuit. The Indians, crossing a difficult mountain range, came out in the Bitter Root Valley to find a force of United States troops under Captain Rawn intrenched and ready to check their further progress. Joseph parleyed with Rawn, who told the Indian that he would be permitted to proceed only if he surrendered his arms, ammunition, and horses. During the conference Joseph noted the weakness of Rawn's force. The following day the redskin leader marched down the valley in plain view of the American trenches, completely ignoring Rawn's force. Howard was several days behind. Ten days after Joseph crossed the valley of the Bitter Root he stopped to rest his band at Big Hole near the Idaho-Montana line. His thoughts were only upon the pursuing Howard. He was, therefore, taken completely by surprise when a heavy rifle fire opened one morning upon his camp. General Gibbon, sent from Montana to intercept the fleeing Indians, broke cover and rushed the village. The hostiles scattered and Gibbon captured the tipis. He was preparing to destroy them when Chief Joseph delivered a murderous counter attack. Gibbon fell back to a defensive position and fought off the Indians far into the night. Then Chief Joseph abandoned the fight and hastened to rejoin the women and children who were already far on the trail. Gibbon himself was so severely wounded that he had to be relieved. His troops had suffered too heavily to pursue. Howard, meanwhile, kept doggedly on, adding Gibbon's force to his own. On the night of August 20 his camp was thrown into confusion. Shadowy mounted figures darted here and there. Rifles cracked. Then Howard's herd of horses, urged on by yelling Indians, were swallowed up by the darkness. Chief Joseph with supreme audacity had immobilized his enemy.

THE END OF THE TRAIL

WHILE Howard was waiting for new horses, Joseph hastened northeastward across the mountain country of Montana toward the plains and Canada. The wary chieftain estimated correctly that the few passes which led out of the eastern side of the uplands would be closely guarded. By a brilliant feint Joseph eluded Colonel Sturgis who was posted at the outlet of Clark's Fork. Toward the end of September the band came to rest in the Bear Paw Mountains of northern Montana thinking, according to some reports, that they were safe on Canadian soil. Here General Miles surprised them and fought a bloody battle in which he was repulsed with heavy losses. He then entered upon siege operations. Five days later Chief Joseph surrendered. "Chief Joseph," remarked Miles, "was the highest type of the Indian I have ever known, very handsome, kind, and brave."

522 The Surrender of Chief Joseph, from a painting by Frederic Remington, in Nelson A. Miles, *Personal Recollections*, The Werner Company, Chicago, 1897

523 General Oliver Otis Howard, 1830–1909, from an engraving after a photograph by Brady, in *The Century Magazine*, September 1886. © The Century Co., used by permission

GENERAL HOWARD'S REPORT

General Howard reported that from "the beginning of the Indian pursuit across the Lolo trail, until the embarkation on the Missouri River for the homeward journey, including all halts and stoppages, from July 27th to October 10th, my command marched one thousand three hundred and twenty-one miles in seventy-five days. Joseph, the Indian, taking with him his men, women, and children, traversed even greater distances, for he had to make many a loop in his skein, many a deviation into a tangled thicket, to avoid or deceive his enemy." Joseph's message of surrender was in keeping with his character. ". . . Our chiefs are all killed . . . the old men are all dead. . . . It is cold and we have no blankets. The little children are freezing to death. My people . . . have no blankets, no food. . . . I want to have time to look for my children and see how many of them I can find. Maybe I shall find them among the dead. Hear me, my chiefs: I am tired; my heart is sick and sad. From where the sun now stands, I will fight no more forever." The Indians were removed, first to Fort Leavenworth and then to Indian Territory. Ultimately some, though not Chief Joseph, were permitted to return to their beloved mountains.

RECOMMENDATIONS OF THE TAYLOR COMMISSION

"In making treaties it was enjoined on us to remove, if possible, the causes of complaint on the part of the Indians. This would be no easy task. We have done the best we could under the circumstances. . . . We are aware that the masses of our people have felt kindly toward them, and the legislation of Congress has always been conceived in the best intentions, but it has been erroneous in fact or perverted in execution. Nobody pays any attention to Indian matters. This is a deplorable fact. . . . Naturally the Indian has many noble qualities. He is the very embodiment of courage. Indeed, at times he seems insensible of fear. If he is cruel and revengeful, it is because he is outlawed and his companion is the wild beast. Let civilized man be his companion, and the association warms into life virtues of the rarest worth. Civilization has driven him back from the home he loved; it has often tortured and killed him, but it never could make him a slave. As we have had so little respect for those we did enslave, to be consistent, this element of Indian character should challenge some admiration. . . . It is useless to go over the history of Indian removals. If it had been done but once, the record would be less revolting: from the eastern to the middle states, from there to Illinois and Wisconsin, thence to Missouri and Iowa, thence to Kansas, Dakota, and the plains; whither now we cannot tell. Surely the policy was not designed to perpetuate barbarism, but such has been its effect. . . . But one thing then remains to be done with honor to the nation, and that is to select a district or districts of country, as indicated by Congress, on which all the tribes east of the Rocky mountains may be gathered. For each district let a territorial government be established, with powers adapted to the ends designed. The governor should be a man of unquestioned integrity and purity of character; he should be paid such salary as to place him above temptation; such police or military force should be authorized as would enable him to command respect and keep the peace; agriculture and manufactures should be introduced among them as rapidly as possible; schools should be established which children should be required to attend; their barbarous dialects should be blotted out and the English language substituted. . . . Aside from extermination, this is the only alternative now left us." — Report of the Secretary of the Interior, 1868, 40th Congress, 3d Session, Executive Documents No. 1, 502–05.

524 A Reservation Indian, from a painting by Frederic Remington, in *Drawings by Frederic Remington*. © R. H. Russell, New York, 1897

THE PEACE POLICY

525 Sioux Indians Receiving Provisions from United States Agents near Fort Randall, from an engraving after a photograph, in *Frank Leslie's Illustrated Weekly*, November 9, 1867

SOME years before Custer's defeat the United States had begun developing a new policy with respect to the Indians of the plains. To attempt to defeat these hardy and skillful warriors was both vastly expensive and futile. The area over which the tribes ranged was very great. Their method of fighting was to pounce upon and destroy isolated detachments of soldiers and settlements. Chief Joseph had demonstrated that an Indian village might be as mobile as a military force. When the problem of dealing with the Indian was fully comprehended at Washington, the policy of war was abandoned. Peace at almost any price was preferable. By his fighting the red man had saved himself from annihilation. The Government decided to purchase peace by feeding him. Pushed by the westward advance of the frontier into a subarid country where agriculture was scarcely possible and where the whites had destroyed the bison, starvation awaited the redskin until the Government consented to provide subsistence. The end of the Indian wars did not mean that the white man of the frontier developed any more kindly feeling toward his red neighbor. The traditional attitude of the border that the only good Indian was a dead Indian was unchanged. Though in the East and at the National Capital some viewed the peace policy from a humanitarian point of view, the average westerner saw it in no such light, and the average American citizen paid no attention to what was going on. The new policy of the Government was to confine the nomadic Indians of the plains on reservations and to supply them with rations as long as might be necessary. For the Indian this meant that their old freedom was gone. Their villages could no longer be moved from place to place. Crude shacks, in which frequently many families were crowded, began to take the place of the old tipis. The Indian, like most undeveloped peoples, had no idea of sanitation. This had made little difference when their camps were frequently moved. When the habitations were fixed, however, disease appeared. Tuberculosis began to ravage; pneumonia took a heavy toll. Wild children of the plains suffered the mental anguish which resulted from their loss of liberty. They were like caged animals who sickened and died. Where once they had hunted the bison, they now went to the agent's office to draw their rations. Frequently the flour and bacon were unfit for use. Frequently also the agents were ignorant and corrupt men. The decade of the 'seventies was notorious for the low moral tone of its public life. Few white men cared if the Indian did die. After all, was not the redskin an obstacle in the way of the advance of civilization?

TREATIES

IN 1871 Congress passed a measure which marked a turning point in the long history of the relations of the National Government with the Indian. The tribes should no longer be recognized as nations with whom treaties could be made. The act struck a blow at the hereditary authority of the chiefs, and it did not give the Indian agents magisterial powers. Before 1871 the attitude of the Government had been that the Indian tribe, however loose its organization, was competent to punish its own members who committed offences against other Indians. After 1871 there was no semblance of authority for the punishment of any crime which one Indian might commit against another. No mode of procedure was recognized by statute or treaty for the regulation of matters between the Government and the several tribes. The Indians were not made citizens. Complete anarchy was only prevented by the powerful influence of custom and public sentiment in the remarkably homogeneous Indian communities. Slowly and painfully out of the legal chaos emerged the concept that uncivilized redskins are wards of the nation.

526 Satisfying the Demands of Justice, from a drawing by Frederic Remington, in *Drawings by Frederic Remington*, R. H. Russell, New York, 1897

527 From a painting *The Twilight of the Indian*, by Frederic Remington, in *Drawings by Frederic Remington*. © R. H. Russell, New York, 1897

INSECURITY

The problem which confronted the defeated Indian was to acquire the white man's way of getting a living; to assimilate if possible within a generation the culture and way of life which the white man had been a thousand years and more in developing. The white man emphasized individualism; the Indian had for countless generations followed a communal way of life. Only under the most favorable circumstances could the redskin be expected to make this abrupt transition. Actually the Indian was pauperized. He tended to lose his pride of race as his old freedom was taken from him. The status of tribes had changed from that of dependent nations exercising control over their own soil to that of individual subjects holding their lands by sufferance. The redskin, according to the ruling of the Supreme Court, had only the right to occupancy on his reservation, and the powers of Congress were only limited by their sense of justice in dealing with a weaker and helpless people. The Indian might be moved from place to place at the will of the Government. In the 'seventies fear of removal was one of the most potent influences tending to prevent the red man from adopting the white man's ways and improving the soil which he was expected to cultivate. Many times the Indian found himself dispossessed merely because white people had found that his lands were unexpectedly fertile and coveted them. So were driven "back into sullen apathy spirits in which the Promethean spark of enterprise had been for a moment elicited."

A CENTURY OF DISHONOR

In 1881 the attention of the people of the nation was focused on the long history of wrongs which the Indian had suffered at the hands of the white man. *A Century of Dishonor* by "H. H." was widely read and made a powerful impression. President Cleveland in his first administration read Mrs. Helen Hunt Jackson's book and was deeply moved by it. In a sense the book overstated the case for the Indian, a fault almost inevitable in a person who felt deeply the wrongs which the weaker race had suffered. Mrs. Jackson proposed no solution for the problem which she called to the attention of the American people. In her conclusion, however, she noted certain things which must disappear. "Cheating, robbing, breaking promises — these three are clearly things which must cease to be done. One more thing, also, and that is the refusal of the protection of the law to the Indian's rights of property, 'of life, liberty, and the pursuit of happiness.' When these four things have ceased to be done, time, statesmanship, philanthropy, and Christianity can slowly and surely do the rest. Till these four things have ceased to be done, statesmanship and philanthropy alike must work in vain, and even Christianity can reap but small harvest."

A CENTURY OF DISHONOUR

A SKETCH

OF THE UNITED STATES GOVERNMENT'S
DEALINGS WITH SOME OF THE
NORTH AMERICAN TRIBES

By H. H.

AUTHOR OF "VERSES" "BITS OF TRAVEL" ETC.

"Every human being born upon our continent, or who comes here from any quarter of the world, whether savage or civilized, can go to our courts for protection—except those who belong to the tribes who once owned this country. The cannibal from the islands of the Pacific, the worst criminals from Europe, Asia, or Africa, can appeal to the law and courts for their rights of person and property—all, save our native Indians, who, above all, should be protected from wrong"

Gov. Horatio Seymour

LONDON
CHATTO & WINDUS, PICCADILLY
1881

528 From the title-page of the original by Helen Hunt Jackson, in the New York Public Library

INDIAN RIGHTS ASSOCIATION

Mrs. Jackson's book lead directly to the founding, in 1882, of the Indian Rights Association. This organization has interested itself in seeing that justice is done the Indians and in the furthering of their interests. It has been accused of sentimentality and of meddlesomeness. It has, however, served the nation well by assisting materially the unfortunate race, whom the white man had dispossessed, to make progress in the assimilation of the white man's civilization.

THE FIRST ANNUAL REPORT

OF THE

EXECUTIVE COMMITTEE

OF THE

INDIAN RIGHTS ASSOCIATION,

FOR THE YEAR ENDING DECEMBER, 1883.

PRINTED BY ORDER OF THE
EXECUTIVE COMMITTEE,
1884.

PHILADELPHIA:
OFFICE OF THE INDIAN RIGHTS ASSOCIATION,
1316 FILBERT STREET,
1884.

529 From the title-page of the original in the New York Public Library

CAUSES FOR THE SIOUX OUTBREAK OF 1890

"The time seemed now to have come to take a further step and divide the great Sioux reservation up into separate reserves for each important tribe, and to open the surplus land to settlement. The needs of the white population, with their business and railroads, and the welfare of the Indians, seemed alike to demand this. Commissioners were therefore sent out to treat with the people for the accomplishment of this end, and an agreement which, after much debate, had won general approval was committed to them for presentation to the Indians. The objections of the Indians to the bill, however, were many and they were ardently pressed. Some preferred their old life, the more earnestly because schools and churches were sapping and undermining it. Some wished delay. All complained that many of the engagements solemnly made with them in former years when they had surrendered valued rights had been broken, and here they were right. They suspected that present promises of pay for their lands would prove only old ones in a new shape . . . and demanded that no further surrender should be expected until former promises had been fulfilled. They were assured that a new era had dawned, and that all past promises would be kept. So we all thought. . . . But the requisite number, three-fourths of the Indians, signed the bill, and expectation of rich and prompt rewards ran high. The Indians understand little of the complex forms and delays of our government. Six months passed, and nothing came. Three months more, and nothing came. A bill was drawn up in the Senate under General Crook's eye and passed, providing for the fulfillment of the promises of the commission, but it was pigeon-holed in the House. But in the midst of the winter's pinching cold the Indian learned that the transaction had been declared complete and half of their land proclaimed as thrown open to the whites. Surveys were not promptly made; perhaps they could not be, and no one knew what land was theirs and what was not. The very earth seemed sliding from beneath their feet. Other misfortunes seemed to be crowding on them. . . . No doubt the people could have saved themselves from suffering if industry, economy, and thrift had abounded; but these are just the virtues which a people emerging from barbarism lack. The measles prevailed in 1889 and were exceedingly fatal. Next year the grippe swept over the people with appalling results. Whooping cough followed among the children. Sullenness and gloom began to gather, especially among the heathen and wilder Indians. A witness of high character told me that a marked discontent amounting almost to despair prevailed in many quarters. The people said their children were all dying from diseases brought by the whites, their race was perishing from the face of the earth, and they might as well be killed at once. Old chiefs and medicine men were losing their power. The old ways which they loved were passing away. In a word, all things were against them, and to add to the calamity, many Indians, especially the wilder element, had nothing to do but to brood over their misfortunes. While in this unhappy state, the story of a messiah coming, with its ghost dance and strange hallucinations, spread among the heathen part of the people. . . ." — Bishop W. H. Hare, quoted in James Mooney, *The Ghost-Dance Religion and the Sioux Outbreak of 1890*, 840–42.

530 An Indian Chief, from the bronze statue by Alexander Phimister Proctor (1862–), in the Brooklyn Museum

531 The Ghost Dance, from a painting by Mary Irvin Wright, courtesy of the Bureau of American Ethnology, Washington

THE GHOST DANCE RELIGION

IN Nevada about 1888 appeared among the Indians a new religion. A young Piute, Wovoka by name, became a John the Baptist, proclaiming the advent of an Indian Messiah and the ushering in of the millenium. He told his people: "When the sun died I went up to Heaven and saw God and all the people who had died a long time ago. God told me to come back and tell my people they must be good and love one another, and not fight, or steal, or lie. He gave me this dance to give to my people." The dance and the songs which accompanied it were to prepare the Indians for that glorious day soon to dawn when they would be reunited with the loved ones who had gone ahead and when the Indian's paradise would begin. The new religion, like that of Handsome Lake, was a blend of Christian and Indian elements. It did not incite the redskins to war against the whites. It was evidence of the hopelessness of a conquered race. Their power broken, their old mode of life threatened, the Indians turned to religion whence they derived hope that they themselves together with their old ways of life would be saved. They believed that a flood of lava, rushing from a volcanic eruption, would flow eastward and wipe out the whites, leaving the red men in sole possession of their ancient heritage. The new religion spread swiftly among the tribes of the Central Basin, crossed the Rocky Mountains, and made its way among the villages on the plains. Religion had always been of vast importance in the lives of the Indians and this new teaching, with its new dance, led swiftly to fanaticism. In the Ghost Dances of the years 1889 and 1890 were reënacted scenes reminiscent of the great revival on the Kentucky and Tennessee frontier in 1800. Like the whites at the Cane Ridge and other camp meetings, the Indians fell into trances, saw visions, and worked themselves into frenzy.

THE SIOUX AND THE GHOST DANCE

As the Messiah craze swept through the Sioux villages of the northern plains it developed menacing possibilities. The battle of the Little Big Horn had occurred only a decadeand a half before. Bitter memories of that last great war still lingered. The Sioux to a peculiar degree had fallen upon hard times. Disgruntled and discontented persons among them began to seek to turn the new religion to private ends. Particularly the old shaman, Sitting Bull, dreamed of using this wave of excitement as a means to throw off the yoke of the whites and restore the dominion of the Indians. In December 1890, the situation on the Sioux reservations, Pine Ridge and Rosebud, became tense. The great majority of the Indians were peaceful and friendly. The voice of the revered Red Cloud was raised for peace. Bands of hostiles, however, were slipping off the reservations into the Bad Lands to practice the rites of the Ghost Dance. Sitting Bull, with his village, had determined to follow them. On December 15 he was arrested by a force of Indians who were members of the agency police. As the old leader was about to be led away to agency headquarters he called upon his excited followers to resist. Immediately began a bloody fight, and when the village had fled, the body of Sitting Bull was found among the slain. So passed the most tenacious of the Irreconcilables.

532 A Sioux participating in the Ghost Dance, from a photograph in James A. Mooney, *The Ghost Dance and the Sioux Outbreak of 1890*, Bureau of Ethnology, *Fourteenth Annual Report*, Washington, 1896

THE BATTLE OF WOUNDED KNEE

533 Sioux Camp at the Battle of Wounded Knee, from a photograph in the United States Army Signal Corps, War Department, Washington

The death of Sitting Bull brought panic to the Sioux, large numbers of whom fled from their villages. Through the efforts of friendly Indians and of white troops the bands were gradually brought back to the reservation. Thirteen days after the death of Sitting Bull, Major Whitside, in charge of the Seventh Cavalry, came upon a band led by Big Foot that was making its way toward the Pine Ridge Agency. Whitside demanded successfully the unconditional surrender of the Indians. The united force proceeded toward the Agency and camped on the evening of December 28 on the banks of the Wounded Knee. Whitside, having warned his superiors, was promptly reinforced and the command of the troops was taken over by Colonel Forsythe. On the morning of December 29, the colonel, having carefully placed his troops in an arc about the camp and having located a battery of Hotchkiss guns in such a position as to be able to command the tipis, demanded that Big Foot's warriors give up their arms. The braves, concealing their weapons under their blankets, assembled outside the camp and showed unwillingness to disarm themselves. The soldiers then searched the tipis, finding few weapons of value. A tense situation developed. Colonel Forsythe did not desire a battle but was prepared for such an emergency. Not understanding the Sioux language he did not realize the purport of the excited exhortations of a shaman, Yellow Bird, who was telling the braves that when they were disarmed they would be killed. Suddenly Yellow Bird threw a handful of dust in the air. The Indian rifles flashed forth and the battle was on. One of the fiercest fights in border history ensued, with a heavy loss of life on both sides. Hardly had the rifles begun to crack when the Hotchkiss guns laid down a heavy fire on the tipis where the women and children were concealed. Mooney, who investigated the episode, has left an account of what followed. "The terrible effect may be judged from the fact that one woman survivor, Blue Whirlwind, with whom the author conversed, received fourteen wounds, while each of her two little boys were also wounded by her side. In a few minutes two hundred Indian men, women and children, with sixty soldiers, were lying dead and wounded on the ground, the tipis had been torn down by the shells and some of them were burning above the helpless wounded, and the surviving handful of Indians were flying in wild panic to the shelter of the ravine, pursued by hundreds of maddened soldiers and followed up by a raking fire from the Hotchkiss guns, which had been moved into position to sweep the ravine. There can be no question that the pursuit was simply a massacre, where fleeing women, with infants in their arms, were shot down after resistance had ceased and when almost every warrior was stretched dead or dying on the ground." — Quoted in W. K. Moorehead, *The American Indian*, 127–28.

THE SIGNIFICANCE OF WOUNDED KNEE

Wounded Knee was the last pitched battle between the Indians and the whites within the limits of the United States. It marks the end of an epoch. The conquest of the redskin had been completed and his resistance crushed. Not without significance is the fact that this concluding fight displayed in its worst phases the enmity which had existed for so long between the races. The Indians were suspicious of the white man. They feared and hated him. The white soldier on his part, borrowing his savageness from the untamed son of the wilderness, treated his Indian enemy as though the adversary were a beast. Wounded Knee was the terrible revenge of the Seventh Cavalry for Custer's defeat.

534 From a painting *Pursuing the Indians*, by Frederic Remington, in Nelson A. Miles, *Personal Recollections*, The Werner Co., Chicago, 1897

CHAPTER XII

THE FRONTIER ON THE PLAINS

IN the 'twenties Calhoun and Monroe had planned for a permanent Indian frontier on the grasslands east of the Rockies. They believed that the snowy peaks which marked the western edge of the Sioux and the Pawnee hunting grounds would also become the permanent boundary of the United States. In days before men grasped the capacities of the railroad to bind remote regions together the incorporation of the Pacific Coast country into the American Union seemed altogether beyond the realm of possibility. Yet the 'forties saw the banner of the Republic flying over both Oregon and California and also a flood of immigrants crossing the grasslands and the mountains to the fertile valleys and the shining gold fields of the Far West. In 1850 California, foreign soil scarcely three years before, took a place at the council table of the nation on a footing of equality with Massachusetts and Virginia whose history and traditions ran back into the seventeenth century. In the 'sixties the calamity of the Civil War checked, although it did not stop, the taming of the American wilderness. During the war men, dominated by the lust for gold, rushed headlong from "strike" to "strike" in the mountain country and squalid shanties and unsightly diggings marred the majestic uplands. When North and South put away the sword and musket and turned to the tasks of peace, American hearth-fires burned in the larger part of that vast extent of territory, across which the map makers wrote the name, "United States."

The white frontier, however, in its westward advance had leaped the grasslands west of the Father of Waters. Insufficient rainfall played a determining part in the adjustments of the American people to the western half of the Great Plains, where precipitation was not sufficient to support agriculture, particularly of the unscientific type practiced in the middle of the nineteenth century. Major Long's exaggerations concerning the "Great American Desert" east of the Rockies contained an element of truth. While rich soil in sheltered and well-watered valleys was to be had on the Pacific Coast, few Americans were willing to risk experimentation on the grasslands in the rain shadow of the mountains. For men who adventured into the country west of Iowa or the eastern towns of Kansas in the middle of the century the societal environment was even more forbidding than the natural. In this region the desperate redskin was consciously making his last stand against civilization. Not until the fear of major wars between the races had been allayed would men bring their families to the wind-swept western plains. When, however, conditions became favorable, population quickly flowed into empty spaces capable of supporting human life. Many of the pioneers were part of that immigrant tide from Europe which characterized the second half of the nineteenth century. Americans came also to the grasslands — men trained on older frontiers or tenderfeet from the distant East. Close to the foothills of the Rockies the "Cow Country" appeared where the nomadic cowboy "punched" cattle that grazed at will over the national domain. Great herds were driven northward from the feeding grounds in Texas to Wyoming and Montana. From the direction of the Mississippi farmers worked their way westward, taking up homesteads and replacing the buffalo grass with crops of corn and wheat. The redskin was compelled to give up his wandering. His day of freedom had passed forever.

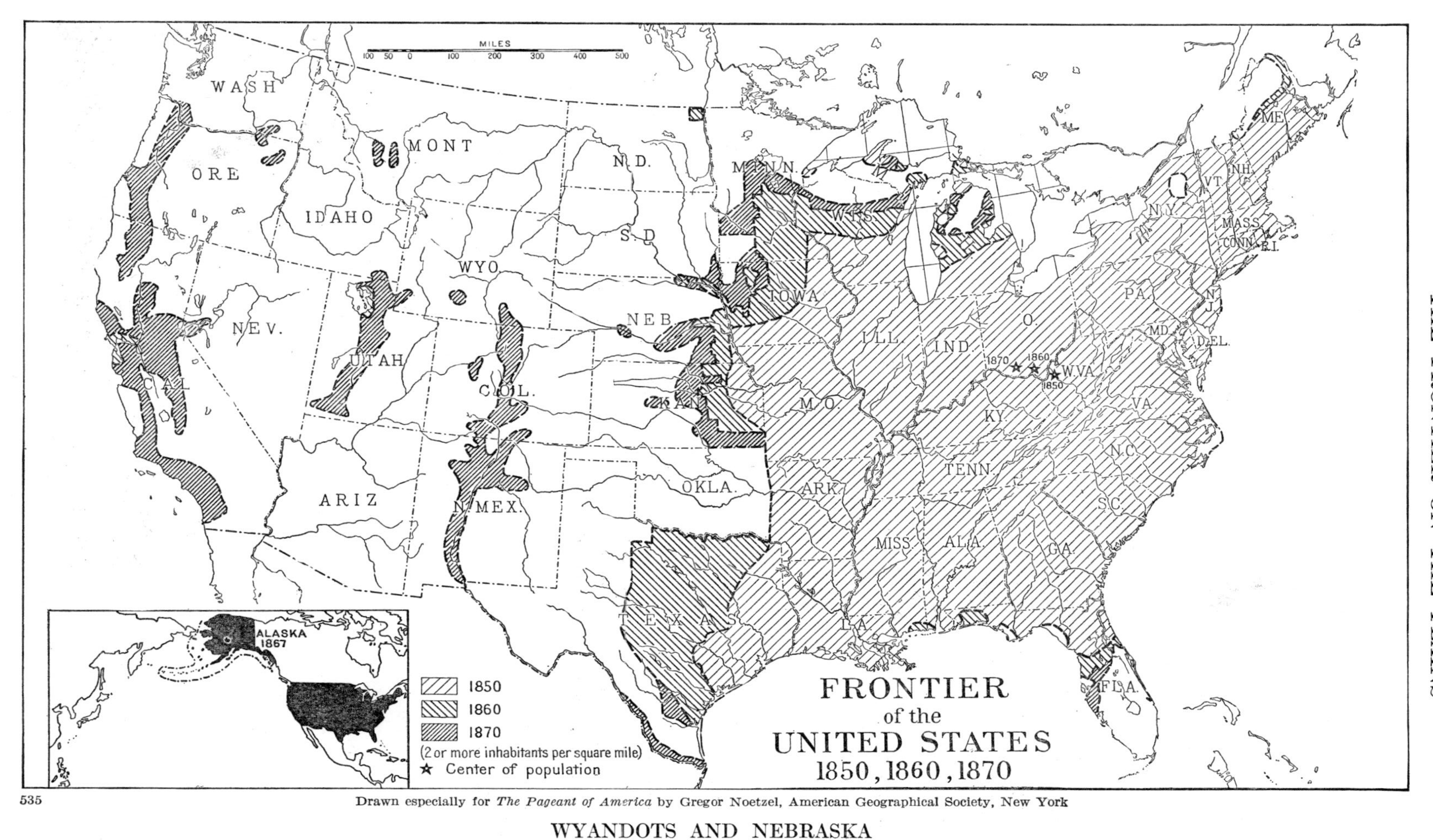

535 Drawn especially for *The Pageant of America* by Gregor Noetzel, American Geographical Society, New York

WYANDOTS AND NEBRASKA

A GROUP of emigrant Indians assembled in July, 1853, on the site of the present Kansas City, Kansas. The Wyandots present, together with some Delawares and Shawnees, set up without legal authorization a "provisional government" for the Territory of Nebraska. They elected "provisional governor," William Walker, a white man who had always lived with the Wyandots and who had been a chief. The Wyandot convention was an astute political move to hasten the organization of the Nebraska Territory and to strengthen the hands of those who favored a central route for the proposed railroad across the continent. In the following year the Kansas-Nebraska Act, fathered by Stephen A. Douglas, organized the region as two territories.

536 From the mural painting *Westward the Star of Empire Takes its Way*, by Emanuel Leutze (1816-68), in the Capitol, Washington. Photograph © Underwood & Underwood, New York

KANSAS, AN EXCEPTION

THROUGHOUT the history of the United States men have been attracted to the fringe of settlement for the most part for economic reasons. They have seen in empty or undeveloped regions opportunities to better themselves. The hunter-pioneer made either wages or a profit from the fur trade. The gold seeker dreamed of sudden wealth. The farmer-pioneer sought independence and the benefits which would accrue from rising land values. The speculator as always hoped to reap where he had not sown. In the different stages of its frontier history Kansas saw all these types, although the gold seeker did not linger within its boundaries. Yet Kansas was unique; the motives behind its settlement were often political. Many a Kansas pioneer left his old home and put his fortune to the hazard on the edge of the Indian country for an ideal. Oftentimes, whether from the North or the South, he was first of all a sectional man firmly convinced of the righteousness of the stand of his own section of the country on the vexed problem of negro slavery and bent on winning Kansas for the cause he espoused

PROPAGANDISTS FOR THE NORTH

IN 1854 the Reverend C. B. Boynton and T. B. Mason, "Committee from the 'Kansas League' of Cincinnati" journeyed through Kansas and in the following year published a book. "In considering the magnitude of the interests which are at stake — the extent and value of the region to be lost or won for freedom — by the action of this generation, the question ought to present itself to every mind, What can I do; what ought I to do; how can Kansas, Nebraska and that great adjoining West, be most effectually secured? Especially should every Christian make this a subject of prayerful inquiry. . . . Will the friends of freedom be justified in leaving the settlement of Kansas to the operation of the common causes which have governed emigration elsewhere, or are they called upon, in the emergency which has suddenly arisen, to improve, by unusual measures, the opportunity which has been presented in the providence of God." — *A Journey through Kansas*, 209. "The Indian lands now form but an inconsiderable portion of the Territory in quantity, but they embrace some of the most desirable parts of the country, and in particular, a large proportion of the timber of the Kansas river, and on the mouth of its tributaries. . . . So far as the great ends of civilization and Christianity are concerned, the most of these Indian lands are so occupied by the tribes as to be useless to the world, or rather they are obstacles in the progress of the country. . . . Among the Delawares, Shawnees, and Pottawatomies are some whom civilization and Christianity have reached, but this is not true of the mass, and we fear will never be. How their Territory is, without injustice to them, to pass into the possession of the whites, is a question we cannot answer, and yet we cannot doubt that the transfer will ere long be made." — *Ibid.*, 151, 154-55. The authors quite evidently did not extend to the red man that solicitude which they professed for the black.

537 River steamer passing Kansas, Missouri, 1850, from an engraving after a drawing from nature, in Charles A. Dana, *The United States Illustrated*, New York, 1853

IMMIGRATION TO KANSAS

THE story of the efforts of northern people through organizations like the Emigrant Aid Society to fill Kansas with "free state" settlers, of the efforts of Southerners, particularly Missourians, to counteract or neutralize this tide, and of the resulting disorder and bloodshed in Kansas has been told in another volume (Volume VIII). In 1857 a correspondent of the *Missouri Republican* writing from St. Joseph pictured what happened: "The emigration to Kansas reminds me of that to California, in the days of its greatest allurements. Trains upon trains are pouring in from every quarter, but particularly from the Free States. I had once thought, as I used to write you, that Kansas would be a Slave State; but I am now forced to alter my opinion from the overwhelming evidences to the contrary that force themselves upon me every day. Our ferry boats are busily engaged, from daylight until dark, in carrying over trains, and the proportion of Free-Soil to Pro-Slavery emigrants is as fifteen to one. This is not confined alone to our point of crossing, but it is so at every other that I can hear from; and it satisfies me that the political destiny of Kansas is fixed beyond all question, and that another year will fill all her prolific plains with a thrifty population. Wars and rumors she will know no more, but peace will brood over her beautiful prairies and prosperity will reign within her borders. I am a Pro-Slavery man, and would prefer to see my favourite institution established there; but I am, nevertheless, convinced that the energetic, enterprising Yankee will develop the resources and build up the country sooner than we could do, and that, by living in harmony with them, as our neighbors, they will do us no injury in our peculiar property." — Quoted in N. H. PARKER, *Kansas and Nebraska Handbook*, 1857, 50–51. During the Civil War Kansas became a state.

538 Pilgrims of the Plains, from a drawing by A. R. Waud in *Harper's Weekly*, December 23, 1871

NEBRASKA ORIGINS

THE territory of Nebraska was organized simultaneously with Kansas in the hope, on the part of some national statesman, that ultimately Kansas and Nebraska could be admitted to the Union as slave and free state respectively. Anti-slavery elements in the North, however, defeated this plan by concentrating their energies on aiding emigration to Kansas. Slavery was obviously impossible on the plains of Nebraska. The flow of population into that country depended, therefore, primarily upon the attractiveness of the region itself. The Missouri River, that ancient highway of the fur traders, marked its eastern boundary. From the rich alluvial plains which bordered that stream the territory stretched westward into the region of deficient rainfall. Across these plains, flower-bedecked in the summer months, wound a trail of bones. Skeletons of horses and cattle and bits of rotting equipage comprised the prairie record of the folk movement of the 'forties into Oregon and California. Thousands of Americans whose homes were on the Pacific Coast and other disappointed thousands who had returned to the East knew the Nebraska plains at first hand from journeying across them. In the memories of such men and women were recorded images of grasslands blackened with bison herds, of antelopes disappearing behind the sky line, of villages of prairie dog burrows, of swift-riding bands of Indians decked out in all the splendor which a barbaric imagination could devise. Immediately upon the organization of the territory some of these persons who knew the opportunities of Nebraska began entering the region to exploit the rich soil which lay beyond the Missouri River.

539 The First Claim Cabin in Nebraska, built by Daniel Norton, between Omaha and Bellevue, 1853, from an engraving after a drawing by George Simons in the frontier sketchbook of N. P. Dodge, in Julius S. Morton and Albert Watkins, *Illustrated History of Nebraska*, Western Publishing and Engraving Co., Lincoln, 1918

540 Nebraska Settlers Viewing their New Land, from an engraving after the painting *The Founders of a State*, by Thomas Hovenden, in *The Illustrated American*, April 11, 1896

THE FIRST PHASE

"THE tract of bluff land immediately west of the Missouri was first occupied for about ten miles inland. The earliest settlers encountered the usual hardships of frontier life. They really passed beyond civilization when they crossed the Missouri. They were in a land where the Indians ruled. They had to build their houses, cultivate their farms, and contest for supremacy with the Indians. . . . There was gradual steady growth along the river. Towns were founded and flourished; and the land brought under cultivation made fertile farms. A few pioneers pushed out forty, fifty, or sixty miles from the Missouri, but their difficulties in making things comfortable about them were generally very great. I met one of these pioneers sixty miles from the Missouri. His house was built of lumber that he had carted all that distance from the river. His means were small; he could not go into the stock business and let his produce transport itself; there was little for it but to work and wait. . . . My friend waited. . . . The railway came, and he attained a . . . fortune with which, in the restless spirit proverbially belonging to the pioneer, he departed to fight with fate in other regions." — O. A. MULLEN, *Nebraska* (1875), 192–93.

THE FREIGHTER OF THE PLAINS

FAR to the west of the towns that dotted the banks of the Missouri lay some trading centers, scattered forts and other military outposts for the protection of the frontier. Isolated as they were in a region practically untouched by civilization, they had not entirely lost touch with the world. Through their gates from time to time in the summer months creaked the freight wagons. Then the holds of these schooners of the prairies gave up their cargoes of supplies ranging all the way from ammunition to occasional luxuries. There were bales of goods for the Indian trade, uniforms from the quartermaster for the soldiers of the garrison, food, and sacks of precious mail. The freighter had loaded his wagon at one of the river towns on the Missouri. Day after day in company with other wagons he had plodded toward his destination, his eye ever searching the horizon's circle alert for the feathered silhouette of a mounted figure. The Indians had mixed feelings toward the freighter. He reminded them constantly of the strengthening hold of the white man upon their country, but he made it possible for them to obtain the much desired white man's goods. Toward the inn-keepers at whose rude and isolated ranches the freighter stopped for the night the redskins felt only enmity. They were white men who had established strongholds in hunting grounds of the red race and frequently these became the centers of little settlements. To pounce upon such settlements was a duty but one which should not be rashly undertaken. In these rough frontiersmen who had ventured so far beyond the fringe of settlement seemed to be concentrated all the brutal aggressiveness and sheer fighting ability which has enabled the white race to seize for itself a share of the earth's surface out of all proportion to its numbers. After a brief day the freighter's schooners gave way to the railroad and the inn-keeper transformed his hostelry into a "hotel" beside a "depot."

541 A Caravan on its Way to the West, from a mural painting by Edward J. Holslag, in the First National Bank, St. Louis

THE SECOND PHASE OF NEBRASKAN SETTLEMENT

542 Laying the Tracks of the Pacific Railroad, from a drawing in Samuel C. Bowles, *Our New West*, Hartford, 1869

The "fifty-niners," following the lure of gold in Colorado, ushered in the second phase of the settlement of Nebraska. "This second pilgrimage for gold was terrible, earnest, mad. . . . The road to the holy land of gold again lay through Nebraska. The men of the southeast found their best starting point at St. Joseph, in Missouri. Another stream of migration struck Nebraska at Brownville, another at Nebraska City, and yet another at Omaha. The St. Joseph and Brownville contingents met in the Little Blue Valley. . . . The pilgrims by way of Omaha all traversed the Platte Valley on its northern bank. The first objective point was Fort Kearny. There all the streams converged, and thence flowed on together in the valley of the Platte turning south to their destination at about meridian one hundred and five west of Greenwich. This gold-seeking movement bruited abroad the fame of Nebraska as an agricultural community. Some of the voyageurs stopped by the way, and opened up farms. Some others, whose expectations came to nothing in the gold country, returned in a style of rough comfort as good as that in which they went out, but many came back in a most pitiable plight, having endured hunger, nakedness, and many dangers by the way, and having been nearly devoured by the mosquitoes in the under-brush on the islands of the Platte, where they had hidden in the daytime, traveling by night through fear of Indians. . . . Others who took the back track and 'busted,' settled in the Platte Valley, the valley of the Big Blue, and the valley of the Little Blue; and their success attracted still others who joined with them in possessing the land. . . . The territory, which had hitherto been merely traversed by nomads, was settled by residents. . . ." — Mullen, *Nebraska*, 193–94.

THE CIVIL WAR

In April 1861, frontiersmen in Nebraska and Kansas on sweaty mustangs brought news to the neighbors that Sumter had been fired upon and that war had broken out between North and South. In a few weeks they saw officers and enlisted men of the Regular Army hurrying eastward to new posts of danger. The frontier was left virtually defenseless. The Indians would not be slow to take advantage of their opportunity. If the nation should be rent asunder and the military power of the Federal Government destroyed, the redskin might drive back the frontier and repossess his ancient heritage. Nebraska, where Americans had scarcely yet gained a firm foothold, raised two regiments. One went east to help save the nation; the other gave the Indians blow for blow and held them off. To frontier communities who were profoundly anxious as the fate of the nation hung in the balance and who mourned many dead on both eastern and western fronts, came in 1862 the reassuring news of the passing of the Homestead Act (see Vol. III) and in 1863 word of the incorporation of the Union Pacific Railroad Company (see Vol. IV). In the month after Grant crushed Bragg at Lookout Mountain and Missionary Ridge, ground was broken for the new railway. These shovelfuls of prairie soil and the rising prices of farm produce renewed the heart of the pioneer settler. Before his eyes was concrete evidence that one of the most terrible wars in the nineteenth century could not stop the economic growth of the nation.

543 Indian Alarm on the Cimarron River, from an engraving by A. L. Dick after a drawing by E. Didier, in Joshua Gregg, *Commerce of the Prairies*, J. W. Moore, Philadelphia, 1849

544 Colonists' Reception House on the Northern Pacific Railroad, from a wood engraving in *Führer durch die länderein der Nördlichen Pacific eisenbahn in Minnesota*, Northern Pacific Railroad Co., New York, 1872

MINNESOTA

DURING the years in which Kansans and Nebraskans were driving a salient into the Indian country, Minnesota folk were turning its northern flank. Years before the first white settlers had taken up homes in Kansas and Nebraska, cabins dotted the Minnesota woodlands. The first comers were refugees from an old Canadian settlement along the Red River. Three river systems, the Red, the Mississippi, and the St. Lawrence, all penetrate this plains country of Minnesota. Americans used the latter two avenues of communication to enter the region before the Civil War. In 1838 the first American settlement had its origin a little below the falls of the St. Croix. Somewhat later other settlements sprang up about the falls of St. Anthony. Growth was slow before 1850. Minnesota communities were islands beyond the margin of continuous settlement. They were doubly isolated in winter, when the Mississippi was frozen. In 1849, the year in which territorial government was established, less than five thousand people lived in Minnesota. On April 28 of this year the *Minnesota Pioneer* commented on the problem of isolation. "During five months the communication between this part of the country and our brethren in the United States has been difficult and infrequent. A mail now and then from Prairie du Chien was brought up on the ice in a 'train' drawn sometimes by horses and sometimes by dogs, containing news so old that the good people in the country below had forgotten all about it. . . . When the milder weather commenced and the ice became unsafe, we were completely shut out from communication for several weeks."

BOOM DAYS IN MINNESOTA

THE establishment of the territory of Minnesota in 1849 brought settlers. As usual the Indians were in the way. The years of 1851 and 1852 found white officials haranguing the Sioux whose hunting grounds lay west of the Mississippi. The proud Dakotas yielded to pressure and sold out. Not until the autumn of 1853 did the Indians finally leave their extinguished lodge fires. Ere they departed, however, they saw the white tide sweep over the land which had once been theirs. Before the Sioux treaty was proclaimed in 1853 some twenty thousand whites had rushed into the southern counties of Minnesota. Practically all of the newcomers were trespassers without vestige of legal rights to the lands they occupied. The "Suland" which the Indians evacuated was not legally open to settlement until the late summer of 1854 and another year rolled around before the first installment of land went on sale. But enforcing laws on a distant frontier was a difficult business; the settler would not be denied; the land was his by right of actual possession. He even thought of himself as a public benefactor when he read a vigorous defense of himself by Alexander Ramsey, Governor of the territory. "These hardy pioneers, who at the sacrifice of many of the comforts of life, have passed the frontiers of the Union . . . constitute the rank and file of that great army of peaceful progress, which has shed brighter lustre on our name than all the fields, red with carnage, that have witnessed the triumph of our flag. They bring with them to the wilderness, which they embellish and advance, maxims of civil liberty, not engrossed on parchments, but inscribed in their hearts — not as barren abstractions, but as living principles and practical rules of conduct. They cost their Government neither monthly pay, nor rations, — they solicit no bounty . . . but they make the country, its history and its glory."

545 St. Paul, Minnesota, from a colored lithograph by J. Queen after a drawing by Strobel, published in Philadelphia in 1853, in the collection of I. N. Phelps Stokes, New York

MINNESOTA IN THE CIVIL WAR

546 New Ulm, Minnesota, in 1860, from a lithograph in the Minnesota Historical Society, St. Paul

THE cloud of war which cast a shadow over the nation in 1861 had for Minnesota a silver lining. In the years from 1860 to 1865 population increased from one hundred and seventy-two thousand to slightly more than two hundred and fifty thousand. In the same period the wheat harvest yielded an increase of from slightly more than five million one hundred thousand bushels to just under nine million five hundred thousand bushels. While marching armies were bringing poverty and desolation to the South, Minnesota, profiting by enhanced agricultural prices resulting from the war, was becoming one of the granaries of the nation. This prosperity, however, should be set against the somber background of an Indian uprising. Some of the Sioux, bowing to the inevitable, became farmers and by so doing aroused the animosity of their wild kindred who would not assume the white man's yoke. The feeling among the Indians became tense. In 1862 an accidental row in which some whites were killed led to an outburst of frenzy on the part of the Indians. When the bloody tomahawk dropped from the hands of the hostiles, defeated by powerful military forces which had been rushed against them, sorrowful rescue parties found the bodies of hundreds of men, women, and children beside the ashes of their habitations. The Sioux, humbled for the moment by their own terrible losses, were driven from Minnesota at the point of the bayonet. Four years later occurred an event which symbolized the passing of an era on the grasslands of the West.

THE PASSING OF KIT CARSON

IN May 1868, a feeling of warmth in the air and the sight of greening prairies cheered the little garrison at Old Fort Lyon on the Arkansas some miles east of Bent's Fort. Yet an anxious winter merged into an anxious spring. The Indians were restless. As they left their winter camps to wander over the western grasslands in search of the game which was already nearing extinction, they were sullen and angry. The completed transcontinental railroad had brought them face to face with starvation. Red Cloud in the north was still defying the United States. At Old Fort Lyon Kit Carson, not yet sixty, lay on his bed, broken in body and spirit. Kit had been no weakling. With firmness and courage he had met life on the frontier, life that contained all the hard cruelty of a primitive struggle for existence. The frontier killed him, as it did so many other Americans, prematurely. He had been badly hurt while on a hunting trip just before the Civil War and had never fully recovered from his internal injuries. Mourning the loss of his wife, he derived what solace he could from the love and admiration which the little garrison at Old Fort Lyon heaped upon him. Before May, 1868, had fully roused the grasslands to new life, the soldiers of the fort stood stiffly at attention beside a new grave into which was reverently lowered a coffin of rough planks containing the body of General Christopher Carson. The ceremony marked an epoch. Before another spring revived the flowers on Kit's grave, Red Cloud had made peace and the Government had formulated a new Indian policy. For the Great Plains west of Minnesota and west of the Kansas-Nebraska salient, the day of the hunter and his wild, free life had passed forever. That of the settler was at hand.

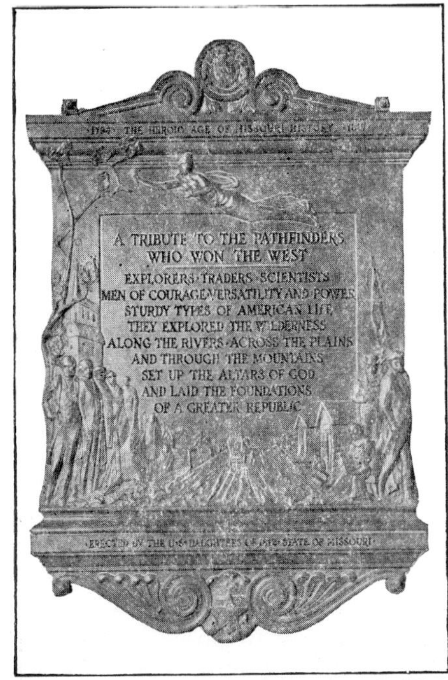

547 Tablet to the Pathfinders Who Won the West, erected in St. Louis by the Daughters of the State of Missouri, courtesy of the Missouri Historical Society, St. Louis

548 Railroad Building on the Great Plains, from a drawing by A. R. Waud, in *Harper's Weekly*, July 17, 1875

RAILROAD BUILDING

THE years which followed immediately upon Lee's surrender saw feverish railroad building in the Great Plains. In 1866 the first transcontinental line was completed. It followed the central route. Almost immediately three other ventures were launched, each having as its objective the crossing of the plains and the mountains. Two proposed to follow the southern route through New Mexico to California. The third aimed to connect Lake Superior with Puget Sound. Jay Cooke, patriotic financier of the Civil War, directed the last attempt. A buoyant enthusiasm, in part the result of that old American malady, a speculative craze, was in the air. The judgment of so wise a man of affairs as Cooke himself was clouded. Carried away by his dream of populous communities springing up over night in the northern grasslands, he urged his railroad builders westward and still westward. He established Duluth. He brought sudden prosperity to St. Paul. He called into being Fargo on the Red River. Between 1865 and 1873 thousands of settlers, taking advantage of the offer of free land contained in the Homestead Act and of the opportunities offered by the new railroads, established farms in the eastern portion of the Great Plains. Cooke's laborers were spiking rails to ties in Bismarck in 1873 when his Philadelphia banking house suddenly closed its doors. On the next day panic swept the nation.

THE HOMESTEADER

JAMES D. BUTLER, writing in 1873 a pamphlet on Nebraska for the information of emigrants, described the homesteader. "A majority of homesteaders are men of family. Some of them enter Nebraska, bring their wives and children in their own wagons, lodging on the way, and for a while on their farms in those wagons. If they have money they buy, at the nearest railroad station, lumber for house-building, already so far manufactured that they need no carpenter to set up their dwellings. But poorer men throw up sod-houses. The green sward turned up by the breaking plow is so 'matted and massed together' as to form better brick than the Hebrews turned out for Pharaoh, even before he denied them straw. Out of this material, and with no tool but a spade, many a man by ten days' labor has completed a house, roof and all, (15 × 15 feet inside) — a Nebraska 'brown front' both warmer in winter and cooler in summer than any house which can be made of lumber. Doors and windows are for sale in all stores, and trees alongside every brook afford rafters. Many pioneers leave their families in the old home, until they have prepared the new one. Few can leave their farms and go to them, but westward trains are full of wives carrying children to their husbands. Sixteen babies have been counted in a single car on this pilgrimage — Japhets in search of their Fathers. But while most pioneers drop many a comfort on their long march, some Yankees are shrewd enough to go west, and yet not go out. A Massachusetts man chartered a freight car on Cape Ann, put on board his household stuff, provisions, wife and children, and traveled without change to Nebraska, keeping house all the time till he and his were landed at the nearest station to Plymouth colony. The rapidity of settlement has been largely owing to the recent extension of railroads through these land districts. But those roads could not have thus developed the country, had they not run on the parallel along which settlement naturally flows." — *Nebraska*, 17.

549 A Sod House on a Claim in Kansas, from a photograph in F. H. Barrington, *Kansas Day*, Topeka, 1892

THE FRIENDLY PRAIRIES

550 An Early McCormick Reaper, courtesy of the International Harvester Company of America, Chicago

When American pioneers reached for the first time the margins of the prairies in the valley of the Ohio, they distrusted the fertility of these open stretches where grew no trees. Experience proved, however, that grasslands could bring forth bountiful crops. Even so, settlers were slow to push beyond the edge of the forest. The forest was familiar; for generations Americans had been learning to adjust their lives to it. The prairie presented new conditions. Wood for building and, what was even more important, for fuel, was difficult to get. The familiar plow could not cope with the age-old sod. By the time the Civil War came to a close most of the forested areas of the public domain had been taken up. On the last frontier men must adjust themselves to the peculiar conditions of the grasslands or return to the East. By this time, however, the problems of the prairie had been largely solved. The railroad modified the great distance of the open country and brought it into contact with the older settlements. The prairie plow was a special tool for turning the virgin sod. McCormick's reaper and binder enabled the husbandman to harvest broad fields with little additional help. The inventions of man made the grasslands attractive.

THE BLACK HILLS

In the summer of 1875 rumors ran through the West of gold in the Black Hills. Many prospectors hastened to the region although it was on the reservation of the Sioux. The Government of the United States had the country examined with the result that gold in paying quantities was discovered. Again was repeated the stampede of adventurers dominated by the lust for the yellow metal. Overnight in the winter of 1875–76 Custer grew into a city only virtually to disappear a few months later. In June, 1876, Deadwood became the El Dorado of the Black Hills. Scenes so familiar in California and the Rocky Mountains were reënacted. "Reached Deadwood at 12m," wrote a fortune-hunter in his diary. "We camped on Discovery about one-half mile below Elizabeth City. . . . There are four whiskey shops here but no provisions for sale in the town. . . . We went on up the Creek to the mouth of the Deadwood. Here we found about sixty or seventy miners gathered. They came for the purpose of adjusting some difficulty about a claim between two men. They were all armed with rifles and revolvers. Some were drunk and made considerable noise." A few days later the diarist, disappointed and disillusioned, left the Hills "broke." Visions of wealth gave place to anxiety as to whether he would be able to get home. On the way out he met a party coming in from Cheyenne. One was Calamity Jane, a camp follower. "She was riding horseback attired as a man with a Winchester rifle across her saddle bow." — "Holmes Diary," *Collections of the State Historical Society of North Dakota*, V, 73, 77.

551 Calamity Jane, from a photograph, courtesy of J. H. Sears & Co., New York

552 South Deadwood in 1877, from a photograph, courtesy of J. H. Sears & Co., New York

553 The Exodus from the Black Hills, from a drawing by William de la Montagne Cary, in *Harper's Weekly*, November 6, 1875

THE AFTERMATH OF THE GOLD RUSH

The gold rush brought thousands of people to the Black Hills. The limited opportunities for placer mining were quickly exhausted. Leaving the Hills, many disappointed in the search for wealth took up ranches or farms on the Dakota plains. Capitalistic mining speedily took the place of the primitive efforts of the individual, and gold mines sunk deep into mountain walls of rock replaced the prospector's cradle. Mining communities assumed an air of permanence. They offered a market for the produce of the agricultural country about the Hills. The rush had precipitated the last war with the Sioux, and in 1877 that fierce people lay prostrate beneath the heel of the conqueror. Men could now bring their wives and children to Dakota without a constant dread of the war whoop and the humming bullet. By 1879 the hard times of 1873 were only an unpleasant memory and the nation, buoyant and prosperous, was pushing on to undreamed-of material conquests. An incredible number of miles of railroad were laid down in the 'seventies and the 'eighties. New railroads covered the Great Plains with a devouring breed of speculators. The Dakota boom was in full swing.

A MINGLING OF PEOPLES

Land — empty, limitless in extent, and to be had for the asking — was the lodestone drawing to the Great Plains pioneers from far and near. Farmers came over from Iowa or Minnesota into the unoccupied country. Younger sons and daughters of the Ohio Valley decided to try their luck in the "West." Folk from the eastern seaboard struck out for the frontier. Clerks and laborers in numberless English and Scotch cities and towns perused with kindling eyes glowing accounts, usually prepared by railroad companies, setting forth the opportunities of the plains which had once been the bison country. Germans, long familiar with migration to America, began to think less in terms of Wisconsin, Iowa, and Missouri and to discuss the possibilities of Dakota and Nebraska. Swedes and Danes left their tiny farms and quiet villages to test their fortunes in the prairies. Norwegians packed their families and few belongings aboard little boats docked at the head of some fjord from which their forefathers had once set forth to win Iceland and Greenland for civilization. They looked for the last time upon the crags above and beyond them to the mountains rising range on range. A few months later these astonished newcomers began life afresh on plains where the flat horizon is reminiscent of the sea. All their lives the Scandinavian pioneers had conceived that the farmer's lot in life was to make a meager living from a few much cultivated acres. In America they suddenly found themselves in a land where farms were measured in hundreds and sometimes thousands of acres. A new freedom and a new vision stirred their souls as they put their hands to the sod-breakers.

554 Fargo, North Dakota, from a drawing by W. A. Rogers, in *Harper's Weekly*, August 27, 1881

THE SPECULATOR AND HIS TOWN

People hurrying to occupy an empty country are bound to distribute themselves unevenly over its surface. The problem of the speculator is to guess what their adjustments to the new conditions will be. In the first half of the nineteenth century, when rivers and canals were the principal avenues of communication, the speculator gravitated naturally to junctions of waterways and gambled in town lots in Pittsburgh, Buffalo, Cincinnati, or St. Louis. The railroad after the middle of the century added a difficult factor to the speculator's calculations. When the tracks ran for hundreds of miles across a rolling grassland where there was relatively little variation from place to place, the problem of guessing where the population of the future would cluster in towns was past solution. As always the speculator sought to solve it by assisting destiny. In the boom days after the depression of 1873 had passed, the plains from the Dakotas to Kansas became covered with towns whose existence was largely in the minds of men. Each was confidently expected to become a center of trade for the flourishing farms that would surround it. Churches were to rise; stores, dazzling department stores, were to display their wares; mills and factories were to bring the industrial age to the agricultural prairies. Enough of such fantastic dreams came true to give hope to every adventurer among the many who sought to profit by luck rather than by labor.

THE LAND OF GOLDEN GRAIN.

NORTH DAKOTA.

The Lake-Gemmed, Breeze-Swept Empire of the New Northwest.

HOMES FOR THE HOMELESS.

By P. DONAN.

PUBLISHED BY
CHARLES R. BRODIX,
CHICAGO, ILL.
1883.

555 Booming North Dakota, from the title-page of a pamphlet in the New York Public Library

WINDSOR

An emigrant from England who took up land in the Dakota territory in the early 'eighties has left a description of a typical speculator's town. "This small group of wooden buildings beside the track constituted the 'town' of Windsor, and comprised a saloon, hotel, and provision stores and post-office combined. Depot there was none at the period of our visit, the railway company not deeming the embryo-city of sufficient importance to warrant the erection of accommodation in this respect, so that passengers were forced to alight upon the tracks. This 'flourishing City of Eden' was mainly the property of a single speculative individual, who was then engaged in 'running up' the monster wooden hotel in the hope no doubt of attracting immigrants, and so raising the district and his own income at the same time — disinterested benefactor of humanity: To reach the door of the saloon, where resided the man of property upon whose shoulders rested the burdens and responsibilities of a young town, you had to cross a swampy tract by means of a single raised plank. In this resort was transacted by its frequenters all the business there was to be done in Windsor, concerning sale and barter. Here every newcomer, whether he sought to slake his thirst or find a man . . . would be requested to stand up and drink with the rest when a sign was given by a member of the company. . . . In the store at Windsor they have hung a map of the town, as it is planned out. It recalls that of Jamestown previously referred to, save that in this case the absurdity of the thing is rendered more apparent by the almost total absence of the town itself. There are more square meshes of a network of blocks and avenues, all named as usual; and a depot into the bargain. Quite a big town the map shows. . . ." — F. J. Rowbotham, *A Trip to Prairie Land*, 124–25.

NORTHERN DAKOTA

AS

A FIELD FOR EMIGRATION

AND

INVESTMENT.

LIVERPOOL.
NORTHERN PACIFIC RAILROAD AGENCY. LAND DEPARTMENT.
1882

556 A Bid for the English Emigrant, from the title-page of a pamphlet in the New York Public Library

557 From the painting *Where Tracks Spell Meat*, by Charles M. Russell, courtesy of the artist

CATTLE IN MONTANA

BETWEEN the Black Hills and the Bighorn Mountains lay in 1880 a stretch of grassland that was still an Indian and bison country. In the summer of that year Granville Stuart, already by turns gold miner, trader, and merchant, decided to make a venture in the cattle business. He brought a herd to a range east of the Judith Mountains and near the newly-established Fort Maginnis. In January a terrible blizzard gripped the country but was broken at last by chinook winds. "The first year on the range we had no neighbors and as we had watched the cattle closely but few strayed from the range. We rounded up alone, beginning May 25. Our losses all told, this first year were thirteen percent, five percent from Indians, five percent from predatory animals and three percent from storms. The small loss from storms was because there were so few cattle on the range; that feed was unlimited; and the creeks, and brush, and tall rye grass furnished them dry beds and shelter equal to a good stable and our cattle were northern range stock. The same summer [1880] an English company drove five thousand head of cattle from Texas and located their home ranch at the mouth of Otter creek in Custer county. The cattle did not reach Montana until late in the fall and they were thin and worn from the long drive. Practically the entire herd perished." — STUART, *Forty Years on the Frontier, II*, 160. For a discussion of the cattle business see Volume III.

THE COW COUNTRY OF THE NORTH

STUART has described the transformation that came to Montana in the early 'eighties. "In 1880 the country was practically uninhabited. One could travel for miles without seeing so much as a trapper's bivouac. Thousands of buffalo darkened the rolling plains. There was deer, antelope, elk, wolves and coyotes on every hill and in every ravine and thicket. In the whole territory of Montana there were but two hundred and fifty thousand head of cattle, including dairy cattle and work oxen. In the fall of 1883 there was not one buffalo remaining on the range and the antelope, elk and deer were indeed scarce. In 1880 no one heard tell of a cowboy . . . but in the fall of 1883 there were six hundred thousand head of cattle on the range. The cowboy, with leather chaps, wide hats, gay handkerchiefs, clanking silver spurs, and skin fitting high heeled boots . . . had become an institution. Small ranches were . . . along all the streams and there were . . . log schoolhouses in all the settlements." "Here," wrote Theodore Roosevelt in 1888, "there are no fences to speak of, and all the land north of the Black Hills and the Big Horn Mountains and between the Rockies and the Dakota wheat-fields might be spoken of as one gigantic, unbroken pasture, where cowboys and branding-irons take the place of fences." — *Ranch Life and Hunting Trail*, 1.

558 The Round Up, from an engraving after a drawing by Frederic Remington, in *The Century Magazine*, March 1888

THE CATTLE KINGS

559 From the painting *Smoking Them Out*, by Charles M. Russell, courtesy of the artist

The railroad was the primary factor which covered the plains of eastern Montana and western Dakota so suddenly with cattle. In 1883 the eastern and western divisions of the Northern Pacific were united at Gold Creek, Montana, and the country which for so many years had been the isolated hunting grounds of the Sioux and the Crows felt the magic touch of a market. Americans, Englishmen and Frenchmen rushed into the new business in the north. Those who succeeded became for a day cattle kings. Granville Stuart was one of these as was his close friend the Marquis D'Mores. The year in which the Northern Pacific was completed the Marquis invested two hundred and fifty thousand dollars in a packing plant at Medora in the Dakota territory. Here were slaughtered many of the cattle of the northern range and the expense of the long haul of live stock to Chicago was saved. While the Mores plant was going up, young Theodore Roosevelt was founding not far away his Elkhorn ranch on the Little Missouri. In the same year Pierre Wibaux from France located the later famous W-bar ranch on the Big Beaver in Dakota. In a sheltered river bottom he built a log house, fourteen by sixteen feet in size. Here he brought Madame Wibaux from their old home not far from Calais. On Christmas day in a typical American frontier cabin, which under the touch of the mistress of the house was made to express a little of the culture of the Old World, M. and Mme. Wibaux entertained their neighbors with a dinner famous in the frontier annals of Dakota. Wibaux, though practically ruined, was able to survive the slump of 1886 in the cattle business. In 1890 the erection of a magnificent White House, a landmark of the western prairies, symbolized the return of his prosperity. The cattle business, however, had entered a new phase. Pasturing on the public domain came to an end and the privately-owned ranch became the normal method of conducting the industry.

CATTLE RUSTLERS

The western cattle range in the late 'seventies and early 'eighties was a vast region on which grazed property worth hundreds of thousands, and sometimes millions, of dollars. Hiding places were many. The arm of the law was weak. The cattle rustler was an inevitable parasite whose appearance was practically contemporaneous with that of the first herds. He stole unbranded calves. If fortune smiled upon him, he added branded stock to his ill-gotten herds. He often posed as a wolfer, excusing his wanderings over the range on the ground that he was making his rounds. When rustling began seriously to threaten the profits of the cattle business and when the cattle men discovered that the law was unable to cope with the situation, the vigilantes of the cattle range appeared. The methods of these alert, swift-riding posses were summary and effective. They gave a first offender a sharp warning to quit the country. They hung the second offender to the nearest tree or shot him down if he pulled his gun. The protective associations of the cattle men which lay behind the vigilantes served to check the depredations of thieves who otherwise might have destroyed the very business which they preyed upon.

560 Cattle Rustlers Hunted Down by Montana Vigilantes, from a painting by Marchand, in *Munsey's Magazine*, May 1901

561 Cowboys Coming to Town for Christmas, from a wood engraving after a drawing by Frederic Remington, in *Harper's Weekly*, December 21, 1889

THE HEYDAY OF THE OLD RANGE

THE early 'eighties saw the range fill up with herds of cattle. Besides the cattle kings, individuals or companies who owned thousands of head of stock, many small ranchers appeared who raised hay to feed animals in winter. Here and there also farmers, "nesters" as the cowboys called them, fenced in the homesteads which they took up. Flocks of sheep also cropped the grasslands. In spite of the "nesters" and the sheep men, the cattle business boomed. The early 'eighties saw the cow country, where herds grazed over the public domain, reach its zenith. The nation was increasing rapidly in population. Hundreds of thousands of emigrants were pouring into the United States to swell the numbers of the swiftly growing industrial cities of the East. To the cattle men of the West the market for meat seemed unlimited. Yet some persons in Montana in the summer of 1886 saw all too clearly that the range was overstocked, that there was no way to prevent new herds from being brought upon it, that disaster impended.

THE TERRIBLE WINTER

THE winter of 1886–87 was marked by a succession of devastating blizzards. On January 9, it "began to snow and snowed steadily for sixteen hours. . . . The thermometer dropped to twenty-two degrees below zero . . . and on the night of January 15 stood at forty-six degrees below zero, and there was sixteen inches of snow on the level. It was as though the Arctic regions had pushed down and enveloped us. . . . The cattle drifted before the storm and fat young steers froze to death along their trails. . . . We kept plenty of men on the range to look after them as best they could, keeping them back from the rivers, and out of air holes and open channels in the ice, helping them out of drifts and keeping them in what shelter the cut banks and ravines offered. . . . The herds that were driven up from the south and placed on the range late in the summer, perished outright. Others lost from seventy-five to eighty percent of their cattle. . . . The large outfits were the heaviest losers as they could not feed or shelter their immense herds. Most of the big outfits had borrowed large sums of money at a high rate of interest and the cattle that they had left would hardly pay their indebtedness. They had to stay in the business and begin all over again. Eastern men who had large sums of money invested closed out the remnant of their herds and quit. The rancher with a good body of hay land and from one hundred to two hundred head of cattle was the man that profited. . . . In the spring of 1887 the ranges presented a tragic aspect. Along the streams and in the coulees everywhere were strewn the carcasses of dead cattle. Those that were left alive were poor and ragged in appearance, weak and easily mired in the mud holes. . . . In the fall of 1886 there were more than one million head of cattle on the Montana ranges and the losses in the 'big storm' amounted to twenty million dollars. This was the death knell to the range cattle business on anything like the scale it had been run on before."
— STUART, II, 235–37.

562 Cattle Drifting Before the Storm, from a wood engraving after a drawing by Frederic Remington, in *The Century Magazine*, March 1888. © The Century Co.

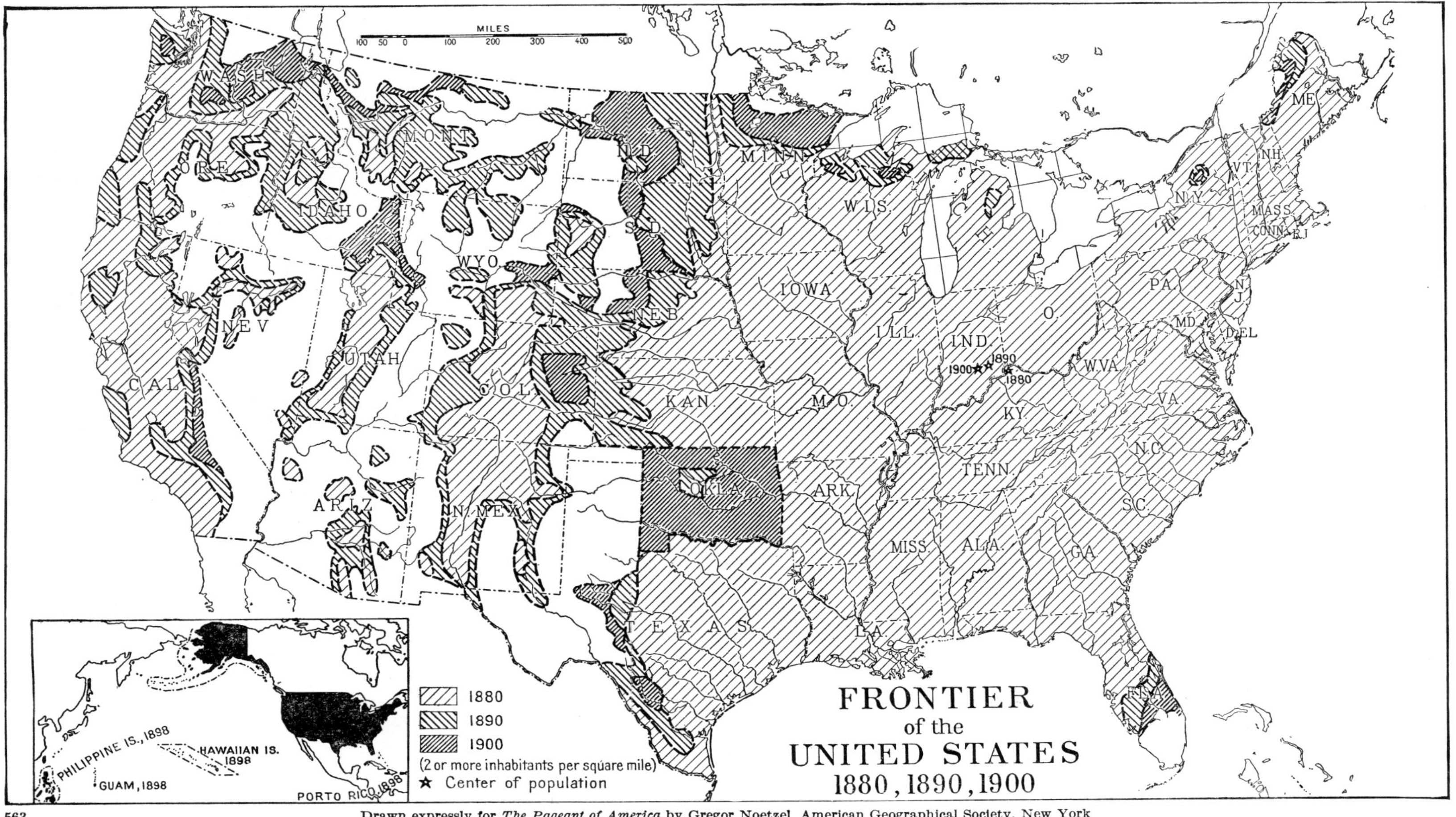

563 Drawn expressly for *The Pageant of America* by Gregor Noetzel, American Geographical Society, New York

THE "BONANZA" FARM

Counterparts of the Montana cattle kings were the "bonanza" farmers of Dakota. Railroads held great blocks of cheap land given to them to encourage the extension of their tracks. With industrialism striding rapidly forward in the East, experimenting with the factory system on great western farms was almost inevitable. The average "bonanza" farmer operated from three to ten thousand acres. He used the highly efficient labor-saving machinery of the new age and got his summer labor from the lumber camps of Wisconsin and Minnesota. The smaller farms, however, have increased in number and importance with the passing years. Their owners, horny-handed husbandmen, dominate the plains. The day of the frontier has passed.

CHAPTER XIII

MEETING THE CHALLENGE OF THE DESERT

THE folk who hastened westward to California in search of gold in 1849 and who followed the route through New Mexico, found it one of striking contrasts. From the grasslands of Kansas many turned southwestward through the Trans-Pecos highlands. Sharp-edged ridges ran roughly north and south. The more observant pioneer noted that this was a region of fault-block mountains. In a distant geologic age the Trans-Pecos country had been flat, its surface underlain by horizontal rock strata. Tremendous natural forces had then broken the region with faults and had heaved up and tilted great blocks of stone. These were the ridges and mountains. The steep faces invariably faced the west, the rock layers exposed by the erosion of streams dipping to the eastward. American trappers had known this country in Mexican days better than they knew the Colorado plateau which rises to the northwest. Climbing to the latter vast upland, as large as the United Kingdom, the early adventurer found himself in a country strangely flat. Here and there above the surface rose isolated mesas, buttes, or even mountain masses. The appearance of flatness, however, was deceptive. Rivers had carved deep gorges which incised the great tableland with a bewildering pattern of canyons. The greatest of these is that superb example of nature's handiwork, the Grand Canyon. The Colorado plateau is in many places almost inaccessible. On its southwest side it is bordered by the Arizona highlands. The picturesque boundary between the two physiographic areas is a line of cliffs. In the Arizona highlands the steep faces of the tilted blocks of stone which make the mountains, and which are reminiscent of the Trans-Pecos country, face the great plateau. The Arizona highlands are a labyrinth of mountains and valleys drained by the Gila River system. As in the Trans-Pecos region and the Colorado plateau, the country is dry, save where mountain slopes are sufficiently elevated to precipitate moisture from the winds. West of the Arizona highlands is a basin of the lower Colorado, a true desert which merges into the Mohave desert of southern California. Through this bewildering confusion of mountain plateau, valley, and sandy desert, thousands of people made their way in the rush to the California gold fields.

In the dry and tumbled country of the Southwest the nineteenth-century American pioneer, searching eagerly for opportunity, his thoughts absorbed with problems of the future, came suddenly face to face with antiquity. He found the Southwest a land of ruins and of mystery. In the heart of the Colorado plateau in the canyons of the San Juan and its tributaries he stumbled upon great pueblos into whose empty rooms had drifted the sand and dust of uncounted centuries. Adventurers in search of pelts or gold paused to gaze with awe upon the high walls and vast extent of Pueblo Bonito in Chaco canyon. Looking up to the cliffs which rise sheer above the floor of valleys etched in Mesa Verde they beheld the Cliff Palace. As the bright sun shining through the clear atmosphere of the Southwest lighted up the walls and towers of those silent masses where wild birds built nests in empty rooms, even the dullest mind could not escape the sense of mystery pervading the region. Other travelers, following the course of the lower Gila, stopped a moment to stand before that great pile of adobe which the early Spaniards had called Casa Grande. Unrolled on the lap of the desert the American newcomers found unexpectedly a record of the past.

A PARADOX

564 The Ruins of Casa Grande, from a lithograph, in Lieutenant-Colonel W. H. Emory, *Notes of a Military Reconnoissance from Fort Leavenworth, in Missouri, to San Diego, in California*, Washington, 1848

The archæologist has followed upon the heels of the pioneer. With infinite labor he has explored Casa Grande. He has worked patiently for many years to unravel the long and strange story of Pecos beside the river which bears its name. From the rooms of Pueblo Bonito he has removed the accumulated débris of centuries and recovered hidden treasures ages old. He has scaled dizzy cliffs, and the voice of man has echoed once more through the silent habitations of the caves. His labor, not yet completed, has brought to light the sure outlines of the human history of the Southwest. In this parched and mountainous country modern men can peer far back along the corridor of time. Increasing knowledge brings a paradox. That part of the United States last reached by the American frontier is the very country in which the record of unfolding human culture in the United States can with assurance be traced farthest into antiquity.

UP FROM SAVAGERY

Once upon a time — no one can say exactly when — nomads lived in the canyon country in the very heart of the inaccessible Colorado plateau. For moderns they are still a shadowy, even a hypothetical, people, for they left no remains. They cultivated no crops, made no pottery, and lived in temporary shelters long since destroyed by the forces of nature. Like the nineteenth-century Digger Indians of the Central Basin to the northwest of them, they managed to wrest a precarious living from their environment by catching rabbits and prairie dogs and by gathering grass seeds, berries, and roots. "Remains of these aborigines have not yet been discovered, nor will they be easy to distinguish from those of such modern nomads as the Apache and Piute, unless they are found buried below the relics of later cultures." In course of time a knowledge of agriculture came to them from the plateaus of Mexico and Central America where American agriculture originated. "At some early time, then, [probably 1500 to 2000 B.C.] the Southwestern nomads took up the practice of corn-growing; but at first their agriculture sat lightly upon them; their crops were not of sufficient importance, nor had their methods of cultivation become intensive enough, to tie them very closely to their fields. Eventually, however, better care brought fuller harvests, and it became necessary to provide storage places for the garnered grain. Where caves were available they were used, holes being dug in the floor for caches. The population undoubtedly increased, and the leisure acquired from the possession of surplus food-stuffs, and the consequent partial release from the exacting requirements of the chase, allowed the people to work at, and to perfect, their arts, and to lavish time upon elaborate sandal weaves, fine basketry, and carefully made implements. But they were as yet ignorant of pottery. Such were the Basket Makers." — A. V. Kidder, *Southwestern Archeology*, 119–20.

565 Basket Makers Storage and Burial Cave, from a photograph, courtesy of the Museum of The American Indian, Heye Foundation, New York

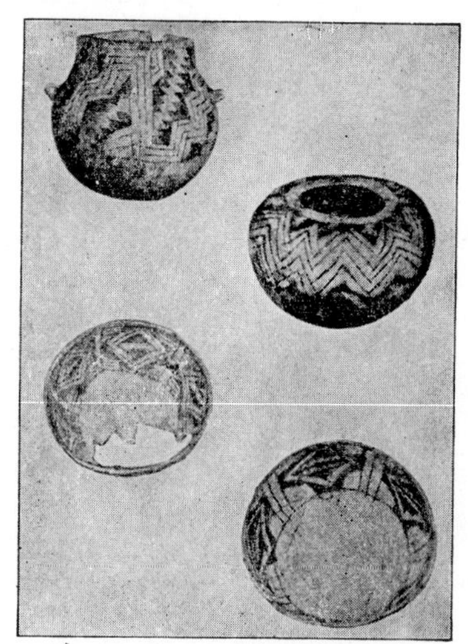

566 Pre-Pueblo Pottery, from a photograph, courtesy of the Peabody Museum, Boston

POST-BASKET MAKERS AND PRE-PUEBLOS

Population was sparse in the Colorado plateau and the maze of canyons made difficult the invasion of the region by war parties from tribes outside the area. The center of the Basket Maker culture lay in the San Juan valley. Sheltered by nature from foreign wars the Basket Makers advanced through the passing years toward a higher type of culture. They came to depend more and more upon their cornfields. The development of agriculture checked the wandering of the old days and caused the Indians to bethink themselves of better houses. The stone-sided cists in which maize had been stored were enlarged into dwellings built of slabs and roofed with poles and brush. The art of making pottery was discovered or learned from their Indian neighbors on the south. A new culture emerged in the valley of the San Juan and spread a little way both eastward and southward. For want of a better name it has been called post-Basket Maker culture. Development continued. Archæologists, working with spade and trowel in the remains of the final phase of the post-Basket Maker period, find in the graves evidence of the coming of a stranger people, easily identified because of their habit of skull deformation. They brought with them the cotton plant, the art of making cotton cloth, and perhaps the bow and arrow. Perhaps also they brought traditions and rituals which in modified form still persist in the Southwest. For the most part, however, they accepted the culture of the post-Basket Makers and made it their own. In course of time descendants of the newcomers, known to history as the pre-Pueblos, became the dominant people in the country of old Basket Makers. Ultimately, after a long period in which they dwelt in the slab structures of the post-Basket Makers, the pre-Pueblos finally achieved the brilliant Pueblo culture of the Southwest.

A NEW TYPE OF DWELLING

The evolution of agriculture in the heart of the arid Colorado plateau through the Basket Maker, post-Basket Maker, and pre-Pueblo periods presents an extraordinary example of adjustment to environment. Centuries of selection produced grain that could be planted deep in the soil to reach what little moisture the earth contained and that would mature quickly after the brief period of summer rains. The almost individual care given to every growing plant and the utilization and conservation of every possible drop of water which characterized the agriculture of the Pueblos were also results of age-long adjustment. The evolution of husbandry turned the pre-Pueblo of the slab house into the early Pueblo farmer. In the valley of the San Juan a new type of abode appeared. A small cluster of rectangular rooms with masonry walls housed the agriculturists. Nearby was a kiva, a circular room sunk in the earth and entered from above by the same opening which served as smoke vent. This was used for ceremonies in the worship of the rain gods and the deities of water upon whose friendliness and favor depended life itself. Prayers, dances, and ritual were as important for the growing corn as selecting the seed or cultivating the crop.

567 Section of a Kiva and Dwelling House, from a photograph of Dr. Prudden's model, courtesy of the American Museum of Natural History, New York

FARMERS AGAINST HUNTERS

The early Pueblo farmers had achieved an adjustment to the life conditions of the dry country superior to that of any other people. As they waxed prosperous, their culture spread throughout the arid Southwest. Over an area which extended from Great Salt Lake on the north to eastern New Mexico, little groups of farmers built their circular underground kivas and their rectangular dwellings. But their wealth brought them anxiety and suffering as well as comfort. Doubtless hunter tribes had occasionally troubled the forerunners of the Pueblos. When the latter, however, spread beyond the sheltered valleys where their culture had evolved, they came into contact with the hunter peoples who ranged over the mountain and plains country to the north and east of the plateau. These strangers discovered that the food supply derived from the pursuit of game could be profitably supplanted by raids upon the unprotected granaries of the Pueblo farmers.

UTAH
COLORADO
ARIZONA
NEW MEXICO
DISTRIBUTION OF POPULATION DURING THE VARIOUS PERIODS OF PUEBLO HISTORY. EARLY PERIOD - *UNSHADED* GREAT PERIOD - *LIGHT DOT SHADING*. LATE PREHISTORIC PERIOD - *LINE SHADING*. PERIOD OF THE CONQUEST - *BLACK*. PRESENT-DAY PUEBLO VILLAGES - *SHOWN BY WHITE DOTS*.

568 Distribution of Population during Various Periods of Pueblo History, redrawn from a map in Alfred V. Kidder, *Southwestern Archæology*, Yale University Press, New Haven, Conn., 1927

THE HEYDAY OF THE PUEBLOS

After a time the expansion of the culture of the Pueblo farmers over the arid Southwest slowed down and halted, before the frontiers of that country had been reached. War seems to have been the cause. Perhaps for a space a rough balance was achieved in the conflict between the huntsmen and the corn planters. Then the contraction of the agriculturists began. Scattered farm groups coalesced into ever larger compact communities isolated from one another. The little cluster of rooms of the early farmers grew into the pueblo, a great apartment house, built usually about one or more courts. The pueblo was a fortress, now set in a recess in the face of towering cliffs, now lifting its defiant walls above the flood plains of a canyon bottom. Conflict with their enemies forced the Pueblos to more perfect communal effort, and communal effort brought to its acme the Pueblo culture. "The difficulties confronting them [the Pueblos] were sufficient to spur them to their best endeavors, but not great enough to stunt their progress. Life was not too easy, nor yet too hard. They had reached that vital moment in their history when opportunity and necessity were evenly balanced." — Kidder, 128. In this golden age great pueblos and cliff dwellings were constructed. The arts flourished and were expressed in shapely pottery beautifully decorated and in jewels of turquoise. But the hunters would not be denied. Their rapacity grew with the wealth of the Pueblos. The great structures even in the San Juan region had to be abandoned. The culture area of the Pueblos sharply contracted, and a new center appeared in the valley of the Rio Grande in New Mexico. Adversity began to bring retrogression. The Pueblos had passed their zenith. They were, however, a vigorous people with a highly developed culture which represented an almost perfect adjustment to the conditions of their habitat when in 1540 they first looked upon the face of a white man.

569 Ceremonial Dance in a Zuñi Pueblo, from a photograph by John Hillers

570 A Navajo Family in the Canyon de Chelly, Arizona, detail from a group in the American Museum of Natural History, New York

NAVAJOS

When the sixteenth-century Spaniard, bearing the cross and the sword, entered the domain of the Pueblos, he soon discovered that the Navajos were one of the most important hunter peoples who were making predatory war upon the descendants of the cliff-dwellers. Linguistic and physical evidence suggests that the Navajo tribe is the result of the combination of many elements. The sub-arid Southwest was a melting pot, and the aggressive, up-standing Navajos were one of its best products. They were good fighters but had no genius for agriculture, never adopting this culture trait of their Pueblo enemies. They were content to wander from place to place in search of the scanty game of the desert or an opportunity for a successful raid upon their agricultural neighbors. Their hogan or habitation (see No. 118, Vol. I) was a simple structure though erected with much ceremony. Usually conical in form, the framework was of poles covered with branches, grass, and earth. The dwelling was often so low that a man could not stand erect within it. Their greatest artistic achievement, cloth weaving, was doubtless taught them by Pueblo women whom they captured. Parasites though they undoubtedly were, they were strong people carrying on with success their struggle for existence in their desert environment. An American observer in 1846 commented on the fact that they "are celebrated for intelligence and good order . . . the noblest of American aborigines." — Quoted in Hodge, *Handbook of American Indians*, 11, 43.

APACHES

Central and northern Arizona was the principal country of the Navajos when the whites found them. The Apaches ranged for the most part over New Mexico and western Texas. The name Apache, the Zuñi word for "enemy," is given to a complex of tribes and bands of diverse origin but displaying a common culture. These nomads of the desert practiced a very primitive agriculture, but for the most part lived on the game they caught and on roots and berries. Their habitations were rough huts of brush, well adapted to their dry country. Again and again they raided the peaceful and sedentary Pueblos and carried off rich booty. The Pueblos could not strike back effectively. If a war party of farmers sallied forth from the walls of a communal fortress, the Apache attackers vanished in a vast and confused terrain where concealment was easy and ambush the universal mode of warfare. Against the swift and sudden raids of the marauders the Pueblos could only defend themselves by eternal vigilance and, when necessary, a hasty retreat within the walls of their dwellings. For the Apaches the warfare of the raid was the breath of life. When the white men entered the region, the Apaches and the Navajos were slowly but surely bringing down the great Pueblo culture. The parasite was killing its host.

571 Apaches Ready for the War Path, from a photograph in the collection of Dwight Franklin, New York

THE SPANISH ERA

572 Spanish Houses — Isleta, New Mexico, from an engraving after a photograph by Charles F. Lummis, in *Memorial of Fra Alonzo Benavides*, edited by Mrs. E. E. Ayer, R. R. Donnelly & Sons, Chicago, 1916

The Indians through the centuries had developed two types of adjustment to the dry Southwest, that of agriculture and that of hunting coupled with predatory warfare. The Spaniards, entering the country from the south, established a third. During the long period of the Spanish and Mexican occupation of the Southwest agriculture was but little practiced. The mineral resources of the region were left largely unexploited. The white men in whose veins ran Spanish blood depended for life for the most part upon their flocks and herds. They extended into New Mexico the ranch industry of the northern plains of old Mexico. With the rancher came the Spanish system of vast landed estates and also the Mexican cowboy. For the first time the scanty grasslands of the Southwest were dotted with grazing domestic animals, horses, goats, sheep, and cattle. In New Mexico the Spaniards lived mostly in the valley of the Rio Grande. They dwelt in towns for the same reason that the Pueblos lived in their great apartment houses. The Spaniards were, moreover, much influenced by Pueblo models in fashioning their houses; for in dwellings as in agriculture the Pueblos had achieved an almost perfect adjustment to their sunny, dry, and hot environment. The houses of the Spaniards often resembled roughly the room clusters of the early Pueblo farmers before the days of the great communal dwellings.

THE DECLINING PUEBLOS

The Pueblos, long accustomed to battle with the Navajos and the Apaches, were unwilling to bow their necks to the Spanish yoke without a struggle. They disliked the regulations of their Spanish Governors but they hated more the religion taught by the gentle friars. In the kivas the shamans danced furiously, performing the ancient ritual with meticulous detail in an effort to ward off the anger of the Pueblo gods at the coming of a strange religion. Centuries of evolution had created for the Pueblo man a culture that controlled his life with an iron discipline. The conservatism of the agriculturist, strengthened by an ancient faith, chained him to the customs of the past. In 1680 the Pueblos in a bloody uprising drove the Spaniard from the upper Rio Grande. The white man came back and resumed his rule, but the Pueblos continued their ancient mode of life. The diseases which the European brought ravaged the Pueblo villages. The continuing raids of the Apaches and Navajos and occasional struggles with the whites aided the retrogression. When Coronado marched through New Mexico, Pecos, on the river which bears its name, was the greatest of all the pueblos. In the eighteenth century wars with the fierce Comanches of the plains reduced its fighting strength. Then in 1788 smallpox emptied the rooms of Pecos. Forty odd years later when the pallor of death lay over the place, an American pioneer described Pecos. ". . . it contained a population of fifty to a hundred souls, the traveler would often times perceive but a solitary Indian, a woman, or a child, standing here and there like so many statues upon the roofs of their homes, with their eyes fixed on the eastern horizon or leaning against a wall or a fence, listlessly gazing at the passing stranger. . . ." — Gregg, *Commerce of the Prairies*, 1830, 1, 272. In 1838 seventeen survivors of Pecos trudged away to the northwest to join some kinsmen.

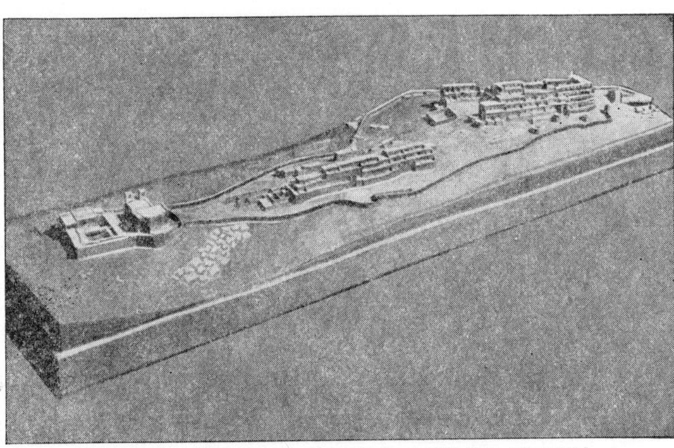

573 The Pueblo of Pecos, as it appeared about 1700, from the model in the Museum of New Mexico, Santa Fé

574 Apaches on the Banks of the San Carlos River, Arizona, detail from a group in the American Museum of Natural History, New York

CONTACT WITH THE WHITES

The Spaniard coming into the Southwest brought good as well as evil to the Indian. Wheat began to grow in the fields of the Pueblos, while vineyards and peach and apple orchards appeared. Domestic animals, the horse, ass, sheep, goat, and cow, came into the hands of the Indians. Pueblo economy was modified and its agricultural foundation broadened. To the Navajos and Apaches the white settlements offered alluring new opportunities for raids which continued through the whole Spanish period. So profitable was raiding for the Apaches that, after the coming of the whites, they grew in prosperity and increased in numbers. To the end of the Spanish period, however, they remained essentially parasites, the terror alike of the Spaniards and the Pueblos. Their predatory expeditions, moreover, were pushed southward near to the heart of old Mexico. The Apaches were at their zenith when the American frontier reached the Southwest. The evolution of their Navajo neighbors had been slightly different. Contact with the whites enabled them to advance from the hunting to the pastoral stage of culture. They became, as well as raiders, the Bedouins of the Southwest.

THE COMING OF AMERICANS TO THE SOUTHWEST

When Mexico in 1821 slipped from the palsied hand of Spain, American frontiersmen began to enter the Southwest. Almost immediately the Santa Fé trade (see No. 396) sprang into vigorous life. The trapper followed hard upon the heels of the trader. Men of the type of Bridger and Jedediah Smith, who counted no obstacle of desert or mountain too hazardous, paid scant heed to international boundaries. The empty mountain country to the south of Great Salt Lake which lay within the domain of Mexico was as familiar to Carson or Bill Williams as was that traversed in the 'forties by the Oregon Trail. Traders and trappers, however, made few settlements; they were the harbingers of the settlement. In 1846, in the first year of the Mexican War, General Kearny broke the power of the Mexican in the Pueblo country. The treaty of Guadalupe-Hidalgo in 1848 and the Gadsden Purchase in 1853 extended American sovereignty not only to California but to the vast region between the Sierras and the Continental Divide. In 1849 and 1850 gold-seekers flocked across the dry Southwest to the El Dorado in the Sacramento Valley. The gold rush brought American settlers to the valley of the upper Rio Grande. Only a handful of immigrants, however, stopped in New Mexico and few came after the rush. The country was dry. No railroads brought the Southwest into contact with life-giving American markets. Indian parasites, who melted into the desert at the first show of force, were as ready to prey upon the American as upon the Mexican or the Pueblo. Before the American flag was raised at Santa Fé, men of Spanish blood had acquired title to the desirable farming and grazing land and these titles had been confirmed by the treaty which brought the Mexican War to an end. Such were the more important reasons why New Mexico and Arizona during the 'fifties, 'sixties, and 'seventies remained in fact largely a Mexican and Indian country.

575 Cliffs near Jacob's Pool, Arizona, from a photograph in the collection of Dwight Franklin, New York

576 Navajo Raiders, from a painting by Maynard Dixon, courtesy of the artist

WAR ON THE FRONTIER

THE war between the North and South had repercussions in the land of deserts and canyons. In 1862 an army of Texans sought to conquer New Mexico for the Confederacy only in the end to be expelled with heavy loss. The average New Mexican hated the Texan more than he loved the Union, but he did effective service for the cause to which Lincoln dedicated his life. Sectional warfare in New Mexico and farther east caused the withdrawal of federal troops from Arizona, leaving for the moment that country almost completely at the mercy of the Navajos and the Apaches. In 1863, however, the year in which the Confederacy reached its flood tide, the Navajos were suddenly brought to the end of the predatory epoch of their history. Carson, five years before his death, led a determined American force into their country, defeated them, rounded them up as though they had been wild cattle, and brought most of them off as prisoners. So the Bedouins of the Southwest felt the mailed fist of the Americans. When several years later they were permitted to build again their hogans in their old haunts and were given flocks of domestic animals, they returned to their former independence but they were parasites no longer.

INDIAN HERDSMEN

THAT spot where New Mexico, Arizona, Utah, and Colorado all touch lies within the reservation of the Navajos. The Navajo remains a wandering herder. Vastly different from that of the Pueblos is his way of living. For their communalism he substitutes extreme individualism. There are no Navajo villages in any important sense. The traveler through the reservation will come occasionally upon a lone family beside their primitive hogan, while near by a flock of sheep grazes on the scanty grass. The women still weave their famous blankets but incline more and more to import their yarn from the East. Only in the sale of these and a few other small commodities and in the purchase of a few simple necessities do the Navajos touch the life of the outside world. They live in isolation in their elevated habitat, free from any considerable mixture of white blood, independent, self-supporting, asking only to be left alone.

577 Navajo Sheep at a Drinking Pool, Guando, Arizona, from a photograph.

578 Roosevelt Dam, Arizona, from a photograph. © Wide World Photos, New York

THE AMERICAN PERIOD

In the 'eighties the first trains roared through the canyons of the Southwest. The coming of the railroad marked the passing of an epoch. The land of sage brush and cactus was isolated no longer; through the very heart of it ran two of the new trade routes binding together the eastern and western coasts of the nation. The railroad brought settlers and capital. Mining engineers followed trails which prospectors had blazed into the mountains of southern Arizona. The exploitation of the mineral wealth of the desert by the methods of industrialism began. The American newcomers faced the maze of land titles inherited from the Spanish régime. The central government created a special court to adjudicate conflicting claims and to determine hazy boundaries. When these judges, in the early 'nineties, adjourned *sine die*, the individual landowner for the first time in the history of the Southwest felt secure in his possessions. Vast areas of fertile soil had been turned to the uses of civilization. National leaders began to plan the reclamation by irrigation of desert soil. So passed the last frontier.

THE FUTURE OF THE PUEBLOS

The Apaches, who had prospered during the easy-going Spanish days and who for three decades had successfully stood off the Americans, after the coming of the railroad felt at last the full power of the United States. Victorio, the greatest Apache leader, was brought to bay and killed. In the 'eighties General Crook and General Miles fought the last of the desert marauders to exhaustion. The Apache tribes were forced to settle and remain on reservations allotted to them. The ancient scourge of the sedentary folk of the dry country was quieted. For the first time in their long history the Pueblos could cultivate their fields in peace. Theirs is the peace of the desert. The clamor of American civilization comes but dimly to the mesas. The flood of white population which has inundated most of the ancient habitat of the Indians within the United States has not overspread the dry Southwest. The climate, to which the Pueblo culture is an almost perfect adjustment, protects it somewhat from the domineering Caucasian. Intermarriage with the whites is rare. Yet the Pueblos are the wards of the nation and the Indian bureau has attempted to force them, as all other Indians, into the American mold. Schools bring to their children the white man's learning and religion. An unsuccessful attempt was once made to destroy their ancient religion. But the Pueblos have found among the white race wise friends who are seeking to protect them from the melting pot and who vision a renaissance, the result of spiritual growth from within rather than enforced culture changes from without. The Pueblos share in the artistic genius of their race and the opening years of the second quarter of the twentieth century brought the dawning of a new day in their art life. Perhaps in the Southwest a fragment of the "first Americans" will through the years develop as Indians, sharing in and contributing in their peculiar way to the thought life of the world. Perhaps this dream of their friends will turn out to be only another mirage of the desert.

579 A Modern Pueblo in Arizona, from a photograph. © Underwood & Underwood, New York

THE DAWES SEVERALTY ACT

580 An Indian Farm House on the Crow Reservation, Montana, from a photograph. © Underwood & Underwood, New York

THREE years before the massacre at Wounded Knee (see No. 533) the National Government had formulated its Indian policy in the Dawes Severalty Act of 1887. The principle which underlay this measure was that the Indian's social and political organization should be abolished. Tribal governments should disappear. Community life should be given up. The Indian should come under the sole jurisdiction of the National Government. His reservation should be divided into farms and these farms should be distributed among the members of the tribes. Such land as was left over might be sold to the whites and the money held in trust for the Indian. For twenty-five years an Indian who received a farm should be unable to sell or alienate his land. He should, however, be a citizen of the United States. At the end of the quarter century he was to be free to do what he would with his own. The President at his discretion could apply the Dawes Act to the different tribes. The measure, however, did not apply to the so-called Five Civilized Tribes, the Cherokees, Chickasaws, Choctaws, Creeks, and Seminoles.

RESULTS OF THE DAWES ACT

IN 1895 the Dawes Act was applied to those hardy northern mountaineers, the Nez-Percés. More than two thousand Indians, men, women and children were given farms. A considerable section of prairie land was also reserved for grazing purposes for the tribesmen. The surplus land was sold to the whites for more than a million and a half dollars, the income from which was distributed annually among the Indians. The Nez-Percés found themselves a prosperous, almost rich, people. They were among the most promising of the mountain Indians and the Government looked forward to their quick absorption into the nation. Twenty-five years passed. In 1920 the Nez-Percés received their farms in full possession. Within five years the lands were mostly gone and a landless and impoverished generation faced the tasks of life. Twenty-five years had proved too short a period to enable this mountain people to develop to such a point as to be able to compete with their white neighbors. Unwonted prosperity had impaired somewhat their moral fiber. The younger generation, brought up on the farms, was observed to be not so independent or trustworthy as the old people who had once maintained themselves in the wild life of the mountains. Not all the Indians, however, were foolish enough to dispose of their lands, and those who held fast enjoyed good homes. In 1923 was established among those redskins an "Indian Home and Farm Association" for the purpose of awakening in the younger members of the tribe an ambition to become useful citizens to abandon idleness and gambling, and to become independent farmers. The Nez-Percés are learning from the school of adversity. Their experience makes clear one of the most serious difficulties confronting those charged with responsibility for the Indians.

581 Indian Farmers Harvesiing Oats, from a photograph. © Underwood & Underwood, New York

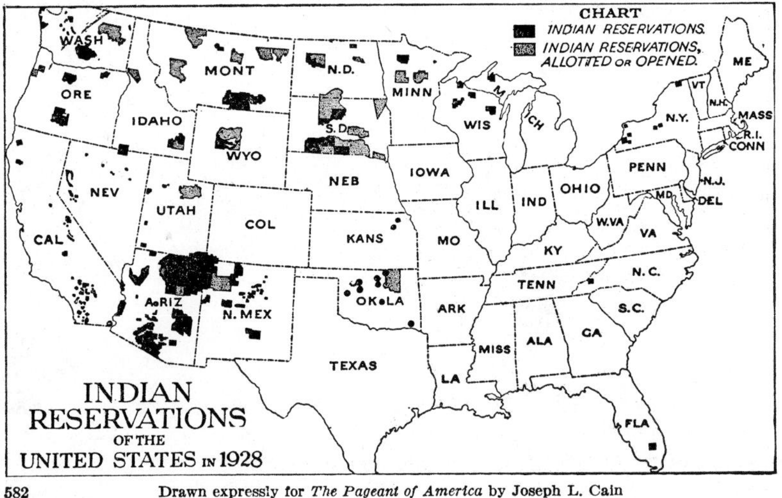

582 Drawn expressly for *The Pageant of America* by Joseph L. Cain

THE BURKE ACT

LONG before catastrophe had befallen the Nez-Percés, experience had demonstrated that the Dawes Act was in many respects not a wise measure. In 1906 it was amended by the so-called Burke Act. This law abolished the twenty-five year probationary period and empowered the Secretary of the Interior to give full property rights at any time to individuals whom he considered competent to manage their own affairs. Conversely the Secretary could keep "incompetents" in an indefinite period of dependence. Under the Burke Act citizenship was postponed until the Indian received a certificate of competence. On June 2, 1924, however, was promulgated a law making all Indians born within the national borders citizens of the United States. The act was primarily a sentimental gesture toward the "first Americans," passed when consideration of the restrictive immigration law of the same year was rousing national sentiment. In interpreting this measure the Supreme Court ruled that citizenship is a personal and political right. "Citizenship is not incompatible with tribal existence or continued guardianship, and so may be conferred without completely emancipating the Indians or placing them beyond the reach of Congressional regulations adopted for their protection." In 1929 President Hoover appointed the president of the Indian Rights Association as chief of the Bureau of Indian Affairs. The event closed an era. A cloud which had hung almost continuously over succeeding administrations since the abandonment of the policy of war and to which the scientist, O. C. Marsh, had called attention in his report on the scandals of the Red Cloud agency, was dispelled. A new day of scientific aid in their efforts to adjust themselves to American life dawned for the wards of the nation.

MEDICAL CARE

GUARDIANSHIP of the property of incompetents, medical care, and education are the fundamentals of the American Indian policy of the twentieth century. Confinement on reservations and contact with the whites aggravated disease among the defeated and dispirited redskins in the last quarter of the nineteenth century. Even to many of themselves they seemed a dying race for the medical and hygienic provisions made by the Federal Government were totally inadequate. The year 1911 marked the beginning of annual appropriations for the prevention and treatment of disease. Tribal funds were also used for the work. In 1926 the medical work was reorganized. A surgeon of the Public Health Service was detailed to be in general charge, and the Indian country was divided into four districts, each of which was in charge of a medical director. The policy of hiring local physicians to assist in caring for the health of the Indians was abandoned and full-time men, devoting their whole lives to their work, began to take the place of the contract doctors. The decline of the redskin population has been checked and disease as a handicap to cultural advance is being steadily reduced.

583 Hospital at the San Carlos Indian Agency, Arizona, from a photograph in the Army War College, Washington

584 School Buildings at the San Carlos Indian Reservation, Arizona, from a photograph in the United States Army Signal Corps, War Department, Washington

EDUCATION

In its efforts to train the Indian for citizenship, the Government has laid great emphasis upon education. The Indian must be taught the English language. He must be trained, moreover, in some useful occupation. For the most part the schools are vocational in character, giving instruction in farming, trades, and home economics. Three types of schools have been developed. The younger children go to the reservation day schools where they receive instruction in grammar and prevocational work. The reservation boarding schools train the children in more advanced branches. There are a few non-reservation boarding schools, of which, from 1879 until 1917, Carlisle in Pennsylvania was the most prominent and most important. The advantage of the boarding school over the day school is that the child can be taken out of his home environment, where too often the practices and attitude of the old savage days still continue in modified form. The pupil can be taught cleanliness and manners as well as English and a trade. To be sure, when he returns to his community after his schooling is over, he is more than likely to lapse into the slovenly ways of his parents and to adopt their mode of life and their superstitions. This is particularly true among the Indians of the Southwest, where the power of ancient custom is very strong. Progress toward better things, however, is being achieved. The discouragements which confront the Indian educator and his frequent apparent failure to impress the lives of his pupils, demonstrate in another way the difficulties which confront the red race in trying to absorb the civilization developed by the whites.

585 Charles Curtis, 1860–, from a photograph. © Harris & Ewing, Washington

INDIANS OF THE UNITED STATES

In 1925 the Indian population of the United States numbered three hundred and forty-nine thousand, five hundred and forty-five. Of these one hundred and seventy-five thousand, one hundred and sixty were estimated to be full bloods; sixty-three thousand, three hundred and fifty-two were estimated to have more than half Indian blood; and one hundred and eleven thousand, eighty-three were estimated to have less than half Indian blood. Since 1920 the Indian population has been slowly increasing. The process of amalgamation, however, is going on and the percentage of full bloods is decreasing. In 1916 Dr. Charles A. Eastman, a full-blood Sioux, pointed out what seems to be the ultimate destiny of the American Indian. "It is too late to save his color; for the Indian young men themselves have entirely abandoned their old habits of remaining aloof from the racial melting pot. This cultivation and infusion of new blood has revived the depressed spirit of the first American. . . ." In 1929 Charles Curtis, in whose veins ran the blood of the Kaw Indians of the Great Plains, became Vice-President of the United States.

CHAPTER XIV

ALASKA

IN the summer of 1923 a President of the United States set foot for the first time upon the soil of Alaska. He found the region sparsely populated although for more than half a century the sovereignty of the nation over which he presided had extended to this vast northland. A few thousand white men had built their homes near the foot of mountains from the lofty slopes of which glaciers slide lazily down to the sea. Neighbors of these frontiersmen were Tlingit and Haida Indians. Farther to the north lived other white men scattered along a coast where were also to be found the villages of Aleuts and Eskimos. There were small towns in the interior. The people who greeted the President spoke many languages and the welcome was enthusiastic. Alaskans saw in the journey of the chief executive the end of an epoch marked by governmental neglect and public indifference toward the interests of their homeland. When cheering crowds on the shore waved farewell to the presidential transport steaming slowly southward, they believed that a new day had dawned for Alaska. The future must disclose whether they were right.

Alaska differs from all other American frontiers. It lies in that climatic border zone where the farmer gives place to the herder and the hunter. Roughly equidistant from the Equator are Iceland, whose fields are covered with sheep and cattle, and Newfoundland, whose people for the most part are fishermen. In these two islands and in Alaska climate sharply restricts the activities of men. The southern shore of Alaska is a drowned coast cut by steep-sided fiords and bordered by many islands. From the Alaskan peninsula the Aleutian islands stretch westward toward Kamchatka, stepping stones from North America to Asia. Against the bleak and fog-bound shores of these isles flows the warm Japanese current; thence it bends eastward, and continues down the irregular Alaskan coast. Within a zone whose climate is modified by this current live most of the people of Alaska. North of the Alaskan peninsula the Bering Sea washes the coast and into this *mare clausum* the Yukon dumps its load of silt. The Eskimo, pursuing walrus northward through Bering Strait, comes at last into the Polar Sea. The northern shore of Alaska is remote indeed from the busy life of the modern world. This coast slightly more than a thousand miles from the pole is the habitat of the fish, birds and mammals that find the Arctic a friendly country. To the water's edge cling tiny settlements of Eskimos who support life by hunting and fishing. Fur-clad hunters pushing southward across the plain which lies behind the coast find their way blocked at last by the towering uplands of central Alaska. Varied indeed is the topography of this untamed northland. Prairies, gay with summer flowers, spread for miles beyond the foothills of mountains capped with perpetual snow. Rivers incise deep valleys in the uplands and build up flood plains near their mouths. The climate is as varied as the surface. From the moisture and warmth of the southern coast to the seasonal extremes of the interior where the summers are hot and the winters almost unbelievably cold is a climatic contrast not to be duplicated in North America. To the conditions of this land of contrasts man from remote antiquity has striven to adjust himself.

INDIANS OF THE SOUTHERN ALASKA SHORE

586 A Yakutat (Tlingit) Priest, from a photograph, courtesy of The American Museum of Natural History, New York

The island-dotted shore which extends from the Gulf of Alaska to Puget Sound was the setting for one of the important intellectual achievements of the American Indians. Fish abounded and at certain seasons choked the streams emptying into the ocean. Inevitably the Haidas of the Queen Charlotte Islands and their kinsmen, the Tlingits, who lived to the northward, depended for their living upon the harvest of the sea. Forests reaching down to the water's edge furnished logs which were built into dwellings characterized by taste and fine workmanship. Great fir trees were turned into canoes large enough to carry war parties to enemy villages. But the Haidas and Tlingits inclined more to trade than to war and social position among them depended upon the amount of possessions rather than upon military prowess. Upon fishing as an economic foundation they developed one of the most advanced Indian cultures north of the Rio Grande. A bountiful nature which made life relatively easy gave them leisure to seek and to create beauty. They were wood and stone carvers. Early traders who came in ships to Alaskan villages were astonished at the tall, brightly painted and beautifully carved totem poles which stood before their dwellings, at the carved corner posts and at the well-wrought log cabins in which the fisher folk lived. White men who tarried in the Indian towns found a stratified society with slaves at the bottom and persons of some wealth at the top. These fishing Indians had an elaborate ceremonial trading system known as the potlatch. Their lives were enriched by an unusually abundant oral literature. They were the originators of a culture still developing toward better things when the white trader came like a blight among them.

587 An Athapascan Indian of the Yukon Valley, from a photograph, courtesy of The Museum of the American Indian, Heye Foundation, New York

THE ATHAPASCANS

To the northward of the Tlingits in that mountainous plateau through which flows the Yukon and the Tanana rivers lived the northwestern branch of the great Athapascan family of Indians. At certain seasons they pitched their tents beside the river banks and fed upon the salmon which came up stream for spawning. At other times they struck into the wild interior in search of caribou and other game. Life for them was hard. They were a dirty, wretched, and degraded people. The struggle for a bare existence so completely absorbed their energies that they developed little material culture. They had borrowed from the Eskimos some tools and customs. Culture traits of the Tlingits also appeared among them. They were, however, among the most primitive redskins of the continent. These Athapascans of the Yukon, together with the California and the Digger Indians, were examples of human life lived constantly on the verge of disaster. A slight bit of bad fortune was all that was needed to wipe out a village.

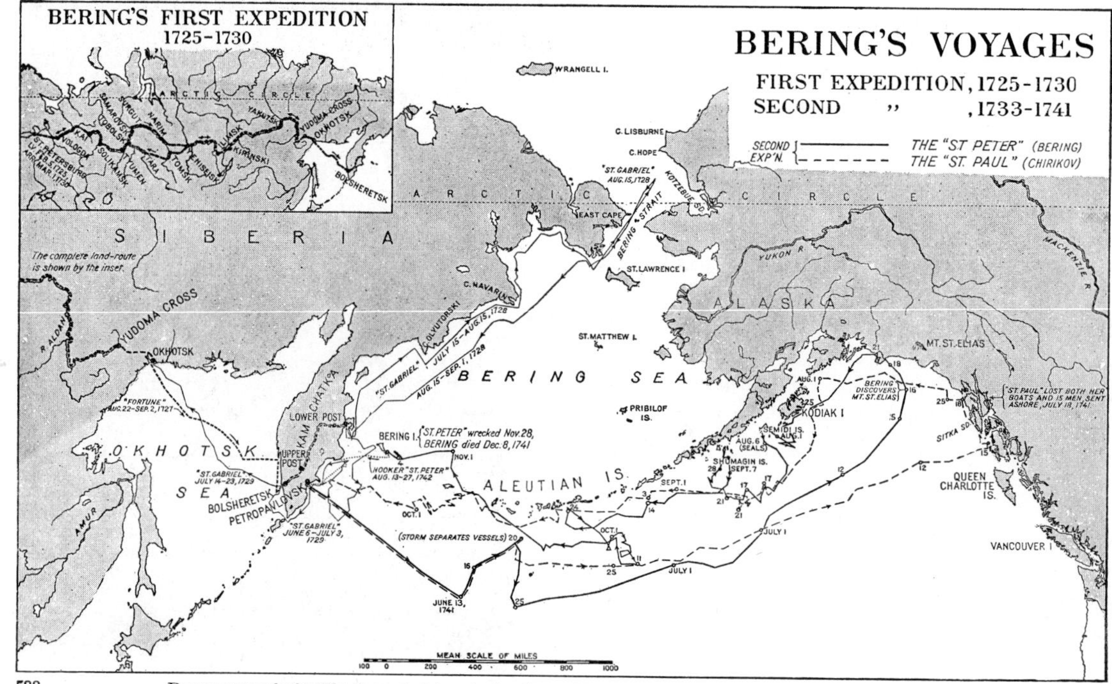

588 Drawn expressly for *The Pageant of America* by Gregor Noetzel, American Geographical Society, New York

THE ESKIMOS AND ALEUTS

WHERE the Bering Sea and the Arctic Ocean break against the shores of Alaska the Eskimos built their huts of sod and driftwood. Through a long period of evolution they had perfected their adjustments to the conditions of their northern habitat. From time immemorial the wild life of the sea and shore and of the vast inland plains had furnished them with all their needs. Their ingenious boats and paddles, their harpoons, their skin clothing, and the oil lamps with which they heated their houses were evidence that they had learned to live with a modicum of comfort in the Arctic. Whales were plentiful before the coming of the whites and walrus roared on every headland. The fleet caribou which grazed on the tundra were without number. Life for the Eskimos was arduous but reasonably secure. They looked forward to the future with no fear of famine. On the Alaskan Peninsula and the Aleutian Islands stretching away to the west lived kinsmen of the Eskimos, the Aleuts. Their language resembled that spoken in the igloos further to the north. Their physical characteristics were much the same. Perhaps they had less individual enterprise. Some observers, however, studying their history, have concluded that they possessed greater intellectual ability than the Eskimos. Before the white man came there were perhaps twenty-five thousand of these Aleuts dwelling on the Aleutian Islands, which divide the Pacific from the Bering Sea. They were fishermen and hunters of the walrus, seal, and sea otter. Like the Eskimos, they had perfected their adjustments to their difficult environment. With a plentiful food supply about them, they, too, looked to the future untroubled by fear. Perhaps Aleut fishermen in Bering Sea in the summer of 1728 saw a ship, sailing from the southwest, disappear over the northern horizon. That hardy Danish mariner, Vitus Bering, sailing for Russia, was on his way to his great discovery. In August he proved that North America and Asia are not connected and gave his name to the strait which separates them. Thirteen years later the Dane, accompanied as on the former voyage by the Russian navigator Chirikof, was again afloat on the waters of the north Pacific. Early on the voyage a storm drove the ships apart and the explorers never again saw one another. Bering made the Alaskan coast under the shadow of Mt. St. Elias. Turning westward he skirted the shore, felt his way along the fog-bound Aleutian Islands, and was finally wrecked near the coast of Kamchatka. There he died, a sacrifice to the cause of geographical exploration. Chirikof, meanwhile, had reached the North American coast near the present Sitka, where the hostile Tlingits fell upon his men. In October 1741, the Russian brought his starving crew back to Kamchatka and gave to the civilized world its first knowledge of Alaska. In southern Alaska soon after the Russian discoveries there met on the opposite side of the globe various elements of the expanding European culture area. Russians, advancing eastward, met Spanish and British traders going west.

A NORTHERN TRAGEDY

ALEUTS who in the summer of 1741 watched with wondering eyes Bering's small ship sail past their villages little realized that disaster impended. They knew of no world outside their islands and the mainland on the east. Yet scarcely a dozen arctic summers had come and gone when Russian fur traders were everywhere among them. The Aleutian world was thrown into chaos. Armed with firearms against which Aleutian darts were of no avail, the intruders compelled the natives to take the prey which the white man sought. Small boats, manned by Aleuts, were sent into dangerous waters while their wives and children were held as hostages on shore. Too often these unfortunates paid the penalty for the death of a Russian or even for an unsuccessful voyage. The traders fought with one another, for the Tsar and his laws were far away. Crime and disorder, robbery and loss were the inevitable result of unregulated trade. The latter half of the eighteenth century saw the Aleuts shrink to perhaps one-tenth of their former number. The remnant of a once numerous people cowered beneath the blows of ruthless masters. Rarely has the impact of white civilization upon a primitive people brought to the latter such immediate and terrible suffering.

589 An Old Russian Blockhouse in Alaska, from a photograph in Joseph Schafer, *The Pacific Slope and Alaska*, Vol. X of *The History of North America*, edited by Guy Carleton Lee, G. Barrie & Sons, Philadelphia, 1904

THE ORGANIZED FUR TRADE

THE year 1788 found certain Russian speculators reading with unconcealed pleasure the terms of a charter creating a company which they had formed and granting it monopolistic privileges in the most important waters of distant Alaska. The new enterprise, known finally as the Russian-American Fur Company, prospered. Its headquarters, first established on Kodiak Island, were later transferred to Sitka in spite of the vigorous opposition of the Tlingits. Ships were built which sailed to China with holds packed with bales of furs which brought fabulous prices at the hongs of old Canton. A trade exchange sprang up, in spite of the restrictive commercial policy of Spain, between Alaska and the Spanish settlements of California. Indelibly written into the history of Alaska are the names of two great managers of the Russian-American Fur Company, Baranof and Wrangell. The establishment of the company brought in course of time peace to the suffering Aleuts as its managers began to understand the importance of the native population for their enterprise. In 1824 came to Alaska Father Veniaminoff, missionary of the Greek Catholic Church. For eighteen years he labored in a parish that stretched along hundreds of miles of coast from the Aleutian Islands to Sitka. He learned the native tongue and devised a Russian-Aleutian grammar to serve as the foundation for the education of the Aleuts. He brought the Christian faith and the inspiring ritual of his church to the simple men and women of the north. His work was generously supported by his compatriots at home. When he returned to honors in his native land, the Russian church had extended its ministry over the whole of the southern Alaskan coast.

590 The Harbour of New Archangel (Sitka) in Sitka or Norfolk Sound, from a lithograph by I. Clark after a drawing by Capt. Lisiansky, in Urey Lisiansky, *A Voyage Around the World in the Years 1803, 4, 5, & 6 etc.*, London, 1814

591 A Family of Fur Seals, showing the bull in the foreground, from a photograph. © Rau Studios, New York

THE FUR TRADE OF SOUTHERN ALASKA

THE Russian-American Fur Company was not permitted to enjoy undisturbed the rich peltries of the northwest coast of North America. Within a decade after the founding of the company British and American traders were driving what bargains they could with the Haidas and the Tlingits. Bloody encounters taught the Indian to respect the power of the white man. Wily traders tempted him with trinkets and liquor. The first half of the nineteenth century witnessed a fierce struggle for profit between men of several nations amid the islands of the southern Alaskan coast. In 1890 Albert P. Niblack, an ensign in the United States Navy, drew a dark picture of the result. "European civilization has borne with crushing force upon the Indians of the Northwest coast. Demoralized and staggered by contact with the whites, the remnant of the former population is just beginning to rally from the blow. Nothing places the Northern tribes (Tlingits and Haidas) higher in the scale of intelligence than the philosophy with which they are adapting themselves to their changed environment, retaining their advantageous native customs and accepting from us only what contributes to their comfort and welfare." The grotesque faces of the totem poles still looked down upon the Indian villages, reminding the people of the faith and ways of their forefathers and of the proud heritage of the nations of the northwest coast.

A FORGOTTEN LAND

IN 1867 a hesitant Senate ratified the treaty of purchase which Secretary Seward had negotiated with the Ambassador of Russia. "Then Alaska was forgotten, just as it had been by the Russian Government after the expedition of Bering. American citizens went into the Territory believing that the laws of the United States would be extended for the protection of life and property. This was not done — the land was literally abandoned. There was no civil law. There were five Army posts established one after another — Sitka, Wrangell, Kenai, Tongass, and Kodiak. In the last two years of the military occupation Sitka and Fort Wrangell only were maintained. The Army had no authority to act in any civil or criminal case. A pandemonium of crime ensued." — J. L. MCPHERSON, in *Alaska, Hearings on H. R. 5694, 67th Congress*, 160. In 1877 the military units were withdrawn, but until 1884 no government was established. The agents of the customs department were left in sole charge but without law of any kind other than that pertaining to the customs and with no means of enforcing their decisions. The situation became intolerable. In 1878 the customs officer at Wrangell resigned in despair. "I have acted in the capacity of arbitrator, adjudicator, and peacemaker until forbearance has ceased to be a virtue. Within the past month one thousand complaints by Indians have been laid before me for settlements, and as I am neither Indian agent nor justice of the peace, I decline the honor of patching up Indian troubles. . . . For quietness to reign . . . there must be some power here beyond that conferred on deputy collectors. . . . What this country wants is law, and without it she will never flourish or prosper." — *Ibid.*, 163–64.

592 A Blockhouse at Fort Wrangell, from a photograph in Joseph Schafer, *The Pacific Slope and Alaska*, Vol. X of *The History of North America*, edited by Guy Carleton Lee. © G. Barrie & Sons, Philadelphia, 1904

THE PLIGHT OF THE ESKIMOS

593 Family Group of the Western Eskimos, from a model in the United States National Museum, Washington

THE years between 1884 and 1897 were marked by a policy of drifting on the part of the Government of the United States. The territory was given a Governor but the people of the region had no share in shaping their own political destinies. Washington paid scant heed to the needs of remote Alaska. Scarcely a member of Congress knew that disaster had befallen the Eskimos. In 1890 Dr. Sheldon Jackson, pioneer missionary in the Alaskan field, wrote to the Department of the Interior. ". . . fifty years ago American whalers, having largely exhausted the supply in other waters, found their way into the North Pacific Ocean. Then commenced for that section the slaughter and destruction of whales. . . . As the great herds of buffalo that once roamed on the western prairies have been exterminated for their pelts, so the whales have been sacrificed. . . . With the destruction of the whale one large source of food supply for the natives has been cut off. Another large supply was derived from the walrus . . . but commerce wanted ivory, and the whalers turned their attention to the walrus, destroying thousands annually for the sake of their tusks. Where a few years ago they were so numerous that their bellowings were heard above the roar of the waves and grinding and crashing of the ice fields, this year I cruised for weeks without seeing or hearing one." Seals, sea lions, salmon, and the game of the interior were being seriously diminished as a result of the activities of the white men. "Thus the support of the people is largely gone, and the process of slow starvation and extermination has commenced along the whole arctic coast of Alaska. Villages that once numbered thousands have been reduced to hundreds; of some tribes but two or three families remain."

SAVING THE ESKIMOS

WITH rare insight Jackson estimated the situation of the Eskimos and devised a solution. In spite of the jeers of his white friends in Alaska he proposed the introduction of domesticated reindeer from eastern Siberia. Congress turned a deaf ear to his earnest plea in 1890 for funds. He then appealed to the American public and several eastern newspapers helped him to raise a little more than two thousand dollars. In 1891 Jackson brought sixteen reindeer to Alaska and in the following year returned from Siberia with one hundred and seventy-one more animals. "In 1893 Congress made an appropriation of six thousand dollars to continue the work. This was twenty-eight years ago. In the succeeding ten years, up to and including the year 1902, we imported to Alaska a total of one thousand, two hundred and eighty reindeer. [In that year Russia forbade further exportation.] From this small beginning the herds now [1921] total in excess of one hundred and eighty thousand, while over one hundred thousand have been killed for food. . . ." McPHERSON, 250. The Eskimos responded to the opportunities offered by the reindeer.

594 A Reindeer Herd at Nome, from a photograph. © Underwood & Underwood, New York

595 An Eskimo with his Prize Reindeer, from a photograph. © Underwood & Underwood, New York

AN ESKIMO INDUSTRY

The reindeer are distributed among the natives under a system of apprenticeship whereby each apprentice receives six, eight, and ten reindeer by the close of the first, second, and third years, and ten more at the close of the fourth year, when, if he has demonstrated his ability, he assumes entire charge of his herd, and must, in turn, employ and similarly distribute reindeer among his apprentices. "Under the governmental regulations no native may dispose of female reindeer to the whites. . . . During the winter of 1917–18, reindeer fairs were held at Mary's Igloo, at Unalaska, at Noatak, and at Noorvik. Hundreds of the natives gathered to compare their experiences . . . to race their deer, pull their draft animals on loaded sleds and learn the latest methods of handling and slaughtering stock. . . . " — McPherson, 250–51. This industry has improved the lot of the Eskimo and has made his future secure.

THE KLONDIKE GOLD RUSH

In 1896 news went out to the world that gold in large quantities had been discovered in Klondike Creek, a small tributary of the Yukon River just east of the boundary of Alaska. Gold had been found in Alaska as early as 1880, when the ore at Juneau was located, but in no such quantities for placer mining as in the Klondike country. The result of this discovery was a gold rush in 1896 and 1897, reminiscent of the days of 1849. Tens of thousands of men hastened to Alaska, seeking the Klondike by every possible route. Many sailed in boats up the Yukon; others crossed the passes near Cook Inlet and Prince William Sound. Some even tried to make their way overland from the Canadian provinces of Saskatchewan and Alberta. Most of those who came knew little or nothing of Alaskan conditions. A few, as in Calfornia, found wealth in the gravel beds, from which the nuggets were panned. Many paid the extreme penalty for their rashness. During the height of the rush, large amounts of gold were taken from the Yukon Valley. The region saw the development of prosperous towns where for a day money flowed freely and swaggering men talked in large terms of the future. Then the accessible gravels gave out. The miners went home and the region once more bore its former aspect of emptiness and isolation. The winter wind whistled through abandoned habitations and made snow piles on the floors. Then dreams of another Klondike lured prospectors into the heart of the Alaskan wilderness. Again and again glittering particles in the sand rewarded their search and small rushes established settlements. But the days of the Alaskan El Dorado were passed. The gold rush of 1896 brought to an end the period of governmental indifference. In the first decade of the twentieth century was developed the policy of conserving Alaskan resources.

596 A Laundry at Dawson City, 1900, from a photograph. © Rau Art Studios, Inc.

597 Prospectors on the Summit of the Chilkoot Pass during the Klondike Gold Rush, from a photograph. © Underwood & Underwood, New York

598 Drawn expressly for *The Pageant of America* by Joseph L. Cain

MODERN ALASKA — A PERMANENT FRONTIER

THE Klondike find brought sharply to the attention of the Federal Government the mineral wealth of Alaska. Almost immediately neglect was replaced by a policy of extreme restriction and conservation. Forests and coal and oil lands were retained in the hands of the Government. The development of the country was retarded. Yet Alaska continued slowly to make progress. In 1906 a delegate from Alaska was permitted to sit in Congress. Six years later a legislature was established. In 1913 the United States began the construction of the now completed railroad from Seward to Fairbanks in the interior. In 1923 the Alaska Agricultural College and School of Mines, the "farthest north" institution of higher learning, opened its doors. In the same year the President of the United States came in person to see what might be done to hasten the sound development of this rich northern country. In 1920 the white persons in Alaska numbered 27,883 of whom 20,586 were males. Alaska displays the disproportion between the sexes which has characterized every former frontier. As the land fills up the disparity between men and women will doubtless be modified. This north country is a land of homes for white men as well as red. But Alaska presents a problem which the American pioneer elsewhere never faced. The home-seeker in the north builds his house in the land of the midnight sun on the edge of the Arctic. Going northward the explorer passes at last the limit of agriculture. So remote is Alaska from great centers of population that many years must pass before the northern farmer can hope to ship abroad any considerable quantity of food stuffs. The immediate future of Alaska depends upon its extractive industries, particularly upon its mines, forests, and fisheries, and upon its growing herds of reindeer. As the years pass it is becoming more and more a playground where men and women seeking release from the artificialities of urban life may come face to face with some of the grandest aspects of nature. During the nineteenth century the American frontier swept westward across the continent until halted by the Pacific. In the twentieth, the pioneer, turning northward, approaches with halting step the ice-bound Polar Sea. Northern Alaska must always remain a frontier where men stand on the edge of a wilderness so unfriendly that few will be willing to make their homes within it.

NOTES ON THE PICTURES

9. The artist, a Virginia illustrator, specialized on scenes of southern life. See Vols. III and IX.

17. Outacite, also known as Wootassitan and Woosatasate, was styled "Governor of the Lower and Middle Settlements of the Cherokees" when Governor Francis Nicholson was in South Carolina in 1721.

19, 21. For Frederic Remington see Vol. XII, pp. 50, 299.

22. For Dwight Franklin see Vol. VII, Notes on the Pictures, 644; also Vols. I, III and VI. See 24, 26, 28, 61.

25. See 19.

30. This map was presented to Governor Francis Nicholson by the Indian cacique who drew it. It shows the Cherokee towns in the southwestern part of North Carolina.

33. For MacNeil see Vol. XII, pp. 190, 207.

39. This portrait by Peale is the only authentic likeness of Sevier known to exist. For an account of Peale's work see Vol. XII, pp. 5, 14.

43. Darley was the most prominent American illustrator of his day. See Vol. XII, pp. 37, 244, 285–287; also see Vols. III and XI.

47. This is an imaginative likeness. No accurate portrait of Logan is known to exist.

52. A pupil of Laurens, Twachtman and MacMonies, White has painted numerous murals of historical subjects. See 55, 57, 62, 78, 80.

53. Enid Yandell studied under MacMonies and Rodin.

54. In his day Bingham enjoyed a great reputation as a painter of contemporaneous life and character. His early work shows the influence of Chester Harding. At the time of his death he was Professor of Fine Arts at the University of Missouri.

60. This is an artist's idealization of Boone. Many ideal pictures of him were painted and figured in wood-cuts published in the 'forties. The only known portrait of Boone made from life was painted by Chester Harding in 1820 when Boone was eighty-six years of age.

67. See 43.

68. See 19.

74. The buildings shown in this engraving were located between the present Wayne and Griswold streets.

75. For Robert Aitken see Vol. XII, pp. 176, 219.

87. Harding wandered widely through the frontier states in the early years of the last century and painted portraits of numerous pioneers. See Vol. XII, pp. 17, 22.

94. Jouett was born in Mercer County, Kentucky, in 1783 and died at Lexington in 1827. He painted about three hundred and fifty recorded portraits, including one of Lafayette made from life at Frankfort, Kentucky, in 1824.

100. See Vol. I, Notes on the Pictures, 26.

103. See Vol. I, Notes on the Pictures, 19.

105. See 22.

107. First known as Mount Johnson. The name was changed to Fort Johnson after a palisade had been built around the old mansion during the French and Indian War.

108, 117. See 39.

123. For Gilbert Stuart see Vol. XII, pp. 16, 18–20.

125. See Vol. IV, Notes on the Pictures, 130.

130, 132, 135. Drawn by an Iroquois Indian.

140. This likeness of Little Turtle is from an old cut reproduced from a painting of the chief made while he was in Philadelphia. The original portrait was destroyed when the British burned the Capitol at Washington during the War of 1812. On the forehead may be seen as part of the headdress the rattles of three rattlesnakes.

142. The De Lancey Gill collection comprises the finest assemblage of modern Indian photographs.

148. For John Trumbull see Vol. XII, pp. 16, 17, 21, 23, 30, 33.

149. Lakeman painted many portraits at Salem, Massachusetts, about 1820.

161. The artist studied under Blashfield and painted numerous murals.

165. Sartain, known principally as an engraver in mezzotint, was skilled in miniature painting and large portraiture.

166. See 39.

178. For Howard Pyle see Vol. XII, pp. 289, 293, 294. Also see Vols. I, III, VI, VIII, X, XI.

186. Inman was a painter, lithographer and illustrator. See Vol. XII, pp. 17, 37, 39, 242, 279.

200. See 125.

207. Pierre E. du Simetiere, a Swiss artist, came to America in 1765. He painted portraits of the most prominent men of the time including George Washington, Baron Steuben, Benedict Arnold, and John Jay. He also painted miniatures and designs for publications. His valuable collection of Revolutionary manuscripts and broadsides is in the Philadelphia Library.

209. For Crèvecœur see Vol. XI, pp. 48, 61, 97.

222. In Trumbull's *Reminiscences* he says that he stealthily penciled the portraits of various southern Indian leaders who came to see Washington in New York in 1790.

233. See 125.

247. For Samuel F. B. Morse as a portrait painter see Vol. XII, pp. 17, 25, 30, 34, 280.

254, 257, 260, 267. See 103.

256, 258. See p. 159.

264, 285. The artist, a pupil of Abbot H. Thayer and George de Forest Brush, has specialized in mural painting.

295. For Thomas Sully see Vol. XII, pp. 17, 27, 28, 242.

297. See Vol. IV, Notes on the Pictures, 359.

300. Cobbett, an English politician and writer, was born in 1766 and died in 1835. A man of strong and often radical convictions, and a turbulent character, he was engaged in controversies throughout his life. On three occasions he was tried and forced to pay heavy fines. In 1809 his attack on the flogging of mutinous militia caused him to be fined a thousand pounds and imprisoned for two years. In 1817, being in debt thirty-four thousand pounds, he fled to the United States. From North Hempstead, now Roslyn, Long Island, he continued his contributions to the *Register*, which he had published in England, and wrote an *English Grammar* of which ten thousand copies were sold in a month. Upon his return to England he was a member of Parliament from 1826 to 1835.

307. See 125.

308. This is said to be the earliest view made of New Orleans.

310, 311. See 123.

316. For Thure de Thulstrup see Vol. IX, pp. 126, 138, 162.

319, 320. See Vol. X, Notes on the Pictures, 359.

322. For Charles Keck see Vol. I, Notes on the Pictures, 643; also Vols. III, VII, IX, XI.

324. See 256.

327. The artist specializes in paintings of Indians and American pioneers. His painting, *Custer's Last Fight*, was exhibited in many cities throughout the country.

328. See Vol. III, Notes on the Pictures, 370.

334, 347. See 19.

338, 349. See 123.

343. See 39.

344, 346. See 254.

351. For Bierstadt see Vol. XII, pp. 42, 47, 48.

352. See 103.

353, 355, 356, 357, 358, 359. See 256.

361. A self-taught artist, Dixon has had success as an illustrator and mural painter of Far West subjects.

371. See Vol. IV, Notes on the Pictures, 183.

372, 373. Seymour, an Englishman, was a landscape painter and engraver who lived in Philadelphia for some years. He accompanied Major Long on the expedition which he illustrated.

374, 380, 381, 384, 385. See 256.

388. See 43.

389, 390. See 19.

391. See p. 198.

392, 393. See 256.

395. A pupil of John La Farge, Holslag has mural paintings in the Library of Congress and other public buildings.

396. True studied under Howard Pyle and Frank Brangwyn, assisting the latter with decorations for the Panama Pacific Exposition of 1915.

401. See 19.

402. See 297.

407, 408. See 256.

421. See 19.

422. See 396.

428. See 19.

433. See 391.

444. See 396.

447. See 19.

468. Thomas, a portrait painter, studied under Chase in New York and under Lefebvre and Constant in Paris.

479. For Thomas Moran see Vol. XII, pp. 42, 47, 49.

483. The artist is a marine painter whose work may be viewed in the Brooklyn Art Institute Museum, the City Museum, St. Louis, and the Toledo Museum.

487. For Bayard Taylor see Vol. XI, pp. 203, 204.

492. See 396.

501, 511, 512, 513, 517, 522, 524, 526, 527, 534. See 19.

530. For Proctor see Vol. XII, p. 203.

536. Leutze painted the familiar *Washington Crossing the Delaware.* See Vol. XII, pp. 30, 35, 280.

538. See Vol. IX, Notes on the Pictures, 80.

541. See 395.

548. See 538.

554. See Vol. IX, Notes on the Pictures, 349.

557, 559. See 328.

558, 561, 562. See 19.

576. See 361.

INDEX

Titles of books under author are in italics; titles of illustrations under producer are in quotation marks.